EMERGING GROWTH POLE

THE ASIA-PACIFIC ECONOMY

EMERGING GROWTH POLE

THE ASIA-PACIFIC ECONOMY

EDITOR
Dilip K. Das

PRENTICE HALL

Singapore New York London Toronto Sydney Tokyo

First published 1996 by
Prentice Hall
Simon & Schuster (Asia) Pte Ltd
317 Alexandra Road
#04-01 IKEA Building
Singapore 159965

Library of Congress Cataloging-in-Publication Data

Emerging growth pole: the Asia-Pacific economy/editor, Dilip K. Das.
     p.   cm.
    "This compendium ... contains [25] abridged papers from several top-of-the-line scholars
in the world"--P.
    Includes bibliographical references and index.
    ISBN 0-13-525841-3
    1. Asia--Economic integration.   2. Pacific Area--Economic integration.   3. Asia--Economic
conditions--1945-   4. Pacific Area--Economic conditions.   I. Das. Dilip K., 1945- .
HC412.E584 1996   95-26812
337.1'5--dc20   CIP

Printed in Singapore

1 2 3 4 5   99 98 97 96

ISBN 0-13-525841-3

Prentice Hall International (UK) Limited, *London*
Prentice Hall of Australia Pty. Limited, *Sydney*
Prentice Hall Canada Inc., *Toronto*
Prentice Hall Hispanoamericana, S.A., *Mexico*
Prentice Hall of India Private Limited, *New Delhi*
Prentice Hall of Japan, Inc., *Tokyo*
Editora Prentice Hall do Brasil, Ltda., *Rio de Janeiro*
Prentice Hall, Inc., *Upper Saddle River, New Jersey*

For
Vasanti, Tanushree and Siddharth
with love and appreciation

CONTENTS

升

Advancement is achieved not by violence but by adaptability and modesty, adapting oneself to obstacles and bending around them, like wood in the earth that grows upward without haste and without rest. Since the individual is borne along by the propitiousness of time, he advances. When one is advancing farther and farther, it is important for him not to become intoxicated by success. Precisely when he experiences great success, it is necessary to remain sober and not to try to skip any stages; he must go on slowly, step by step, as though hesitant. Only such calm, steady progress, overleaping nothing, leads to the goal.

Wisdom of the *I Ching*

PREFACE

A remarkable record of high, sustained and equitable growth in Japan and the East Asian economies has been one of the great human achievements of the recent past. These economies have risen from the ashes of war to become dazzling testaments to David Ricardo and his predecessor Adam Smith. The Southeast Asian economies and China followed suit to become a part of the Asia-Pacific economic whirlwind. Together they generated a stereotypical view of a dynamic East Asia and a mimetic South East Asia and China. The governments of Australia and New Zealand fervently believe that their destiny lies increasingly with the Asia-Pacific because they need its markets, capital and skills. For a decade and a half they have consciously endeavored to integrate themselves with the Asia-Pacific economies. Identifying with their British heritage is gradually receding into their past.

It surprises many that the Asia-Pacific region has succeeded despite its apparent heterogeneity. A 1993 World Bank report, entitled *The East Asian Miracle*, christened the following eight regional economies as the high performing Asian economies (HPAEs): Taiwan, Indonesia, Hong Kong, Singapore, Republic of Korea, Japan, Malaysia and Thailand. Since 1960, these eight economies have grown more than twice as rapidly as the rest of the Asia-Pacific economies, roughly three times as quickly as Latin America and South Asia, and 25 times faster than sub-Saharan Africa. They significantly outperformed the industrial economies and the oil-rich Middle East. Over the 1960–85 period, real income per capita increased more than four times in Japan and the East Asian economies and more than doubled in the Southeast Asian economies. After its third Party Congress in 1978, China adopted the Deng doctrine and recorded remarkably high growth rates, using the same *mutatis mutandis* economic strategy as the HPAEs. The final result was that China, particularly southern China, has been growing like the HPAEs for over a decade. If growth were randomly distributed, there is roughly one chance in ten thousand that success could have been so regionally concentrated.

This superlative economic performance has caused movements in the tectonics of international economy and, as indicated in Chapter 1 of this volume, has turned the region into a growth pole. The expression "growth pole" is being used here in the same sense as it is used for North America and the European Union (EU). By 2000, the region is projected to be the largest market in the world. Little wonder that it is one of the most interesting parts of the international economy for both the academic and business communities alike.

A good deal of the extraordinary growth in the region was due to the superior accumulation of physical and human capital. Private domestic investment and rapidly growing human capital are considered the principal engines of growth for the region. These two kinds of capital were allocated better than in other countries, resulting in highly productive investment in line with their comparative advantage. The agricultural sector, while declining in relative importance, experienced rapid growth and productivity improvement. Population growth rates declined more rapidly in the region than in other parts of the developing world. Some of these economies also got a head start because they had a better-educated labor force and a more effective system of public administration. If all this is true, there is little that could be called miraculous about these economies.

The macroeconomic policies adopted by these economies were generally in accordance with the neoclassical economic doctrines. Macroeconomic management was clairvoyant and, therefore, macroeconomic performance generally stable. This policy milieu turned out to be a boon for private investment. Gradual integration of the banking system also contributed to economic growth. In most of the regional economies, their governments intervened selectively. This succeeded because intervention was within the context of sound, fundamental policies and did not ignore the fact that markets have to function. Add to this the discipline of Confusionism—thrift, hard work, respect for authority, high value of education, and perhaps most of all, the instinct to put the group above the individual—and we see a coalescence into an awesome economic force.

The regional economies have been integrating through mutual trade, investment and economic assistance. This integration has so far been market driven. However, institutional forces started operating in the early 1990s, when the Asia-Pacific Economic Cooperation (APEC) forum considered a timetable for free trade in the region. The institutional initiatives took shape during the APEC meeting in Tokyo in August 1994. Under the APEC plan, the regional members will be allowed to liberalize their economies ahead of the World Trade Organization (WTO) schedule and they will be free to offer the same benefits to countries outside the region as they extend to each other. The APEC plan is to convert the Asia-Pacific region into the most open trading area of the world. Japan is the economic epicentre of the

Asia-Pacific region. It is an economic superpower as well as a regional superpower. By the late 1980s, Japan had become the largest foreign direct investor and aid giver in the world and its financial markets were the most liquid. Although the supernova dimmed during the early 1990s, Japan had by then acquired confidence and assertiveness in the international arena. Under its strategy of *kokusaika* or internationalization, it had begun seeking broader horizons. The absolute regional economic dominance of Japan will seemingly continue into the foreseeable future.

When one starts designing or teaching a course in an area as significant as the Asia-Pacific economies, one is hard put to find suitable teaching material. This is not to say that there is a scarcity of such material. There has been a good deal of intellectual curiosity and, therefore, continual research endeavors in this area. However, apt and fitting pieces that could function as cohesive course inputs are thinly distributed, creating the need for such a book. Every time I teach such a course, I find myself consulting as many as thirty books and articles, and suggesting a smaller number of them to my students. This is a process marked by inefficiency and diseconomy of effort. I, therefore, believe that a volume like this, which covers all major aspects of the Asia-Pacific economies, will have a high utilitarian value for the academic community.

The chapters in this volume are neither overly technical nor excessively specialized. They are at a middle level and should be accessible to MBA students, MA (Economics) students, and those in finance and banking related graduate courses. The book is divided into six logical parts. Sequentially they are well connected. Every section is preceded by an introductory essay which emphasizes the highlights and salient features of each chapter and fills minor gaps. For instance, the introduction to the first part briefly focuses on the economic developments of the immediate past in the Asia-Pacific region. The first part is named "Introduction to Asia-Pacific Economies" and, true to its name, it provides a comprehensive introduction to the reader. The second part deals with the "Issues in International Trade and Investment" while the third traces the movement of the region "Toward an Asia-Pacific Trading Bloc." Next "Exchange Rate, Finance and Banking" related issues are addressed, followed by the "Macroeconomic and Monetary Issues" in the fifth part. The last part deals with the "Economic Studies of Selected Countries" which includes one of the most important regional developments, namely, Japan's rise to be an economic superpower.

Despite the variety of issues covered in this volume, I have tried to make it as cohesive as is feasible. I expect the collection to be a substantive pedagogic aid for students and instructors alike.

Graduate School of Business
University of Sydney   *Dilip K. Das*

Chapter 1

Dilip K. Das

IS ASIA-PACIFIC COMING TOGETHER AS A COHESIVE GROWTH POLE?

1.1 Growth Dynamism

The outstanding feature of the postwar world economy—to honor a cliche—is the Asia-Pacific economic dynamism. A clutch of market-economy states in the region have emerged as the most dynamic component of the world economy. The pioneering growth efforts of these economies will be dealt with at length in Chapter 2. This growth dynamism has attracted a great deal of interest in contemporary international business as well as international economic literature. The export-oriented policy regime adopted by these economies made them the most market responsive in the world and enhanced their ability to compete as well as adjust to external shocks. The saving and investment rates in the region were higher than those in other economies, both developed and developing, and resource allocation was more in accordance with the comparative advantage of the respective economies which coalesced to accelerate growth and heighten economic efficiency. The economic strategy adopted by them was largely in keeping with neoclassical principles. Consequently, the gross domestic product (GDP) of the region expanded at an unprecedented rate and the Asia-Pacific region became the focal point of economic growth. Little wonder that this phenomenon has been studied extensively by scholars (Arndt 1989; Berger and Hsiao 1988; Chen 1986; Cheng and Haggard

1987; Gibney 1992). While Japan is the largest regional economy and the epicentre of the regional economic growth, China is the briskest growing economy. This was the direct consequence of growth-boosting market reforms that were launched in 1978. Over 1980–93, China's GDP soared at an average annual rate of 9.4 percent. For the Republic of Korea, Taiwan and Singapore, this average was more than 7 percent and for Thailand, Hong Kong, Malaysia and Indonesia, it was close to 6 percent. All the regional economies have also recorded impressive increases in their GDP per capita.

Initially, this rapid economic expansion was taken for a transitional phase of the world economy. However, this country group has continued to grow at a faster rate than the other countries or country groups. For the immediate future, global economic scorekeepers and forecasters prognosticate perpetuation of the strong growth trend. Two recent long-term (1990–2000) growth projections are available for the region; the first one was made by FUGI Global Model (Omishi 1991) and the second by the Japan Center for Economic Research (JCER 1992). The first forecast puts the average growth rate of real GDP at 6.1 percent while the second at 5.5 percent. These projections are impressive by any measure. Japan, with GDP growth rate of more than 4 percent, has the highest growth rate among the G-7 countries. A growth rate greater than 6 percent has been forecast for both the Asian newly industrializing economies (ANIEs)[1] and the four large Association of Southeast Asian Nations (ASEAN-4)[2] economies. For China the forecast is 6.5 percent for the 1990–2000 period, which appears to be a trifle conservative. Only Australia and New Zealand have been projected to grow at over 2.5 percent, the lowest growth rate prediction for the region. Other than these formal forecasts, the coastal growth centers in China, such as those in the Guangdong and Fujian regions, are expected to grow at more impressive rates than those stated above for the Chinese economy. Of these growth centers, Shenzhen is the best known. If one predicts the region to grow into an economic power comparable to the U.S. and the Economic Union (EU) by the year 2000, no one will be surprised.

Since these economies adopted outward-oriented policies, several of them, particularly the ANIEs, began to make their presence felt on the international trade scene in a significant manner by the mid-1970s. By the mid-1980s, their deft exploitation of comparative advantage and sharpened competitiveness began to exert pressure on their trading partners, who in turn were forced to structurally adjust their economies. According to the GATT league table of leading exporters, Japan was the third largest trader in the world in 1992, accounting for 9.1 percent of the world trade. The U.S., at this point, was the largest trader, accounting for 12.0 percent of the world trade. Hong Kong was the tenth largest trader with 3.2 percent of the world trade. China and Taiwan were the eleventh and twelfth, respectively, accounting for 2.3 percent and 2.2 percent of the world trade. Singapore stood in the sixteenth position with 1.7 percent of the world trade. Australia, Malaysia and Thailand have also grown into substantial traders, with each accounting for 1 percent or more of the world trade (GATT 1993: Table 1.4). There are few better gauges of the Asia-Pacific's trade boom than the region's crowded docks. Hong Kong and Singapore are two of the busiest ports in the world. In 1993, the former handled 9.20 million TEUs (or 20-feet equivalent units, the standard container measure), while the latter handled 9.04 million TEUs. In comparison, Rotterdam handled 4.30 million TEUs. The two next busiest ports in the region were Kaohsiung in Taiwan and Pusan in South Korea, which handled 4.30 million TEUs and 2.95 million TEUs, respectively, in 1993 (*The Economist* 1994). Other regional ports that have grown enormously during the last five years are Penang, Port Klang and Johor in Malaysia, Batam in Indonesia and Shanghai and Shekon in China.

Two salient and noteworthy features of the region's economic dynamism are: (a) its reliance on market forces and (b) the successful and effective role of the international economic institutions. The region owes its brisk growth to the crucial role played by the market forces. To be sure, activities of the private sector were underpinned by the respective governments, or "administrative guidance" provided to the private sector. A variety of "competing models of capitalism" were in use in the region. They all drew on the Japanese concept of guided capitalism. Secondly, international economic institutions, particularly the General Agreement on Tariffs and Trade (GATT) were highly effective in the Asia-Pacific region. When it was ready for takeoff, GATT, through its various rounds of multilateral trade negotiations (MTNs), succeeded in creating a relatively open international trade regime. This led to the success of the market-driven strategies of the outward-oriented economies of the Asia-Pacific region. Eventually, it made the "economic miracle" feasible. In addition, the activities of the International Monetary Fund (IMF) and the World Bank, although primarily devoted to other objectives, successfully managed to reinforce the global framework of trade and investment liberalization. The Asia-Pacific region benefited the most from it. This is one reason why there are no formal regional integrating institutions in the Asia-Pacific region (APEC 1993). Consequently, the pattern of economic activity that has emerged is quintessentially global rather than regional, both in scope and composition.

1.2 Genesis of Economic Cooperation

The emergence of economic cooperation in Asia-Pacific can be traced back to the 1950s, when *Pax Americana* reigned supreme and the U.S. played the role of a moral guardian and the protector and exemplar of a liberal economic system. The regional interest of the U.S. was largely based on cold war strategic and geopolitical considerations. Expansion of the activities of the GATT, as alluded to above, had provided a framework of regulations within which the erstwhile small regional economies could expand their trade. Add to it the political–strategic security provided by the U.S. dominance, and a healthy ambience for regional economic cooperation is in place. Besides, the countries of the region themselves had high interest in regional economic cooperation, stemming from their highly skewed— if not complementary—resource endowments.

The economic and strategic dominance of the U.S. in the 1950s and 1960s also met the need of a war-ravaged Japan for a patron and mentor. The strategic aspect of the U.S. alliance, with Japan and other regional countries, was formalized in treaties like the Mutual Security Treaty of 1951 and 1960, the Australia–New Zealand–United States Security Treaty (ANZUS) of 1951 and the Southeast Asia Treaty Organization (SEATO) of 1954. These political alliances had a significant impact on the economic development and cooperation of the Asia-Pacific region because they brought both small and large economies closer politically at a time when opportunities for bilateral trade were expanding. The broader framework of international economic policies of each country facilitated the development of extensive economic ties and subsequently a relatively easy acceptance of large-scale economic interdependence (Drysdale 1988). After the end of the Vietnam War, the U.S. hegemony declined considerably and Japan emerged as a regional and, eventually, a global economic superpower. Its economic relationship with the regional economies began to expand. At this point, Australia and New Zealand also effected a huge shift in their focus from the U.K. to Asia-Pacific. The two countries began to make concerted efforts to integrate with the region. Also, the ASEAN countries, after the Bangkok Declaration of 1967, began to gradually galvanize themselves into action for greater security and economic exchange. Viewed in this way, the genesis of close cooperation among the Asia-Pacific countries lies squarely in the realm of geopolitical and strategic expedience.

The forces that were reshaping the global economy during the latter half of the 1960s, and the challenges that were emerging, provided an economic rationale to cooperate. As stated above, it was well recognised in the region that rapid growth and high productivity are attainable by increasing trade, which allows specialization and exploitation of economies of scale. Therefore, expanding markets in the regional settings and market integration will offer wide scope for national and regional growth, and will work toward benefiting all. Acceptance of this logic brought the regional economies together without any institutionalized efforts and also without a great deal of initiative from their respective governments.

A negative development in the international economy also worked towards enhancing regional cooperation. In the 1970s, when the postwar liberal trading system began to make retrograde motion and the GATT discipline began to erode, several regional economies began to feel the pinch of neo-protectionistic measures like voluntary trade restrictions, managed trade practices and other grey area measures. The U.S. trade diplomacy adversely affected the agricultural trade of Australia and New Zealand. This external threat intensified the regional economic cooperation. It was reflected in the strong support provided by the Asia-Pacific economies to the Uruguay Round of the MTNs.

1.3 Increasing Interdependence

The Europoean integration, which is based on treaties, advanced greatly after

1986. Although the Asia-Pacific integration has gone nowhere as far, interdependence among countries has increased considerably in the recent past. A matrix analysis of various economic transactions confirms this (MITI 1992). An examination of the commodity trade matrix indicates increasing trade interdependence. Over the first half of the 1980s, when the growth of world trade was slow, regional trade grew steadily at an average annual rate of 8.4 percent. Between 1986 and 1990, the average annual growth rate of the regional trade was 14.2 percent, which was higher than the overall growth rate of world trade. During the latter half of the 1980, the intra-ANIEs trade grew at the rate of 44.7 percent per year compared to 26.6 percent per year in the first half of the 1980s. Trade between the ANIEs and the ASEAN-4 grew at the rate of 31.7 percent per year in the latter half of the 1980s compared to 10.4 percent per year in the first half. Also, significant increases were observed in trade of these country groups with China.

The degree of export dependence in this region, which is calculated by dividing the value of exports by GNP, increased from 10.0 percent in 1986 to 12.1 percent in 1990. However, the degree of dependence for intra-regional exports rose from 6.5 percent to 7.9 percent over the same period. This shows that the increase in exports directed within the region made up 1.4 percent of the total increase of 2.1 percent in export dependence, which in turn implies increasing interdependence in trade in the region.

Trade in manufactures brings the same trend out more emphatically. The MITI statistics show that exports of manufactured products within the region grew at an average annual rate of 17.2 percent in the latter half of 1980s, which surpassed the growth rate of merchandise trade. Thus trade in manufactured goods has made large contributions to overall trade expansion and mutual interdependence.

Expanding trade in services is another important aspect of deepening interdependence. Trade in services in the region has been expanding at a rate far exceeding that of the world average. This expansion is particularly striking for Japan, the ANIEs and ASEAN-4, where trade in services has expanded at more than 20 percent per year.

Intra-regional capital inflows have also increased considerably, particularly after the liberalization of financial markets in several Asia-Pacific economies, which increased financial integration in the region. Foreign direct investment (FDI) is yet another driving force which brings about interdependence and integration among the economies. A stupendous outflow of direct investment from Japan has underpinned much of the growing economic integration. This surge occurred after 1985, when the appreciating yen forced Japan's exporters to move a lot of their production to lower cost areas in Asia. Several high cost and low technology industries moved offshore. This, in turn, spurred a huge leap in exports back to Japan (Das 1993). In the process, Japan's relationship with the Asia-Pacific region became closer and more productive. Large investments have been made by Japan as well as the ANIEs into the ASEAN-4 economies. In 1989, investment from Japan to ASEAN-4 was more than four times that from the U.S. It was one-third of the total FDI made in the ASEAN-4. The ANIEs made over 20 percent of the total foreign investment in these countries. This had gone a long way toward strengthening ties between Japan, the ANIEs and the ASEAN-4.

Taiwan has become a cash-rich economy with over US$90 billion worth of forex reserves, a staggering sum by any reckoning. It has emerged as a large foreign investor in the region. Between 1987 and 1993, Taiwan invested $12 billion in China, Malaysia, Indonesia, Thailand, Vietnam and the Philippines. It has accepted regional cooperation as an inevitable trend (Baum 1993). It is helping to expand the industrial base of Southeast Asia, thereby, integrating the regional economy. Taiwanese find Southeast Asia alluring because it offers stable governments, relatively open economies, a large reservoir of natural resources, relatively low wage rates and increasingly affluent consumers.

There is another kind of micro-level regional integration which emerged during the 1980s. Its rationale, again, was pure and simple economic expedience. The best known and most talked about example of this is southern China, where economic zones around Guangdong, Fujian and nearby provinces have expanded, with intimate interaction with Hong Kong and Taiwan. The two ANIEs are sources of capital and technology. In future, Hong Kong will integrate more with mainland economy because there is a great deal of scope for Hong Kong to provide high value-added services, like legal, accounting, marketing and financial services. These opportunities will not escape the notice of the business community of Hong Kong. Another fast emerging zone is the so-called "Baht Zone," spreading from Thailand to neighboring Indochinese countries, where the Thai baht, a strong and stable currency, is being increasingly used as the key currency for trade. The third such zone is the Johor–Riau–Batam triangle involving Indonesia, Singapore and Malaysia, which has made considerable progress without any promotional efforts from the three governments, although the concept has their acquiescence. Since the middle of 1992, central bankers and financial authorities from Australia, Hong Kong, Japan and Singapore have been negotiating for the establishing of a cooperative network among the Asia-Pacific region's four major financial centers. In addition, countries like the Republic of Korea, Taiwan and Malaysia are assisting the other smaller economies of the region by not only providing them with foreign currency but also with blueprints for economic development. The smaller economies are getting assistance in accumulating the critical mass of capital, technology and managerial ability needed to launch into sustained growth. These and similar endeavors are afoot in the region and are doing an adequate job of bringing the regional economies together.

The above convincingly establishes that a de facto or non-institutional-aided economic integration has been continuing in Asia-Pacific for nearly two decades, and that to whatever extent it has come into being, it was driven to it by market forces. The active participation of the private sector is integral to the success of further development and integration of the regional economies.

1.4 *Le Mot Juste*

Is "growth pole" the most accurate expression or *le mot juste* to describe the Asia-Pacific region? If a growth pole is defined as a large economy, or a group of interrelated and integrating economies which make their presence felt in the international economy by way of inter alia intragroup and international trade and financial flows, then the Asia-Pacific region has come close to being one, that is, if it is not already one. The size of its GDP and trade and foreign investment performance place the Asia-Pacific region is the same league as the EU and the U.S., the other two growth poles. The distinction, however, is clear. While the Asia-Pacific *vide ut supra* has only integrated de facto, the other two growth poles are integrated in a formal or institutionalized manner. However, as has been amply demonstrated, the integration process is decisively on and, of late, has accelerated.

The combined economic might of the growth poles, measured by the size of their GNPs, is in a comparable range. For instance, according to 1992 statistics, the EU is the largest growth pole with a GNP of US$6.1 trillion, the U.S. comes a close second with $5.5 trillion followed by the Asia-Pacific region at $4.4 trillion. However, we have seen that high growth rates have been forecast for the Asia-Pacific regional economies. The region's size will, therefore, grow relatively to the other two growth poles in the foreseeable future. According to MITI projections, Asia-Pacific will surpass the U.S. economy in terms of GDP by the year 2010 (MITI 1992).

If forex reserves are taken as one of the measures of economic strength, the Asia-Pacific region falls between the other two growth poles, with forex reserves of US$273 billion in 1992. The corresponding figure for the EU was $335 billion while that for the U.S. was $75 billion. The Asia-Pacific growth pole comprises economies that are among the most successful traders in the world, therefore, this growth pole led the other two in international trade. Its exports added up to $703 billion, as against the exports of the EU of $534 billion and that of the U.S. of $394 billion. The same observation applies to the imports, which stood at $654 billion for Asia-Pacific against $585 billion for the EU and $495 billion for the U.S.

The region has now come into its own and in the early 1990s, when the other two growth poles were in the grip of a recession, Asia-Pacific chugged along and posted impressive growth rates. So much so that when the Japanese economy went into a severe downturn in 1992 and 1993 and its real GDP growth rate plummeted to 1.1 percent and 0.3 percent respectively, the rest of the regional economies were unaffected and the growth momentum of the region was maintained. It bears repeating that the Japanese economy is the largest in the region. This implies that this growth pole is capable of playing the "locomotive role" in the international economy, which, until not too long ago, only the U.S. economy was capable of doing. By the early 1990s, Asia-Pacific had cut its umbilical cord of economic dependence upon the other two growth poles. Its economic dynamism has provided it with its own momentum. Growth in intra-regional demand more than compensated for falls in demand in the U.S. and the EU during the early 1990s. Taking the argument a step further, the Asia-Pacific region has become less dependent upon the rest of the world. The observations made earlier in this paragraph corroborate this fact. The elasticity coefficient, measuring Asia-Pacific response to the performance of the rest of the world, slumped from around 1.5 in the early 1970s to 0.3 in 1992 (Rowley 1992). The region will undoubtedly have a demonstration effect over other international economies. The South Asian economies are already trying to emulate it by adopting and promoting private enterprise and "market friendly" strategies of economic growth. Aside from this indirect influence, these economies will directly propagate growth to their trading partners, thus enhancing their salutary influence over the international economy. Viewed in this way, "growth pole" justly describes the Asia-Pacific region.

1.5 Summing Up

The postwar growth dynamism of the Asia-Pacific economies has attracted a great deal of scholarly and professional interest. Their brisk growth was attributed essentially to their export-oriented strategy, high savings and investment rates, and pragmatic resource allocation. This set of policies made them the most market-responsive economies in the world. The result was brisk GDP growth rates in the past two decades. Forecasters prognosticate continuance of this strong growth trend.

Although the Asia-Pacific economies relied essentially on market forces and the private sector for efficient economic growth, their governments did provide "administrative guidance" which did not play a market stifling role. Also, international economic institutions, particularly the GATT, played an effective and supportive role when the regional economies were taking off.

The origin of the Asia-Pacific economic cooperation can be traced back to the *Pax Americana* period of the 1950s. The political–strategic security provided by U.S. dominance created a healthy ambience for economic cooperation. Although regional cooperation had begun from the realm of geopolitical and strategic expedience, it soon spilled over into the economic arena. Since the region recognized that rapid growth and high productivity is attainable through trade, expanding markets in the regional setting was given a conscious priority.

Over the 1980s and early 1990s, interdependence among the Asia-Pacific countries increased considerably. A matrix analysis of trade and foreign investment confirms this beyond doubt. Intra-regional capital flows have also gone up after market liberalization commenced in several regional economies. Central bankers and financial authorities from Australia, Hong Kong, Japan and Singapore have been trying to negotiate for the establishing of a cooperative network among the four major financial centers of the region. Other than this, a microlevel regional integration process is also afoot, enhancing economic bonds. A de facto or noninstitutional-aided economic integration has started in the region as well. To whatever extent the regional integration has come to, it was essentially driven by market forces.

Whether or not the Asia-Pacific economies can be referred to as a growth pole may be answered as follows: The regional economies are integrating fast and, as a group, they are comparable to the EU and the U.S. in terms of GNP, exports, imports and forex reserves. Therefore, they can be called a growth pole as much as the EU and the U.S. Yet, the clear distinction between Asia-Pacific and the EU and the U.S. cannot be ignored. The latter two are integrated in a formal manner while Asia-Pacific is not. Notwithstanding this fact, the region is making its presence felt internationally. It has begun to play the "locomotive role" which until not too long ago only the U.S. economy was capable of playing. The regional economy has also acquired a great deal of independence vis-a-vis the other two growth poles and the rest of the international economy.

Notes

1. Republic of Korea, Taiwan, Hong Kong and Singapore.
2. Indonesia, Malaysia, the Philippines and Thailand.

References

Arndt, H. W., 1989, "Industrial Policy in East Asia," *Industry and Development*, No. 22, United Nations Industrial Development Organization, Vienna, Vol. 2, pp. 40–88.

Asia-Pacific Economic Cooperation (APEC), 1993, *A Vision for APEC*, Report of the Eminent Persons Group to APEC Ministers, Singapore, October.

Baum, J., 1993, "Taipei's Offshore Empire," *Far Eastern Economic Review*, March 18, 44–46.

Berger, P. L. and H. H. M. Hsiao (eds.), 1988, *In Search of an East Asian Development Model*, Transaction Books, New Brunswick, NJ.

Chen, E. K. Y., 1986, "The Newly Industrializing Countries in Asia: Growth Experience and Prospects," in R. A. Scalapino, S. Sato, J. Womomdi, and S. J. Hom (eds.), *Asian Economic Development: Present and Future*, Institute of East Asian Studies, University of California, Berkeley, CA.

Cheng, T. and S. Haggard, 1987, *Newly Industrializing Asia in Transition: Policy Reform and American Response*, Institute of International Studies, University of California, Berkeley, CA.

Das, Dilip K., 1993, *The Yen Appreciation and the International Economy*, Macmillan, London.

Drysdale, P., 1988, *International Economic Pluralism*, Allen & Unwin, Sydney.

The Economist, 1994, "The Rise of Ports Like Klang," April 19, 74–76.

General Agreement on Tariff and Trade (GATT), 1993, *Statistics: International Trade*, Geneva.

Gibney, F., 1992, *The Pacific Century*, Maxwell Macmillan International, New York.

Japan Center for Economic Research (JCER), 1992, *The Coming Multipolar Economy*, Tokyo.

Ministry of International Trade and Industry (MITI), 1992, "Vision for the Economy of the Asia-Pacific Region in the Year 2000 and Tasks Ahead," Tokyo, August 10–11, mimeo.

Omishi, A., 1991, "Outlook for the Asian Pacific Economy in 1990s, FUGI Global Model Simulation", background paper prepared for the New Delhi Conference on the Future of Asia-Pacific Economies, March.

Rowley, A., 1992, "Asia Above the Gloom," *Far Eastern Economic Review*, December 24–31, 52–53.

Part I

Introduction to the Asia-Pacific Economies

After having established in Chapter 1 that the Asia-Pacific economies are as much of a growth pole of the international economy as the EU of the twelve western European economies or the U.S., I set out to introduce the regional economies, their evolution and the process of their coming into their own. Vertiginous economic growth has succeeded in creating a prosperous crescent running from Thailand to Korea. Mutual trade and investment—as alluded to in Chapter 1—has integrated the Asia-Pacific economies in a de facto manner.

A remarkable record of high, sustained and equitable growth in the Asia-Pacific economies has been one of the great human achievements of this period. These economies have risen from the ashes of the war to become dazzling testaments to David Ricardo and his predecessor Adam Smith. The Southeast Asian economies and China followed suit to become a part of the Asia-Pacific economic whirlwind. Together they generated a stereotypical view of a dynamic East Asia and a mimetic Southeast Asia and China. The governments of Australia and New Zealand fervently believe that their destiny lies increasingly with Asia-Pacific because they need its markets, capital and skills. For a decade and a half they have consciously endeavored to integrate themselves with the Asia-Pacific economies. Identifying with their British heritage is gradually receding into their past.

It surprises many that the Asia-Pacific region has succeeded despite its apparent heterogeneity. A 1993 World Bank report, entitled *The East Asian Miracle*, christened the following eight regional economies as the high-performing Asian economies (HPAEs): Taiwan, Indonesia, Hong Kong, Singapore, Republic of Korea, Japan, Malaysia, and Thailand. Since 1960, these eight economies have grown more than twice as rapidly as the rest of the Asia-Pacific economies, roughly three times as quickly as Latin America and South Asia and twenty-five times faster than sub-Saharan Africa. They significantly outperformed the industrial economies and the oil-rich Middle East. Over the 1960–85 period, real income per capita increased more than four times in Japan and the East Asian Economies and more than doubled in the Southeast Asian economies. After its Third Party Congress in 1978, China adopted the Deng doctrine and recorded remarkably high growth rates using the same economic strategy as the HPAEs. The final result was that China, particularly southern China, has been growing like the HPAEs for over a decade. If growth were randomly distributed, there is roughly one chance in ten thousand that success could have been so regionally concentrated.

This superlative economic performance has caused movements in the tectonics of international economy and, as indicated in Chapter 1 of this volume, has turned the region into a growth pole. The expression "growth pole" is being used here in the same sense as it is used for North America and the European Union. By 2000, the region is projected to be the largest market in the world. Little wonder that it is one of the most interesting parts of the international economy for both the academic and business communities alike.

A good deal of the extraordinary growth in the region was due to the superior accumulation of physical and human capital. Private domestic investment and rapidly growing human capital are considered the principal engines of growth for the region. These two kinds of capital were allocated better than in other countries, resulting in highly productive investment in line with their comparative advantage. The agricultural sector, while declining in relative importance, experienced rapid growth and productivity improvement. Population growth rates declined more rapidly in the region than in other parts of the developing world. Some of these economies also got a head start because they had a better-educated labor force and a more effective system of public administration. If all this is true, there is little that could be called miraculous about these economies.

The macroeconomic policies adopted by these economies were generally in accordance with the neoclassical economic doctrines. Macroeconomic management was good and macroeconomic performance generally stable. This policy milieu turned out to be a boon for private investment. Gradual integration of the banking system also contributed to economic growth. In most of the regional economies, their governments intervened selectively. This succeeded because intervention was within the context of sound, fundamental policies and did not ignore the fact that the markets have to function. Add to this the discipline of Confucianism— thrift, hard work, respect for authority, high value of education, and perhaps most all, the instinct to put the group above the individual—and we see a coalescence into an awesome economic force.

The regional economies have been integrating through mutual trade, investment and economic assistance. This integration has so far been market driven. However, institutional forces started operating in the early 1990s, when the Asia-Pacific Economic Cooperation (APEC) forum considered a timetable for free trade in the region. The institutional initiatives took shape during the APEC meeting in Tokyo in August 1994. Under the APEC plan, the regional members will be allowed to liberalize their economies ahead of the GATT schedule and they will be free to offer the same benefits to countries outside the region as they extend to each other. The APEC plan is to convert the Asia-Pacific region into the most open trading area of the world. Japan is the economic epicentre of the Asia-Pacific region. It is an economic superpower as well as a regional superpower. By the late 1980s, Japan had become the largest foreign direct investor and aid giver in the world and its financial markets were the most liquid. Although the supernova had dimmed during the early 1990s, Japan had by then acquired confidence and assertiveness in the international arena. Under its strategy of *kokusaika* or internationalization, it had begun seeking broader horizons. The absolute regional economic dominance of Japan will seemingly continue into the foreseeable future.

Notwithstanding its diversities, the Asia-Pacific region has managed to become a trail blazer in the area of economic growth. Part I comprises two chapters: Chapter 2 (Das) traces the economic growth path of the regional economies over the last three decades while in Chapter 3, Yoshio Suzuki, a doyen among regional economists, shows how the region came to establish itself as a major entity in the world economy. The dynamic trade-oriented growth strategy has allowed as many as six regional economies to double their output in a decade. There were several common strands in their macroeconomic policies. For instance, they all recorded high savings and investment rates and adopted outward-oriented economic policies after an initial, ephemeral, emphasis on import substitution, which led to changes in the structure of production as well as trade. Exceedingly high export growth rates and unusually rapid structural change in trade in manufactures portend the fact that economic policy played a decisive role in these economies, shifting specialization of production toward higher value-added goods. In this process, one cannot undervalue the significance of the supply-side variables and export promotion strategies. These and other causal factors are dealt with at length in the second chapter.

To be sure, the superlative economic performance of the region, in particular, those of the four dragons, namely, the Republic of Korea, Taiwan, Hong Kong and Singapore, has had an impact over the thinking of the macroeconomic managers of the five ASEAN countries and China. They closely watched how the four dragons endeavored to catch up with the industrialized economies of the world and also strengthened economic bonds among themselves. In Chapter 3, Suzuki analyzes five common features of regional growth. He also sheds light on the impact of regional economic expansion on the global economic order, an issue that can potentially turn into a grating one.

After recording a healthy GDP growth rate of 4.6 percent over the 1989–91 period, in real terms, the Japanese economy went into a downswing. The "double bubble burst" or asset deflation brought its growth rate down to 1.1 percent in 1992 and 0.1 percent in 1993. Although fiscal stimulus was applied to jerk the economy out of recession, it proved to be inadequate and the country's economy was static in 1994. For four successive years the economy has trended downward. During 1995, extensive deflationary pressures continued to weigh on recovery, therefore the GDP was expected to grow by 0.8 percent only. This may well be the longest and deepest recession during the postwar period.

Notwithstanding the fact that the industrial economies and the most important regional economy, Japan, were mired in recession during the early 1990s, the Asia-Pacific region continued on its brisk growth path unabated. In the past, the region had depended heavily on the industrial countries for its growth, and for the first time it stopped relying on their economic bouyancy for its own brisk growth. A great deal of economic expansion in the region was being fed by the largest ever growth in foreign direct investment in China and the ASEAN countries. These economies were also receiving substantial portfolio investment, which is based on commercial considerations. During the 1991–93 period, China recorded an average GDP growth rate of 11.3 percent, in real terms. The economy is roaring on. This rapid economic expansion is continuing to force structural changes in the surrounding economies, particularly in the East Asian economies and Hong Kong. These economies are benefiting from productivity raising structural changes linked to the Chinese economic expansion. Australia and New Zealand had performed poorly in 1990. Both these economies had slid into recession in 1991. But over the following two years, the two countries not only came out of recession but also recorded impressive and accelerating growth rates.

Chapter 2

Dilip K. Das

AN INTRODUCTION TO THE REGIONAL ECONOMY

2.1 The Economic Takeoff

To the medieval Europeans, the Asia-Pacific region was something of a cornucopia and for a long time it was admired for the exotic aspects of its life and cultures. To the postwar world, it is the land of effervescent economic growth. Its rise can be traced back to the early 1960s when the Japanese economy came into its own. Since then several fundamental and far-reaching economic changes have taken place in the region and a new era of economic expansion had begun. It has outpaced all the other regions in terms of economic growth over the last three decades. Throughout the 1960s, Japan's GNP grew over 10 percent annually and it successfully exported its way out of all the exogenous economic disturbances of the 1970s. Japan was followed by the "four dragons" whose economic achievements surpassed that of Japan. Other Southeast Asian countries[1] and China followed close on the heels of the dragons. One country's economic growth helped others in the region such that it almost became a self-perpetuating economic expansion. These countries concentrated their energy on economic growth, pursued pragmatic macroeconomic policies and climbed the spiral of industrialization to become the most dynamic region of the international economy in a short time span. They demonstrated to the rest of the world that vigorous economic growth does not take a miracle. Herman Kahn, with some prescience, noted that the Asia-Pacific economies were turning into the center of world economic power. The center of international economic dynamism which used to be in the Mediterranean in the remote past, had moved to northwestern Europe and then to the north Atlantic. During the postwar period it moved again, to the Asia-Pacific region (Kahn 1979). This notion has not only acquired credibility but considerable international support and scholars have begun to use expressions like "the Pacific century" unabashedly (Vogel 1984; Linder 1986; Gibney 1992). In what follows, we trace the growth path of the Asia-Pacific economies from poor, struggling economies to international stardom, analyze the economic characteristics of each subregion and delve into the causal factors underlying their hypergrowth and economic transformation.

2.2 The Region Defined

The Asia-Pacific economies have been the subject of active interest and animated discussion among economists, industrialists, bureaucrats and politicians. Since the mid-1960s, when Professor Kiyoshi Kojima put forward his concept of an Asia-Pacific region, it has been variously defined, with each definition including its proponent's favorite country group, policy coverage and institutional arrangements. Kojima envisioned a two-tier Asia-Pacific region which included the five industrialized countries, namely, the U.S., Canada, Australia, New Zealand and Japan, as the core group. The developing countries of the region were of secondary importance and were to be the secondary partners in the regional economic grouping. He posited a Pacific free trade area (PAFTA) in 1966 involving mutual elimination of tariffs among the member economies while retaining them for nonmembers. Country groupings, and therefore acronyms, that developed over time included: (a) the Pacific Association for Trade and Development (PAFTAD), which had a strong economic flavor; (b) the Organization for Pacific Trade and Development (OPTAD), which was intended to be like the OECD (Organization for Economic Cooperation and Development) and had Sir John Crawford and Subiro Okita as its protagonists; (c) the Pacific Economic Cooperation Conference (PECC), which brought academics, businessmen and government officials informally together for the exchange of views regarding regional and international economies. The PECC publishes several economic and statistical publications regarding the Asia-Pacific region; (d) the Pacific Basin Economic Council (PBEC), which had a completely business community orientation; (e) the East Asia Economic Caucus (EAEC), which was proposed by the ASEAN (Association of Southeast Asian Nations) to economically unite it with Japan, China, Taiwan, Hong Kong, the Republic of Korea, Vietnam, Myanmar and the Pacific island nations but Japan declined to commit itself to the idea; and (f) the Asia-Pacific Economic Cooperation (APEC) forum, which was floated by the former Australian Prime Minister, R. L. J. Hawke, in 1989 and which initially received unenthusiastic support from Japan. By 1992, however, it had grown into a formal body of fifteen regional members, namely, the U.S., Canada, Mexico, Japan, Australia, New Zealand, China, Hong Kong, Taiwan,

South Korea, Thailand, Indonesia, Malaysia, Singapore and the Philippines. By the time of its fourth meeting in 1992, the membership question was still not settled. Questions were being asked such as: Why should Mexico be a member when several nations of Indochina and the Pacific islands are not?

In the background of a surfeit of definitions and concepts of the Asia-Pacific regional groupings, I am venturing to propose my own to include:

- Japan, the largest and pivotal Asia-Pacific economy
- Australia and New Zealand, two prosperous economies
- South Korea, Taiwan, Hong Kong and Singapore—four newly industrializing economies
- Indonesia, Malaysia, Thailand, the Philippines—the ASEAN-4—first three of which are among the better-performing developing economies
- China, a large developing economy which has recorded rather high growth rates over the 1980s.

The groupings of these twelve economies is based on economic norms. It brings together those economies of the East and Southeast Asia and Western Pacific that, with minor exceptions, have experienced dynamic growth in the immediate past because of their liberal, pragmatic and market-oriented macro-economic policies, outward-oriented industrialization strategy, and efficient resource allocation by way of rational prices; and whose governments are consciously committed to economic growth. The second feature of this group of economies is complementarity in terms of natural resources, technology and market size. The third characteristic which vindicates their being grouped together is an increasing dynamic cooperation and deepening interdependence among them since the early 1980s. The economies of Eastern Pacific are excluded because their inclusion will make this compact mutually cooperative and interactive—and therefore symbiotic—group sprawling and cumbersome, both functionally and conceptually. This is not to contend that the Eastern Pacific economies will not interact closely (as do the U.S. and Japan) with those of Asia-Pacific. They will, and some of them do so intensely, but they will relate to the Asia-Pacific group without belonging to it and will remain active external participants.

As seen in Figure 2.1, the Japanese economy, by virtue of its financial prowess, technological lead and the strength of the yen, and by virtue of the fact that it is the largest economy of the region, will be the epicentre of this economic grouping. It is an important determinant of the prosperity of the Asia-Pacific region. A lot of what Japan does will determine the future direction of the regional economy. With the four newly industrializing economies of East Asia and the two industrialized economies of Australasia interacting more closely with Japan than the ASEAN-4 and China, the Asia-Pacific region makes a compact, three-tier growth pole of the international economy. In the foreseeable future, it promises to be as dynamic as the other two growth poles of the international economy, namely, the European Community (EC) and the two North Atlantic economies, namely, the U.S. and Canada.

FIGURE 2.1   The Asia-Pacific economic groups

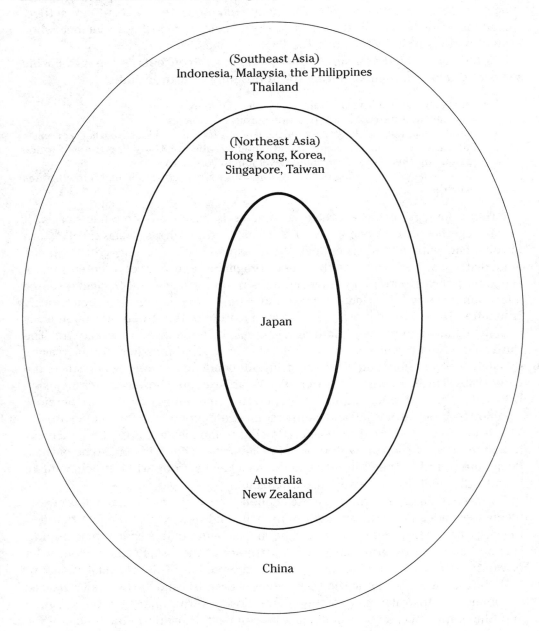

2.3 *Vivre La Difference*

The richness of diversity in the Asia-Pacific region is visible in land area, population, size of GDP and other indicators. For instance, the region includes China which has a huge land area of over 9.5 million square kilometers and a population of 1.1 billion. On the other hand, the region also includes small countries, called microstates, with areas under 1,000 square kilometers and with populations of under 10 million. Japan, the largest economy of the region, is an economic superpower having a per capita income of US$25,430 (Table 2.1). At the other extreme are the small economies like the Philippines, New Zealand, Malaysia, and Singapore, with GDPs of less than $50 million. The Philippines, Indonesia and China are the low income economies with per capita incomes of $730, $570 and $370, respectively. Japan, with 67 percent of the regional GDP, overwhelmingly dominates the regional economic stage. China and Australia are the second and third largest economies, accounting for 8.2 percent and 6.6 percent of the regional GDP, respectively.

Some countries are very densely populated while others are very sparsely populated. Most countries are a contiguous whole, but Indonesia and the Philippines are archipelagos, together having over 20,767 islands, ranging from small reefs to areas about the size of France. Japan, Korea and Taiwan are ethnically homogeneous societies while Malaysia, Indonesia, Singapore and Hong Kong are pluriracial and pluricultural.

TABLE 2.1   GDP and GNP of the Asia-Pacific countries

	GDP in 1990 (US$ million)	GDP as proportion of total regional GDP (%)	GNP per capita in 1990
Japan	2,942,890	66.8	25,430
Korea	236,400	5.4	5,400
Taiwan	144,820	3.3	7,997
Hong Kong	59,670	1.3	11,490
Singapore	34,600	0.8	11,160
Indonesia	107,250	2.4	570
Malaysia	42,400	0.9	2,320
Thailand	80,170	1.8	1,420
Philippines	43,860	1.0	730
Australia	296,300	6.6	17,000
New Zealand	42,760	0.9	12,680
China	364,900	8.2	370
Total	4,396,020	100.0	

Sources: World Bank, *World Development Report 1992*, Washington, DC, 1992. Data for Taiwan come from *Taiwan Statistical Data Book 1992*, Council for Economic Planning and Development, Taipei, Republic of China.

When growth began in the region, during the early 1960s, Japan was reconstructing its war-ravaged economy, China was in the throes of revolutionary turmoil, and Korea and Taiwan were abjectly poor. At this point, Australia and New Zealand were prosperous countries, although they were far from being matured industrial economies. Thus, while the majority of countries started growth from a low level, some started from a high base. There is a striking disparity in natural resource endowments, countries range from very poor to very rich. This diversity has been harnessed to deepen economic interdependence and maintain high growth in the region. As mentioned in Section 2.1, Japan posted high growth rates in the 1960s. In the 1970s and 1980s, it slowed but the four Asian newly industrializing economies (ANIEs) and the ASEAN-4 began to register high growth rates. The expansion of trade and investment in the region during the 1980s further stimulated growth in the ANIEs and the ASEAN-4. In addition, rapid growth in China during the 1980s was achieved through active economic interaction with the market economies of the region, which in turn contributed to the growth of the region. As discussed earlier, an interesting economic symbiosis has developed among the regional economies, with Japan providing capital, technology and markets, Australia, New Zealand and the ASEAN-4 natural resources and markets, and the ANIEs drawing in natural resources and providing capital and exports of manufactured goods. The stark complementarity between the Chinese and Japanese economies is sharply evident and has facilitated collaboration between the two.

2.4 Pioneering Growth

The Asia-Pacific region, particularly Japan and the ANIEs, has established itself as a trailblazer in the arena of economic growth. One active in *haute couture* will naturally be drawn to Paris, a connoisseur of art will head for Florence, while an economist interested in rapid growth and industrialization will find it impossible to take his mind away from Japan and the ANIEs because it is the most interesting and dynamic region of the world economy. Achievements of the Asia-Pacific economies were neglected during the 1960s. Myrdal's *magnum opus*, published in 1968, saw South Asian economies as the prototype of growth and the economies of the future. The world was enthralled by the superficial intricacies of their Five Year Plans and the vigor and direction that their governments were going to impart to these economies. The ANIEs did not come into focus until the publication of the Asian Development Bank's report in 1971. It was an influential work and set a new line of thinking about the Asia-Pacific economies. The superlative performance of Japan and the ANIEs changed what economists knew about economic growth and initiated a new orthodoxy. Adam Smith and classical economists could only partly explain this performance. Standard theories about the rise of capitalism and industrialization, *a la* Garnaut (1988), have begun to appear as inadequate as pre-Galilean astronomy.

The Asia-Pacific economies expanded faster than that of any other region in the world. During the postwar period, four waves of economic dynamism swept through them. The first one swept through Japan in the 1950s and the second one through the ANIEs followed close on its heels in the 1960s. The third wave struck the ASEAN group in the 1970s. The fourth struck and transformed the Chinese economy during the 1980s. Kuznets' (1971) authoritative work has no record of an economy doubling its GDP in a decade. Australia and the U.S. came close to performing this feat when the former averaged a 5.7 percent growth rate between the early 1860s and the mid-1880s and the latter averaged 5.5 percent a year for a period between the late 1860s and the early 1890s. Over the postwar period, five economies of the Asia-Pacific region achieved the rare feat of doubling GDP in a decade. They were Japan, South Korea, Taiwan, Hong Kong and Singapore. During the 1980s, China, through actively reforming its domestic economy and interacting with the market economies, became the sixth economy to achieve this distinction (Garnaut 1988). Thailand has maintained high growth rates for a long time and is heading the same way. While other countries in the Asia-Pacific region were experiencing rapid economic expansion, Australia and New Zealand had achieved the status of matured and industrialized, albeit small economies, growing at a sedate pace.

To be sure, there are considerable differences in the economic policies of the Asia-Pacific countries. For instance, on the one hand, there is the *laissez-faire* Hong Kong and on the other, there is Korea, where significant industrial policy interventionism took place. Yet there are several basic commonalties in macro-economic policies as well as common determinants of rapid growth in these economies. They recorded the highest rates of saving in the world. Government policies and fiscal incentives contributed indirectly to high domestic savings. Real interest rates were positive and from an international perspective, high. The government sector also made direct contribution to saving, particularly in Korea, Taiwan and China. High saving rates was one reason behind strong investment performance. External capital was another. Several Asia-Pacific economies supplemented domestic savings with external capital inflows whenever the resource gap seemed large. These countries, except the Philippines, were careful about not jeopardizing their external stability. High savings leading to high investment soon became a virtuous cycle, with one feeding on the other in a circular causation. Since a large proportion of national income was continually invested, capital stock expanded rapidly. Several Asia-Pacific economies kept a firm grip over their financial markets and forced them to serve the needs of the industrial sector during the initial phases of growth.

High investment certainly leads to technology upgradation and expansion of capital stock and explains better growth performance, but only partly. The classical view that factor input determines economic growth is now considered limited. Studies like those by Denison (1962) and Otani and Villanueva (1988) have shaken the classical view. Capital formation seems to explain only a small part of cross-country differences in growth rates. Cross-country comparisons, while confirming some correlation between high investment ratios and high growth rates, report weak correlation coefficients. In addition, there is the unanswered riddle of the direction of causality. A major part of growth performance is attributed to total factor productivity, generated by all encompassing, albeit ill defined, "residual factors." They include the human factor and Singapore's Senior Minister Lee Kuan Yew's "vital intangible,"[2] macroeconomic policy and improvement in resource allocation, institutional and structural characteristics, absorption of technology, efficiency of investment or incremental capital-output ratio (ICOR), provision of public goods, management and entrepreneurship.

Let us, therefore, turn to the residual factors in the case of the Asia-Pacific region. The high points of policy stance and economic characteristics enumerated below applied, in varying degrees, to all of them. First, an outstanding characteristic of the Asia-Pacific economies was their outward-oriented growth process, that is, growing ratio of foreign trade to GDP and domestic expenditure. International economic orientation contributed to both growth and stability. Economies that are internationally insolvent or have binding international liquidity constraints cannot grow. They are also highly vulnerable to debt traps. Rising exports of manufactures from these countries helped diversify export structures away from primary exports and thereby steadied their terms of trade. Outward economic expansion also established a second virtuous cycle, that of linking trade expansion to technological upgradation of the domestic industrial sector. Exporting firms came to acquire the wherewithal of importing advanced capital goods embodying state-of-the-art technology. Trade exposed them to the newest techniques and helped them focus on the art of the possible. These firms realized the importance of the technological edge necessary to stay competitive in the international markets. Brisk expansion of trade provided them with opportunities to specialize according to comparative advantage which, in turn, encouraged the exploitation of scale economies as well as the maintenance of high capacity utilization (Balassa and Williamson 1990). The Asia-Pacific economies ranging from Japan to the ASEAN-4 have been able to capture these dynamic gains from trade in addition to the static gains that were provided by improved resource allocation. Although only Hong Kong was a free-trading economy, other governments on various occasions supported the expansion of the manufacturing sector including manufacturing exports. Import tariffs were slapped on consumer imports at times for balance of payments reasons, however, the bias introduced by these tariffs was largely offset by export subsidies. Policy neutrality was more or less maintained.

Second, to stimulate export-oriented industrialization, countries of the Asia-Pacific region used both credit subsidies and financial repression (as in Korea) and fiscal subsidies (as in Taiwan). The former had side effects. For instance, with capital costs subsidized, the favored sectors tended to become capital intensive and large scale. In addition to providing loans at below market rates and possibly buying government debts at low interest rates, banks were forced to suppress deposit rates, which discouraged savings in the financial sector. Conversely, a fiscal subsidy on output or exports of favored industries does not have these side effects. Besides, the cost of credit subsidies is hidden in low deposit rates while the cost of fiscal subsidies is explicit in the tax structure (Bradford and Branson 1987).

Third, economic growth in the Asia-Pacific region was accompanied by rapid changes in the structure of production. The agricultural sector declined relatively while the importance of manufacturing and service sectors rose (cf. Section 2.7) and export specialization underwent an identical transformation. Structural changes continued steadily and by the 1970s, the developing economies of the Asia-Pacific region had made a considerable degree of progress in industrialization. Their economies had acquired a significant level of capital intensification.

Fourth, prudent and cautious macroeconomic management was another hallmark of these economies. In general they were low inflation economies. Over the 1980–90 period, in seven of them, the average long-term inflation rate was 5 percent or less. The best performers were Japan (1.5 percent), Malaysia (1.6 percent) and Taiwan (2.2 percent). The Philippines and New Zealand were the poorest performers with average inflation rates of 14.9 and 10.5 percent respectively. The World Bank associated higher growth with lower price distortions. The *World Development Report 1983* contained a price distortion index for 31 countries. It was prepared using measures of distortion of foreign exchange pricing, factor pricing and product pricing. It demonstrated that in the 1970s countries with higher government-induced distortions grew slowly. The *World Development Report 1985* showed that large price distortions also lead to slower growth of exports and greater likelihood of debt-servicing difficulties. Although distortions were there (as in Korea), in general the Asia-Pacific economies were identified with low levels of price distortions. In spite of this, these economies implemented numerous reforms in their industrial and trade policies as well as financial systems. During the 1980s, several of them adopted macroeconomic reforms that were conducive to growth. Some of them (Japan, Taiwan and Korea) had to adjust to external surpluses while others (Australia, New Zealand, Indonesia, Malaysia and Thailand) had to adjust to external deficits. Adoption of reform measures drove these economies to liberalization and efficiency-enhancing macroeconomic policies. Although Australia and Thailand were exceptions in this regard because they were forced to impose controls on capital movement while making structural adjustments, in general, governments in the region saw an opportunity to liberalize the economy while making macroeconomic adjustments. Freeing of market forces helped achieve optimal allocation of resources on the given production possibility curve in these economies and dynamic gains from international orientation of their economies helped in moving this curve outward.

Fifth, governments had high commitments to economic growth in these economies, which is a precondition of economic growth. It was given higher priority than social and welfare objectives. They intervened directly in the economic affairs to promote growth. Yet they were less intrusive in resourced allocation than in other developing economies and did not stifle market forces. Government policy in all these economies, including Indonesia after 1965, rejected public ownership over the means of production and centralized planning. These economies discovered early that the private sector is the high achiever. Market orientation of these economies facilitated the operation of price mechanisms. Therefore resources were able to move with relative ease from less to more productive uses. Reliance on markets for resource allocation also facilitated adjustments to domestic and external economic shocks. An exemplary case of the market and government collaborating is the phasing out of industries that were losing comparative advantage in Japan and ANIEs. These governments did not suffer from the soft state syndrome and were authoritarian in varying degrees, therefore rent-seeking groups were not able to dominate them. These groups have had a powerful influence on policy making in other market economies. Therefore these societies were able to pursue their economic goals in a more determined manner without frittering away their creative energy.

Sixth, much is made of the cultural values of the Asia-Pacific societies as a promoter of economic growth. These societies assign high value to formal education, personal discipline and an attitude of thrift. These proclivities are central to what is popularly described as Confucianism. This cultural tradition is the common property of Northeast and Southeast Asia, more so in the former than in the latter. Several of these traits, such as thrift, higher education and meritocracy, can be easily and closely associated with a capacity to sustain high levels of growth. Individual and social disciplines impart social cohesion and a readiness to accept change. Individuals and families react passively to short-term costs of change for its long-term promise and potential. They tend to rationalize the short-term pain and in the process create an environment of political stability, so necessary for stable economic growth. In addition, for centuries, the Sinic societies—Chinese, Japanese and Koreans—have shown intense respect for bureaucracy and officialdom. This made it possible for their modern governments to get away with their soft authoritarianism. Yet another trait is an almost religious regard for education, scholarship and learning. In the Confucian world the loci of wisdom and virtue were seen to interset. This has helped in creating skilled and well-educated workforces in the region. All these characteristics have decisive economic ramifications.

The rise of the Asia-Pacific countries to economic prominence has given new relevance to the age-old rhetoric enquiry of Simon Kuznets (1966). In the preface of his seminal book he had wondered whether the economic principles devised and followed in the West were suitable for universal application or were culture bound and had meaning and relevance for societies where they were created. In its quest for productive efficiency, the West came upon its rational model through its belief in individualism and successfully harnessed the forces of scientific creativity and technological innovation. As opposed to this, the Asia-Pacific societies traditionally emphasized human relations, group cohesion and harmony. When they launched into economic growth, they borrowed technology from the West through various modes of technology transfer. By marrying machines with their human-centered cultures, the Asia-Pacific countries achieved unparalleled economic growth. Western technology and Eastern ethos produced laudable economic results (Tai 1989). While, on the one hand, this mix is not a sufficient condition for economic growth, on the other, its success insinuates that if Western individualism was appropriate for the pioneering period of industrialization, it is likely that post-Confucianism "collectivism" is better suited to the age of mass industrialization and mass production (MacFarquhar 1990). The East Asian model has emerged as the first alternative to the rational Western model which was born at the dawn of the industrial revolution.

A little-known tendency of the post-Confucian countries, namely, Japan, Taiwan, Hong Kong, Singapore and Korea, is that they are singularly meritocratic, which has decisive economic ramifications. In their belief that people vary in calibre and have inherent genetic differences, these societies are Platonic. Plato categorized people into gold, silver and brass (Dore 1987). Meritocracy begins with children in schools, continues in universities and then in bureaucracies, both public and private. At all levels high performers are separated repeatedly from the mediocres. The system assumes that people legitimately deserve material rewards, prestige and power by virtue of their capabilities. Meritocracy identifies the high achievers, separates wheat from chaff, and rewards the deserving. Academic achievements, although important, are not the only determinants of success in a career. Other qualities like drive, determination and dynamism also play a role. The individuals who belong to the top of the ability spectrum are also judged for these qualities. They differentiate the high flyers on the seniority-promotion fast track from plodders on the slow track. Meritocracy, thus, allows the best possible use of human resources and contributes to institutional efficiency, which becomes easily visible in general efficiency and economic performance. By contrast, in other developing countries, for instance, those in South Asia, an individual of any calibre can be anywhere because these societies are not meritocratic. A capable individual can plod all through his career while a mediocre, low drive, lacklustre individual can be a high flyer on the fast track. The outcome of this tendency is also evident from the tardy economic performance of these resource rich economies.

Japan, the pioneer economy of the region, is so close to the other Asia-Pacific economies that such proximity—and propinquity—has to influence the other economies. They benefit from it both in a tangible and intangible manner; tangibly because they can easily and cheaply benefit from the exchange of goods and services, including financial services, and intangibly because they will be more prone to exchanging ideas and ambitions with a pioneer of their own geographical region than with those that are equally alluring but remotely located.

2.5 Subregional Transformations

Let us now focus on economic metamorphoses of each subgroup in the region and begin with Japan.

2.5.1 Japan

In the early 1950s, the economy had a dualistic structure and it depended heavily on the U.S. military procurement orders. The Engel coefficient for urban households in the mid-1950s was 45 percent, that is, almost half of the disposable income was being spent on food (Kosai 1986). This is considered a characteristic of a developing economy. The first good year that the economy had was 1955 when it recorded a 10 percent growth rate in real terms. This is referred to as Japan's beginning of *suryo* or quantitative prosperity. Industry consciously began to bridge the technology gap that existed between Japan and other industrialized economies and also began to develop export sectors. The earliest success was achieved by the shipbuilding industry. Export success gradually began to spread to other sectors and with that, domestic consumption and investment began to boom. The sudden rise in plant and equipment investment during the latter half of the 1950s produced a sea of change in the economy and by 1959 Japan had entered a period of prosperity called the Iwato boom. This upswing of the business cycle was durable and lasted for 42 months. It had an all pervading effect over the economy and the Japanese economy found itself on the crest of a technological revolution. Growth and modernization processes moved on a fast clip and facilitated the development of consumer durable sectors like the automobile and electrical machines and appliances sectors. The international economy was entering an era of mass production in several key consumer durable industries and worldwide demand for such products was strong. The establishment of the General Agreement on Tariffs and Trade (GATT) promoted free trade, which was to benefit Japan immensely.

The institutional competitiveness of Japanese exports continually increased because of its well conceived domestic and international strategy in this regard. It was based on properly laid down objectives, clear ideas on how to achieve them and provision of necessary institutional support by the government. The varying degrees of success in international competitiveness are explained by the differences in growth–productivity–resource orientation on the one hand and distribution–security–opportunity orientation on the other (Scott 1985). Japan fell in the former category. Although business and government collaborated closely and purposefully, the vital success ingredient was growth and the productivity orientation of both. It was firstly the growth orientation of *kaisha*, or the corporations, which was strengthened and nurtured by fierce domestic competition. Secondly, they were supported by a well-laid-out government strategy turning them into formidable international competitors (Abegglen and Stalk 1985). The growth–productivity orientation was based on the dynamic comparative advantage

(Higashi and Lanter 1990). Japan's export production was dominated by large firms because they had greater financial, personnel and material resources than small or medium sized firms and could absorb the effects of export price changes while deciding whether to slash prices or to shift into new products or businesses.

After the mid-1960s, Japan maintained its growth momentum and steadily caught up with the other industrialized economies. Measures of total factor productivity growth show (Balassa and Noland 1988) that it outperformed all the major industrial economies during the 1966–73 period. It fell behind France and Germany during the 1973–85 period but remained well ahead of the U.S. However, Japan constantly maintained its lead in capital formation. Its growth rate of capital formation was about double that of the other major industrial economies. By 1980, in the areas of industrial development, technological advancement, trade, managerial and organizational capability, Japan had become a power to reckon with and by the mid-1980s it emerged as the second largest economy, third largest trader and the largest creditor nation in the world. Towards the end of the decade it also became the largest donor and largest foreign investor (Das 1993).

2.5.2 Australia and New Zealand

They are two small, land rich, better off, industrial economies and, like Japan, members of the OECD. They have high per capita incomes and moderate growth rates. Their pattern of trade conforms more to their highly favorable endowment of land. Measured in terms of the volume of GDP, Australia is larger than Sweden and Switzerland while smaller than Spain. Its per capita GNP is comparable to Italy and the Netherlands. The GDP of New Zealand is comparable to that of Ireland while its per capita GNP is close to that of Belgium. Both the countries are sparsely populated. A rich natural resource base, together with domestic and external capital, and a long history of economic growth has helped provide the foundation for high living standards. Yet, the two countries have found it hard to sustain their relative position among the affluent countries. Since they have traditionally relied on agriculture and extractive industries for a great proportion of their export earnings, they found it progressively more difficult to create wealth which is comparable to that being generated by the technological societies into which other industrial countries have transformed themselves. Natural resources and primary products are still a large part of their foreign trade. Australia is a large exporter of coal, wool, wheat, beef and mineral ores, while New Zealand exports are dominated by meat, dairy products, wool and forestry products. Thus, these two economies depend heavily on exports of primary products for earning foreign exchange. Much like developing countries, they export primary goods to finance their imports of capital goods. Both economies have been recipients of foreign direct investment which brought technology and managerial skills with it. Since they relied on the other OECD economies for keeping up with technology, they had to rely on foreign direct investment. During the last three decades, in terms of growth rate and economic performance in general, Australia was far more dynamic than New Zealand.

The two economies have had three distinct eras: the first was the emigrant colonialism of the prewar period when they were providers of food and raw materials for industrial societies, particularly Britain. After 1945, the slow transition towards economic independence began. Traditional dependence on Britain in both trade and finance ended. This second phase was marked by extensive government interference in all aspects of the economy, financial controls and exchange restrictions. The third phase can be dated from the late 1970s when the two economies began to adjust to the international economy and discovered their place in the Asia-Pacific region.

The two economies have had periods of concern because their commodity and foodstuff exports to traditional markets in Europe and North America faced restrictions because of the intensification of protectionistic policies since the mid-1970s. Their exports failed to keep pace with the growing import bills and, therefore, they tended to give in readily to protect their domestic manufacturing sectors, at times at high costs. Japan's rise as a major industrial power changed the scene profoundly for them. With its voracious needs for industrial raw materials, it became a major trading partner of Australia and New Zealand. Japan also saw a large market for its manufactured and durable consumer goods exports in these two regional neighbors. Economic interdependence and common strategic interests has brought the three economies close and the mutual affinity is likely to grow. Over the 1980s, Korea also became a significant trading partner of Australia and New Zealand, and the economic ties were substantially strengthened with China, Taiwan and the ASEAN-4. In the process the two economies have successfully carved a regional niche for themselves. Their future growth prospects largely depend on their success in increasing efficiency within their economies as well as growth in the regional and international economies.

The two countries entered a free trade agreement called the New Zealand–Australia Free Trade Agreement (NAFTA) in 1965 and another one called the Australia–New Zealand Closer Economic Relations Trade Agreement (ANCER) in 1983. The key difference between the agreements is that the latter aimed at freeing trade in all goods across the Tasman from restrictions—although a small number of products were specifically set aside for later consideration—while the objectives of NAFTA were less ambitious. It aimed at progressively liberalizing trade in specified goods. The ANCER had a far larger scope. It was intended to eventually establish a trans-Tasman free trade zone by phasing out all tariff, quantity and other restrictions on trade between the two partners. Subsequently the agreement was extended to free up trade-in services and to consider ways of harmonizing business laws (Australia 1986). Both the partners benefited from the ANCER, with New Zealand deriving greater benefits than Australia. This difference in gains is partly accounted for by the fact that Australia is a much more important trading partner for New Zealand than New Zealand is for Australia (Australia 1989).

2.5.3 Asian Newly Industrializing Economies (ANIEs)

The success of the four ANIEs has attracted a great deal of professional and popular interest. They were extensively studied and immense literature exists on their economic growth and its rationale.[3] As indicated earlier, although the "four dragons" began to breathe fire in the 1960s, their achievements were not recognized until the early 1970s. The publication of *Industry and Trade in Some Developing Countries* (Little et al. 1970) was an important step in this direction. These four economies took a leaf out of the book of Japan's economic success and pursued an export-oriented strategy of deliberate promotion of manufacturing goods exports in keeping with their comparative advantage. They saw wisdom in shunning import-substitution after the initial stages of growth and exploited dynamic gains from trade and reaped the benefits of their comparative advantage. The result was an exemplary economic performance. They recorded very high rates of GDP growth which in turn was associated with their high rate of export volume growth. These countries are poorly endowed with natural resources. Initially their exports were concentrated on traditional and labor-intensive manufactured products, then they progressed to capital- and technology-intensive manufactured goods. By the early 1990s, they had begun to make forays into the knowledge-intensive product markets.

A certain set of preconditions existed in these economies when they began their hypergrowth. They included: a well educated and disciplined labor force, competent bureaucracy, social and governmental commitment to economic growth, market-oriented domestic economic strategy and a dominant role for the private sector. The small public sector that existed was largely regarded as a good performer (Amsden 1989; Chang and Singh 1992). In addition, the international economic environment of the 1950s and 1960s was aptly suited for the outward-oriented growth strategy of the ANIEs. These unusual preconditions assisted their brisk takeoff into high and sustained growth.

The high level of human capital raised the technological level in the ANIEs in a short time span. They also maintained significant growth rates in savings and capital accumulation. However, there were other developing economies that failed to take off despite comparable rates of saving and investment. The ANIEs must have done something extra to achieve what they did. While most other developing economies remained wedded to ideologically oriented development doctrines promoted by institutions like the United Nations Conference on Trade and Development (UNCTAD) and stressed basic needs, income distribution (before growth and production) and other social objectives, the ANIEs were influenced by the resurgence of neoclassical economics in the 1960s and adopted clear, pragmatic neoclassical policy lines. Sound macroeconomic policies and, in general, high quality economic management, were among the basic reasons of their economic success. Their economic strategy and management was characterized by pragmatism and flexibility. Conversely, the outcome of ideologicially oriented economic policies and poor quality economic management can be seen in the shoddy performance of South Asian developing economies, which has continued decade after decade.

The mainstream neoclassical economists and Western model of free enterprise both preclude governments from the running of the economy and spurn government intervention. Three of the ANIEs had all pervasive government presence in their economic affairs, Hong Kong was the only exception. So much so that governments went into such detailed decision making as "picking the winners." However, the intervention was of a rather different kind. It did not replace markets, only guided them. It was not a market subduing or distorting intervention but a market-conforming variety, little understood in the context of Western-style capitalism. The soft authoritarianism of these governments gave the ANIEs basic directions without smothering the market forces and destroying domestic competition. This strategy supported the survival-of-the-fittest kind of industrialization, thereby improving the efficiency of resource allocation. Instead of being counterproductive, this kind of government intervention enhanced economic efficiency because governments adopted policies to compensate for the weaknesses of the free enterprise system. The negative externalities were identified and taken care of by the governments. For instance, an important externality for developing countries is the cost of selling in the world market. The developing country's exports have to counter the quality bias and individual enterprises cannot bear the cost of countering the bias and creating a market niche without government support. Another area which benefits from government intervention was that of the market cost of labor which often tends to be higher than the social cost of labor. Thus, in the ANIEs, intervention lubricated the economies instead of thwarting them.

Lastly, emphasis on private enterprise, concomitantly existing with domestic and international competition, contributed to making ANIEs resilient. Private sector enterprises, without competition, would have resulted in private monopolies which in turn would have been as pernicious as the public sector ones. The experience of the ANIEs buttresses the dictum that competition is value creating.

2.5.4 The ASEAN-4

In the oft used metaphor of "flying geese," Japan leads a formation of Asia-Pacific economies, followed by the ANIEs, with the ASEAN-4 coming last. This subgroup has learned a great deal from the economic and technological experiences of the economies that preceded it in the "flying geese" formation. Japan and the ANIEs were *sui generis* only to a limited extent because the ASEAN-4 were able to replicate their performance to a considerable degree. The ASEAN-4 also gained immensely from economic cooperation with them. Noteworthy in this context is the Malaysian campaigns to "look East" and "learn from Japan." ASEAN was established in a low-key manner in 1967, initially without any economic ambitions. However, it soon began to make economic cooperation related overtures and the federation of the

ASEAN Chamber of Commerce and Industry was established in 1971 for cooperation among private enterprises.

Although they were neighbors, their economic ties were initially tenuous. They were well endowed with natural resources and, therefore, were suppliers of industrial raw materials and foodstuffs. Their exports were strongly specialized in primary products. With rapid industrialization, significant structural change occurred over the 1970s. Growth in manufactured exports began which received impetus from the huge expansion in world trade that took place in the early 1970s. The share of manufactured goods in total exports increased considerably in all of them except Indonesia, where it was negligibly small to begin with. Trade expansion enabled these countries to establish extensive links with a wide range of countries, especially the industrialized economies. While promoting, these economies did not neglect their agricultural sectors because they were essentially land-based economies. Consequently, per capita food production rose steadily. Indonesia recorded the minimum rate of growth of food production.

The economic philosophy of the ASEAN-4 was generally one of pragmatic flexibility, bending with international economic developments and responding to external changes with economic prudence. At an early stage in their industrialization process, they began to show a healthy respect for outward looking strategy. This strategy is known to create pressure for adopting better monetary, exchange rate and labour policies. Nevertheless, the blemish of high tariff rates (in the 30 to 60 percent range) continued in Thailand, Indonesia and the Philippines. In many cases these tariffs were unbound. During the first half of 1993, these economies were attempting to grapple with this distortion. In the ASEAN-4 countries, macroeconomic management is considered high quality (Arndt 1989). These countries increasingly allowed market forces to drive their economies, which, coupled with outward orientation, enhanced functional efficiency and the efficiency of resource allocation. Also, it is generally agreed that external factors influenced the growth process in the ASEAN-4 significantly (Chintayarangsan et al. 1992).

Owing to recession, the early 1980s were lean years for these economies but their decadal average growth rate was the highest for any region in the world. They attracted a good deal of foreign direct investment due to rapid growth and prudent economic management. A major part of foreign direct investment went into high technology industries. By the early 1990s, Malaysia had become the largest exporter of integrated circuits in the world. Their eagerness to emulate the ANIEs and Japan is obvious.

2.5.5 China

During the economic restoration period of 1950–57, the economy grew at an average rate of around 8 percent per year but the brisk growth abruptly collapsed with the "Great Leap Forward" (1958–60). However, despite reversals and the chaos of a decade long (1966–76) cultural revolution, China's economic performance was not abjectly dismal. Long-term average output grew by over 5 percent per year, although the per capita rise was much lower. Initially growth in output was entirely made through contributions from increasing the labor force. The high savings rate helped build capital but the ICOR was also high and the efficiency of investment remained low. Being a neighbor, China could not help being impressed by the achievements of Japan and the ANIEs. Through the socialistic economic haze, it saw the economic benefits potentially attainable from dismantling its myriad price and quantity controls, having a market economy and adopting open trade policies. The realization that the complexities of the socialistic economic system was taking a heavy toll on efficiency and output had set in well by the end of the cultural revolution and 1976 marked the beginning of the implementation of what became the political economy of reform and economic opening. The reform measures were first introduced gingerly but decisively after the third plenary meeting of the Eleventh Communist Party Central Committee in December 1978. This became an epochal point in modern Chinese economic history. This was the beginning of a sweeping set of economic reforms, popularly known as the "open door" policy.

Several liberalization and open market reform measures were initiated in the early 1980s and they were strengthened in a stronger wave of reforms in 1984. The former, import-substituting industrialization, strategy was almost abandoned. Commitment to reform was steady and several missing elements of the Japan–ANIEs formula were eagerly institutionalized. Society supported the new economic ideology and accepted the use of markets for the allocation of resources in lieu of the central planning authority. The operation of market forces first began in the rural economy and after 1984 entered the urban economy. The opening up of the economy enabled the absorption of much needed technology from abroad as well as the inflow of foreign direct investment (World Bank 1985b, 1989). Consequences of liberalization and reforms were clearly visible in China's growth rate. Real GNP grew by an average of almost 9 percent per year over the 1978–91 period, a rate that doubles the size of the economy every eight years. Thus, liberalization and reforms paid off handsomely. The economy acquired a great deal of momentum and by the early 1990s was bursting with life. When the republics of the former USSR next door were close to bankruptcy, China had over US$40 billion in foreign exchange reserves and was attracting plenty of foreign direct investment. More than $1 billion worth of Chinese funds were floated in the West in the early 1990s and investors' response was highly favorable (*The Economist* 1992). China tried to integrate with the surrounding Asia-Pacific economies, especially with Japan.

Hindsight reveals that in spite of commitment to economic reforms, China's course has been a zig-zag one. It needs to stay on course because the part of the economy that is being run by the central planning authorities was operating poorly even in the early 1990s. A third of the state-owned enterprises were money-losers and twice as many were really in the red. Fortuitously, half the industrial output at this point was accounted for by firms that were not state-owned but were owned by market-sensitive lower-tier governments, private individuals and foreign investors. In addition, problems related to poor infrastructure continue to dog the economy. The Fourteenth National Congress of the Chinese Community Party in October 1992 attempted to institutionalize politically the open market reforms and turn China into a "socialist market economy," which appears to be an oxymoron. During the Congress, it was acknowledged that the operating principles should be as follows: that macroeconomic tools are better instruments of economic control, that the plan should be nothing more than strategic targets, that infrastructure investment should be the government's prerogative, that the government should no longer manage industrial enterprises, that bureaucracy must be shrunk as must employment in state enterprises and that more attention should be paid to the services sector for absorbing surplus labor (Byrnes 1992). This is the famous thesis of patriarch Deng Xiaoping and represents the current proclivity of the managers of the Chinese economy. Japan will serve as a key model for the relationship between the government and industry as China switches to a market economy (Mitsumori and Meshino 1992). Indications are that the reform revolution will roll on and in the short term, consumerism will supplant communism.

2.6 Economic Ascension

The long-term growth rate is a good indicator of economic dynamism because: (a) it eliminates short-term variations; and (b) it reveals whether the growth was a sustained feature or a mere period-specific event caused by some favorable internal or external developments. The average GNP growth of the Asia-Pacific economies and that of other country groups over the 1965–90 period is given in Table 2.2. The

TABLE 2.2   **Comparative average annual GNP growth rates, 1965–90**

Country/region	%
Japan	4.1
ANIEs	7.1
ASEAN-4	3.6
Australia and New Zealand	1.5
China	5.8
Asia-Pacific region	**4.6**
Sub-Saharan Africa	0.2
South Asia	1.9
Middle East and North Africa	1.8
Latin America and the Caribbean	1.8
OECD countries	2.4
United States	1.7

Sources: World Bank, *World Development Report 1992*. Data for Taiwan come from *Taiwan Statistical Data Book 1992*, Council for Economic Planning and Development, Taipei, Republic of China.

group average for Asia-Pacific was 4.6 percent. The performance of none of the other country groups is comparable to that of the Asia-Pacific region. The second best performing region, the OECD economies, had an average GNP growth rate of 2.4 percent, which is half of the Asia-Pacific growth rate.

The brisk growth rate of the Asia-Pacific economies led to a more than fourfold economic expansion of their GDP in real terms over the 1965–89 period (Table 2.3). The North American and West European economies, which comprises the other two growth poles of the global economy, doubled their respective GDPs over the same period and the world GDP increased by 2.2 times. This growth pattern enhanced the weight of the Asia-Pacific region in the international economy. Its GDP was 13.6 percent of the total world GDP in 1965. By 1989, its share rose to 25.3 percent, while both the pre-established growth poles lost ground. Rapid economic expansion has established the Asia-Pacific region as the third growth pole of the international economy. However, as seen in Table 2.4, it is still the smallest of the three in terms of the volume of GDP. The future need not be a repetition of the past and economic growth during the 1990s may not be at a fast clip. The expansionary phase of the business cycle that began in Japan in November 1986 ended in 1991. Several indices began to show "plateau condition" and corporate earning rates hit the ceiling. Notwithstanding the slowdown of the dominating Japanese economy, no one expects the region to lose its momentum. Its catching up process with the other two growth poles will therefore continue.

As seen in Table 2.4, there were marked intraregional differences in economic expansion. The mantle of greatest dynamism fell on the ANIEs because their longterm (1965–90) average GNP growth rate was 7.1 percent. Taiwan and Korea recorded an outstanding 8.5 and 7.1 percent respectively. China, as noted earlier, did not do poorly, as this indicator shows, recording a respectable 5.8 percent long-term average. Japan followed with 4.1 percent. By the early 1980s, it had become a matured industrial economy and its growth rate had stabilized at a

TABLE 2.3 Comparative GDP at constant prices, 1965–90 (in 1987 US dollars, in billions)

	1965	1970	1980	1989
Asia-Pacific countries	919	1515	2473	3759
	(13.6)	(17.6)	(20.6)	(25.3)
United States and Canada	2597	3030	4016	5271
	(38.6)	(35.2)	(33.4)	(35.4)
European Community of 12	2252	2821	3771	4548
	(33.5)	(32.7)	(31.3)	(30.6)
World	6719	8618	12030	14867
	(100.0)	(100.0)	(100.0)	(100.0)

Figures in parentheses stand for percentage of total world GDP.

Source: International Economic Data Bank, Australian National University, Canberra.

TABLE 2.4   GDP and GNP growth, 1965–90 (%)

	GDP as a proportion of world GDP				Average annual growth rate of GNP per capita over 1965–90
	1965	1970	1980	1989	
Japan	10.0	13.5	14.9	17.7	4.1
Korea	0.3	0.4	0.6	1.1	7.1
Taiwan	0.2	0.3	0.5	0.8	8.5
Hong Kong	0.1	0.1	0.2	0.4	6.2
Singapore	0.1	0.1	0.1	0.2	6.5
Indonesia	0.3	0.3	0.4	0.6	4.5
Malaysia	0.3	0.4	0.6	1.0	4.0
The Philippines	0.2	0.2	0.3	0.3	4.4
Thailand	0.2	0.2	0.3	0.4	1.3
Australia	1.2	1.3	1.2	1.4	1.1
New Zealand	0.2	0.1	0.1	0.1	1.9
China	0.8	1.1	1.4	2.3	5.8
Regional average	13.6	17.6	20.6	25.3	4.6

Source: International Economic Data Bank, Australian National University, Canberra.

lower level than that in the earlier decades. In addition, it suffered from the *endaka* recession in the mid-1980s (Das 1993). Among the ASEAN-4, the Philippines remained a languorous economy and pulled down the long-term average of the group to 3.6 percent. The other three members averaged 4 percent or higher. Since this group was a late boomer, their decadal average for the 1980s was close to 10 percent. Again, the Philippines was an exception. Australia and New Zealand recorded a sedate 1.5 per cent average annual growth over this period. Table 2.4 also shows that between 1965 and 1989, the share of GDP of the ANIEs in the world GDP quadrupled. It soared from 0.7 percent of the world GDP in 1965 to 2.5 percent in 1989. Korea, Taiwan and Hong Kong all quadrupled their respective shares. China raised its share by a multiple of 2.9 and the ASEAN-4 by a multiple of 2.3. Japan came close to doubling its share of the world GDP. Australia and New Zealand did not expand their share but stood their ground and maintained their share of the world GDP.

Starting from a low economic level, several countries of the Asia-Pacific region achieved per capita income levels comparable to the poorer countries of the European Community. Korea surpassed Portugal in terms of 1990 per capita income and Taiwan came ahead of Greece as well as oil-rich Saudi Arabia. Singapore and Hong Kong were better off than Spain and almost as rich as New Zealand. Living standards of Italy and Britain were not very far those of these two countries. Malaysian per capita income was 71 percent higher than that of Turkey.

The openness of the Asia-Pacific economies progressively increased. If export, as a proportion of GDP, is taken as a measure of openness (Table 2.5), the

TABLE 2.5   Exports as percentage of GDP

	Japan	ANIEs	ASEAN-4	ANZ	China	Regional average
1965	5.2	18.0	26.6	11.9	6.8	8.5
1970	6.6	26.4	26.7	13.4	8.2	9.2
1980	10.8	50.1	31.0	15.4	10.8	15.2
1989	14.2	72.1	35.8	17.7	15.2	21.2

Source: International Economic Data Bank, Australian National University, Canberra.

performance of the ANIEs turns out to be outstanding. In the short time span of a quarter of a century, exports soared from 18 percent of the GDP to 72.1 percent. ASEAN-4 did well but their endeavors on this count were concentrated during the latter half of the 1970s and the 1980s. In 1989, exports were 35.8 percent of their GDP. The ANIEs and the ASEAN-4 became the most open economies in the world. Australia and New Zealand (ANZ), like other industrial economies, were fairly open even in the mid-1960s and have since slowly opened their economies further. As the statistics indicate, China's opening up began in earnest after the adoption of the "open door" policy, that is, over the 1980s. Also, Japan has shown a steady rise in opening up. For the region as a whole, the progress seems steady, appearing to have accelerated after the 1970s.

The openness of an economy must be closely associated with its export growth rate and economic integration with regional and nonregional economies. In conformance with this observation, the ANIEs recorded the highest long-term real growth rate of exports. During the 1965–89 period, their exports grew annually at the average rate of 15.5 percent (Table 2.6). The ASEAN came next with a group average of 7 percent. Indonesia and the Philippines lagged behind because they were slow to open and, therefore, the least open economies in the group. Note that all these economies began their exports from a very low level, therefore, statistics do hide the low base effect. Japan recorded 9.9 percent. Again, the long-term average has been adversely influenced by languid performance over the 1980s. For China, the long-term average was 8 percent and, unlike Japan, this figure has been favorably influenced by its performance over the 1980s. The average growth rate of exports for the Asia-Pacific region was 10.1 percent which is almost twice as high as that for the U.S., the European Community of 12, as well as the developing countries. Thus, the region's export performance was outstanding. Its outward orientation paid off richly. Was the trade-related dynamic growth of the Asia-Pacific countries externally driven or internally generated? Was it the demand-side variables that principally determined the dynamic export growth or the supply-side factors? James Riedel went to considerable length in his statistical investigation to answer these queries and concluded that international trade expansion only worked as "the handmaiden" of growth for the Asia-Pacific region, not the "engine of growth". He found evidence that suggested that it was the supply-side rather

TABLE 2.6   Real growth rate of exports, 1965–89 (exports measured in constant 1987 US dollars)

	%	%
Japan	9.9	
Korea	18.7	
Thailand	9.5	15.5
Hong Kong	11.1	
Singapore	11.3	
Indonesia	5.4	
Malaysia	8.2	7.0
The Philippines	5.5	
Thailand	9.6	
Australia	5.1	4.9
New Zealand	4.2	
China	8.0	
Average for Asia-Pacific countries		10.1
United States and Canada		5.9
European Community of 12		5.6
Developing countries		5.6
World		6.0

Source: International Economic Data Bank, Australian National University, Canberra.

than demand-side factors that were primarily responsible for the dynamic export performance (Riedel 1984). He categorically rejected the premise that the exports performance of the region was externally driven.

Such an aggressive export performance resulted in steep rises in the volume of exports from the region. They doubled to US$37 million between 1965 and 1970 and increased to $291 million in 1980 which was an eightfold increase in a decade (Table 2.7). In 1990, they reached $715 million, which is again two and a half times that of a decade ago. In 1965, the Asia-Pacific countries accounted for a puny 11.4 percent of total world exports. This proportion did not rise much in 1970 but in 1980 they had begun to account for 15 percent of total world exports. In 1990, this proportion was as high as 22 percent. Japan has traditionally dominated exports from the region. In 1965, it accounted for 42.6 percent of total exports from the region. In 1970, the corresponding proportion rose to 52.1 percent and further to 66.1 percent in 1980. Japan's domination of the regional exports kept increasing. However, the situation was reversed in 1990 when Japan's dominance came down to 40.1 percent of the total exports of the Asia-Pacific region. Other large exporters in the region are China, Taiwan, Korea and Singapore.

Between 1965 and 1990, Japan doubled its share in world exports and accounted for 8.81 percent of the total (Figure 2.2). The ANIEs expanded their share of the

Dilip K. Das

TABLE 2.7 Export expansion from the Asia-Pacific economies, 1965–90

Country	1965		1970		1980		1990	
	Exports (US$ million)	As proportion of total world exports (%)	Exports (US$ million)	As proportion of total world exports (%)	Exports (US$ million)	As proportion of total world exports (%)	Exports (US$ million)	As proportion of total world exports (%)
Japan	8,452	4.87	19,319	6.61	129,542	6.67	286,768	8.81
Korea	175	0.10	830	0.28	17,446	0.90	64,837	1.99
Taiwan	450	0.26	1,428	0.49	19,837	1.02	67,040	2.06
Hong Kong	880	0.51	2,037	0.70	13,672	0.70	29,002	0.89
Singapore	981	0.57	1,554	0.53	19,375	1.00	62,627	1.62
Indonesia	722	0.42	1,055	0.36	21,909	1.13	25,553	0.78
Malaysia	1,206	0.69	1,687	0.58	12,939	0.67	31,505	0.97
Philippines	766	0.44	1,060	0.36	5,751	0.30	9,134	0.28
Thailand	607	0.35	685	0.23	6,369	0.33	23,002	0.71
Australia	2,971	1.71	4,482	1.53	21,279	1.10	35,973	1.10
New Zealand	979	0.56	1,203	0.41	5,262	0.27	9,045	0.28
China	1,643	0.95	1,768	0.60	17,481	0.90	80,529	2.47
Regional average	19,831	11.42	37,108	12.69	290,863	14.98	715,016	21.96

Source: International Economic Data Bank, Australian National University, Canberra.

FIGURE 2.2 Exports of the Asia-Pacific economies as share of total world exports, 1965–90

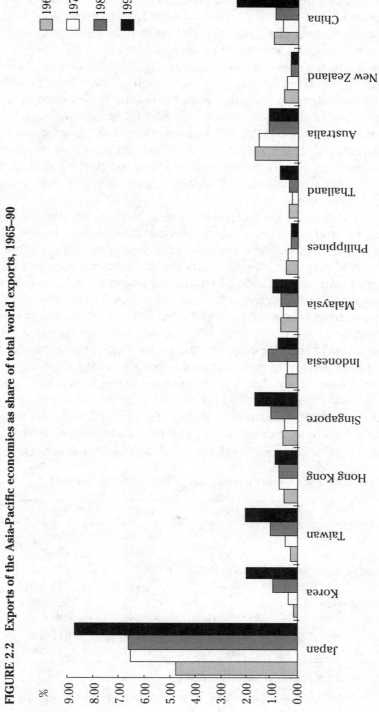

world trade from 1.4 percent of the total to 6.6 percent while the ASEAN-4 expanded its share from 1.9 per cent to 2.7 percent over the same period. These dramatic jumps should be interpreted carefully. The small base effect is obvious for these two subgroups. China succeeded in raising its share of world trade by a multiple of 2.6. Conversely, the share of Australia and New Zealand slipped drastically from 2.3 percent to 1.4 percent because the two countries lacked the drive in exports.

Table 2.8 indicates that the Asia-Pacific economies have gained in international trade at the expense of the U.S. and Canada. The EC has strengthened its position. Until the mid-1970s, the Asia-Pacific region did not hold a position of significance on the international trade scene, although certain countries were doing well. However, largely because of the extraordinarily good performance of the ANIEs, Thailand and China during the 1980s, the region gained a high profile on the international trade scene.

Initially, a dominant part of their exports comprised labour-intensive and resource-based products. This is how industrialization begins. However, soon these economies began to export light manufactured products. Manufactured goods are high value-added goods and their exports are an important indicator representing the competitive strength of the industrial sector and economic maturity in general. In 1965, the Asia-Pacific region accounted for a mere 10.85 percent of the total exports of manufactures in the world (Table 2.9). In 1990, this proportion was 24.78 percent or a quarter of total world exports of manufactures. In the early years these exports were heavily dominated by Japan. For instance, in 1965, it accounted for 73 percent of manufactured exports from the region and in 1970 for 74.4 percent. However, by 1980, other countries in the region were participating more actively and Japan accounted for only 61.1 percent of the total. In 1990, this proportion had further plummeted to 46.9 percent due to active manufactured export drives by China, Taiwan, Korea and to a lesser extent by Singapore and Hong Kong. Over the 1965–90 period, the ANIEs raised their share of world markets

TABLE 2.8   Comparative export performance, 1965–90 (US$ million)

	1965	1970	1980	1990
Asia-Pacific countries	19,831	37,108	290,863	715,016
	(11.42)	(12.69)	(14.98)	(21.96)
United States and Canada	35,110	58,775	275,992	496,522
	(20.22)	(20.10)	(14.22)	(15.25)
European Community of 12	65,885	116,125	687,847	1,349,580
	(37.94)	(39.70)	(35.43)	(41.45)
World	173,650	292,475	1,941,181	3,255,825
	(100.0)	(100.0)	(100.0)	(100.0)

Figures in parentheses stand for percentage of total world trade.

Source: International Economic Data Bank, Australian National University, Canberra.

TABLE 2.9 Export of manufactures from the Asia-Pacific economies, 1965–90

Country	1965		1970		1980		1990	
	Export of manufactures (million US$)	As % of total world exports of manufactures	Export of manufactures (million US$)	As % of total world exports of manufactures	Export of manufactures (million US$)	As % of total world exports of manufactures	Export of manufactures (million US$)	As % of total world exports of manufactures
Japan	7,704	7.92	18,024	9.92	124,028	11.32	279,436	11.63
Korea	104	0.11	635	0.35	15,686	1.43	60,675	2.53
Taiwan	187	0.19	1,087	0.60	17,441	1.59	62,112	2.59
Hong Kong	823	0.85	1,954	1.08	13,194	1.20	27,784	1.16
Singapore	336	0.35	474	0.26	10,452	0.95	38,315	1.60
Indonesia	27	0.03	15	0.01	533	0.05	9,061	0.38
Malaysia	73	0.07	125	0.07	2,464	0.22	17,263	0.72
Philippines	43	0.04	80	0.04	2,118	0.19	5,905	0.25
Thailand	19	0.02	55	0.03	1,788	0.16	14,783	0.62
Australia	432	0.44	846	0.47	5,588	0.51	13,004	0.54
New Zealand	53	0.05	132	0.07	1,062	0.10	2,255	0.09
China	752	0.77	797	0.44	8,517	0.78	64,693	2.69
Regional average	10,552	10.85	24,224	13.33	202,872	18.51	595,289	24.78

Source: International Economic Data Bank, Australian National University, Canberra.

in manufactured goods from 1.5 percent to 7.9 percent while the ASEAN-4 raised theirs from 1.6 percent to 2.9 percent. As in the case of exports, the low base effect is obvious for these two subgroups. Australia and New Zealand did not capture markets in manufactures in 1990 to any greater extent than they had in 1965. Conversely, China, after a poor performance up till 1980, succeeded in raising its market share by three and a half times during the 1980s (Figure 2.3).

Growing participation of the Asia-Pacific economies in international trade in manufactures is apparent from Table 2.10. Their significance grew considerably over the 1980s. At the beginning of the decade, the Asia-Pacific economies and the North American growth pole were neck to neck in terms of volume of manufactured exports. However, by 1990, the Asia-Pacific region had left North America far behind and had almost 70 percent higher exports. The EC maintained its position of strength, essentially due to intratrade in manufactures.

Japan, Taiwan and Korea have emerged as net foreign investors in the international economy. Of course, Japan is the largest foreign investor. Going by the *International Financial Statistics*, net foreign direct investment made by Japan in 1980 was a skimpy US$2.1 billion. It soared to $46.3 billion in 1990, making Japan the largest foreign investor in the world. In 1991, the investment level fell to $29.4 billion because of financial turmoil in Japan. Korea recorded a tiny net foreign investment of US$7 million in 1980. This amount rose to $105 million in 1990 and to $241 million in 1991. Taiwan also turned into a substantial net investor during the latter half of the 1980s. Its investments rose and reached US$5.3 billion in 1990.

Table 2.11 shows that Japan turned into a net exporter of capital through portfolio investment in 1983. Taiwan, Korea, Malaysia and Singapore also began to make portfolio investment abroad in a relatively small way during the latter half of the 1980s. China began to do so in 1989, although investments were not substantial until 1991.

TABLE 2.10   Comparative performance in export of manufactures (US$ million)

	1965	1970	1980	1990
Asia-Pacific countries	19,831	37,108	290,863	715,016
	(11.42)	(12.69)	(14.98)	(21.96)
United States and Canada	35,110	58,775	275,992	496,522
	(20.22)	(20.10)	(14.22)	(15.25)
European Community of 12	65,885	116,125	687,847	1,349,580
	(37.94)	(39.70)	(35.43)	(41.45)
World	1,736,050	292,475	1,941,181	3,255,825
	(100.0)	(100.0)	(100.0)	(100.0)

Figures in parentheses stand for percentage of total world trade in manufactures.

Source: International Economic Data Bank, Australian National University, Canberra.

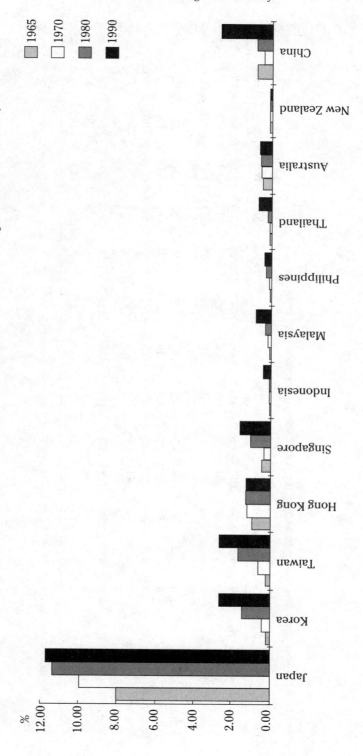

FIGURE 2.3 The Asia-Pacific economies' exports of manufactures as share of total world exports of manufactures, 1965–90

Dilip K. Das

TABLE 2.11 Portfolio investment in and by the Asia-Pacific economies (US$ million)

Country	1965	1970	1975	1980	1981	1982	1983	1984	1985	1986	1987	1988	1989	1990	1991
Japan	80	250	2590	9430	7670	840	-2900	-23960	-41750	-102040	-91330	-51750	-32530	-14490	35450
Korea	0	0	0	40	60	15	188	333	982	301	-113	-482	-29	811	–
Taiwan	–	–	–	45	85	145	41	-50	-46	69	-371	-1711	-902	-1006	45
Hong Kong															
Singapore	0	0	-2	13	-48	-29	-49	-151	175	-549	252	-293	324	287	232
Indonesia	0	0	0	46	47	315	368	-10	-35	268	-88	-98	-173	0	0
Malaysia	88	-28	268	-11	1131	601	668	1108	1942	30	140	-448	-107	-255	170
Thailand	0	13	1	96	44	68	108	155	895	-29	346	530	1486	-38	–
The Philippines	–	3	27	4	3	1	7	-3	5	13	19	50	280	-50	110
Australia	128	456	417	1896	673	2399	1183	736	2144	1188	4325	5834	377	1970	4842
New Zealand	0	0	0	0	0	0	0	0	0	0	0	0	88	30	–
China	–	–	–	–	–	41	20	83	742	1567	1051	876	-180	-241	-7558

Source: International Economic Data Bank, Australian National University, Canberra.

The foregoing exposition has convincingly established that the Asia-Pacific region has emerged as the third growth pole of the international economy. Unprecedented growth in GDP, fast clip expansion in exports (especially exports of manufactured products) expansion in foreign direct investment and portfolio investment, and other economic achievements indicate that a new actor is entering the stage of the international economy. The economic dynamism of the Asia-Pacific economies is rejuvenating the global economy. Some countries see new threats rather than new opportunities in the phenomenon of the Asia-Pacific growth because they suffer from severe constraints on factor mobility and have a limited capacity to make the necessary structural adjustments.

2.7 Structural and Industrial Transformation

As mentioned earlier, economies in the Asia-Pacific region consistently maintained high rates of investment. The only exception to this rule is the Philippines which could not maintain its investment during the 1980s due to noneconomic reasons (Table 2.12). The ANIEs were the highest investors, recording average investment rates of 12.8 percent for the period 1965–80 and 5.8 percent for the 1980–90 period. The ASEAN-4 recorded average investment rates of 10.5 percent for the first period and 6.2 percent for the second period, if the Philippines is excluded from the group average. China recorded an average investment rate of 10.7 percent for the first period, which is as high as the rate recorded by the ASEAN group. For the second period, China recorded an average rate of 13.7 percent, which is the highest rate of investment not only in the Asia-Pacific region but in the world. Australia and New Zealand, particularly the latter, increased their rate of investment

TABLE 2.12 Gross domestic investment average annual growth rate (%)

	1965–80	1980–90
Japan	6.9	5.7
Korea	15.9	12.5
Taiwan	12.9	3.4
Hong Kong	8.6	3.6
Singapore	13.3	3.6
Indonesia	16.1	7.1
Malaysia	10.4	2.9
Thailand	8.0	8.7
The Philippines	7.6	–2.5
Australia	2.7	3.0
New Zealand	0.8	4.4
China	10.7	13.7

Sources: World Bank, *World Development Report 1992*, Washington, DC. Data for Taiwan come from *Taiwan Statistical Data Book 1992*, Council for Economic Planning and Development, Taipei, Republic of China.

during the 1980s. The average rate of investment for the Asia-Pacific region over the period 1965–80 was 9.5 percent and 9.0 percent during the 1980–90 period. Both of these averages are higher than those for any other region in the world. The 1980s were a difficult period and several regions recorded negative growth in their investment. Latin America recorded negative growth of 2 percent and sub-Saharan Africa –4.3 percent. The developing economies of Europe recorded a growth rate of –0.1 percent over this period. Before 1980 many countries in the region faced a resource gap and had to borrow from external sources. In contrast, during the 1980s several countries not only financed investment out of their own savings but also generated a surplus over investment. The principal surplus generating countries were Japan, Taiwan, Hong Kong, Singapore and China.

Growing investment leads to accumulation of physical capital and thereby to an economy's transition from a less developed to a more developed one. The implicit assumption is that the incremental capital-output ratio (ICOR) is not inimical. The central feature of this transition is the transformation of the production structure and, therefore, the GDP composition. The structural changes occur in the following sequence: (a) the share of industry in total output rises while the agricultural sector shrinks both in relative and absolute terms; and (b) with the continued rise in investment and income, the share of the services sector begins to expand largely at the expense of the manufacturing sector. The causal factors behind this transition are, first, changes in comparative advantage resulting from ongoing accumulation of physical and human capital. Secondly, Engel's law posits a decline in relative expenditure on food and necessities with rising income and a concomitant increase in the share of manufactured products and services. Third, the choice of macroeconomic policies and trade orientation of the economy also influences the structural transformation (Chenery and Syrquin 1975). As seen in Table 2.13, the relative contribution of the agricultural sector has contracted considerably in the region over the 1965–90 period. In Japan the agricultural sector contributed only 3 per cent of the GDP in 1990. In Korea and Taiwan the relative contribution of this sector was also reduced considerably while in Hong Kong and Taiwan it disappeared. In the ASEAN countries the relative decline of the agricultural sector was significant, except for the Philippines where the relative decline was only marginal. In Australia the agricultural sector shrank further, while in New Zealand it still contributed 9 percent to GDP in 1990. In China there was a marked reduction but the agricultural sector still contributed over a quarter of the GDP. Being a highly populous country, it will need to maintain a substantial agricultural sector, although agriculture's relative contribution to GDP will continue to decline. For the region, the contribution of the agricultural sector fell by more than a half, which implies that the regional economic structure was swaying towards industrial and services activities.

In Japan, the relative contribution of the industrial and manufacturing sectors declined because at its stage of development the services sector is more important and grows faster. The services sector's contribution to GDP grew by 10 percent

TABLE 2.13 Structure of production

	Distribution of GDP (%)							
	Agriculture		Industry		Manufacturing		Services	
	1965	1990	1965	1990	1965	1990	1965	1990
Japan	10	3	44	42	34	29	46	56
Korea	38	9	25	45	18	31	37	46
Taiwan	26	4	30	46	21	37	44	49
Hong Kong	2	0	40	26	29	18	58	73
Singapore	3	0	24	37	15	29	74	63
Indonesia	51	22	13	40	8	20	36	38
Malaysia	28	–	25	–	9	–	47	–
Thailand	32	12	23	39	14	26	45	48
Philippines	26	22	27	35	20	25	47	43
Australia	9	4	39	31	26	15	51	64
New Zealand	–	9	–	27	–	19	–	64
China	38	27	35	42	28	38	27	31
Regional average	24	11	30	37	20	26	47	52

Sources: World Bank, *World Development Report 1992*, Washington, DC. Data for Taiwan come from *Taiwan Statistical Data Book 1992*, Council for Economic Planning and Development, Taipei, Republic of China.

over the 1965–90 period. In Korea and Taiwan, the industrial, manufacturing and services sectors expanded. All three sectors expanded at the expense of the agricultural sector. Hong Kong recorded a decline in the industrial sector and virtually became a service economy. However, in Singapore the contribution of the industrial sector expanded at the cost of the services sector, which contributed 11 percent less to GDP. Rapid industrialization in the ASEAN-4 countries is evident from the considerable expansion of the industrial and manufacturing sectors. Their relative contribution to GDP virtually doubled. The Philippines was an exception—here industrial sector growth was slow. The ASEAN-4 countries only recorded minor expansion in the contribution of the services sector to GDP. Again, the Philippines was an exception because the relative contribution of the services sector declined. Like Japan, Australia has grown to become an economy where the services sector dominates the rest. Its relative contribution expanded at the expense of other sectors. Like the ASEAN-4, China industrialized fast and its efforts are visible in the change in distribution of its GDP over the 1965–90 period. The relative contribution of the manufacturing sector rose by 10 percent. For the region, the manufacturing and services sectors have expanded while the agricultural sector has declined in importance.

Although statistics for the latter half of the 1980s are incomplete, Table 2.14 illustrates reasonably well the progress made by various industrial subsectors during the 1980s. Countries having high levels of per capita value added in

TABLE 2.14   Share of value added in manufacturing industries (%)

	Year	Resource processing	Food processing	Labor intensive	Capital intensive	Machinery
Japan	1980	17.2	9.7	12.5	24.4	36.2
	1988	15.2	10.0	9.8	23.6	41.4
Korea	1980	19.9	17.3	23.3	20.5	19.0
	1988	17.1	11.8	21.0	19.3	30.0
Taiwan	1980	24.5	12.5	26.9	21.4	20.6
	1988	24.1	10.3	16.0	22.9	26.6
Hong Kong	1980	11.7	5.3	47.0	11.3	24.7
	1988	11.7	6.4	47.6	8.9	25.9
Singapore	1980	24.7	5.1	10.3	11.6	48.3
	1988	11.6	5.8	5.9	20.2	56.4
Indonesia	1980	14.4	30.3	23.5	18.3	13.5
	1988	14.6	26.5	26.8	21.9	10.1
Malaysia	1981	23.6	23.7	18.0	11.5	23.2
	1987	19.4	19.6	16.5	21.4	23.0
Thailand	1982	16.3	54.1	12.0	8.3	9.3
	1986	15.6	35.6	24.0	8.6	7.2
Philippines	1980	17.8	31.0	17.1	22.9	11.1
	1987	19.8	43.5	13.6	15.4	8.6
Australia	1980	19.1	18.6	14.4	23.9	24.0
	1987	19.5	20.4	15.8	23.0	21.0
New Zealand	1981	17.4	27.7	20.3	16.2	18.4
	1986	22.3	26.9	18.6	14.9	17.3
China	1980	12.3	12.4	22.2	25.1	27.9
	1986	20.7	11.9	18.4	22.2	26.9

Source: MITI (1992: Table 1.4).

manufacturing, such as Japan, Australia, New Zealand, Singapore and Taiwan, show a higher proportion of value added in machinery and capital-intensive industries. In Japan, the combined share of machinery and capital-intensive industries reached 65 percent. Conversely, countries having relatively low per capita value added in manufacturing, such as Indonesia, Malaysia, Thailand, the Philippines and China, have a higher proportion of value added in labor-intensive and food processing industries. The resource abundant countries show a higher concentration in resource-processing and food processing industries. Among the ANIEs, Singapore has a high concentration in the machinery and capital-intensive industries. This is a country-specific example of concentration. Hong Kong is characterized by an emphasis on labor-intensive manufacturing.

Both Korea and Taiwan briskly expanded the machinery sectors over the 1980s. The share of value added in labor-intensive and food processing industries declined in both countries while the share in machinery and capital-intensive industries exceeded 50 percent. Among the ASEAN-4, Malaysia has a 45 percent concentration in machinery and capital intensive industries. A doubling of the share of value added in capital intensive industries has a lot to do with this. As opposed to this, Malaysia's natural resource production and food production shares fell rapidly. In Thailand, Indonesia and the Philippines the share of food processing industries has traditionally remained large due to abundant food resources in these countries. However, in Indonesia and Thailand the share of this industry declined over the 1980s and that of labor-intensive industries has risen. It should be remembered that a great deal has happened in Thailand since 1986, the last year for which the statistics are included. The share of value added in the capital intensive and machinery industries in China is close to 50 percent. These two subsectors were large and state-controlled (MITI 1992). In most Asia-Pacific countries the industrial sector has climbed several rungs up the ladder of comparative advantage. With steadily rising investment and an increasing stock of physical and human capital, the ability of these economies to export new products and compete successfully in the international markets has increased markedly.

Along with the physical capital, human capital also accumulated fast in the region. Japan and the ANIEs have attained high general literacy levels and the result is remarkable human capital endowment in the labor force. These countries have also trained a good number of scientists and engineers and have ensured an indigenous capacity for technological adaptation, which is vitally essential for successful industrialization. In the ASEAN-4 countries the situation is far from uniform. The Philippines has a strong educational tradition but trains an inadequate number of science and technology related personnel. Thailand has made impressive strides in the past in this regard. As much as 30 percent of Malaysia's adult population is illiterate. However, the number of Malaysian college graduates in various disciplines has soared impressively. Among the ASEAN countries, Indonesia's educational achievements are the least impressive. These countries have one common feature—they have the lowest proportion of technically trained people in the Asia-Pacific region. This feature is liable to slow the efficient adaptation of technology from abroad in the future (Noland 1990). In urban China the labor force is not as well trained as in the ANIEs. China is also expected to face shortages of science and technology related personnel.

2.8   Conclusion

Over the last three decades, the Asia-Pacific region developed into the third growth pole of the international economy and scholars began to wonder if this was the beginning of a Pacific century. During this period, several informal groupings and fora involving varying combinations of the Asia-Pacific countries emerged. The Asia-Pacific countries are far from institutionalizing these arrangements in the manner of an Asian OECD. No matter how the region is defined, the Japanese economy has to be its hub. A great deal of diversity exists in the economic and social indicators of these countries. The Asia-Pacific region has established itself as a trail blazer in the area of economic growth. Six regional economies doubled their output in one decade. Their dynamic trade-oriented growth poses an intellectual challenge. They appear to be an alternative model of development, a model which is more relevant and therefore more successful, than the standard neoclassical model in which the world had put its faith. There were considerable differences in the macroeconomic policies pursued by these countries, yet there were several basic commonalities. For instance, they all recorded high savings and investment rates and adopted outward-oriented economic strategies after an initial spell of import-substitution. The shift to outward-oriented strategies led to a change in the structure of production as well as that of trade. High export growth along with unusually rapid structural change in manufactured trade suggests that economic policy played a decisive role, shifting specialization of production towards higher value-added goods. The supply push and export promotion strategies were among the key elements underpinning dynamic transitional growth. The other causal factors included lower levels of price distortions, adoption of pragmatic liberalization measures, market orientation, high commitment to economic growth of both the governments and the societies and Confucionist cultural orientation. Proximity to Japan, the pioneer regional economy, stimulated the other regional economies both directly and indirectly. Despite striking similarities in the growth process, each economy or group had its own characteristic growth path. The ultimate result, for the majority of them, was the same.

The brisk growth rate led to a more than fourfold economic expansion of GDP for the Asia-Pacific region in real terms over the 1965–89 period. North America and the EC, which comprised the other two growth poles of the global economy, doubled their respective GDPs over the same period. This growth pattern enhanced the weight of the Asia-Pacific region in the international economy. To be sure, there were marked intra-regional differences in economic expansion. The mantle of greatest dynamism fell on the ANIEs. These countries opened their economies considerably. Some of the ASEAN countries are an exception in this regard. In a region which in general was highly successful in export expansion, these two country groups also recorded the highest long-term average growth rates of exports. This trade-related dynamic growth was principally supply driven, although demand-side factors did assist. Such an outstanding export performance resulted in a steep rise in the volume of exports from the region and by 1990 the region accounted for almost a quarter of total world exports. In terms of volume, Japan dominated the regional exports. However, over the decade of the 1980s this domination markedly declined. China, Taiwan, Korea and Singapore developed as substantial exporters in their own right. The export of manufactured products has special significance because it represents the competitive strength of the industrial sector. In the mid-1960s, the region accounted for 11 percent of total exports of manufactures. Almost all of the region's manufactured exports were from Japan. By 1990, the region accounted for as much as a quarter of total exports of manufactures. Japan no longer dominated these exports but it remained the largest exporter of manufactured products in the region. Exports from China, Taiwan, Korea—and to a lesser extent from Singapore and Hong Kong—had expanded significantly. In terms of the value of manufactured exports, by 1990 the Asia-Pacific region had left North America far behind. Japan, Taiwan and Korea have emerged as net foreign investors. These countries, along with Malaysia and Singapore, and to a lesser extent China, have also begun to make portfolio investments abroad.

The structure of the economies of these countries has undergone considerable transformation. The relative contribution of agriculture to GDP has contracted considerably in the region. The regional economic structure has swayed towards the industrial and services sectors. In as many as five economies, the services sector has become the dominant sector. Countries having high levels of per capita value added in manufacturing, such as Japan, Australia, New Zealand, Singapore and Taiwan, showed a higher proportion of value added in machinery and capital-intensive industries. Other countries recorded a marked expansion in the food processing and labor-intensive industries. In addition over the last three decades considerable accumulation of human capital endowment has taken place in the labor force in this region.

Notes

1. The term "country" is being used somewhat loosely for expositional convenience, although not all the Asia-Pacific countries qualify for it. Korea without exception stands for the Republic of Korea.
2. That is, the people's determination to pull their country up by its bootstraps.
3. For instance, see Berger and Hsiao (1988); Corbo et al. (1985); Lau (1990); Mutoh (1986); Smith et al. (1985); and Woronoff (1986). This list is far from exhaustive.

References

Abegglen, J. C. and G. Stalk, 1985, *Kaisha: The Japanese Corporations*, Basic Books, New York.

Amsden, A., 1989, *Asia's New Giant*, Oxford University Press, New York.

Arndt, H. W., 1989, "Industrial Policy in East Asia," *Industry and Development*, No. 22, United Nations Industrial Development Organization, Vienna, Vol. 2, pp. 40–88.

Asian Development Bank, 1971, *Southeast Asia's Economy in the 1970s*, Longman, London.

Australia, 1986, *Fourth Report, Senate Standing Committee on Industry and Trade*, Australian Government Publishing Service, Canberra.

———, 1989, *The Impact of the Australia–New Zealand Closer Economic Relations Trade Agreement*, Bureau of Industry Economics, Research Report No. 29, Australian Government Publishing Service, Canberra.

Balassa, B. and M. Noland, 1988, *Japan in the World Economy*, Institute for International Economics, Washington, DC.

Balassa, B. and J. Williamson, 1990, *Adjusting to Success: Balance of Payments Policy in the East Asian NICs*, revised edition, Institute for International Economics, Washington, DC.

Berger, P. L. and H. H. M. Hsiao (eds.), 1988, *In Search of an East Asian Development Model*, Transaction Books, New Brunswick, NJ.

Bradford, C. I. and W. H. Branson (eds.), 1987, "Pattern of Trade and Structural Change," in *Trade and Structural Change in Pacific Asia*, University of Chicago Press, Chicago, pp. 3–24.

Byrnes, M., 1992, "China Faces Sweeping Changes," *Financial Review*, October 24.

Chang, H. J. and A. Singh, 1992, *Public Enterprises in Developing Countries and Economic Efficiency*, UNCTAD Discussion Paper No. 48, UNCTAD.

Chenery, H. B. and M. Syrquin, 1975, *Patterns of Development, 1950–70*, Oxford University Press, London.

Cheng, T. and S. Haggard, 1987, *Newly Industrializing Asia in Transition: Policy Reform and American Response*, Institute of International Studies, Berkeley, CA.

Chintayarangsan, R. et al., 1992, "ASEAN Economies: Macro-economic Perspective," *ASEAN Economic Bulletin*, March, 353–75.

Corbo, V. et al., 1985, *Export Oriented Development Strategies: The Success of Five Newly Industrializing Countries*, Westview Press, Boulder, CO.

Das, Dilip K., 1993, *The Yen Appreciation and the International Economy*, Macmillan, London.

Denison, E. F., 1962, *The Sources of Economic Growth and the Alternatives Before US*, Committee for Economic Development, New York.

Dore, R., 1987, *Taking Japan Seriously*, Athlone Press, London.

The Economist, 1992, "Deng's Last Show," October 10, 13–14.

Garnaut, R., 1988, *Asia's Giant*, University of Adelaide, Adelaide.

Gibney, F., 1992, *The Pacific Century*, Maxwell Macmillan International, New York.

Higashi, C. and G. P. Lanter, 1990, *The Internationalization of the Japanese Economy*, Kluwer Academic Publishers, Boston, MA.

Kahn, H., 1979, *World Economic Development: 1979 and Beyond*, Croom Helm, London.

Kosai, Y., 1986, *The Era of High-Speed Growth*, University of Tokyo Press, Tokyo.

Kuznets, S., 1966, *Modern Economic Growth: Rates, Structure and Spread*, Yale University Press, New Haven, CT.

————, 1971, *Economic Growth of Nations: Total Output and Production Structure*, Harvard University Press, Cambridge, MA.

Lau, L. J. (ed.), 1990, *Models of Development: A Comparative Study of Economic Growth in South Korea and Taiwan*, Institute for Contemporary Studies Press, San Francisco, CA.

Linder, S. B., 1986, *The Pacific Century*, Stanford University Press, Stanford, CA.

Little, I. M. D., T. Scitovsky, and M. Scott, 1970, *Industry and Trade in Some Developing Countries: A Comparative Study*, Oxford University Press, New York.

MacFarquhar, R., 1990, "The Post-Confucian Challenge," *The Economist*, February 9, 67.

Ministry of International Trade and Industry (MITI), 1992, "Vision for the Economy of the Asia-Pacific Region in the Year 2000 and Tasks Ahead," Tokyo, August 10–11, mimeo.

Mitsumori, K. and K. Meshino, 1992, "China Maps Capitalist Road on Japan's Economic Model," *Nikkei Weekly*, October 19.

Mutoh, H. et al., 1986, *Industrial Policies for Pacific Economic Growth*, Allen & Unwin, Sydney.

Myrdal, G., 1968, *Asian Drama: An Enquiry into the Poverty of Nations*, Pantheon Books, New York.

Noland, M., 1990, *Pacific Basin Developing Countries*, Institute of International Economics, Washington, DC.

Otani, I. and D. P. Villanueva, 1988, *Determinants of Long-term Growth Performance in Developing Countries*, International Monetary Fund Working Paper 88/97, Washington, DC.

Reidel, J., 1984, "Trade as the Engine of Growth in Developing Countries Revisited," *Economic Journal*, 94(373): 56–73.

Scott, B. R., 1985, "National Strategies: Key to International Competitiveness," in B. R. Scott and G. C. Lodge (eds.), *US Competitiveness in the World Economy*, Harvard Business School Press, Boston, MA, pp. 96–128.

Smith, M. et al., 1985, *Asia's New Industrial World*, Methuen, London.

Tai, H. C. (ed.), 1989, "The Oriental Alternative," in *Confucianism and Economic Development*, Washington Institute Press, Washington, DC, pp. 114–44.

Vogel, E. F., 1984, "The Advent of the Pacific Century," *Harvard International Review*, 6(5): 174–222.

World Bank, 1983, *World Development Report 1983*, Washington, DC.

———, 1985a, *World Development Report 1985*, Washington, DC.

———, 1985b, *China: Economic Structure in International Perspective*, Washington, DC.

———, 1989, *Economic Prices for Project Evaluation in China*, Washington, DC.

———, 1992, *World Development Report 1992*, Washington, DC.

Woronoff, J., 1986, *Asia's 'Miracle' Economies: Korea, Japan, Taiwan, Singapore and Hong Kong*, M.E. Sharpe, New York.

CAUSES BEHIND THE EMERGENCE OF ASIA-PACIFIC AS THE THIRD MAJOR AREA OF THE WORLD ECONOMY

3.1 Introduction

The superlative economic achievements of the Asian newly industrializing economies (ANIEs) had an impact over the thinking of the macroeconomic managers of the ASEAN (Association of Southeast Asian Nations) countries and China. Those countries in East Asia have been vigorously endeavoring to catch up with the industrialized economies and in the process have been trying to develop strong economic ties among themselves. These economies have been endeavoring to integrate, that is, if integration is defined as a fairly free flow of goods, capital, ideas and people across national boundaries. To take an example, Taiwan and mainland China have not only transformed their economies over the decade of the 1980s, they have come considerably closer than they ever were in the past, albeit the difference in the stages of growth and development. Chow (1992) pointed out five commonalities in their economic transformation. First, in both countries, government intervention in economic affairs declined while private sector initiatives were encouraged. The post-"open door" economic reforms of China are well known.

In Taiwan, the government liberalized economic activity by encouraging private investment by providing the financial services of government banks, establishing a stock market, giving tax exemptions for certain industries and relaxing controls over the establishment of factories. The second common feature was the importance given to the agricultural sector during the early stages of growth. In both Taiwan and China, the increase in agricultural productivity was achieved mainly by redistributing land to farmers. The third commonality was the adoption of an export-promotion regime. Increase in exports contributed a great deal to the growth of GDP. The fourth common element was emphasis on price stability. Conscious efforts were made and the two economies by and large succeeded in attaining their objective. The fifth common element was the gradual decontrol of restrictions on imports and the setting of an official exchange rate close to the market clearing level. The currency overvaluation was gradually eliminated. By 1992, the official exchange rates and the free market rates converged and almost coincided.

In the following section, the author intends to point out that all the five common features identified by Chow are also common to the rest of the East Asian countries, but not to those countries playing catch-up outside of East Asia. Section 3.3 discusses the mechanisms underpinning the rapid pace of development in the East Asian economies and intra-trade in East Asia in recent years. Section 3.4 examines the expanding share of East Asia, or the Western Pacific (including East Asia and Oceania), in the world economy. It also discusses the impact of this expansion on the global economic order. Finally, Section 3.5 asks that readers consider whether the recent development of East Asia constitutes merely an extension of Western models of development, or whether it constitutes a new Asian model of development.

3.2   The Commonality in Features

Interestingly enough, most of the features identified by Chow were also present in Japan during its reconstruction and high-growth period between 1946 and 1973, in the ANIEs in the 1960s and 1970s, and in the ASEAN countries in the 1980s.[1]

In Japan's case, in particular, all five features were definitely present. After the end of World War II Japan entered a period of reconstruction that lasted from 1946 to 1954. This period was characterized by (Feature 1) the phased reduction of government intervention and strong regulation, which had been features of the war-time economy, and (Feature 2) the redistribution of agricultural land from landlords to farmers, with the result that all tenant-farmers became owner-farmers, and nonfarming landlords disappeared. These two reforms strengthened private initiatives in the market economy, which resulted in the subsequent period of high economic growth.

In the period from 1955 to 1973 Japan achieved an average growth rate of 10 percent. The features of this period were growth driven by exports (Feature 3), and an emphasis on domestic price stability (Feature 4) under the balance-of-payment discipline of the Bretton-Woods system. Indeed, the average inflation rate of wholesale prices between 1955 and 1972 was only 1 percent. The fifth feature, the decontrol of imports and foreign exchange, was implemented only gradually (Feature 5) and was not completed until 1980, when the control of international capital flow was totally abolished.

The same five features are also present in the growth strategies of other East Asian countries. For instance, deregulation (Feature 1) in various sectors of the economy has always been implemented gradually but steadily (Feature 5) in most Asian economies. Export-led growth (Feature 3) with private initiative is also common in all countries in the region. Land reform (Feature 2) was implemented in Korea and other countries in the region, and with the exception of the Philippines and Brunei, farmers are today landowners rather than tenants. The priority given to price stability (Feature 4) is confirmed by the fact that inflation rates in East Asian countries have generally remained in single figures.

This contrasts with the situation in the countries playing catch-up in Latin America, West Asia, the Middle East and Africa. Although deregulation (Feature 1) and export promotion (Feature 3) are common features in the development strategies of these countries, there is still widespread domination of the agricultural sector by a few large landowners with many small tenants (Feature 2). In addition, inflation rates (Feature 4) are rarely in single figures. Further, "radicalism" rather than "gradualism" (Feature 5) is usually a feature of deregulation and reform processes in these countries.

Interestingly, this contrast between "gradualism" and "radicalism" is also found in the process of market-oriented reform in communist China and Russia. As Professor Chow has noted, China's reform process started with the household responsibility system in the agricultural sector, with private initiatives gradually being extended to the manufacturing and service sectors in urban areas. The decontrol of prices has also been very gradual and is still incomplete after ten years. In Russia, however, the abolition of government intervention and the introduction of private initiative were implemented simultaneously in all sectors of industry, while the decontrol of prices in January 1991 resulted in radical price movement.

3.3   The Dynamism of Rapid Development in Domestic Economies and Intra-Trade in East Asia

In addition to these common features, the development of the East Asian economies has also been characterized by interaction among the region's countries. This has resulted in the rapid development of intra-trade in East Asia, particularly since the Plaza Accord of September 1985 (Das 1993). The enhanced interaction and intra-trade among Taiwan, Hong Kong, and mainland China is part of a phenomenon that affected the whole of East Asia.

The traditional trade structure of East Asia was that Japan and the ANIEs—Korea, Hong Kong, Taiwan and Singapore—imported raw materials from ASEAN countries and mainland China, produced manufactured goods from those materials, and exported the manufactured goods to Western developed countries. For Japan and the ANIEs, therefore, the biggest source of imports was East Asia, and the largest export markets were North America and Western Europe. This type of "vertical" trade structure limits the industrialization of material-supplying countries and is not conducive to the development of intra-trade based on the exchange of finished goods. It is also characterized by trade friction with the Western developed countries due to the structural trade surpluses of Japan and the ANIEs.

This trade structure has changed dramatically since the Plaza Accord of 1985. Today, East Asia or the Western Pacific, including Oceania, is not only Japan's largest source of imports, but also its biggest export market. In 1991 this region's share of Japan's export trade reached 38.9 percent, compared with 29.1 percent for the United States. The contribution of growth in intra-trade to total growth in the trade of all East Asian countries[2] has risen from 36.4 percent in 1981–85 to 44.6 percent in 1986–90. The contribution of the United States to total growth in the exports of East Asian countries fell from 61.6 percent in 1981–85 to 20.7 percent in 1986–90 (see Table 3.1).

This dramatic change is the result of the development of "horizontal trade" in the form of exchanges of manufactured goods within East Asia. Faced with the appreciation of the yen, which has doubled in value from 240 to 120 against the U.S. dollar since the Plaza Accord of 1985, Japan has shifted its production bases

TABLE 3.1   Increase in exports of East Asian countries by destinations (US$ million)

From	To	East Asia	U.S.	EC	Total (including others)
Japan	1981–85	9,932	34,389	3,003	46,316
	1986–90	41,371	25,082	33,017	111,820
NIEs	1981–85	13,449	20,661	−595	37,624
	1986–90	65,473	31,857	25,232	146,683
ASEAN	1981–85	3,643	294	−970	−1,172
	1986–90	19,952	7,499	7,822	38,147
China	1981–85	6,461	1,353	−80	9,190
	1986–90	23,022	5,119	4,437	39,189
Total (of the above four)	1981–85	33,485 (36.4%)	56,697 (61.6%)	1,358 (1.4%)	91,958 (100.0%)
	1986–90	149,818 (44.6%)	69,557 (20.7%)	70,508 (20.9%)	335,839 (100.0%)

Source: International Monetary Fund, *Direction of Trade Statistics Yearbook*, Washington, DC, various issues.

for less technology-intensive manufactured goods to the ANIEs, ASEAN and the coastal areas of mainland China. This has been accomplished through enormous direct investment involving the export of capital goods and parts, as well as technology transfers. Between 1986 and 1989, Japan's direct investment in the ANIEs increased threefold, and there was a fivefold increase in Japanese direct investment in ASEAN. Total investment in both regions during this period reached US$20.8 billion. This is greater than the total for the entire period from 1951 to 1985, when investment amounted to US$19.1 billion.

Like the yen, the currencies of the ANIEs have also been revalued against the U.S. dollar since 1988. In addition to the dramatic increase in direct investment, exports of capital goods and parts, and technology transfers from Japan, those from the ANIEs to ASEAN and mainland China have also started to increase since 1988 and surpassed those from Japan in 1990 (see Figure 3.1).

This process has made an enormous contribution to the stimulation of industrialization in Thailand, Indonesia, Malaysia, the Philippines, and the coastal areas of mainland China, resulting in steady growth in their exports back to Japan and the ANIEs. Economic interaction is reflected in economic growth rates of more than 10 percent in the ANIEs between 1986 and 1988. The ASEAN countries registered growth of almost 10 percent between 1988 and 1991 (see Figure 3.2). Japan also enjoyed high growth, with an average growth rate of 5 percent between 1987 and 1991.

This dynamism results from the rapid development of economies and intra-trade in East Asia today.

3.4   Emergence of East Asia as the Third Economic Zone

According to an estimate published by the Japan Research Center in February 1992, the Americas' share of world GDP reached 29 percent in 1990, with North America contributing 26.1 percent and Latin America 2.9 percent. Europe's share stood at 32.9 percent, which was divided between 30.4 percent for Western Europe and 2.5 percent for Eastern Europe. The share of the Western Pacific, defined as Asia and Oceania, amounted to 20.9 percent, or only two-thirds as much as the Americas and Europe. Japan contributed 12.8 percent of this share, China 1.6 percent, other Asian countries 5 percent, and Oceania 1.5 percent.

However, if we assume that the present differential of growth trends in the three zones will continue for the next 20 years, then the Western Pacific's share of world GDP will reach 30.2 percent by 2010, with Japan contributing 17.5 percent, China 2.6 percent, other Asian countries 8.8 percent, Oceania 1.3 percent. This compares with figures of 26 percent for the Americas and 28.7 percent for Europe.

This is just an estimate based on a rough assumption, and whether or not the share of the Western Pacific will surpass those of the Americas and Europe is not the key issue here. What is important is that if the present trend in East Asia continues, the world economy will come to consist of three major zones: the

FIGURE 3.1   Direct foreign investment in the ASEAN countries

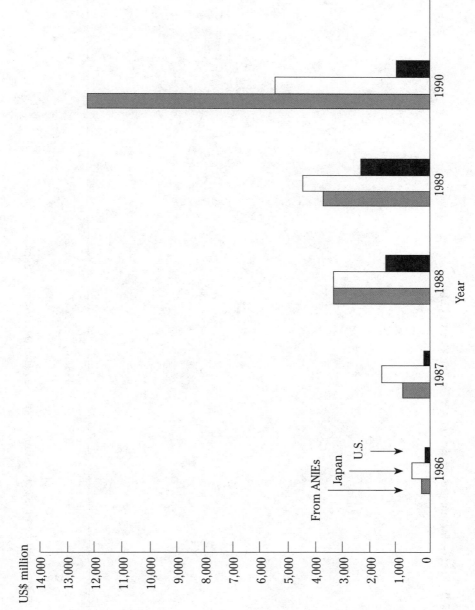

Source: Nomura Research Institute, Tokyo.

FIGURE 3.2   Real economic growth rate of ANIEs, ASEAN and China

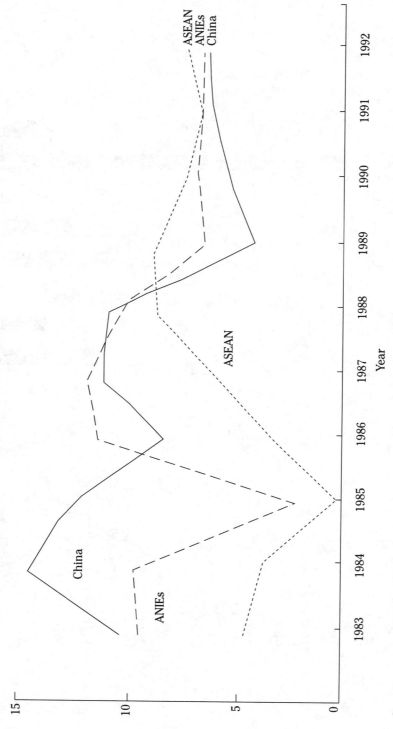

Growth rates for 1991 and 1992 are estimated by the Asian Development Bank

Americas, Europe and the Western Pacific. All three will be similar in scale, and each will have substantial intra-trade. In other words, the world economy is moving from the two-polar system of the past 200 years toward a three-polar system.

The development of the East Asian economies has doubtless owed a great deal to the global free trade system maintained by the Western industrialized nations. From the viewpoint of the Western front-runner nations, whose shares of world markets have been eroded by the countries playing catch-up, it seems unfair for East Asian countries to maintain a gradual approach to the reduction of government intervention and the deregulation of imports and exchange rates. Western front-runner nations are also dissatisfied with the slow pace of political reform from "development dictatorship" to democracy in many East Asian countries.

If frustration with the "gradualism" that characterizes Asia's progress toward free economies and democracy causes the Western front-runners to discriminate against exports from Asian countries through the formation of regional free trade systems in the Americas and Europe, international trade will be dominated not by free trade and globalism, but by managed trade and regionalism. East Asia and the Western Pacific would then be forced to respond in kind, and the world economy would eventually be divided into three trade blocs. From the author's perspective, this would be an utterly imprudent solution to the problems that exist, and the resulting order would be extremely inefficient.

The front-runners should treat the "voluntary export restraints" and "voluntary import promotion" proposed by the U.S. for the East Asian countries as temporary measures, to be implemented on a limited basis and abolished as soon as possible. The two regional free trade systems, based on the integrated markets of the EC in Europe and on the U.S.–Canada–Mexico Free Trade Treaty in the Americas, should not be allowed to evolve into trade blocs. Instead these systems should be used as steps toward the formation of a global free trade system through approaches that ensure consistent openness to the rest of the world. The GATT rules and negotiations in the Uruguay Round should take precedence over regional trade rules and negotiations.

For their part, the countries in Asia-Pacific playing catch-up should implement deregulation and open up their markets in line with the GATT rules. They should not form a third trade bloc in the Asia-Pacific region. Several regional economic groupings have been proposed in the past. They have been discussed elsewhere in this book. These country groups should limit themselves to forums for exchanges of views among the ASEAN countries, Japan, Korea, Taiwan and China. They must not be used as the framework for a trade bloc. (Part III discusses this issue in more detail.)

3.5   Is East Asia's Development Something New?

To conclude this chapter, the author would like to ask readers to consider whether the development of Asia-Pacific is merely a transmission of Western civilization, or whether something new is emerging.

In the author's judgment, liberalism, equity and humanism, which are the core values of Western civilization, have certainly been transmitted as supreme virtues to the East Asian countries. Their economic reforms toward free market economies and their political reforms toward democracy are without doubt based on these values. The economic development of East Asia in recent times is clearly the fruit of Western civilization as it has existed since the Industrial Revolution.

However, the people of Asia-Pacific are inclined to interpret the bounds and demands of such values as liberalism, equity and humanism against the context of long-term relationships, and to implement reforms gradually and step by step. Even profit maximization in a market economy takes longer in Asia-Pacific than in the West. Moreover, fair competition in a market does not necessarily mean equal opportunity in spot transactions—sometimes it can mean equal opportunity in long-term relationships with good customers. Such longer-term networks are particularly important today, when companies invest substantial amounts of time and money in the development of advanced technology, the application of technology to new products, and the establishment of production and distribution bases for those products. The high growth of productivity in the Asia-Pacific region would not have been possible without the gradual and long-term contribution of many companies across political borders. This "gradualism" and emphasis on a long-term relationship, which are essential aspects of Asian culture, may have their roots in the traditional way of thinking of ancient agricultural peoples.

To encourage the emerging Asia-Pacific economy to integrate with the world economy, which has been dominated solely by the Western front-runners, we must recognize that while East and West both share the same values of Western civilization, their approaches (and maybe their cultures) are different. The differences between East and West are between long-term and short-term approaches, between gradualism and radicalism, and between an emphasis on networks and individual needs and interests.

The author hopes that the Western front-runners will be patient enough to understand that the countries playing catch-up in East Asia have different approaches to liberalism and democracy. Ultimately, the East Asian countries will be able to satisfy the Western front-runners by taking gradual steps toward liberalization and democratization. One cannot help but wonder whether the recent development of the Asia-Pacific region has something new to add to our global framework for civilization.

Notes

1. The four ANIEs are Korea, Hong Kong, Taiwan and Singapore. The ASEAN consists of Brunei, Indonesia, Malaysia, the Philippines and Singapore. Since Singapore is a member of both groups, in discussions and statistics in this paper it is included only in the NIEs and not in ASEAN.

2. The East Asian countries here are being defined as Japan, Korea, Hong Kong, Taiwan, Singapore, Indonesia, Thailand, Malaysia, the Philippines and China.

References

Chow, G. C. 1992, "The Integration of China and Other Asian Countries into the World Economy," paper presented at the Mont Pelerin Society General Meeting, Vancouver, Canada, September 4.

Das, Dilip K. 1993, *The Yen Appreciation and the International Economy*, Macmillan, London.

Part II

ISSUES IN INTERNATIONAL TRADE AND INVESTMENT

The neo-classical trade theory posited that countries trade with each other largely in response to differences among countries in factor endowments and, therefore, production capabilities. As noted earlier, there are significant differences in the stages of economic development among the Asia-Pacific economies. These economies form a *ganko keitai* or a flying geese paradigm. This in turn leads to significant differences in production capabilities, resulting in enhanced trade probabilities. In addition, intra-industry trade occurs due to each country's variety of products and differences in consumer tastes and preferences. Analogously, foreign direct investment occurs in response to the market opportunities provided by the production capability differences among countries. There are wide differences in per capita gross national product (GNP) in the Asia-Pacific region which can be taken as a proxy for differences in per capita capital stock. The trade dynamism of the Asia-Pacific region is a well known cliche. Its export growth rate for the decade of the 1980s was twice that of the other two growth poles, that is, North America and the Economic Union (EU). Intra-regional trade has also expanded fast. It was dominated by Japan and the four ANIEs, the five economies at the upper end of the GNP ladder. Among the sub-groups in the region, intra-ANIE trade is the largest. Likewise, Japan and two of the ANIEs, namely, Taiwan and Korea have emerged as large foreign investors. Chapter 4 (Riedel) presents an in-depth tableau of trade and investment related issues.

Two significant trade and investment-related issues have been taken up in Chapter 5 (Anderson) and Chapter 6 (Tejima). The former deals with the importance of trade in fibers, textiles and clothing in the region and its impact on economic growth. The latter focuses on Japanese foreign direct investment in the region. It also compares it to Japanese foreign direct investment in the other regions. Toward the end it makes an attempt to prognosticate investment trends, taking into account the radically changed financial environment in Japan.

In Chapter 7 Chi-Hung Kwan elaborates on the process whereby ASIAN countries and China follow the same route as the Asian Newly Industrializing Economies (ANIEs) with the help of foreign direct investment from Japan and the ANIEs. Foreign direct investment in the Asia-Pacific region has had a substantive economic impact. It has substantially influenced both the growth rate of the recipient countries and the regional integration pattern. To maintain the growth of the region, Japan and the ANIEs should continue to contribute to this process through positive industrial adjustment, that is, diversifying into newer industries and relocating the older and declining ones into those countries that are on a lower economic rung. Kwan reaches a bold and important conclusion, namely, "Japan should abandon the mercantilist view that production and exports are good, while consumption and imports are bad." His prognostication is that regional industrial restructuring will proceed at an unprecedented scale in the future. Both investing and receiving countries stand to benefit from restructuring. The recent appreciation of the yen has buttressed his hypothesis.

In Chapter 8 Kym Anderson juxtaposes regional trade trends against an international backdrop. Developments in the world trading system and in global trade are becoming ever-more important to the East Asian region, partly because the region's share of world trade is growing so rapidly but also because of the continuing high dependence of the region on markets outside Asia and the absence of free trade within the region. True, the share of East Asia's trade that is intra-regional has been rising, as have the intra-regional trade shares of both Western Europe and North America. But all three regions remain strongly interdependent, each with more than one-eighth of their GDP traded extra-regionally. Thus all three regions have a huge and still-growing interest in ensuring that prosperity flourishes outside their own geographic region and that extra-regional trade remains open, which is what a healthy multilateral trading system is able to provide. The latter is especially important for Asia because, unlike in Western Europe and now North America, this region does not have a free trade agreement or customs union. Therefore, the GATT/WTO is important for maintaining and increasing openness not only of Asia's trade with other regions but also of intra-Asian trade. Yet East Asian governments have been much less assertive than those of the U.S. or EU in the GATT/WTO process. There is considerable scope for East Asia to increase its influence on world trade policies, for the betterment of its own welfare as well as that of the rest of the world.

In the immediate term the key task is to ensure the ratification and implementation of the Uruguay Round. But even if the Round were to be implemented without major problems during the remainder of this decade, the GATT rules–based multilateral trading system under the WTO will continue to come under strain. The irony is that the challenges to that system—regionalism, environmentalism, concern about labor standards, competition policy, and aggressive unilateralism—are in part a result of the GATT's very success in fostering global economic integration over its 47-year lifetime.

What might East Asia do to minimize the risks and maximize the opportunities arising from these recent and prospective challenges facing the WTO rules–based global trading system (to which China and Taiwan hope to become members soon)? It is unlikely to be in the economic interests of this region to form its own trading bloc, because of the risks of losses from not only trade diversion but also retaliatory closure of export markets outside the region. Even if it was, it is not likely that the entire East Asian, Western Pacific, or broader Pacific rim would form a free trade area: the high degree of potential (as distinct from actual) trade complementarity that exists between freely trading resource-rich and resource-poor Pacific rim countries works against its political feasibility. Instead, the interests of the East Asian economies generally will continue to be served best by the maintenance and strengthening of an open multilateral trading system under the WTO. That can be facilitated in various ways. One is by promoting unilateral trade liberalization in the Asia-Pacific region itself. Another is to play a leading role in shaping the debate on trade policy and the new issues on the WTO's agenda. The APEC region is a microcosm of the world with a rich variety of economies (rich, poor, resource-abundant, resource-scarce) and yet there is a great deal of goodwill among them, so the chances of examining and sorting out the new issues calmly is much greater in an APEC forum than in the larger-number forum of the WTO. Recently an investment code was developed through APEC, in conjunction with PECC. A similar process might be used to develop positions on the interactions between trade and environment, labor standards, and/or competition policy.

Chapter 9 (Hawawini and Probert) focuses on the feeble trade and investment relationship between the EC and the Asia-Pacific region. European business interests have remained largely unimpressed by the heady growth of the region. If anything, trade friction with Japan has risen, specially in the auto sector. Of late, acrimonious exchanges with Korea have also taken place. Efforts were afoot to cultivate business relations with the ASEAN countries, however, no noteworthy success has been in sight. To be sure, two-way trade has increased, but this was more an outcome of the Asian firm's aggressive foreys than of initiatives taken by the EC firms. As regards foreign direct investment, the European firms preferred trade to investment. Besides, Asia-Pacific was not one of the favorite areas of investment for the European firms. Their preferences lay in other regions like the Mediterranean and the East European countries. In the ultimate analysis the West European economies and corporations have remained rather preoccupied with the EC integration process. They have missed out on the opportunities of mutual interaction with the Asia-Pacific economies and firms and in the process missed out on mutual economic gains.

Chapter 4

James Riedel

Intra-regional Trade and Foreign Direct Investment in the Asia-Pacific Region

4.1 Introduction

The purpose of this chapter is to explain the level and pattern of intra-Asian trade and foreign direct investment. The approach is positive rather than normative in that the aim is to explain the facts and not to suggest what should be the level and pattern of intra-Asian trade and direct investment. We shall therefore eschew making policy recommendations to promote intra-Asian trade and direct investment.

The chapter first examines the theory of international trade and investment as it pertains to the intraregional dimension of these flows. There is in fact no separate theory of trade and investment between countries of a given geographical region apart from the general theory of trade and investment. Essentially, the theory argues that where there are complementarities between economies, international trade and investment arise to exploit the profit opportunities they provide, subject always to the proviso that obstacles not be placed in their way. What is true generally should hold equally for trade and investment among countries of the Asian region.

The chapter then briefly surveys the potential for intra-Asian trade, focusing on the main complementarities which exist among the Asian economies and the barriers to trade in the Asian countries. This is followed by an overview of the level and pattern of intra-Asian trade and by an examination of some special features of intra-Asian trade, in particular the role of Japan, trade among the newly industrializing economies (NIEs), among the countries of the Association of Southeast Asian Nations (ASEAN) and among the South Asian countries, and finally the role of entrepôt trade in Asia.

Subsequently, the chapter examines intra-Asian direct investment and assesses how well it conforms to the pattern one would predict from the theoretical principles. Finally, it briefly considers the future prospects of intra-Asian trade and direct investment.

4.2   Theoretical Considerations

It is convenient to consider the theory of trade and the theory of foreign direct investment separately. However, the relationship between these flows, in particular the question of whether they are complements or substitutes, will be addressed.

4.2.1 International Trade Theory

The theory of international trade is founded on the principle of comparative advantage. As Ricardo first explained it, for a nation to gain from trade, all that is necessary is that its relative cost of producing different goods differ from the relative cost of producing the same goods in other countries. No matter whether a country is absolutely more (or less) efficient in producing all goods, it will gain from trade, exporting those goods whose relative cost of production at home is low and importing those goods whose relative cost is high. Since virtually every country in the world has a comparative advantage in something (and hence comparative disadvantage in something else), every country in the world should gain from trade.

The commodity pattern of trade is explained by the determinants of comparative advantage. The most widely applied hypothesis, the Heckscher-Ohlin theorem of neoclassical trade theory, posits that comparative advantage derives from differences among countries in relative endowment of resources. The theorem as it is generally formulated rests on several key assumptions: constant returns to scale, a common worldwide stock of technological knowledge, common tastes and preferences among countries, and no country-specific resources or factors of production. Under these assumptions it follows that a country will find a comparative advantage in those goods which use the relatively abundant factor of production relatively intensively. In other words, relatively labor-abundant (developing) countries are predicted by the theory to have a comparative advantage in relatively labor-intensive goods, while relatively capital-abundant (developed) countries find a comparative advantage in capital-intensive goods. The theory can be extended to allow for many factors of production and many countries without losing much of its generality (Jones and Neary 1984). For example, in a multicountry model in which countries' relative endowment of labor and capital are on a continuum, it can be shown that a country in the middle of the continuum will trade in both directions, exchanging its exports for more capital-intensive goods in relatively capital-abundant countries and for more labor-intensive goods in relatively labor-abundant countries (Krueger 1977).

The Heckscher-Ohlin hypothesis has been tested empirically for many countries and found generally to hold, especially for trade in manufactures between countries at different per capita income levels. The hypothesis naturally fails when its key underlying assumptions are seriously at odds with reality. For example, the assumption of no country-specific resources clearly does not apply to natural resources which are distributed very unevenly around the world. Obviously, if a country does not have certain natural resources, it will import them regardless of the capital or labor-intensiveness of their extraction.

Another assumption which has been called into question is that there is common worldwide stock of technological knowledge to which all countries have equal access. However, even if technology is ultimately diffused around the world, it takes time for this to happen. Therefore, countries which are better able to generate new technologies gain a comparative advantage, albeit a temporary one, in producing new goods which use newly minted technology, what are often called "high-tech" goods. Over time, as new products become standardized for mass consumption, their production may shift from the country which created them to other countries with lower production costs. That products have a life cycle and that countries specialize at different stages in the product life cycle has been offered as an alternative to the Heckscher-Ohlin hypotheses (Vernon 1966). However, the product cycle theory fails as a separate theory of trade because it begs the question of why some countries are better able than others to create new products and new technologies. If the reason is that some countries have more skilled labor and scientific resources to devote to research and development, then the product cycle theory comes close to being nothing other than an extended version of the Heckscher-Ohlin proposition.

Trade based on the principle of comparative advantage, whether it derives from an abundance or scarcity of natural resources, from differences in relative endowment of labor and capital, or from leads and lags in technology, is a market response to international differences in production capabilities. The greater these differences, the greater the potential gains and the larger the potential scope of international trade. And yet it has been observed that the largest proportion of international trade is among the developed countries, which are very similar in terms of per capita income and relative resource endowment. Furthermore, a large proportion of trade among the developed countries involves the simultaneous export and import of similar goods (or at least goods classified for statistical purposes in the same commodity categories), what is known as intra-industry trade. On the face of it, intra-industry trade appears to be something quite distinct from trade based on comparative advantage since it appears to be motivated by similarities rather than differences among countries.

Several theories have been advanced to explain intra-industry trade. Naturally, they rest on assumptions very different from the Heckscher-Ohlin theorem. The Heckscher-Ohlin assumption of common tastes and preferences, for example, has been challenged by Linder who suggests instead that tastes and preferences differ among countries according to per capita income (Linder 1961). On this assumption, it is argued that as per capita income differences among countries decline, as they did, for example, in Europe, trade will expand rather than diminish because of a growing overlap of demand for each country's variety of products. The empirical implication of this proposition is that intra-industry trade should be greatest among countries at similar income levels. This is essentially what the data show, although intra-industry trade is largely confined to trade among developed countries. There is little intra-industry trade among developing countries of similar per capita income (Havrylyshyn and Civan 1985).

To sum up, traditional theory argues that trade occurs largely in response to differences among countries in production capabilities. The possible exception to this is intra-industry trade which occurs predominantly among the developed countries and in any case may be more an aggregation phenomenon than a fundamental contradiction of the traditional theory. The implications of trade theory for intra-Asian trade are obvious—where significant differences in production capabilities exist among the Asian countries, international trade is likely to arise, provided that there are no significant barriers to these flows, such as high transportation costs or policies restricting trade.

4.2.2 Theory of Direct Investment

International trade and foreign direct investment have much in common; most importantly, both are market responses to opportunities provided by differences among countries in production capabilities. Since both serve the same purpose, evening out consumption possibilities in a world of different production capabilities, a central question that arises in regard to direct investment is why it takes place at all. The most comprehensive answer to this question is given by the "eclectic theory" of foreign direct investment (Dunning 1981a, 1981b).

According to this theory, there are three sets of determinants of foreign direct investment, each relating to an advantage of direct investment over alternative modes of serving the firm's customers at home and abroad. The first necessary condition for foreign direct investment is that foreign firms have an ownership advantage over their rivals or potential rivals in the host country. The ownership advantage is necessary to outweigh the disadvantage of being foreign. It may take the form of either a monopoly over a product or brand name, a patent on a production process or technology, or a superior knowledge of the market and of marketing techniques. In most empirical studies of U.S. multinational corporate investment, the ownership advantage is associated with research and development expenditure, but this is only one potential source of ownership advantage and may not be the most important for firms of smaller, less-developed countries which invest abroad.

The second requirement for foreign direct investment is that the host country must have some locational advantage in terms of serving the market of the host country or as an export base. The locational advantage may derive from a fundamental comparative advantage, such as an abundance of high-quality, low-wage labor, from relatively low transportation costs, or from policy-determined costs arising from trade restrictions, labor legislation, pollution controls and direct incentives to or restrictions on direct investment. In the absence of a locational advantage, the firm would choose exporting over direct investment as the way to exploit its ownership advantage in foreign markets.

Finally, even when there is an ownership advantage and a locational advantage, there must be an internalization advantage that induces the firm to choose direct investment over other arms-length arrangements, such as production licensing. In many developing countries there is an expressed desire to unbundle foreign direct investment so as to obtain the technology that comes with foreign investment without yielding control over production to foreigners. However, except in the natural resource field where service contracts, production-sharing agreements and technical assistance agreements are not uncommon, foreign investors have generally resisted unbundling the direct investment package. Often it has proved difficult to define the component to be sold, such as a technology, and to agree upon a price (Frank 1980).

It is useful to consider how this theory applies to the three broad forms of foreign direct investment in developing countries: (a) natural resource investment; (b) investment to serve the host-country market; and (c) export-oriented investment. In the case of natural resource investment, the locational advantage is obvious. The ownership advantage of firms from developed countries derives from the high capital-intensity and technology-intensity of natural resource extraction. This advantage has not, however, always proved enduring, as evidenced by the nationalization of foreign firms in the natural resource sector of developing countries. The internalization advantage for natural resource investment is also not as strong as in the other sectors, as already noted.

The first wave of postwar direct investment in developing countries aimed at serving the host-country market occurred in the 1950s and 1960s in response to the adoption of the import-substitution industrialization strategy by many developing countries. That producers in developed countries possessed some ownership advantage over domestic firms in developing countries was apparent from the fact that they dominated the market for manufactured goods in developing countries. The premise of the infant industry argument on which the import-substitution strategy was founded was that manufacturers in developing countries could acquire the ownership advantage if only given time. However, import barriers themselves provided the missing locational advantage to direct investment in developing countries, and thus direct investment became a means of circumventing trade restrictions. In recent years foreign investment aimed at the domestic market has been concentrated in the service sector, in such branches as banking, insurance and tourism. In this sector the locational advantage derives not so much from government policies as from the nature of the services themselves, which often require a local presence in order to provide the service.

The third form of foreign direct investment is the export-oriented investment, which acquired special importance in East Asia in the 1970s and 1980s. The locational advantage of export-oriented investment derives primarily from comparative advantage, in particular from a relative abundance of low-wage labor and from policy-induced advantages, such as the establishment of export processing zones within which foreign firms could operate under essentially free-trade conditions. The ownership advantages of the foreign firms, which initially were exclusively from the developed countries, derived in the case of labor-intensive consumer goods from the foreign firms' inside knowledge of the market for labor-intensive products in developed countries, and in the case of manufactured components from the foreign investors' ability to identify labor-intensive processes within the vertically integrated production structure of the multinational firm which could be relocated to developing countries. One important consequence of export-oriented direct investment was in inducing local firms to emulate the export-oriented foreign firms, with the result that indigenous firms, especially in the Asian NIEs, have acquired an ownership advantage that allowed them to become foreign investors themselves.

The theory of foreign direct investment pertains to intra-regional investment flows in the same way that trade theory pertains to intra-regional trade. Where there are ownership, locational and internationalization advantages to foreign direct investment among the Asian countries, investment should follow, provided barriers are not placed in its way. Furthermore, to the extent that direct investment flows are motivated by comparative advantage considerations, as in the case of natural resource investment and export-oriented investment, a complementary relationship should be observed between direct investment flows and trade flows. Even import-substituting direct investment may complement trade, since foreign firms operating in sheltered markets often make heavy use of imported capital goods and intermediates from the home country. The expectation is, therefore, that where conditions favor intra-Asian trade, they will also favor complementary flows of foreign direct investment between the Asian economies.

4.3   Complementarities among the Asian Economies

The most comprehensive indicator of relative resource endowment is per capita income. Generally, the higher per capita gross national product (GNP), the larger the per capita stock of physical and human capital and/or the greater the per capita endowment of natural resources. By this measure, the relative resource endowments of the Asian economies vary enormously, perhaps more than in any other region (see Figure 4.1). Between Japan and Hong Kong and Singapore there is about 12 years' growth of per capita income at 5 percent, with a similar gap between the latter and Taiwan; between Taiwan and the Republic of Korea; between the Republic of Korea and Malaysia, and so on down the income ladder to Indonesia.[1] It is only among the South Asian countries and the People's Republic of China that one finds similarity in the level of per capita income, and even that is more apparent than real, since within the large continental economies of India and the People's Republic of China there are wide regional disparities in per capita income. For example, after ten years of emulating the Asian NIEs Guangdong Province is now sometimes referred to as the "fifth little tiger."

Japan is of course the predominant economy in Asia, with an income more than double all the rest of Asia combined (see Figure 4.2). Interestingly, the "four little tigers," as the Asian NIEs are often called, when measured by income, are not so little after all, with a combined income equal to that of the People's Republic of China or South Asia, each with population exceeding one billion. The four ASEAN countries constitute the smallest bloc in Asia, with a combined income only 7 percent of that of Japan.[2]

FIGURE 4.1   Per capita gross national product, 1988 ($'000)

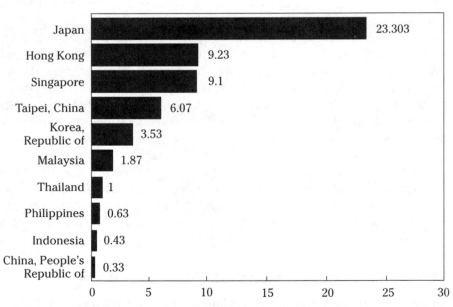

Sources: ADB (1990); International Monetary Fund, *International Financial Statistics*, Washington, DC, December 1990.

FIGURE 4.2   Gross national product, 1988 ($ billion)

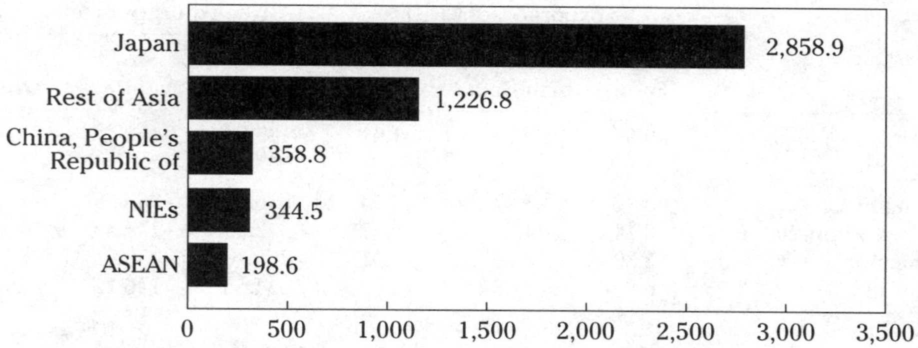

NIEs include Hong Kong, Republic of Korea, Singapore and Taiwan. In this figure, ASEAN includes Indonesia, Malaysia, Philippines and Thailand.

Sources: ADB (1990); International Monetary Fund, *International Financial Statistics*, Washington, DC, various issues.

To what extent are the vast differences in per capita income among the Asian economies due to differences in per capita endowment of natural resources, and to what extent due to differences in the accumulated stock of physical and human capital per person employed? An indication of the relative abundance of natural resources in the Asian economies is given in Table 4.1 and Figure 4.3. Table 4.1 reports the net exports (exports minus imports, the equivalent of production minus consumption) of the three broad categories of traded primary products, food, primary raw materials and mineral fuels, expressed as ratios to GNP and population. Figure 4.3 shows the net resource trade balance of the Asian regional groupings.

Interestingly, the highest and the lowest income countries in Asia are found to have the poorest natural resource endowment. Only two of the countries, Malaysia and Indonesia, are significant net exporters of oil, the most important source of new wealth from natural resources in recent years. Malaysia is also the only major net exporter of primary raw materials. The ASEAN countries are the only significant net exporters of food, the rest either being broadly self-sufficient or, as in the case of Japan, Hong Kong and Singapore, major net importers of food. While the differences among the Asian economies in natural resource endowment are significant, and no doubt give rise to intra-regional trade opportunities, they are certainly not sufficient to explain the large differentials in per capita income among the Asian economies.

The differences in per capita income among the Asian countries derive primarily from differences in the per capita stocks of physical and human capital. The wealthier countries invest a larger proportion of gross domestic product (GDP) and invest it more effectively than the poorer countries (see Table 4.2). Many reasons

TABLE 4.1   Net exports of primary products as a percentage of GNP and per capita, 1987

	Export (% of GNP)			Net export per capita ($)		
	Food	Raw materials	Mineral fuel	Food	Raw materials	Mineral fuel
Japan	−0.95	−0.78	−1.61	−185.50	−152.47	−314.12
NIEs						
Hong Kong	−8.16	−3.62	−2.54	−650.85	−288.90	−202.50
Korea, Republic of	0.11	−4.63	−4.67	2.96	−124.45	−125.61
Singapore	−3.39	1.79	−6.91	−265.10	139.91	−540.65
Taiwan	0.63	−2.66	−2.90	34.66	−146.32	−159.67
ASEAN						
Indonesia	1.55	1.40	9.29	6.78	6.15	40.72
Malaysia	4.26	12.74	9.01	74.62	223.20	157.96
Philippines	2.22	0.76	−2.67	12.14	4.16	−14.57
Thailand	8.11	0.25	−3.68	66.62	2.08	−30.20
China, People's Rep. of	0.73	0.10	1.25	2.15	0.30	3.68

NIEs include Hong Kong, Republic of Korea, Singapore and Taiwan. In this table, ASEAN includes Indonesia, Malaysia, Philippines and Thailand.

Source: U.N. Series-D Trade Tapes.

TABLE 4.2   Real growth rates and gross domestic investment as a percentage of gross domestic product

	Real GDP growth (%)		GDI as % of GDP	
	1971–80	1981–89	1971–80	1981–89
Japan	6.30	4.20	33.00	30.30
NIEs	9.23	7.87	31.55	30.79
Hong Kong	9.50	7.21	25.60	27.48
Korea, Republic of	8.70	9.28	28.90	29.82
Singapore	9.00	6.91	41.10	42.86
Taiwan	9.70	8.08	30.60	23.00
ASEAN	8.00	4.86	24.48	26.17
Indonesia	7.90	5.16	24.80	28.76
Malaysia	8.00	5.41	20.50	30.31
Philippines	6.20	1.74	26.70	20.17
Thailand	9.90	7.11	25.90	25.43
China, People's Rep. of	6.50	9.44	34.20	34.39

NIEs include Hong Kong, Republic of Korea, Singapore and Taiwan. In this table, ASEAN includes Indonesia, Malaysia, Philippines and Thailand.

Sources: ADB (1990); International Monetary Fund, *International Financial Statistics*, Washington, DC.

FIGURE 4.3   Net exports, 1987 ($ million)

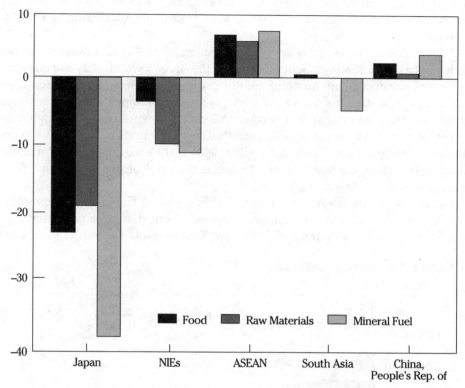

NIEs include Hong Kong, Republic of Korea, Singapore and Taiwan. In this figure, ASEAN includes Indonesia, Malaysia, Philippines and Thailand.

Sources: U.N. Series-D Trade Tapes.

have been offered to explain international differences in the quantity and quality of investment, including environmental conditions, cultural factors and type of political organization, but by far the most important is economic policy (Reynolds 1983). This is not to imply that environment, culture and type of government are not important, but only that given these factors, the choice of economic policies is critically important. This is evident from the fact that major shifts in economic policy have been associated with major changes in economic performance in countries operating in vastly different environments, cultures and political systems, for example, Republic of Korea in the 1960s, Tunisia in the 1970s, Turkey in the 1980s, and the People's Republic of China in the 1980s.

Of the policies which have been found to have a significant effect on economic performance, trade policies are among the more important. Trade restrictions are the principal instrument of industrial policy since the alternative of promoting industry through direct subvention is often politically and financially unacceptable.

Since trade restrictions have significantly influenced intra-Asian differences in production capabilities and constitute the principal obstacle to intra-Asian trade, it is useful to survey briefly the barriers to trade that exist among the Asian countries.

Unfortunately, there is no accurate measure of the restrictiveness of trade policies because of the prevalence of non-tariff barriers which defy measurement. Tariff rates, although an incomplete indicator of the level of protection, are nonetheless indicative both because they constitute an important barrier to trade in their own right and because it is often the case that countries with higher than average tariff rates also impose more quantitative restrictions on trade. The average tariff rate in the Asian countries in the early 1980s is shown in Figure 4.4. Particularly striking is the close correspondence between the level of per capita income and the level of the average tariff.

During the 1980s trade was liberalized in most of the Asian economies to some degree. Hong Kong and Singapore were, of course, already virtually free-trade economies. The Republic of Korea and Taiwan, on the other hand, still have

FIGURE 4.4   Average tariff rate (%)

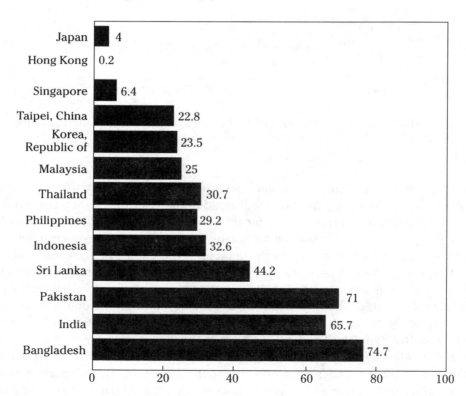

Sources: James et al. (1989: 33); Riedel (1992).

not removed all the barriers to trade erected during their earlier phase of import-substitution industrialization. Nevertheless, both have, since the mid-1960s, been steadily reducing the number of quantitative import restrictions and lowering tariff rates. However, trade liberalization in the Republic of Korea and Taiwan was accelerated in the 1980s as a result of their growing trade surpluses and in response to intensified pressure from the United States to unilaterally reduce their levels of protection. The Republic of Korea, for its part, raised the number of products exempt from quantitative restrictions from 60 percent in 1977 to 80 percent in 1985 and set a target of 95 percent by 1988. In addition, the average tariff rate in the Republic of Korea was reduced from 41 percent in 1978 to 22 percent in 1985, with a target of 18 percent in 1988 (World Bank 1989). Taiwan undertook even more ambitious trade reforms, eliminating almost all quantitative restrictions and lowering the average tariff rate below 20 percent by the end of the 1980s. Indeed, in January 1990, Taiwan applied for accession to the General Agreement on Tariffs and Trade (GATT) as a developed country, promising to make its trade practices consistent with GATT principles and with the practices of other developed economies.

Among the ASEAN economies under this discussion, Malaysia has been the most open, with lower levels of protection and greater reliance on free-trade zones to promote manufactured exports and attract foreign direct investment. Thailand and the Philippines have a strong legacy of import-substitution industrialization, though in recent years both have undertaken to liberalize imports and to promote manufactured exports. In 1980 Thailand embarked on a course of structural adjustment, combining fiscal retrenchment with vigorous export promotion, and it achieved considerable success. The volume of Thai-manufactured exports grew at 25 percent per annum from 1980 to 1988 and rose as a share of total merchandise exports from 22 percent in 1980 to 55 percent in 1988. Import liberalization, however, has progressed more slowly. The Philippines, on the other hand, launched a more ambitious program of trade liberalization in the 1980s, with a tariff reform in the early 1980s and substantial reduction in quantitative restrictions in the mid-1980s. However, because of serious macroeconomic difficulties, exacerbated by political upheaval, the Philippines' trade reform program has achieved only modest success.

Indonesia probably accomplished more trade liberalization in the 1980s than any of the other ASEAN economies, both because its policy objectives were more ambitious and because its initial level of protection was higher than in the other economies. In 1985 the government announced across-the-board reductions in nominal tariffs and introduced a package of measures to provide inputs to exporters at international prices. A year later the government announced its intention to remove quantitative restrictions altogether. Under this policy the overall value of imports subject to controls fell from 43 percent in mid-1986 to 21 percent in December 1988 (World Bank 1990).

The People's Republic of China has followed a fitful course of trade liberalization, sometimes described as "two steps forward and one step backward" (Srinivasan 1990). The major policy shift in the 1970s was to view trade no longer as a necessary evil, but as an essential part of economic modernization. The reforms themselves, which included the creation of new agencies to promote exports and attract foreign investment, have brought forth new problems, including inflation and growing indebtedness. As a result, the process of trade reform has from time to time been slowed or halted while the associated problems were tackled. Nevertheless, the aim of opening the economy to freer trade remains a priority, even though the measures taken to achieve it appear rather ad hoc and uncoordinated.

4.4   Overview of Intra-Asian Trade

4.4.1 Level and Growth of Intra-Asian Trade

The renowned dynamism of Asia is reflected in Table 4.3. In the 1980s incomes in Asia grew more than twice as fast as the rest of the world. Given the growth rate differential between Asia and the rest of the world, before the year 2000 Asia will constitute the world's largest market, with purchasing power exceeding either North America or Europe.

Naturally, with production during the 1980s growing twice as fast as elsewhere, the exports of the Asian countries also expanded at about double the rate in North America and Europe. In the first half of the 1980s, North America was the principal market for Asian exports. However, beginning in 1986, a profound shift occurred in the geographic pattern of Asian exports, with Asia becoming its own most important and most rapidly expanding market. The acceleration of intra-Asian trade occurred among the Asian developing economies as well as between the Asian developing economies and Japan (see Figure 4.5).

Numerous factors are behind the rapid growth in intra-Asian trade since 1986, though it is impossible to determine their relative importance. Certainly, the currency realignments which took place in 1985 and 1986 were of prime importance. From

TABLE 4.3   Regional income (1988) and export growth rates (1982–88)

	Gross national product ($ billion)	Gross national product growth rate (%)	Export growth rate (%)
North America	5,352.1	2.3	5.1
Europe	5,000.0	2.2	5.7
Asia	4,084.8	4.8	10.0

Sources: International Monetary Fund, *World Economic Outlook* (Washington, DC, 1989); General Agreement on Tariffs and Trade, *International Trade* (1988–89).

FIGURE 4.5   Dynamics of intra-Asian trade, 1983–89 ($ billion)

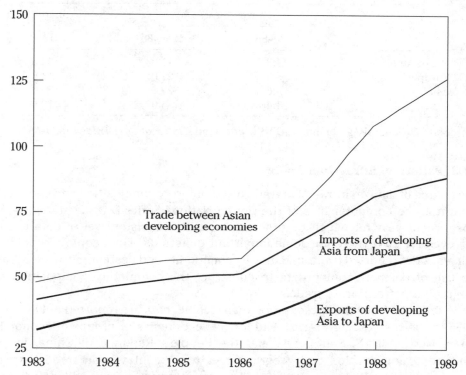

Source: International Monetary Fund, *Direction of Trade Statistics Yearbook 1990*, Washington, DC, 1990.

1980 to 1985 the U.S. dollar appreciated in real terms by some 40 percent, making the United States a relatively attractive market to Asian exporters. However, after the Plaza Accord the U.S. dollar fell steadily, thereby reducing the relative profitability of exporting to the United States in favor of Japan, Germany and other members of the European Monetary System.[3] In addition, the increasing threat of protectionism in the United States and Europe, occurring at the same time most Asian countries were unilaterally liberalizing trade, no doubt gave impetus to intra-Asian trade. And, of course, with income growing more rapidly in Asia than elsewhere, one would expect intra-regional trade to be relatively strong. However, the share of intra-Asian trade in total Asian exports, which stood at 38 percent in 1988, considerably exceeded Asia's share in world income, which was only about 25 percent (see Table 4.4). On the face of it, therefore, there would appear to be a bias in favor of intra-regional over inter-regional trade. In order to explore this, however, it is necessary to examine the commodity composition and geographic pattern of intra-Asian trade.

TABLE 4.4   Asian exports by destination (%)

	Growth rate (%)		Share (%)
	1980–86	1986–88	1988
North America	14.3	11.9	29.5
Europe	5.8	27.0	18.6
Asia	4.6	27.7	38.0
Other	–1.4	5.0	13.9

Source: General Agreement on Tariffs and Trade, *International Trade (1988–89)*.

4.4.2 Pattern of Intra-Asian Trade

The source of data on intra-Asian trade by commodity composition and geographic pattern is the computer files of the United Nations Series-D trade statistics. The most recent year for which there is a reasonably consistent set of data is 1987, and even for 1987 there are some important omissions. The People's Republic of China has not reported trade statistics by commodity and destination, necessitating the use of partner-country data to construct the commodity composition and geographic pattern of its trade.

In order to make the presentation manageable, data are reported only for 1987 (1985 in the case of South Asia), and for five economies or groups of economies: Japan, NIEs, ASEAN, South Asia and the People's Republic of China. In fact, commodity composition and geographic pattern of intra-Asian trade have not changed significantly in recent years. Three broad questions are addressed in this overview: (a) How important is intra-regional trade for the various Asian economies and groups? (b) What is the commodity composition of intra-regional trade for the various economies and groups? and (c) What is the geographic pattern of intra-regional trade by commodity category?

The answer to the first question is given in Table 4.5, which presents the percentage share of exports to Asia in total exports by commodity for each economy or group. As the table shows, around the average share of intra-Asian exports for all goods and all economies (34 percent in 1987), there is a great deal of variation both among the individual economies or groups and across commodity categories. Intra-Asian exports are more important to the ASEAN economies and the People's Republic of China than to the other countries or groups. This derives, it is suspected, from the dependence of the ASEAN economies and the People's Republic of China on the entrepôt services of Singapore and Hong Kong, an issue which subsequently will be considered in more detail. Also observed in Table 4.5 is a greater share of intra-Asian trade in primary products than in manufactures. This is probably due to the fact that market opportunities outside the Asian region are greater for manufactures than for primary products, since North America is relatively abundant in natural resources and Europe has relatively high barriers to agricultural imports.

TABLE 4.5 Exports to Asia as a percentage of total exports by economy group and commodity, 1987

	Japan	NIEs	ASEAN	South Asia[a]	China, People's Rep. of	Asia
All goods	26.4	31.5	56.8	20.5	63.9	33.9
Primary	56.3	71.8	66.2	27.7	68.8	64.0
Food	42.7	69.0	46.1	18.2	77.7	54.4
Raw materials	57.9	78.5	81.1	9.2	67.4	74.9
Mineral fuel	68.3	64.6	65.5	55.4	54.1	62.1
Nonferrous metals	57.7	75.2	76.5	35.8	78.7	67.7
Manufactures	25.6	26.5	40.9	15.2	62.3	28.7
Chemicals	51.2	66.2	74.4	32.8	59.2	56.6
Basic manufactures	46.3	42.0	52.1	18.2	70.4	46.1
Machinery and transport equipment	21.3	24.7	42.6	19.7	117.8	23.5
Miscellaneous	18.4	17.3	16.3	3.4	51.0	21.6
Selected products						
Textiles and yarn	49.3	54.4	35.4	15.7	–	–
Iron and steel	54.5	51.2	60.0	34.8	–	–
Nonelectrical machinery	28.4	23.7	62.1	21.9	–	–
Electrical machinery	33.1	28.9	38.2	10.5	–	–
Transport equipment	8.7	11.7	63.0	23.1	–	–
Motor vehicles	7.3	6.1	60.4	22.2	–	–
Ships and boats	11.8	14.5	76.9	60.2	–	–
Clothing	13.6	14.8	8.4	2.5	–	–
Footwear	43.9	9.3	8.8	2.8	–	–
Scientific instruments	20.4	27.5	41.8	6.0	–	–

– = not available
a. 1985.
NIEs include Hong Kong, Republic of Korea, Singapore and Taiwan. In this table, ASEAN includes Indonesia, Malaysia, Philippines and Thailand.
Source: U.N. Series-D Trade Tapes.

The economies least integrated into the Asian region are the South Asian economies. Japan and the NIEs appear to be about equally dependent on the Asian region, but the data are misleading. The reason is, of course, that the NIEs face an export market in Asia that is more than twice the size of the market Japan faces (which excludes Japan itself). The 26 percent of NIE-manufactured exports destined for Asia is roughly equal to the share in world income of their Asian market (which includes Japan). Japan, on the other hand, exports about 26 percent of its manufactured exports to developing Asia, whose share in world income is only about 8 percent.

The commodity composition of intra-Asian exports by country of origin is shown in Table 4.6. The bulk of intra-Asian exports are manufactures, accounting for 72 percent of the total. Primary products are an important part of intra-Asian exports only for the South Asian and ASEAN economies, which in the case of the latter is dominated by the oil exports of Malaysia and Indonesia. Japan and the NIEs export mainly manufactures, which, in accordance with their respective comparative advantages, are concentrated, in the case of Japan, in iron and steel, machinery and transport equipment and, in the case of the NIEs (and the People's Republic of China), in the more labor-intensive branches of textiles, clothing and electrical machinery.

The geographic pattern of intra-Asian exports is shown in Table 4.7. The striking feature about the geographic pattern is the overwhelming importance of

TABLE 4.6   Commodity composition of intra-Asian exports by economy or group, 1987

	Japan	NIEs	ASEAN	South Asia[a]	China, People's Rep. of	Asia
All goods	100.0	100.0	100.0	100.0	100.0	100.0
Primary	5.3	25.3	73.1	57.6	36.1	27.9
Food	1.1	10.7	15.8	22.5	14.7	8.8
Raw materials	1.7	9.3	36.8	2.3	12.1	6.4
Mineral fuel	0.7	3.9	17.8	32.3	7.8	10.9
Nonferrous metals	1.7	1.2	2.6	0.4	1.3	1.6
Manufactures	94.6	74.7	26.8	42.3	63.8	72.0
Chemicals	9.9	7.0	3.0	5.2	5.2	7.1
Basic manufactures	21.9	22.1	11.3	30.2	22.7	20.5
Machinery and transport equipment	53.1	25.7	9.7	4.2	8.1	30.1
Miscellaneous	9.6	19.8	2.7	2.5	27.7	14.2
Selected products						
Textiles and yarn	4.5	12.3	1.8	13.1	17.6	8.5
Iron and steel	11.4	3.3	1.0	0.8	1.0	5.5
Nonelectrical machinery	21.2	7.6	1.7	2.3	1.7	10.7
Electrical machinery	22.5	16.2	7.1	0.5	5.9	15.2
Transport equipment	9.3	1.8	0.8	1.3	0.4	4.2
Motor vehicles	7.0	0.4	0.1	0.6	–	2.7
Ships and boats	0.8	0.5	0.6	0.3	0.1	0.6
Clothing	0.1	6.7	0.8	1.4	14.6	4.5
Footwear	–	1.2	–	–	1.2	0.5
Scientific instruments	–	2.4	–	0.1	1.7	2.7

– = nil.

a. 1985.

NIEs include Hong Kong, Republic of Korea, Singapore and Taiwan. In this table, ASEAN includes Indonesia, Malaysia, Philippines and Thailand.

Source: U.N. Series-D Trade Tapes.

Japan and the NIEs, which account for two-thirds of total intra-Asian exports and more than 80 percent of intra-Asian exports of manufactures. The lack of integration of the South Asian economies into the Asian economy is remarkable, in spite of the apparent complementarities between the South Asian economies and Japan and the NIEs.

Apart from South Asia, the commodity composition and geographic pattern of intra-Asian exports described in the tables reflect clearly the complementarities which exist among the Asian economies. There are, however, several aspects of intra-Asian trade which merit a closer examination: (a) the role of Japan; (b) the intra-group trade of the NIEs, the ASEAN economies and the South Asian economies; and (c) the entrepôt role of Hong Kong and Singapore.

TABLE 4.7   Geographic pattern of Intra-Asian exports by commodity category, 1987

	Japan	NIEs	ASEAN	South Asia[a]	China, People's Rep. of	Asia
All goods	36.9	29.5	16.2	1.7	15.5	100
Primary	7.1	26.7	42.4	3.6	20.0	100
Food	4.8	35.7	29.0	4.4	25.8	100
Raw materials	2.5	25.3	54.4	0.3	17.2	100
Mineral fuel	9.9	17.8	44.6	8.7	18.8	100
Nonferrous metals	38.1	22.5	25.9	0.4	12.8	100
Manufactures	48.5	30.6	6.0	1.0	13.7	100
Chemicals	51.4	29.0	6.8	1.3	11.4	100
Basic manufactures	39.4	31.8	8.9	2.5	17.2	100
Machinery and transport equipment	65.0	25.2	5.2	0.2	4.1	100
Miscellaneous	25.1	41.1	3.1	0.3	30.2	100
Selected products						
Textiles and yarn	19.7	42.3	3.4	2.6	31.8	100
Iron and steel	76.0	17.8	2.9	0.2	2.9	100
Nonelectrical machinery	73.2	21.1	2.7	0.3	2.5	100
Electrical machinery	54.7	31.4	7.6	–	6.0	100
Transport equipment	81.6	13.0	3.1	0.5	1.5	100
Motor vehicles	93.0	5.1	0.8	0.4	0.5	100
Ships and boats	53.3	26.6	16.1	0.9	2.8	100
Clothing	1.2	44.4	3.1	0.5	50.6	100
Footwear	1.7	62.8	2.5	0.1	32.6	100
Scientific instruments	–	26.2	–	0.1	9.6	100

– = nil.
a. 1985.
NIEs include Hong Kong, Republic of Korea, Singapore and Taiwan. In this table, ASEAN includes Indonesia, Malaysia, Philippines and Thailand.

Source: U.N. Series-D Trade Tapes.

4.5   Special Aspects of Intra-Asian Trade

4.5.1 Predominant Role of Japan

Japan as the largest and most advanced economy in Asia dominates intra-Asian trade. It is instructive, therefore, to consider the magnitudes of Japanese exports to and imports from the Asian economies. The commodity composition of Japanese exports and imports by group is shown in Table 4.8. The largest single flow recorded is Japanese exports of manufactures to the NIEs, the bulk of which is machinery and transport equipment. ASEAN and the People's Republic of China together account for another 8 percent of Japanese exports, also mainly machinery and transport equipment. The second largest flow recorded is Japan's imports of primary commodities from ASEAN. Japan also imports a substantial amount of manufactures from the NIEs. The East Asian developing countries are both an important market for Japanese exports and an important source of Japanese imports.

The ASEAN economies have a reciprocal, albeit more dependent, relationship with Japan. Japan is the destination for about 37 percent of ASEAN exports of primary products, and it is the source of about 34 percent of ASEAN imports of manufactures. In the NIEs, however, the trade relationship with Japan is not so balanced. Japan supplies about 42 percent of NIE imports of machinery and transport equipment but absorbs less than 10 percent of NIE exports of manufactures, the major market for which is the United States. This pattern of importing capital goods and industrial inputs from Japan and exporting final products mainly to the United States places the NIEs in a vulnerable position during periods of exchange rate realignment among the major currencies. For example, a depreciation of the U.S. dollar against the yen can have a significant, negative effect on the NIEs' terms of trade unless they are able to redirect exports from the weak-currency to the strong-currency country. In the mid-1970s the NIEs were not very successful in avoiding the terms-of-trade loss from the dollar depreciation against the yen, because exchange rate policy was mainly aimed at maintaining parity with the U.S. dollar so as to relieve pressure on exporters in adjusting to the currency realignment. In the mid-1980s, however, when the dollar fell against the yen, the Republic of Korea and Taiwan allowed their currencies to appreciate against the dollar along with the yen, inducing significant rise in exports to Japan.

4.5.2 Trade within the Groups

The importance of trade within each of the three groups, that is, NIEs, ASEAN and South Asia, is indicated in Table 4.9. The relatively large proportion of intra-NIE trade is also not remarkable, given that two of the four NIEs, Hong Kong and Singapore, are entrepôt centers for the People's Republic of China and Southeast Asia, respectively. The Republic of Korea and Taiwan direct most of their trade with the People's Republic of China through Hong Kong; however, trade between the Republic of Korea and Taiwan is negligible, since their economies are far more

TABLE 4.8 Japanese exports to and imports from Asia by economy/group and commodity, 1987 ($ billion)

	NIEs		ASEAN		South Asia		China, People's Rep. of	
	Exports	Imports	Exports	Imports	Exports	Imports	Exports	Imports
All goods	38.8	18.3	9.4	16.2	3.4	2.2	8.2	7.2
Primary	2.3	6.5	0.4	14.6	0.1	1.3	0.3	4.5
Food	0.5	4.0	0.1	2.1	–	0.4	–	1.5
Raw materials	0.7	0.7	0.1	3.9	0.1	0.7	0.1	0.9
Mineral fuel	0.3	1.5	0.1	8.1	–	1.1	–	2.1
Nonferrous metals	0.8	0.2	0.1	0.5	–	–	0.1	0.1
Manufactures	36.5	11.8	9.0	1.6	3.3	0.9	7.9	2.6
Chemicals	4.0	0.9	1.0	0.2	0.2	–	0.7	0.4
Basic manufactures	7.4	2.7	2.0	1.0	0.7	0.8	2.9	1.0
Machinery and transport	20.4	2.2	5.5	0.2	2.1	–	3.7	–
Miscellaneous	4.7	5.9	0.4	0.2	0.2	–	0.5	1.1

– = nil.

Source: U.N. Series-D Trade Tapes.

TABLE 4.9   Intra-exports as share of total exports, 1987 (%)

	All goods	Primary products	Manufactures
Intra-NIEs	8.9	12.1	8.5
Intra-ASEAN	3.7	3.9	3.5

Source: U.N. Series-D Trade Tapes.

competitive with each other than complementary. What is more interesting is the small proportion of intra-ASEAN trade, since the ASEAN economies are the only ones in Asia which give each other trade preferences.

The failure of the ASEAN preferential trade arrangement to create much trade is mainly because the scheme is very modest in scope (Langhammer and Hiemenz 1990). Preferences are negotiated on a commodity-by-commodity basis, with ample allowance for countries to claim exemptions. The result is that most generous preferences are given on products which are not imported, such as snow ploughs in Indonesia and rubber in Malaysia (Balasubramanyam 1989). In addition, since each country maintains its own separate tariff schedule on trade with the rest of the world and further since the average tariff rate varies widely among the ASEAN countries (see Figure 4.4), it has been necessary to impose strict rule-of-origin restrictions, which greatly hamper the effectiveness of the preferences.

The failure of the preferential trade arrangement to generate more intra-ASEAN trade is, however, probably a blessing in disguise. The largest of the ASEAN countries (Indonesia, Philippines and Thailand) have built up sizable industrial sectors many of which are sheltered from international competition and not particularly efficient. Given the high average tariff level in these countries, it is quite possible that more generous and effective trade preference could cause a significant amount of trade diversion from more efficient, lower-cost suppliers in the rest of the world to the ASEAN countries. In these circumstances, the cost of creating trade among ASEAN countries could well exceed the benefits.

4.5.3 Entrepôt Trade in Asia

The two richest developing economies in Asia, Hong Kong and Singapore, until the mid-1950s earned their livelihood primarily as entrepôt centers to the hinterlands of the People's Republic of China and Southeast Asia. The manufacturing boom which propelled them into the front ranks of the developing economies in the 1960s and 1970s was induced in part by the decline in entrepôt trade opportunities in the mid-1950s, in Singapore's case because of its confrontation with Indonesia, and in the case of Hong Kong because of the closing up of the People's Republic of China at the time of the Korean war. In recent years, however, entrepôt trade has regained its lost importance both in Singapore and Hong Kong, although for Singapore it is difficult to get an accurate picture since statistics are not reported on trade with Indonesia. This discussion, therefore, focuses on Hong Kong's entrepôt trade, which in any case is far greater than Singapore's.

The proximate cause of the resurgence of entrepôt trade in Hong Kong, which grew at an annual rate of about 30 percent in the 1980s, was the initiation of the "open door" policy of the People's Republic of China in 1979. In the explosion of international trade which followed, Hong Kong played a major role as an intermediary. The shares of Chinese exports and imports which flowed through Hong Kong as entrepôt trade (as opposed to transshipment through Hong Kong) increased significantly, rising from about 4 percent to about 30 percent of exports and from about 1 percent to 22 percent of imports (see Figure 4.6). From Hong Kong's perspective, this constituted an even more dramatic shift, with the share

FIGURE 4.6   People's Republic of China trade via Hong Kong: percentage share of total exports and imports

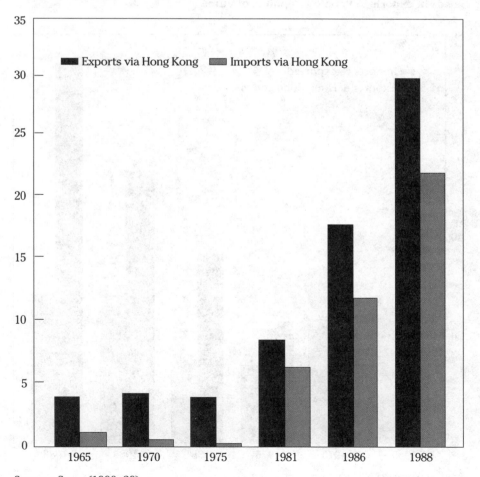

Source: Sung (1990: 29).

of imports from the People's Republic of China being re-exported, rising from about 20 percent to 74 percent. Along with the rapid increase in re-exports to the People's Republic of China was an even more rapid expansion in exports of domestic (Hong Kong) goods, as indicated by the modest rise in the share of domestic exports in total exports to the People's Republic of China (see Figure 4.7).

The rise in exports of domestic goods to the People's Republic of China has been mainly attributed to the massive investments made by Hong Kong firms in processing and assembly operations in Guongdong Province, which make heavy use of Hong Kong-made raw materials and components. The rise in Hong Kong re-exports to the People's Republic of China—and its growing reliance on the Hong Kong middlemen—is more difficult to explain. In part it has occurred because two

FIGURE 4.7   Hong Kong's trade with People's Republic of China: share of imports from People's Republic of China re-exported and share of Hong Kong goods in exports to People's Republic of China

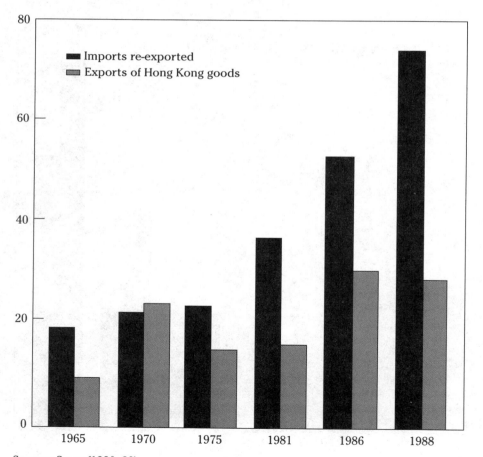

Source: Sung (1990: 29).

of the People's Republic of China's trading partners, the Republic of Korea and Taipei, China have bans on direct trade with the People's Republic of China. However, a significant proportion of the People's Republic of China's trade with North America, Europe and Asia is conducted through Hong Kong (see Table 4.10).

There is, however, an explanation for this seeming paradox (Sung 1990). The essence of the argument is that demand for Hong Kong's entrepôt services has increased because economic reforms in the People's Republic of China and the diversification of its commodity composition of exports and imports have increased transactions costs. In addition, Hong Kong has diversified the composition of exports away from homogenous raw materials to more heterogeneous manufactured goods, which also increases transactions costs and raises the demand for intermediation. With continued expansion and diversification of trade in the People's Republic of China and Southeast Asia, it is likely that entrepôt trade through Hong Kong and Singapore will increase further, becoming an even more important part of intra-Asian trade.

TABLE 4.10   Share of indirect trade through Hong Kong with selected partners, 1988 (%)

	Exports	Imports
Australia	51.9	n.a.
Canada	51.9	n.a.
Germany	39.1	7.7
Indonesia	53.8	23.4
Japan	15.4	21.2
Singapore	16.5	18.0
United States	62.1	15.6
United Kingdom	49.7	18.7

n.a. = not available.

Source: Sung (1990).

4.6   Intra-Asian Direct Investment

Unlike trade, foreign direct investment mainly flows in one direction, from the richer to the poorer countries. The richer countries tend to have the ownership advantage required for direct investment by virtue of their capital abundance, technological lead and marketing know-how, while the poorer countries offer the locational advantages of abundant, low-wage labor and/or unexploited natural resources, advantages which can be negated by restrictions on foreign direct investment or an unstable political environment. This pattern of direct investment, from the richer to the poorer countries, is well illustrated in Asia.

James Riedel

4.6.1 Japanese Investment in Asia

Japan, as the largest and richest country in Asia, is the main source of direct investment from within the region. The geographic distribution of Japanese investment in Asia is shown in Table 4.11. Not surprisingly, the NIEs claim the largest share of Japanese investment, which is largely concentrated in manufacturing, where Japan's ownership advantage is strongest. The ASEAN economies have also been major recipients of Japanese investment, both because of the advantages they offer in terms of low-cost labor for export manufacturing and because of their abundance of natural resources, especially in Indonesia and Malaysia (see Figure 4.8). Since 1979 the People's Republic of China has attracted a growing proportion of Japanese direct investment, which by 1988 amounted to more than US$2 billion. The South Asian economies, in spite of the large market they offer, have not attracted Japanese direct investment, mainly because of the restrictions they impose on direct investment, international trade and business generally (James et al. 1989: 122).

4.6.2 NIE Investment in Asia

The ownership advantage, as noted above, is something that can be acquired in

TABLE 4.11   Japanese overseas direct investment in Asia, 1951–88

	Cumulative total, 1951–88 ($ million)	Percentage distribution
NIEs	15,018	46.8
Hong Kong	6,167	19.2
Korea, Republic of	3,248	10.1
Singapore	3,812	11.9
Taiwan	1,791	5.6
ASEAN	14,750	46.0
Indonesia	9,804	30.6
Malaysia	1,834	5.7
Philippines	1,120	3.5
Thailand	1,992	6.2
South Asia	270	0.9
Bangladesh	11	–
India	148	0.5
Pakistan	18	0.1
Sri Lanka	93	0.3
China, People's Republic of	2,036	6.3

– = nil.

NIEs include Hong Kong, Republic of Korea, Singapore and Taiwan. In this table, ASEAN includes Indonesia, Malaysia, Philippines and Thailand.

Source: Ministry of Finance, Government of Japan, February 25, 1990.

FIGURE 4.8 Japanese direct investment motives (percentage cited as one of the three most important motives for foreign direct investment)

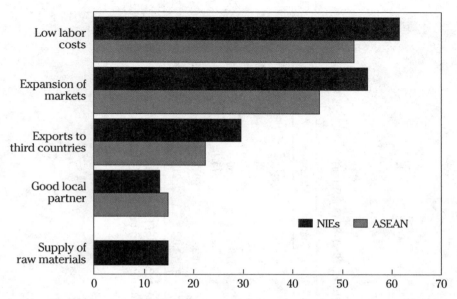

Source: Ministry of International Trade and Industry, Government of Japan, *White Paper on International Trade (1987).*

the process of economic development. Perhaps the best examples of this are the NIEs which in recent years have become major investors in export-oriented, labor-intensive manufacturing in the ASEAN economies and the People's Republic of China. Unfortunately, the only data available on the NIEs' direct investment in Asia are for investment approvals, not the actual investment amounts. Table 4.12 presents data on the cumulative total from 1980 to 1988 of direct investment approvals in the ASEAN economies, Republic of Korea, and Taiwan.

There are several interesting findings in Table 4.12. First, Asian economies are the source of almost half the direct investment in the NIEs and ASEAN economies, a much greater proportion than the region's share in world income or investment, suggesting that being from the region may give Asian investors an advantage over their counterparts from outside the region. The table also illustrates the predominant role of Japan, especially in the NIEs. However, in the ASEAN economies, the NIEs are themselves major investors, especially the richest and most open of the NIEs, Hong Kong. Singapore is important in neighboring Malaysia and Indonesia, but in the region as a whole it is far behind Hong Kong, in part because many of the largest Singapore firms are state-owned. Taiwan has emerged as a major investor in the ASEAN economies, especially in the Philippines. Its comparative advantage in labor-intensive manufactures is becoming rapidly eroded by rising real wages. Nevertheless, Hong Kong and Taiwan possess valuable knowledge gained over

TABLE 4.12 Foreign direct investment approvals, cumulative total, 1980–88 ($ million)

From \ To	Korea, Rep. of	Taiwan	Indonesia	Malaysia	Philippines	Thailand
Japan	2,070.3	1,843.6	1,209.8	512.6	302.7	1,245.3
Hong Kong	155.2	400.5	932.9	123.1	81.7	359.7
Korea, Republic of			212.3	19.8	4.4	14.4
Singapore	Negative	67.9	410.5	250.8	13.7	170.3
Taiwan			117.5	75.4	122.0	49.8
Asia	2,264.6	2,320.7	3,759.4	918.7	630.3	1,999.2
World	4,108.2	5,464.8	9,374.0	2,213.7	2,095.4	3,331.7

Sources: Taiwan: Ministry of Economic Affairs; Republic of Korea: Ministry of Finance; Malaysia: Ministry of Finance; Thailand: Bank of Thailand; Philippines: Board of Investments; and Indonesia: Central Bureau of Statistics, *Monthly Statistical Bulletin*, November 1989.

many years, about the world market for labor-intensive manufactures, which is an asset they can continue to exploit profitably by investing in export-oriented manufacturing activities in lower-wage countries. In this way, direct investment facilitates movement up the ladder of comparative advantage both in the investing countries, whose resources are freed up to move into more capital-intensive activities, and in the host countries, whose industrial employment and nontraditional (manufactured) exports expand.

The process of relocating labor-intensive manufacturing from higher to lower wage economies in Asia has gained particular momentum among the People's Republic of China; Hong Kong; and Taiwan. During 1979–88 direct investment from Hong Kong to the People's Republic of China accounted for about two-thirds of an estimated US$30 billion, a part of which probably originated in third countries (mostly from Taiwan) (Sung 1990). Also, the number of workers employed by Hong Kong firms in the People's Republic of China now substantially exceeds the number employed in manufacturing in Hong Kong.

4.6.3 Link between Intra-Asian Investment and Trade

It was noted above that intra-regional trade in Asia is of a magnitude that is greater than would be expected on the basis of the relative size of the Asian market. One possible explanation for the apparent bias in favor of intra-Asian trade is the growing importance of intra-Asian foreign direct investment, which from the fragmentary evidence that is available appears to be highly export-oriented.

The best evidence of the export-orientation of Asian foreign direct investment comes from Japan. There has been a dramatic rise in Asia's share of Japanese foreign direct investment in the developing world. There has also been a corresponding rise in the export-orientation of Japanese investment in developing countries (see Figure 4.9). However, data are not available on the export orientation of Japanese foreign direct investment by region. However, the direction of change both in the relative importance of Asia as a destination for investment and in the share of exports in total sales of Japanese affiliates in developing countries suggests that the export orientation of Asian affiliates is considerably higher than those elsewhere in the developing world.

It is interesting to consider the export-orientation of Japanese affiliates by sector (see Table 4.13). Export-orientation is, not surprisingly, highest in the natural resource-based sectors (such as food processing, wood processing and nonferrous metals) and is lowest in the heavy capital-intensive manufacturing sectors (such as chemicals and iron and steel). The relatively labor-intensive sectors such as textiles, electrical machinery and precision machinery are also highly export-oriented, with shares of exports in total shares exceeding 50 percent. Interestingly, the increase in the export-orientation of Japanese affiliates in developing countries is across the board, wood processing being the exception to this general trend.

FIGURE 4.9   Japanese foreign direct investment in developing economies:
the roles of Asia and of exports (%)

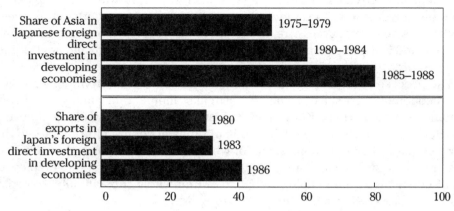

Source: Takouchi (1990).

TABLE 4.13   Share of exports in total sales of Japanese affiliates in
developing countries (%)

	1980	1983	1988
Manufacturing	33.0	35.1	42.3
Food processing	63.1	41.0	76.7
Textiles and apparel	33.8	34.7	51.6
Wood processing	62.8	65.3	57.1
Chemicals	16.0	16.4	27.5
Iron and steel	16.0	16.4	16.5
Nonferrous metals	45.8	38.8	63.8
General machinery	21.9	25.1	43.8
Electrical machinery	37.5	57.0	53.1
Transportation equipment	7.7	10.6	22.9
Precision equipment	41.6	80.2	51.6

Source: Takouchi (1990).

It is likely that foreign affiliates of Hong Kong and Taiwanese firms in Asia are
at least as export-oriented as their Japanese counterparts. Hong Kong and
Taiwanese investors followed the Japanese into those branches in which the
Japanese affiliates produce largely for export. Moreover, many of the Hong Kong
and Taiwanese firms investing in the People's Republic of China and Southeast
Asia established themselves by producing for world markets.

4.7   Future Prospects for Intra-Asian Trade and Investment

Will intra-Asian international trade and foreign direct investment continue to expand as rapidly as they have in the recent past? There are good reasons to expect they will. First, as long as the Asian countries continue to liberalize unilaterally their trade policies and to maintain current high levels of investment, the Asian market will continue to outpace growth in the other major export markets, principally North America and Europe. It is also likely that real wages in Japan and the Asian NIEs will continue to increase faster than elsewhere in Asia, and that as a result the flow of direct investment from the higher wage Asian countries to the lower wage Asian countries will be maintained for some time to come. Since intra-Asian direct investment appears to complement and reinforce intra-Asian trade, the bias which was observed in favor of intra-regional over inter-regional trade is likely to grow stronger.

Another potential source of bias in favor of intra-Asian trade is the negative force of protectionism in Asia's traditional markets, principally the United States and Western Europe. In recent years both the United States and the European Community have relied more and more on nontariff, discriminatory trade restrictions to protect domestic markets and have resorted increasingly to bilateral and regional trade arrangements to promote trade liberalization. Asian exporters have undoubtedly been victims of both of these developments. The Asian countries, especially Japan and the Asian NIEs, are the most frequent targets of anti-dumping duties, countervailing subsidy measures and so-called safeguard restrictions applied by the United States and the European Community. It is also likely that Asia, more than any other part of the world, is likely to be hurt by the proposed North American Free-Trade Agreement.

As for Europe-1992, it is difficult to foresee how Asia's trade prospects will be affected. To the extent that the 1992 measures achieve their stated goals of improving European efficiency and intensifying competition within the European Community, they will expand opportunities for trade with Asia. On the other hand, if the price for liberalization within the European Community is more protection from foreign competition, then Asian interests will clearly suffer. The Asian countries' best hope for relief from the discriminatory trade policies of the United States and Europe was the promise of the Uruguay Round of a renewed strength and an expanded role for the GATT system. However, if the Uruguay Round fails, it is more likely that the international trading system will slide further in the direction of regionalism. While this would undoubtedly give greater scope to intra-Asian trade, it would do so at a high cost to the Asian countries.

Notes

This article was adapted from James Riedel, 1991, "Intra-Asian Trade and Foreign Direct Investment," *Asian Development Review*, 9(1): 111–46, with the permission of the Asian Development Bank.

1. References to Taiwan are to the Republic of China.
2. In this discussion, the Asian NIEs include Hong Kong, Republic of Korea, Singapore

and Taiwan and the ASEAN countries include Indonesia, Malaysia, Philippines and Thailand.
3. The Plaza Accord was reached by the Group of Five (France, Germany, Japan, United Kingdom and United States) in their September 1985 meeting at the Plaza Hotel, New York, to seek an orderly appreciation of the major non-dollar currencies.

References

Asian Development Bank (ADB), 1990, *Asian Development Outlook 1990*, Manila.

Balasubramanyam, V. N., 1989, "ASEAN and Regional Trade Cooperation in Southeast Asia," in D. Greenaway, T. Hyclak and R. Thornton (eds.), *Economic Aspects of Regional Trading Arrangements*, Wheatsheaf, Brighton, UK.

Dunning, John D., 1981a, *International Production and the Multinational Enterprise*, George Allen & Unwin, London.

————, 1981b, "Explaining the International Direct Investment Position of Countries: Towards a Dynamic or Developmental Approach," *Weltwirtschaftliches Archiv*, 117: 30–64.

Frank, Isaiah, 1980, *Foreign Enterprises in Developing Countries*, Johns Hopkins University Press, Baltimore, MD.

Havrylyshyn, Oli and E. Civan, 1985, "Intra-industry Trade Among Developing Countries," *Journal of Development Economics*, 18: 40–58.

James, William E., Seiji Naya, and Gerald M. Meier, 1989, *Asian Development: Economic Success and Policy Lessons*, University of Wisconsin Press, Madison, WI.

Jones, Ronald W. and J. Peter Neary, 1984, "The Positive Theory of International Trade," in R. W. Jones and P. B. Kenen (eds.), *Handbook of International Economics*, Vol. 1, Elsevier Science Publishers, Amsterdam, pp. 1–62.

Krueger, Anne O., 1977, *Growth, Distortions and Patterns of Trade Among Many Countries*, Princeton Studies in International Finance, No. 40.

Langhammer, Rolf J. and Ulrich Hiemenz, 1990, *Regional Integration Among Developing Countries*, Kieler Studien no. 232, J.C.B. Mohr (Paul Siebeck), Tubingen.

Linder, S. B., 1961, *An Essay on Trade and Transformation*, Almqvist och Wiksell, Stockholm.

Reynolds, L. G., 1983, "The Spread of Economic Growth to the Third World," *Journal of Economic Literature*, 21(3): 941–80.

Riedel, James, 1992, "International Trade in Taiwan's Transition from Developing to Mature Economy," in Gustav Ranis (ed.), *Taiwan: From Developing to Mature Economy*, pp. 253–304.

Srinivasan, T. N., 1990, "External Sector in Development: China and India, 1950-89," *American Economic Review*, 80(2): 113–17.

Sung, Yung-Wing, 1990, "The Marketization of a Command Economy and International Trade in Intermediary Services: The Case of China and Hong Kong," Harvard-Yenching Institute, Cambridge, MA, mimeo.

Takouchi, Kenji, 1990, "Does Japanese Direct Foreign Investment Promote Japanese Imports from Developing Countries?" paper presented at the Second Convention of the East Asian Economics Association, Bandung, August.

Vernon, R., 1966, "International Investment and International Trade in the Product Cycle," *Quarterly Journal of Economics*, 80: 190–207.

World Bank, 1989, "Strengthening Trade Policy Reform," Washington, DC, mimeo.

————, 1990, *Trends in Developing Economies 1990*, Washington, DC.

Chapter 5

Kym Anderson

Fibers, Textiles and Clothing in Asia-Pacific's Economic Development

5.1 Introduction

One of the most conspicuous signs in Western economies of the beginnings of export-oriented industrial growth in East Asia has been the appearance in Western markets of clothing from that region. Japan was the first contributor, but was followed and eventually replaced in the 1960s and 1970s by Hong Kong, South Korea and Taiwan. And then in the 1980s that second generation of newly industrialized economies also has begun to be overshadowed—at least at the low-priced end of international markets—by China and some of the ASEAN countries, most notably Thailand. This very visible development is but a small part of the changing pattern of production and international trade in fibers, textiles and clothing that provide a classic case study of the process of industrial growth and of the dynamics of our interdependent world economy. Nowhere has that pattern changed more dramatically than in East Asia during the past few decades. For centuries Asia had supplied the textile factories of Europe with natural fibers, including silk from East Asia along the so-called Silk Road. That began to change late last century with the opening up and modernization of Japan. This change has been reinforced since the late 1950s by the export-oriented industrialization of subsequent generations on natural resource-poor, densely populated economies such that today East Asia exports virtually no natural fibres and instead has become the most important region of the world both as an importer of raw cotton and wool and as an exporter of manufactured textile products and clothing.

Will advanced industrial countries continue to make room for further generations of newly industrializing countries seeking to export their way out of poverty? Or will the recent growth in textile exports from countries such as China simply cause high-wage countries to raise their import barriers to late developers such as Vietnam? To answer that properly requires first addressing questions such as the following:

- ☐ How is the relative importance of fiber, textile and clothing production and trade in an economy likely to change as that economy and the rest of the world grow?
- ☐ To what extent has the economic growth of first Japan and then East Asia's advanced developing economies altered the location of production of textile products and the pattern of global trade in fibers, textiles and clothing?
- ☐ Have China and Southeast Asia's market economies been able to follow a similar development path to their more advanced Northeast Asian neighbors, particularly since the dramatic reforms began in China in the late 1970s?

These questions are addressed sequentially before attention is turned to future prospects for further structural adjustments and the policy responses necessary in the advanced and newly industrialized economies to facilitate further export-led growth of the less-developed economies of East Asia and elsewhere.

5.2 The Changing Importance of Fibers, Textiles and Clothing as Economies Grow

Standard trade and development theory suggests that a poor country opening up to international trade will tend to specialize in the production and export of primary products, though less so the more densely populated the country. If its domestic incomes and stocks of industrial capital per worker grow more rapidly than the rest of the world's (for example, because of a high domestic savings ratio or large borrowings from abroad), relative wages increase and labor is attracted to the manufacturing sector. As a result, its export specialization will gradually move away from primary products (in raw or lightly processed form) to manufactures. Labor begins to be attracted to manufacturing at an earlier stage of economic development, and the nonresource-based manufactured goods initially exported use unskilled labor relatively more intensively, the lower the country's stock of natural resources per worker and hence initial real wage rate. This is because the relatively low wage will give the resource-poor country an international comparative advantage initially in labor-intensive, standard-technology manufactures.[1]

Since many (though by no means all) processes in textile and clothing production tend to be intensive in the use of unskilled labor, this theory suggests they would be among the items initially exported by a newly industrializing, densely populated country. And as the demands for textile raw materials by that country's expanding textile industry grow, so the country's net exports of natural fiber would diminish, or net imports of natural fiber would increase, *ceteris paribus*. On the other hand, since synthetic fiber production is an extremely capital-intensive activity, those fibers will tend to be imported by the newly industrializing country from relatively more capital-abundant countries. If this newly industrializing country is growing more rapidly than other countries, it will initially increase its shares of world production and exports of textiles and clothing and of world imports of fibers at the expense of more mature industrial economies.

In time, another generation of newly industrializing countries would duplicate this process, so gradually displacing the former in world markets for labor-intensive textiles and clothing but providing a growing market for exports of capital-intensive goods and services from more advanced economies.[2] Those latter goods would gradually change from ones whose production is moderately capital intensive (including yarns and fabrics among the textile items) to goods produced with very capital-intensive methods (including synthetic fibers).[3] Meanwhile, economies which are slower growing and/or are relatively richly endowed with natural resources per worker will tend to retain an export specialization in natural fibers and/or other primary products and import textiles, clothing and other labor-intensive manufactures from densely populated, lower-wage economies.

This theory has strong empirical support from both cross-sectional and time-series evidence. For example, the theory suggests the share of primary products in total exports (PRI) would be negatively related to both per capita income (Y, a crude index of the endowment of nonnatural capital per worker) and population density (PD, a proxy for the endowment of natural resources per worker), and this is what is obtained in estimating OLS regression equations from cross-sectional data. Using World Bank data available for the year 1983 for 69 countries with populations exceeding one million, Anderson and Park (1989) obtain the following regression result (*t*-values in parentheses):

$$PRI = 180.4 - 9.75 \ln Y - 11.52 \ln PD, \qquad\qquad R^2 = 0.54$$
$$\quad\;\; (5.7) \qquad\;\; (7.2)$$

The theory suggests also that the share of labor-intensive goods such as textiles and clothing in total exports of manufactures would be very high at first at low levels of per capita income and industrialization and then would fall, and would tend to be higher the greater the population density of the country. Data from the World Bank (1988) provide 1986 shares of textiles and clothing in manufactured exports (TEX) as well as Y and PD data for 1986 for 63 countries, from which the following regression equation is obtained:

$$TEX = 25.6 + 7.77 \ln Y - 0.523 (\ln Y)^2 + 0.0013 PD, \qquad\qquad R^2 = 0.52$$
$$\quad\;\; (5.6) \qquad\;\; (5.7) \qquad\qquad (6.3)$$

These regression equations are clearly consistent with the theory of changing comparative advantage presented earlier, with the latter equation suggesting that after it peaks the share of textiles and clothing in manufacturing exports declines at an increasing rate as income per capita rises.

The four key conclusions that can be drawn from these statistical relationships are confirmed also in the first three columns of Table 5.1. They are:

☐ that the shares of primary products in total exports and of textiles and clothing in manufactured exports are higher in developing economies than in advanced industrial economies
☐ that these shares tend to decline over time in all growing economies
☐ that the declines are faster in economies that are growing relatively rapidly
☐ that within both developing and advanced economies, relatively densely populated economies tend to have lower shares of exports due to primary products and higher shares due to textiles and clothing

The experiences of Japan and Northeast Asia's newly industrialized economies especially illustrate the latter two points, given that they have been the world's fastest growing economies for decades and are very densely populated.

There are two other indicators of changes in comparative advantage that are useful for present purposes. One is an index of export specialization, or what Balassa (1965) called an index of "revealed" comparative advantage, defined as the share of a product group in an economy's exports as a ratio of that commodity group's share of world exports. Columns 4 to 9 of Table 5.1 shows this index over time for all primary products, natural fibers, textiles, clothing, other labor-intensive products (as defined by Balassa (1979)), and synthetic fibers. At least four points can be made from these data. First, export specialization is stronger in textiles than in clothing for advanced industrial countries, while the opposite is typically true for developing economies (although China prior to its recent reforms was an exception). Second, the export specialization index for both commodities tends to fall over time in high-wage countries, to rise over time for rapidly industrializing low-wage countries, and to reach a peak for middle-income economies that is at a later stage for textiles than for clothing. Third, export specialization in other labor-intensive manufactures follows a similar pattern to textiles and clothing, suggesting that textiles and clothing are not unusual but rather just an important example of the process of shifting comparative advantage associated with global economic development. And fourth, synthetic fibers represent one of many capital-intensive activities in which advanced industrial countries have a high but declining comparative advantage, while capital-scarce developing economies have a very low but rising comparative advantage in such products (column 9 of Table 5.1).

Japan, being very densely populated, has a much stronger comparative disadvantage (advantage) in primary products (manufactures) than the average industrial country. Hence its export specialization index in the 1960s was much lower for primary products including natural fibers and much higher for textiles and clothing than other industrial countries. And, since Japan's economy has

TABLE 5.1 Export specialization and net exports as a share of world trade in primary products, fibers, textiles and clothing,[a] industrial and developing economies, 1965 to 1990

	Primary products[a] share (%) of total exports (1)	Textiles and clothing's share (%) of		Index of export specialization[b] in:						Net exports as a % of world trade in:			
		Total exports (2)	Manufactured exports (3)	All primary products (4)	Natural fibers (5)	Textiles (6)	Clothing (7)	Other labor-intensive manufactures[c] (8)	Synthetic fibers (9)	Natural fibers (10)	Textiles (11)	Clothing (12)	Synthetic fibers (13)
All advanced industrial economies													
1965–69	29	6	9	0.70	0.64	1.03	0.98	1.19	1.29	−29	11	−10	38
1970–79	27	5	7	0.64	0.70	1.05	0.79	1.20	1.34	−17	6	−32	39
1980–87	25	4	6	0.66	0.80	0.95	0.60	1.07	1.25	−4	2	−44	37
1990	19	4	5	n.a.	n.a.	n.a.	n.a.	n.a.	n.a.	n.a.	n.a.	n.a.	n.a.
All developing economies													
1965–69	84	6	38	2.02	2.23	0.93	1.05	0.30	0.11	38	−9	9	−22
1970–79	80	6	32	1.98	1.73	0.90	1.50	0.40	0.09	24	−3	28	−30
1980–87	68	9	27	1.76	1.42	1.20	1.98	0.84	0.37	10	0	40	−30
1990	51	12	24	n.a.	n.a.	n.a.	n.a.	n.a.	n.a.	n.a.	n.a.	n.a.	n.a.
Japan													
1965–69	7	15	16	0.17	0.14	2.60	1.81	3.18	2.96	−15	13	10	16
1970–79	5	7	7	0.13	0.07	1.59	0.44	2.56	2.79	−18	8	−1	19
1980–87	4	4	4	0.12	0.05	1.12	0.15	1.64	1.66	−15	6	−3	14
1990	2	2	2	n.a.	n.a.	n.a.	n.a.	n.a.	n.a.	n.a.	n.a.	n.a.	n.a.
Northeast Asian NIEs[d]													
1965–69	20	38	47	0.48	0.40	2.89	14.40	3.19	0.01	–	−1	15	−5
1970–79	11	35	39	0.29	0.44	3.11	12.10	2.68	0.39	−1	1	25	−7
1980–87	8	26	29	0.21	0.19	2.84	7.51	3.49	1.20	−4	2	25	−1
1990	5	22	23	n.a.	n.a.	n.a.	n.a.	n.a.	n.a.	n.a.	n.a.	n.a.	n.a.
ASEAN[e]													
1965–69	89	2	18	2.19	0.70	0.30	0.29	0.19	0.01	1	−4	−0	−3
1970–79	80	3	17	2.03	0.41	0.46	0.69	0.41	0.02	−1	−3	2	−4
1980–87	64	5	15	1.75	0.21	0.59	1.20	0.75	0.05	−3	−1	4	−5
1990	42	8	14	n.a.	n.a.	n.a.	n.a.	n.a.	n.a.	n.a.	n.a.	n.a.	n.a.
China													
1965–69	56	20	47	1.40	2.18	3.76	1.77	1.13	0.02	0	3	1	−3
1970–79	52	21	44	1.32	4.34	4.38	2.82	1.25	0.02	−1	3	2	−4
1980–87	45	28	51	1.22	4.89	4.76	5.44	1.61	0.07	2	4	7	−11
1990	26	27	37	n.a.	n.a.	n.a.	n.a.	n.a.	n.a.	n.a.	n.a.	n.a.	n.a.

a. All primary products are SITC 0 to 4 plus 68 less 266; natural fibers are SITC 26 less 266; textiles are SITC 65; clothing is SITC 84, and synthetic fibers are SITC 266.

b. The index of export specialization is the share of a commodity group in an economy's exports as a ratio of that commodity group's share of world exports, following Balassa (1965).

c. Other labor-intensive manufactures are defined by Balassa (1979) to be SITC 632, 633, 664, 665, 666, 722, 735, 821, 831, 894, 895 and 899.

d. The newly industrialized Northeast Asian economies of Hong Kong, South Korea and Taiwan.

e. The Association of Southeast Asian Nations, made up of Brunei, Indonesia, Malaysia, Philippines, Singapore and Thailand.

Source: International Economic Data Bank, *Trade Data Tapes*, Australian National University, Canberra, 1992.

grown faster than other industrial economies its "revealed" comparative advantage in these products has declined faster too, as indicated in Table 5.1.

The newly industrialized economies (NIEs) of Northeast Asia, namely Hong Kong, South Korea and Taiwan, also are endowed with few natural resources per worker and so their rapid economic growth also has resulted in a much lower level of, and sharper decline in, their index of export specialization in primary products compared with other developing economies, while their indexes of export specialization in textiles and clothing are very high. Note, however, that the latter indexes have been declining since the 1960s for labor-intensive clothing. These indexes also began to decline in the 1970s for textiles. By contrast, these indexes have been rising rapidly for capital-intensive synthetic fibers. These changes reflect the fact that the comparative advantage of these NIEs is gradually moving away from unskilled labor-intensive manufacturing towards more capital-intensive processing. The ASEAN economies too have been following the same general pattern, though somewhat less rapidly because they are somewhat less densely populated, and have not been growing as fast as, Northeast Asia's NIEs.

Notice also from Table 5.1 that, in industrial countries, textiles have a higher and a less rapidly decreasing index of export specialization than clothing, and conversely in developing economies, reflecting the fact that clothing production is more intensive in the use of unskilled labor than textile production on average (see note 3).

This export specialization index is less than ideal as an indicator of comparative advantage because it ignores what is happening to a country's import pattern. An indicator which better captures both trade patterns is shown on the right hand side of Table 5.1, namely, net exports as a percentage of world trade for a particular commodity. The story suggested by that index is much the same, however. Industrial (developing) economies as a group are net importers (net exporters) of natural fibers and net exporters (importers) of clothing. Textiles are an in between commodity in that developing economies as a group switched in the mid-1980s from being a net export item to a net import item for industrial countries.

It should be kept in mind that textiles and clothing comprise a heterogeneous set of commodities which not only use a wide range of production techniques in terms of their labor or capital intensity but also face widely varying elasticities of demand. The former explains why France until the mid-1970s had remained a net exporter of clothes, in terms of value, by exporting high priced fashion clothing, and why Italy still is a net clothes exporter, given the strong demands elsewhere in Northwest Europe for fashionable clothing. Nonetheless, by the late 1980s, developing countries were supplying more than half the world's exports of clothing and a third of global textile exports, double their shares of the late 1960s. The dramatic increase in the penetration of imports into industrial country markets for these products attests to this. Anderson (1992: Table 2.9) report that the shares of developing country imports in domestic sales in industrial countries doubled (to 6 percent) for textiles and quadrupled (to 18 percent) for clothing between the early 1970s and the mid-1980s, compared with an increase for manufactures in total from 1.5 to 3.1 percent. It is this inexorable increase in import penetration by developing country producers of textiles and clothing that makes these items important for newly industrializing countries and at the same time of concern to politicians in high-wage countries who are worried about job losses in their constituencies.

Brief though this evidence is, it strongly suggests that the theory presented earlier is helpful in explaining the changing pattern of world production and trade in fibers, textiles and clothing, notwithstanding the prevalence of trade-distorting barriers provided by the Multifiber Arrangement (MFA) and related policies. The experiences of Japan and East Asia's more recently industrializing economies, reflected in Table 5.1, are especially dramatic and are deserving of closer attention. Hence they are examined in a longer historical perspective in the next two sections.

5.3   The Experience of Japan in Historical and International Perspective

Japan's rapid economic growth began with the Meiji Restoration in the 1860s. The deregulation and opening up of the largely agrarian economy at that time was followed by a century of growth in Japanese incomes and capital formation at rates that were more than twice as fast as in the more mature economies (Kuznets 1966; Maddison 1982). The share of Japan's GDP that was exported also rose dramatically such that Japan's trade grew almost ten times as fast as world trade between the 1870s and the 1930s. Also, Japan was then and still is one of the most densely populated large economies in the world with a very poor endowment of agricultural land and mineral resources per worker. From the above theory it is therefore not surprising to find the following:

  ☐ The primary sector's shares of GDP, employment and exports in Japan have fallen from high levels around 1870 (columns 1 to 3 of Table 5.2).
  ☐ The shares of textiles and clothing in Japan's manufacturing and especially total GDP, employment and exports have risen from 1870 but subsequently have fallen, and their shares of imports have fallen and then risen, as comparative advantage moved towards more capital-intensive manufactures (columns 4 to 10 and 12 of Table 5.2).
  ☐ The share of natural fibers in Japan's exports have fallen continually and its share of Japan's imports have grown initially before falling,[4] along with the relative rise and demise of textiles (columns 3, 11 and 13 of Table 5.2).

This hill-shaped development pattern is also reflected in the changing trade dependence of Japan's textile/clothing sector. Table 5.3 shows the clear increase and then decrease in the share of Japan's production of textiles and clothing that are exported, starting from zero prior to 1870, peaking at around 30 percent in the 1930s and falling to below 10 percent in the latter 1980s (primarily synthetic fibers and yarns, which are extremely capital intensive). Table 5.3 also shows that imports

TABLE 5.2 Importance of textiles, clothing and fibers in production, employment and trade, Japan, 1874–90 (percentage shares in value terms)

	Primary products' share of:			Textiles and clothing's share of total:				Textile and clothing's share of manufacturing:			Natural fiber's share of total imports	Index of export[c] specialization in textiles and clothing	Index of import[c] specialization in natural fibers
	GDP[b] (1)	Employment (2)	Exports[a] (3)	GDP[b] (4)	Employment (5)	Exports (6)	Imports (7)	GDP[b] (8)	Employment (9)	Exports (10)	(11)	(12)	(13)
1874–79	45	73	83 (38)	–	–	4	54	10	–	25	1	–	–
1880–89	44	71	77 (37)	2	–	9	44	18	–	36	6	–	–
1890–99	43	67	55 (29)	4	–	23	19	26	–	51	21	1.2	1.1
1900–09	35	65	45 (26)	5	7	28	11	26	62	51	26	–	–
1910–19	34	59	34 (23)	7	8	34	8	28	61	52	32	1.5	1.4
1920–29	30	50	38 (32)	8	9	34	5	30	55	56	27	1.9	1.5
1930–39	18	45	20 (13)	9	6	35	3	28	37	44	25	3.4	2.4
1950–59	18	39	12 (1)	3	4	36	0	11	22	38	23	5.4	3.5
1960–69	10	24	7 (0)	2	3	19	1	7	14	19	10	2.9	1.5
1970–79	5	13	3 (0)	1	2	6	3	5	11	6	3	1.2	0.9
1980–85	3	9	2 (0)	1	2	4	3	4	8	4	2	0.9	0.8
1986–90	2	8	1 (0)	1	2	3	3	3	8	3	2	0.5	0.8

a. Numbers in parentheses are for raw silk (the only natural fiber exported).

b. Gross domestic product shares in the prewar period are at constant 1934–36 prices, thereafter at current prices.

c. Indexes of import and export specialization are the share of these items in Japan's trade as a ratio of the share of those items in world trade. Textiles and clothing are SITC items 65 and 84; natural fibers are SITC items 26 less 266. Over the pre-1950 period these indexes are those for the single years 1899, 1913, 1929 and 1937, global data for which are from Maizels (1963).

Source: Updated from Park and Anderson (1991: Table 1).

TABLE 5.3   The trade dependence of Japan's textile and clothing manufacturing industries, 1874–90 (%, value based)

	Share of production exported	Share of domestic sales supplied by imports
1874–81	2	42
1882–91	5	29
1892–01	13	16
1902–11	26	15
1912–21	27	5
1922–31	27	7
1932–39	29	3
1951–55	24	1
1956–60	23	1
1961–65	18	1
1966–70	17	2
1971–75	14	5
1976–80	13	7
1981–85	13	8
1986–90	8	11

Source: Updated from Park and Anderson (1991: Table 2).

accounted for more than a third of domestic textile and clothing consumption in the early years of Japan's industrial development (primarily cotton yarns and fabrics needed as inputs for producing finished textiles and clothing), that this import dependence fell to almost zero in the 1950s and early 1960s with the growth in domestic production, but that it has since grown to more than one tenth as low-cost imports of labor-intensive items have become available from nearby newly industrializing economies.

Not only have developments within Japan itself been consistent with theory, but so too has the country's changing role in international markets. In particular:

☐ The shares of world exports of textiles and clothing from (and world imports of natural fibers by) older industrial economies, such as the United Kingdom, France and the United States, have fallen as Japan's shares expanded (Table 5.4), one consequence of which is the declining importance of these items in, for example, United Kingdom trade (Table 5.5).[5]

☐ Japan's shares of world exports of textiles and clothing and world imports of natural fibers have grown until the takeoff of other generations of newly industrializing economies (Asia's NIEs from the 1960s, mainland China from 1978—see Figure 5.1 and Anderson 1992: Fig. 3.2).

☐ The subsequent decline in Japan's importance in international markets for textiles and clothing have occurred first for labor-intensive clothing and last for capital-intensive synthetic fibers (Anderson 1992: Fig. 3.3).

That is, in addition to the relative importance of textiles and clothing in Japan's *domestic* economy rising and then falling, the shares of Japan in world exports of

TABLE 5.4   Major countries' shares in world exports of textiles and clothing, 1899–90 (%)

	Japan	United Kingdom	France	Other Western Europe	United States	Others[a]	Total
1899	2	47	15	29	2	5	100
1913	4	43	15	29	3	6	100
1929	9	43	14	23	5	6	100
1937	22	37	6	23	3	9	100
1955	15	21	11	30	12	10	100
1965	13	8	8	38	6	27	100
1975	8	5	7	42	5	33	100
1985	7	3	5	36	4	45	100
1990	3	3	4	35	3	52	100

a. Since Canadian and Australasian exports were minimal, and East European exports are not included for the postwar period because of lack of data, this column from 1955 almost entirely refers to developing countries.

Source: Updated from Park and Anderson (1991: Table 4).

TABLE 5.5   Importance of textiles, clothing and fibers in United Kingdom trade, 1750–91 (% in value terms)

	Share of textiles and clothing in total exports	Share of natural fibers in total imports
1750–99	52	12
1800–19	64	11
1820–39	71	21
1840–59	64	28
1860–79	61	27
1880–99	46	20
1900–19	38	18
1920–29	34	14
1930–38	24	10
1950–59	11	9
1960–69	7	5
1970–79	6	2
1980–91	4	1

Source: Updated from Park and Anderson (1991: Table 5).

textiles and clothing and world imports of natural fibers also trace out a hill-shaped path over time, the latter being part of a landscape in which the hill for older economies is to the left of Japan on this time path and that for more recent industrializers is to the right.

FIGURE 5.1   East Asia's shares of world exports of textiles and clothing, 1954–90[a]

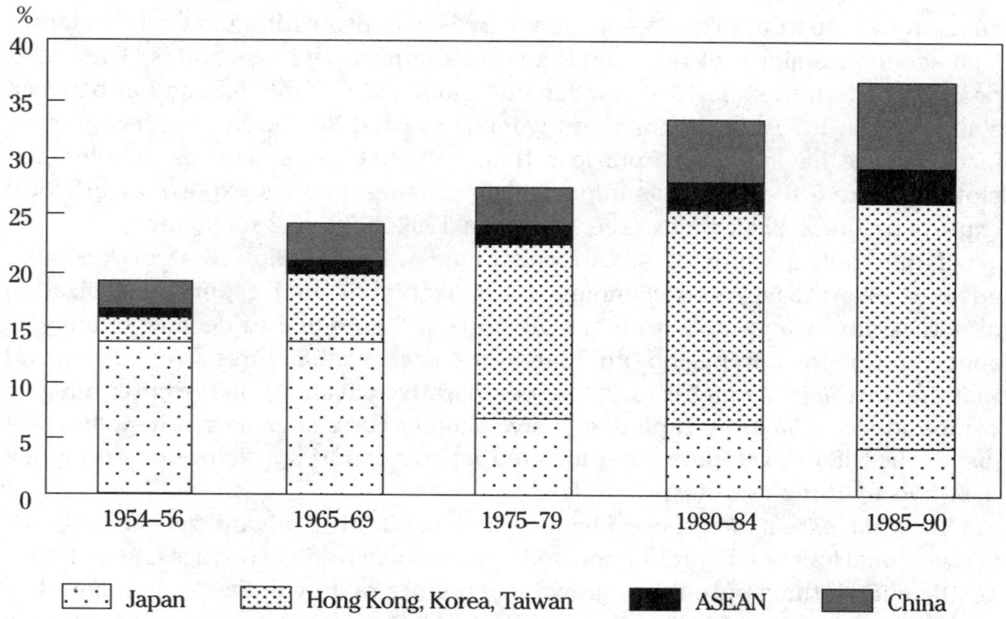

a. Textiles and clothing cover SITC divisions 65 and 84.

Sources: Internationl Economic Data Bank, *Trade Data Tapes*, Australian National University, Canberra, 1992; and United Nations, *Yearbook of International Trade*, New York, 1956 and 1957.

5.4   The Impact of Growth of Asia's Developing Economies

The newly industrialized economies of Hong Kong, South Korea and Taiwan are, like Japan and China, among the world's most densely-populated countries. They also have had the enviable reputation for a long time of enjoying extremely rapid rates of economic growth, as has China since 1978. Thus the above theory suggests that all of these economies should lose their comparative advantage in primary products at a relatively early stage of their economic development and have an initial strengthening of comparative advantage in unskilled-labor-intensive manufactured products, such as finished textiles and clothing, which will eventually diminish. And this is indeed what the historical record shows in Table 5.1, with the greater primary export share for ASEAN than for Northeast Asia reflecting the fact that the ASEAN economies are much more resource-rich and less densely populated than the latter economies.

Of more importance from the point of view of this chapter is the change in comparative advantage in (rather than just export shares of) textiles and clothing. Even though the share of textiles and clothing in manufactured exports has been

falling, those goods' share of total exports from newly industrializing Asian economies, relative to the global export share, kept rising for some time after each
economy's industrial take-off—despite increases in protection in advanced industrial economies aimed at reducing the latter's imports of these goods. This index
peaked at 5.5 in the mid-1950s for Japan (column 12 of Table 5.2) and at between
5 and 9 in the 1970s for the three newly industrialized Northeast Asian economies,
in each case having risen from less than half that value. That is, textiles and
clothing were 5 to 9 times as important in Northeast Asia's exports as in world
exports at those peak times (see Anderson 1992: Table 3.2 for details).

If the trade pattern of ASEAN and China were to follow that of the more
advanced Northeast Asian economies, it is likely that their export specialization
in natural fibers and other primary products will continue to decline steadily as
specialization in clothing and other labor-intensive manufactures strengthens, and
that the Northeast Asian NIEs will lose comparative advantage in the latter but gain
competitiveness in more capital-intensive manufactures such as synthetic fibers—
just as the NIEs' development has affected Japan's export specialization during the
past two or three decades.

To what extent are these changes in comparative advantage affecting the
international location of production and international trade in textiles and clothing?
Textile and clothing output has grown much more rapidly in East Asia than it has
in the rest of the world. The share of East Asia in world exports of textiles and
clothing has therefore grown dramatically. Notwithstanding the decline in Japan's
share, Northeast and Southeast Asia now account for almost 40 percent of that
trade, double the share of three decades ago and now similar to the combined
share of Western Europe and North America (Figure 5.1). This has occurred despite
the fact that within the textile industry grouping there are some industries which
through technological change have become extremely capital-intensive and thereby
expanded in some of the advanced industrial countries (Yamazawa 1983).

The large jump in China's share since 1978, together with export growth from
ASEAN (and South Asia), may well slow the growth in the share of the three newly
industrialized Northeast Asian economies during the next decade or so, as happened
for Japan from the mid-1960s—although the new capital-intensive technologies
being developed by textile firms in advanced industrial countries will no doubt be
adopted by Hong Kong, Korean and Taiwanese firms which will slow the decline
in their market share.[6] But even with a slowdown in the growth of the East Asian
NIEs' share, it is probable, given the likelihood of ASEAN's and China's strengthening
comparative advantage in labor-intensive manufactures, that East Asia's total share
of world exports of textiles and clothing will continue to expand through the 1990s.

A corollary to the increasing importance of East Asia in world production of
textiles and clothing and to the region's declining comparative advantage in primary
products is the growth in the region's share of world imports of natural fibers.
Japan's share of global imports of natural fibers has declined somewhat since the
early 1970s, but this has been more than compensated for by the steady growth

in natural fiber imports by the newly industrialized economies of Northeast Asia since the early 1960s and by China and ASEAN since the 1970s. That region's combined share of world imports of natural fibers is now more than 35 percent compared with half that in the mid-1950s. Less than half of the current share is due to Japan. Yet Japan accounted for more than three quarters of the region's share of world fiber imports in the 1950s (Anderson 1992: Figure 3.2).

Just as the expansion in East Asia's production of finished textiles and clothing is stimulating its domestic demand for natural fibers, so too is it stimulating a greater demand for synthetic fibers. The question arises as to who will supply that growing demand for man-made fibers. Since their production tends to be much more capital-intensive than yarn and fabric production and, even more so, than finished textiles and clothing (see note 3), one would expect late-developing economies to find it less costly to import those fibers at early stages of their development than to produce them domestically. This is in fact what Northeast Asia's NIEs found in the 1960s and early 1970s: they imported them from Japan, so that while Japan lost out in international markets for labor-intensive finished textiles and clothing (and at a later stage for synthetic yarns and fabrics) it gained market share in capital-intensive synthetic fibers. Similarly, the Northeast Asian NIEs became exporters of synthetic yarns and fabrics somewhat later than was the case with clothing and only now are they becoming significant exporters of synthetic fibers (see column 13 of Table 5.1), while growth in their share of the international market for more labor-intensive items such as clothing is leveling off as China's share grows (Anderson 1992: Figure 3.3). Thus by successful structural adjustments both Japan and the Northeast Asian NIEs are making way for China, ASEAN and other less developed economies in world markets for labor-intensive goods and at the same time are benefiting, as Europe also may do, from the latter's growing import demands—even within the textile and clothing group of commodities—for capital-intensive intermediate goods.

5.5   Lessons, Future Prospects and Policy Implications

5.5.1   Lessons from East Asia's Experience

The clearest lesson to emerge from the above analysis is that textiles and clothing are industries which tend to first increase and then decrease in relative importance to an economy as it gradually transforms from being largely agrarian to being a modern industrial state. This rise and demise will not occur uniformly across economies as they develop and their comparative advantages change, because the latter changes will depend heavily on changes in a country's relative factor endowments as compared with average global endowment ratios. Specifically, industrial competitiveness will begin with more labor-intensive products, and will occur at a lower level of industrial capital per worker, the more poorly is an economy endowed with natural resources per worker. It is therefore not surprising that the economic growth of densely populated Japan, following the opening up of that economy in the 1860s, was accompanied by growth in production and exports of labor-intensive manufactures such as textiles and clothing. Nor is it surprising, given the large size and rapid expansion of Japan's economy, that its textile exports gradually eclipsed those from the United Kingdom and Europe in international markets.

Furthermore, in the 1950s/early 1960s the newly emerging economies of Hong Kong, South Korea and Taiwan—which are even more densely populated than Japan—began to duplicate the Japanese development pattern. Following their economic liberalization and opening up, the production and import of textiles and clothing from those economies grew very rapidly, as did their demand for imports of natural fibers. As a group these newly industrializing economies (NIEs) made substantial inroads into international markets for textiles and clothing. Just as Japan in earlier decades had put competitive pressure on the United Kingdom, continental Europe and North America which brought about the relative demise of their textile and clothing industries, so these Northeast Asian NIEs began to reduce the competitiveness of these industries in Japan.

However, the competitiveness of the Northeast Asian NIEs grew so rapidly, and Japan's response to their growth was so prompt and positive (e.g. developing new labor-saving technologies for these industries, specializing in the more capital-intensive processes within these industries and subcontracting other processes offshore—see Yamawaki 1992), that Northeast Asia's aggregate shares of the world's textile and clothing exports and natural fiber imports continued to increase despite some decline in Japan's share. Moreover, this expansion occurred in spite of the increasingly protectionist policies of the more advanced industrial economies, beginning with the barriers to Japan's exports in the 1930s and escalating steadily from the 1950s with the Short-term Cotton Textile Trade Agreement (STA) which became the Long-term Cotton Textile Trade Agreement (LTA) and then four successive Multifiber Arrangements (MFA).[7]

Since the late 1970s a third generation of export-led NIEs has emerged—most notably including China, but also including countries in Southeast Asia, especially Thailand and Indonesia. Their contributions, which have been boosted considerably by their trade liberalizations, have added further to the relocation of textiles and clothing production to, and exports from, East Asia. And while the competitive pressure on high-income countries from newly emerging exporters such as China will be offset to some extent by reduced pressure from the East Asian NIEs, this offset will occur only at the labor-intensive end of the spectrum. As firms in the Asian NIEs upgrade to more capital-intensive textile processes in response to competitive pressure from ASEAN and China, the NIEs in turn will put competitive pressure on Japan, the United States and Western Europe at the more capital-intensive and design-intensive end of the spectrum of textile and clothing activities. Thus total exports of textiles and clothing from the East Asian region are likely to continue to increase through the 1990s. That is, there is a high probability China's and ASEAN's industrial development will ensure East Asia's share of world exports of these manufactures—and the region's share of world imports of fibers—keeps growing.

5.5.2 Future Prospects and Policy Implications

This historical experience of the East Asian region does not suggest there is reason to be pessimistic about the export growth prospects for would-be newly emerging exporters of textiles and clothing, particularly when the international relocation of production and trade has occurred despite very high and rising levels of protection against imports of these products into advanced industrial economies. Those protectionist policies have simply slowed the process of adjustment to long-term changes in comparative advantage (as well as slowing the rate of growth of incomes in both advanced and emerging industrial economies).

How the rest of the world responds to this competitive pressure from East Asia will have a critical bearing on the future of poor agrarian economies contemplating their development strategy at the close of this century and beyond. For such economies to increase their share of world markets for labor-intensive textiles and clothing in line with their changing comparative advantage, as they accumulate or import industrial capital, it is essential that advanced industrial countries allow the penetration of increasing volumes of imports of these products. Without that market access, export growth prospects for newly emerging economies will be thwarted, which in turn will dampen their overall economic performance.

In the case of China, the current Multifiber Arrangement (MFA-IV) negotiated in 1986 between industrial and developing countries, and related agreements, allow for very little export growth from China relative to China's potential—even though China used its economic and political might to obtain larger quotas than normal MFA restrictions allowed.[8] If China's market access is not revised upwards, particularly in the United States where as much as one-third of China's textile and clothing exports have been destined in recent years, one or both of the following outcomes seems likely. First, China could redirect its export production to rely more on other labor-intensive manufactured goods in which it already is a competitive exporter (see Table 5.1 above). This would result in (a) a transfer of increasing import competition from one to another group of manufacturing firms in industrial countries, (b) a reduced demand for American, Australasian and developing country cotton and wool, and (c) a reduced demand for synthetic fibers from Western Europe, Japan and Korea. So while restrictions on China's textile and clothing exports serve one special interest group in rich countries, they directly harm others, in both manufacturing and agriculture.

The second possibility is that China may become pessimistic about export-led growth prospects based on manufactures and return to a more insular development strategy, which would result in even slower overall economic growth than the first option. A reduction in growth and in the share of production that is traded necessarily would reduce the rest of the world's economic growth. It would affect exporters of primary products not only because it would reduce demand for specific raw materials needed by China's export manufacturing industries but also because China's own mobile resources (particularly labor) would be attracted less rapidly out of primary production. And it would reduce the sales by Western Europe, the United States, Japan and gradually Northeast Asia's advanced NIEs of capital-intensive manufactured goods, services and technologies to China. This second possibility would be especially unfortunate for the world economy, not to mention for China itself.

If China were to be given unrestricted access to industrial country markets for textiles and clothing, to what extent might those markets be swamped by Chinese exports? Having seen China's share of world exports of these products grow from 3 to 7 percent during the 1980s, many observers understandably have been concerned at the prospect of widespread unemployment of textile workers in industrial countries as Chinese goods flood in. The degree of concern is much greater than the evidence would suggest is appropriate, however, for two reasons. One is that China's exports to some extent are simply replacing exports of other, more advanced economies. As is clear from Figure 5.1 above, Japan has made way for the Asian NIEs since the 1950s, just as the United Kingdom and other European countries did for Japan earlier this century. These countries can reasonably be expected to do likewise for China, as indeed is predicted by Trela and Whalley's (1990a, b) general equilibrium modelling results. That is, industrial country imports, and those from China's Northeast Asian neighboring economies, would increase by less than the gross expansion in China's exports.

The second reason to discount the expressed fear of a potential flood of textile and clothing products from China has to do with the current degree of China's import penetration. It is true that China's share of textile, clothing and footwear sales in advanced industrial economies has quadrupled since the mid-1970s, and that its penetration has been uniformly spread across all major regions. But this growth has been from a low base, so the share of Chinese goods is still very small both in absolute terms and relative to other supplies. As of 1986, China supplied only 1.6 percent of domestic sales of textiles and clothing in all industrial market economies, which is similar to the shares held by Northeast Asia's NIEs or all other developing economies in the early 1970s (Anderson 1992: Table A1). Even if China's exports of these products were to grow at the same frenetic pace as those from Hong Kong, South Korea and Taiwan during the 1970s, China by the turn of the century would be supplying barely 5 percent of textile and clothing sales in advanced economies.

On the other hand, if China's access to textile and clothing markets were to continue to be limited, its desperate need to earn foreign currency would simply force it to expand exports of other light manufactures. China's share of those product markets in industrial countries also has been growing rapidly, more than trebling since its implementation of economic reforms (Anderson 1992: Table A1).

Thus trying to prevent any disruption to one group of manufactures in industrial countries will simply transfer the pressure to another group.

In short, a great deal hangs on whether textile trade is liberalized in the early 1990s. Should the opportunity be provided for China to substantially expand its exports during this decade, that may be just what is needed to reaffirm the Chinese government's resolve to push on with its economic reforms, to open that economy further, and thereby to promote political stability there and hence in the world at large, not to mention the boost it would give to global economic welfare. On the other hand, if current restrictions were to continue, China's capacity to expand may well be seriously thwarted. Moreover, other densely populated economies which are looking to become more outward-oriented, such as in South Asia or the centrally planned economies of Vietnam or North Korea, also would be discouraged from doing so if markets in rich countries are not opened up more.[9]

5.5.3 What Impact will Developments in Europe Have?

The political changes that began to sweep Eastern Europe in the late 1980s, together with the "1992" program and the European Economic Area initiative for greater economic integration within Western Europe, will have important implications for East Asia's prospects in European and indeed global markets for textiles and clothing. Should the European Community accommodate the wish of the three most recent entrants to the EC (Greece, Portugal and Spain) in retaining high barriers to external imports of textiles and clothing into that bloc, these low-wage Southern European countries would be more able to supply the rest of Western Europe with such goods, albeit at a higher cost than East Asia. And if Turkey and other Mediterranean suppliers also were to be given greater preferential access to Western European markets by being granted associate membership to the EC, Asian and other suppliers would be further squeezed out of European markets (Hamilton 1990b, 1992).

The recent political developments in Eastern Europe will have a less certain and less immediate impact than the completion of the economic integration of Western Europe. But in the longer run these developments in Eastern Europe may have a much more profound impact. Eastern Europe and some of the Soviet republics are as densely populated as Western Europe as a bloc (that is, twice as densely populated as the rest of the world). Should East European economies begin to specialize their production in order to exploit their comparative advantages to the full, the likelihood is that the region would use its low wage levels to compete at the labor-intensive end of the manufacturing spectrum (Hamilton and Winters 1992; Anderson 1993). And if Western Europe provides preferential access for goods from Eastern Europe, as seems likely, this would further reduce European sales prospects for East Asian and other suppliers. On the other hand, if Europe were to open its markets and East European economies were to grow rapidly as a consequence of economic reforms, at least the volume if not the share of sales in Europe supplied by East Asia and other developing countries would be likely to continue to rise.

5.5.4 How Liberal will Textile and Clothing Trade be in the 1990s?

In assessing the prospects for substantial liberalization of industrial country markets for textiles and clothing, several points need to be made. First, the perceived growth during the 1970s and 1980s in import barriers facing developing country exporters may be more apparent than real. Certainly the trade from developing to industrial countries has continued to grow rapidly, as demonstrated by the import penetration data in Table 5.2. This supports the contention of Hughes and Waelbroeck (1981), Yoffie (1983), Bhagwati (1988) and others that protection policies are somewhat porous. The porosity results partly from the ingenuity of producers in developing countries in finding ways around barriers by altering their export product mixes, by relocating production in countries with unfilled export quotas, and so on. But it can also be the result of authorities in the importing countries turning a blind eye to the overfilling of trade quotas in situations where to not do so would be against the countries' broader foreign policy interests. The dramatic import penetration by China during the 1980s may be a case in point (Cline 1987). Thus while it is generally true that quantitative limitations on trade are more inefficient policy instruments than ad valorem trade taxes, there are situations where the administrative flexibility offered by import quotas and "voluntary" export restraints can actually result in more rather than less trade.

This is not to downplay the harm done by the MFA and related barriers to textile and clothing trade. As modelling results show (e.g., Trela and Whalley 1990a, b; Suphachalasai 1992), the MFA does cause wasteful trade restrictions and diversions, and its removal would benefit virtually all developing countries—not to mention the boost it would give to incomes in the liberalizing advanced industrial economies themselves. Moreover, the covert nature of quantitative trade restrictions used under the MFA are such that consumers and other would-be opponents in high-income countries are less informed about the extent and hence cost of these trade barriers than they would be with, say, a tariff, and hence are less active lobbyists against the MFA. Rather, the point is that newly and would-be emerging economies should not be discouraged by the MFA from adopting an export-led, open-economy industrialization strategy because, as China and ASEAN in the 1980s and East Asia's more advanced NIEs in earlier decades have demonstrated, rapid and equitable economic growth based on such a strategy is clearly possible.

5.5.5 Ways to Enhance the Prospects for Trade Liberalization

An important way in which the prospects for reforming the MFA can and indeed have been recently improved is through the dissemination of more information on the costs and distributional consequences of existing policies. The global, general equilibrium modelling work of Trela and Whalley's, for example, is able to add greatly to the quantitative information on the costs of these policies. More such work is needed, however, particularly on the distributional consequences within countries. Such models can demonstrate clearly that volume-dominated quotas under the MFA hurt poorer consumers in importing countries disproportionately by raising most of the prices of low value standard clothing items, and causing job losses elsewhere in their country that may more than offset the jobs saved in declining textile and clothing firms, and by reducing the foreign exchange earnings of those other industries. Disseminating more widely the results of such studies, as the World Bank has been doing recently for example (Hamilton 1990), can add significantly to the political pressure for reform from within protected economies.

There are also ways of adding external pressures for reform. China has unilaterally been able to successfully seek greater access for its textile goods by threatening to otherwise reduce its grain and other imports from those protecting countries. While most other developing economies are too small individually to be able to so threaten, they would have some prospect of doing so if they were to become more active and cohesive participants in the multilateral trade negotiation process. Moreover, exporters of fibers, both natural and synthetic, have a common interest in an expanding, less restricted trade in textiles and clothing. As tolerance for high protectionist barriers weakens in high-income economies it may pay fiber exporters to act together to lobby in multilateral and national fora for such liberalization, in a manner similar to that adopted by the so-called Cairns group of non subsidizing, food-exporting countries. The conversion of bilateral import quotas to global quotas for each importing country, as proposed during the Uruguay Round of multilateral trade negotiations, would certainly help that process. It would also save the newly developing NIEs having to export via the more advanced NIEs because the former but not the latter countries had filled their quotas.

Efforts might also be intensified to disseminate in Southern and Eastern Europe the results of analyses which show the virtues of an export-led industrial development strategy which is based on an open economy approach rather than being dependent on discriminatory preferential access to a protected European Community. While the latter preferential approach may seem attractive in the short run, its effects in the longer run will not be as great as an approach based on exploiting their global as distinct from protected regional comparative advantage. The same applies to Mexico in the context of the NAFTA proposal to include Mexico in a North America free trade area. Now is a particularly opportune time to intensify the dissemination of such liberal ideas, with (a) MFA-IV due to expire at the completion of the Uruguay Round, (b) the further liberalizing of trade within both Western Europe and North America,[10] and (c) the reconstruction of Eastern Europe's economies getting underway at long last.

To conclude, further research is still required to improve our understanding of the reasons for the persistence of protection against textile and clothing imports. Like the agricultural sector, textiles and clothing are classic declining industries in advanced industrial countries. In fact they are typically the first significant manufacturing industries to come under pressure to decline in a growing economy. Being reasonably concentrated geographically and being major employers, firms in these industries have found it worthwhile investing in lobbying for the raising and maintaining of high trade barriers. While this may continue to be the case for a while yet, the time may well come when the benefits to politicians in these countries from protecting these producers is more than offset by the political benefits foregone from other constituents harmed by the protection (Cassing and Hillman 1986; Hillman 1989). A better understanding of the reasons for existing policies and their changes can only help in identifying ways to facilitate reform, and thereby in boosting the prospects for poorer developing countries to repeat the East Asian process of exporting their way out of poverty.

Notes

This paper draws on and updates parts of Anderson (1991 and 1992).

1. A clear exposition of this theory can be found in Krueger (1977). The theory combines modifications to the standard Heckscher-Ohlin trade model, synthesized by Johnson (1968) in his Wicksell Lectures to explain the inter-country pattern of manufacturing trade specialization, with the Ricardo-Viner model popularized by Jones (1971). The latter is necessary to explain the differences between countries in their comparative advantages in primary products relative to manufactures. For further elaboration of the theory see, for example, Deardorff (1984), Eaton (1987) and Leamer (1987). On the usefulness and limitations of population density as a proxy for the stock of agricultural land and minerals per worker, see Keesing and Sherk (1971) and Bowen (1983).
2. For more on these changes in manufacturing comparative advantage that accompany economic growth, and their effects on global patterns of production and trade, see Akamatsu (1961), Balassa (1979), Leamer (1984) and Balassa and Bauwens (1988).
3. Perhaps the best single indicator of (physical and human) capital intensity of production is value added per worker (Johnson 1968; Lary 1968). According to Japan's 1980 data for industry value added(from the input-output table published by the Bank of Japan in its *Economic Statistics Yearbook*, Tokyo, 1984), and for number of employees (published by the Ministry of International Trade and Industry in its *Textile Statistics Yearbook*, Tokyo, 1981), the value added per worker in 1980 in Japan's clothing industries averaged 4.0 million yen, while in the natural-fiber spinning and weaving industries it averaged 4.8 million yen, and in the synthetic fiber and spinning industries it was 24.1 million yen. Similar data for Korea (from the Bank of Korea's *1985 Input-Output Table*, Seoul, 1986) also show value added per worker to be highest in synthetic fiber production (12.8 million won), intermediate for yarns and fabrics (4.6 million won) and lowest for finished textiles (3.9 million won) and clothing (2.4 million won).
4. By about 1920, cotton and wool accounted for almost one-third of Japan's total import bill (column 11 of Table 5.2), a share that is comparable to the importance of energy products in Japan's imports around 1980.
5. The high peak share of textiles and clothing in total exports of 70 percent for the United Kingdom (Table 5.5) compares with subsequent peaks of less than 50 percent for Japan and its newly industrialized neighbors (Tables 5.1 and 5.2). Progressively lower peaks over time are to be expected given the increasing array of labor-intensive manufacturing

possibilities that face newly industrializing economies as new products come onto the market and their production processes become standardized.

6. This process of international technology transfer was first discussed in detail by Vernon (1966). A more explicit explanation for this phenomenon is provided by Grossman and Helpman (1991).

7. On the history of the MFA see, for example, Keesing and Wolf (1980), Cline (1987), Giesse and Lewin (1987), and Hamilton (1990).

8. Cline (1987: 142–3). China also benefited before the 1986 renegotiation of the MFA from a loop-hole in the import-restrictive arrangements which allowed Chinese firms to export clothing based on ramie (Cable 1987: 623–4).

9. South Asia began moving in this direction recently: the value of clothing exports from Bangladesh, India, Pakistan and Sri Lanka grew at a very impressive 18 per cent per year in nominal US dollar terms during the 1980s, increasing the region's share of global clothing exports from 1.9 per cent in 1979 to 3.9 per cent in 1990.

10. There are legitimate concerns that the increased use of anti-dumping actions by the EC and rules of origin provisions in the NAFTA agreement could effectively raise barriers to textiles and clothing imports by Western Europe and North America as those regions move toward closer regional integration. See, for example, Hindley and Messerlin (1993).

References

Akamatsu, K., 1961, "A Theory of Unbalanced Growth in the World Economy," *Weltwirtschaftliches Archiv*, 86(2): 196–217.

Anderson, K., 1991, "Textiles and Clothing in Global Economic Development: East Asia's Dynamic Role," World Competition, 14(3): 97–117.

———— (ed.), 1992, *New Silk Roads: East Asia and World Textile Markets*, Cambridge University Press, Cambridge.

————, 1993, "Intersectoral Changes in Transforming Socialist Economies: Distinguishing Initial from Longer Term Responses," in I. Goldin (ed.), *Economic Growth and Agriculture*, Macmillan, London.

Anderson, K. and Y. I. Park, 1989, "China and the International Relocation of World Textile and Clothing Activity," *Weltwirtschaftliches Archiv*, 125(1): 129–48.

Balassa, B., 1965, "Trade Liberalization and 'Revealed' Comparative Advantage," *Manchester School of Economic and Social Studies*, 33(2): 99–124.

————, 1979, "The Changing Pattern of Comparative Advantage in Manufactured Goods," *Review of Economics and Statistics*, 61(2): 259–66.

Balassa, B. and L. Bauwens, 1988, *Changing Trade Patterns in Manufactured Goods: An Econometric Investigation*, North-Holland, Amsterdam.

Bhagwati, J. N., 1988, *Protectionism*, MIT Press, Cambridge, MA.

Bowen, H. P., 1983, "Changes in the International Distribution of Resources and Their Impact on U.S. Comparative Advantage," *Review of Economics and Statistics*, 65(3): 402–14.

Cable, V., 1987, "Textiles and Clothing in a New Round of Trade Negotiations," *World Bank Economic Review*, 1(4): 619–46.

Cassing, J. H. and A. L. Hillman, 1986, "Shifting Comparative Advantage and Senescent Industry Collapse," *American Economic Review*, 76(3): 516–23.

Cline, W. R., 1987, *The Future of World Trade in Textiles and Apparel*, Institute for International Economics, Washington, DC.

Deardorff, A. V., 1984, "An Exposition and Exploration of Krueger's Trade Model," *Canadian Journal of Economics*, 17(4): 731–46.

Eaton, J., 1987, "A Dynamic Specific-Factors Model of International Trade," *Review of Economic Studies*, 54(2): 325–38.

Giesse, C. R. and M. J. Lewin, 1987, "The Multifiber Arrangement: 'Temporary' Protection Run Amuck," *Law and International Policy in International Business*, 19(1): 51–170.

Grossman, G. M. and E. Helpman, 1991, "Endogenous Product Cycles," *Economic Journal*, 101(408): 1214–29.

Hamilton, C. B. (ed.), 1990a, *Textile Trade and Developing Countries: Eliminating the MFA in the 1990s*, World Bank, Washington, DC.

———, 1990b, "European Community External Protection and 1992: Voluntary Export Restraints Applied to Pacific Asia," *European Economic Review*, 35: 377–87.

———, 1992, "The New Silk Road to Europe: New Conditions for Old Trade," in Anderson (1992), Ch. 7.

Hamilton, C. B. and L. A. Winters, 1992, "Opening up International Trade in Eastern Europe," *Economic Policy*, 14: 78–116.

Hillman, A. L., 1989, *The Political Economy of Protection*, Harwood Academic, New York.

Hindley, B. and P. Messerlin, 1993, "Guarantees of Market Access and Regionalism," in K. Anderson and R. Blackhurst (eds.), *Regional Integration and the Global Trading System*, Harvester Wheatsheaf, London, Ch. 17.

Hughes, H. and J. Waelbroeck, 1981, "Can Developing-Country Exports Keep Growing in the 1980s?" *World Economy*, 4(2): 127–48.

Johnson, H. G., 1968, *Comparative Cost and Commercial Policy Theory for a Developing World Economy*, Almqvist and Wiksell, Stockholm.

Jones, R. W., 1971, "A Three-Factor Model in Theory, Trade and History," in J. Bhagwati et al. (eds.), *Trade, Balance of Payments and Growth*, North Holland, Amsterdam, Ch. 1.

Keesing, D. B. and D. R. Sherk, 1971, "Population Density in Patterns of Trade and Development," *American Economic Review*, 61(5): 956–61.

Keesing, D. B. and M. Wolf, 1980, *Textile Quotas Against Developing Countries*, Thames Essay No. 23, Trade Policy Research Centre, London.

Krueger, A., 1977, *Growth, Distortions and Patterns of Trade Among Many Countries*, International Finance Section, Princeton University, Princeton, NJ.

Kuznets, S. S., 1966, *Modern Economic Growth: Rate, Structure and Spread*, Yale University Press, New Haven, CT.

Lary, H. B., 1968, *Imports of Manufactures from Less Developed Countries*, Columbia University Press, New York.

Leamer, E. E., 1984, *Sources of International Comparative Advantage: Theory and Evidence*, MIT Press, Cambridge, MA.

———, 1987, "Paths of Development in the Three-Factor, n-Good General Equilibrium Model," *Journal of Political Economy*, 95(5): 961–99.

Maddison, A., 1982, *Phases of Economic Development*, Oxford University Press, London.

Maizels, A., 1963, *Industrial Growth and World Trade*, Cambridge University Press, Cambridge.

Park, Y. I. and K. Anderson, 1991, "The Rise and Demise of Textiles and Clothing in Economic Development: The Case of Japan," *Economic Development and Cultural Change*, 39(3): 531–48.

Suphachalasai, Suphat, 1992, "Thailand's Growth in Textile Exports," in Anderson (1992), Ch. 4.

Trela, I. and J. Whalley, 1990a, "Global Effects of Developed Country Trade Restrictions on Textiles and Apparel," *Economic Journal*, 100(403):1190–205.

———, 1990b, "Internal Quota Allocation Schemes and the Costs of the MFA," University of Western Ontario, mimeo.

Vernon, R., 1966, "International Investment and International Trade in the Product Cycle," *Quarterly Journal of Economics*, 80(2): 190–207.

World Bank, 1988, *World Development Report 1988*, Oxford University Press, New York.

Yamawaki, H., 1992, "International Competition and Japan's Domestic Adjustments," in Anderson (1992), Ch. 7.

Yamazawa, I., 1983, "Renewal of the Textile Industry in Developed Countries and World Textile Trade," *Hitotsubashi Journal of Economics*, 24(1): 25–41.

Yoffie, D. B., 1983, *Power and Protectionism: Strategies of the Newly Industrializing Countries*, Columbia University Press, New York.

Chapter 6

Shigeki Tejima

FOREIGN DIRECT INVESTMENT BY JAPANESE FIRMS IN THE ASIA-PACIFIC REGION

6.1 Introduction

The principal focus of this chapter is, as indicated by the title, Japanese foreign direct investment (FDI) in the Asia-Pacific region. In places, references have been made to other Asian economies. The chapter first provides a comparison between Japanese investment in this region and investment in other regions. The chapter then looks at the basic features of Japanese investment in this region, and compares these basic features with those of Japanese investment in other regions. This analysis is based on a 1991 survey conducted by the Export-Import Bank of Japan (EXIM Bank). An attempt is then made to prognosticate future investment trends, taking into account the results of the 1991 survey and the recent financial environment and changes in Japan.

6.2 Japanese FDI in the Asian Region

In the recent past, the economic growth of the Asia-Pacific countries has been exceptionally high, far beyond all other developing and developed countries, although the developed countries enjoyed a stable expansion of their economies in the "boom" period of 1983–89. This vigorous economic growth of the Asia-Pacific countries was stimulated by the dramatically expanding international trade and foreign investment inflow of those countries. Along with European and American FDI, Japanese FDI has contributed to the recent development of the Asia-Pacific countries.

The absolute level of Japanese FDI in Asian countries increased remarkably in the 1980s. In the 1980 fiscal year Japanese FDI in the Asian region was US$1,186 million. It reached US$8,238 million in the 1989 fiscal year—an amount seven times larger than the 1980 figure. In the 1989 fiscal year total Japanese FDI reached its historically highest level, although the importance of Japanese FDI in the Asia-Pacific region has declined in the 1980s in comparison with Japanese FDI in the developed countries.

Japanese FDI in the latter half of the 1980s was characterized by the following movements (see Table 6.1):

☐ Rapid increase of Japanese FDI to North America (about 50 percent of the total) and Europe (about 20 percent of the total) (see Figures 6.1 and 6.2).
☐ Increase of Japanese FDI to the Asian newly industrialized economies (ANIEs) (up to 1989) and the ASEAN (Association of Southeast Asian Nations) countries (since 1987).
☐ Rapid expansion of FDI in the service sector as well as the manufacturing sector.

These three features are rather different from those characterizing Japanese FDI in the 1970s, when it mainly flowed into the manufacturing sectors of Asian and Latin American countries, and often took advantage of the import-substitution policy of those countries in those days. Previously, in the total notified cumulative amount of Japanese FDI for the period of the 1951–79 fiscal year, FDI in the Asia-Pacific region held the largest share (27.2 percent) followed by North America (25.8 percent). Today, however, if we take the same cumulative amount for the period of the 1951–90 financial year, FDI in Asia-Pacific occupies the third position (15.3 percent) behind North America (43.8 percent) and Europe (19.1 percent)(see Table 6.1(b)).

At the beginning of the 1990s we find a new movement pattern for Japanese FDI. In the 1990 and 1991 financial years, Japanese FDI in the Asia-Pacific region was stable, especially in the manufacturing sector, although FDI to North America dramatically declined during these two financial years, especially in the non-manufacturing sector.

If we look at the top recipients of Japanese FDI, major host countries in the Asia-Pacific region are ranked high in the 1991 fiscal year. Australia was the third largest host country followed by Indonesia (the sixth), Hong Kong (the eighth), Malaysia (the ninth), Thailand (the twelfth), Singapore (the fourteenth), China (the fifteenth), Taiwan (the sixteenth), South Korea (the twenty-first) and the Philippines (the twenty-fourth) (see Tables 6.2 and 6.3).

It should be noted that FDI in Indonesia, Malaysia and China increased in the 1991 fiscal year over the amount of the previous year, while almost all other

TABLE 6.1 Japanese foreign direct investment by region
(a) Annual outflow by region ($ million, %)

Region	1987 Total Value	%	1987 Manufacturing Value	%	1988 Total Value	%	1988 Manufacturing Value	%	1989 Total Value	%	1989 Manufacturing Value	%	1990 Total Value	%	1990 Manufacturing Value	%
North America	15,357	46.0	4,848	61.9	22,328	47.5	9,191	66.6	33,902	50.2	9,585	58.9	27,192	47.8	6,793	43.9
U.S.A.	14,704	44.1	4,378	55.9	21,701	46.2	8,836	64.0	32,540	48.2	8,874	54.5	26,128	45.9	6,388	41.3
Latin America	4,816	14.4	161	2.1	6,428	13.7	443	3.2	5,238	7.8	196	1.2	3,628	6.4	648	4.2
Asia	4,868	14.6	1,679	21.4	5,569	11.8	2,371	17.2	8,238	12.2	3,220	19.8	7,054	12.4	3,068	19.8
NIEs	2,581	7.7	878	11.2	3,264	6.9	775	5.6	4,902	7.3	1,347	8.3	3,354	5.9	804	5.2
Korea	647	1.9	247	3.2	483	1.0	254	1.8	606	0.9	251	1.5	284	0.5	147	0.9
Taiwan	368	1.1	255	3.3	372	0.8	263	1.9	494	0.7	302	1.9	446	0.8	274	1.8
Hong Kong	1,072	3.2	108	1.4	1,662	3.5	85	0.6	1,899	2.8	116	0.7	1,784	3.1	114	0.7
Singapore	494	1.5	268	3.4	747	1.6	173	1.3	1,902	2.8	678	4.2	840	1.5	269	1.7
ASEAN	1,030	3.1	704	9.0	1,967	4.2	1,360	9.9	2,782	4.1	1,554	9.5	3,241	5.7	2,028	13.1
Indonesia	545	1.6	295	3.8	586	1.2	298	2.2	631	0.9	166	1.0	1,105	1.9	536	3.5
Thailand	250	0.7	210	2.7	858	1.8	626	4.5	1,276	1.9	789	4.8	1,154	2.0	714	4.6
Malaysia	163	0.5	148	1.9	388	0.8	346	2.5	673	1.0	471	2.9	724	1.3	582	3.8
Philippines	72	0.2	51	0.7	135	0.3	90	0.7	202	0.3	128	0.8	258	0.5	196	1.3
China	1,227	3.7	69	0.9	296	0.6	203	1.5	438	0.6	207	1.3	349	0.6	161	1.0
Middle East	63	0.2		0.0	260	0.6	13	0.1	66	0.1	3	0.0	27	0.0	1	0.0
Europe	6,576	19.7	852	10.9	9,117	19.4	1,547	11.2	14,808	21.9	3,089	19.0	14,294	25.1	4,593	29.7
England	2,473	7.4	289	3.7	3,956	8.4	335	2.4	5,239	7.8	1,174	7.2	6,805	12.0	1,999	12.9
Germany	403	1.2	109	1.4	409	0.9	82	0.6	1,083	1.6	530	3.3	1,241	2.2	386	2.5
France	330	1.0	78	1.0	463	1.0	148	1.1	1,136	1.7	304	1.9	1,257	2.2	491	3.2
Spain	283	0.8	261	3.3	161	0.3	76	0.6	501	0.7	149	0.9	321	0.6	100	0.6
Netherlands	829	2.5	37	0.5	2,359	5.0	702	5.1	4,547	6.7	572	3.5	2,744	4.8	1,318	8.5
Africa	273	0.8	2	0.0	653	1.4	1	0.0	671	1.0	6	0.0	551	1.0	0	0.0
Oceania	1,413	4.2	290	3.7	2,668	5.7	239	1.7	4,618	6.8	184	1.1	4,166	7.3	383	2.5
Total	33,366	100.0	7,832	23.5	47,023	100.0	13,805	29.4	67,540	100.0	16,284	24.1	56,911	100.0	15,486	27.2

Source: EX-IM Bank of Japan with the Ministry of Finance's statistics.

TABLE 6.1 (continued)
(b) Cumulative investment amount by region ($ million, %)

Region	1991 Total		1991 Manufacturing		1951–90 Total		1951–90 Manufacturing		1951–79 Total		1951–79 Manufacturing	
	Value	%	Value	%	Value	%	Value	%	Value	%	Value	%
North America	18,823	45.3	5,868	49.7	136,185	43.8	40,322	49.4	8,202	25.8	2,030	18.7
U.S.A.	18,025	43.3	5,558	45.1	130,529	42.0	37,744	46.2	7,394	23.2	1,734	16.0
Latin America	3,338	8.0	365	3.0	40,483	13.0	6,281	7.7	5,580	17.5	2,583	23.8
Asia	5,936	14.3	2,928	23.8	47,519	15.3	18,659	22.9	8,643	27.2	3,847	35.4
NIEs	2,202	5.3	641	5.2	23,274	7.5	7,695	9.4	3,160	9.9	1,802	16.6
Korea	260	0.6	157	1.3	4,138	1.3	1,987	2.4	1,102	3.5	757	7.0
Taiwan	404	1.0	186	1.5	2,731	0.9	2,049	2.5	323	1.0	300	2.8
Hong Kong	925	2.2	121	1.0	9,850	3.2	722	0.9	939	3.0	165	1.5
Singapore	613	1.5	177	1.4	6,555	2.1	2,937	3.6	796	2.5	580	5.3
ASEAN	3,083	7.4	1,945	15.8	20,773	6.7	9,852	12.1	5,298	16.7	1,983	18.2
Indonesia	1,193	2.9	578	4.7	11,540	3.7	3,657	4.5	3,894	12.2	1,202	11.1
Thailand	807	1.9	595	4.8	4,422	1.4	2,959	3.6	363	1.1	269	2.5
Malaysia	880	2.1	613	5.0	3,231	1.0	2,403	2.9	504	1.6	324	3.0
Philippines	203	0.5	159	1.3	1,580	0.5	833	1.0	537	1.7	188	1.7
China	579	1.4	308	2.5	2,823	0.9	717	0.9	14	0.0		0.0
Middle East	91	0.2	55	0.4	3,431	1.1	1,277	1.6	2,101	6.6	975	9.0
Europe	9,371	22.5	2,690	21.9	59,265	19.1	12,540	15.4	3,893	12.2	683	6.3
England	3,588	8.6	904	7.3	22,598	7.3	4,280	5.2	1,823	5.7	91	0.8
Germany	1,116	2.7	341	2.8	4,689	1.5	1,384	1.7	387	1.2	58	0.5
France	817	2.0	237	1.9	4,156	1.3	1,339	1.6	355	1.1	55	0.5
Spain	378	0.9	287	2.3	1,867	0.6	1,049	1.3	151	0.5	136	1.3
Netherlands	1,960	4.7	395	3.2	12,816	4.1	2,828	3.5	257	0.8	30	0.3
Africa	748	1.8	1	0.0	5,826	1.9	231	0.3	1,306	4.1	86	0.8
Oceania	3,278	7.9	405	3.3	18,098	5.8	2,302	2.8	2,078	6.5	664	6.1
Total	41,584	100.0	12,311	34.4	310,808	100.0	81,613	100.0	31,804	100.0	10,867	100.0

Source: EX-IM Bank of Japan with the Ministry of Finance's statistics.

FIGURE 6.1   Japan's overseas direct investment trends by industry

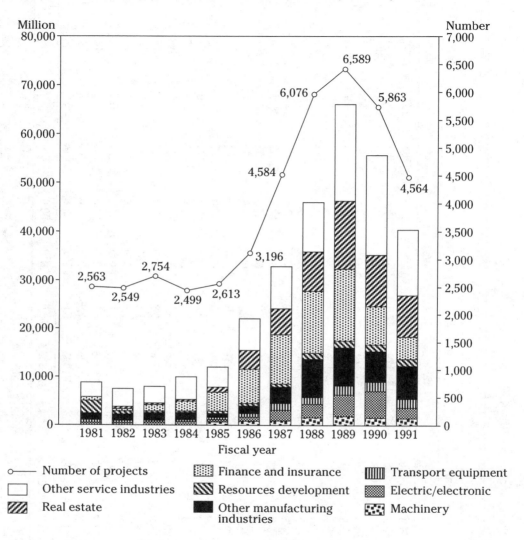

Source: EX-IM Bank of Japan with the Ministry of Finance's statistics.

FIGURE 6.2   Japan's overseas direct investment trends by region

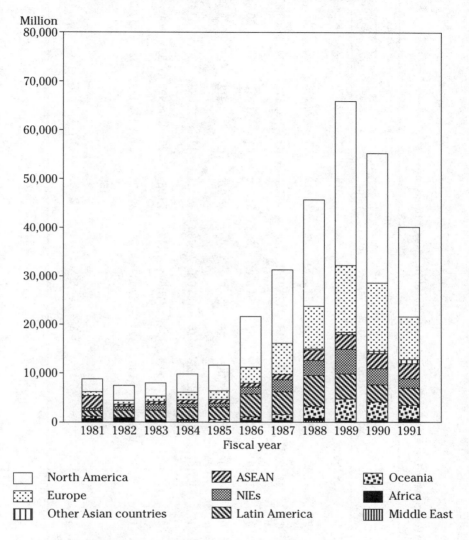

Source: EX-IM Bank of Japan with the Ministry of Finance's statistics.

Shigeki Tejima

TABLE 6.2 Overseas direct investment in the Asia-Pacific countries (number of cases, $ thousand)

	1970		1971		1972		1973		1974		1975		1976	
	No.	Value	No.	Value	No.	Value	No.	Value	No.	Value	No.	Value	No.	Value
Korea	77	17,449	96	28,180	196	146,049	315	210,811	98	17,015	37	92,959	44	102,436
Taiwan	61	24,756	22	12,405	37	10,394	119	34,057	52	32,612	44	24,203	46	28,217
Hong Kong	49	9,260	72	41,192	123	29,459	216	123,275	148	50,706	102	105,172	114	68,866
Singapore	26	8,927	47	15,107	72	42,183	82	81,292	55	51,469	64	51,651	83	26,740
Thailand	21	12,656	34	8,646	62	29,582	76	33,991	60	30,978	26	14,312	27	19,306
Malaysia	33	14,008	17	12,147	45	13,435	116	125,630	78	48,411	43	52,083	36	52,186
Indonesia	34	48,634	48	112,409	61	118,809	143	341,308	113	375,286	120	588,997	85	930,749
Philippines	11	28,999	17	4,519	23	9,746	74	42,932	55	59,220	64	149,188	50	14,703
China									2	158				
Brunei			2	155			1	688	1	2,348	1	595	1	325

TABLE 6.2 (continued)

	1977 No.	1977 Value	1978 No.	1978 Value	1979 No.	1979 Value	1980 No.	1980 Value	1981 No.	1981 Value	1982 No.	1982 Value	1983 No.	1983 Value
Korea	33	95,062	51 (30)	222,134 (172,570)	45 (30)	94,760 (60,209)	23 (17)	35,083 (22,604)	33 (19)	73,194 (34,882)	26 (16)	103,165 (24,947)	45 (24)	129,042 (31,028)
Taiwan	54	17,611	102 (84)	39,549 (38,259)	92 (68)	38,667 (34,521)	75 (54)	47,217 (43,119)	98 (69)	54,437 (49,080)	65 (46)	54,645 (46,093)	92 (62)	103,023 (75,939)
Hong Kong	110	108,517	135 (27)	158,494 (9,973)	225 (55)	224,716 (19,619)	158 (30)	155,805 (19,519)	178 (31)	329,101 (19,851)	162 (27)	401,013 (10,885)	178 (20)	562,524 (11,876)
Singapore	89	65,862	161 (96)	173,946 (130,907)	166 (97)	255,382 (185,184)	132 (60)	139,888 (107,228)	164 (88)	266,338 (170,492)	154 (91)	180,256 (151,393)	184 (88)	322,065 (267,789)
Thailand	38	49,157	50 (31)	31,648 (17,256)	68 (41)	54,544 (36,318)	58 (40)	33,297 (22,488)	52 (32)	30,638 (18,419)	66 (40)	94,175 (79,845)	73 (33)	71,667 (37,626)
Malaysia	33	68,807	30 (18)	47,942 (22,096)	38 (36)	33,458 (132,188)	48 (17)	146,337 (34,041)	41 (32)	31,047 (18,103)	77 (31)	82,534 (59,276)	95 (37)	139,637 (111,293)
Indonesia	83	425,303	84 (47)	610,182 (409,585)	65 (38)	149,781 (35,491)	96 (63)	529,396 (325,095)	88 (61)	2,434,148 (329,390)	84 (55)	409,650 (144,460)	89 (52)	373,562 (178,012)
Philippines	58	26,931	44 (18)	53,477 (36,071)	43 (12)	102,200 (47,853)	36 (23)	78,318 (43,226)	28 (7)	71,947 (36,575)	19 (7)	34,139 (17,810)	20	64,948 (4,839)
China					1	13,500	6	11,863	9 (3)	25,795 (4,305)	4 (3)	18,493 (3,493)	5	2,955
Brunei	3	4,668			1	300			(3)	4,700 (4,700)			7 (3)	1,896 (1,592)

TABLE 6.2 (continued)

	1984 No.	1984 Value	1985 No.	1985 Value	1986 No.	1986 Value	1987 No.	1987 Value	1988 No.	1988 Value	1989 No.	1989 Value	1990 No.	1990 Value	1991 No.	1991 Value
Korea	57	106,702	75	133,767	111	435,533	166	646,858	153	482,904	81	605,826	54	284,339	48	260,425
	(43)	(37,492)	(55)	(36,921)	(93)	(142,563)	(137)	(247,239)	(115)	(253,935)	(65)	(250,654)	(32)	(146,864)	(28)	(157,311)
Taiwan	68	64,691	68	114,142	178	290,525	268	367,401	234	372,367	165	494,007	102	445,712	87	404,544
	(54)	(57,579)	(53)	(109,262)	(142)	(273,485)	(177)	(254,919)	(99)	(262,715)	(90)	(302,120)	(50)	(274,605)	(40)	(185,464)
Hong Kong	119	411,723	105	131,068	163	502,301	261	1,072,488	335	1,661,781	335	1,898,411	244	1,784,770	178	925,025
	(10)	(5,669)	(24)	(14,046)	(51)	(52,433)	(58)	(108,014)	(71)	(84,797)	(67)	(116,269)	(37)	(113,524)	(41)	(120,597)
Singapore	108	224,810	110	338,969	85	302,176	182	494,399	197	747,102	181	1,902,436	139	839,809	103	613,314
	(32)	(74,641)	(32)	(92,315)	(36)	(104,493)	(106)	(268,126)	(80)	(173,223)	(67)	(677,594)	(35)	(269,717)	(32)	(176,853)
Thailand	76	118,623	51	48,413	58	123,749	192	249,961	382	858,887	403	1,275,534	377	1,154,336	258	806,789
	(40)	(79,435)	(27)	(25,324)	(26)	(87,293)	(153)	(210,198)	(281)	(626,115)	(272)	(789,095)	(245)	(714,297)	(184)	(594,816)
Malaysia	63	142,143	60	79,296	70	158,035	64	163,324	108	387,135	159	673,101	169	724,775	136	879,795
	(34)	(114,071)	(32)	(32,790)	(46)	(64,568)	(42)	(147,796)	(91)	(346,202)	(111)	(470,586)	(119)	(582,257)	(92)	(612,722)
Indonesia	82	373,825	62	408,266	46	249,769	67	545,445	84	585,507	140	630,975	155	1,105,056	148	1,192,881
	(46)	(90,955)	(24)	(66,050)	(16)	(26,481)	(35)	(294,918)	(35)	(297,851)	(66)	(165,839)	(72)	(535,847)	(89)	(578,535)
Philippines	12	45,655	9	60,654	9	20,581	18	72,379	54	134,480	87	201,988	58	258,461	42	202,673
	(6)	(16,544)	(3)	(42,335)	(2)	(14,813)	(8)	(51,325)	(32)	(89,557)	(46)	(127,580)	(31)	(195,845)	(18)	(158,623)
China	66	114,194	118	99,858	85	226,356	101	1,226,499	171	296,234	126	438,193	165	349,001	246	579,198
	(30)	(20,666)	(51)	(21,997)	(38)	(22,838)	(58)	(70,136)	(117)	(202,679)	(85)	(206,268)	(113)	(160,976)	(178)	(308,775)
Brunei	3	4,545		745	1	974	1	74		457		214			1	351
										(457)					(0)	(1)

TABLE 6.3 Japanese foreign investment by country and industry in Asia-Pacific ($ million)
(a) NIEs

Industry	NIEs			Hong Kong			Singapore			Korea			Taiwan		
	1989	1990	1991	1989	1990	1991	1989	1990	1991	1989	1990	1991	1989	1990	1991
Foodstuffs	487	42	30	11	10	12	438	3	8	11	11	4	27	18	6
Textiles	32	119	25	16	4	3	2	101	15	5	7	1	9	6	6
Lumber and pulp	9	24	4	1	1	0	4	23	0	1	0	0	3	0	4
Chemicals	138	121	138	7	0	0	42	53	45	41	28	57	48	40	36
Iron and steel/nonferrous metal	96	80	40	10	9	5	14	10	7	15	13	13	57	48	15
Machinery	97	60	97	19	3	50	30	10	14	19	11	12	29	36	21
Electric/electronic	261	207	142	26	70	14	91	54	54	66	22	14	78	61	60
Transport equipment	80	47	38	0	0	1	0	0	0	68	35	34	12	12	3
Others	150	101	127	27	15	36	58	14	34	25	19	22	40	53	35
MANUFACTURING TOTAL	1,350	804	641	116	114	121	678	269	177	251	147	157	302	274	186
Agriculture and Forestry	0	3	4		2	4		1	0			0			0
Fisheries	4	0	1	3	0	0	1	0	0			1			
Mining	0	5	1		0	0		5	0						1
RESOURCES DEVELOPMENT TOTAL	4	8	6	3	2	4	1	6	0			1			1
Construction	162	44	24	68	32	18	91	2	2		1		3	9	4
Commerce	563	1,123	659	390	752	331	70	265	154	3	5	7	100	101	167
Finance and Insurance	805	485	416	425	398	307	339	87	97	39		9	2	0	3
Services	688	333	172	239	102	56	148	86	37	260	117	41	41	28	38
Transportation	354	81	69	122	31	10	228	46	58		1		4	3	1
Real Estate	893	426	161	528	348	62	345	52	83	12		12	8	26	4
Others	2	1	0	2	0	0		1	0						
COMMERCE AND SERVICES TOTAL	3,467	2,493	1,501	1,774	1,663	784	1,221	539	431	314	124	69	158	167	217
BRANCHES	85	51	56	6	6	16	3	25	6	42	14	34	34	6	0
TOTAL	4,900	3,354	2,204	1,898	1,784	925	1,902	840	614	606	284	261	494	446	404

Source: Ministry of Finance

TABLE 6.3 (continued)
(b) ASEAN

Industry	ASEAN			Indonesia			Malaysia			Thailand			Philippines		
	1989	1990	1991	1989	1990	1991	1989	1990	1991	1989	1990	1991	1989	1990	1991
Foodstuffs	34	65	110	3	10	14		2	8	30	49	86	1	4	2
Textiles	60	157	121	17	65	57	1	4	8	41	88	54	1	0	2
Lumber and pulp	50	49	30	32	15	10	8	23	16	10	10	3	0	1	1
Chemicals	140	399	419	26	241	314	49	96	41	55	50	58	10	12	6
Iron and steel/ nonferrous metal	208	130	196	20	12	21	45	52	94	134	58	41	9		40
Machinery	211	152	128	2	8	21	26	81	26	181	59	77	2	4	4
Electric/electronic	586	581	598	15	5	83	273	261	283	243	177	202	55	138	30
Transport equipment	60	316	135	27	170	25	3	10	27	17	117	18	13	19	65
Others	203	176	208	24	9	33	65	53	110	78	105	56	36	9	9
MANUFACTURING TOTAL	1,554	2,028	1,945	166	536	578	471	582	613	789	714	595	128	196	159
Agriculture and Forestry	20	29	22	1	2	1	4	3	2	12	17	18	3	7	1
Fisheries	12	13	21	8	12	9	1	0	10	3	1	1	0	0	1
Mining	208	207	237	177	170	202	25	6	32	2	1	0	4	30	3
RESOURCES DEVELOPMENT TOTAL	240	249	280	186	184	212	30	9	44	17	19	19	7	37	5
Construction	123	46	70	1	11	2	71	6	22	47	23	44	4	6	2
Commerce	87	91	45	0	19	3	25	11	5	56	60	34	6	1	3
Finance and Insurance	264	156	373	211	84	283	40	22	58	12	49	32	1	1	0
Services	241	400	150	57	234	23	10	33	71	150	126	33	24	7	23
Transportation	29	31	24	0	2	3		6	11	28	22	10	1	1	0
Real Estate	220	204	180	3	36	89	26	51	56	159	109	24	32	8	11
Others	7	5	0	7	0	0		5	0	0	0	0		0	0
COMMERCE AND SERVICES TOTAL	971	933	842	279	386	403	172	134	223	452	389	177	68	24	39
BRANCHES	16	33	16			0		2	0	16	31	16	0	0	0
TOTAL	2,782	3,241	3,083	631	1,105	1,193	673	724	880	1,276	1,154	807	202	258	203

Source: Ministry of Finance

TABLE 6.3 (continued)
(c) China, India and Pakistan

Industry	China 1989	China 1990	China 1991	India 1989	India 1990	India 1991	Pakistan 1989	Pakistan 1990	Pakistan 1991
Foodstuffs	13	9	19		0				
Textiles	11	21	70		2		82		
Lumber and pulp	1	2	1						
Chemicals	11	12	11	4	2	3		1	
Iron and steel/ nonferrous metal	6	14	11			1			
Machinery	42	50	29	1	1				
Electric/electronic	80	22	123	7	14	7		0	
Transport equipment	1	1	9	1	1			5	9
Others	40	30	35	4		4		6	
MANUFACTURING TOTAL	206	161	308	17	20	15	82	6	9
Agriculture and forestry	0	2	2						
Fisheries	6	4	3						
Mining	4	20	1						
RESOURCES DEVELOPMENT TOTAL	10	26	6	0	0		0	0	
Construction	4	7	1					1	
Commerce	9	3	6				1	1	
Finance and Insurance	10	2	11						
Services	174	136	189				0	1	
Transportation	15	0	2						
Real Estate	8	9	16						
Others		0	0						
COMMERCE AND SERVICES TOTAL	220	157	225	1	10		1	2	
BRANCHES	1	3	40	0			0	1	4
TOTAL	438	349	579	18	30	14	83	9	14

Source: Ministry of Finance

countries recorded decreases of Japanese FDI in that same year. In Korea and China, Japanese investors recorded the highest annual investment outflow in the 1987 fiscal year. In Taiwan, Hong Kong, Singapore and Thailand, Japanese FDI reached a peak in the 1989 fiscal year. The Philippines experienced a peak of Japanese FDI in the 1990 fiscal year, while in the case of Malaysia it was achieved in the 1991 fiscal year. Rather exceptionally Indonesia received the highest level of investment in the 1981 fiscal year. FDI to Indonesia in the 1991 fiscal year was still less than half of the amount recorded in the 1981 fiscal year, although Japanese FDI had gradually increased through the entire period of the 1980s after the sudden decrease in 1982. In Thailand, Japanese FDI reached its peak in the 1989 fiscal year at US$1,275 million. This amount was about 40 times the amount recorded in the 1980 fiscal year (US$33 million). In China, Japanese FDI in the 1991 fiscal year was US$579 million, or about 50 times the FDI recorded in the 1980 fiscal year (US$12 million). In the case of Malaysia, FDI in the 1991 fiscal year was US$880 million, which was more than six times the amount recorded in the 1980 fiscal year (US$146 million).

If we look at Japanese FDI by industry in each Asian country, it is notable that about 50 percent or more of the FDI was oriented toward the manufacturing sector, except in Hong Kong, Singapore and Indonesia. This concentration in the manufacturing sector was a trend quite opposite from that for Japanese FDI in North America and Europe, where the major portion of investment was oriented toward the nonmanufacturing sector. FDI in Thailand and Malaysia, in particular, was highly concentrated in the manufacturing sector. In both countries the electric/electronic industry has held the largest share of Japanese FDI for the past several years, while the machinery, chemicals, iron/steel/other metals and transport equipment industries have been popular industries among Japanese investors as well. Indonesia has a long history as a recipient of Japanese investment in its mining sector. But in recent years FDI in the manufacturing sector has increased in the chemical, transport equipment, and textile industries. Investment in the finance and insurance sector and the services sector has also increased.

Traditionally, in Hong Kong and Singapore, FDI in nonmanufacturing sectors has been dominant. Commerce, finance/insurance, services, transportation and, in recent years, real estate, have been major recipients of Japanese investment from time to time. In Korea and Taiwan the electric/electronic, iron/steel/other metals and chemicals industries are major recipients of Japanese FDI in the manufacturing sector. In Australia, a major portion of Japanese FDI has been oriented toward the mining and service sector, but in recent years, Japanese FDI in the manufacturing sector has gradually increased. In recent years Japanese FDI in the commerce sector has been noticeable in Taiwan, while Japanese investment in the service sector has been prominent in South Korea. In China, the services industry and electric/electronic industry have been the principal recipients of Japanese FDI. The textiles and machinery industries have been the second largest recipients of Japanese FDI in China.

6.3 Japanese Firms' Investment Strategy and Performance

6.3.1 Japanese Firms' FDI Strategy by Region

In the 1980s, Japanese FDI was extraordinarily accelerated by the sudden appreciation of the Japanese yen after the Plaza Accord in 1985. Clearly, the appreciation of the yen lowered the price of foreign real estate and financial assets and labor costs in terms of the yen, and increased the export price of Japanese goods in terms of other currencies.

The appreciation of the yen coupled with two basic investment motives—the desire to decrease trade friction and to pursue a long-term globalization strategy— stimulated a rapid expansion of Japanese FDI in North American, Western European and Asian countries. In the 1980s, many Japanese firms invested in North America and Western Europe in order to decrease trade friction with the U.S., Canada and European countries. Major Japanese automobile, electric/electronics and steel companies built large-scale manufacturing plants in North America and Europe in an attempt to decrease such trade friction. Later, however, many large Japanese firms also invested in North America and Europe as part of a long-term globalization (or global management) strategy. This investment motive was similar to the investment motive held by American and European multinational corporations.

Through the "globalization" or "global management" strategy Japanese firms sought the most effective production and sales bases for the world market. In order to contribute more effectively to international markets, Japanese firms strove to build effective worldwide network systems of production, sales and financing. This effort is sometimes called a "tri-polar strategy" or a "three-legged strategy" by Japanese firms. It involves establishing a regional headquarter in Europe, America and Asia, and giving each regional headquarter the autonomy to build more effective production and sales networks. The policy or strategy to be pursued by the firm is tailored to the varying characteristics of each region.

The special theme of the 1991 survey conducted by the EXIM Bank was "Globalization of Japanese firms in the 1980s and its prospect for the 1990s." Under the survey a questionnaire was sent to 551 major Japanese firms and 298 respondent firms (see Table 6.4). The questionnaire asked firms to identify the "most important" market or purchaser for existing production bases in every region (see Table 6.5). We received answers from 225 Japanese firms about the 1,274 production bases owned, at least partly, by those Japanese firms. Out of the 1,274 production bases, 300 were located in ANIEs, 322 in ASEAN, 50 in other Asian countries, 365 in North America, and 232 in Europe.

According to the survey results, the local market is the most important for existing production bases in every region. These results also held for production bases in ASEAN and the ANIEs, even though sometimes these regions are regarded as export bases for third countries. Out of 300 responding Japanese production subsidiaries established in ANIES, 74 percent were mainly oriented toward the local market. In the ASEAN countries, 62 percent of the 322 production firms owned by Japanese firms were oriented toward the local market.

In Asia the import-substitution policies of host countries in the 1970s have deeply influenced the policies of Japanese investors. Moreover, in recent years the significance of local consumption markets has grown dramatically, forcing Japanese investors to become more positive toward Asian local markets.

Yet, in the ANIEs and ASEAN countries, export to Asia, including Japan, as well as export to the U.S. and Europe, is a significant aspect of the activities of Japanese production bases. For example, 15 percent of the 300 subsidiaries in the ANIEs aimed their activities toward Asia including the Japanese market (8 percent), ASEAN (6 percent) and other Asian countries (1 percent), while 12 percent aimed their activities toward North America (10 percent) and Europe (2 percent). Similarly, 25 percent of the 322 subsidiaries in the ASEAN countries were oriented toward the markets of Japan (15 percent), the ANIEs (10 percent) and other Asian countries (1 percent). The remaining 13 percent of these subsidiaries targeted their activities at North America (8 percent) and Europe (5 percent).

On the other hand, 92 percent of the 420 Japanese subsidiaries in North America and 95 percent of the 232 Japanese subsidiaries in Europe served the local market. Exports to other countries are relatively less significant for the production bases in developed countries.

Similar responses were obtained when firms were asked to identify "important" markets, that is the most or second most important market for each firm. Generally speaking, Japanese firms have extended FDI to North America and Europe in order to sell to the local market. They have set up production and sales bases to respond to, and better serve, the changeable, diversified and sophisticated demands of developed countries. American and European investors have extended FDI in Europe and the U.S. for similar reasons. However, Japanese investors have also invested in North America and Europe in order to avoid trade friction with host countries.

In Asia-Pacific, networks have often been developed not only to serve Japanese and other Asian markets, but to serve North American, European and local markets. These networks have taken advantage of effective and relatively low-cost Asian suppliers.

Japanese regional networks in Asia-Pacific comprise some affiliates in some Asian countries that produce labor-intensive components and assemble final goods; other affiliates in other countries that produce relatively capital- or technology-intensive components; still other affiliates that function as the regional headquarters, and control financing, procurement of spare parts and regional marketing; and a Japanese headquarter that supplies capital, capital goods and key components not available elsewhere. This regional "hierarchy" or diversification strategy among Japanese investors can be better understood when viewed in relation to the motives underpinning investment by region.

TABLE 6.4   Survey methodology and profile of respondent firms

(a) Capitalization

Capital	Number of firms	Percentage
Below ¥100 mil.	6	2.0
¥100 mil.–500 mil.	24	8.1
¥500 mil.–1 bil.	4	1.3
¥1 bil.–5 bil.	52	17.4
¥5 bil.–10 bil.	43	14.4
over ¥10 bil.	169	56.7
Total	298	100.0

(b) Annual sales

Capital	Number of firms	Percentage
Below 50 bil.	77	25.8
¥50 bil.–100 bil.	53	17.8
¥100 bil.–200 bil.	49	16.4
¥200 bil.–300 bil.	35	11.7
¥300 bil.–500 bil.	30	10.1
¥500 bil.–1 tril.	29	9.7
over ¥1 tril.	25	8.4
Total	298	100.0

(c) Number of employees

Number of employees	Number of firms	Percentage
0–300	18	6.0
301–500	19	6.4
501–1,000	29	9.7
1,001–2,000	60	20.1
2,001–5,000	84	28.2
5,001–10,000	45	15.1
10,001–30,000	32	10.7
30,001–	11	3.7
Total	298	100.0

(d) Number of overseas affiliates by region

	NIEs	ASEAN	U.S.	EC	Others	World total
Production bases	438	498	453	281	335	2,005
(Joint ventures)	(236)	(324)	(137)	(90)	(185)	(972)
Sales bases	252	108	323	556	254	1,493
Others	52	43	687	210	127	1,119
Total	742	649	1,463	1,047	716	4,617

TABLE 6.4 (continued)
(e) Number of overseas affiliates by industry

		Total number by industry					Average per company				
			of which:					of which:			
	Number of firms	Production bases	Joint venture	Sales bases	Other FDI positions	Total number of FDI positions	Production bases	Joint venture	Sales bases	Other FDI positions	Total number of FDI positions
Foodstuff	16	80	57	24	26	130	5.0	3.6	1.5	1.6	8.1
Textiles	13	77	60	25	21	123	5.9	4.6	1.9	1.6	9.5
Wood, wood product	4	9	5	5	1	15	2.3	1.3	1.3	0.3	3.8
Pulp, paper	4	24	21	1	2	27	6.0	5.3	0.3	0.5	6.8
Chemical	43	254	163	146	73	473	5.9	3.8	3.4	1.7	11.0
Chemical excluding pharmaceuticals	34	235	152	119	53	407	6.9	4.5	3.5	1.6	12.0
Pharmaceuticals	9	19	11	27	20	66	2.1	1.2	3.0	2.2	7.3
Petroleum and rubber products	6	41	12	65	24	130	6.8	2.0	10.8	4.0	21.7
Ceramics, earthenware and stone products	11	86	61	31	16	133	7.8	5.5	2.8	1.5	12.1
Iron and steel	13	75	51	22	80	177	5.8	3.9	1.7	6.2	13.6
Nonferrous metals	9	150	39	40	25	215	16.7	4.3	4.4	2.8	23.9
Metal products	6	23	24	3	2	28	3.8	4.0	0.5	0.3	4.7
General machinery	32	169	70	206	63	438	5.3	2.2	6.4	2.0	13.7
Assembled	25	133	53	148	50	331	5.3	2.1	5.9	2.0	13.2
Parts	7	36	17	58	13	107	5.1	2.4	8.3	1.9	15.3

Electrical machinery	67	526	133	502	640	1,668	7.9	2.0	7.5	9.6	24.9
Assembled	35	351	95	352	618	1,321	10.0	2.7	10.1	17.7	37.7
Parts	32	175	38	150	22	347	5.5	1.2	4.7	0.7	10.8
Transportation equipment (excludes automobiles)	3	18	10	32	8	58	6.0	3.3	10.7	2.7	19.3
Automobiles	33	292	202	113	98	503	8.8	6.1	3.4	3.0	15.2
Assembled	10	134	98	77	75	286	13.4	9.8	7.7	7.5	28.6
Parts	23	158	104	36	23	217	6.9	4.5	1.6	1.0	9.4
Precision instruments	16	91	19	160	16	267	5.7	1.2	10.0	1.0	16.7
Assembled	11	52	13	121	15	188	4.7	1.2	11.0	1.4	17.1
Parts	5	39	6	39	1	79	7.8	1.2	7.8	0.2	15.8
Others	22	90	45	118	24	232	4.1	2.0	5.4	1.1	10.5
Total	298	2,005	972	1,493	1,119	4,617	6.7	3.3	5.0	3.8	15.5

Definitions of regional groups:
NIEs: Korea, Taiwan, Hong Kong and Singapore
ASEAN: Thailand, Indonesia, Malaysia and the Philippines
EC: Belgium, Denmark, France, Germany, Great Britain, Greece, Holland, Ireland, Italy, Luxembourg, Portugal and Spain

Definitions of industry groups:
Materials industries: Textiles, wood and wood products, paper and pulp, chemicals, iron and steel, non-ferrous metals
Processing and assembly industries: General machinery, electronic equipment (assembly, parts), transportation equipment (excluding automobiles), automobiles (assembly, parts), precision instruments (assembly, parts)
Other: food products, pharmaceuticals, petroleum and rubber products, ceramics and cement products, metal goods, others
Ratios of composition were calculated using only valid responses to each question. The number of valid responses to each question may differ from question to question.

TABLE 6.5   The most important purchaser of existing production bases by region (%)

Recipient of investment	Purchaser						Total number of companies
	NIEs	ASEAN	Other Asian countries	Japan	North America	EC	
NIEs	73	6	1	8	10	2	300
ASEAN	10	62	1	15	8	5	322
Other Asian countries	10	2	58	22	6	2	50
North America	4	–	–	4	92	0	365
EC	2	–	–	1	2	95	232

6.3.2   FDI Motivation by Region

The most commonly cited reason for investment by firms in all regions was "preservation and/or expansion of market share" (Figure 6.3). This result is compatible with the survey results relating to the most important markets for existing and planned production bases. This indicates that the most important purchaser for both existing and planned production centers in every region is the local market. On the other hand, we find that the regionally specific reasons cited for investing in the EC, U.S. and Canada included "development of a new market," "countermeasures against trade friction," and "development of products adapted to the local markets," while the reason cited for investing in the ANIES was "diversification of overseas production bases." The reasons cited for investing in the ASEAN countries included "securing the advantage of low labor costs," "reverse exports to Japan" and "exports to a third country." These responses reflect the local market-oriented attitude of Japanese firms toward the U.S., Canada and Europe, as well as the importance of Asian countries as production and export bases. (These results are again compatible with the survey results relating to the most important market.)

However, a comparison between the 1991 and 1990 survey reveals some marked changes in the frequency with which some reasons for investing in the U.S., Canada and ASEAN were cited. First, the number of firms which cited "to offset trade friction" as a reason for investing in Canada and the U.S. decreased from 20 percent in 1990 to 9 percent in 1991. (Compare column "C" for the U.S. and Canada in Figure 6.3a with column "C" in Figure 6.3b.) This decrease was probably due to the fact that the major investment projects in the U.S. and Canada have already been completed. Secondly, the number of firms that cited "taking advantage of low labor" as a reason for investing in ASEAN fell from 37 percent in 1990 to 26 percent in 1991. (Compare column "D" for ASEAN in Figure 6.3a with column "D" in Figure 6.3b.) This decrease reflects the fact that wage rates in the ASEAN countries have been pushed up by the rapid expansion of FDI flows to the ASEAN countries.

FIGURE 6.3   Motivation for foreign direct investment in the 1991 and 1990 surveys
(a) 1991 survey

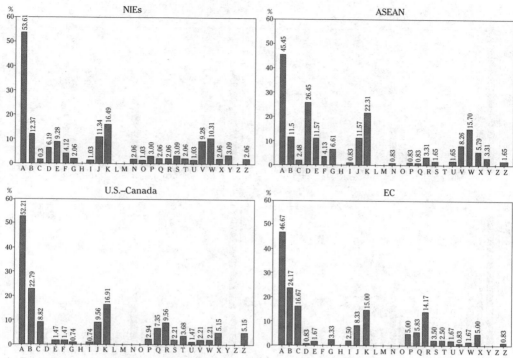

A. Preservation and/or expansion of market share
B. Development of a new market
C. Response to voluntary export restraints, dumping tariffs, and other trade regulations by the host country
D. Taking advantage of low cost labour
E. Securing stable supply of raw materials and natural resources
F. Requests from the host country
G. Taking advantage of favourable tax treatment and other preferences in the host country
H. Taking advantage of benefits available in tax havens
I. Avoiding foreign exchange risk
J. Promotion of specialization within the firm
K. Diversification of production facilities overseas
L. Enforcement of the reguration for foreign capital
M. Release of the incentive for foreign capital
N. Wage increase in the host country
O. Political unstability of the host country
P. Maximization of global financing
Q. Utilizing skills of talented foreign researchers
R. Development of products adapted to the local market
S. Obtaining business information
T. Obtaining know-how from the joint venture partner or the firm we have taken over or obtained shares in
U. Shifting existing overseas investment bases
V. Reverse exports to Japan
W. Exports to a third country
X. Supplying parts to an assembly manufacturer
Y. Response to the domestic labor shortage in Japan
Z. Bottleneck of the infrastructure in the host country
Z. Other

FIGURE 6.3 (continued)
(b) 1990 survey

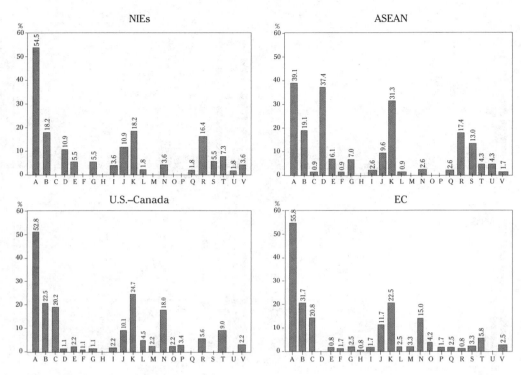

A. Preservation and/or expansion of market share
B. Development of a new market
C. Response to voluntary export restraints, dumping tariffs, and other trade regulations by the host
   country
D. Taking advantage of low cost labor
E. Securing stable supply of raw materials and natural resources
F. Requests from the host country
G. Taking advantage of favorable tax treatment and other preferences in the host country
H. Taking advantage of benefits available in tax havens
I. Avoiding foreign exchange risk
J. Promotion of specialization within the firm
K. Diversification of production facilities overseas
L. Maximization of global financing
M. Utilizing skills of talented foreign researchers
N. Development of products adapted to the local market
O. Obtaining business information
P. Obtaining know-how from the joint venture partner or the firm we have taken over or obtained
   shares in
Q. Shifting existing overseas investment bases
R. Reverse exports to Japan
S. Exports to a third country
T. Supplying parts to an assembly manufacturer
U. Response to the domestic labor shortage in Japan
V. Other

6.3.3 Self-evaluation by Japanese Firms of the Past Performance of FDI

As noted in the above section, the marketing strategy and investment motivation of Japanese firms differs by region. After the rapid increase of Japanese FDI in the 1980s, Japanese firms are now in a position to review the past performance of FDI by region and to plan for the 1990s. In the EXIM survey we asked Japanese companies to evaluate the past performance of their own FDI by region with respect to four performance categories, that is, profitability, sales, localization and the final aggregate score for all items (see Figure 6.4). In Figure 6.4 profitability is measured in the upward direction of the vertical axis and localization is measured in the downward direction of the same axis. Annual gross sales are measured in the right hand direction of the horizontal axis and general performance is measured in the left hand direction of the same axis. All the evaluations for the different performance categories have been ranked from "one" to "five." The ranking "one" means insufficient, "five" means fairly sufficient, and "three" means in-between. The localization category takes into account the local content of the components used in the production process in the host country, as well as progress made in increasing the number of local management staff and technology transfers to the local economy.

Investment in the ANIE and ASEAN countries had outstanding rankings in all four performance categories. On the other hand, investment in Europe and North America came in third and fourth place respectively. The relatively low rankings given to investment in the developed countries seems to have been due to relatively low profitability rankings. The low profitability rankings, in turn, are hardly surprising given that most of the large-scale production facilities in the developed countries have just been very recently inaugurated. Japanese FDI in Europe and North America has a relatively short history. In recent years it has been characterized by the investment of large amounts in large-scale production facilities. Japanese FDI in Asia has a long history and involves relatively small investment amounts for each project. These traits have facilitated the better profit performance of FDI in Asia.

Furthermore, Japanese FDI in the Asian countries has been motivated by purely economic reasons. In the Asian countries, Japanese firms have sought to take advantage of effective and low cost production and expanding local consumption markets. In contrast, Japanese FDI to the developed countries is strongly influenced by the desire to ease trade frictions—a rather political factor. It may take a few more years before investments in North America and Europe bear fruit. However, Figure 6.4 shows that the companies rated localization in North America and Europe as being on a par with that in the ANIEs and ASEAN countries. This suggests that Japanese firms made considerable efforts to become truly local firms all over the world.

Figure 6.5 summarizes the results of another survey on the profitability of Japanese FDI. It provides information on the percentage of foreign subsidiaries recording deficits or surpluses as well as cumulative deficits or surpluses by region.

FIGURE 6.4   Each company's self-evaluation of the past performance of their own FDI by region

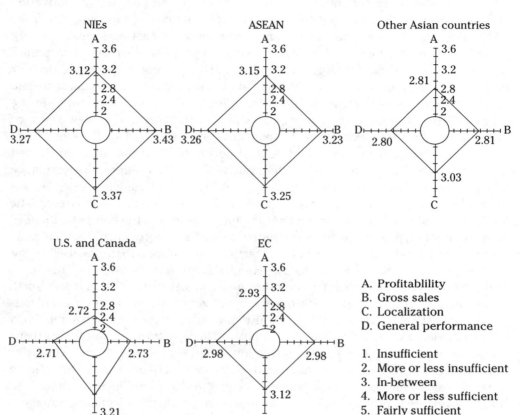

A. Profitablility
B. Gross sales
C. Localization
D. General performance

1. Insufficient
2. More or less insufficient
3. In-between
4. More or less sufficient
5. Fairly sufficient

In the ANIEs, the companies which recorded a surplus in the 1990 financial year, and which did not have a cumulative debt, accounted for 74 percent of foreign subsidiaries. Companies recording a surplus accounted for 61.1 percent of the foreign subsidiaries in ASEAN, 47.1 percent of the foreign subsidiaries in Europe and 33.5 percent of the foreign subsidiaries in North America.

On the other hand, the companies which recorded a deficit in the 1990 financial year, and a cumulative debt at the end of the 1990 financial year accounted for 11.5 percent of foreign subsidiaries in the ANIEs, 22.2 percent in ASEAN, 32.6 percent in Europe and 47.5 percent in North America.

The survey results shown in Figure 6.5 mirror the survey results in Figure 6.4, that is, they show the good profit performance in ASEAN and the ANIEs and the poor profit performance in North America and Europe.

Figure 6.4 (and Figure 6.5) show that the general performance evaluation was different for the Asian, European and North American region, and was strongly

FIGURE 6.5   The profitability of production firms by region

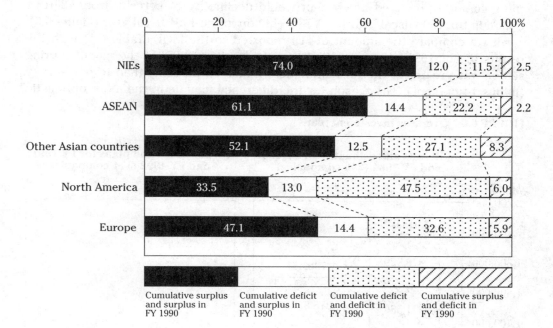

influenced by the profitability evaluation. This suggests that Japanese firms have not yet achieved the goals set forth in their global management strategy. If these firms had fully met the goals of the globalization strategy, each region would have had the same general performance evaluation.

In short, in the 1980s Japanese firms invested in Europe and the U.S. mainly in order to avoid trade friction. "Globalization" goals were of secondary importance in these regions. This motivation hierarchy helps explain the poor evaluation for FDI in North America and Europe. In the Asian countries, where investments have been driven by "globalization" goals, the general performance evaluation for FDI has been good.

The future investment strategy of Japanese firms will be influenced by the evaluations of the past performance of their own FDI. A balanced global management strategy will be preferred in the 1990s over investments to avoid trade friction.

6.4   New Japanese FDI Trends and Prospects for the 1990s

6.4.1   Short-Term and Medium-Term Prospects

In the 1990 fiscal year, the annual amount of Japanese FDI reported to the Ministry of Finance (MOF) showed its first decline in nine years. This trend toward decreasing FDI amounts was further strengthened in the 1991 fiscal year (Table 6.1) and can be expected to continue in the 1992 fiscal year.

In the 1991 survey conducted by the EXIM Bank, 240 respondents stated that the volume of projected investment would decline by 14 percent, from ¥2,013.1 billion in the 1990 fiscal year to ¥1,730.5 billion in the 1991 fiscal year (Figure 6.6).

If we compare the amount of FDI reported to the MOF (Table 6.1) with the results of our 1991 survey, we find that the decline in FDI in the manufacturing sector was greater in the MOF statistics (minus 20 percent) than in our survey (minus 14 percent). The reason for the difference may lie in the more optimistic

FIGURE 6.6   Overseas investment plans

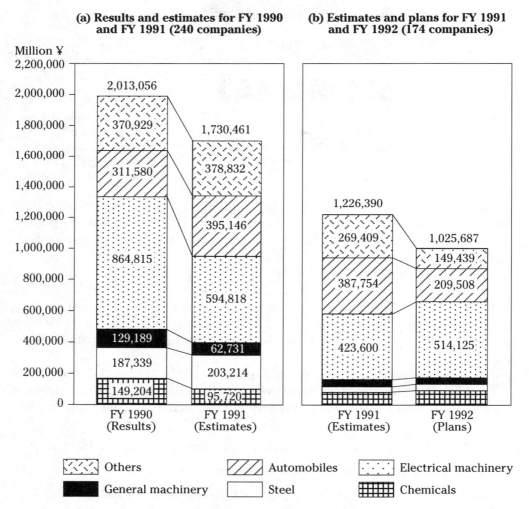

(a) Results and estimates for FY 1990 and FY 1991 (240 companies)

(b) Estimates and plans for FY 1991 and FY 1992 (174 companies)

Notes: 240 companies: Respondents of FY 1990 results and FY 1991 estimates
174 companies: Respondents of FY 1991 estimates and FY 1992 plans

attitude that prevailed among Japanese investors during the August–October 1991 period, when we conducted our survey.

The responses we received from 174 firms in our survey also indicate that FDI will continue to decline in the 1992 fiscal year. Taken as a group, these 174 firms plan to invest ¥1,025.7 billion overseas during the 1992 fiscal year. This represents a 16.6 percent drop over expected actual investment for the 1991 fiscal year by the same 174 firms (Figure 6.6).

Similarly, companies seem to be generally cautious about investing over the next three years through the 1994 fiscal year. An increasing number of firms do not have a medium-term investment plan. In the 1991 survey, 31 percent of the respondents indicated that they did not plan to invest overseas up to and through the 1994 fiscal year. This constitutes a 6 percentage point increase from the 1990 survey result (25 percent) for the three year period 1991–93 and a 14 percentage point increase from the 1989 survey result (17 percent) for the period 1989–91. The continuously rising percentage of firms with no FDI plans deserves attention (see Figures 6.7a, b and c).

6.4.2 Reasons for the New Japanese FDI Trends

Several reasons can be cited for this new FDI trend. The first is that Japanese firms have already carried out their major production projects in the U.S. automobile and steel sectors. In the near future, the mainstream of investment in those sectors will shift to the completion of ongoing projects and the expansion or renewal of existing production facilities and R&D activities. Therefore, FDI flows to the U.S. will grow more moderately than in previous years. The 1991 survey asked firms which did not have medium-term FDI plans for the next three years to indicate their reasons for not investing (Figure 6.7d). Out of these firms, 53 percent indicated that past FDI flows had allowed them to establish an adequate position overseas that enabled them to meet business opportunities over the next three years. The number of firms citing the need for "countermeasures against trade friction" as an investment motivation decreased more for North America than for Europe. This suggests that new projects aimed at avoiding trade friction in North America will decrease in future.

The second reason for the new FDI trend is that slower growth rates in the developed countries have made potential Japanese investors view with pessimism the future potential of the markets in those countries. In our survey, 19 percent of the companies that do not plan to make overseas investments maintain a wait-and-see attitude because global business conditions are unpredictable (Figure 6.7d). Moreover, 6 percent of the companies with no investment plan intend to preserve the status quo since they do not expect the market to expand.

Significantly, no firm in the 1991 survey stated that they had no medium-term FDI plan because they were "focusing resources on the strong domestic demand." However, in the 1990 survey, 8 percent of the firms had indicated that they were

FIGURE 6.7   Surveys of firms with or without medium-term foreign direct investment plans for FY 1994, FY 1993 and 1989–91

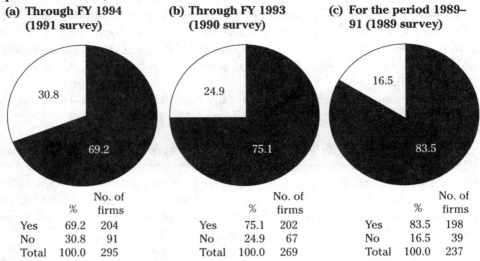

(a) **Through FY 1994**
    (1991 survey)

(b) **Through FY 1993**
    (1990 survey)

(c) **For the period 1989–**
    91 (1989 survey)

	%	No. of firms
Yes	69.2	204
No	30.8	91
Total	100.0	295

	%	No. of firms
Yes	75.1	202
No	24.9	67
Total	100.0	269

	%	No. of firms
Yes	83.5	198
No	16.5	39
Total	100.0	237

(d) **Reasons for absence of overseas direct investment plans (1991 survey)**

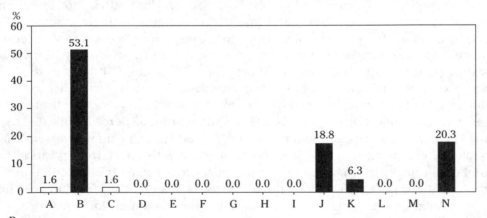

Reasons:
A. Overseas investments made to data have not yielded the expected results
B. Sufficient market position obtained with investment to date to meet future business opportunities
C. Business performance of parent company is shaky
D. Focusing resources on responding to strong domestic demand
E. Lack the technological competitiveness to survive overseas
F. Insufficient qualified personnel in the parent company to send overseas
G. Sufficient response to business environment possible with OEM production
H. Difficulty procuring necessary capital from financial institutions
I. Difficulty procuring necessary capital from capital markets
J. Uncertain economic conditions recommend caution for the time being
K. Further expansion of the market not foreseen
L. Difficulty obtaining sales and service outlets in local market
M. Excessive burden of responding to investment frictions
N. Other

focusing their resources on the strong domestic demand. Japanese investors have become more conservative in their assessment of the future expansion of the Japanese economy as well as other economies.

Previously, in the second half of the 1980s, the economic recovery in the developed countries stimulated expansion in mutual FDI flows among the developed countries. Now, the rather poor prospects for these countries in the early 1990s have reduced, to some extent, the enthusiasm of Japanese firms.

The third reason for the new FDI trend is that financial resources for investment have been squeezed tight by the monetary situation and stagnant stock market in Japan. In the late 1980s, the "boom" in the stock market offered huge opportunities for Japanese firms to obtain extremely low-cost financing through convertible bonds and warrant bonds. However, the "collapse" of the stock market has wiped out this kind of cheap funding.

6.4.3 A Short Transitional Period in FDI Flows

Recent decreases in Japanese FDI do not signal the end of the "globalization" or "global management" strategies of Japanese firms. They merely signal the end of a period of rapid Japanese FDI expansion, which was stimulated by the appreciated yen and by the desire to avoid trade friction with developed countries.

Decreasing Japanese FDI may indicate the beginning of a short-term transitional stage of "wait and see," preceding a stage of stable expansion. In the short transitional period of the early 1990s, the expansion of existing production and sales bases should become the mainstream of Japanese FDI throughout every region in the world.

According to our 1991 survey, investment in strengthened capacity via the expansion of "existing" production facilities forms the core of planned investment for the next three years in all four regions (including ASEAN and the EC). In contrast, our 1990 survey indicated that investment in "new" manufacturing facilities would occupy the largest share of investment plans in ASEAN and the EC (see Figures 6.8a and b).

6.4.4 Future FDI and Motives by Region

According to our 1991 survey, the attitude of Japanese firms toward investment plans will differ by region in the early 1990s (1992–94) (see Figure 6.9a). Of the 121 companies that had investment plans for the next three years (1992–94) in ASEAN, 68 percent indicated a plan for an "increase" or a "large-scale increase." Of the 120 companies that have investment plans in the EC, 61 percent indicated a plan for an "increase" or "large-scale increase" in the next three years. In North America 49 percent of the 136 companies with plans indicated plans to increase investment, while in the ANIEs 40 percent of the 97 companies with plans indicated that they planned to increase investment.

FIGURE 6.8   (a) Content of investment in the 1991 survey

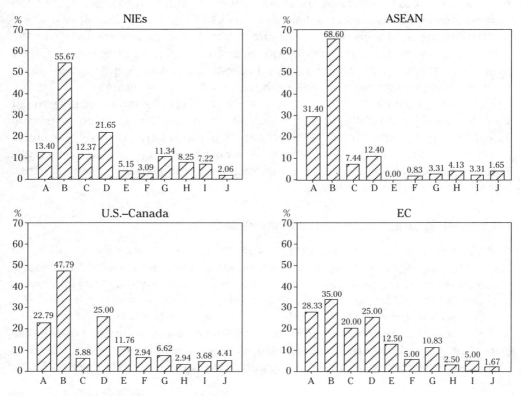

A. Establishment of production bases
B. Expansion of production bases
C. Establishment of sales and service bases
D. Expansion of sales and service bases
E. Establishment/expansion of research and development bases
F. Establishment/expansion of financial bases
G. Establishment/expansion of regional headquarters
H. Establishment/expansion of parts procurement bases
I. Establishment/expansion of engineering bases
J. Others

Japanese firms indicated a strong interest in China and other Asian countries. Among the 38 companies which have investment plans in China, more than 70 percent intend to increase investment. Among the 17 companies with plans for other Asian countries, about 60 percent want to increase investments·in these countries. Positive investment attitudes towards ASEAN, China and the other Asian countries seem to be grounded in the good performance of past investments in this region, and the possibility that the future will see significant growth in the local Asian markets.

FIGURE 6.8   (b) Content of investment in the 1990 survey

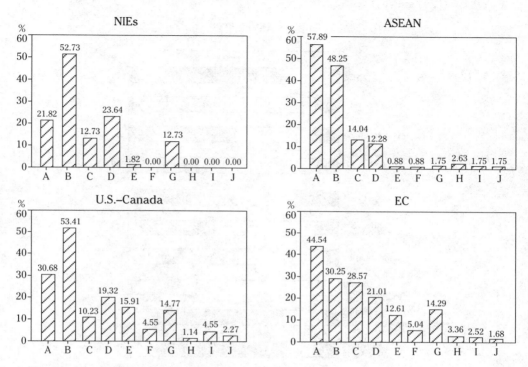

A. Establishment of production bases
B. Expansion of production bases
C. Establishment of sales and service bases
D. Expansion of sales and service bases
E. Establishment/expansion of research and development bases
F. Establishment/expansion of financial bases
G. Establishment/expansion of regional headquarters
H. Establishment/expansion of parts procurement bases
I. Establishment/expansion of engineering bases
J. Others

6.4.5 Future FDI by Industry and by Region

In the early 1990s, we will see a variety of different investment attitudes among Japanese firms. These attitudes will differ by industrial sector as well. For example, major firms in the electric and electronics industries may steadily increase their FDI to maintain their international competitiveness, regardless of the short-term prospects for the developed countries' economies. In our 1991 survey, 60 percent of electric equipment companies indicated that they have plans to increase investment levels for the next three years (1992–94) (see Figure 6.9b). In the 1990 survey, 52.4 percent of these companies had planned to increase investment.

FIGURE 6.9   Overseas investment plans through FY 1994 in comparison with actual FDI for FY 1990 (1991 survey)

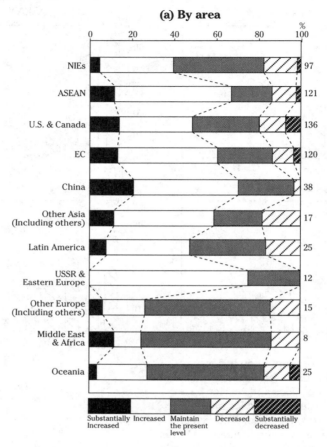

(a) By area

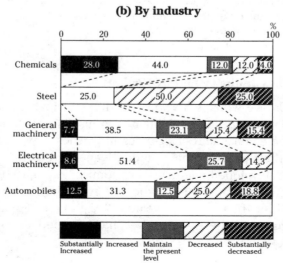

(b) By industry

FIGURE 6.9 (continued)

(c) Electrical machinery

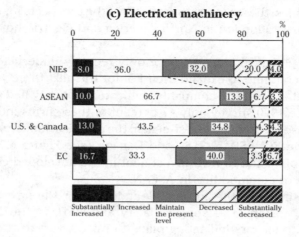

(d) Chemicals

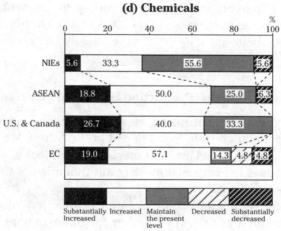

(e) Automobiles

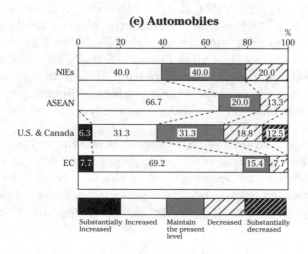

Investment in the electric and electronic industries can be expected to increase in ASEAN and North America (see Figure 6.9c). According to interviews conducted at several companies, these increases may reflect the prospects for stable expansion in semiconductor production in North America and electric home appliances in ASEAN.

Firms in the chemical industry have only recently undertaken FDI activities. These firms will continue to expand their FDI for the next three years. In the 1991 survey 72 percent of chemical companies indicated that they had plans to increase investment. In the 1990 survey only 47 percent of these firms indicated that they planned to increase investment. Investment in the chemical industry can be expected to increase in the EC, ASEAN, U.S., and Canada (see Figure 6.9d). This flow of investment may be linked to R&D investment in the developed countries and the mass-production of commodities in ASEAN.

Foreign investment in the automobile industry for the next three years may focus on the expansion of existing capacity and R&D. In the 1991 survey, the percentage of auto makers indicating plans to raise investment dropped sharply to 44 percent from 74 percent in the previous survey. Investment in the automobile industry can be expected to increase in the EC and ASEAN, but not in the U.S. and Canada, where major large-scale projects have already been completed (see Figure 6.9e).

6.4.6 Future Investment Plans: Production Bases and Principal Markets

In the 1991 survey, we asked firms to identify the most important markets for production bases scheduled to be established in the future. We received answers from 105 firms (see Table 6.6). The local market is the most important market for future production bases in every region—a result that mirrors the responses given for existing production bases.

Significantly, the total number of planned production bases in the ASEAN countries (81) is far greater than the number for other regions (55 in Europe, 54 in North America, 36 in the ANIEs, and 27 in the other Asian countries), while the number of existing production bases is almost the same for the ANIEs (300), ASEAN (322), North America (365) and Europe (232) (see Table 6.5). In addition, FDI to the other Asian countries (including China) will likely increase in the future.

Another interesting point is that 28 percent of the future production bases in the ANIEs are oriented toward the ASEAN markets, although only 6 percent of the "actual" production bases in the ANIEs are oriented toward the ASEAN markets (compare Table 6.5 with Table 6.6).

In the ASEAN countries, the percentage of production bases oriented toward the local markets will remain at 62 percent for the next three years (1992–94). However, in the ANIEs the percentage of production bases oriented toward the local market decreased from 73 percent to 58 percent. Japanese production bases in the ANIEs will see sales to the other Asian countries (including Japan and

TABLE 6.6 The most important purchaser of future production bases by region in the plan for the next three years (1992-94) (%)

Recipient of investment	Purchaser						Total number of companies
	NIEs	ASEAN	Other Asian countries	Japan	North America	Europe	
NIEs	58	28	–	3	6	6	36
ASEAN	6	62	1	22	7	1	81
Other Asian countries	–	4	67	19	7	4	27
North America	–	2	–	6	93	–	54
Europe	–	–	–	4	4	93	55

ASEAN) increase to 31 percent from the present 15 percent. Production subsidiaries in the ASEAN countries will likewise see the share of sales to other parts of Asia increase to 30 percent from the present 25 percent. Exports to Japan alone will increase from 15 percent to 22 percent in the ASEAN countries.

Similar results were obtained for the question relating to the "important" markets for each firm. The results suggest the future continuing growth of ASEAN consumption markets as well as increasing investment into both ASEAN and the ANIEs (oriented toward the ASEAN markets). The ANIEs, ASEAN and Japan will become increasingly important as export destinations for Japanese subsidiaries in the Asian countries. Japan will become a more important purchaser for the products manufactured by the ASEAN subsidiaries of Japanese parent companies.

6.5 Conclusion

Given the rather poor evaluation that Japanese FDI in North America has received from Japanese firms, and the bias toward greater investment in the Asian countries in future, Japanese FDI flows in the 1990s will be more balanced than in the 1980s. The shift toward Asia has been motivated by the advantages the Asian countries present as production bases and potential consumption markets. Japanese FDI and foreign portfolio investment have maintained stable outflow amounts for 1991, whereas the long-term capital accounts as well as the current accounts for 1991 showed large surpluses, with large foreign capital inflows to the Japanese stock market.

This Balance of Payments position is quite different from that of the 1980s when the current account surplus was surpassed by the long-term capital account deficit caused by the large FDI outflow and portfolio investment outflow.

The current account surplus of 1991 was stimulated by increasing international competitiveness. Japan's increasing international competitiveness in turn has hinged on rapid increases in domestic investment in capital goods and equipment by Japanese firms for the past three years (1988-90), shrinking Japanese imports, and the relatively stable yen—which was in the range of 120–140 yen per U.S. dollar for the period 1987–91.

This state of affairs suggests that in future market pressure to appreciate the Japanese yen (and the resulting yen appreciation) will further stimulate Japanese FDI. Capital account surpluses (without large declines of Japanese capital outflow) are supplying the financial resources that Japanese firms need to achieve indispensable FDI projects. At the beginning of the 1980s, Japanese outward FDI was about one-tenth of U.S. FDI in terms of stock. After the rapid expansion of the 1980s, the stock of Japanese FDI amounted to 40 percent of U.S. FDI in 1989. Taking into account the scale of the Japanese economy, which is about 60 percent of the U.S. economy, there is no doubt that Japanese FDI will further increase in the 1990s.

Stable increases in Japanese FDI on a worldwide basis, that respond to long-term global management strategy (as opposed to a desire to avoid trade friction) will strengthen the host countries' economies. It will contribute to high economic growth in the host countries, and introduce new production systems and management skills.

Finally, in light of their experiences in the 1980s, Japanese firms will want to become more "local" in orientation, and contribute to the local society. Japanese FDI will play a truly important role in promoting a more open international economy by contributing to the increase of international trade, the diffusion of effective production systems, technology transfer, philanthropy and the restructuring of Japanese parent companies and Japan's economy itself.

Note

This chapter is mainly based on Tejima (1992) and Tejima et al. (1992).

References

Tejima, Shigeki, 1992, "Japanese Foreign Direct Investment in the 1980s and its Prospects for the 1990s," *EXIM Review*, 11(2): 26–51.

Tejima, Shigeki et al., 1992, "Report on Results of FY 1991 Foreign Direct Investment Survey," *Kaigai Tooshi Kenkyusho Ho* (Research Institute for International Investment and Development), 18(1): 35–65.

Chapter 7

Chi-Hung Kwan

A New Wave of Foreign Direct Investment in Asia

7.1 Introduction

Boosted by a massive inflow of foreign direct investment (FDI) in the latter half of the 1980s, the ASEAN countries and China have transformed themselves into major offshore production bases for multinationals, as the Asian newly industrializing economies (ANIEs) did before them. Although the foreign direct investment boom was disrupted in 1990 and 1991 by the yen's depreciation and the global recession, it started to recover in 1992, thanks to the acceleration of economic reform in China and the yen's appreciation since early 1993. Recent investment in Asia by multinationals has been characterized by a greater emphasis on selling into local markets, rather than merely using the region as a base for exporting, and includes a larger proportion of high-value-added products and processes.

The inflow of foreign direct investment has been a major factor supporting economic growth in Asia. To maintain this economic growth in the region, investing countries such as Japan and the ANIEs should continue to contribute to this process through positive industrial adjustment, that is, diversifying into new industries while at the same time relocating declining industries to countries catching up from behind. On the other hand, developing countries should seek to improve their investment environment. The flow of foreign direct investment has been and will remain a major force in regional industrial restructuring. Both investing and receiving countries should benefit from this dynamic pattern of division of labor.

7.2   Diversified Objectives of Investment

Foreign direct investment in Asia has until recently been concentrated in labor-intensive industries to take advantage of cheap labor costs. With income in the Asian countries rising rapidly, more and more foreign investment has come to focus on penetrating local markets.

7.2.1 Four Major Types of Foreign Direct Investment

Foreign direct investment in Asia can be broadly classified into four categories, according to the objective of investment: (1) outsourcing, (2) trade-barrier-circumventing, (3) market- and technology-accessing, and (4) round-tripping.

Outsourcing has been by far the most important objective of companies from more advanced countries investing in the developing countries of Asia. This type of investment is common for labor-intensive products and processes such as textile manufacturing and electronics products assembly. Production tends to be relocated in stages from the more advanced countries to the less developed ones, and is motivated by the search for lower production costs. This pattern of investment flow (and the dynamic changes in the pattern of trade accompanying it) has come to be known as the flying-geese pattern. In most cases, output from the Asian production bases is exported, either back to the countries of origin of the investors or to third countries. Most of the investment by Hong Kong companies in the mainland, and Japanese investment in Asia during the second half of the 1980s, falls into this category. In a broader sense, investment in the development of natural resources such as oil can also be classified into this category.

Trade-barrier-circumventing investment aims at substituting local production for the export of goods from an investing country to a receiving country. Many developing countries adopt a policy mix of granting preferences to foreign direct investment while levying high import tariffs as a means of promoting infant domestic industries. It goes without saying that this kind of investment presupposes a large or potentially large domestic market. The bulk of investment by Japanese, Korean and Taiwanese companies in the United States and Europe can be classified as trade-barrier-circumventing, and more and more Japanese investment in China also falls into this category.

Investment that aims at gaining access into markets and technology is common among the developed countries. Investment of this type is usually concentrated in the service sector, such as wholesale and retail trades and research and development, rather than in manufacturing: its goal is to nurture markets and collect fresh ideas. Many Japanese companies have been building marketing networks and R&D facilities in the United States under this system of investment. They have been followed by companies in Korea and Taiwan.

Round-tripping investment refers to domestic investment made under the disguise of foreign investment, and is aimed at taking advantage of fiscal and other benefits available in a given country to foreign investors. A rising proportion of foreign direct investment in China is believed to be of this nature: investment capital originates in China, flows to Hong Kong and then reenters China as foreign investment. Round-tripping investment does not involve a net flow of funds between investing and receiving countries, and should be distinguished from the capital flight common in developing countries.

7.2.2 Factors Promoting Direct Investment

Foreign direct investment of the outsourcing variety usually takes place when companies in an advanced country are being forced to restructure to cope with a fast changing business environment. Such a restructuring involves shifting some resources out of declining sectors and into promising domestic sectors within the advanced country (diversification), while shifting other resources abroad in the form of foreign direct investment. Corporate headquarters thereafter become linked to overseas subsidiaries via intra-firm trade (Figure 7.1). The choice of resources (management know-how, labor, capital stock, technology, and so forth) to be diversified domestically and to be relocated overseas depends on both the cost of relocation and the expected return on resources after relocation. For example, labor (with the exception of engineers and managers) is likely to be shifted to other sectors at home, since the cost accompanying the relocation of labor overseas is

FIGURE 7.1   Industrial restructuring and foreign direct investment

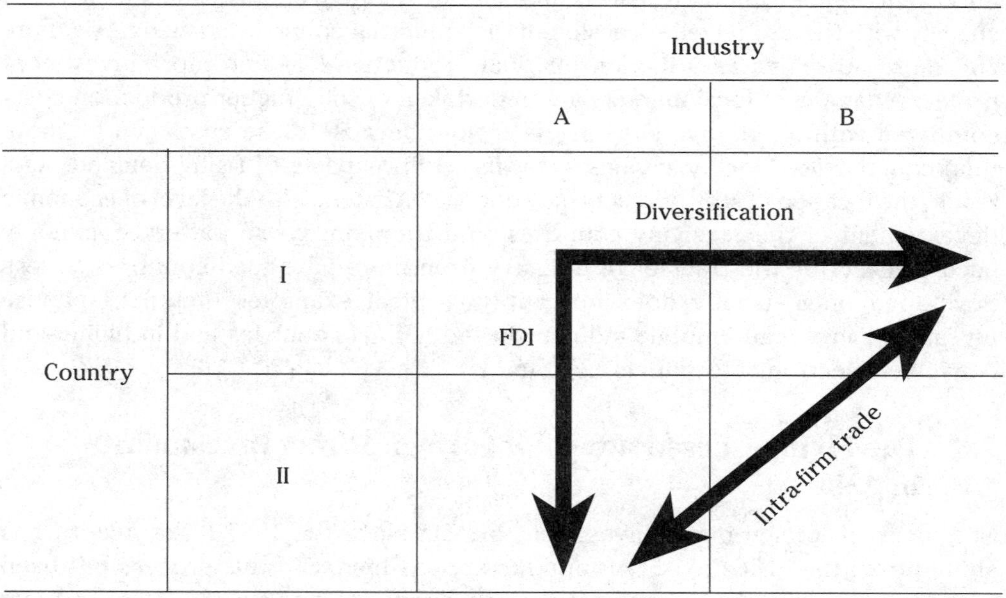

Source: Based on Hara (1992) with adaptations.

usually high. On the other hand, industry-specific resources such as technology and capital stock are likely to be shifted overseas, where the rate of return is expected to be higher (even taking into account the cost of relocation).

Factors promoting foreign direct investment of the outsourcing variety include rising costs in the investing countries (push factors) and an improving investment environment in the receiving countries (pull factors). Among them, currency appreciation in Japan and the ANIEs, the economic "catching up" process of developing countries and a general liberalization in FDI policies seem to have been the most important factors sustaining FDI flows in Asia over the last ten years.

A stronger yen, for example, widens the gap between the cost of production in Japan and production in the Asian countries, giving Japanese companies more incentive to relocate facilities to the latter. The flow of foreign direct investment has the effect of boosting the Asian countries on both the demand side and the supply side. The economic growth rate in the Asian countries follows closely the trend in the inflow of direct investment from Japan, which in turn follows closely the ups and downs in the yen–dollar rate (Figure 7.2).

At the same time, liberalization of FDI policy, as exemplified by China's open door policy, has provided immense and unexploited opportunities for investors. The economic catching up of developing countries, particularly the ASEAN countries and China, has also made a division of labor within the manufacturing sector possible among countries in the Asia-Pacific region.

In addition to investment that aims at outsourcing (first type), investment emphasizing access to local markets (second and third types) has grown in importance. High economic growth in Asia's developing countries has contrasted sharply with the prolonged recession of the industrial countries, making Asia more and more attractive as a market for final products. More and more investment projects that aim at local markets are undertaken despite higher production costs compared with alternative sites in the region, because these costs can be more than compensated for by savings in tariffs and prospects of rising demand. As a result, the location of such projects may not be consistent with the level of economic development of the receiving countries, and the flying-geese pattern commonly used to describe the transfer of industry from more advanced countries to less developed ones usually does not apply. Typical examples include Japanese investment in the automobile industry in the ASEAN countries and in higher-end consumer electronics products in China.

7.3 The Flying-Geese Pattern of Foreign Direct Investment in Asia

The focus of foreign direct investment in Asia since the 1985 Plaza Accord has shifted from the ANIEs to ASEAN and further to China, and this process has been broadly in line with the flying-geese pattern. Keener competition for foreign direct investment has led to a convergence of FDI policy among Asian countries.

FIGURE 7.2   The yen–dollar rate and Asian economic growth

Year-on-year, %

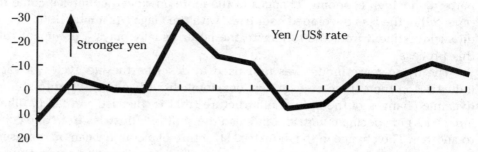

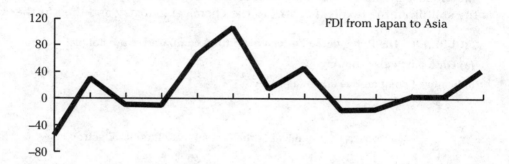

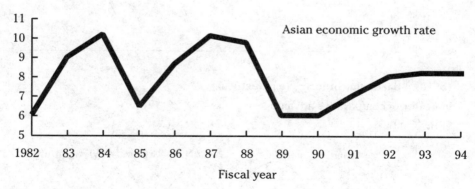

Fiscal year

Asia = NIEs + ASEAN + China

Source: Compile by NRI based on official statistics.

7.3.1 The Flying-Geese Model of Changing Comparative Advantage

Dynamic changes in the Asian economy can be characterized by the flying-geese pattern, in which economic changes in the more advanced countries come to be repeated in the less developed countries, with time lags (Akamatsu 1962). Foreign direct investment from the former to the latter usually plays a dominant role in this process.

The flying-geese model was first used to describe the life cycles of various industries in the course of economic development. It has been used to study the dynamic changes of the industrial structure (that is, the rise and fall of different industries) in specific countries, and also the shift of industries from one country to another. The change in the industrial structure of a country can be represented by a set of inverted V-shaped curves which chart the changing competitiveness of individual industries over time (upper part of Figure 7.3). A typical sequence is the shift from the textile industry to the chemical industry and then further to

FIGURE 7.3   The flying-geese pattern of shifting comparative advantage

(a) For a particular country

Indicator of comparative advantage

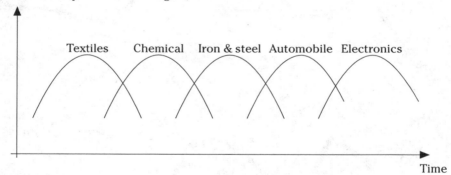

(b) For a particular industry (e.g. textiles)

Indicator of comparative advantage

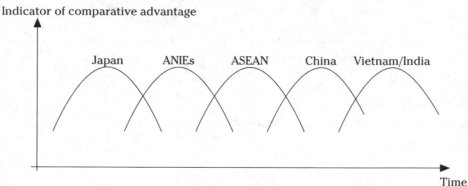

Source: Based on Yamazawa (1990) with adaptations.

the steel and the automobile industry. The "international version" is shown in the lower part of Figure 7.3, with the inverted V-shaped curves now representing the same industry in different countries (instead of different industries in the same country). A typical example is the shifting of textile production from Japan to the ANIEs and then further to the ASEAN countries and China.

Foreign direct investment has played a dominant in the emergence of new industries and the withering away of old ones. In the case of the ANIEs, for example, inflows of foreign direct investment laid the foundation for the textile and garment industry in the 1960s. On the other had, outflows of foreign direct investment helped Japan to reduce the size of its textile industry and release resources for new industries. In a similar evolutionary process, the ANIEs are now relocating their labor-intensive industries to ASEAN and China.

The flying-geese model explains the shifting competitiveness of an industry over time by focusing on the dynamic changes in factor endowments (labor and capital) that countries usually experience during the course of economic development. Foreign direct investment, in addition to triggering an indigenous improvement in the availability and quality of factor endowments in the countries catching up from behind, also helps promote the transformation of trade structures by transferring factors of production (capital, technology and management know-how) from the more advanced countries to the less developed ones. The flying-geese model should be distinguished from the product cycle theory (Vernon 1966) which emphasizes changes in the production process (particularly the combination of factors of production) over time, taking factor endowment in the countries involved as given.

7.3.2 The Yen's Appreciation and Japanese Investment in Asia

The yen's sharp appreciation since early 1993 is paving the way for another wave of Japanese investment in Asia. According to Japan's Ministry of Finance, Japanese FDI in Asia jumped 43.2 percent in the 1994 fiscal year, after declining for four consecutive years between the 1990 and 1994 fiscal years (Table 7.1). The increase is particularly marked for investment in Asia's manufacturing sector, which has surpassed Japanese manufacturers' investment in North America (Figure 7.4).

The shift of Japanese investment to Asia largely reflects the high profitability of investment in the region compared with Europe and America. According to a survey conducted by the Japanese Ministry of Trade and Industry (MITI), the ratio of recurring profits to sales has been consistently higher for Asia than the rest of the world. The gap widened sharply in 1991 and 1992, thanks to the recession in the industrial countries (Figure 7.5).

In contrast with the yen's appreciation after the 1985 Plaza Accord, the yen's current rise favors the member states of ASEAN and China more than the ANIEs.

For the ANIEs, the range of industries that can benefit from the high yen has narrowed because of growing competition from the ASEAN countries and China

TABLE 7.1 Japan's direct investment in the Asian countries

	FY 1989		FY 1990		FY 1991		FY 1992		FY 1993		FY 1994		
	$ mil.	% share	$ mil.	% share	$ mil.	% share	$ mil.	% share	$ mil.	% share	$ mil.	% share	Year-on-year %
ANIEs	4,900	7.3	3,355	5.9	2,203	5.3	1,922	5.6	2,419	6.7	2,865	7.0	(18.4)
South Korea	606	0.9	284	0.5	260	0.6	225	0.7	245	0.7	400	1.0	(63.3)
Taiwan	494	0.7	446	0.8	405	1.0	292	0.9	292	0.8	278	0.7	(−4.8)
Hong Kong	1,898	2.8	1,785	3.1	925	2.2	735	2.2	1,238	3.4	1,133	2.8	(−8.5)
Singapore	1,902	2.8	840	1.5	613	1.5	670	2.0	644	1.8	1,054	2.6	(63.7)
ASEAN	2,782	4.1	3,242	5.7	3,083	7.4	3,197	9.4	2,398	6.7	3,888	9.5	(62.1)
Indonesia	631	0.9	1,105	1.9	1,193	2.9	1,676	4.9	813	2.3	1,759	4.3	(116.4)
Malaysia	673	1.0	725	1.3	880	2.1	704	2.1	800	2.2	742	1.8	(−7.3)
Philippines	202	0.3	258	0.5	203	0.5	160	0.5	207	0.6	668	1.6	(222.7)
Thailand	1,276	1.9	1,154	2.0	807	1.9	657	1.9	578	1.6	719	1.8	(24.4)
China	438	0.6	349	0.6	579	1.4	1,070	3.1	1,691	4.7	2,565	6.2	(51.7)
ANIEs + ASEAN + China	8,120	12.0	6,946	12.2	5,865	14.1	6,189	18.1	6,508	18.1	9,318	22.7	(43.2)
U.S.	32,540	48.2	26,128	45.9	18,026	43.3	13,819	40.5	14,725	40.9	17,331	42.2	(17.7)
Europe	14,808	21.9	14,294	25.1	9,371	22.5	7,061	20.7	7,940	22.0	6,230	15.2	(−21.5)
World total	67,540	100.0	56,911	100.0	41,584	100.0	34,138	100.0	36,025	100.0	41,051	100.0	(14.0)

Figures do not include reinvestment.

Source: Japanese Ministry of Finance.

FIGURE 7.4 Shift of Japanese FDI from North America to Asia (manufacturing)

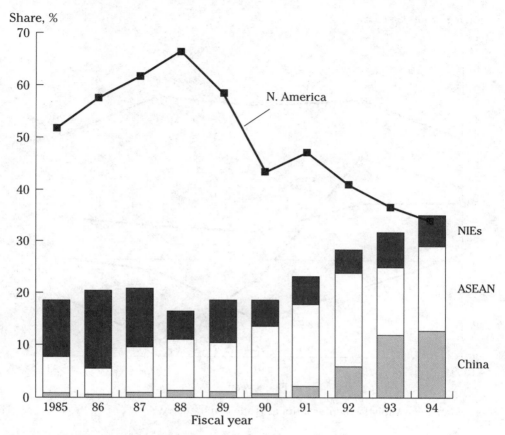

Source: Japanese Ministry of Finance.

(Figure 7.6). In the case of South Korea, for example although heavy industries and high-tech industries that compete with Japan have been picking up, labor-intensive industries have been suffering a chronic recession and are unlikely to recover their attractiveness to foreign investors, even with the strong yen.

In contrast, the ASEAN countries are in a better position to benefit from the yen's appreciation this time, as the large inflow to the region of Japanese investment since the late 1980s has laid a foundation for further development. Like the ANIEs in 1986–87, the ASEAN countries are enjoying an inflow of investment from Japan and an acceleration of exports on the back of a stronger yen. Japanese companies, particularly those in the electronics industry, are speeding up the transfer of capital and technology to the ASEAN countries. The current surge in Japanese investment includes a larger proportion of investment in high-value-added products and processes than in the past, thanks to improved productivity

FIGURE 7.5   Profitability of Japanese FDI by receiving region (manufacturing)

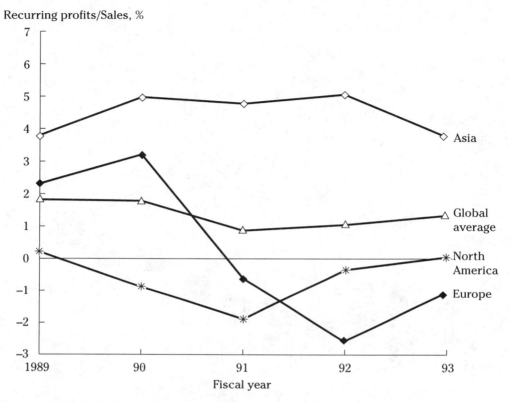

Source: Japanese Ministry of International Trade and Industry.

and the development of supporting industries in the host countries. More and more electronics companies, for example, are raising the local content of their products while reducing their dependence on the supply of parts and components from their headquarters in Japan. A virtuous cycle between the inflow of foreign direct investment and industrial development seems to be firmly in place.

China, which failed to ride the tide of the yen's appreciation in the latter half of the 1980s, has turned out to be the largest winner this time around. According to a recent survey by the Japan External Trade Organization, Japanese companies have ranked China as the most attractive place in which to set up a new plant in every major industry from textiles to precision machinery (Table 7.2). Statistics compiled by the Ministry of Finance show that Japanese investment in Asia has been shifting from the ANIEs to ASEAN and further to China. More and more Japanese companies favor China over the ANIEs and even the ASEAN countries because China, with its large population and high growth rate, promises to become an important market over the medium-term. This factor has become all the more

TABLE 7.2 Attractive countries and regions for new Japanese investment (625 companies polled, multiple answers; polling scores in percentages)

Rank	1	2	3	4	5	ANIEs	ASEAN
All Industries	China 58.1	EC 15.8	U.S. 15.7	Indonesia 13.4	Malaysia 13.3	15.7	30.9
Foods	China 72.0	U.S. 16.0	Indonesia 14.0	EC 12.0	Thailand 10.0	20.0	20.0
Textiles	China 83.3	Indonesia 27.8	EC 11.1	H.K. 11.1	Other Asia 11.1	11.1	27.8
Clothing	China 72.2	U.S. 16.7	Other Asia 11.1	EC 5.6	Thailand, Indonesia 5.6	–	11.1
Pulp/papers	China 60.0	U.S. 60.0	Thailand 20.0	Indonesia 20.0	–	–	40.0
Chemicals	China 45.5	EC 25.8	Indonesia 25.2	U.S. 22.7	Malaysia 18.2	18.2	43.9
Pharmaceuticals	China 44.4	EC 33.3	U.S. 22.2	–	–	33.3	22.2
Rubber products	China 62.5	U.S. 12.5	EC 12.5	Thailand 12.5	Malaysia 12.5	–	12.5
Ceramics	China 45.0	Other Asia 30.0	EC 20.0	U.S. 15.0	Thailand 15.0	20.0	30.0
Iron/steel	China 70.6	Indonesia 41.2	Malaysia 29.4	Singapore 17.6	Philippines 17.6	23.5	52.9
Nonferrous metals	China 61.5	Malaysia 30.8	Other Asia 30.8	Thailand 23.1	Indonesia 23.1	15.4	69.2
Metal products	China 58.8	Thailand 17.6	Malaysia 17.6	EC 15.7	Indonesia 15.7	19.6	39.2
Machinery	China 47.9	EC 19.7	U.S. 16.9	Taiwan 12.7	Thailand 12.7	25.4	26.8
Electronics/ electrical	China 51.3	EC 20.0	U.S. 16.3	Malaysia 15.0	Indonesia 10.0	12.5	28.8
Electronics (parts)	China 77.4	Philippines 16.1	U.S. 12.9	EC 12.9	Malaysia 12.9	–	35.5
Transportation machinery	China 70.0	Malaysia 20.0	U.S. 15.0	EC 15.0	Other Asia 15.0	15.0	30.0
Transportation machinery (parts)	China 51.4	Thailand 21.6	U.S. 18.9	Malaysia 18.9	EC 16.2	8.1	35.1
Precision machinery	China 65.1	U.S. 20.9	EC 18.6	Malaysia 11.6	Thailand, Singapore 9.3	16.2	25.6
Others	China 55.9	Indonesia 14.7	U.S. 11.8	Other Asia 11.8	Taiwan, Malaysia 8.8	14.7	22.1

Source: Japan External Trade Organization, July 1993.

FIGURE 7.6   Stronger yen favoring exports of heavy-industry products (South Korea)

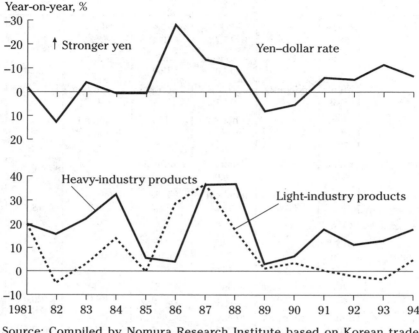

Source: Compiled by Nomura Research Institute based on Korean trade statistics.

important as rising protectionism and the prolonged recession in the industrial countries (including Japan itself) prompts Japanese companies to develop new markets.

7.3.3   Shift of Foreign Direct Investment to China

The foreign direct investment boom in China that started in 1992 has continued (Table 7.3). China received US$27.5 billion (on an implementation basis) in foreign direct investment in 1993 and US$33.8 billion in 1994, up from US$11.0 billion in 1992. Foreign direct investment in China has been dominated by the overseas Chinese. In 1994, Hong Kong (and Macau) invested US$20.2 billion in China, accounting for 60 percent of the total, followed by Taiwan's US$3.3 billion (10 percent of the total). Major overseas Chinese conglomerates have started to invest in mega infrastructure projects in China, ranging from superhighways to container ports and power plants. The overseas Chinese are said to be very conservative people, particularly when it comes to political risks. Their aggressive strategy in China shows that they now look at China more and more as a business opportunity rather than a risk factor.

TABLE 7.3   Foreign direct investment in China by country (implementation basis) (US$ billion)

	1990	1991	1992	1993	1994
Hong Kong/Macau	1.9	2.5	7.5	17.3	20.2
Taiwan	0.2	0.5	1.1	3.1	3.3
Japan	0.5	0.5	0.7	1.3	2.1
U.S.	0.5	0.3	0.5	2.1	2.5
Others	0.4	0.6	1.2	3.7	5.7
Total	3.5	4.4	11.0	27.5	33.8

Source: Chinese Ministry of Foreign Trade and Economic Cooperation.

Apart from Hong Kong and Taiwanese companies, overseas Chinese interests that have supported the ASEAN economies have also sharply increased their investment in China. Many of them have set up regional headquarters in Hong Kong which serve as bases for expanding business in China. Singapore is also promoting itself as the gateway to China, while its government is taking initiatives to build industrial estates in various parts of China.

The shift of investment to China has caused some anxiety within ASEAN over the adverse effects it might have on regional economic development. To enhance their attractiveness to foreign investors, the ASEAN countries are undertaking new measures to deregulate industries and redress domestic structural problems. For example, since June 1993 Indonesia has implemented a series of measures to ease regulations governing the establishment of wholly foreign-owned enterprises, and the access of these enterprises to the domestic market; Malaysia is reducing its corporate tax rate in steps from 34 percent to 30 percent in the 1995 fiscal year.

In 1992, ASEAN decided to establish an ASEAN Free Trade Area (AFTA) within the next 15 years, starting in 1993. This schedule was shortened to ten years during the ASEAN ministerial meeting held in September 1994. AFTA will cover trade in manufactured goods and processed agricultural products. By liberalizing trade in the area, AFTA should encourage horizontal division of labor in industrial goods by making it attractive for multinationals to build production networks across national borders.

The ANIEs are also taking positive steps to reverse the shift of foreign direct investment to China. South Korea, which has so far been quite cautious in its approach toward the inflow of foreign direct investment, for example, has shifted to a more aggressive approach. In November 1993, it announced liberalization measures to promote investment from abroad that brings in the latest technology.

7.3.4 Emerging New Frontiers

In this fashion, the flow of foreign direct investment to the Asia-Pacific region over the last ten years has spread from the ANIEs to the ASEAN countries, and further to China. Aware of this trend, other developing countries in Asia such as Vietnam and India are trying to join the flying-geese formation by improving their own investment environment.

The open door policy and economic reform now taking place in Vietnam and India have followed closely the Chinese model. On the external front, the focus has been on promoting the inflow of foreign direct investment and exports; on the domestic front, there has been a shift from reliance on central planning to the market mechanism in organizing economic activity. While in China this process started in the late 1970s, Vietnam's Doi Moi policy started in 1986 and India's economic reform under Prime Minister Rao started in 1991.

The investment environment of both Vietnam and India has improved substantially over the last few years. Macroeconomic stability has been achieved; inflation rates in both countries have dropped to single digit levels while economic growth has recovered from the troughs. Progress has been made in liberalizing rules governing foreign direct investment. Against this background, substantial increases have been recorded since 1992 in the inflow of foreign direct investment to both Vietnam and India. While U.S. companies have dominated foreign investment in India, overseas Chinese companies from Hong Kong and Taiwan are the major foreign players in Vietnam. Japanese companies have so far lagged behind in investing in Vietnam and India, but their interest in these countries has been growing fast. Most Japanese companies seem to prefer Vietnam over India when considering where to invest, due to geographical and cultural proximity.

7.4 Foreign Direct Investment and Regional Industrial Restructuring

The flow of foreign direct investment has been a major force shaping the division of labor among Asian countries. In this section, we study the dynamic changes in the comparative advantages of Asian countries by tracing the development of each country's trade structure over time. To supplement our macroeconomic analysis, we also take a closer look at the electronics industry, which has become the major recipient of Japanese investment.

7.4.1 Industrial Restructuring and Changing Trade Structure

The flying-geese pattern can be applied to an examination of changes in the commodity trade composition of the Asian countries. In the course of economic development, a country's comparative advantage usually shifts from the production of primary commodities to labor-intensive manufactured goods and, later on, to capital- and technology-intensive products. This shift is reflected in the trade structure which progresses from that of a developing country to that of a newly industrializing country and, finally, to one typical of an industrialized country. The flow of foreign direct investment has promoted this process.

Changes in the (revealed) comparative advantage of a country's industries can be shown by calculating the specialization indexes of each of the involved industries. For a particular industry, the specialization index is defined as the trade balance standardized by the volume of two-way trade for the industry concerned. That is,

$$\text{Specialization index} = \frac{\text{Exports} - \text{Imports}}{\text{Exports} + \text{Imports}}$$

From this definition, the value can range from −1 to +1; a higher value implies stronger international competitiveness.

A country's trade structure can be classified into one of four categories, using as criteria the relative magnitude of the specialization indexes of the country's primary commodities, labor-intensive manufactures and machinery. Because a country typically passes from one category to the next in a certain sequence (from developing country to young NIE to mature NIE and finally to industrialized country), we refer to our classification as the four stages of the trade structure (Figure 7.7).

A nation at the developing country stage usually has a weak industrial base and must depend on imports not only for capital goods but also for labor-intensive manufactures. The manufacturing sector as a whole runs a large deficit that must be financed by earnings from exports of primary commodities. For this pattern of trade, the specialization index is high for primary commodities and low for machinery and labor-intensive manufactures.

Early in the process of industrialization, progress is made in the import substitution of labor-intensive manufactures, and the specialization index of labor-intensive manufactures begins to rise. As that index surpasses the index of primary commodities, the trade structure enters the young NIE stage.

As economic development gathers pace, progress is also made in the import substitution of machinery, and the specialization index of that item begins to rise. At the same time, as labor flows into the industrial sector, the importance of the agricultural sector begins to fall. Shrinking exports of agricultural products and rising imports of raw materials (to support the expanding manufacturing sector) cause the specialization index of primary commodities to decline faster. When the specialization index of machinery surpasses that of primary products, the trade structure enters the mature NIE stage.

As income continues to rise, an increase in labor costs reduces the export competitiveness of labor-intensive manufactures, and the comparative advantage shifts to capital- and technology-intensive products. Declining industries are relocated overseas to release resources for expanding industries. Thus, the specialization index of machinery surpasses that of labor-intensive manufactures and the trade structure reaches its final stage, the industrialized country stage.

FIGURE 7.7   Four stages of trade structure

	Specialization index				Examples
I. Developing country stage	Primary commodities	>	Labor-intensive manufactures	> Machinery	Indonesia, Thailand
II. Young NIE stage	Labor-intensive manufactures	>	Primary commodities	> Machinery	China
III. Mature NIE stage	Labor-intensive manufactures	>	Machinery	> Primary commodities	Hong Kong, Korea
IV. Industrialized country stage	Machinery	>	Labor-intensive manufactures	> Primary commodities	Singapore, Japan

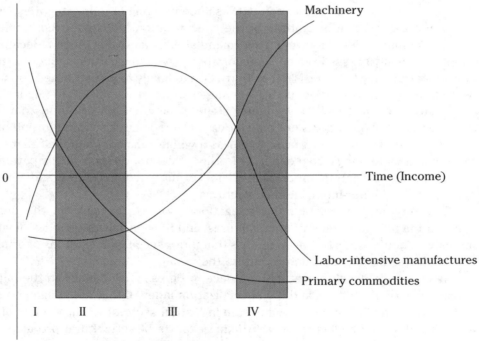

$$\text{Specialization index of industry K} = \frac{\text{Exports} - \text{Imports in industry K}}{\text{Exports} + \text{Imports in industry K}}$$

Source: Nomura Research Institute.

In what follows, we trace the changing trade structures of the Asian countries using this "stage approach" (Table 7.4).

In the mid-1960s, Japan's trade structure was at the mature NIE stage, with labor-intensive manufacturing as the leading export sector. This was broadly in line with Japan's stage of economic development at the time. The subsequent surge

TABLE 7.4   Asian countries' stages of trade structure

	Stage of trade structure			
	Developing country	Young NIE	Mature NIE	Industrialized country
South Korea		□————	—△——	————O
Taiwan	□————	————	————	—△-O
Hong Kong			□-△-O	
Singapore			□————	—△-O
Thailand	□——△——		————O	
Malaysia	□——△——	————O		
Philippines	□————	——△-O		
Indonesia	□-△-O			
China		△-O		
(Australia)	□-△-O			
Japan			□————	—△-O

□ = 1965; △ = 1992; O = 2000 (forecast).
Source: Nomura Research Institute.

in exports of machinery, particularly automobiles, and the decline of labor-intensive industries moved Japan's trade structure into the industrialized country stage.

The ANIEs are following Japan's footstep in upgrading their trade structure. The trade structures of South Korea and Taiwan were at different stages in the mid-1960s, but both are now at the mature NIE stage. Hong Kong and Singapore took advantage of their geographical locations (they are trading hubs with good harbors) and led Korea and Taiwan in the process of industrialization in the 1960s. Both countries' trade structures had reached the mature NIE stage by 1965. Subsequently, Hong Kong developed into a major exporter of labor-intensive manufactured goods while Singapore pursued a development strategy based on promoting capital- and technology-intensive industries. Singapore's trade structure has now reached the industrialized country stage, but Hong Kong has lagged behind in upgrading its trade structure.

The appreciation of the NIEs' currencies since 1986 has prompted the relocation of their labor-intensive industries to the ASEAN countries, and helped shift their own comparative advantage to higher-value-added products. Both Taiwan and South Korea are expected to reach the industrialized country stage within the next few years. In Hong Kong, the availability of cheap labor across the Chinese border has helped maintain export competitiveness, but has also delayed the transformation of the trade structure, which will probably remain in the mature NIE stage by the year 2000.

Most of the ASEAN countries still have trade structures typical of developing countries. In recent years, however, the massive inflow of foreign direct investment from Japan and the ANIEs has paved the way for radical change. Unlike in the past, recent foreign direct investment has concentrated in the manufacturing sector instead of the resource sector. The ASEAN countries are seizing this chance to reduce their dependence on exports of primary commodities, and industrialization is accelerating. Thailand's trade structure, which is now similar to that of Taiwan in the late 1960s, should reach the young NIE stage in the next few years and the mature NIE stage before the year 2000. Malaysia and the Philippines, but not oil-dependent Indonesia, will reach the young NIE stage by the turn of the century.

China's trade structure has undergone drastic changes in recent years, thanks to the inflow of direct investment from Hong Kong and Taiwan. By 1992, the specialization index of labor-intensive manufactures had overtaken that of primary commodities, qualifying China as a young NIE by our classification. Given its current pace of industrialization, China should come close to the mature NIE stage by the year 2000.

Noting that China is a big country with a population of 1.2 billion, the flying-geese pattern can be used to describe the spread of industrialization from the mainland's more advanced regions to less developed ones. Indeed, part of China's coastal region, such as Guangdong Province, has already reached the mature NIE stage. Investment from the coastal region to inland areas should help sustain China's export competitiveness on one hand, and narrow the income gap between different parts of the country on the other.

The above analysis has focused on merchandise trade, but attention should also be paid to the service sector, which tends to increase in importance as countries reach an advanced level of economic development. The flow of foreign direct investment also plays a major role in this process. In the case of Japan and the ANIEs, industrial restructuring will not be limited to expanding one industry at the expense of another within the manufacturing sector. Rather, it will be accompanied by massive transfer of resources, including land and labor, from the manufacturing sector to the service sector. Hong Kong and Singapore have developed into trading and financial centres for the Asia-Pacific region. In the case of Japan, companies will also find new business opportunities in the service sector, thanks to changing patterns of consumer demand and progress in deregulation. The shift of the center of gravity from manufacturing to services may lead to a breakdown of the "full-set" industrial structure (the ability to produce domestically everything that is needed) that characterizes the Japanese economy. Regional industrial restructuring allows Japan to concentrate on high value-added products, leaving standardized and lower-end products to Asia's developing countries.

7.4.2 A Closer Look at the Japanese Electronics Industry

The yen's appreciation since early 1993 has led to a decline in the export competitiveness of Japan's electronics industry, prompting Japanese electronics makers to relocate production facilities overseas. Most of these companies are concentrating their investment in Asia, and the electronics industry has become the leading sector of Japanese investment in the region.

The flying-geese pattern of shifting production in the Asia-Pacific region can also be observed in the electronics industry. Thanks to the yen's appreciation, production of higher-end products (for example, computer peripherals) that have lost their cost advantage in Japan is being shifted to the ANIEs, while production of standardized products (large color TVs and air conditioners) is being shifted to the more advanced ASEAN countries, such as Malaysia. At the same time, lower-end products (for example, cassette recorders) that have been produced so far in the ANIEs and the more advanced ASEAN countries, are moving to Indonesia and China.

Meanwhile, a division of labor seems to be emerging between Japanese subsidiaries in the ASEAN countries and China, with the former emphasizing exports and the latter oriented towards the domestic market. Thus there are more and more investments in relatively high-tech products (such as portable video cameras) in China which cannot be rationalized by cost considerations alone.

To cope with the rising cost of procuring parts and components from Japan accompanying the current round of the yen's appreciation, subsidiaries of Japanese electronics companies throughout Asia are raising the local content of their products. In some cases, 100 percent of the production process is now located outside Japan. The process of industrialization in the host countries is thus further moved forward by rising investment on the part of Japanese makers of parts and components.

The increase in investment by Japanese electronics companies in Asia has been accompanied by the formation of production networks across national borders. Division of labor along product lines and processes has allowed maximum exploitation of the resources available in different locations. Network formation among different subsidiaries has been accompanied by a substantial increase in intra-firm trade, which has become a major factor contributing to rising intra-regional trade in the region. The operations of the various corporate members of these networks are coordinated through regional operational headquarters, which provide such services as procurement of parts and components, research and development, fund raising and training. Most companies have found Singapore the ideal place to locate such operational headquarters.

Investment by Japanese electronics companies in Asia is expected to accelerate. With more and more Japanese investment being earmarked for overseas rather than home, the importance of exports from Japan should decline while that of overseas production should increase. According to a survey undertaken by Nomura Research Institute in December 1993, the overseas share of Japanese production (overseas production/global sales) is projected to rise from 29.2 percent in 1993 to 38.2 percent for five major electronics giants; from 35.9 percent to 56.8 percent for five medium-sized electronics companies; and from 33.1 percent to 45.5 percent for 25 major parts makers (Figure 7.8). On the other hand, the share of exports

FIGURE 7.8   Growing importance of overseas production for Japanese electronics companies (Overseas production/global production)

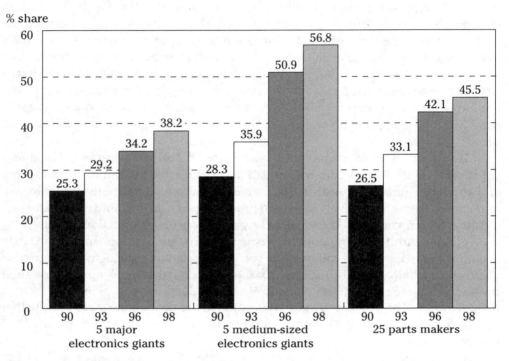

Source: Nomura Research Institute.

as a percentage of overseas sales is expected to drop sharply for all three categories.

With overseas investment rising, production in Japan will specialize more and more in high-value-added products and research and development, while the manufacturing of standardized products will be shifted to the Asian countries. Japan has become a net importer of refrigerators and color TV sets, and more products are expected to join this list. Indeed, a larger and larger proportion of home electrical appliances sold in Japan is being imported from (Japanese subsidiaries) in Asia (Table 7.5). Electronics companies thus face the need to restructure their traditional system of mass production at home.

7.5   How to Keep the Geese Flying

The emergence of Asia as a major player in the global economy has given rise to both challenges and opportunities for the industrial countries. Low labor costs and rising productivity in the Asian countries have boosted Asian exports. This rise in exports, in turn, threatens some sectors in the industrial countries. As a result,

TABLE 7.5 Rising share of imported home electrical appliances in Japan

	Import/Domestic sales (%)								Major import sources		
	1988	1989	1990	1991	1992	1993	1994	1995 (1st half)	1st	2nd	3rd
Copying machines	0.4	2.2	2.1	0.5	3.6	9.6	20.3	29.7	China	Thailand	Hong Kong
Calculators	38.2	38.8	36.2	37.7	39.3	52.9	65.4	88.9	Thailand	China	Malaysia
Color TV sets	8.1	16.0	10.6	17.2	23.3	34.5	54.3	61.5	Malaysia	South Korea	Thailand
Video tape recorders	3.6	5.1	4.4	3.5	8.0	11.6	25.2	28.2	Malaysia	South Korea	Thailand
Microwave ovens	4.8	12.2	5.6	2.5	2.6	6.2	16.2	24.5	South Korea	Thailand	China
Electrical irons	8.1	14.7	10.3	18.9	12.1	14.9	27.2	31.6	China	Taiwan	Singapore
Hair dryers	13.6	17.0	18.4	21.3	23.6	27.5	46.2	55.2	Thailand	China	South Korea

Source: Japanese Ministry of International Trade and Industry.

trade friction between the Asian and industrial countries has escalated, while concerns of a hollowing out of industry are rising in the industrial countries. On the other hand, more and more multinationals have found the Asian countries attractive markets and destinations for investment.

To maintain the vitality of the global economy and to realise the benefits of the international division of labor, countries at more advanced levels of economic development should upgrade their own industrial structures by diversifying into new areas, and should relocate declining industries abroad. Imposing barriers on trade because of fears of a hollowing out of domestic industry and rising unemployment will do more harm than good in the long run. Such measures will only delay an upgrading of industrial structures in both the advanced countries and the developing countries. There are no instances in which declining industries in advanced nations have recovered their competitiveness through protective policies. Protectionist measures may also lead to trade wars and a disintegration of the free trade system.

This is particularly true for economic relations between Japan and its neighbors. Faced with the yen's sharp appreciation, Japanese companies are relocating their production facilities to the Asian countries. This should help promote economic development in the Asian countries while freeing up resources for emerging industries in Japan. So far, Japan has contributed to economic development in the Asian countries on the supply side, by providing the necessary funding and technology through investment and trade. From now on, Japan should play a larger role on the demand side, as an "absorber" of Asian exports.

Needless to say, the only way for Japan to prevent a hollowing out is to cultivate new growth fields. Hong Kong's experience in relocating the bulk of its industrial base to China in recent years provides an instructive example. Despite a sharp reduction of employment in the Hong Kong manufacturing sector, the territory's unemployment rate has remained low as new jobs at higher pay have been created in the service sector. The economic boom in Southern China also supports Hong Kong on the demand side, by absorbing some of the territory's goods and services. The lesson to be learned here for Tokyo: Japan should pay more attention to the service sector and strengthen its links to the fast growing economies of Asia.

Japan, however, seems to be wavering between protectionism and positive industrial adjustment. It was recently reported, for example, that MITI planned to help Japanese petrochemicals makers transfer their excess production capacity to China, making effective use of official development assistance (ODA) such as financing by the Export-Import Bank of Japan and related technological aid. The plan is in perfect agreement with the spirit of positive industrial adjustment, and should be extended to other industries and other developing countries in the future. On the other hand, MITI is considering imposing restrictions on textile imports from Asian countries, citing the market disruption in Japan caused by the rapid growth in imports.

Following the successful "catching up" of Japan in the 1960s, the United States and European countries imposed trade barriers in the form of tariffs and quantitative restrictions on Japanese products. The same measures were applied later to the ANIEs and other developing countries in Asia. It is truly regrettable and ironic that Japan, which has firmly opposed such measures, is going to adopt a similar policy towards developing countries now that the country's position has been reversed.

Japan should abandon the mercantilist view that production and exports are good, while consumption and imports are bad. Instead, Tokyo should adopt policies that promote an international division of labor according to comparative advantage. By relocating declining industries abroad and liberalizing imports, Japanese producers and consumers should realise gains in real income by lowering the nation's costs of production and imports. More importantly, the resulting growing prosperity among Asian countries will promote stability in the Asia-Pacific region, and thus Japan's national security.

The same policy is also desirable for countries in the process of catching up with Japan, and major steps have already been taken in the right direction. South Korea, for example, has broadened the list of domestic industries that are eligible to invest abroad, and has expanded the amount of credit available to help relocate declining industries overseas. Likewise, Singapore is building an "external wing" to complement the domestic economy; the government has been playing an active role in developing the Growth Triangle that comprises Singapore, Riau Province in Indonesia and Johor in Malaysia, while at the same time promoting investment in China. Thailand is strengthening its economic ties with neighboring countries in Indochina. Hong Kong does not pursue an active industrial policy, but has upgraded its industrial structure by relying on the market mechanism.

Regional industrial restructuring is expected to proceed with an unprecedented scale from now on. Asian countries should participate actively in this process by promoting the two-way flow of direct investment across national borders. Foreign direct investment is not a zero sum game; both investing and receiving countries should benefit from the advantages that result from a better allocation of social resources (MacDougall 1958).

References

Akamatsu, K., 1962, "A Historical Pattern of Economic Growth in Developing Countries," *Developing Economies*, preliminary issue 1 (March–September): 3–25.

Hara, M. , 1992, *Foreign Direct Investment and the Japanese Economy*, Yuhikaku, Tokyo (in Japanese).

MacDougall, G. A. D., 1958, "The Benefits and Costs of Private Investment from Abroad: A Theoretical Analysis," *Economic Record*, 36: 13–35.

Vernon, R., 1966, "International Investment and International Trade in the Product Cycle," *Quarterly Journal of Economics*, 80 (May): 190–207.

Yamazawa, I., 1990, *Economic Development and International Trade: A Japanese Model*, University of Hawaii Press, Honolulu.

Chapter 8

Kym Anderson

WORLD TRADE DEVELOPMENTS FROM AN EAST ASIAN PERSPECTIVE

8.1 Introduction

Developments in the world trading system and in global trade are crucially important to the East Asian region in general, and to China in particular as it seeks to trade its way to a higher standard of living. A healthy global trading system is essential for a continuation of East Asian economic growth not only because the region's share of world trade more than doubled during the past three decades, but also because of the continuing high dependence of the region on markets outside Asia and the absence of free trade within the region. True, the share of East Asia's trade that is intra-regional has been growing, as have the intra-regional trade shares of both Western Europe and North America. But Section 8.2 of this chapter shows that all three regions remain strongly interdependent, each with one-seventh or one-eighth of their GDP traded extra-regionally.

An important consequence of East Asia's share of world trade increasing from less than 10 percent in the early 1960s to more than 20 percent today is that its potential for influencing world trade policy developments is growing. Indeed continued prosperity in East Asia depends not just on how well people there respond to changes in the world economy, but also on how well their firms and governments manage to influence the evolution of policies affecting world trade, be they multilateral, regional, or unilateral.

At the multilateral level, successful implementation of the Uruguay Round is obviously of crucial importance. As mentioned in Section 8.3, the new World Trade Organisation (WTO) will have a full work program from day one, not least in monitoring that implementation and arbitrating disputes arising from it. But even if the Round were to be implemented without major problems during the remainder of this decade, the General Agreement on Tariffs and Trade (GATT) rules-based multilateral trading system under the WTO will continue to come under strain. The irony is that the challenges to that system—regionalism, environmentalism, concern about labor standards, competition policy—are in part a result of the GATT's very success in fostering global economic integration over its 47-year lifetime. These challenges are discussed in Section 8.4

Regional integration initiatives in Europe and North America, in addition to influencing the multilateral trading system, also are having direct impacts on East Asian trade and investment. These effects are analysed briefly in Section 8.5. Unilateral trade policy initiatives, particularly by the United States, are also being keenly felt in East Asia. Section 8.6 touches upon some of these policies. The final section examines what East Asia might do to minimize the risks and maximize the opportunities arising from these recent and prospective challenges facing the GATT rules-based global trading system to which China hopes to soon become a Contracting Party.

8.2   East Asia's Expanding Role in World Trade

In the early 1960s, East Asia accounted for less than one-tenth of the world GDP and trade. Today its shares of world GDP and trade are more than one-fifth. East Asia's growth in importance has been primarily at the expense of North America in terms of output and income, and at the expense of other developing countries with respect to trade (Table 8.1). This follows from the fact that the share of GDP traded internationally has grown relatively rapidly for North America.

East Asia's interdependence with the rest of the world is even greater than these shares suggest because much of Europe's large trade volume is with other European countries as a result of the preferential regional trading arrangements of the European Community (EC)/European Union (EU), the European Free Trade Association (EFTA) or, until it was disbanded in 1991, the Council for Mutual Economic Assistance (COMECON). When intra-bloc trade is ignored, it is clear from Figure 8.1 that East Asia is a much larger participant in world trade outside those blocs, dominating both Europe and the Americas. Indeed if the European Union were to be treated as a single trader, now that it has implemented much of the Single Market Act to remove remaining barriers to trade in goods and services

TABLE 8.1   Importance of Europe, North America and East Asia in the world economy, 1963 and 1992–93

	GDP (%)		Merchandise trade[a] (%)	
	1963	1992	1963	1993
Europe (incl. the CIS)	34	37	50	46
North America (incl. Mexico)	45	29	18	20
East Asia	9	21	9	22
Rest of world	12	13	23	12
WORLD	100	100	100	100

a. Merchandise exports plus imports.

Sources: World Bank (1994) and GATT (1994).

within the EU, then six East Asian economies appear in the list of the world's top nine exporters in 1993, with three more close behind (Table 8.2).

How regionalized has East Asia's trade become over the post-war period, compared with Europe's and North America's trade? In part (i) of Table 8.3 it is clear that Asia's intra-regional trade[1] share had grown relatively little until the 1980s and only by a fifth during the 1980s (which brought its share back to the levels experienced during the inter-war period of Japanese imperialism in Northeast Asia). This change has been minor despite the greater regionalization of Europe's and (to a lesser extent) North America's trade and the large increase in Asia's share of world trade. The effect of changes in the regions' shares of world trade on intra-regional trade shares can be netted out by calculating the intensity of the intra-regional trade index, which is (roughly) the intra-regional trade share divided by the region's share of world trade. Part (ii) of Table 8.3 shows those indexes for Asia, Western Europe, North America, and the world as a whole (comprising also four other regions, not listed). Those data confirm that Asia's regional trade pattern is different: while the intensity of intra-regional trade in Europe and North America has been steadily increasing over the inter-war and post-war periods, East Asia's intra-regional trade intensity has been decreasing since the 1960s.

Do those differences in intra-regional trade intensity indexes mean Asia has become more dependent on the rest of the world while Western Europe and North America have become more inward-focused? The answer is no, because what also needs to be taken into account is the overall extent to which each region's GDP is internationally traded. In this regard Asia has changed relatively little compared with Europe and America (part (iii) of Table 8.3). Indeed that share for Japan has grown hardly at all in recent decades (while doubling for North America and

FIGURE 8.1 Regional shares of world merchandise trade, 1963 and 1993 (exports plus imports as a percentage of global exports plus imports)

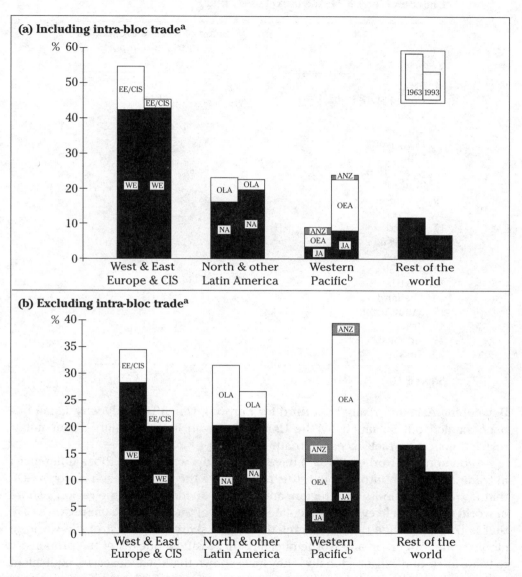

a. Figure (b) is distinguished from Figure (a) in that it excludes from regional and global trade totals the value of trade between countries in Western Europe; between East Europe/ CIS former COMECON members; between Canada, Mexico and the United States; and between Australia and New Zealand.

b. Japan; the market economies of Northeast and Southeast Asia plus China (collectively Other East Asia); and Australia and New Zealand (ANZ).

Sources: GATT (1987, 1994).

TABLE 8.2   The 20 leading traders internationally when the European Union (formerly Community) is treated as a single trader and intra-EU trade is excluded, 1993

	Share of world merchandise exports and imports (%)
1. EU-12	19.1
2. United States	18.0
3. Japan	10.2
4. Canada	4.8
5. Hong Kong	4.7
6. China	3.3
7. Korea, Rep.	2.8
8. Taiwan	2.8
9. Singapore	2.7
10. Switzerland	2.1
11. Mexico	1.6
12. Malaysia	1.6
13. Sweden	1.5
14. Australia	1.5
15. Austria	1.5
16. Thailand	1.4
17. Saudi Arabia	1.2
18. Brazil	1.1
19. Indonesia	1.1
20. Russia	1.1

Source: GATT (1994).

Developing Asia and rising by a third for Europe), which is partly why Japan has been singled out so much by the United States in its complaints about unfair restrictions on market access abroad.[2]

Anderson and Norheim (1993) have suggested a way to take those differences in trade orientation into account. It is to calculate the share of each region's GDP that is traded within its own region, and then to divide that by the region's share of world trade; and likewise to calculate the ratio of the share of each region's GDP that is traded outside that region relative to the share of the rest of the world in global trade. Anderson and Norheim called these ratios indexes of the propensity to trade intra- and extra-regionally. They have shown that the indexes are equivalent to the product of the trade intensity index and the trade-to-GDP ratio. The calculated values for these propensity indexes are shown in parts (iv) and (v) of Table 8.3. What they reveal is that on average Western European countries have a *greater* propensity to trade extra-regionally than do Asian countries and that this difference has narrowed but not greatly during the past three or four decades. Those indexes also reveal that in the 1970s North America in this respect had been rapidly catching up with Asia—and *has* caught up with Japan—despite the much larger

TABLE 8.3   Trade shares and the intensity and propensity of regionalization in world merchandise trade, 1928–90

	1928	1938	1948	1958	1968	1979	1990
(i) INTRA-REGIONAL TRADE SHARE (%)[a]							
Western Europe	51	49	43	53	63	66	72
North America incl. Mexico	29	25	37	38	40	35	40
Asia	46	52	39	41	37	41	48
Japan[f]	63	68	60	36	32	31	35
Australasia[f]	16	16	14	25	31	49	51
Developing Asia[f]	47	55	44	47	45	48	56
WORLD, total	39	37	33	40	47	46	52
(ii) INTENSITY OF INTRA-REGIONAL TRADE INDEX[b]							
Western Europe	1.13	1.14	1.21	1.38	1.51	1.57	1.60
North America incl. Mexico	2.21	2.33	2.24	2.72	2.90	3.09	3.21
Asia	2.61	2.83	2.74	3.15	2.84	2.77	2.31
Japan[f]	4.17	4.65	4.29	3.28	3.81	3.08	2.33
Australasia[f]	0.97	0.93	1.08	2.00	2.47	3.32	2.47
Developing Asia[f]	2.66	2.96	3.10	3.56	3.37	3.17	2.64
WORLD, total[c]	1.85	1.92	2.43	2.65	2.81	2.64	2.62
(iii) SHARE (%) OF GDP TRADED[a]							
Western Europe	33	24	35	33	34	48	46
North America incl. Mexico	11	8	11	9	10	19	20
Asia	32	27	25	26	21	27	29
Japan[f]	35	29	8	19	17	20	18
Australasia[f]	38	32	47	31	25	29	30
Developing Asia[f]	30	25	25[e]	29	26	37	47
WORLD, Total[c]	24	19	22	22	22	35	34
(iv) INDEX OF PROPENSITY TO TRADE INTRA-REGIONALLY[d]							
Western Europe	0.38	0.27	0.30	0.46	0.50	0.75	0.73
North America incl. Mexico	0.24	0.18	0.25	0.26	0.28	0.60	0.63
Asia	0.83	0.76	0.67	0.83	0.60	0.76	0.67
Japan[f]	1.37	1.57	0.28	0.53	0.31	0.55	0.42
Australasia[f]	0.39	0.21	0.43	0.57	0.71	1.03	0.89
Developing Asia[f]	0.82	0.72	0.84	1.07	1.09	1.23	1.21
WORLD, total	0.45	0.37	0.54	0.57	0.61	0.91	0.88

TABLE 8.3 (continued)

	1928	1938	1948	1958	1968	1979	1990
(v) INDEX OF PROPENSITY TO TRADE EXTRA-REGIONALLY[d]							
Western Europe	0.30	0.21	0.31	0.26	0.21	0.28	0.23
North America incl. Mexico	0.09	0.06	0.08	0.07	0.07	0.14	0.13
Asia	0.21	0.16	0.18	0.18	0.15	0.19	0.19
Japan[f]	0.14	0.10	0.04	0.13	0.12	0.15	0.13
Australasia[f]	0.37	0.31	0.46	0.27	0.19	0.17	0.19
Developing Asia[f]	0.25	0.21	0.16	0.17	0.16	0.23	0.26
WORLD, total	0.21	0.16	0.19	0.16	0.15	0.23	0.21

a. Throughout the table, "trade" refers to the average of merchandise export and import shares or intensity indexes, except that the share of GDP traded and the propensity index refer to exports plus imports of merchandise. All values are measured in current U.S. dollars. Turkey and Yugoslavia are included in Western Europe. North America refers to Canada, Mexico and the United States, and Australasia refers to Australia and New Zealand.
b. The intensity of trade index for regions is defined (roughly) as the share of one region's trade with another region relative to that other region's share of world trade (see Anderson and Norheim (1993) for a more precise definition of the indexes of intra- and extra-regional trade intensity).
c. The world total intensity index is the weighted average across the seven regions (Africa, Eastern Europe, Latin America and the Middle East are not shown), using the regions' shares of world trade as weights.
d. The propensity to trade index is defined as the intensity index multiplied by the ratio of exports plus imports to GDP (see Anderson and Norheim 1993). The world total refers to the weighted average for the seven regions (Africa, Eastern Europe, Latin America and the Middle East are not shown), using the regions' shares of world GDP as weights.
e. In the absence of reliable estimates of GDP prior to the 1950s for developing countries and until 1989 for Eastern Europe, "guesstimates" have been made of the trade-to-GDP ratio for those regions. Given their small weights in world trade, the aggregates for the world nonetheless will be reasonably reliable. The ratio is estimated at current prices.
f. The rows for Japan, Australasia and Developing Asia differ from the other rows in that they are treated not as regions themselves but as part of their sum which is the Asian region including South Asia.

Source: Anderson and Blackhurst (1993: Appendix).

size and greater range of resource endowments and hence lesser need for the U.S. economy to trade internationally.[3]

In short, there are at least three things to note from these data and from Table 8.4 (which shows simply the share of each region's GDP that is traded extra-regionally—this share has since the 1960s averaged about one-seventh for Western Europe and Japan and has risen to one-eighth for North America). First, they reveal that East Asia has become a more significant—indeed a major—participant in world trade, with its importance now exceeding Europe's and North America's when

TABLE 8.4   Share (in %) of GDP traded extra-regionally, Western Europe, North America and Asia, 1928–90[a]

	1928	1938	1948	1958	1963	1968	1973	1979	1983	1990
Western Europe	17	12	21	16	12	13	14	16	15	13
North America incl. Mexico	8	6	7	6	6	6	8	13	11	12
Asia	17	8	15	16	11	14	14	16	15	15
Japan[f]	24	4	3	12	11	12	14	14	15	12
Australasia[f]	37	20	45	29	27	23	27	27	22	28
Developing Asia[f]	22	18	16	19	13	20	19	28	24	31
WORLD, Total[c]	15	12	15	13	12	12	14	19	17	16

See notes a, c and f of Table 8.3.

Source: Anderson and Blackhurst (1993: Appendix Table A7).

intra-bloc trade is excluded. But secondly, this region's interdependence through trade with other regions is roughly matched by that of North America and Western Europe, notwithstanding the common claim that the latter are inward-looking trading blocs. That is, all three regions have a huge and still-growing interest in ensuring that prosperity flourishes outside their own geographic region and that extra-regional trade remains open, which is what a healthy multilateral trading system is able to provide. Thirdly, a healthy multilateral system is especially important for Asia because, unlike in Western Europe and now North America, this region does not have a free trade agreement or customs union and so the GATT/WTO is important for maintaining and increasing openness not only of Asia's trade with other regions but also of intra-Asian trade. Yet, despite East Asia being as important, or even more important than Europe and North America in trade between regions, Asian governments have been much less assertive than those of the U.S. or EU in the GATT/WTO process. It is argued below that there is considerable scope for East Asia to increase its influence on world trade policies, both in the immediate future and in the longer term, for the betterment of its own welfare as well as that of the rest of the world. In the immediate term the key task is to ensure the ratification and implementation of the Uruguay Round, to which attention now turns.

8.3   Ratifying and Implementing the Uruguay Round Agreements

For all its faults, the GATT rules-based multilateral trading system (MTS) has served the world—and especially East Asia—very well. In particular, as a result of seven previous rounds of trade negotiations, import tariffs on manufactures have been wound down for most commodities to negligible levels in industrial countries. It is true that many non-tariff barriers are still in place and some have risen in response to tariff cuts. But the fact remains that the share of world GDP that is traded internationally has risen from just over one-fifth in the 1950s and 1960s to more than one-third since the latter 1970s (part (iii) of Table 8.3),[4] only a part of which is likely to be due to the fall in international transport and communication costs and in the value-added share of output.

The signing of the Uruguay Round agreements in Morocco in April 1994 brought to an end a record-breaking seven and a half arduous years of trade negotiations. Those agreements represent a momentous achievement worthy of much celebrating. National legislatures have been ratifying them, during 1994–95 so that the World Trade Organisation (WTO) could come into effect in 1995. It then remains for the agreements to be implemented during the next six to ten years.

Not surprisingly, numerous commentators had declared GATT to be dying with the passing of one deadline after another for concluding the Uruguay Round. It is therefore worth asking why it proved to be so difficult to bring the Uruguay Round to a successful conclusion, particularly at a time when many countries were clearly interested in trade policy reform (as witnessed, for example, by numerous countries' unilateral reforms of recent years and the formation and extension of various free trade areas/customs unions).

The struggle to reach agreement in the Uruguay Round was not so much a sign of a crisis in the MTS as a sign that, having reduced manufacturing tariffs so much in previous rounds, the time had come to turn to non-tariff barriers and in particular to the trade policies of politically more sensitive sectors (agriculture, textiles and clothing, and services) and to trade-related policies. These were the difficult items that had often been ignored also in unilateral and minilateral reforms. Certainly it is not very surprising that agreement on the extent and speed of farm and textile trade reform was difficult to reach. After all, assistance to textile and clothing producers has been in place for decades and agricultural protection has been growing for centuries, so even a moratorium on further increases in protection levels for these traditional declining industries would be a significant change. And with trade in services also being brought under the discipline of the GATT/WTO for the first time, not to mention progress in such trade-related areas as intellectual property and investment, the Round has to be seen as involving the relinquishing of a considerably greater degree of national sovereignty over policy.

Even assuming the Uruguay Round is ratified soon, that will not allow complacency with respect to the MTS. The new World Trade Organisation will have a full work program from day one on relatively routine matters, in addition to some major new challenges on the immediate horizon. Four routine activities are worth mentioning by way of illustration, before turning in the next section to a discussion of some of the WTO's new challenges.

First, monitoring the implementation of the Uruguay Round agreements will be a major task in itself. Since there is plenty of scope in the agreements for different interpretations of what is required to comply,[5] a greater degree of policy transparency is required than the GATT's Trade Policy Review Mechanism has, with its very limited resources, been able to deliver to date. Two aspects of the agreement on agriculture provide particularly striking examples. One is that since countries have had to replace all non-tariff import barriers with bound tariffs, and they have done so by setting tariffs at rates well (sometimes several times) above the tariff equivalent of the previous non-tariff barriers, it may well be that actual import barriers on some items will be higher at the end than the beginning of the decade. The other is that while the Aggregate Measure of Support (AMS) via domestic farm policies is to be reduced under the agreement, increased price supports for industries that are "supply constrained" (for example, by land set-asides or dairy herd quotas) do not count in measuring changes in the AMS, even though we have clear evidence that higher prices induce higher yields per hectare or per cow. Thus in addition to measuring the AMS there is a continuing need for the estimation of producer subsidy equivalents (PSEs) and related indexes of actual protection, not least so that a proper evaluation of the leakiness of the Uruguay Round agreement can be used to negotiate a tighter outcome in the next round of farm policy talks, to begin in 1999 (Anderson 1994).

Second, because there is plenty of scope in the agreements for different interpretations of what constitutes compliance, as well as a large backlog of unresolved issues that have been left on the back burner pending the Uruguay Round's completion, the revamped dispute settlement mechanism for the WTO will be extremely busy as countries test the new rules and procedures.

Third, the WTO will have to cope with the flood of recent and prospective applications for membership. At present there are about 125 members, so potentially more than 50 countries could line up. The most important to cope with first is China, and that would then allow Taiwan to join immediately. Of Europe's former Communist countries only the Czech and Slovac republics are full members; so a score of applications are or will soon be forthcoming from that region too.

And fourth, the task of tidying up unfinished business in the Uruguay Round (for example, in services) and beginning preparations for the next round of multilateral trade negotiations needs to get under way. Traditionally there is a honeymoon period before the task begins again, but that will not be the case this time. Indeed the task may have to get under way as early as this year if the U.S. Congress proves reluctant to ratify the Uruguay Round agreements. As with the NAFTA agreement, which was perceived to require side agreements on environmental and labor standards before the U.S. Congress would ratify it, so too the U.S. may insist on a specific work program not only for a WTO committee on trade and environment but also for one on labor standards, discussed below.

8.4   Other Challenges Ahead for the WTO

The GATT's very successes since the late 1940s, together with rapid technological changes, mean that traditional barriers to international trade have become increasingly less important as determinants of international competitiveness. Those barrier reductions include not only governmental ones such as import tariffs but also natural ones such as transport and telecommunication costs, the latter being especially important in lowering the transactions costs of the banking/foreign exchange aspects of trade.

The resulting extra exposure of national economies to competition from abroad has caused attention to focus much more sharply on domestic policies that influence the international competitiveness of firms and industries. Two responses to that have been calls for (a) other microeconomic reforms which would increase competition domestically and lower firms' production costs, and (b) restraint on introducing further social policies that add to private costs of production. In the case of the first, if they are implemented multilaterally rather than unilaterally, those additional reforms are less painful for the groups that stand to lose (for example, trade unionists in the case of labor market deregulation, monopolies in the case of antitrust policies, favored domestic firms in the case of opening up government procurement). The reason is that the more other countries are reforming, the faster will be global market growth and hence the less need for contraction of any one sector absolutely (even if it were to decline relatively).

The same is true in the case of governments needing to respond to calls for cost-raising social policies. For example, raising environmental, labor or other social standards is less threatening to producers of tradables in one country if standards are similarly raised in countries with firms competing with those producers. This is especially true when a significant new player with lower standards enters the scene, as has happened increasingly during the past 15 years with the opening up of China and is now beginning to happen (albeit much less spectacularly) with Vietnam and some of Europe's former Communist countries.

Not surprisingly, achieving agreement among countries to coordinate such reforms is easier when the tastes and preferences in the countries concerned are more similar. Hence their greater success among similar countries in a region than globally. Witness, for example how Western European countries were able to use the EC (now EU) to expand their social charter via Maastricht. When the countries of a region are dissimilar, regional agreements tied to market access provide a vehicle. The United States, for example, was able to convince Mexico to sign side agreements on environmental and labor standards in the course of getting the U.S. Congress to approve the main NAFTA trade agreement.

When viewed in this light, the greater promise, as well as potential problems associated with the deepening and widening of regional integration agreements, become more apparent (Lawrence 1993). At one extreme there are those who seek to emphasize the problems, the biggest being the potential for the world to break up into three inward-looking trading blocs. And at the other extreme there are those who claim these initiatives to encourage greater regional integration will, over time, be embraced at broader multilateral levels. The latter analysts would argue that regionalism is therefore a stepping stone rather than a stumbling block to an improved multilateral trading system and thereby to enhanced economic welfare.

Certainly the pessimistic view that "GATT is dead" will be credible once the Uruguay Round agreements are ratified by national governments only in the sense that the GATT Secretariat will be replaced by a more substantive World Trade Organisation next year. But the optimistic view about regionalism and the associated minilateral agreements on social issues such as environmental and labor standards needs to be tempered also. In the discussion that follows the author will first consider regionalism and then environmental and labor issues. This is followed by a brief discussion of competition policy and trade.

8.4.1 Regionalism and the WTO[6]

There are several ways in which the proliferation of regional economic integration initiatives may be more of a stumbling block than a stepping stone towards freer world trade, even leaving aside for the moment the question of social issues. For one, regional integration agreements can be more trade diverting than trade creating. The history of the West European arrangements as reported in Table 8.3 suggests this has not been a major problem in the past at least, in the sense that the propensity for Western Europe to trade with other regions has grown rapidly since the 1950s. Whether it will be a problem in the future is a moot point, however.

Supporters of NAFTA believe there is no cause for concern. They point, for example, to the effect that President Bush's offer to other Latin American countries (to consider forming a free trade area with the United States) has had in encouraging those developing countries to push ahead unilaterally with their macro- and micro-economic reforms (which would be necessary before the U.S. would consider their application). And Central and Eastern Europeans also know that before significant agreement to free up trade with Western Europeans could be reached, those formerly planned economies have to become much more market-oriented.

However, people outside those regions believe there *are* causes for concern, not least because the text of recent regional integration agreements tend to be many hundreds of—rather than just a few dozen—pages. That is, they contain so many qualifications and exceptions that these agreements fall a long way short of creating literally free trade areas.

Snape, Adams and Morgan (1993) argue that a preferential trade agreement is more likely to complement and facilitate liberal multilateral trade the more it involves (a) full liberalization of trade between participants in at least all products if not also in productive factors; (b) no raising of external barriers to trade and investment on formation or subsequently, and a willingness and capacity to negotiate external barrier reduction thereafter; (c) homogeneous rules of origin and dispute settlement procedures; and (d) openness to new members on the same conditions as those faced by existing members.

Clearly, not even EFTA or the EU, let alone NAFTA and the more recently negotiated and prospective regional integration agreements in Europe and America, are close to fulfilling all these conditions. In fact the latest ones are more like "hub-and-spoke" agreements, involving an ever larger number of separate bilateral deals between the main or "hub" economy (the U.S., the EU-12, or Russia) and smaller "spoke" economies. The likelihood is that the "spokes" to be added in the future will be increasingly less natural trading partners than those added to date. And such agreements then may require those smaller spoke economies to also negotiate separate bilateral deals with other spokes. At the same time rules of origin and dispute settlement procedures become ever more important elements in the administration of such trade agreements. The proliferation of hub-and-spoke RIAs not only would increasingly distract participants' attention away from the multilateral trading system, but also would increase friction both among participants and between them and outsiders. It is difficult to imagine the world going very far down such a path without the global trading system coming under the sort of stress experienced in the 1930s.

Another way in which regional integration initiatives can be stumbling blocks to freer global trade is that their protagonists, by focusing on deeper and wider regional integration, divert the attention of government leaders and officials away from improving the broader MTS. Certainly the Uruguay Round suffered from Western Europe's preoccupation with furthering the EC Single Market and Maastricht processes during the past decade and with deciding on how to proceed with the next enlargements and association accords. The Round suffered not just directly but also indirectly in the sense that American frustrations over getting the EC to the negotiating table led first to the Canada-U.S. Free Trade Agreement and then to NAFTA, both of which absorbed time that might otherwise have been spent speeding up progress on the Uruguay Round.

And finally, as they widen and deepen, the regional trading blocs tend to become more assertive towards other countries and blocs. Whether that helps or hinders progress toward freer world trade is an empirical question. In the early post-war years when the U.S. dominated the GATT, it was helpful that its inclination was predominantly (with some notable exceptions) in support of freer trade. Now that the U.S. has declined in relative importance and influence in the GATT and has become more protectionist in its rhetoric than in previous decades, and that the EU has risen to become a counter-weight economically but is unable because of its diverse membership to take up the leadership vacuum left by the U.S., progress in liberalizing trade multilaterally is more difficult.

This state of affairs suggests that there is scope for a third group of countries—most obviously (as shown in Figure 8.1) one centered on the Western Pacific with or without North America—to take the initiative and contribute to the GATT/WTO process. This possibility is discussed in the final section below. But, before going into that, consider the possible ramifications of extending beyond regional discussions and into the WTO the entwining of trade policy with social issues and competition policy.

8.4.2 Environmentalism and the WTO[7]

The greening of world politics accelerated substantially in the 1980s and is now much more pervasive in its effects on the world economy. Insofar as it has increased uncertainty (hopefully only temporarily) about the future profitability levels of firms, it has probably contributed to the current recession. It has also changed comparative advantages of different countries as the implementation of stricter environmental standards and higher taxes on polluters takes effect in some countries more so than in others.[8] But because many of the more recent concerns of environmentalists go beyond national boundaries and in some cases have to do with the global commons, they raise several questions about the roles for trade policy.

One, which arose initially with the first wave of concern for the environment in the 1960s, has to do simply with the concern of firms in advanced industrial economies that their competitiveness is being eroded by the imposition of, say, stricter pollution abatement standards at home than abroad. Where the environmental damage caused by production is purely local, the calls by disadvantaged firms for trade restrictions or subsidies to offset the decline in their international competitiveness, because standards have been raised, has no economic logic: such assistance would tend to offset the desired effect of limiting by-product pollution. Nor is it reasonable to conclude that other countries are engaging in "eco-dumping" if the imports they are able to supply are produced with laxer environmental standards, in so far as those lower standards are consistent with the preferences and natural resource endowments of those exporting countries (for example, because those countries are poorer and/or less densely populated and less urbanized). Even so, claims for protection against "eco-dumping" have political appeal and may result in higher import barriers or export subsidies than would otherwise be the case in advanced economies.

Trade policy actions of this kind are more likely to occur, and to be more difficult to dismiss as inappropriate, when environmentalists in such countries view particular damage to the environment as unacceptable *regardless of the nation in which the damage occurs*. This case is even more problematic if the damage is not just psychological (as with animal rights) but also physical (for example, pollution blown across national borders by the prevailing winds), for then the relocation of production to a country with laxer environmental standards may *worsen* animal welfare, or pollution at home, in addition to reducing the profitability of the home firms. The infamous U.S.–Mexico dispute over the use of dolphin-unfriendly nets by tuna fishermen comes to mind. In that case the GATT ruled against the U.S. ban on imports of tuna from Mexico, partly because the ban did not discriminate according to which type of net was used—as it cannot, because an aspect of the production process rather than the final traded product itself is what is considered objectionable. The GATT panel ruled against the ban because to do otherwise would have created a huge loophole in the GATT for any country unilaterally to apply trade restrictions as a means of imposing its environmental standards on other countries. Such a loophole would work against the main objective of the multilateral trading system which is to provide stable and predictable market access opportunities through agreed rules and disciplines and bound tariffs on imports.

Another concern is that, in addition to proposing the use of trade restrictions, some environmentalists also oppose trade liberalization. They oppose the GATT's attempts to lower trade barriers on at least two grounds: that freer trade means more output and income which they presume would mean more degradation of the natural environment; and that freer trade encourages the relocation of environmentally degrading industries to countries with lower environmental protection standards and/or more fragile natural environments.

Neither of these assertions is unambiguously supported by empirical evidence, however. The first, that income increases mean greater damage to the natural environment, may be true for some poorer countries (in which case any additional environmental damage has to be weighed against the marginal economic benefits of higher incomes for poor people), but once middle-income status is reached people tend to alter their behavior in ways that reduce pressures on the environment. One is that population growth tends to decline as incomes rise (Baldwin 1995). Another is that education investment expands, and with it comes more skillful management of all resources including the environment. And thirdly, modernizing communities with rising incomes and improving education tend eventually to improve private property rights and put more stringent environmental policies in place (Radetski 1992; Grossman 1995). Clear-cut examples include Japan in the post-war period and Korea and Taiwan during the past decade or so.

The second assertion by environmentalists, that the relocation of production following trade liberalization necessarily worsens the global environment, is even more questionable, for at least two reasons. First, we know from the law of comparative advantage that not *all* industries will be relocated from rich to poor countries when the former's trade barriers are lowered: some industries in the North will expand at the expense of those industries in the South. In any case, it cannot be assumed that relocating production in the South is necessarily worsening the environment. A recent examination of the likely environmental effects of reducing government assistance to two of the North's most protected industries, coal and food, revealed that in both cases the global environment may well be improved by trade liberalization (Anderson and Blackhurst 1992: Chapter 8). But evidently many more empirical studies will be required before the more extreme environmental groups alter their perception of and publicity against the GATT/WTO as an environmentally unfriendly institution.

There is, however, one further way in which trade policy is being called upon to help achieve environmental objectives that has somewhat more validity. It is as a carrot or stick to entice countries to sign international environmental agreements. In the case of combatting global environmental problems such as ozone depletion or climate change, the free-rider problem arises. One of the more obvious and possibly more cost-effective ways to reduce the free-rider problem is to write trade provisions into the agreement, as was done in the 1987 Montreal Protocol on reducing the use of CFCs and halons to slow ozone depletion (see Anderson and Blackhurst 1992: Chapter 7). To date no GATT contracting party has formally objected to that use of trade policy. Nor have they objected to the bans on trade in ivory and rhino horn that are part of the Convention of Trade in Endangered Species (CITES), or to the trade provisions in the Basel Convention on trade in hazardous substances and waste. Conflicts may arise in the future, however, if trade provisions are drafted into more contentious international environmental agreements (for example, to impose a global carbon tax).

8.4.3 Labor Standards and the WTO

An even more recent and reluctant entrant on the WTO's potential agenda is the issue of labor standards. Like environmental standards, the linking of labor standards with trade originates with concerns in high-standard countries that lower costs of employing labor in other countries gives them a competitive advantage, from which producers in the high-standard countries (particularly unionized workers in low-skill industries) would like to be protected if those standards abroad are not to be raised. The protection could come in the form of import barriers on the goods in question, or fines (as in NAFTA's side agreement), or the denial of preferential market access (as the U.S. does with respect to its Generalized System of Preferences to developing countries), or potentially even trade sanctions against countries not prepared to raise their labor standards. The concern in high-standard countries ostensibly is not so much with the average wage level difference but rather with such things as occupational health and safety standards, worker rights to form unions and seek a minimum wage level, the use of child or prison or forced labor, and the derogation from national labor laws in export processing zones. Human rights activists and development NGOs often add support to these calls, believing that such action could reduce poverty and improve the quality of life in developing countries (even though in fact the raising of labor standards in the formal sector is more likely simply to drive employment into the informal sector, where labor standards are even lower, and/or to lengthen the queues of people seeking high-paid, high-standard formal sector jobs). As with environmental standards, traditional protectionist forces are prompt to support any such calls for import restraint by high-standard countries against goods from lower-standard countries.[9]

The International Labor Organization has been writing labor standards for 75 years. Why has this issue suddenly become entangled with the GATT/WTO and trade policy issues? In fact it has been there for a long time,[10] but it has been kept on the back burner and raises its head mainly when the trading system is in the news, such as when the ITO was being conceived in 1947, at the end of the Tokyo Round, and now that the WTO is about to be born. It is also coming under increasing discussion partly as a result of falling communication costs, which have enabled citizens of high-standard countries to get information on labor (and environmental) standards in other countries more easily. That, together with the ever greater sense of integration among the world's people (the "global village" idea), allows and encourages the concern for human (as with animal) rights to spread beyond national boundaries. The trend toward increasing discussion of social issues such as labor standards might therefore be expected to continue indefinitely as global economic growth and integration proceed. Around that general upward trend in concern we will see fluctuations that are opposite to the business cycle:[11] the worse the labor market is performing in high-wage countries (especially in the lower-skill categories), the more likely it is that imports from low-wage countries will be blamed (Lawrence 1994). And that likelihood is exacerbated by the computer and information revolutions which are increasing the demand for skilled relative to unskilled workers (Wood 1994).

Yet another reason why the issue has become more prominent now is because it became the subject of a side agreement to the NAFTA.[12] That side agreement was a price President Clinton paid to buy off opposition from labor groups to the NAFTA's passage through the U.S. Congress. Having been encouraged by their success in that regional trade liberalization setting, and before that in some minor trade and investment agreements in the 1980s (see Lawrence (1994) for details), the advocates for that side agreement are now, like the environmental lobby groups, seeking to have an influence at the multilateral trade level. In both situations, the desire to reach agreement on trade liberalization is to some extent simply being used opportunistically by these groups to further their own causes, despite the somewhat tenuous connection with trade. And their relative success to date is in large measure due to the superficial popular appeal of their causes and the less apparent downside of their causes in terms of the potential risk to the global trading system.

8.4.4 Competition Policy and the WTO

Among the reasons given for adding competition policy to the WTO's agenda are concerns about differences across countries in antitrust rules and their degree of enforcement, about exemptions to those rules (for example, export cartels, monopoly commodity boards, state-owned enterprises), and about conglomerates with substantial market power that operate globally and are therefore beyond the reach of national antitrust jurisdictions. The European Union has developed supranational institutions to cope with some of these concerns in Western Europe, but that model is unlikely to be replicable on a global scale. GATT rules aimed at increasing competition through market access already offer some protection against anti-competitive practices; the issue is whether more use could be made of those rules or whether additional rules are possible (Hoekman and Mavroidis 1994). The consequences for East Asia are far from clear at this stage, so if the issue is likely to come under active consideration by the WTO there will need to be a burst of research and analysis undertaken in the region (Richardson 1994).

In short, the demands for greater harmonisation of domestic policies for competitiveness reasons, coupled with the greening of world politics and the growing interest in worker and other human rights beyond national borders, are likely to put the WTO and trade policy under pressure to perform tasks for which they were not designed and are not well suited—and at a time when the WTO needs first to consolidate its role in the world and ensure the implementation of the Uruguay Round before moving into these new and much more controversial issues.

In addition to being affected *indirectly* by these new challenges to the multilateral trading system, Asian economic growth is also being affected *directly* by several trade policy developments abroad. Two developments in particular deserve attention and are discussed below: the regional integration initiatives of Europe and North America, and the aggressive unilateral tactics of the United States.

8.5 Direct Effects on Asia of European and American Regional Integration Initiatives[13]

Apart from their systemic effects on the multilateral trading system, the deepening and widening of economic integration in Europe and North America have at least three important direct effects on excluded economies. The rest of the world's trade with those regions is affected by what the integration initiatives do to the integrating regions' rates of economic growth, to their comparative advantages, and—the focus of much attention in Asia—to their external trade and foreign investment barriers. Each of these effects will be considered in turn.

8.5.1 Effects on Economic Growth Rates

It is impossible to be precise about the effects of closer economic integration on output and income growth in Western Europe and North America. But it is noteworthy that between the late 1950s and the late 1980s, Western Europe's share of global GDP rose from a quarter to a third. While this is less than the spectacular growth achievement of East Asia's market economies, it clearly outperforms much of the rest of the world. At least some of that superior achievement may be attributable to the trade liberalizations associated with the formation of the EC and EFTA. Furthermore, a simulation exercise by Baldwin (1989) suggests, under various assumptions, that the EC1992 Single Market program could raise the EC's GDP growth rate by at least a further 0.6 of a percentage point per year. Even more impressive gains are being suggested for Mexico as a result of NAFTA. Both Kehoe (1992) and McCleary (1992), for example, suggest Mexico's GDP growth rate could be raised because of NAFTA by more than 1.5 percentage points per year (see also McKibbin (1994)). Mexico's economy is too small for its addition to the Canada–U.S. FTA to have a significant effect on U.S. and Canadian growth rates, but the effect nonetheless is likely to be positive.[14]

8.5.2 Effects on Comparative Advantages

These regions' faster economic growth, more efficient location and use of productive factors, and induced investment will be accompanied by changes in comparative advantages. Standard trade and development theory, such as provided by Leamer (1987), offers a guide as to what to expect from the growth in their effective availability of man-made capital relative to labor time and natural resources. Other things being equal, their integration initiatives are likely to strengthen their comparative advantages in capital-intensive (including skill-intensive) industrial and service activities at the expense of primary production and labor-intensive manufacturing.

Such changes would appear to be good news for resource rich Australasia and for East Asia's developing countries which export either primary products or labor-intensive manufactures in exchange for capital-intensive goods and services: both their volume and terms of trade would improve. These changes would tend to have the opposite effect on many of Japan's firms, however, for Japan would face stronger competition from Western Europe and North America. A few empirical studies are available to provide estimates of the orders of magnitude that might be involved. One is by Stoeckel, Pearce and Banks (1990). It uses a straightforward non-dynamic computable general equilibrium model of the world economy to estimate the welfare effects of the EC1992 Single Market program. That study suggests that Australasia would gain about 0.2 percent of its GDP, that East Asia's developing countries would gain 0.1 percent of their GDP, and that Japan would lose 0.07 percent of its GDP. A more recent and more detailed simulation study by Haaland and Norman (1992) provides almost the same result for Japan (a 0.08 percent loss). But these studies ignore an important change in the past decade, namely, the emergence of Northeast Asia as a major net exporter of capital. Insofar as integration initiatives provide new foreign investment opportunities for excluded economies, this increased demand for its surplus savings would more or less offset the loss to Japan from greater competition in markets for capital-intensive goods and services.

8.5.3 Effects on External Trade and Investment Barriers

There are legitimate concerns that the above potential benefits for the Western Pacific, from faster economic growth and changes in comparative advantages in Western Europe and North America, may be offset by the raising of external barriers to trade and investment—a "fortress Europe" or "fortress America" fear. Even the current external barriers create incentives for trade diversion as internal barriers are lowered. In the case of North America, for example, NAFTA effectively will provide the U.S. and Canada with a larger supply of low-priced labor. As a consequence, Mexico will be able to provide a home for a greater share of those footloose industries that are able to supply the expanding North American market and are attracted by low wages.

What is the likelihood of barriers to imports from the Western Pacific being raised by these blocs? In the case of Western Europe, strengthened internal competition will impose structural adjustment pressures on numerous industries. The better organised among those industries (including textiles and motor vehicles) may well be successful in seeking protection from the full force of the adjustment pressures. And insofar as Eastern European producers are insulated via Association Accords from such increased protection, most of the burden would fall on East Asia.

In the case of North America, since it is a free trade area rather than a customs union, the main fear is a rise in U.S. external barriers, including the use of strict interpretations of rules of origin.[15] Whether U.S. trade barriers rise depends in part on how well the U.S. perceives it is being treated by its trading partners, a point to which attention is now turned.

8.6   Aggressive Unilateralism, Particularly by the U.S.

The past decade is full of examples of occasions when the U.S. has blamed declining U.S. competitiveness on external factors. The introduction of NAFTA during a recession has added a further reason for U.S. protectionists to demand higher external trade barriers, and for battling U.S. exporters to demand the greater use of aggressive unilateral tactics to obtain greater market access overseas, most notably in the trade-surplus economies of East Asia.

Japan is an especially obvious target for unilateral action unnder Section 301 and Super 301 of the U.S. trade acts. Japan not only has an overall trade surplus but a strong bilateral trade surplus with the U.S.. Moreover, as noted above from part (iii) of Table 8.3, its trade-to-GDP ratio has grown very little relative to that of other industrial countries, leaving it vulnerable to the criticism that it has been opening up its markets less than have other countries. Japan may well claim that the share of GDP traded extra-regionally is no different for Japan than for North America or Western Europe (see Table 8.4), but such claims are likely to have much less impact in improving U.S. perceptions of Japanese trade policies than would increases in import penetration ratios. That fact, unfortunately, has led to calls for the setting by the U.S. of quantitative import targets to be achieved by Japan, with failure to do so triggering punitive restrictions on imports by the U.S. of Japanese goods. The possibility of U.S. policy moving further down this path of managed trade is justifiably worrying not just for Japan but for all supporters of a non-discriminatory, open, rules-based multilateral trading system (Bhagwati and Patrick 1991).[16] This is especially so because U.S. demands are typically not for more access for imports in general (for example, of cellular phones or beef) under freer trade but for particular imports of U.S. products (for example, Motorola phones and grain-fed beef) under quantitatively managed trade.

And of course China has been vulnerable to U.S. demands for such things as improved human rights before the U.S. Congress would renew its extension of most-favored-nation treatment to U.S. imports from China each June.

Even if the enhanced dispute settlement mechanism of the WTO and China's membership in the Organization help to reduce the frequency and severity of U.S. unilateral actions of these types, there are at least two other worrying aspects of U.S. trade policy trends. One is the possibility of the U.S. signing "free" trade agreements with other countries, Chile being the most likely candidate in the medium-term. That hub-and-spoke development is likely to be much less beneficial or more harmful to excluded economies than a clean customs union or multi-country FTA, for the reasons mentioned earlier (see Snape, Adams and Morgan (1993)). Even the idea of a discriminatory Asia-Pacific FTA that has been promoted by the U.S. recently is still inferior economically to the idea of open regionalism characterized by unilateral or regional trade liberalization on a most-favored-nation basis. And the other worrying aspect of U.S. policy is the interest in putting social issues such as environmental and labor standards on the WTO's already overcrowded work agenda, despite the fact that the countries of Latin America, Asia and Africa would rather see those issues debated elsewhere than in the WTO.

8.7   How should East Asia Respond?

Just as there are three levels of trade challenges facing East Asia (multilateral, regional, and unilateral), so too are there opportunities to act and react at these three levels. The most obvious immediate priority at the multilateral level was for the Uruguay Round to be ratified in 1994–95 so that the WTO could come into being during 1995 ready to deal with not only its enlarged routine work program but also the potentially damaging threats to it from the promotion of regionalism, environmentalism, labor standards, and aggressive unilateralism. A necessary condition for that will be a substantial expansion in the budget of the WTO. Considerably more (permanent or consultant) staff will be needed to cope with (a) the ever growing work load of the Trade Policy Review Body and others charged with monitoring the implementation of the Uruguay Round agreements, (b) the backlog of disputes postponed during the Round, not to mention the inevitable testing of the new rules under the enhanced dispute settlement mechanism, (c) the flood of applications for WTO membership, particularly from the former centrally planned economies, and (d) the need for more legal and economic research on the new agenda items mentioned above plus others such as competition policy.[17] With respect to research on the trade/environment and trade/labor standards issues, it is especially important for the trade policy community to be immediately proactive, for to not do so runs the risk that open trading regimes and the WTO will be made scapegoats for perceived problems whose causes and hence solutions lie elsewhere. More research is needed on the effects both of liberalizing trade in products and capital on the environment and workers, and of raising environmental and labor standards on trade and economic welfare in poor as well as rich countries.

To the more specific issue of the proliferation of regional integration agreements in Europe and America, the excluded economies of East Asia and Australasia could respond in one or more of several ways. One response is simply to continue to search imaginatively for ways to circumvent these blocs' import barriers and to meet the rules of origin associated with direct foreign investment within the bloc. Non-tariff barriers to trade have been found to be porous in the past (Yoffie 1983), and they are likely to continue to be so in the future. A second obvious response is to invest more both in lobbying for better market access and in actual manufacturing within Western Europe and North America. A more radical third possibility is to take up former President Bush's offer to seek membership in NAFTA or in an FTA with the U.S.—although it might be more desirable for North American and East Asian countries to join ANZCERTA since the latter is a much "cleaner", less distorting agreement!

Outsiders are also likely to consider forming closer links and perhaps even new regional integration agreements with other excluded economies. Within East Asia we have already seen in recent years a deepening integration of the economies of mainland China, Hong Kong and Taiwan (Chia and Lee 1993; Jones, King and Klein 1993), the signing of the AFTA free trade agreement by the ASEAN countries, the proposal for an East Asian Economic Caucus (EAEC), and various attempts to give more life to the Asia-Pacific Economic Co-operation (APEC) concept. The hope is that all of these initiatives will lead to a strengthening of the MFN-based open regionalism that has characterized the East Asian region in recent decades and set it apart from the more discriminatory regionalism elsewhere (Young 1993).

It is unlikely to be in the economic interests of this region to form an inward-looking trading bloc, because of the risks of losses from not only trade diversion but also retaliatory closure of export markets outside the region. Nor is it likely to be politically feasible for an entire East Asian, Western Pacific, or broader Pacific rim free trade area to form, for the following reasons. First, the smaller East Asian countries would be unlikely to form a trade bloc with Japan alone for fear of Japanese domination in the absence of a North American counterweight. And for domestic political reasons it is unlikely North America would be able to join such a bloc in the near future—after all, much of U.S. trade policy during the past two decades has been aimed at *reducing* imports from East Asia and Australasia. Similarly, governments in Northeast Asia have found it difficult politically to reduce their barriers to agricultural and other processed primary products from North America or even just from Australasia. In short, the high degree of potential (as distinct from actual) trade complementarity that would exist between freely trading resource-rich and resource-poor Pacific rim countries works against the political feasibility of creating a free trade area in the region (Drysdale and Garnaut 1989).

Instead, the interests of the Chinese and East Asian economies generally will continue to be served best by the maintenance and strengthening of an open multilateral trading system under the WTO. That can be facilitated in various ways. One is by promoting trade liberalization in the Asia-Pacific region itself. Fortuitously, even if this is done on a non-discriminatory, most-favored-nation basis as discussed in APEC circles, most of the benefits would be reaped within the region because of strong intra-regional trade bias (for reasons of economic and cultural proximity) and strong (and potentially much stronger) trade complementarity among the economies of the region.[18]

Finally, one other way for APEC countries to strengthen the multilateral trading system is to play a leading role in shaping the debate on trade policy and the new issues on the WTO's agenda. The APEC region is a microcosm of the world with a rich variety of economies (rich, poor, resource-abundant, resource-scarce). And yet there is a great deal of goodwill among them, so the chances of examining these issues calmly is much greater in an APEC forum than in the larger-number forum of the WTO. The November 1994 meeting of APEC Heads of Government in Bogor, Indonesia, offers an opportunity to encourage that. Recently APEC, in conjunction with PECC, developed an investment code; a similar process might be used to develop positions on the interactions between trade and environment, labor standards, and/or competition policy. For that to be successful, further (including quantitative) research efforts on the new issues may be necessary. The challenge will be to use that research output to convince the wider community that trade and payments liberalization can be consistent not only with economic growth but also with sustainable development, improved labor and environmental standards, and even improved political freedom and other human rights.

Notes

This chapter was prepared for a conference on China and East Asian Trade Policy, Australian National University, Canberra, September 1–2, 1994. An earlier version was presented at a conference on Challenges and Opportunities for East Asian Trade, ANU, July 13–14, 1994. Thanks are due to Hugh Corbet, Andrew Elek, David Robertson and other conference participants for helpful comments, and to ANU's Australia–Japan Research Centre and National Centre for Development Studies, and the Australian Research Council, for financial support.

1. The Asian data in Tables 8.3 and 8.4 include South Asia and Australasia, but their shares are quite small so the general trends for East Asia are very similar to those shown for Asia.
2. This is not to say those complaints are fully justified, although it is telling that the share of Japan's GDP that was traded during the inter-war period, when it had closer to free trade with its colonised neighbors, was up to twice as large as its share in recent decades. For discussions on the extent to which the trade-to-GDP ratio for one country relative to the rest of the world can be used as a measure of openness, and in particular on the extent to which it indicates the degree of openness of the Japanese economy, see, for example, Leamer (1988), Srinivasan (1991), and Lawrence (1992).
3. Again a comparison between the interwar-period and present-day indexes for Japan provides some striking results: its propensity to trade intra-regionally is no higher now than in the late 1920s, and its index of propensity to trade extra-regionally in 1990 was less than one-third that of the inter-war period.
4. These data refer only to merchandise trade; the increase would be even greater if services trade were to be included.
5. The Japanese might call them *tama-mushi* agreements, after the *tama-mushi* beetle which has translucent wings that appear as different colors depending on the angle of the viewer and the sunlight.
6. For a more detailed discussion of this issue see the volume of papers prepared as background for the special coverage of this topic by the GATT Secretariat (Anderson and Blackhurst 1993).
7. For further discussion of this issue see the 1992 GATT annual report and the volume of papers prepared as background for the special coverage of this topic in that report (GATT 1992; Anderson and Blackhurst 1992).
8. Since the services of the natural environment are normal (and possibly superior) goods in the sense that more of them is demanded as incomes rise, and since the supply of many of those services is limited to differing extents across countries depending on population density, the degree of enforcement of property rights, and so forth, it is not surprising that environmental standards differ across countries and change at different rates over time (Anderson 1993).
9. For a more detailed discussion on the phenomenon of the capture of proponents of these

issues by traditional protectionists, see Anderson and Blackhurst (1992: Chapters 10 and 11).

10. The history is patchy but goes back a hundred years (Charnovitz 1987).

11. This is opposite to the case of the environment, where concerns tend to fluctuate pro-cyclically.

12. France has also been encouraged to seek the addition of this issue to the WTO's agenda following its qualified success in getting a "social charter" signed by EU member governments at Maastricht.

13. This section draws on Anderson (1991) and Anderson and Snape (1994). See also the paper at this conference by Snape (1994).

14. An important caveat to keep in mind with ex ante empirical studies, however, is that typically they ignore the rules of origin and anti-dumping and countervailing duty provisions to be applied within the bloc, the effects of which (a dampening of intra-regional trade and GDP growth) become clear only well after the agreement has been passed into law.

15. For a discussion on the risk of rules of origin effectively raising an integrating region's external trade barriers to the highest tariff equivalent in the region, see Krueger (1992).

16. The motivation for U.S. unilateral trade policy action unfortunately is not restricted to claims of unfair trading practices. It has also been triggered by, for example, concerns about human rights in China which led to threats to withdraw China's most-favored-nation status as an exporter to the U.S.; by concerns about lack of progress on resolving missing-in-action cases in Vietnam, which until this year had prevented trade and investment by Americans in Vietnam; and by Norway's decision to resume some limited whaling in the light of evidence presented to the International Whaling Convention that Minky Whale numbers are no longer endangered, which led to U.S. threats to violate its GATT obligations to provide market access for Norwegian fish. The latter action is similar to but less subtle (more obviously GATT illegal) than the unilateral action the U.S. took against Mexico in its dispute over the use of dolphin-unfriendly tuna nets.

17. The research challenges include looking for ways to harness the energy of groups seeking higher environmental and labor standards such that these groups support, rather than oppose, trade liberalization. The cases of coal and food trade liberalization were mentioned in section 8.4.2 as examples of cases when trade liberalization is likely to be environmentally friendly (Anderson and Blackhurst 1992: Chapter 8). But convincing agnostics and skeptics that trade liberalization does not necessarily worsen the global environment is sure to require much more quantitative economic/environmental modelling, a task that will make conventional economic modelling appear simple (Powell 1993; Anderson and Strutt 1995).

18. The trade complementarity among Asia-Pacific economies traditionally had been strongest in inter-sectoral trade (raw materials for finished manufactures), and then also in inter-industry trade (labor-intensive for capital-intensive manufactures), but most of the trade growth now is in intra-industry trade in manufactures and services as the economies develop and their economic integration deepens.

References

Anderson, K., 1991, "Europe 1992 and the Western Pacific Economies," *Economic Journal*, 101(409): 1538–52.

———, 1993, "Economic Growth, Environmental Issues, and Trade," in M. Noland (ed.), *Pacific Dynamism and the International Economic System*, Institute for International Economics, Washington, DC, Ch. 11.

————, 1994, "Agricultural Policies and the New World Trading System," in G. Raby (ed.), *The New World Trading System*, OECD, Paris, Ch. 16.

Anderson, K. and R. Blackhurst (eds.), 1992, *The Greening of World Trade Issues*, Harvester Wheatsheaf, London, and University of Michigan Press, Ann Arbor, MI.

———— (eds.), 1993, *Regional Integration and the Global Trading System*, Harvester Wheatsheaf, London, and St. Martin's Press, New York.

Anderson, K. and H. Norheim, 1993, "Is World Trade Becoming More Regionalized?" *Review of International Economics*, 1(2): 91–109.

Anderson, K. and R. H. Snape, 1994, "European and American Regionalism: Effects on and Options for Asia," *Journal of the Japanese and International Economies*, 8(4): 454–77.

Anderson, K. and A. Strutt, 1995, "On Measuring the Environmental Impacts of Agricultural Trade Liberalization," in M. E. Bredahl (ed.), *Agriculture, Trade, and the Environment: Discovering and Measuring the Critical Linkages*, Westview Press, Boulder, CO.

Baldwin, R., 1989, "On the Growth Effects of 1992," *Economic Policy*, 9 (Fall): 247–81.

————, 1995, "Does Sustainability Require Growth?" in I. Goldin and L. A. Winters (eds.), *The Economics of Sustainable Development*, Cambridge University Press, Cambridge.

Bhagwati, J. and H. T. Patrick (eds.), 1991, *Aggressive Unilateralism: America's 301 Trade Policy and the World Trading System*, University of Michigan Press, Ann Arbor, MI.

Charnovitz, S., 1987, "The Influence of International Labor Standards on the World Trading Regime: An Overview," *International Labor Review*, 126(5): 565–84.

Chia, S. Y. and T. Y. Lee, 1993, "Subregional Economic Zones: A New Motive Force in Asian-Pacific Development," in M. Noland (ed.), *Pacific Dynamism and the International Economic System*, Institute for International Economics, Washington, DC, Ch. 7.

Drysdale, P. and R. Garnaut, 1989, "A Pacific Free Trade Area?" in J. Schott (ed.), *Free Trade Areas and U.S. Trade Policy*, Institute for International Economics, Washington, DC.

GATT, 1987, *International Trade 1986–87*, GATT Secretariat, Geneva.

————, 1992, *International Trade 1991–92*, GATT Secretariat, Geneva.

————, 1994, *International Trade Statistics 1994*, GATT Secretariat, Geneva.

Grossman, G. M., 1995, "Pollution and Growth: What Do We Know?" in I. Goldin and L. A. Winters (eds.), *The Economics of Sustainable Development*, Cambridge University Press, Cambridge.

Haaland, J. I. and V. D. Norman, 1992, "Global Production Effects of European Integration," in L. A. Winters (ed.), *Trade Flows and Trade Policy After '1992,'* Cambridge University Press, Cambridge, Ch. 3.

Hoekman, B. M. and P. C. Mavroidis, 1994, "Competition, Competition Policy, and the GATT," *World Economy*, 17(2): 121–50.

Jones, R., R. King, and M. Klein, 1993, "Economic Integration Between Hong Kong, Taiwan and the Coastal Provinces of China," *OECD Economic Studies*, 20 (Winter): 114–44.

Kehoe, T. J., 1992, "Modelling the Dynamic Impact of North American Free Trade," in *Economy-wide Modelling of the Economic Implications of a FTA with Mexico and a NAFTA with Canada and Mexico*, Publication 2508, U.S. International Trade Commission, Washington, DC.

Krueger, A. O., 1992, "Free Trade Agreements as Protectionist Devices: Rules of Origin," Duke University, Durham, NC, mimeo.

Lawrence, R. Z., 1992, "How Open is Japan?" in P. Krugman (ed.), *Trade with Japan: Has the Door Opened Wider?* University of Chicago Press, Chicago, IL, Ch. 1.

————, 1993, "Regionalism, Multilateralism and Deeper Integration," draft monograph for the Brookings Institution project on "Integrating the World Economy," Washington, DC, mimeo.

————, 1994, "Trade, Multinationals, and Labor," in P. Lowe and J. Dwyer (eds.), *International Integration of the Australian Economy*, Reserve Bank of Australia, Sydney, pp. 233–65.

Leamer, E. E., 1987, "Paths of Development in the Three-Factor, n-Good General Equilibrium Model," *Journal of Political Economy*, 95(5): 961–99.

———, 1988, "Measures of Openness," in R. E. Baldwin (ed.), *Trade Policy Issues and Empirical Analysis*, University of Chicago Press, Chicago, IL.

McCleary, R. K., 1992, "An Inter-temporal, Linked, Macroeconomic CGE Model of the United States and Mexico, Focusing on Demographic Change and Factor Flows," in *Economy-wide Modelling of the Economic Implications of a FTA with Mexico and a NAFTA with Canada and Mexico*, Publication 2508, U.S. International Trade Commission, Washington, DC.

McKibbin, W. J., 1994, "Dynamic Adjustment to Regional Integration: Europe 1992 and NAFTA," *Journal of the Japanese and International Economies*, 8(4): 422–53.

Powell, A. A., 1993, *Integrating Econometric and Environmetric Modelling*, General Paper No. G-102, Centre of Policy Studies and the Impact Project, Melbourne.

Radetski, M., 1992, "Economic Growth and Environment," in P. Low (ed.), *International Trade and the Environment*, Discussion Paper 159, World Bank, Washington, DC.

Richardson, J. D., 1994, "Competition Policies as Irritants to Asia-Pacific Trade," paper presented at the ANU Conference on Challenges and Opportunities for East Asian Trade, Canberra, July 13–14.

Snape, R. H., 1994, "Impact of NAFTA on the East Asian Economies," paper presented at the ANU Conference on China and East Asian Trade Policy, Canberra, September 1–2.

Snape, R. H., J. Adams, and D. Morgan, 1993, *Regional Trade Agreements: Implications and Options for Australia*, Australian Government Publishing Service for the Department of Foreign Affairs and Trade, Canberra.

Srinivasan, T. N., 1991, "Is Japan an Outlier Among Trading Countries?" in J. de Melo and A. Sapir (eds.), *Trade Theory and Economic Reform: Essays in Honour of Bela Balassa*, Basil Blackwell, Oxford, Ch. 11.

Stoeckel, A., D. Pearce, and G. Banks, 1990, *Western Trading Blocs: Game, Set or Match for Asia Pacific and the World Economy*, Centre for International Economics, Canberra.

Wood, A., 1994, *North-South Trade, Employment and Inequality: Changing Fortunes in a Skill-driven World*, Clarendon Press, Oxford.

World Bank, 1994, *World Development Report 1994*, Oxford University Press, New York.

Yoffie, D. B., 1983, *Power and Protectionism: Strategies of the Newly Industrializing Countries*, Columbia University Press, New York.

Young, S., 1993, "East Asia as a Regional Force for Globalism," in K. Anderson and R. Blackhurst (eds.), *Regional Integration and the Global Trading System*, Harvester Wheatsheaf, London, and St. Martin's Press, New York, Ch. 6.

Chapter 9

Gabriel Hawawini
Jocelyn Probert

EC TRADE AND INVESTMENT RELATIONS WITH THE DEVELOPING ASIA-PACIFIC ECONOMIES: EVOLUTION IN THE 1980s

9.1 Introduction

When Eastern European countries emerged from central economic planning systems at the turn of the 1990s, fears were expressed in the developing countries of Asia[1] that the trade and investment of the European Community (EC) would be diverted away from Asia in favor of these newly opened countries on the doorstep of the world's largest trading block. These fears seem somewhat overdrawn, considering that EC trade and investment patterns hardly reveal a profound interest in developing Asia. European business interests appear to be largely unimpressed by the heady growth rates of the major economies of Asia during the last two to three decades, to judge by their seeming failure to rise to the challenges and opportunities presented by the increasing flow of goods, technology, services and investments within the Asia-Pacific region. A clear discrepancy has emerged between, on the one hand, the earnest declarations at the individual government or European Commission level of the importance of the Asian region, and, on the other, of the steps taken either politically or economically to demonstrate this belief.

The European presence in Asia dates as far back as the days of the spice traders in the thirteenth century. Until 50 years ago, European firms dominated the economic scene in Southeast Asia. Since then American and, more recently, Japanese interests have overtaken European shares of foreign investment in practically every country in the region. The enunciation of Malaysian Prime Minister Mahathir's "Look East" policy in late 1981 has hastened this trend and ensured that no "special relationship" endures between any EC member country and its former territory. More recently, Korean, Taiwanese and Hong Kong companies have themselves emerged as major investors in Southeast Asia, further challenging the position of European business interests. Although individual home country statistics for certain EC members may indicate absolute growth in investments in developing Asia, the decline in the relative share for European countries continues. Today, European investment is underrepresented throughout Asia with the possible exception of Singapore.

Reasons for the relative decline in European activity can be found at the political, economic and business level. The creation of a framework to achieve harmonization of individual country regulations and the removal of barriers to internal trade within the European Community has dominated European affairs. The effect of this preoccupation with intra-EC affairs, which has included a lack of attention to the potential impact on extra-EC nations of a single European market, has been a benign neglect of relationships with regions which are neither principal trading partners nor enjoy a special relationship with the EC (such as the African–Caribbean–Pacific (ACP) country grouping).

The reluctance of European countries to develop business relationships with developing Asian countries is not, however, mirrored by these countries' efforts to build trading links with Europe. From the viewpoint of the members of the Association of Southeast Asian Nations (ASEAN)[2] and the three Asian newly industrialising economies (ANIEs),[3] the EC is an important business partner. Whereas the ANIEs and ASEAN account for 2.4 percent and 1.6 percent, respectively, of EC total trade, the reverse relative flow is more significant: the EC accounts for slightly less than 14 percent of the ANIEs' total trade, and for just under 15 percent of trade for ASEAN[4] in 1991. Although the United States remains the most important destination for ANIEs capital, increasingly investments by Korean and Taiwanese firms are taking place within the EC. These investments within the EC are generally defensive investments undertaken to avoid perceived or actual EC barriers to imports.

The rest of this chapter is organized as follows. After a review in Section 9.2 of the EC's external trade relations, this chapter examines trade patterns and trends between the EC and the ANIEs (Section 9.3), ASEAN (Section 9.4), and China

(Section 9.5). Policy issues in EC–Asian trade are discussed in Section 9.6. Section 9.7 looks at the competitiveness of EC exporters and Section 9.8 examines the foreign direct investment policies and patterns in the developing countries of Asia. Asian foreign direct investment in the EC is covered in Section 9.9 and concluding remarks make up the final section.

9.2 EC External Trade Relations

The 12 countries of the EC together form the largest economic grouping in the world, with a combined GDP more than twice the size of Japan's and 12 percent greater than that of the United States. In 1991, combined exports (including intra-EC trade) amounted to US$1,370 billion, compared with imports of US$1,470 billion. Stripping out trade between EC member states, EC exports to the world, at US$525 billion, are nearly 25 percent greater than those of the United States and two-thirds greater than Japan's, while imports of US$610 billion are greater by 20 percent and 160 percent, respectively.

In per capita terms, however, West European trade with third countries is modest. The biggest trading partner for each individual EC member country is a fellow EC member. The proportion of intra-EC trade has grown significantly since the formal establishment of the European Community in 1957, and is expected to continue to expand as internal barriers to trade within the Community are removed. In the year after the Treaty of Rome was signed, intra-EC exports accounted for slightly more than a third of total EC trade; by 1979 54 percent of exports came from other EC countries, and in 1991 that share had reached 62 percent. The same trend can be seen in intra-EC imports, which rose from 33 percent in 1958 to 50 percent in 1979 and 58 percent in 1991.

The net result of the EC's growing preoccupation with its internal affairs has been a decline in share, experienced by developed and developing countries alike, for third party trade with the EC. Despite a growing preference among industrialized nations to trade with each other, the United States share of EC imports has fallen sharply, to just under 8 percent in 1991 from 11 percent in 1958, although the United States remains the largest external supplier of goods to the EC. This decline has been partially offset by the increased penetration of Japanese imports in the EC market over the last three decades (a development which has not been reciprocated by increased EC exports to Japan), 4.5 percent of the goods imported by the EC in 1991 came from Japan, compared with 0.7 percent in the year the foundations of the EC were laid.

In light of these trends, developing countries as a whole have been significant losers: they accounted for a mere 17 percent of EC imports in 1991, down from 30 percent in 1958; and for 16 percent of exports against 29 percent in 1958. Within the developing countries grouping, however, Asian nations—China, the ANIEs and ASEAN—have substantially outperformed competing developing economies, increasing their share in EC imports from non-OECD countries to over 30 percent by 1991, from just 16 percent in 1970. This has been achieved by maintaining competitiveness in more traditional manufactures such as clothing and textiles, while becoming newly competitive in such sectors as electronic machinery and transport equipment. Table 9.1 shows the trade pattern between the EC and developing East Asia in 1985 and 1990. Other developing regions have been less able to emulate this performance.

The year 1991 was the first time trade between Western Europe and the Asia-Pacific region surpassed transatlantic trade, suggesting strong and growing links between the two regions. All the same, in that same year total EC imports from the 11 major economies of East Asia (Japan, China, the three ANIEs and the six members of ASEAN) totalled US$143 billion, roughly equivalent in value only to the EC's imports from France. Excluding Japan from the equation, imports from East Asia fall to US$77 billion.

9.3   EC–ANIEs Trade Relations

In 1991 the ANIEs' exports to and imports from the EC totalled nearly US$70 billion. As pointed out above, this represents slightly less than 14 percent of the ANIEs' total trade and 2.4 percent of EC world trade. In 1985, the shares were 10.4 percent and 1.4 percent, respectively, suggesting healthy growth in the relationship. Yen appreciation against the dollar after the Plaza accord in 1985 allowed the ANIEs to challenge some of Japan's export market shares, principally in Asian markets. Europe became a target for exports, both as a result of attempts to diversify export markets away from the United States, and because of the attractiveness of the EC as a market in its own right.

South Korea, Taiwan and Hong Kong together run large and growing trade surpluses with the EC. The trade balance in their favor exceeded US$10 billion in 1991 (including some overlap between Hong Kong and China trade, as mentioned above), against US$1.2 billion in 1985. The size of their surplus with the United States, however, was more than US$22 billion. The ANIEs trade account with Japan, on the other hand, shows a substantial deficit of close to US$30 billion. Although superficially the deficit with Japan is erased by the surpluses with the EC and the United States, the critical factor for the ANIEs, and particularly Korea, is their ability to reduce dependence on Japan for high technology components. While trade negotiators in Korea demand greater access to Japanese markets and help to reduce their deficit, officials in the EC and the United States request more favorable trading conditions for their products in Asian markets and restraint on exports from Asia to the West.

Relations between Korea and the EC have been strained by the concentration of 60 percent of EC-bound Korean exports in just four sectors: textiles and apparel, electrical and electronic machinery, steel, and transportation equipment. Korean reluctance to extend to the EC the same guarantees on intellectual property rights

TABLE 9.1   EC/developing East Asia trade, by SITC single-digit classification, 1985 and 1990 (US$ million)

	EC imports		EC exports	
	1985	1990	1985	1990
EC/ASEAN				
SITC 0 Food and live animals	1,719.4	2,778.9	254.2	580.6
1 Beverages and tobacco	110.8	126.1	155.0	516.7
2 Crude materials, excl. fuels	1,381.7	1,951.3	49.4	213.6
3 Mineral fuels	190.6	153.9	37.8	163.6
4 Animal and vegetable oils	698.4	772.4	8.9	21.3
5 Chemicals	147.5	302.3	1,254.0	2,725.4
6 Manufactures class. by material	1,022.5	2,605.5	1,073.1	2,899.3
7 Machinery and transport equipment	1,910.4	7,798.5	3,750.3	10,298.9
8 Misc. manufactures	863.4	5,296.8	709.5	1,789.5
9 Other	64.1	110.2	168.1	250.0
Total	8,108.8	21,896.3	7,459.6	19,459.2
EC/China				
SITC 0 Food and live animals	341.1	770.9	65.1	279.9
1 Beverages and tobacco	5.9	15.5	7.0	1.3
2 Crude materials, excl. fuels	722.8	962.8	241.7	215.2
3 Mineral fuels	132.3	163.9	4.8	12.0
4 Animal and vegetable oils	43.1	46.4	8.9	136.1
5 Chemicals	320.2	785.8	782.0	743.0
6 Manufactures class. by material	622.1	1,895.2	1,417.0	678.3
7 Machinery and transport equipment	51.1	1,654.8	2,624.3	4,067.5
8 Misc. manufactures	699.4	5,837.3	264.1	310.0
9 Other	27.1	30.2	42.3	142.2
Total	2,965.0	12,162.8	5,457.3	6,585.3
EC/ANIEs				
SITC 0 Food and live animals	135.2	244.4	198.5	558.9
1 Beverages and tobacco	7.3	77.6	159.1	653.7
2 Crude materials, excl. fuels	123.8	183.4	190.7	507.5
3 Mineral fuels	5.2	9.4	25.0	68.1
4 Animal and vegetable oils	1.3	1.8	25.8	46.2
5 Chemicals	114.3	485.3	1,402.7	3,671.1
6 Manufactures class. by material	1,232.6	3,579.7	1,381.5	3,991.1
7 Machinery and transport equipment	2,798.6	12,030.9	2,911.7	8,780.1
8 Misc. manufactures	5,228.7	13,018.1	870.1	2,916.5
9 Other	66.1	153.5	56.6	367.1
Total	9,779.0	29,784.3	7,221.8	21,560.2

Source: OECD, *Trade by Commodity*, Series C, 1990.

as it has granted to the United States has further soured the relationship. Taiwan, however, has escaped strong criticism by virtue of its more diversified export structure—and the absence of formal diplomatic relations.

A government-led campaign in Korea in the mid-1980s to reduce dependence on Japan for imports diverted some import trade away from Japan, but largely in favor of the United States, which has pressed more aggressively than the EC for the opening of Korean markets. European firms, on the other hand, were penalized by another government-inspired crusade to readjust the balance of payments in Korea's favor by limiting "unnecessary and luxurious imports," since European exports included such items as cars (the Korean market first opened to foreign car imports in 1987) and whisky (on which higher duties were payable than for locally produced alcohol). All the same, European exports to Korea trebled in 1985–89.

European exports of machinery and transport equipment to the ANIEs exceeded imports from the same region in 1985, but by 1990 imports were 50 percent higher. The small surplus the EC runs with Korea is about to disappear, since rapid growth in exports to the EC have not been matched by a similar surge in EC exports. Taiwanese exports of machinery have outstripped EC exports since the end of the 1970s: Taiwan is the largest supplier outside the OECD of specialized machinery (SITC[5] 72), metalworking machinery (SITC 73), and office machinery including computers (SITC 75). It was overtaken by Korea in 1985 as the main supplier of telecommunications and sound recording equipment (SITC 76), and now both Singapore and China have larger exports to the EC in this category. U.K. trade statistics show that the ANIEs plus Singapore increased their share of the office machinery imports from 9 percent to 11 percent of the market between 1989 and 1991, rivalling Japan's share, and accounted for 13 percent of telecommunications and sound recording equipment imports, compared with Japan's 10 percent and the United States' 29 percent.

The EC deficit with Taiwan and Korea in textile yarns is widening, whereas Hong Kong is a net importer of textiles from the EC for processing and re-export. Hong Kong and Korea are, respectively, the first and third largest contributors to the EC deficit in clothing with the region, which trebled to US$9.6 billion between 1985 and 1990. The overall growth rate in the ANIEs' textile industry has slowed in recent years, reflecting rising labor costs at home and currency appreciation which has brought smaller comparative advantages. Restructuring of the industry has encouraged the relocation of production facilities to ASEAN and, more recently, to lower labor cost countries such as China and Vietnam.

European, particularly German, firms have successfully penetrated the Korean market for various chemical goods, including tanning and dyeing materials (SITC 53). The ANIEs and the region as a whole are large buyers of chemical products from Europe. EC exports of professional and scientific instruments (SITC 87) continue to surpass ANIEs imports.

9.4   EC–ASEAN Trade Relations

9.4.1 Global Trade Patterns and Trends

The EC is ASEAN's third largest trading partner, behind Japan and the United States. The United States has traditionally been the principal export market for Asia-Pacific economies, including Japan. This reliance on the United States intensified in the early years of the 1980s. During the later years of the decade the trading relationship between ASEAN and the EC became significantly more important, as ASEAN countries sought to diversify their markets and reduce their dependence, particularly on Japan, as a source of industrial inputs. Although two-way trade with the EC saw a threefold increase in volume during the decade and now accounts for 14.4 percent of ASEAN's trade worldwide—against 11.4 percent in 1984, when world commodity prices were low, and both Europe and ASEAN were in recession. This share is still *below* the level of the 1970s, when trade with the EC exceeded 15 percent of all ASEAN trade. From the EC point of view, however, the weight of ASEAN trade in the EC total is very small, hovering between 1.15 percent and 1.25 percent in the early years of the 1980s though expanding more rapidly since 1988. By 1991, the ASEAN share of EC combined imports and exports had climbed to 1.63 percent (Table 9.2).

The pattern of trade between Europe and the member states of ASEAN during the 1960s and 1970s conformed to the typical North–South relationship. ASEAN was a supplier of primary commodities (natural rubber, palm oil, tapioca, timber, tin) to the EC, from which it imported machinery and other capital goods as well as consumer products. Thus, there was a clear distinction at that time between the composition of ASEAN's imports and its exports. ASEAN trade with the EC during this period was mostly in surplus, but because of the greater importance to ASEAN of trade with the EC than vice-versa (a situation which endures today) the trade relationship was one of "significant dependence" rather than inter-dependence (Harris and Bridges 1983). The promising size of the EC market for ASEAN primary products afforded the EC considerable influence over quantity and price, such that economic slowdown in Europe in the opening years of the 1980s exerted a noticeable direct and indirect effect on the economies of Southeast Asia.

Growing manufacturing competence among ASEAN members as a result of individual governments' progressively more export-oriented trade and investment policies have in recent years wrought significant changes in the composition of trade with the EC. The success of ASEAN and the ANIEs in taking share from other developing countries is in large measure attributable to these policies. Agricultural and raw materials, which in 1973 represented nearly 70 percent of ASEAN exports to the EC, by 1990 accounted for barely a quarter of the total, while in the decade 1980–1990, the share of manufactured goods in ASEAN exports to the EC more than doubled to 73 percent. This is a considerably higher share of manufactures than appears in ASEAN's worldwide export composition.

TABLE 9.2 EC exports to and imports from ASEAN countries, 1980–91 (US$ million)

EC exports to:	1980	1981	1982	1983	1984	1985	1986	1987	1988	1989	1990	1991
Indonesia	1,738	2,330	2,952	2,178	1,918	1,734	1,845	1,977	2,266	2,236	3,548	3,902
Malaysia	1,441	1,547	1,292	1,493	1,548	1,182	1,286	1,358	1,617	2,226	3,177	3,609
Philippines	824	821	819	973	531	482	642	941	1,068	1,307	1,533	1,356
Singapore	2,386	2,353	2,525	2,499	2,733	2,878	2,830	3,686	4,706	5,507	7,056	6,959
Thailand	1,008	1,027	881	1,151	1,043	1,259	1,474	1,895	2,436	3,042	4,374	4,703
ASEAN total (A)	7,397	8,078	8,469	8,294	7,773	7,535	8,077	9,857	12,093	14,318	19,688	20,529
yr/yr growth (%)	23.7	9.2	4.8	−2.1	−6.3	−3.1	7.2	22.0	22.7	18.4	37.5	4.3
World total (US$bn) (B)	666	637	615	599	613	650	797	958	1,065	1,136	1,368	1,368
yr/yr growth (%)	15.3	−4.3	−3.5	−2.6	2.4	5.9	22.6	20.2	11.2	6.7	20.4	0.0
ASEAN share (%)	1.11	1.27	1.38	1.39	1.27	1.16	1.01	1.03	1.14	1.26	1.44	1.50

EC imports from:	1980	1981	1982	1983	1984	1985	1986	1987	1988	1989	1990	1991
Indonesia	1,637	1,359	1,212	1,249	1,284	1,438	1,544	1,920	2,478	2,741	3,547	4,317
Malaysia	2,470	2,106	1,812	1,987	2,363	2,246	2,281	2,909	3,550	4,177	4,974	5,917
Philippines	1,156	1,130	1,048	1,011	1,086	959	1,155	1,369	1,539	1,520	1,694	1,896
Singapore	1,997	1,589	1,524	1,765	1,898	1,778	2,203	2,965	3,883	4,976	6,689	7,169
Thailand	1,752	1,737	1,852	1,507	1,606	1,675	2,142	2,891	3,523	3,957	5,031	6,294
ASEAN total (C)	9,012	7,921	7,448	7,519	8,237	8,096	9,325	12,054	14,973	17,371	21,935	25,593
yr/yr growth (%)	17.7	−12.1	−6.0	1.0	9.5	−1.7	15.2	29.3	24.2	16.0	26.3	16.7
World total (US$bn) (D)	729	687	656	628	637	664	781	957	1,083	1,168	1,416	1,456
yr/yr growth (%)	19.3	−5.8	−4.5	−4.2	1.3	4.3	17.7	22.4	13.2	7.8	21.3	2.9
ASEAN share (%)	1.24	1.15	1.14	1.20	1.29	1.22	1.19	1.26	1.38	1.49	1.55	1.76

Trade balance:	1980	1981	1982	1983	1984	1985	1986	1987	1988	1989	1990	1991
with ASEAN (US$m)	−1,615	157	1,021	775	−464	−561	−1,248	−2,197	−2,880	−3,053	−2,247	−5,064
with world (US$bn)	−63.2	−49.8	−41.4	−29.5	−23.3	−14.4	15.1	0.7	−18	−31.8	−48.1	−88.3
ASEAN share of total EC trade (A+C/B+D)	1.18	1.21	1.25	1.29	1.28	1.19	1.10	1.14	1.26	1.38	1.50	1.63

Sources: IMF, *Direction of Trade Statistics*, various issues.

ASEAN exports of manufactured goods (SITC 5–8) to the EC quadrupled over the second half of the 1980s to US$16 billion by 1991, while trade in manufactured goods in the opposite direction rose 2.5 times, to US$18 billion. Substantial increases in United States imports of ASEAN manufactured goods have similarly been registered. In the case of Japan, however, ASEAN countries have found the manufactured goods market considerably more difficult to penetrate. Thus, the EC represents ASEAN's second largest market, behind the United States, for manufactured goods, while Japan is the largest supplier of all goods to the region.

EC exports to ASEAN countries have tended to grow more slowly than EC imports from ASEAN, in part because of the closer attention paid by the EC to export markets near to home and increased competition from Japan and elsewhere. ASEAN imports from the EC are primarily of machinery and transport equipment, but also chemicals and basic manufactures. Since the EC is not a supplier of mineral fuels to the region, manufactured goods make up approximately 90 percent of the total, against a 60 percent share of manufactured goods in all ASEAN imports.

Trade between the EC and ASEAN in the early 1980s showed a steady surplus for the EC, reversing the deficits of the late 1970s. Since 1986, however, the EC has again been importing more from ASEAN than it has managed to export, although the annual deficit has thus far been relatively small. This may change if the effect of German reunification is to continue to suck in large volumes of imports, which ASEAN and other Asian countries are well placed to supply. The United States in recent years has seen a marked increase in its trade deficit with ASEAN. Part of this trade diversion is due to increased activity in the ASEAN region by companies from the ANIEs which seek to deflect intensifying United States criticism over the substantial trade surplus they run with the United States. Europe, too, is experiencing this trend, as ANIEs firms seek to exploit unused ASEAN quotas for EC markets. Japan, on the other hand, runs a significant trade surplus with ASEAN reflecting demand from its locally based manufacturing operations for equipment and components. Little of the output from these plants is reimported to Japan, witness the low level of ASEAN manufactures exported there (and the decline in all nonoil exports to Japan from ASEAN, except for food products and nonferrous metals). Most production is instead destined for local consumption or for third markets, primarily the United States and Europe.

9.4.2 A Closer Look at Bilateral Trade Relations

Regional data mask significant inter-country variations in trade flows. In the early 1980s, exports from the Philippines and Singapore found their biggest market in the United States. Thailand exported principally to the EC, while Malaysia and Indonesia—by virtue of their oil and gas resources—sent most exports to Japan. By the end of the decade the United States had become the most important market for all ASEAN members except Indonesia, for whom Japan continues to be an important buyer of oil: over 40 percent of all Indonesian exports go to Japan.

The EC is the second largest buyer of goods from Singapore, Thailand and Indonesia.

On the reverse side of the trade coin, Japan is the principal source for imports by Singapore, Thailand, Malaysia and Indonesia, while the United States maintains its traditional role as main supplier to the Philippines. The EC has for more than a decade been the second largest supplier to Indonesia, and since 1985 has overtaken the United States to become the second largest exporter to Thailand.

Table 9.3 underlines the importance of Germany as an EC trading partner for ASEAN, and a growing one by virtue of the demand created by reunification. Together with the U.K. and the Netherlands, these three countries account for 75 percent of EC–ASEAN trade. Conspicuous is the minor role of France in trade with

TABLE 9.3   ASEAN's imports from and exports to major EC countries, 1987–91 (US$ million)

	Year	Indonesia M	Indonesia X	Malaysia M	Malaysia X	Philippines M	Philippines X	Singapore M	Singapore X	Thailand M	Thailand X
Germany	1987	836	361	538	616	282	291	1,122	927	771	573
	1988	908	456	647	723	342	297	1,625	1,367	1,090	737
	1989	918	487	857	893	436	333	1,807	1,645	1,311	818
	1990	1,522	750	1,254	1,147	557	390	2,172	2,130	1,653	1,194
	1991	2,061	907	1,468	1,141	490	502	2,115	2,509	2,000	1,495
U.K.	1987	325	213	546	574	148	245	1,034	815	409	417
	1988	342	349	812	738	170	326	1,274	1,145	600	588
	1989	359	371	1,215	943	181	326	1,396	1,554	651	746
	1990	441	517	1,600	1,160	267	351	1,870	1,683	907	937
	1991	603	654	1,698	1,503	225	372	1,905	1,796	898	1,076
France	1987	392	102	204	238	129	125	750	439	198	284
	1988	479	165	256	306	129	164	789	654	491	380
	1989	411	203	276	378	175	151	1,113	703	410	442
	1990	662	286	438	414	161	144	1,468	863	809	563
	1991	544	386	467	476	148	165	1,698	692	601	745
Netherlands	1987	316	493	103	619	92	310	244	530	154	776
	1988	266	646	122	639	136	314	342	675	216	870
	1989	260	679	248	895	215	327	471	719	220	975
	1990	572	723	222	775	181	357	536	1,132	242	1,115
	1991	505	838	328	828	154	338	571	1,551	314	1,086
Italy	1987	237	175	125	177	36	36	438	332	168	218
	1988	251	221	155	226	118	40	655	569	241	293
	1989	351	243	242	254	72	48	808	602	371	296
	1990	410	276	402	269	94	61	957	698	426	421
	1991	536	381	569	435	106	79	912	561	544	508

M = imports, X = exports

Sources: IMF, *Direction of Trade Statistics*, various issues.

ASEAN, particularly considering the prominent position it holds within the EC, and that of Italy. Except for Malaysia, where it is second to the U.K., Germany is the principal export destination for individual ASEAN countries, and their major supplier. Reflecting past ties, over 60 percent of the U.K.'s ASEAN imports come from, and two-thirds of its exports go to, Singapore and Malaysia.

Individual ASEAN countries tend to be viewed by European exporters as marginal markets, too small despite their growth to expend much effort on. The degree of separation between the markets is reflected in the very low levels of intra-ASEAN trade (equivalent to a mere 19 percent of total ASEAN trade at the end of the 1980s, compared with 14.7 percent in 1970). Malaysia and Singapore, which represent just 6 percent of the total population of the region, accounted for 74 percent of all intra-ASEAN trade in 1990. These two countries also account for just over 50 percent of EC exports to the region, a figure that has changed little since 1980.

Germany, the principal EC exporter to all ASEAN except Malaysia, traditionally runs a surplus with each of these countries. The exception is Malaysia. However, German exports exceeded Malaysian imports in 1990 and 1991. In contrast, Singapore moved into surplus with Germany for the first time in 1990, suggesting some diversion of trade between the two countries. Italy has been particularly successful in the last 2–3 years, increasing exports to each country while holding down imports. Italy, France and Spain operate the largest number of national quota restrictions to protect local markets and producers.

EC exports to Malaysia in 1990 accounted for little more than 6 percent of machinery and transport equipment, behind not only Japan (32 percent) and the United States (26 percent), but also Singapore (13 percent) and Taiwan (6 percent). In the chemicals trade, the U.K. and Germany together accounted for 14 percent of Malaysia's imports, the same share as the United States though less than Japan's 20 percent share. In basic manufactures (SITC 6), the U.K. and Germany's combined 8 percent share was again dwarfed by Japan's (26 percent) and Taiwan's (11 percent) shares.

German exports to Thailand are highly concentrated: 62 percent are capital goods (43 percent is nonelectrical machinery). By comparison, 55 percent of Japan's exports to Thailand are capital goods, while electrical machinery (12 percent), chemicals (9 percent) and road vehicles and parts (9 percent) contribute most of the rest. Germany represents some 6 percent of all Thai imports.

The German share of Indonesian imports is slightly higher, at around 7 percent. Machinery, chemicals and road vehicles are the main import categories, both for Germany and for the U.K. (which accounts for only 3 percent of total imports). The U.K., the Netherlands and France all export similar amounts to Indonesia.

The last 20 years have seen significant changes in the relative importance of individual ASEAN members in EC imports from the region (Table 9.4). The greatest advances have been made by Singapore and Thailand (which in 1990 became for the first time a larger supplier to the EC than Malaysia). On the other hand, ASEAN's most populous country, Indonesia, has seen its share decline by a third between

TABLE 9.4   Composition of EC imports from ASEAN countries (%)

	1970	1975	1980	1985	1990
Indonesia	24.8	18.4	18.2	17.8	16.2
Malaysia	39.3	32.5	27.4	27.7	22.7
Philippines	9.6	16.2	12.8	11.8	7.7
Singapore	12.2	17.8	22.2	22.0	30.5
Thailand	14.0	15.0	19.4	20.7	22.9
	100.0	100.0	100.0	100.0	100.0

Sources: IMF, *Direction of Trade Statistics*, various issues.

1970 and 1990, to slightly more than 16 percent. This is the direct result of the increasing share of oil and gas in Indonesia's export trade composition: by the mid-1980s oil and gas accounted for 70 percent of the country's exports to the industrialized world. Indonesia has been slower than its fellow ASEAN members to diversify into electronics, although it has recently taken away from Thailand part of its share in EC textile and clothing imports. Significant increases in Indonesian-made garments did not appear on world export markets until 1987. Until relatively recently neither Indonesia nor the Philippines, whose share in EC imports has halved over the last 15 years, had provided suitable investment conditions to encourage the development of export-oriented industries.

Thailand's principal exports to the EC are tapioca, canned seafood, textiles and garments, footwear, and gems and jewellery. Tapioca was Thailand's largest export to the EC in 1987, but further trade creation is impossible owing to the strict control on EC imports through voluntary export restraints. A bilateral agreement covering the years 1991–94 sets a four-year total EC quota on tapioca pellets for animal feed from Thailand of 21 million tonnes, with import duties not exceeding 6 percent. Most of this enters the EC via the Netherlands, accounting for 44 percent of Thailand's trade with that country. The tapioca trade pushes the Netherlands into second position as an EC importer of Thai produce, and gives the Netherlands the EC's largest bilateral trade deficit with Thailand. Germany, which is Thailand's biggest EC destination, accounts for 5 percent of its total exports. A quarter of German imports are textile manufactures.

Malaysian exports have evolved over the past twenty years away from commodity products, such as rubber, tin and palm nuts, towards mineral oil and oil products (though these do not find a significant market in the EC), coffee, cocoa, yarns and textiles, apparel and electronic components. Like Thailand, Malaysia is affected by EC farm trade policy by virtue of the importance of its palm oil exports to the EC. Between 1985 and 1990, the share of manufactures in Malaysia's exports to the EC rose from 45 percent to 63 percent, while its share of manufactured exports to the world rose from 27 percent to 49 percent. Apparel (SITC 84—classified at the two-digit level) represents 15 percent of the EC's imports of

Malaysian manufactures, while electrical and electronic machinery (SITC 75 + 76 + 77) accounts for 55 percent, or 40 percent of all EC imports from the country. Taking the developing Asia region as a whole, Malaysian exports to the EC of SITC 77 products ("electrical machinery and appliances", which includes semiconductors and components) are now second only to those of Taiwan, largely due to the activities of multinational corporations in Malaysia. It boasted a 5 percent share of U.K. imports in this category, the largest share of any Asian nation and twice the size of Hong Kong's. A nascent export industry is motor vehicles, which has grown from effectively zero in 1987 to EC- (mostly U.K.-) bound exports three years later of US$90 million (less than 2 percent of all exports to the EC).[6]

Indonesia's main export destinations in the EC are Germany, the U.K., the Netherlands and France, which together account for nearly 10 percent of its total exports. Clothing is the main import category for each of these countries, with textiles also going to Germany and the U.K. Indonesian apparel exports to Germany totalled nearly US$320 million in 1991, from just US$23 million in 1986. Not only is Indonesia rivalling Thailand's apparel exports to Germany (US$350 million), but in 1990 it overtook Thailand as a supplier of textile yarns. Cork and wood manufactures find important markets in Germany, the U.K. and France.

9.5 EC–China Trade Relations

Chinese dependency on the triad EC–United States–Japan for either imports or exports appears low relative to other Asian countries. However, its dependency on other Asian countries appears proportionately higher since substantial trade passes through the Hong Kong entrepôt and increasing amounts of processing work for re-export to third countries is carried out in mainland China. The EC and the United States each absorbed around 9 percent of China's exports in 1990, according to United Nations (UN) data, while exports to Japan, which include some mineral fuels, account for a further 15 percent (down from 23 percent in 1990). The export share to other Asian countries has risen from one-third to over half of China's total.

International Monetary Fund (IMF) direction of trade (DOT) data clearly demonstrate the interlinkage between China and Hong Kong, particularly since 1988 (Table 9.5). Corresponding data for exports to China (and Hong Kong) indicate no such discrepancy. OECD figures on trade by product classification bear out the general trend of the IMF statistics, while appearing to understate the Chinese position. They show that in 1990 China ran a US$4.5 billion surplus on trade with the EC, while the IMF data implies an EC deficit on trade with China amounting to US$8.4 billion. Although smaller than the size of its surplus with the United States, China's trade position is sufficiently large to be the butt of intense criticism with the European Community.

On the basis of OECD data, China's exports to the EC have quadrupled since 1985 (exports of manufactures have risen 5.9 times), while EC exports to China

TABLE 9.5   Hong Kong and China trade with the EC, U.S. and Japan (US$ million)

	1985	1986	1987	1988	1989	1990	1991
				Exports to EC			
Hong Kong	3,709	5,155	7,680	9,918	11,149	13,959	17,184
China	2,283	4,017	3,916	4,746	4,880	5,920	6,826
				Exports to U.S.			
Hong Kong	9,301	11,108	13,511	15,689	18,505	19,817	22,391
China	2,336	2,633	3,030	3,399	4,414	5,314	6,192
				Exports to Japan			
Hong Kong	1,279	1,651	2,470	3,696	4,525	4,680	5,307
China	6,091	5,079	6,392	8,046	8,395	9,210	10,265

	1985	1986	1987	1988	1989	1990	1991
				Imports from EC			
Hong Kong	3,984	5,905	7,395	8,772	8,687	9,664	10,481
China	2,971	4,106	5,945	7,719	9,159	12,312	16,902
				Imports from U.S.			
Hong Kong	8,994	9,474	10,490	10,815	10,238	9,951	9,740
China	4,224	5,241	6,910	9,261	12,901	16,296	20,305
				Imports from Japan			
Hong Kong	774	1,080	1,578	2,111	2,207	2,182	2,066
China	6,534	5,727	7,478	9,861	11,083	12,057	14,248

Import figures are CIF, exports are FOB.

Sources: IMF, *Direction of Trade Statistics*, various issues.

have risen just 1.2 times. The country has emerged rapidly as a major exporter of basic and other manufactured goods.

Reverting to the UN data, which in this instance is supported by the IMF DOT statistics, Chinese imports appear rather evenly balanced now between the EC, the United States and Japan, but there has been a noticeable decline in the developed world's share of China's imports, from nearly 70 percent in 1984 to just below 50 percent in 1990. Erratic annual growth rates in imports from the EC reflect the stop-go pace of development in the Chinese economy since 1984 and the, at times, acute shortage of hard currency. Growth in imports from the EC averaged 6.2 percent in 1985–91, compared with global import growth of 7.7 percent.

Germany's share of EC imports into China hovers around 40 percent, while France, which has made better inroads here than elsewhere in the Asia region, has become the second largest EC supplier. Imports of French goods have risen fairly steadily throughout the late 1980s, shrugging off the downturns of 1987 and 1989 to emerge at the start of the 1990s with a near 20 percent of the EC's China market. Italian exporters have also performed better in China than either the U.K. or the Netherlands, in a reversal of usual rankings.

China's imports from the EC reveal the same intensity of demand for manufactures as can be seen in ASEAN and ANIEs imports. While still relatively small in absolute terms (some US$4 billion in 1990) the share of machinery and transport equipment is noticeably above average, accounting for over 60 percent of all imports from the EC in 1990, compared with a little over 50 percent for ASEAN countries and 40 percent for the ANIEs. Among industrialized countries the EC has emerged at least temporarily as the largest supplier of such goods to China.

EC imports of manufactured goods from China, which in the mid-1980s were divided evenly between basic manufactures, especially textile yarns, and other manufactures, were by 1990 heavily concentrated in the latter category. With a value of US$5.8 billion, they exceeded miscellaneous manufactured goods (SITC 8) imports from both ASEAN and the ANIEs. Imports are primarily made up of apparel items (SITC 84), worth US$2.5 billion, more than half of which enter the EC through Germany. (A proportion of the EC's clothing imports from Hong Kong, worth US$3.5 billion in total, is undoubtedly also China trade: Germany and the U.K. are the main importers of Hong Kong despatched garments.) Textile yarn (SITC 65) imports from China are by far the largest from the region, creating for the EC a near US$1 billion deficit in 1990 equivalent to half the EC's deficit with the Asian region for the category.

Chinese-made footwear exports (SITC 85) to the EC are currently smaller than those arriving from longer-standing Asian producers such as Korea and Taiwan, but from a low base the growth rate is high. Disagreement among individual EC countries over proposals to subject Chinese shoes and bicycles to an EC wide quota is reportedly causing widespread confusion among importers, who face outright bans in some countries while Germany has lifted all controls.[7]

9.6   Policy Issues in EC–Asian Trade Relations

9.6.1 EC Trade Policy toward Developing East Asian Countries

EC trade policy has a bearing on the future development of Asian countries. The export structure of these nations has changed substantially over the last decade, and Europe represents an important and growing marketplace for their electrical and electronic machinery, textiles and footwear industries. The low level of inter-industry trade between Asia and the EC (as opposed to intra-industry trade, where exports and imports between the two partners would take place within the same industry) leaves Asian exporters vulnerable to nontariff barriers that enjoy strong political support in individual EC member countries. The textile and garment industry, footwear, and a wide variety of consumer electronics sectors—in all of which Asian firms are highly competitive—are among the most affected.

The most tendentious issues for the EC to handle with regard to Asian imports concern textiles, including garments, and electrical and electronic products. The latter are the subject of numerous anti-dumping suits; trade in the former is restricted by quotas under the Multifibre Arrangement (MFA).

EC trade policy is highly complex, and the network of special preferences extensive. Five broad groupings of preferences exist, with different subgroups and different trade objectives: the General System of Preference (GSP);[8] the Lomé Convention, which essentially maintains links with former colonies;[9] the EFTA[10] free trade arrangement; the Mediterranean agreements, which give concessionary access to the EC in an effort to bring the Mediterranean countries into the EC sphere of influence while influencing trade and immigration flows; and the most recently agreed Europe Agreements with Poland, Hungary and the Czech/Slovak Republics.

South Korea, Hong Kong and the ASEAN countries enjoy preferences under the GSP,[11] though Taiwan does not. Otherwise, Asian nations are not eligible for additional preferences under EC trade policy, despite former Commonwealth links between the U.K. and Singapore, Malaysia and Hong Kong. Even the GSP scheme, which includes rules of origin, tariff quotas and a variety of bureaucratic hurdles (Davenport and Page 1991), has proved frustratingly restrictive compared with the United States and Japanese GSP programs.

The GSP in fact seems to have relatively little influence over the ability of a country to expand its trade with the EC (Langhammer 1986). Taiwan is a noteworthy example of how to expand trade without the help of preferential treatment. Price is clearly only one determinant of competitiveness; marketing and distribution skills, product quality, and after-sales service also determine a firm's ability to compete. In any case, only a proportion of Asian exports to the EC fall into GSP-covered trade categories, and Asian countries themselves have demonstrated greater flexibility and more skill in entering new markets with new products than African–Caribbean–Pacific, Mediterranean or Latin American countries.

The effect of multilateral trade negotiations, primarily the GATT, has been to induce a shift in EC trade protectionism from tariff to nontariff barriers (NTBs) controlled by individual member governments (Hiemenz 1991). From 10 percent in 1966, when the EC–6 pursued relatively liberal policies, the EC's NTB coverage on manufactures increased fivefold to levels similar to those found in Japan and the United States (56 percent) by 1986 (Winters 1993). Sensitive products such as textiles and clothing are excluded from the GSP and instead face obligatory quotas and optional ceilings. On textile and clothing, the maximum tariff is 16 percent versus an average of 6 percent on imported manufactures; electronics products can attract a maximum tariff of 14 percent. Nontariff barriers, some of which are of dubious legality in the GATT framework, range from quantitative restrictions through voluntary export restraints to anti-dumping charges. The brunt of these barriers has been borne by Asian producers. National quotas and restrictions, of which there are several thousand, present a major obstacle to successful exporters and continue to do so even beyond the starting date for the single European market. An estimated 40 percent of Korea's trade with the EC, for example, is subject to some form of export restriction.

More troublesome than the exclusion of Asian developing countries from additional EC preferences, is the interplay of individual EC member country interests and industry-specific protectionist measures. Aside from individual country quotas, for example under the Multifibre Arrangement (MFA), Article 115 of the Treaty of Rome could be invoked to achieve the temporary suspension of common trade policies (that is, the free movement of goods within the boundaries of the EC, one of the basic principles on which the foundation of the Community rests) in order to uphold national interests. Use of this Article has generally been made against Asian developing countries.

Little has been done to quell the impression among Asian countries that a "fortress Europe" aims to force out their products as each new success arrives on European markets. The ANIEs must conduct individual bilateral trade negotiations, while ASEAN's negotiating stance with the EC is handicapped by the lack of a strong mechanism within ASEAN[12] to handle such tasks on behalf of all members. Combined with the overall low level of importance of ASEAN trade within the context of total EC trade, plus the lack of a "champion" among EC members to promote its cause, ASEAN is in a weak position to influence EC trade policy. Because the structure of its exports leaves it vulnerable to protectionist action at the national or European Community level, it is incumbent on ASEAN to work to achieve a minimum level of cooperation and understanding.

The removal of internal trade barriers inside the EC will intensify price competition for Asian manufactures, since on the one hand some EC producers are expected to achieve economies of scale and greater levels of efficiency, while on the other a degree of trade diversion will take place to lower-cost countries of the EC, particularly Spain, Portugal and Greece. Most likely industrial sectors affected will be standardized products including textiles, clothing, footwear, leather goods, electronic components, toys and steel (Page 1992). ANIEs, already the target of several anti-dumping measures, may find themselves vulnerable to

Community-wide quotas on footwear and electronics which should eventually replace national quotas. EC trade officials are demanding as a *quid pro quo* for progress in eliminating some of these nontariff barriers the opening of Asian markets in such sectors as leather goods. Greater efficiency among EC producers of many different manufactures could ultimately lead to increased competition with Asian producers outside the EC, as cost advantages come into play.

The harmonization of product standards throughout the EC in the run-up to the Single Market has been identified as an important new barrier to market entry (for internal EC producers, as well as external ones) from the organizational, rather than the trade, point of view. While some regulations are self-evident, there are many subtle differences in requirements for packaging sizes, form of labelling, and so on, which do not apply to all products. The need is to acquire timely information on regulatory changes, and to have access to the standard setting process. Potentially problematic is the failure of customs officials in one country to give credence to proof of acceptance by officials in another.

Reaching product safety standards may be a costly business initially, particularly for small scale producers such as Hong Kong and Taiwanese toy makers. However, since the EC standard is applicable to all European trading partners once attained it should give the products access to markets worldwide. In the attempt to reach EC standards, exporters' own quality standards will rise. Some Asian producers, however, may not find it a financially viable prospect to go through the process. Health and safety standards for fish and shellfish imports—coming mainly from Thailand and Taiwan—will also affect domestic industries.

9.6.2 Textiles

Table 9.6 shows the relative importance of textile and apparel imports to the EC from individual Asian countries. Together worth US$13 billion, they accounted for nearly 14 percent of all EC textile imports. Although both China and the ANIEs are larger clothing exporters to the EC than individual ASEAN countries, the EC represents one of ASEAN's most important textile and garment markets. As in other areas of trade, ASEAN is not an important source of imports for the EC since the EC itself is both a major importer and a major exporter of textiles and clothing, the bulk of this trade taking place between EC member countries.

Growth in clothing production in ASEAN, as in other developing countries, tends to be faster than textile production, because of the greater labor intensity of garment manufacturing. The EC is an exporter of semi-finished, capital-intensive fabrics to ASEAN, and ASEAN producers predominantly export finished clothing items to the EC. There is relatively little bilateral trade between the two regions, in other words, the exchange of differentiated products is small. Rather rapid increases in textile fabric imports (not only from the EC) among ASEAN countries reflects the development of their clothing industry.

The MFA, first introduced in 1974, is the main policy under which the flow of

TABLE 9.6   Textile and apparel˙ imports by the EC from developing East Asia

	SITC 65 + 84 imports				SITC 65 + 84 imports as % of manufactures imports from Asian countries	
	1985		1990		1985	1990
	(US$ m)	(%)	(US$ m)	(%)	(%)	(%)
Thailand	279.9	44.0	1,088.2	33.5		
Malaysia	105.0	16.5	554.6	17.1		
Brunei	0.5	–	1.1	–		
Singapore	54.6	8.6	286.0	8.8		
Indonesia	82.2	12.9	940.1	28.9		
Philippines	114.4	18.0	380.1	11.7		
ASEAN (A)	636.6	100.0	3,250.1	100.0	15.9	20.2
Share of EC imports (%)	1.7		3.4			
China (B)	851.0		3,485.3		49.5	34.2
Share of EC imports (%)	2.2		3.6			
Korea	951.7	30.6	1,799.4	27.3		
Taiwan	493.9	15.9	1,068.1	16.2		
Hong Kong	1,663.6	53.5	3,719.5	56.5		
ANIEs (C)	3,109.2		6,587.0	100.0	32.9	22.5
Share of EC imports (%)	8.2		6.8			
Region (A + B + C)	4,596.8		13,322.4			
Share of EC imports (%)	12.1		13.8			
Japan	501.2		1,079.6			
Share of EC imports (%)	1.3		1.1			
World	37,993.7		96,613.9			

˙SITC 65 + 84. SITC 65 comprises textile yarns and fabrics; SITC 84 comprises apparel and clothing accessories.

Source: OECD, *Trade by Commodity*, Series C, 1990.

world textile trade is regulated. It has become more restrictive over time, the result of failure by developed countries to adjust their industries to the effect of competition from low cost developing countries. The EC operates both an EC-wide quota and national or regional quotas. National or regional quotas will continue until 1995, when the EC-wide quota system should prevail. Article 115 has been used to restrict the import of products under quotas from other EC countries. Global ceilings on sensitive items have frozen imports from all sources.

"Dominant" countries such as the ANIEs tend to be large quota holders in consideration of their past growth performance. Among the ASEAN countries Thailand and Singapore also have relatively high quota allocations. Indonesia, as a late starter in the textile industry, was not put under any quota restriction until

MFA2 (1978–81), and then only in a limited way. Its relatively small quotas now reflect that late start (Pangestu and Hasni 1991). Quota utilization by NIE countries in low value-added items is declining as they move into the production of more sophisticated items. While these quotas are being freed up for use by ASEAN and other less advanced textile producers, ANIEs firms themselves are moving to use them by relocating to these areas.

Asian textile exporters are vulnerable to loss of share to internal market producers (Spain and Portugal), even though labor costs are higher, because of their advantage in being "insiders," or to the Mediterranean countries (especially Turkey, Morocco) which enjoy higher quotas and greater flexibility provisions, or to East European countries. Each of these latter two categories could attract outward processing by EC firms, or some industry relocation by ANIEs firms preferring proximity to the greater familiarity of ASEAN.

EC policy with respect to textile and clothing awaits the conclusion of the Uruguay Round of multilateral trade talks, which envisages the integration of the textile industry into GATT. Since the main theme of the talks is reciprocity of access, fundamental changes are required to the present MFA system and a lengthy transition period is likely.

9.6.3 Electronics

From Table 9.7 it is clear that the European market has become a significantly more important destination for Asian machinery (SITC 7) exports in the last decade. Some inroads have been made into the Japanese market, but Japan remains by far the least important (though not undesired) purchaser. ANIEs firms began their diversification to Europe by the end of the 1970s, and were able to win some small share of the Japanese market only in the latter half of the 1980s as yen appreciation encouraged their entry into the lower end of the price and quality range. Over 40 percent of ASEAN countries' exports of manufactures to the EC are now of electrical and electronic machinery. The ANIEs, which have a less concentrated export pattern, nevertheless count 34 percent of their manufactures in the same industry— a level which is rising as exported products become more sophisticated and as marketing efforts expand.

EC imports from the Asian region of SITC 75 + 76 + 77 goods, covering computers, office machinery, TVs, video recorders and home electrical appliances, rose by 4.5 times between 1985 and 1990, to US$18.4 billion. Nevertheless, they remain below the level of imports from Japan (US$23.5 billion). China emerged rapidly during this period as the third largest supplier behind Korea and Singapore to the EC— primarily Germany—of SITC 76 goods (TVs, radios, sound recorders, and parts and accessories). Table 9.8 shows the evolution of market share for individual countries within their subgroups, most noticeably the advance of Thailand and the relative decline of Malaysia's position. Particularly in the ASEAN countries output of electronics has in the past been heavily biased towards semiconductor assembly

TABLE 9.7   Export destinations within OECD markets for developing East Asian countries' exports of machinery and transport equipment (SITC 7) (% share)

	EC					U.S.					Japan					Total SITC 7 exports to the OECD (US$ million)				
	1970	1975	1980	1985	1990	1970	1975	1980	1985	1990	1970	1975	1980	1985	1990	1970	1975	1980	1985	1990
Thailand	75.0	56.4	12.6	21.2	20.7	25.0	18.2	83.0	60.5	53.8	–	12.7	2.1	16.0	20.1	0.4	5.5	107.0	363.7	3,260.5
Malaysia	60.7	15.9	19.3	27.1	31.1	39.3	71.0	72.4	66.8	55.2	–	8.5	3.8	2.7	7.2	2.8	293.1	1331.4	2,230.0	6,105.5
Brunei	–	–	100.0	97.7	95.9	–	–	–	–	1.7	–	–	–	–	2.5	–	–	1.7	4.3	12.1
Singapore	25.2	35.2	32.4	22.9	32.8	71.4	49.5	55.2	67.8	5.3	0.6	5.9	4.2	3.7	5.6	51.2	553.2	2,390.1	4,376.7	14,696.9
Indonesia	83.3	45.6	20.3	38.5	39.6	–	47.4	65.0	52.0	32.5	–	7.0	14.1	1.4	18.9	0.6	5.7	80.1	49.4	159.4
Philippines	50.0	14.8	15.0	22.5	19.0	11.8	69.3	71.3	72.4	60.5	38.2	7.1	9.4	2.3	14.9	3.4	42.0	593.7	915.2	1,761.2
China	–	62.0	53.0	28.1	32.0	–	3.0	15.1	53.3	49.0	40.0	5.0	10.5	8.5	8.9	1.5	10.0	41.1	181.8	5,168.1
Korea	3.4	11.5	22.1	15.4	22.7	80.7	50.2	49.6	57.6	50.9	14.5	3.5	18.1	8.4	12.9	37.9	452.1	1791.1	5,125.8	15,261.7
Taiwan	7.2	17.2	23.5	14.4	30.6	79.3	65.0	60.6	72.3	47.6	10.1	3.8	8.4	5.3	9.4	178.4	751.4	3,282.3	7,890.5	19,815.0
Hong Kong	16.0	30.3	32.7	25.2	42.4	76.1	55.1	53.1	64.9	39.4	3.4	3.8	1.3	1.3	4.7	218.3	580.2	2,002.5	3,437.1	5,898.1

EC figures for 1970 and 1975 refer to the EC 6 plus the U.K.; East Asian exports to OECD markets other than the EC, U.S. and Japan are not shown separately.

Sources: OECD, *Trade by Commodities*, Series C, various issues.

TABLE 9.8   Electronics* imports by the EC from East and Southeast Asia

	Electronics imports				Electronics imports as % of manufactures imports from Asian countries	
	1985		1990		1985	1990
	(US$ m)	(%)	(US$ m)	(%)	(%)	(%)
Thailand	70.3	4.2	542.4	7.7		
Malaysia	545.0	32.9	1,759.9	25.0		
Brunei	1.8	0.1	0.4	–		
Singapore	852.1	51.4	4,371.0	62.1		
Indonesia	14.5	0.9	41.6	0.6		
Philippines	173.0	10.4	324.4	4.6		
ASEAN (A)	1,656.7	100.0	7,039.7	100.0	41.3	43.7
Share of EC imports (%)	2.6		4.2			
China (B)	19.4		1,301.9		1.1	12.8
Share of EC imports (%)	–		0.8			
Korea	634.0	26.8	2,961.6	29.4		
Taiwan	969.6	40.9	4,779.9	47.4		
Hong Kong	764.2	32.3	2,337.6	23.2		
ANIEs (C)	2,367.8	100.0	10,079.1	100.0	25.1	34.4
Share of EC imports (%)	3.8		6.0			
Region (A+B+C)	4,043.9		18,420.7			
Share of EC imports (%)	6.5		11.0			
Japan	8,993.7		23,462.7			
Share of EC imports (%)	14.4		14.0			
World	62,534.0		168,161.2			

*SITC 75 + 76 + 77

SITC 75: computers (751), office machines (752), parts and accessories.

SITC 76: TVs (761), radios (762), gramophones and sound recorders (763), parts and accessories.

SITC 77: electrical power machinery (771), electrical circuit breakers (772), electrical distribution equipment (773), medical electrical apparatus (774), household electrical apparatus (775), thermionic, cold- and photo-cathode valves and tubes (776), electrical machinery (777).

Source: OECD, *Trade by Commodity*, Series C, 1990.

under the domination of multinationals (Wong 1991). There is evidence to suggest that this is now changing, as production shifts to more sophisticated finished products including office equipment and computers. Singapore leads in this technological upgrading process, and a number of indigenous firms are beginning to emerge. Table 9.9 breaks out exports by each Asian country to the five main EC members in the same SITC categories.

TABLE 9.9   **Imports of electrical and electronics goods by selected EC member country, from Asian countries (US$ million)**

	Germany		U.K.		France		Netherlands		Italy	
	1985	1990	1985	1990	1985	1990	1985	1990	1985	1990
SITC 75										
Thailand	1.8	57.7	–	16.4	0.3	16.7	–	9.2	–	11.5
Malaysia	2.8	15.4	3.9	7.7	0.9	4.7	0.2	0.2	1.3	9.3
Brunei	–	–	–	0.2	–	0.2	–	–	–	–
Singapore	65.9	619.8	146.9	490.6	26.3	235.1	3.0	189.2	31.4	192.1
Indonesia	0.4	0.5	0.1	0.4	–	–	0.1	0.3	0.2	0.3
Philippines	0.6	9.6	–	1.8	–	4.0	–	1.3	0.2	0.4
China	–	39.0	0.7	6.0	0.4	19.2	–	2.7	0.9	18.8
Korea	37.5	132.2	60.0	176.4	58.6	152.4	6.7	59.5	5.2	31.9
Taiwan	77.5	824.0	92.5	415.3	48.9	448.8	30.3	293.0	20.8	234.9
Hong Kong	59.4	446.2	128.4	141.0	17.0	43.3	6.8	89.2	21.3	32.4
World	5,623.6	14,890.8	5,814.2	13,754.2	4,090.0	10,026.0	2,573.8	7,992.6	2,659.0	5,695.8
SITC 76										
Thailand	–	77.2	0.7	68.7	–	27.4	–	7.3	1.5	16.9
Malaysia	41.0	276.2	28.4	134.8	33.8	138.7	8.4	46.0	8.4	29.6
Brunei	–	–	1.3	0.5	–	–	–	–	–	–
Singapore	51.3	364.4	59.5	308.7	61.9	251.0	25.2	109.5	32.1	108.3
Indonesia	–	21.2	0.3	1.2	–	2.7	0.2	3.8	–	0.9
Philippines	2.9	9.3	0.5	1.9	0.3	14.1	–	2.1	0.3	5.9
China	2.0	470.1	4.8	52.4	3.7	199.3	0.3	26.6	0.6	113.2
Korea	81.0	559.1	53.7	197.9	26.3	192.7	12.5	77.6	33.4	136.3
Taiwan	82.4	338.8	80.6	150.7	14.6	106.1	14.7	57.9	28.3	81.3
Hong Kong	52.4	193.1	79.5	329.2	15.5	62.5	16.9	103.1	31.7	18.6
World	2,857.8	9,766.0	2,744.3	6,215.7	1,432.6	5,089.6	1,196.5	3,425.5	1,327.1	4,426.7
SITC 77										
Thailand	14.2	78.7	13.6	83.7	20.1	19.6	15.5	10.1	0.3	3.5
Malaysia	99.7	256.0	209.4	559.3	72.9	97.6	0.6	2.7	8.0	20.8
Brunei	–	–	0.1	0.1	0.1	–	–	–	–	–
Singapore	104.3	382.7	59.9	233.2	32.1	287.5	7.8	28.5	94.9	104.5
Indonesia	8.9	2.5	–	0.8	3.7	0.3	–	0.4	0.1	0.1
Philippines	45.9	110.8	44.0	89.4	38.5	27.0	28.1	6.8	5.8	18.8
China	0.5	101.1	0.8	20.2	0.6	53.2	0.4	9.5	0.6	33.5
Korea	51.7	396.4	53.0	171.4	48.0	146.7	24.6	22.3	13.7	47.9
Taiwan	123.7	554.2	57.4	189.6	55.1	235.9	101.4	70.0	30.3	81.6
Hong Kong	82.7	208.3	72.3	255.4	33.4	69.2	49.7	48.6	11.1	41.4
World	6,576.1	17,960.8	5,495.8	12,344.9	4,330.6	11,925.1	2,582.9	5,721.1	2,775.1	8,565.8

SITC 75: computers (751), office machines (752), parts and accessories.
SITC 76: TVs (761), radios (762), gramophones and sound recorders (763), parts and accessories.
SITC 77: electrical power machinery (771), electrical circuit breakers (772), electrical distribution equipment (773), medical electrical apparatus (774), household electrical apparatus (775), thermionic, cold- and photo-cathode valves and tubes (776), electrical machinery (777).

Source: OECD, *Trade by Commodity*, Series C, 1990.

What is clear from Table 9.9 is the dramatic expansion of the electronics export business in Asia. Between 1980 and 1990, ANIEs doubled their share of OECD machinery imports from 2.3 percent to 4.6 percent and ASEAN countries raised theirs from 1.5 percent to 2.9 percent. By the end of the decade the Asian region, including China, accounted for 8.1 percent of the OECD total. This has caused strains within the EC (and the United States), particularly in light of the inroads made by Korean producers. Frequent anti-dumping charges have been brought against Asian producers on a wide variety of electronic products, ranging from TVs and video recorders to semiconductors and printed circuit boards.

9.7 Competitiveness of EC Exporters

Several studies have shown the declining share of EC exporters in Asian markets to be the result of loss of international competitiveness by European export industries (Harris and Bridges 1983; Langhammer and Hiemenz 1985). Winters (1993) shows that the EC's share of world engineering markets fell from 45 percent in 1970 to 35 percent in 1985. While this in itself is not surprising given the rise of technological skills particularly in Asia, he points to the significance of European declines concentrated in the more advanced technological goods and the apparent rise in share for the least technical engineering exports.

Market proximity may be a factor in encouraging development of trade relations (the degree of contact between Eastern and Western European companies is far greater than between United States and East European companies, for example, and Latin America is largely served by North American firms). Signals from governments, including the granting of aid to a country or region, and the provision of export credit guarantees also have a role to play. Japanese companies, already enjoying location-specific advantages, interpreted their government's granting of large aid packages to Southeast Asian nations as a tacit guarantee underwriting their own business activities. European firms, lacking any proximity advantage or the security of substantial government aid programs, have seen losses of market share outside the EC though less marked ones within (suggesting that protectionist policies rather than competitive strength support local producers inside the EC).

Table 9.10 demonstrates the relative position of European and German exporters of the relatively advanced technology SITC 7 machinery and transport equipment, vis-a-vis United States and Japanese exporters in each ASEAN country.[13] It is clear that EC exporters have lost most ground in Thailand (to both the United States and Japan) and Malaysia (to Japan). Japan, meanwhile, has gained in all markets.

Table 9.11 gives a more detailed perspective on changes in European and German shares of OECD exports of advanced industrial goods to various regions of the world. Although EC shares to the world have increased in all categories

TABLE 9.10   Trends in composition, by origin, of SITC 7 goods imported from OECD by individual Asian countries (%)

	OECD	EC	U.S.	Japan		OECD	EC	U.S.	Japan
Thailand					Korea				
1970	100	29.4	14.9	50.5	1970	100	21.8	22.9	53.1
1975	100	27.1	12.6	54.1	1975	100	23.8	24.9	47.2
1980	100	24.8	20.8	47.4	1980	100	17.9	26.3	51.5
1985	100	29.0	16.6	50.4	1985	100	13.4	31.0	50.8
1990	100	20.5	16.0	56.5	1990	100	19.0	27.6	49.4
Malaysia					Taiwan				
1970	100	51.9	12.9	29.8	1970	100	13.2	23.2	61.2
1975	100	34.5	28.8	29.1	1975	100	19.2	37.7	40.6
1980	100	30.3	16.6	46.9	1980	100	13.3	34.8	49.9
1985	100	17.3	32.4	41.4	1985	100	16.8	31.1	49.0
1990	100	20.3	29.5	45.7	1990	100	17.3	28.2	50.2
Singapore					Hong Kong				
1970	100	33.6	32.6	28.4	1970	100	34.2	29.2	30.3
1975	100	22.0	33.5	36.8	1975	100	30.0	28.7	34.4
1980	100	22.1	31.6	39.3	1980	100	27.0	22.2	47.1
1985	100	21.5	36.1	37.9	1985	100	21.1	18.4	56.1
1990	100	21.7	28.4	45.1	1990	100	19.5	19.5	56.8
Indonesia					China				
1970	100	31.6	27.7	34.9	1970	100	38.4	–	49.6
1975	100	30.3	20.8	41.9	1975	100	40.2	7.6	43.4
1980	100	29.2	15.1	50.8	1980	100	29.6	9.6	54.7
1985	100	40.6	12.3	43.4	1985	100	22.2	16.2	57.0
1990	100	31.1	13.5	49.3	1990	100	41.8	19.8	27.6
Philippines									
1970	100	26.9	30.7	35.8					
1975	100	20.6	30.5	42.0					
1980	100	20.3	38.9	34.3					
1985	100	15.0	51.3	31.5					
1990	100	20.5	34.4	41.3					

The SITC 7 classification covers machinery and transportation equipment. See Table 9.11 for a more detailed definition of SITC 7 categories.

Sources: OECD, *Trade by Commodity*, Series C, various issues.

except SITC 75 (office machines) and 79 (other transport equipment) between 1985 and 1990, the performance with respect to ASEAN, where Japan dominates in most sectors, is noticeably less impressive. The impact of the internal market's tendency toward protectionism can best be seen in the increase in market share for intra-EC exports of office machinery, although data which included non-OECD exports would indicate the advances made by ANIEs producers in Europe.

TABLE 9.11 Share of industrialized countries in total OECD exports of advanced industrial goods to the world, EC, ANIEs and ASEAN (2-digit SITC categories, 1985 and 1990, %)

		World								EC							
		EC		Germany		US		Japan		EC		Germany		US		Japan	
SITC	Division	1985	1990	1985	1990	1985	1990	1985	1990	1985	1990	1985	1990	1985	1990	1985	1990
71	Power generating machinery	39.5	43.9	13.5	14.6	24.7	22.5	8.2	9.6	52.0	51.8	18.0	15.5	23.1	22.5	3.1	4.4
72	Specialised machinery	54.3	60.2	24.7	26.8	15.6	10.4	11.0	9.5	68.2	68.5	28.1	27.3	9.3	6.9	5.0	5.8
73	Metalworking machinery	43.6	51.4	22.0	25.2	10.7	7.8	22.5	16.5	55.2	56.9	25.0	24.5	7.8	5.8	11.4	11.4
74	General industrial machinery	53.7	58.0	23.1	23.9	16.2	12.4	10.3	8.5	66.2	69.3	25.6	24.9	13.0	8.2	4.5	4.9
75	Offices machines & automatic DP	34.3	33.8	8.8	7.2	28.4	21.9	20.9	19.9	47.5	48.4	11.6	9.3	30.2	22.6	11.8	13.3
76	Telecom. & sound recording eq't	16.6	24.5	6.5	7.3	6.1	6.6	47.1	29.6	38.3	39.3	14.9	10.9	7.5	5.4	32.1	24.3
77	Electrical machinery & appliances	38.4	41.3	14.8	16.1	15.8	13.7	14.7	12.8	56.7	57.8	18.8	19.5	15.6	10.4	9.1	9.2
78	Road vehicles	37.4	51.9	19.5	21.9	14.4	8.2	25.8	20.3	78.8	79.1	33.2	27.6	1.2	1.7	11.4	10.7
79	Other transport equipment	40.1	32.9	4.6	5.2	35.4	31.4	4.8	2.5	48.1	36.9	5.7	6.1	33.8	25.8	4.3	1.7
87	Professional scientific instruments	41.0	44.4	17.0	18.8	30.6	25.8	10.0	9.6	48.1	50.5	17.6	18.7	29.4	23.9	5.7	7.3
88	Photographic, optical goods, watches	36.0	37.5	11.2	11.3	13.3	10.5	25.8	22.5	46.4	44.7	13.4	13.2	14.7	10.7	18.3	18.9

		ANIEs								ASEAN							
		EC		Germany		US		Japan		EC		Germany		US		Japan	
SITC	Division	1985	1990	1985	1990	1985	1990	1985	1990	1985	1990	1985	1990	1985	1990	1985	1990
71	Power generating machinery	24.1	22.6	4.2	8.0	32.1	31.4	40.2	42.6	34.0	26.3	11.0	9.5	25.6	20.0	37.1	48.7
72	Specialised machinery	24.9	30.0	12.2	10.5	18.3	14.5	50.9	47.7	28.1	30.8	10.9	15.2	31.7	14.3	28.0	46.9
73	Metalworking machinery	14.7	19.3	8.3	12.3	11.8	15.8	67.9	59.4	21.7	16.3	5.7	6.2	13.8	9.9	25.7	45.3
74	General industrial machinery	22.3	26.2	8.0	12.8	16.3	18.9	55.1	49.7	31.9	28.2	11.1	11.3	13.6	14.3	48.2	50.3
75	Offices machines & automatic DP	9.3	8.2	1.4	2.5	49.8	37.3	39.0	52.3	13.1	15.2	3.1	3.3	58.5	45.8	25.2	36.3
76	Telecom. & sound recording eq't	8.6	6.7	3.0	1.4	19.2	21.7	65.8	67.1	18.5	13.8	6.1	5.9	9.9	10.7	60.8	67.7
77	Electrical machinery & appliances	10.8	12.0	3.2	4.2	26.5	25.8	60.6	60.0	17.7	19.1	5.3	7.6	46.4	35.9	34.0	42.7
78	Road vehicles	24.7	24.4	11.6	11.7	4.9	22.2	67.3	48.4	19.2	20.3	8.3	12.0	4.0	3.3	74.4	72.2
79	Other transport equipment	18.8	19.1	0.4	5.4	64.0	66.6	9.6	10.0	30.6	19.6	3.8	2.7	39.8	61.4	22.6	8.9
87	Professional scientific instruments	18.8	22.8	8.6	9.2	38.1	32.4	37.6	39.4	32.3	29.3	9.9	9.6	35.5	30.5	23.8	32.3
88	Photographic, optical goods, watches	9.3	10.5	3.7	4.4	3.5	4.8	68.4	56.2	14.9	15.8	5.0	5.3	8.5	11.2	47.7	37.5

Sources: OECD, *Trade by Commodity*, Series C, various issues; own calculations.

9.8 Foreign Direct Investment (FDI) in Developing East Asia

9.8.1 Overview of FDI in Developing East Asian Countries

At least until the mid-1980s the developing countries of Asia did not attract the strong investment flows from industrialized countries which could have been anticipated in view of the strength of economic growth there. Developed country FDI was directed either to other industrialized countries or, among the developing countries, to Latin America. The global slowdown in FDI in the early 1980s affected developing countries more than developed ones, although Asian countries fared relatively well. Economic slowdown in 1982–86 reduced flows to Indonesia and the Philippines more than to Singapore, Malaysia and Thailand. The Latin American debt crisis helped to divert United States and Japanese attention to the developing Asian countries. In 1988–89, Asia attracted more than 50 percent of all FDI flows to developing countries, and, in an important new trend, the ANIEs emerged as significant investors in the region in their own right. This latest development assures Asian developing countries that they will at least maintain their share of developing country FDI receipts, particularly since the slowdown of the Japanese economy has sharply reduced Japanese flows of FDI since 1991. European firms, however, have contributed little to the investment boom which has taken place in Asia in the last few years

On average 90 percent of FDI flows from European countries in recent years have been directed to other developed countries, including fellow EC countries. Firms have persisted with investment in Latin America also, in the hope of defending their competitive positions against rising wage costs and administrative controls (Hiemenz 1992). In the future, eastern European countries may exert a similar unfavorable impact, as the bleak economic scenario there demands frequent new defensive investments to protect positions acquired earlier.

United States and Japanese firms have more readily invested in Asia-Pacific than European firms in order to reduce costs (as well as for the more traditional reasons of sourcing raw materials or supplying local markets) driven up by high income levels at home. Greater familiarity with the requirements of managing decentralized operations because of a large home market may also have made United States firms more comfortable with the idea of overseas investment. Further, both American and Japanese firms enjoyed more substantial cost advantages than European firms due to the strength of the U.S. dollar in the 1970s and the Japanese yen in the late 1980s (Page 1987, Davenport and Page 1991).

The ability of countries to attract inward FDI is dependent on a variety of factors, including political and social stability and the overall business environment—the availability and cost of production factors and raw materials, market accessibility, and the presence of a government policy which is both pro-business and pro-FDI. Policy also needs to be consistent over time.

In Asia there was a relatively early shift in FDI priorities from import substitution to export-oriented production, as a means of stimulating economic growth. Singapore was first among Southeast Asian countries to make the move, and looked to Japan rather than the West as its model for development. Additionally, foreign investors were recognized to play an important role in the securing of overseas markets. Free trade principles have increasingly become the vehicle to promote industrialization and modernization. A deepening division of labor within the region has emerged, leading to greater opportunities for regional specialization and the spread of intra-regional investment.

9.8.2 Foreign Investment Policies in the ANIEs: Incentives, Priorities and Restrictions

The governments of Korea, Taiwan and Hong Kong have taken very different approaches towards foreign investment, and the relative amounts invested by foreign partners (Tables 9.12 and 9.13) indicate which offer the more favorable environment.

Hong Kong. Rough FDI per capita calculations show that Hong Kong is the favored destination, in part a result of the territory's long history of overseas involvement, but also of the *laissez-faire* nature of the government approach to business as a whole. The downside of keeping investment regulation to a minimum is that the system has provided no incentives for industrial upgrading. Realization that Hong Kong risks losing its competitive edge in the 1990s unless high technology enterprise develops, is for the first time inducing discussion over the provision of fiscal incentives. Political risk has increased over the last decade, but the flight of talent in the mid to late 1980s has apparently reversed. Hong Kong remains the preferred service centre for companies with business activities in China, but Singapore is

TABLE 9.12   Direct foreign investments and export trade to Pacific Asia

	Cumulative DFI (end 1990)				Yearly average imports (1988–90)			
Countries	Total ($ bn)	Percentage share invested by			Total ($ bn)	Percentage share from		
		U.S.	Europe	Japan		U.S.	Europe	Japan
China	38.95	10.2	6.3	8.4	57.7	12.0	17.6	17.0
Taiwan	11.30	29.1	17.8	32.6	52.6	24.1	15.0	29.9
Indonesia	38.68	5.7	17.6	24.9	17.3	12.5	21.1	24.5
Malaysia	6.50	4.9	17.6	35.3	22.8	17.1	16.5	23.8
Thailand	8.13	16.7	9.6	41.1	25.1	12.2	19.6	31.2
Philippines	3.30	55.8	11.5	15.4	10.9	19.7	12.7	18.4
Singapore	12.97	35.9	26.6	28.8	49.5	16.9	15.5	21.9
Hong Kong	3.96	30.6	15.3	31.5	72.8	8.2	12.5	17.0
Korea	8.10	28.7	14.7	48.2	60.0	24.8	13.1	29.4
Japan	18.40	48.3	27.1	–	210.8	22.7	17.2	–

Sources: Host country statistics; IMF, *Direction of Trade Yearbook*, 1992.

TABLE 9.13   Direct foreign investments—cumulative total, end 1990 (US$ billions)

To:	From:	U.S.	Europe	Japan	Total
China	Amount invested	4.48	2.76	3.66	38.95
	Percent	10.20	6.30	8.40	100.00
	Relative share	1.21	0.62	0.82	
Taiwan	Amount invested	3.29	2.01	3.68	11.30
	Percent	29.10	17.80	32.60	100.00
	Relative share	0.89	0.55	1.12	
Indonesia	Amount invested	2.19	6.81	9.64	38.68
	Percent	5.70	17.60	24.90	100.00
	Relative share	0.23	0.71	1.41	
Malaysia	Amount invested	0.32	1.15	2.29	6.55
	Percent	4.90	17.60	35.30	100.00
	Relative share	0.14	0.50	2.01	
Thailand	Amount invested	1.36	0.78	3.34	8.13
	Percent	16.70	9.60	41.10	100.00
	Relative share	0.41	0.23	2.46	
Philippines	Amount invested	1.84	0.38	0.51	3.30
	Percent	55.80	11.50	15.40	100.00
	Relative share	3.62	0.21	0.28	
Singapore	Amount invested	4.66	3.45	3.74	12.97
	Percent	35.90	26.60	28.80	100.00
	Relative share	1.25	0.74	0.80	
Hong Kong	Amount invested	1.21	0.61	1.25	3.96
	Percent	30.60	15.30	31.50	100.00
	Relative share	0.97	0.49	1.03	
Korea	Amount invested	2.32	1.19	3.90	8.10
	Percent	28.70	14.70	48.20	100.00
	Relative share	0.60	0.30	1.68	
Japan	Amount invested	8.90	5.00	–	18.40
	Percent	48.30	27.10	–	100.00
	Relative share	1.78	0.56	–	
TOTAL excluding Japan	Amount invested	21.67	19.14	32.01	131.94
	Percent	16.40	14.50	24.30	100.00
	Relative share	0.67	0.60	1.48	
TOTAL including Japan	Amount invested	30.57	24.14	32.01	150.34
	Percent	20.30	16.10	21.30	100.00
	Relative share	0.95	0.76	1.05	

Sources: Host country statistics, own calculations.

now a more attractive location for those with greater involvement in Southeast Asia.

Taiwan. The Taiwanese government has for many years maintained a positive stance to foreign business participation in the local market, in the belief that it encourages healthy competition. The transition from military rule to democratically elected government in 1989 was managed smoothly and without disruption to economic growth, allowing foreign capital to flow steadily into the country. Taipei offers investment incentives, but without discrimination between domestic and foreign capital, and in recent years has shifted away from the promotion of specific industries and toward the creation of the right environment for general technological advancement. Investment tax credits, the principal type of benefit offered, are granted to projects involving investments in R&D and in human resource development. This style of management has proved relatively attractive to foreign investors, although the pace of development in capital market structures severely lags behind industrial economic progress. It is noticeable that one of the few sectors still rather closed to foreigners (despite intense lobbying from the United States and the EC)—financial services—remains unsophisticated compared with the highly developed financial services sectors in Hong Kong and Singapore.

Korea. The most difficult investment environment for foreigners in East Asia appears to be Korea, which has undergone stormy periods of labor unrest over the last decade. Sharply rising wage costs and high interest rates are contributing to the factors behind the decision of some foreign firms to leave the country. On a more fundamental basis, however, surveys (Lasserre and Probert 1992a, b) have shown that European investors find the competitive climate in Korea more difficult to come to terms with than elsewhere in the region. The interventionist stance of the government, a sense that foreign firms are discriminated against in official (and less overt) regulations, and the importance given to having a good network of "contacts" in order to succeed tend to discourage Western investment.[14]

Korea may be the least understood business environment, but the government has tried in the last five years to create better conditions for foreign investment. The aim is to attract foreign technology, in order to reduce technological dependence on Japan. However, its weak record on protection of intellectual property rights suggests that it will not be a goal easily reached.

9.8.3 Foreign Investment Policies in ASEAN: Incentives, Priorities and Restrictions

Notwithstanding upheavals in the Philippines, an important factor in the political stability of Southeast Asia over the last 25 years has been the ASEAN organization. A semblance of unity has been preserved on all issues, no matter how great the behind-the-scenes discord. This has helped to create a friendly environment for investors, even though hard economic achievements by the Association to date are few. National interests have tended to prevail over the broader scene where proposed joint projects have been concerned. The recent moves to create an ASEAN Free Trade Zone (AFTA) signal a stronger imperative toward economic cooperation.

Since ASEAN in no sense pretends to economic union, each government pursues its own investment policies. Each has become more liberal over the last decade, but at its own pace, reflecting differences in economic structure and stage of development. Some competition has emerged between countries to attract projects that might otherwise go to a neighboring nation. This has led some commentators (for example, Guisinger 1991) to suggest the adoption of a common investment policy, much as the EC has done, limiting total incentive packages to a certain percentage of the investment value. Despite the impetus created by AFTA, such a move at the official level seems unlikely. Some evidence of an opposite trend can be seen in the discouragement of certain types of investment in some countries: Singapore and, increasingly, Malaysia now positively discourage labor-intensive FDI. In other respects, convergence of ASEAN governments' policies appears to be taking place, as restrictions on investment and performance requirements are lowered.

The volume of inward investment flows experienced by the region as a whole since 1985 has brought bottlenecks into the system and highlighted infrastructural weaknesses. This has prompted a reassessment of FDI priorities by some governments, particularly of the need to spread industrial development more evenly throughout the country. In some cases the role of the national investment board has been redefined away from the original requirement to act as controller of proposed investment to a more genuine support agency.

The investment environment in Singapore is widely regarded as one of the most attractive in the region. Policy has been remarkably consistent over the years. Limited recourse to official development aid (high domestic savings rates rendering the country ineligible) and little need to resort to external financing for investment make Singapore more heavily dependent on FDI than other ASEAN countries as a source of management and marketing expertise, and of technology (Chia 1991). The small scale of the domestic economy required an early shift from labor-intensive manufacturing up the technological ladder into more capital intensive projects and high value-added services. Initiation of the "growth triangle" concept has speeded the process of transferring labor-intensive activities to neighboring countries.

Malaysian social and economic planning has been colored by the perceived need to protect the franchise of the *bumiputra* Malay population. Foreign equity rules for this reason have been more restrictive than in Singapore, where there are no controls on foreign ownership. In Thailand the emphasis now lies on qualitative rather than quantitative assessment of FDI projects and the role of the Board of Investments has been redefined. Indonesia and the Philippines, where structural changes have followed more slowly, have each undertaken in the last five years sweeping changes to FDI application procedures in an effort to speed the pace of development. Both countries now operate simple negative lists where foreign investment is barred; in "open" sectors 100 percent foreign capital is now permitted.

9.8.4 Foreign Investment Policies in China: Incentives, Priorities and Restrictions

Chinese government attitudes to FDI have pursued an erratic course in the last decade, and political risk will remain relatively high compared with the rest of the region as long as the leadership succession issue is unresolved. Commitment to the "capitalist road" is nevertheless firmer, and the ten-year experiment with the coastal provinces' Special Economic Zones (which prevented foreign investment tainting the whole country) is now to be expanded to the interior. Lacunae in the legal framework are slowly being filled, but the lack of transparency in the application of many regulations renders the environment a difficult one for foreigners. Joint venturing is still very much the government's preference for foreign involvement although technically foreigners have been allowed for some time to operate a wholly owned venture. Faster liberalization in the ASEAN countries and the emergence of new FDI destinations such as Vietnam, create competition for the type of FDI projects China wants to attract.

9.8.5 Patterns of Foreign Investment

A lack of comprehensive data by home or host country[15] precludes detailed examination of sectoral FDI, as numerous commentators have indicated in the past. Some general trends are discernible. The overall preference among European firms has been to export rather than invest, or, if investment did take place the motive was to defend share in large protected markets (for example in Latin America) or to secure raw material inputs.[16] The primary motivation to invest in Asia for European (particularly British and Dutch) and, to a lesser extent, American firms has been oil-related. More recently the service industry has attracted attention, in commerce—which seems to reflect the preference for exporting—and in banking as financial sectors have been liberalized.

Table 9.12 shows the relationship between individual Asian countries' imports and cumulative investment stock by origin of exporter/investor. The European preference for exports emerges clearly. European firms' relative under-representation as investors in the region is shown in Table 9.13. In no country does the EC appear as the top investor; only in Malaysia and Indonesia is it ranked second.

The greater challenge to EC relative shares in Southeast Asia is presented by the wave of investment in ASEAN by ANIEs firms seeking to maintain their competitive edge. Taiwan overtook Japan as the top investor in the Philippines (since 1988), Malaysia (since 1990) and Indonesia (since 1991). Singapore alone among ASEAN countries attracts little ANIEs manufacturing investment since wages are similar to home country levels, but Hong Kong has a long history of involvement in the services sector. This wave of ANIEs FDI in ASEAN is partly the result (though not for Taiwan) of the loss of GSP status in the United States, particularly for such industries as electrical equipment and food processing, and the need to find new investment locations where GSP privileges could continue to be enjoyed (United Nations 1992). Production of textiles and clothing, footwear, watches, steel and other manufactured goods either excluded from the GSP or facing NTBs was relocated to Southeast Asia to take advantage of lower labor costs.

In contrast to Western company FDI, Japanese firms concentrated on manufacturing investments in the latter part of the 1980s. Manufacturing accounts for around 40 percent of Japanese investment in the region, compared with just 25 percent of American FDI (or 17 percent if nonresource related manufacturing activities are included). Where Europeans have entered the manufacturing sector, activity is concentrated in the foods and chemical industries, both of which serve local markets. In other industries, local populations have tended to be dismissed as potential consumers of European firms' products (European firms were mostly too late to participate as investors in the import-substitution phase of Asian countries' economic development); this is in direct contrast with the strategy of Japanese firms, which now, in addition to exporting from Asia to third markets including the United States and Europe, focus on the increasingly wealthy domestic consumer market.

A distinguishing feature of intra-Asian FDI is the involvement of small and medium-sized companies in the relocation of production facilities to other countries. The bulk of European and United States investors are multinationals, which, to judge from host country investment data, seem to prefer large scale investments and 100 percent or at least majority ownership of a venture. Many Western firms have discovered that majority shareholdings do not necessarily confer the same degree of management control in Asia that they do at home. Host countries which have insisted strongly on joint participation between foreign and local parties have generally proved less successful in attracting major foreign (Western) projects than those with more liberal policies. The approval of a 100 percent owned project is not necessarily the advantage investors may believe, since they are voluntarily cutting themselves off from a potentially highly beneficial network of local contacts such as the Chinese "common market" which spreads throughout most of the region.

Approximately 90 percent of European FDI in ASEAN is made by Germany, the U.K. and the Netherlands, all of which are major investors in other parts of the world outside the EC. French firms, with one or two notable exceptions, are strikingly absent from the Asian investment scene.[17] Singapore attracts the largest amount of European FDI, while Thailand appears to be the least popular destination.[18] Bank of Thailand data suggest the U.K. is the largest EC investor in the country.

British firms also invest most in the Malaysian manufacturing sector, followed by the Netherlands and Germany. Between 1980 and 1988, approximately 30 percent of U.K. investment stock was in food manufacturing and a further 20 percent in chemicals; only 6 percent had been invested in the electrical and electronics sector, whereas 43 percent of Japanese FDI, 31 percent of American and 23 percent of Taiwanese investment capital had been directed into this industry over the same period.

Philippine Central Bank statistics show the Netherlands to be the top EC investor, with the U.K. ranked second. Neither had cumulative stock of more than US$150 million for the 20 year period 1970–March 1990; no other European country even topped the US$100 million mark. The pattern is similar in Taiwan, despite the more favorable environment—although Netherlands FDI stock exceeded US$500 million. Electricals, chemicals and the motor industry have been the magnet for recent EC investments.

Singapore is the one ASEAN country where European firms—Dutch, French and German—have achieved a reasonable presence in the electronics sector, albeit smaller than either that of the United States or Japan. German firms are involved in precision instrument production in addition to electronics. Sophisticated infrastructure and the open financial services sector has attracted the bulk of German banking investment to Singapore. The government's fiscal inducements have successfully encouraged several European firms to locate regional service center activities there.

In absolute terms EC investment in Asia remains far behind that of Japan and the United States. British and German FDI stocks have increased (Wagner 1989), but cannot match the doubling of Japanese cumulative investment in the region in 1981–87. Since 1985 the relative share of Japanese FDI flows destined for Asia has declined, but increased rapidly in absolute terms at least until 1989. The impact of this flood of Japanese capital has been far greater on the relatively small Asian economies than the larger flows which have gone to the industrialized world.

Singapore alone has seemed to maintain its relative share of EC investment. The U.K. and Germany sustained or even increased FDI to Singapore relative to total FDI while shares to other Asian countries—particularly Malaysia—have slipped. Singapore and Korea boast a 5 percent share of Germany's total FDI stock; 1 percent to 1.5 percent is held in Taiwan and Thailand, and negligible shares are in other Asian countries.

Since the second half of 1991 Germany has increased FDI flows to eastern Europe at the probable expense of some investment in Asia. Since host country investment policies apply equally to all foreign investors and Asia has managed to improve or at least maintain its attractiveness relative to other developing countries, the only conclusion to be drawn is that EC developing country investment priorities will continue to lie elsewhere than in Asia.

9.9   Asian Foreign Direct Investment in the EC

While EC companies may be able to afford to shun opportunities in Asia, the importance of the EC for Asian companies cannot be underestimated. They must adopt strategies which allow them to cope with the barriers erected by EC trade policy.

Practically all instances of manufacturing investment by Asian firms in the EC to date are defensive in nature,[19] established to evade voluntary export restraints or in response to anti-dumping charges. Until 1988 outward investment decisions by Korean and Taiwanese firms (who constitute the vast majority of Asian investors in the West) were hardly influenced by EC moves toward the single market; 80 percent of FDI stock held by these countries was in North America. General or specialized trading accounted for more than four-fifths of Korean investment in the EC prior to 1988; the only three production investments were in electronics.

Responses of Korean and Taiwanese companies to the challenge of the EC have been rather different. Korean firms moved rapidly after 1988 to establish manufacturing plants in order to circumvent the NTBs raised against their imports. By the end of 1990, more than ten Korean companies had established 20 factories and a further 30 were at the planning stage. An element of self-defeating competition appears to have entered the decision-making process: half the plants were involved in the production of TVs, video recorders, car stereos and compact disc players. Samsung (in Portugal), Daewoo (in France) and Lucky-Goldstar (in Germany) are all involved in both TV and video production; all three have manufacturing operations in the U.K. as well. This has done little either to reduce friction with the authorities, which believe it suggests market targeting, or to generate product differentiation leading to improved brand recognition among European consumers. The strategy for market entry has been overwhelmingly in favor of greenfield manufacturing projects; very few have involved local partners and acquisition activity is minimal.

The much smaller Taiwanese firms tend to occupy high technology niche markets, with higher product differentiation than Korean firms. They have concentrated on developing distribution networks, often through acquisition since perceived time constraints prevent the building from scratch of marketing channels. Over-dependence on OEM (original equipment manufacturing) in the past left computer firms without internationally recognized brand names, though this seems to be changing. The move into European manufacturing is coming more slowly.

Outside high technology industries such as office and computer-related equipment where some competitive advantages even in Europe are held, Taiwanese companies must struggle to make a case for investment in the EC. The same difficulty affects Hong Kong and ASEAN clothing and toy manufacturers. Very few cases exist of FDI from other Asian countries.[20] Leaving aside the problems caused by locating in an expensive developed country, Asian firms lack depth of management experience overseas, particularly in European countries.

The "East European option," siting manufacturing or distribution operations in countries with special access to the EC market, has been pursued aggressively by Korean firms and to a lesser extent by Taiwanese companies. Few examples exist of Asian investment in other countries which enjoy EC special preferences.[21]

9.10 Problems, Prospects and Conclusions

The EC has largely ignored the effect its longer-term objectives of economic and political union might have on developing countries. Trade policy remains backward looking, in the sense that protection is given to ailing domestic industries in order to sustain them rather than force restructuring, and therefore it is discriminatory toward dynamic newcomers.

Trade friction has concentrated historically on the relationship with Japan, but is becoming increasingly acrimonious with Korea. Political dialogue between the EC and ASEAN is of long-standing origin but has a history of failure to stimulate interest in developing inter-regional relationships at the private business level. Two-way trade between the EC and Asia has increased, but more as a result of efforts by Asian firms to increase their presence in the European market. Asia's share of the EC's total trade remains extremely underdeveloped compared to the contribution it makes to world GNP. Evidence suggests that European firms are losing competitiveness on world markets but are beguiled by performance inside the boundaries of the EC.

The European preference for exporting rather than undertaking foreign direct investment, and for developed country rather than developing country FDI does not promise much potential for a resurgence of interest in Asia. Proximity to East European and Mediterranean countries coupled with political imperatives suggest greater attention accruing to these regions. In any case, potential economies of scale for EC firms arising from the creation of the single market may lessen the perceived need for cost-motivated FDI in third countries altogether. This would further encourage a swing in investment and production back to the home region.

Alternatively, the positive scenario for economic growth in the Asian region compared with non-EC countries closer to home may be sufficient to continue to attract European investors to look to Asia as an investment location. The investment climate is undoubtedly more favorable there.

For Asian countries the trading relationship with the EC will remain difficult but must be managed. The onus lies on Asian firms and governments to reduce the gap since the imbalance in the importance of the relationship lies firmly in favor of the EC. Despite considerable fears among Asian countries about the impact of the Single European Market on trade, on balance satisfactory completion of the Uruguay Round of the GATT negotiations and the effects it will have on the MFA seem likely to be of far greater significance to long-term trade relations.

Notes

1. All references to Asia, developing Asia, or developing East Asian countries in this chapter refer to the members of ASEAN, the ANIEs and China (see notes 2 and 3 below).
2. The six members are Brunei, Indonesia, Malaysia, the Philippines, Singapore and Thailand. Brunei is excluded from the discussions here, unless otherwise stated, since non-oil trade and investment is small.
3. In this chapter, the ANIEs are the Republic of China (referred to throughout as Taiwan), South Korea (referred to as Korea) and Hong Kong.
4. If Singapore were to be included among the ANIEs, trade with the EC would represent 13.7 percent of this grouping's total trade.
5. The Standard International Trade Classification allows international comparison of product categories, ranging from the broadest, single-digit classification to the most detailed, eight-digit category.
6. Perusahaan Otomobil Nasional, known as Proton, produced its first car in 1985 as a joint venture between the Malaysian government's heavy industrial holding company and Mitsubishi Motors of Japan. Following partial privatisation in 1992 the government controls slightly less than 50 percent of the company. Mitsubishi Motors' stake has fallen to 20 percent. Cumulative exports to the U.K. of Proton cars, which carry no import duties under the GSP, totalled 45,000 units by September 1992. Much of the additional production capacity scheduled for 1993–95 is planned for export to the U.K. and Europe.
7. "Un-common Market", *Far Eastern Economic Review*, February 25, 1993, 42–43.
8. The GSP offers nonreciprocal and nondiscriminatory trade preferences to eligible developing countries, as well as duty-free access for semi-manufactured and manufactured goods, and tariff reductions or exemptions on eligible products.
9. The 70 or so signatories of the Convention are otherwise known as the African–Caribbean–Pacific (ACP) countries.
10. The European Free Trade Association includes Austria, Finland, Iceland, Lichtenstein, Norway, Sweden and Switzerland.
11. The EC is expected to withdraw GSP status from South Korea, Hong Kong and Singapore. The U.S. withdrew these countries' GSP status in 1989.
12. This is the result of the wide variations in income level, degree of economic development, and trade and investment policy goals encompassed by the grouping.
13. Brunei is omitted owing to the small scale of exports involved.
14. A good network of contacts is important in any country, but the results of the survey indicate that this need is particularly acute in Korea.
15. Most host countries exclude investments in the oil and gas industry from their FDI data. There is good reason to believe, therefore, that European interests in Singapore are understated by a wide margin. Petroleum refining attracted the bulk of FDI in Singapore up to the early 1970s, and although new investments are few, foreign firms continue to spend considerable funds on the technological upgrading of their facilities.
16. EC political priorities and the thrust of EC government incentives for natural resources have been clearly concentrated on sub-Saharan Africa, with implicit advantages for European firms investing there.
17. Former French interests in Southeast Asia were heavily concentrated in Indochina. The emergence of Vietnam as a destination for foreign investment is recognised as the last chance for France to build a presence in the region.
18. Investment data throughout is based on host country statistics, though they are notoriously incomplete and difficult to compare—for developed as well as developing countries—owing to differing criteria for recording data (approvals, actual investment, investment in priority sectors for which incentives are given, inclusion of reinvestment,

and the like). Rather than relying on dollar amounts, figures given should be regarded as indicative of trends.
19. A rare exception is the Taiwanese firm Tatung, which acquired Decca TV's plant at Bridgnorth, U.K., in 1981.
20. Several Asian companies are pursuing internationalization by deliberately remaining regional players, where competitive advantage can be maintained.
21. The Thai group Charoen Pokphand has an investment in Turkey.

References

Chia, Siow Yue, 1991, "The EC Internal Market and ASEAN–EC Direct Investment Flows," in Norbert Wagner (ed.), *ASEAN and the EC: The Impact of 1992*, Institute of Southeast Asian Studies, Singapore, pp. 289–317.

Davenport, Michael and Sheila Page, 1991, *Europe: 1992 and the Developing World*, Overseas Development Institute, London.

Guisinger, Stephen, 1991, "Foreign Direct Investment Flows in East and Southeast Asia: Policy Issues," *ASEAN Economic Bulletin*, 8(1): 29–46.

Harris, Stuart and Brian Bridges, 1983, *European Interests in ASEAN*, Routledge & Kegan Paul, London.

Hiemenz, Ulrich, 1991, *The Future of Asia-Pacific Economies—A View from Europe*, Kiel Working Paper No. 460, Kiel Institute of World Economics, Kiel.

———, 1992, "European FDI in the Asia-Pacific Region," paper presented at the LVMH-Sponsored Conference on Europe, United States and Japan in the Asia-Pacific Region, Current Situation and Perspectives, Fontainebleau, 14–15 February.

Langhammer, Rolf, 1986, "EEC Trade Policies towards Asian Developing Countries," *Asian Development Review*, 4(2): 93–113.

Langhammer, Rolf and Ulrich Hiemenz, 1985, "Declining Competitiveness of EC Suppliers in ASEAN Markets: Singular Case or Symptom?" *Journal of Common Market Studies*, 24(2): 105–19.

Lasserre, Philippe and Jocelyn Probert, 1992a, *Strategic and Marketing Intelligence in Asia-Pacific*, Euro-Asia Centre Research Series No. 8, Fontainebleau.

———, 1992b, *Strategic Logic and Competitive Climate in the Asia-Pacific Region*, Euro-Asia Centre Research Series No. 12, Fontainebleau.

Page, Sheila, 1987, "The Structure of Foreign Investment," in Christopher Stevens and Joan van Themaat (eds.), *EEC and the Third World: A Survey: International Division of Labour*, Hodder and Staughton for Overseas Development Institute and Institute of Development Studies, London, pp. 44–69.

———, 1992, *Some Implications of Europe 1992 for Developing Countries*, OECD Development Centre Technical Paper No. 60, OECD, Paris.

Pangestu, Mari and Ida N. Hasni, 1991, "The EC Internal Market and the ASEAN Textile and Clothing Industry," in Norbert Wagner (ed.), *ASEAN and the EC: The Impact of 1992*, Institute of Southeast Asian Studies, Singapore, pp. 190–240.

United Nations, 1992, *World Investment Directory*, Vol. 1: *Asia and the Pacific*, New York.

Wagner, Norbert, 1989, *ASEAN and the EC: European Investment in ASEAN*, Institute of Southeast Asian Studies, Singapore.

Winters, Alan, 1993, *The European Community: A Case of Successful Integration*, Centre for Economic Policy Research Discussion Paper No. 755, London.

Wong, Poh Kam, 1991, "The EC Internal Market and the ASEAN Electronics Industry," in Norbert Wagner (ed.), *ASEAN and the EC: The Impact of 1992*, Institute of Southeast Asian Studies, Singapore, pp. 153–89.

Part III

TOWARD AN ASIA-PACIFIC TRADING BLOC

Part III deals with the to-be-or-not-to-be dilemma of regional integration. The export success of the Asia-Pacific economies, discussed in the preceding section, has generated trade tension with the Asia-Pacific economies' large trading partners such as the U.S. and the EC. The Asia-Pacific economies, and particularly Japan, are competitive in several products in which the U.S. and the EU manufactures are losing comparative advantage. Interestingly, the region's increased exports have been coupled with substantial growth of imports of raw materials and capital equipment. However, the growth of imports in the region has been overlooked. Every now and then interest in economic regionalism increases. Concerns have been raised as to whether the world economy will break into three discriminatory trade blocs. Economists, policymakers and the business community in the region, however, have overwhelmingly favored maintenance of an open world trading system in conformity with Article 1 of the World Trade Organization (WTO). So far the idea of a regional trading bloc has been consciously spurned. Among the bilateral and regional trade initiatives promoting liberalization in the recent past, the Asia Pacific Economic Cooperation (APEC) forum offers the best prospects for cooperation. APEC's guiding principles stipulate that cooperation should be outward-looking, and that consensus should be built on a gradually broader range of economic issues. APEC was established in 1989 and includes 15 economies from both sides of the Pacific. Andrew Elek (Chapter 10) has followed the concept of outward-looking regional cooperation with a missionary zeal for over a decade. He proposes four pragmatic options for profitable cooperation: (1) improving market access, (2) reducing uncertainty regarding future market access, (3) reducing physical bottlenecks, and (4) harmonizing domestic legislation and rules.

To be sure, it will not be easy to realize economic gains from nondiscriminatory trade liberalization but progress should be possible in some sectors where complementarity among the APEC economies is obvious. Preferential or discriminatory arrangements are sure to have a deleterious impact on the multilateral trading system which, in turn, will be injurious to the regional prosperity of the Asia-Pacific. The region gained enormously while international trade was being liberalized under the aegis of the GATT. Elek, therefore, recommends an evolutionary approach, seeking early consensus on less contentious issues in order to build a sense of trust and understanding needed for more effective cooperation among economies on both sides of the Pacific, without discrimination against extra-regional economies.

A good deal of progress has been made toward regional trade liberalization. At the APEC officials meeting in June 1993, participating government officials agreed to:

1. Conduct a viability study of the development of a pilot tariff database project, which would provide timely and detailed information on tariff levels.
2. Initiate a survey on regional tariff policies with a view to the development of an APEC tariff manual.
3. Prepare an APEC customs guide.
4. Hold an APEC customs fair.
5. Publish an investment regulation guidebook.

They also agreed to circulate a survey of regional standards and conformance practice, developed by Australia in collaboration with Japan and New Zealand. This progress is reasonable, even significant, given the short life of APEC.

The last significant development regarding APEC was the 1994 Bogor summit, which, according to aficionados like C. Fred Bergsten, was not only an important economic event but the "biggest trade agreement in the history." Notwithstanding the fact that it was not a binding agreement, it is sure to have an enormous impact on the regional trade and economies. C. Fred Bergsten (Chapter 11), who is the chairman of the APEC Eminent Persons Group (EPG), sees in the Bogor summit possibilities for the next—the ninth—round of the multilateral trade negotiations. His reason is that since APEC has adopted the maxim of open regionalism, the trade liberalization that takes place in the APEC region will be extended to the rest of the world. The APEC countries' enthusiasm to accelerate the implementation of the Uruguay Round is another meaningful achievement of the Bogor summit. Together these countries account for more than half of the world trade and include the two largest exporters in the world. An agreement accelerate the implementation of the Uruguay Round by the two largest exporters would augur well for the Uruguay Round as well as the newly formed World Trade Organization (WTO). In addition, during the summit participants strongly encouraged further unilateral trade liberalization, a notion which sounded alien even to the United States which has played the role of a pioneer in the area of free trade and liberalization in the past.

The progress of the Uruguay Round did not resemble a legato, if anything it was a staccato passage. It causes more than the usual amount of concern in economies that have been successful traders, and promoted regional integration notions. Since the failure of the Round was a real probability, these economies needed a ready alternative. Yamazawa (Chapter 12) posits that despite the lack of Japanese effort and absence of a formal, institutionalized framework, the Asia-Pacific economies are uniting—integrating if you please—in a weak form of regional framework which is not intended to discriminate against outsiders (Cf. Chapter 10). Not only regional but also sub-regionally economic ties have emerged and gradually strengthened in an informal manner. There is a wide consensus in the region that a weak form of regional integration or "open regionalism" will help the region realize its high growth potential.

Chapter 13 (Petri), using long-term historical data, examines whether the region is a trading bloc in the sense that its trade is more regionally oriented than would be expected on the basis of a random trade pattern. The analytical base of this chapter is a simple model of bloc formation. This chapter concludes that although regional interdependence has intensified since the Plaza accord in 1985, the increase is small in an historical context. A long-term perspective reverses the usual belief of increasing economic affinity and interdependence among the regional economies. The principal element of the long-term story is a shift of linkages from the regional partners to a more diversified group of partners, including the United States. This conclusion, however, does not vitiate the significance of the watershed point reached in 1985. Large changes have taken place in investment linkages since then. This development, along with the anecdotal evidence on how individual agents and governments are stepping up investments in regional linkages, suggest that from now on the formation of an Asia-Pacific bloc may catch momentum.

During the post-Plaza Accord period, Japanese firms strengthened their economic ties with the ASEAN countries. In this respect they soon surpassed American firms which had a dominant presence in the past. The Japan–ASEAN economic bond is developing along the same lines as the Japan–ANIEs bond did in the past. Japan's exports to this subgroup of regional economies are dominated by capital and intermediate goods while imports are largely nonmanufactured goods, that is, if "boomerang exports" are excluded (Das 1993: Ch. 4).

Chapter 14 (Ishigami) points out that Japanese firms have been relocating to the ASEAN region as the yen appreciated, wages in the ANIEs rose, the won and the NT dollar appreciated, industrial relations in Korea deteriorated and environmental problems in Taiwan worsened. This led to an intra-firm and intra-regional division of labor between Japan and the ASEAN countries. The Japanese firms began to forge an economic area in this region by erecting design and R&D facilities. Japanese firms have also entered into joint ventures with local firms, enabling them to technologically update and diversify their product lines. They also made it possible for the ASEAN firms to enter into new lines of businesses, hitherto unknown in their domestic economies and to train their manpower. These developments augur well for the new division of labor in the Asia-Pacific region.

Reference

Das, Dilip K., 1993, *The Yen Appreciation and the International Economy*, Macmillan, London.

Chapter 10

Andrew Elek

Pacific Economic Cooperation: Policy Choices for the 1990s

10.1 Introduction

The remarkable recent growth of most East Asian economies, and of their trade with each other and with North America, has been extensively documented (for example, Drysdale 1989; Lee Kuan Yew 1990; Roh 1991). The Asia-Pacific economies now account for over half of world GDP.[1] Close to 65 percent of their trade is with each other; put differently, the 19 percent share of the world trade that takes place among the Asia-Pacific Economic Cooperation (APEC) economies is similar to the 17 percent share of world trade among the twelve members of the European Community.

Until quite recently, this growth of production and trade among a very diverse group of economies has taken place with almost no intergovernmental regional institutions, contrasting sharply with the European experience. Spectacular trade growth has sometimes occurred between economies whose political leaders have no diplomatic channels of communication (for example, China's recently burgeoning trade with Taiwan and with South Korea well before the establishment of inter-government relations).

Against this background, there is some skepticism about recent initiatives for intergovernmental cooperation in the Pacific. Is such cooperation just a make work junket (Hughes 1991)? Could regional economic cooperation actually prove harmful, by getting in the way of a successful trend, or even cut across prospects for an open global trading system? To answer these questions, it is useful to assess why governments in the Pacific region have invested so much recent effort in cooperative initiatives.

10.2   Motives for Pacific Economic Cooperation

The conservative motive for cooperation—to sustain the recent trend toward mutually beneficial interdependence—has been important. The success of East Asian economies has been based on good economic management and high saving rates which allowed these economies to invest massively in human and physical capital, leading to spectacular and sustained increases in productivity. Success has also stemmed from their ability and willingness to take advantage of changing international market opportunities. But, perhaps most importantly, their growth has been sustained by the relatively open multilateral trading system during recent decades.

While the system of international trade under the General Agreement on Tariffs and Trade (GATT) is deficient in several important respects, it has made it possible for Japan and other Western Pacific economies to exploit their comparative advantage. Success in exporting, initially light manufactures, followed by an increasingly sophisticated range of goods and services, has been the key to the growing prosperity of these economies (Drysdale 1989).

10.2.1   Rising Trade Tensions

The rapid growth in East Asian exports led to rising trade tensions during the 1980s. East Asia's trading partners tended to overlook the very substantial matching growth of imports, especially of raw materials and capital equipment (Okita 1992: 5, 6). Attention tended to focus on the capture of market share by East Asian exporters and the pressure this placed on sectors where North American and European economies no longer held comparative advantage. These economies and, until recently, Australia tended to react defensively, often imposing selective import restrictions or demanding "voluntary" export restraints. Trade tensions across the Pacific have also been exacerbated by high and persistent U.S. trade deficits. Although overwhelmingly due to macroeconomic imbalances rather than East Asia's remaining trade barriers, the deficits provided the U.S. with an excuse for threats of retaliation using the "Super 301" section of the 1988 U.S. trade legislation.

Another defensive response to intensive competition has been a widespread drift away from nondiscriminatory multilaterism toward discriminatory, bilateral or regional, solutions to trade problems (Tan et al. 1992). The European community's (EC's) movement toward a unified market by the end of 1992 has been followed by the U.S.–Canada Free Trade Area (FTA), then the North American Free Trade Agreement (NAFTA), which may lead toward a wider FTA including a progressively greater part of Latin America (Baker 1991). Several other FTA options were under consideration in the late 1980s (Schott 1989). These initiatives were designed to be consistent with Article XXIV of the GATT,[2] but they represent marked departures from the fundamental GATT principle of non-discrimination and inevitably imply some diversion of trade from optimal sources and directions.

The difficulties encountered in the Uruguay Round of trade negotiations, combined with the trend towards selective import restrictions and discriminatory FTAs, constitute a serious threat to the open global trading system and therefore to East Asian economies which rely heavily on global markets. East Asia's leaders are aware that, prior to the Uruguay Round, they had not played a significant part in shaping the GATT-based trading system. None of them acting alone, not even Japan, can have much influence on the evolution of rules for world trade. To forge alliances to preserve and gradually enhance rules providing for a stable open global environment for trade and investment is another important motive for economic cooperation in the Pacific region.

10.2.2 Beyond Trade in Goods

The widening range of economic transactions in the Pacific region has also exposed the multiplicity of impediments that increase the cost of such transactions, sometimes prohibitively. As Harris (1991: 302) notes, an important objective of economic cooperation is to reduce such barriers, not just to trade but to travel, payments, and capital and labor movements.

At the end of the Uruguay Round, GATT rules cover, at least in principle, trade in all goods and services. But even the Uruguay Round has hardly begun to consider the obstacles to international trade, investment and payments that are imposed by divergences in the domestic policies of trading partners. Some of these are being addressed by sectoral bodies such as the International Telecommunications Union. However, as in GATT negotiations, it is difficult to reach consensus when over 100 governments are involved. Issues such as the physical impediments to trade (for example, inadequate or incompatible port facilities or air traffic control systems) are much more conveniently addressed by the groups of economies that trade intensively with each other. Therefore, despite the conclusion of the Uruguay Round, interest in closer, more effective cooperation will remain strong in the Pacific, building on bilateral, subregional as well as region-wide efforts.

The self-confidence generated by the spectacular economic growth of most regional economies in the past few decades provides a promising basis for further fruitful cooperation during the 1990s. There are, nevertheless, substantial risks. While the security environment has been transformed with the break-up of the USSR, threats to security remain, including the potential development of nuclear weapons by North Korea. The trust required for effective region-wide economic cooperation could also be severely damaged if any future U.S. political leadership succumbed to the substantial pressure to adopt the isolationist and protectionist policies advocated by some influential politicians.

10.3   Recent Developments

Since 1989, there have been many new initiatives for closer economic cooperation and integration around the Pacific.[3] The diversity of these initiatives, in terms of issues addressed and partners involved, reflects the diversity of the region itself.

Possibly the most significant recent region-wide initiative has been the ministerial-level APEC forum, launched in Australia in November 1989. APEC has evolved from the work of the Pacific Economic Cooperation Council (PECC),[4] which began in 1980, and a close working relationship has been forged between them. Both are designed to improve information about trade and investment links in the region, with task forces and working groups set up to identify common regional economic interests in fields ranging from trade policy, human resource development and technology transfer to energy and telecommunications.

APEC's guiding principles stipulate that cooperation should be outward looking, building consensus on a gradually broader range of economic issues. Regional trade liberalization is to be promoted, provided it is consistent with GATT principles and not to the detriment of other economies.[5] APEC participants include the six members of ASEAN, New Zealand, Australia, Papua New Guinea, China, Hong Kong, Taiwan, South Korea, Japan, Chile, Mexico, Canada and the USA.[6] Participation is to be open-ended, based on the strength of economic linkages; Mexico is the likely next participant. Since 1991, PECC has broadened its coverage even further, to include Russia, Mexico, Peru and Chile. The Pacific Islands are represented by the South Pacific Forum as observers in both APEC and PECC.

10.3.1   ASEAN

At the subregional level, a late 1990 proposal by Malaysia for an East Asian Economic Group received a mixed reception and has been steered, by ASEAN, to an East Asian Economic Caucus within the APEC framework (Tan et al. 1992: 328). The Singapore Summit of ASEAN in January 1992 marked a new phase of economic cooperation in Southeast Asia. The ASEAN Free Trade Area (AFTA), which is to evolve over the next 15 years, will include provision for a Common External Preferential Tariff (CEPT) scheme. In addition, the Framework Agreement for AFTA provides for cooperation in sectors such as minerals and energy, transport and communications, technology transfer, human resource development, finance and banking. The scope of the new proposals, described in detail in Pangestu et al. (1992) as well as in ASEAN (1992a, b, c), is considerably more ambitious than anything contemplated up to the late 1980s (Rieger 1989).

10.3.2 Other Regional Initiatives

The emerging "growth triangle," linking Singapore to the Malaysian state of Johor and the nearby Riau islands of Indonesia, including Batam, is based on less formal understandings about the rights of investors and the provision of infrastructure to link the three economies (Lee Tsao Yuan 1991). The rapidly increasing integration of Hong Kong, Taiwan and Southeast mainland China is a vivid example of subregional integration driven by economic logic rather than intergovernmental agreements (Sung 1991).

Recent developments in bilateral economic cooperation in the Pacific region include the 1990 Structural Impediments Initiative (SII) discussions between the U.S. and Japan. Both participants agreed to review some of their domestic economic policies in order to reduce impediments to trade and investment between them; and to do so in such a way as to avoid cutting across the interests of other economies. The terms of the SII included undertakings by Japan to expand public sector infrastructure investment and to liberalize its retail distribution system. The U.S. *inter alia* undertook to improve savings and educational standards. In contrast, an agreement made during then President George Bush's January 1992 visit to Japan to increase purchases of automotive components from the U.S. paid no regard to the interests of other suppliers and could damage them substantially.

The last few years have also seen a further development of the Closer Economic Relations (CER) arrangements between Australia and New Zealand, substantially unifying those two markets, and stimulating two-way trade while reducing barriers to trade with the rest of the world. An even greater acceleration of trade took place during the last three years between South Korea and mainland China, leading to informal cooperation and the establishment of "unofficial" trade promotion offices.

10.3.3 Next Steps

The challenge facing policy makers in the region is to build on all these regional, subregional and bilateral initiatives, consistently with the region's overriding interest in a more open global trading system.[7] The key to success will be to avoid divisive or discriminatory options, focusing instead on nondiscriminatory, confidence-building steps such as:

- ☐ enhanced exchange of information about trading patterns
- ☐ increased transparency of trade and investment policies
- ☐ reducing uncertainty in international transactions
- ☐ harmonization and/or mutual recognition of policies, regulations and standards
- ☐ nondiscriminatory lowering of tariffs and barriers to labor and capital movements

There are grounds for optimism about moves along these lines. Cooperative initiatives are taking place against a background of substantial unilateral steps by almost all East Asian nations to deregulate their economic systems and to liberalize their trade policies. Japan, Australia and New Zealand have been at the forefront of all OECD economies in terms of the scope of structural reform. The Newly Industrialized Economies (NIEs) of Asia and most ASEAN economies have substantially liberalized their trade regimes.[8] China's rapid growth during the 1980s was made possible by outward-looking economic reform (Raby 1991). Russia and Vietnam have also embarked on deregulation. Mexico's and Chile's advance to a less regulated, more open system of economic management has encouraged similar moves throughout much of Latin America.

Significant trade barriers still remain. The bans on rice imports by Japan and Korea, for example, continue to impose considerable costs on consumers in those countries. These barriers, as well as a large number of "informal" resistances to imports by several Asian economies, are continuing to exacerbate trade tensions across the Pacific.[9] Despite these problems, the dominant trend in East Asia—most spectacularly by China since the late 1970s has been one of "opening to the outside world."

10.4   Scope for Cooperation

Choices about matters on which to cooperate, and with whom, need to be considered concurrently. Given the diversity of the region, any Pacific economy wishing to reach understandings on a comprehensive range of issues would have to deal with just one or two economies at a time. But if issues can be broken up into discrete components a region-wide consensus on some well-defined matters may be possible.

A strategy for future cooperation that insisted on agreement on a comprehensive set of issues would create a risk that bilateral or subregional groupings might form, but would then prove difficult to link with each other. For example, if Australia decided that it would engage in economic cooperation only with economies prepared to reach understandings on *all* the topics covered by the CER agreement with New Zealand, it would not easily find new partners. It would be no less risky to adopt a strategy whereby Pacific regional cooperation had to proceed at the pace of those least interested. APEC participants have agreed, in principle, to look for areas of cooperation involving all of them. They have already agreed to exchange information about trade patterns and to standardize, and provide for full electronic interchange of, trade documentation. However, it will not be easy to find many initiatives which all 15 participants are willing to adopt simultaneously.

Fortunately, there is no need to follow either of these rather restrictive strategies. The following paragraphs outline what could prove to be a pragmatic, evolutionary approach to effective and reasonably broad-based regional cooperation. It aims to tackle four kinds of impediments to economic transactions in the region:

☐ *Market access barriers*: These include the heavy protection of some aspects of agriculture in North East Asia and North America, and the protection of textiles and clothing producers by Australia and North America.
☐ *Uncertainty about future market access*: The increasing resort to arbitrary and discriminatory measures to deal with losses of market share to imports and the

recent threats of unilateral trade retaliation, mostly aimed at East Asia, have increased uncertainty about regional trade prospects.

☐ *Physical bottlenecks*: Shortfalls in infrastructure (ranging from harbors to telecommunications) are serious impediments to trade in the most rapidly growing parts of the region, including coastal China, Indonesia and Thailand.

☐ *Differences in domestic rules and legislation*: Divergent standards relating to safety, quality and environmental matters and different approaches to commercial legislation can introduce distortions to regional trade and investment.

Market access barriers are well defined, but often intractable. The GATT has grappled with them for four decades. The protectionist sentiments that generate trade distortions are, all too often, also well entrenched within the APEC region. In order to develop the momentum of substantive regional cooperation, APEC's trade liberalization agenda should cover a wider range of trade problems than those imposed by tariffs or quotas.[10]

10.4.1 Reducing Physical Impediments

Reducing physical impediments to trade may be a pragmatic starting-point, since the potential for mutual benefit is readily appreciated. Exchange of information about patterns and trends in trade and tourism can pinpoint the investments needed to avoid infrastructure bottlenecks. Harmonization, or mutual recognition, of standards and procedures can also lead to more efficient use of infrastructure capacity. Analysis by APEC working groups, such as those dealing with human resource development, energy, transport, telecommunications, tourism and environment, is directed to this end; each can draw on the accumulated analysis of sectoral policy issues by the corresponding working groups of the PECC. For example, the use of existing transport infrastructure will be improved by APEC's project to achieve total electronic exchange of trade documentation by the end of the decade. It may take some time before APEC can agree on reducing any customs duties; meanwhile, progress can be made on standardizing customs documentation and clearance procedures.

More generally, the relevant working groups of APEC could review the range of standards that are being adopted by the EC. The EC's basic principle of mutual recognition of standards could also prove useful in Asia Pacific. That experience can point to products or processes where broad-based agreements may be relatively easy to achieve. Product labelling and safety standards, for example, could be considered at an early stage. Reaching agreement on environmental standards would almost certainly prove more sensitive; uniform standards may in any case not be appropriate for a group of economies with very different degrees of industrialization and population densities. But it may be possible to agree to share modern techniques for reducing the environmental side effects of some production processes; the dissemination of clean coal technology for power generation is already under consideration by APEC.

10.4.2 Harmonization of Legislation and Regulations

The harmonization of legislation and regulations affecting international transactions in the region will need to grapple with the sometimes radical differences in legal frameworks, compounded by the frequent lack of a clear definition of administrative rules. However, a potentially productive start can be made on rules influencing investment. For example, a common approach to defining the basic rights and responsibilities of foreign investors could avoid the laborious negotiation of scores of bilateral investment protection agreements. A more ambitious objective would be to work towards a more uniform approach to tax concessions offered to investors, avoiding wasteful and distorting "competition" for investment through subsidization.

The substantial harmonization of competition policies between Australia and New Zealand has led to agreement that anti-dumping action will no longer be taken by either partner against exports from the other. This example suggests that progressively closer harmonization of competition policies by a broader group of economies could be encouraged by a corresponding reduction in the scope for anti-dumping actions against those who participate in such harmonization. Such a trade-off could reduce an important source of uncertainty facing exporters in the Asia-Pacific region.

10.4.3 Dispute Settlement

Another useful step toward reducing uncertainty in regional trade would be for APEC participants to agree to adhere strictly to the new procedures and timetables for dispute settlement that are part of the final Uruguay Round outcome.[11] It may also be useful to consider wider access to the dispute settlement mechanism which may be included in the proposed North American Free Trade Agreement (NAFTA). A streamlined region-wide approach to dispute settlement should reduce resort to unilateral retaliation to resolve trade disputes.

10.4.4 Building Consensus

The foregoing list is by no means exhaustive, but indicates the pragmatic trade liberalization agenda that APEC could begin to consider. The issues considered so far have some important common features:

- ☐ In each case, there is scope for breaking down broad sets of issues into manageable policy options and grading them from less contentious to more difficult.
- ☐ Progress can be made on each separate issue, without any conflict with GATT principles and without detriment to others outside the region.[12]
- ☐ Nonparticipants would not be disadvantaged, but neither would they get an obvious "free ride": the benefits of an enhanced dispute settlement process within APEC, for example, would be of advantage to others only if they also agreed to adopt such better standards of behavior.

Progress could be made on individual issues by some APEC participants, ahead of others. Agreements on (say) product labelling standards among some subgroup of APEC participants need not be to the detriment of others, provided that the standards were well-defined (or "transparent"). Nonparticipants to the original understandings could then choose to adopt the same standards informally, possibly leading to subsequent, more formal endorsement.[13]

The preferable approach to tackling the above agenda would be to initiate discussions among all APEC participants. However, there is no reason to discourage or prevent progress by subgroups within APEC on the issues discussed so far, provided that provision is made for others to join a broadening consensus on particular issues over time. In other words, there is a substantive agenda on which progress need not be restricted to the "lowest common denominator" among participants.

ASEAN has adopted such a strategy in the AFTA Framework Agreement (ASEAN 1992b): ASEAN-wide discussions are to start on many facets of economic cooperation. At the same time, the agreement provides explicitly for some members reaching agreements on some matters earlier than others (ASEAN 1992b: Article 1.3; Sadli 1992). There is an underlying assumption that the nature of agreement reached among some members of ASEAN would be designed to facilitate subsequent endorsement by the other members. Moreover, the emphasis in the agreement on maintaining and strengthening ASEAN's economic linkages with its other trading partners suggests that agreements on some substantive issues could be broadened to include some other regional economies (see ASEAN 1992b: Article 5).

Parallel discussions of issues, such as harmonization or mutual recognition of certain standards or policies by ASEAN and by APEC working groups could well lead to some quite broadly-based (possibly APEC-wide) agreements during the 1990s. Such a process could then develop the sense of trust and common purpose required to tackle the wider and currently more contentious issues of cooperation.[14]

10.4.5 APEC IV

Following the adoption of outward-looking principles for regional economic cooperation at APEC III in 1991, the fourth Ministerial-level meeting of APEC in September 1992, in Bangkok, set the stage for substantial trade liberalization. The work program endorsed by Ministers at APEC IV provides for the development of a computerized database of tariff schedules of APEC participants, the harmonization of customs procedures and regulations affecting foreign investment within the APEC region. Considerable emphasis is to be placed on reducing impediments to trade and investment due to divergent or uncoordinated administrative rules affecting market access. Administrative measures which are expected to be addressed include:

- [ ] sanitary regulations
- [ ] labelling and packaging requirements
- [ ] technical standards and certification

☐ rules and marks of origin
☐ visa issue procedures
☐ transparency of trade regulations
☐ anti-dumping procedures
☐ environmental measures affecting trade[15]

This work will be supervised by an ad-hoc group of senior officials who will make recommendations to the next Ministerial-level meeting which will be chaired by the United States in 1993. The ten sectoral working groups of APEC, working in close cooperation with the task forces of the PECC, will continue to identify additional options for reducing impediments to international transactions. Importantly, a small group of eminent statesmen and economists from the region has been established following APEC IV. Their task is to take a longer-term view of economic cooperation in the Asia-Pacific region, to identify future opportunities and to anticipate potential impediments and sources of friction. They will make an initial set of recommendations to the 1993 Ministerial-level meeting of APEC.

APEC IV also agreed to establish a small permanent secretariat, to be based in Singapore, to support the ongoing work of all of APEC's working groups. This marks the end of the establishment phase of the new organization. It is now important to avoid the creation of an overly large new bureaucracy. Emphasis should remain on the policy oriented sectoral working groups to develop a broad-ranging and pragmatic agenda for trade liberalization.

APEC V, in 1993, led to wider participation in the process. Many economies have applied for consideration ranging from the Russian Federation to Papua New Guinea, Chile and Vietnam. There is some concern about diluting the effectiveness of a process if participation expands too rapidly. However, as long as it is understood that cooperative initiatives can be taken by some APEC economies ahead of others, then expanded membership can be consistent with promoting substantive economic cooperation. As discussed below, it is important for APEC to help avoid the emergence of tensions across the Pacific. Therefore, the early admission of some outward-looking Latin American economies is desirable. Mexico and Papua New Guinea joined APEC in 1993, with Chile joining in 1994.

10.5   Improving Market Access

In addition to the wide range of issues already discussed, considerable mutual benefit could also be derived from the reduction of traditional market access barriers such as tariffs and quotas. Drysdale and Garnaut (1989) noted that the remaining barriers to trade in the region, for example, in agriculture, textiles, clothing and processed minerals, tend, perversely, to be highest where there is most complementarity in terms of resource endowments and cost structures.

These barriers stand in the way of the efficient location of production around the region and preclude potential gains from greater specialization. By far the greatest share of benefits from further nondiscriminatory liberalization by the Asia-

Pacific region would accrue to the region itself, a conclusion that has been validated by experience. Liberalization and deregulation contributed to the spectacular growth of trade by APEC economies during the 1980s; no attempt was made to discriminate against the rest of the world, but the relative proximity, complementarity and dynamism of the Asia-Pacific economies ensured that much the largest part—76 percent—of trade growth from 1980 to 1990 was among APEC participants.

Market-opening measures everywhere face the political cost of reducing the protection of internationally uncompetitive sectors. The long-term benefits outweigh the short-term costs of adjustment, but the gains are delayed and widely spread while the costs are concentrated and immediate. To counter this strong resistance to trade liberalization, governments often seek to outflank the vested interests of protected sectors by negotiating for the simultaneous reduction of trade barriers by others, thereby offering immediate offsetting gains to some efficient export sectors.

The political pain involved in liberalization also tempts negotiators to keep trade barriers as bargaining counters, offering to liberalize market access for only those trading partners which are also lowering some of their barriers. There is great reluctance to allow other economies to "free-ride" on the liberalization that might be negotiated among a limited (for example, regional) group of economies. Such reluctance leads, all too often, to preferential or discriminatory trading arrangements which are contrary to GATT's fundamental principle of non-discrimination.

Most Pacific economies have accepted that the long-term economy-wide benefits of liberalization outweigh any short-term costs. The spectacular recent success of East Asian economies, in contrast to the highly protectionist economies of South Asia, the former USSR and Eastern Europe, vindicates this strategy. By acting unilaterally they have accepted, sensibly, that, in addition to their own long-term benefits, all other economies stand to gain; they have not allowed dog-in-the-manger concerns over gains by others to preclude relatively larger gains to themselves.

10.5.1 Priorities for Liberalization

The same logic could be extended to nondiscriminatory liberalization by *groups* of economies—once again they would achieve gains that were relatively greater than those accruing to the rest of the world. It is therefore useful to consider whether Pacific economies could identify sectors in which nondiscriminatory trade liberalization might prove possible, at a pace faster than is feasible in the Uruguay Round.[16] Appreciation of the difficulties involved in gaining support for such initiatives suggests a search for sectors where:

☐ complementarity among regional economies is evident
☐ the net gains from liberalization can be estimated

☐ the original reasons for protection have been weakened by changes in circumstances
☐ natural resource endowments and transport costs limit effective competition from outside the region

10.5.2 Processed Minerals

A potential candidate for early liberalization might be trade in processed minerals, including steel products. Import barriers to coal and other basic raw materials tend to be quite low, but to rise with the degree of processing. This tends to give a high degree of effective protection to processing in particular countries, distorting the economically efficient location of additional or replacement capacity for activities such as steel or aluminium production. The original reasons for the domestic processing of imported minerals by Japan, for example, are now essentially obsolete. Employment in these industries is now an even more trivial part of the workforce, while the high cost of industrial land and the considerably greater cost of meeting more rigorous environmental standards have reduced interest in such industries. The same considerations are increasingly relevant in South Korea and Taiwan. It is becoming clearer that the economy-wide benefits that would be generated by reducing costs to other industries would greatly outweigh the adjustment costs of phasing out aspects of mineral processing. The biggest gains from liberalization would accrue to the resource-poor industrial economies of the region by reducing the costs of inputs to industry; resource-abundant economies such as Australia, Canada and Indonesia would also benefit.[17]

Another option would be for all APEC participants to remove any barriers to trade in tropical products. As in the case of minerals, not only would consumers benefit, but the region would be likely to seize most of the new trade opportunities created by liberalization.

10.5.3 Textiles

Rapid liberalization of trade in textiles and clothing would have considerable benefits for regional consumers: directly for the labor-abundant participants in APEC, such as Indonesia and China, as well as indirectly for efficient raw material producers like Australia. The Uruguay Round outcome will phase out the trade-distorting Multifiber Arrangements by a gradual liberalization of all quota limits. But only marginal increases in access have been agreed upon for the next five years. APEC could contribute substantially to regional growth by agreeing to increase quota limits more rapidly than the minimum pace agreed upon in Geneva. However, it will be very difficult to overcome the resistance of textile producer lobbies in some industrialized economies.

10.5.4 Services

It may also prove difficult to promote rapid regional trade liberalization in services, where trade policy issues are less well understood and where the relative weakness of trade data precludes detailed quantitative analysis of the potential benefits and costs of liberalization. The Uruguay Round has led to an agreement in principle for all trade in services to be brought ultimately under GATT rules, but applying these principles to particular sectors will be a task for the rest of the 1990s and beyond. APEC could accelerate this process by developing sectoral codes for some services of particular interest, such as telecommunications and transport. APEC could then promote the GATT-wide adoption of such codes or consider adopting them within the region, pending wider acceptance.

These examples suggest that options for the nondiscriminatory trade liberalization of products can also be graded in terms of the likely difficulty in several trading partners reaching agreement. As discussed in the previous section, the absolute benefits from liberalization would be greater if all Pacific economies lowered particular trade barriers at the same time. However, so long as all trade liberalization is on a nondiscriminatory basis, no economy would be disadvantaged if some moved faster than others.

10.6 Avoiding Discriminatory Trade Blocs

Confrontations over ideologies and systems have by and large ended, and a new world order based on economic capabilities is about to emerge. The world's future and the destiny of mankind will largely depend on whether the new order fosters exclusive and self-centered regional economic blocs or whether it develops in the direction of promoting openness and cooperation among the regional economies (Roh 1991).

The strong commitment, enshrined in its statement of principles (*Seoul APEC Declaration 1991*, particularly Article 1[d]), to open regionalism and strong support for the GATT-based nondiscriminatory global trading system is an important feature of the new forum. APEC participants can give effect to this commitment directly by the joint pursuit of liberalizing proposals in GATT-based trade negotiations. They can also do so indirectly, by setting positive examples of nondiscriminatory ways to reduce obstacles to international trade and investment, without detriment to other economies, possibly by following up some of the options discussed above. But APEC is a new regional forum and, for the foreseeable future, most trade negotiations in the Pacific will not be APEC-wide but on a bilateral or subregional basis. Care will therefore be needed to ensure that decisions taken in the course of such negotiations do not destroy prospects for subsequent region-wide liberalization by creating tensions and divisions among groups of regional economies. To quote from President Roh's speech again:

In view of the vastness and diversities of the Asia-Pacific, the appearance of subregional groups may perhaps be inevitable for purposes of increased economic efficiency. Subregional groups, however, must also seek to develop in harmony with the open and cooperative order of the region. Asia-Pacific cooperation should not, in any case, develop into a competing relationship between East Asia and North America. On the contrary, it should play a central role for the promotion of a harmonious and balanced development of trans-Pacific relations (Roh 1991).

The U.S. is still the main export market for East Asia, and the U.S.–Japan bilateral economic relationship is among the most intense in the global, let alone the regional, economy. One of the objectives of APEC must be to encourage the two largest Pacific economies to have regard to the interests of their other regional trading partners; as noted by Drysdale (1991), APEC provides 'a convenient regional framework within which Japan can move toward a position of shared policy leadership with the United States, in buttressing and extending the GATT-based trade regime'.

Open global trade *can* be promoted through bilateral negotiations. The 1988 U.S.–Australia–Japan beef negotiations, for example, ensure that Japanese consumers benefit from cheaper beef and all producers can compete for their customers. Both the U.S. and Japan will benefit by implementing their 1990 Structural Impediments Initiative undertakings, but no other economy will be worse off. Provided bilateral or subregional trade negotiations lead to such nondiscriminatory outcomes, trade liberalization efforts by subgroups such as ASEAN can proceed in step with APEC-wide and global economic initiatives. Lee Kuan Yew (1990: para 13) described this process as "concentric circles of cooperation."

In contrast, bilateral or subregional efforts that lead to outcomes detrimental to the interests of others not directly involved will prove divisive, undermining prospects for region-wide liberalization. The pressure placed by the U.S. on Japan in early 1992 to agree to raise imports of motor components from the U.S., without regard to the interest of other suppliers, was clearly inconsistent with the pursuit of a nondiscriminatory global trading system as well as contrary to GATT rules. Preferential FTAs may be consistent with the letter (though not the spirit) of the GATT, but their proliferation in the Pacific region would create quite serious risks for region-wide cooperation.

Discriminatory trade liberalization does create additional trade among the participants and improved growth prospects may generate some new trade opportunities for outsiders. But some trade is bound to be diverted from more efficient directions, reducing the *absolute* gains from trade liberalization. The *relative* share of the reduced gains going to participants is increased, but the benefits to nonparticipants are considerably less and can even be negative. The higher political value often placed on relative as against absolute gains lies behind the conventional trend towards preferential trading arrangements.

The EC has been the most prominent example of postwar regional and preferential trade arrangements legitimized by GATT Article XXIV. The early phase of European economic cooperation involved a preferential reduction of market access barriers. But the EC has also demonstrated that free trade in goods leaves plenty of scope for further steps to reduce transaction costs in order to create a genuinely unified EC market. More recent initiatives for close economic relations, such as NAFTA and the Australia–New Zealand CER, also provide for a much wider range of agreements than the elimination of barriers to trade in goods. A central feature of the U.S.–Canada agreement is a process for consultation on and resolution of bilateral trade disputes. The CER goes further than any other existing economic cooperation arrangement in reducing obstacles to trade in services and harmonizing competition policy legislation. Similarly, as noted above, ASEAN's next steps toward closer economic cooperation extend well beyond the creation of a system of preferential tariffs.

Such broadening of the scope of economic cooperation arrangements reflects the substantial changes in the pattern of international transactions that have occurred since the inception of the GATT over 40 years ago. At that time, international transactions were dominated by trade in physical goods. Since then, trade in services has expanded much more rapidly, trade in electronically stored information is the fastest growing segment of all trade, and movements of various types of labor and capital are closely associated with most trade in goods and services. Yet, despite the rapidly shrinking relative importance of trade in goods, the setting up of an FTA often tends to be regarded as the natural starting-point for closer economic cooperation between pairs or regional groups of economies.

An important disadvantage of a preferential FTA-based approach is that, for consistency with GATT Article XXIV, a large set of issues has to be tackled at the same time. If a preferential FTA is treated as the first phase of closer economic cooperation, trade-related issues cannot be tackled individually, paying regard to their relative sensitivity as well as importance. Since vested interests and protectionist sentiments are most deeply entrenched against free trade in goods, the need to resolve all of these issues simultaneously at the outset may preclude steps to reduce impediments and uncertainties relating to a much wider range of international transactions. Therefore, it is not surprising that existing preferential FTAs have been negotiated among economies with rather similar structures; similarity in cost structures has meant that only relatively minor reallocation of resources was required, hence less resistance to liberalization.

The EC, European Free Trade Area (EFTA), U.S.–Canada and Australia–New Zealand FTAs all link fairly similar economies. The diversity of economic structures and levels of human resource and technological development within ASEAN have proved serious obstacles to substantive cooperation to date (Tan et al. 1992). The U.S.–Canada–Mexico FTA is the first to link economies of quite a different nature. Against that background, it is difficult to envisage FTAs linking many of the remarkably diverse Pacific economies; that is one of the major risks of an FTA-driven strategy for closer cooperation in the Pacific.

A further disadvantage of discriminatory FTAs is that the broader set of issues discussed above, such as the exchange of information reducing physical bottlenecks, harmonizing standards and reducing uncertainties, cannot be tackled simply by a comprehensive set of preferential reductions to barriers to trade in goods. The Singapore–Johor–Riau "Growth Triangle" represents a clear, more imaginative, contrast to the preferential FTA approach to effective subregional economic integration. No discriminatory trade policies are to be involved; in fact, trade policy issues are marginal. Instead, emphasis is placed on reducing physical obstacles to trade through heavy investment in infrastructure and on reducing barriers to investment. The interdependence of these economies will be boosted rapidly, while old-fashioned issues of discrimination against the rest of the world will not arise.

10.7 Economic Cooperation with North America

Despite the disadvantages of discriminatory FTAs it is likely that the U.S. will consider following up the expected finalization of NAFTA in 1993 with negotiations of further FTAs. Negotiations with other Latin American economies were fore-shadowed in President Bush's Enterprise for the Americas initiative in 1991 (see Baker 1991). In September 1992, President Bush raised the prospect of negotiating FTAs with economies in East Asia. The Miami Summit of Western Hemisphere leaders endorsed the concept of Free Trade Agreement of the Americas, to be achieved by 1995. However, it is important for both the U.S. and its East Asian trading partners to recognize the risks of such an approach and steer policymakers toward less divisive options for regional economic cooperation.

One of the concerns for East Asian economies, which has been raised by NAFTA, is the immediate prospect of trade and investment diversion which will result from preferential market access granted to Mexico and potential new participants in NAFTA or any other parallel arrangements with the United States. Another concern is the potential discriminatory impact of future U.S. trade policies on nonparticipants. During the past decade or so, there has been increasing resort by the U.S. to trade policies which are inconsistent with the spirit of the GATT. One example is the insistence on "voluntary" export restraints, primarily directed against East Asian economies which are capturing increased market shares in sensitive sectors of the U.S. economy. Another is the use of Section 301 of U.S. trade legislation to make unilateral judgments about the trade policies of others, combined with the threat of trade retaliation.

A reasonable concern has arisen that, in future, such measures or threats will be directed at those not part of, or linked to NAFTA. While that arrangement, as such, is not raising any new barriers to access to North American markets, a greater degree of uncertainty has been introduced about potential future access, especially to the U.S. market. In addition to the problems of trade diversion, the complex rules of origin (which occupy almost 200 pages of the draft NAFTA documents) will create considerable scope for uncertainty and friction. The increased competition among North American economies across the full range of sectors may promote productivity and growth, creating new trade opportunities for nonparticipants; however, in at least these two large sectors of textiles and automobiles, the rest of the world will be disadvantaged.

A further cause for concern is the potential dilution or interest by the U.S. in defending and enhancing the GATT-based multilateral trading system. As noted by Drysdale and Garnaut (1992), there is a limit to the capacity of the U.S. administration to negotiate trade liberalization during the next few years. If substantial effort is devoted to extending the coverage of preferential trade arrangements like NAFTA, then less will be available for U.S. leadership of new efforts to develop multilateral approaches to issues such as rules for investment, links between trade and competition policy and the trade policy implications of environmental concerns. It would be unfortunate if these new issues were taken up *only* in conjunction with discriminatory bilateral or subregional arrangements for trade in goods, rather than in ways which could enhance global economic linkages.

Against this background, it is important for East Asia to engage the U.S. in discussions aimed at improving trade and other economic links across the Pacific. There is a particularly urgent need to reduce the extent of uncertainty which might otherwise emerge about future access to North American markets. At the same time, it is vital to seek ways to reduce impediments to trans-Pacific trade which do not cut across the highly beneficial process of market-driven economic integration which is under way in East Asia. Care should be taken to ensure that any agreements or understandings reached with the U.S. do not introduce needless new uncertainties or discrimination into trade and investment among Asian economies.

In order to avoid the emergence of a series of hub-and-spoke bilateral trade arrangements with North America, it would be useful for East Asian economies to find ways of raising their interests and concerns in economic links with North America collectively, rather than individually. This would increase the chances of a balanced dialogue, rather than a series of negotiations dominated by the single largest economy. A collective, but not confrontational, approach to the U.S. would also be much more effective in diverting attention from what might otherwise become a preoccupation by the U.S. with economic relations within Latin America.

The United States, on its part, also needs to focus on the future of its trading links across the Pacific. This trade already exceeds U.S. trade across the Atlantic and is vastly greater than trade with all of Latin America. The U.S.'s long-term trading interests beyond the Uruguay Round will not be met simply by a sequence of FTAs with Lating American economies beyond Mexico. Moreover, priority on such arrangements would be increasingly difficult to reconcile with assurances that East Asian interests are not being damaged. Even if East Asia were not clearly disadvantaged in net terms, it would hardly be conducive to economic cooperation across the Pacific. If U.S. strategy for such cooperation remained focused on preferential trading arrangements in its own hemisphere, possibly accompanied by continued threats of retaliation against East Asian exporters, interest in an East Asian economic bloc might well revive. At worst, this could lead to the emergence of three defensive trading blocs dominating the world economy.[18]

Nor would it be feasible or desirable for the U.S. to see its trans-Pacific trade strategy simply in terms of negotiating hub-and-spoke arrangements of FTAs with

ASEAN or some individual East Asian economies. There appears to be very little likelihood of negotiating GATT-consistent FTA arrangements with either China or Japan in the foreseeable future. Other East Asian economies are unlikely to be attracted to preferential trading arrangements with the U.S. which discriminate against China or Japan.

Accordingly, rather than devote excessive negotiating resources to an attempt to negotiate a hub-and-spoke set of FTAs, it would be more constructive for the U.S. to lend its weight to APEC-based efforts to reduce impediments to closer economic integration. Such a positive approach to trans-Pacific trade policy would reinforce the region's common interest in shoring up a nondiscriminatory global trading system.

As discussed in the preceding section, there is a broad potential agenda for APEC which can reduce impediments to trade or investment. Issues such as the reduction of uncertainties, the removal of physical barriers to trade, reducing administrative barriers and achieving greater harmonization of standards or regulations can be addressed in ways which do not introduce new, needless discrimination into economic relations in the broader Asian-Pacific region. Pursuit of this agenda can benefit from the experience gained in negotiations between the U.S. and Mexico. NAFTA's provisions extend beyond discriminatory arrangements for trade in goods, dealing with issues yet to be covered by the GATT. For example, trade in financial services is to be substantially liberalized. NAFTA also provides for the protection of intellectual property rights and reduces distortions to investment (for example, through local content and export performance requirements). It also begins to address region-wide environmental issues as well as providing for more speedy and effective dispute settlement procedures (see Schott 1992).

An important way of reducing uncertainty in trans-Pacific trade would be to adopt a collective approach to dispute-settlement procedures, similar to those to be embodied in NAFTA. An effective dispute-settlement mechanism among all APEC participants could defuse trade frictions more rapidly and reduce the rationale for resort to unilateral trade retaliation. The growing incidence of preferential trade arrangements also suggests the importance of a clearer, region-wide understanding about the definition and application of rules of origin.

It should also be possible for East Asian economies to take up sectoral trade issues with North America without being restricted to negotiating FTA arrangements. For example, North American economies could be involved in possible discussions about nondiscriminatory liberalization of trade in iron and steel products. There could also be early discussion of region-wide liberalization of air-traffic rights; the current complex web of bilateral arrangements will not be able to cope for long with the pressures generated by rapid traffic growth, increasing density of routes and international strategic alliances among carriers.

APEC provides a convenient forum within which economies from the western side of the Pacific can take up all of these issues in a cohesive manner with their

North American partners. As discussed earlier, quite a few important economic cooperation issues are already on APEC's trade liberalization agenda. Purposeful pursuit of that agenda can avoid what could otherwise become parallel, uncoordinated negotiations by Asian economies with the U.S. and/or NAFTA, which would be needlessly divisive. It is in the overwhelming interests of all regional economies to avoid economic confrontation across the Pacific. At a time when the U.S.'s capacity and interest in leading the defence of a nondiscriminatory global system is faltering, there is an urgent need to foster cooperative structures which can strengthen links with the U.S. and provide for collective leadership of the global trading system.

10.8   Conclusion

There is a substantive agenda for nondiscriminatory trade liberalization in the Pacific region. Relatively noncontroversial steps, such as the exchange of information and harmonization of customs documentation, can build the sense of cohesion and trust required to tackle harder issues such as reducing market access barriers.

Tackling substantive economic issues in carefully graduated steps could enhance the effectiveness of APEC during the 1990s, set a positive example of open regionalism, reduce the risk of fragmentation of the world economy into rival trading blocs, avoid escalation of trade tensions across the Pacific and allow APEC to begin to set priorities for future negotiations to improve the global trading system.

Notes

1. In this chapter the Pacific region is defined to include all economies with a Pacific Ocean coastline, from New Zealand through Japan and the Russian Far East in a clockwise direction to Chile, as well as all the Pacific Islands. Asia-Pacific economies are defined as all Pacific economies other than Latin America. East Asia is defined broadly to include Northeast Asia (Japan, Korea, Russia's Far East and the Chinese economies), countries in the Association of Southeast Asian Nations (ASEAN) as well as Australia and New Zealand.

2. Article XXIV of the GATT allows some discriminatory lowering of trade barriers among economies forming an FTA, provided that a substantial share of goods becomes freely traded among the FTA participants. The article requires that no new barriers be erected against nonparticipants, but there is no requirement to improve their access sufficiently to ensure the gains to nonparticipants from trade creation outweigh losses from trade diversion.

3. Harris (1991) defines the distinction between cooperation and integration, by noting that cooperation involves agreements to reduce impediments to international trade in goods and services, while integration goes further to facilitate factor movements (e.g. of labor and capital) across national boundaries.

4. The PECC International Standing Committee, meeting in Honolulu in January 1992, decided to change the name of the organization from Conference to Council. This was done in order to reflect the importance of the work of the PECC's sectoral task forces and forums between the 18 monthly plenary conferences.

5. Elek (1991) analyzes the early evolution of APEC, its principles, objectives and work program as well as its links with PECC. Kim (1990) and Woolcott (1991) cover more recent developments, including APEC's third ministerial level meeting in Seoul in November 1991.

6. The three Chinese economies, with Taiwan designated as Chinese Taipei, joined APEC in November 1991. It is the first international organization in which they are all represented by ministers in their official capacities.

7. Preeg (1992) emphasizes the importance of consistency between unilateral, regional and bilateral strands of trade policy. His article focuses on policy choices for the U.S., but the need to ensure consistency among these options applies to all Pacific economies.

8. Drysdale (1989) describes trade policy liberalization in East Asia, noting that, while some liberalization has been forced during negotiations, more reform is being carried out unilaterally, driven by the economic logic of large potential net gains. George (1990) provides a valuable insight into agricultural reforms in Japan.

9. Prestowitz (1988) provides one of many accounts of the frustrations of U.S. trade negotiators. While their claims of "unfair trade" are somewhat exaggerated, there is considerable scope for further liberalization of all Pacific economies, including the U.S.

10. An earlier version of a potential agenda for regional trade liberalization was presented in Elek (1992a). CSIS (1991) also suggests a broad potential agenda for APEC-wide economic cooperation.

11. Even if there were no final outcome from the Uruguay Round, the draft Dunkel declaration text on dispute settlement could have been used as the basis for an APEC-wide understanding (Dunkel 1991: Section S).

12. Consistency with GATT is not relevant in many cases since GATT does not cover most issues of standardization and harmonization. In matters such as dispute settlement, where GATT is already involved, the steps suggested would all be fully consistent with minimum GATT requirements.

13. The concept of adopting common standards or similar approaches to certain policies is similar to the adoption of OECD or GATT codes in other contexts. In the case of GATT, codes are binding, but there is no need for all participants to adopt them simultaneously. In the case of APEC, adherence to codes would be voluntary, rather than formally binding.

14. Some non-APEC participants could join existing understandings; in other words, APEC is a convenient initial forum for the discussion of options for region-wide cooperation, without permanently excluding others, such as Latin-American economies.

15. The proposed regional trade liberalization program of APEC is set out in the Report to Ministers by the APEC Informal Group on Regional Trade Liberalization (see APEC IV, particularly in Annex 4 to that report).

16. Sector-by-sector liberalization *must* be undertaken on a nondiscriminatory basis to be consistent with Article XXIV of the GATT.

17. Drysdale (1992) outlines a constructive proposal for nondiscriminatory liberalization of trade in iron and steel products in the region.

18. The case against the emergence of a separate East Asian economic grouping was put forcefully by Lee Kuan Yew in his keynote address to APEC II (1990: 1518).

References

APEC II, 1990, *Asia Pacific Economic Cooperation Ministerial Meeting Joint Statement*, Singapore, July 31.

APEC IV, 1992, *APEC Informal Group on Regional Trade Liberalisation, Report to Ministers*, Bangkok, September.

ASEAN, 1992a, *Singapore Declaration of 1992*, Fourth ASEAN Summit, Singapore, January 27–28.

———, 1992b, *Framework Agreement on Enhancing ASEAN Economic Cooperation*, January.

———, 1992c, *Agreement on the Common Effective Preferential Tariff (CEPT) Scheme for the ASEAN Free Trade Area (AFTA)*, Singapore.

Baker, J. A. III, 1991, "America in Asia: Emerging Architecture for a Pacific Community," *Foreign Affairs Quarterly*, Winter.

CSIS, 1991, *A Policy Framework for Asia-Pacific Economic Cooperation*, Report by the CSIS U.S.–Japan Working Group, Washington, DC.

Drysdale, P., 1989, *International Economic Pluralism: Economic Policy in East Asia and the Pacific*, Allen & Unwin, Sydney.

———, 1992, *East Asia: The East Asia Steel Industry*, Economics Division Working Paper 92/6, Research School of Pacific Studies, Australian National University, Canberra.

Drysdale, P. and R. Garnaut, 1989, *A Pacific Free Trade Area?* Pacific Economic Paper 171, Australia–Japan Research Centre, Australian National University, Canberra.

———, 1992, "The Pacific: An Application of a General Theory of Economic Integration," paper prepared for the 20th Pacific Trade and Development Conference, Washington, DC, September 10–12.

Dunkel, A., 1991, *Draft Final Act Embodying the Results of the Uruguay Round of Multilateral Trade Negotiations*, Trade Negotiations Committee, December 20.

Elek, A., 1991, "Asia Pacific Economic Cooperation (APEC)," in *Southeast Asian Affairs 1991*, Institute of Southeast Asian Studies, Singapore.

———, 1992a, "Trade Policy Options for the Asia Pacific Region in the 1990s: The Potential of Open Regionalism," *American Economic Review*, 82(2).

———, 1992b, "Pacific Economic Cooperation: Policy Choices for the 1990s," *Asian-Pacific Economic Literature*, 6(1).

George, A., 1990, *The Politics of Liberalisation in Japan: The Case of Rice*, Pacific Economic Paper 188, Australia–Japan Research Centre, Australian National University, Canberra.

Harris, S., 1991, "Varieties of Pacific Economic Co-operation," *Pacific Review*, 4(4).

Hughes, H., 1991, "Does APEC Make Sense?" *ASEAN Economic Bulletin*, November.

Kim, C., 1990, "Regional Economic Cooperation in the Asia-Pacific: Working Mechanisms and Linkages," in Suh Jang-Won and Ro Jae-Bong (eds.), *Asia Pacific Economic Cooperation: The Way Ahead*, Korea Institute for International Economic Policy, Seoul.

Lee, Kuan Yew, 1990, Asia Pacific Economic Cooperation Ministerial Meeting, Opening Address, Singapore.

Lee, Tsao Yuan (ed.), 1991, *Growth Triangle: The Johore–Singapore–Riau Experience*, Institute of Southeast Asian Studies, Singapore.

Okita, S., 1992, "Transition to Market Economy: Implications for India," Fifteenth Madon Memorial Lecture, Bombay.

Pangestu, M., H. Soesastro, and M. Armad, 1992, "A New Look at Intra-ASEAN Cooperation," *ASEAN Economic Bulletin*, 8(3).

Preeg, E. H., 1992, "The U.S. Leadership Role in World Trade: Past, Present, and Future," *Washington Quarterly*, 15(2).

Prestowitz, C., 1988, *Trading Places*, Basic Books, New York.

Raby, G., 1991, "The 'Neither This Nor That Economy': Decisions, Goals and Process in Chinese Economic Reform, 1978–91," paper presented at the Conference on China's Reforms and Economic Growth, Economics Division, Research School of Pacific Studies, Australian National University, Canberra.

Rieger, H. C., 1989, "Regional Economic Cooperation in the Asian Pacific Region," *Asia Pacific Economic Literature*, 3(2).

Roh, Tae Woo, 1991, Keynote Address to the Third Asia Pacific Economic Cooperation Ministerial Meeting, Seoul, Korea.

Sadli, M., 1992, "Regionalism in Asia," Asia Foundation, New York, mimeo.

Schott, J. (ed.), 1989, *Free Trade Areas and U.S. Trade Policy*, Institute for International Economics, Washington, DC.

Schott, J. J., 1992, "North America Integrates," *International Economic Insights*, 3(5).

Seoul APEC Declaration, 1991, Seoul, November 14.

Sung, Y. W., 1991, "The Economic Integration of Hong Kong, Taiwan and South Korea with Mainland China," paper prepared for the 19th PAFTAD Conference on Economic Reforms and Internationalisation: China and the Pacific Region.

Tan, K. Y., M. H. Toh, and L. Low, 1992, "ASEAN and Pacific Economic Cooperation," *ASEAN Economic Bulletin*, 8(3).

Woolcott, R., 1991, *Backgrounder*, Department of Foreign Affairs and Trade, Canberra.

Chapter 11

C. Fred Bergsten

THE APEC: THE BOGOR DECLARATION AND ITS IMPLICATIONS FOR THE FUTURE

11.1 The Bogor Commitment

The 1994 Asia-Pacific Economic Cooperation (APEC) summit at Bogor, Indonesia, produced a substantial outcome that will have an enormous effect on the future of the Asia-Pacific economies: namely the Bogor Declaration, which is the biggest trade agreement in history.

It is a nonbinding agreement that needs to be implemented just as Punta del Este was nonbinding when it launched the Uruguay Round. Commitments to form major trade agreements are not binding in a legal sense. They do represent, nonetheless, the political will to go forward in a decisive manner.

The Bogor Declaration is literally a case of one half of the world's economy agreeing to move to free trade by a certain date. That sets it up to become—over time—the most sweeping trade agreement in history.

It is also quite likely that the APEC process as launched at Bogor is going to produce the next major round of global trade liberalization. This outcome is likely simply because the APEC countries, from the outset of APEC itself, have adopted the principle of open regionalism. Liberalization as it occurs within the APEC will be extended to the rest of the world, probably on a reciprocal basis. Given the fact that one half of the world's economy is committed to the APEC process, this open regionalism is like an offer from the Mafia: it is an offer you cannot refuse because you cannot afford to be blocked out preferentially from half the world economy. Assuming the APEC process does progress along the lines recommended in our EPG (Eminent Persons Group) report, as implicitly adopted in the Bogor Declaration, the APEC commitments should provide the fulcrum for the next round of global trade liberalization. Roughly speaking, that would then double the ante since APEC itself now involves half the world and the APEC liberalization would create the impetus needed to bring in the other half.

The Bogor Declaration includes several other commitments that should further push forward trade liberalization. The Declaration includes a commitment to accelerate the implementation of the Uruguay Round by the APEC countries. This again amounts to half the world agreeing to accelerate the implementation of the liberalization process already agreed upon. This, of course, speeds up the gains of the Uruguay Round.

The Declaration also contains language strongly encouraging further unilateral trade liberalization. This sort of provision sounds strange to the American people since the U.S. has not been inclined to pursue such unilateral trade liberalization efforts. But such unilateral efforts have frequently been undertaken by the countries of East Asia and there is continued support for the expansion of such efforts in the region.

The APEC commitment to liberalization may help push the political process toward greater support for liberalization within the Asian countries. Within all of the Asian countries one finds the same debate one finds in the U.S. between a protectionist faction and a liberalizing faction. The liberalizing faction is always looking for outside advice, impetus, and pressure to help them win the day internally. The commitment by APEC leaders to free trade and investment in the region strengthens the hand of the liberalizers and may therefore further intensify the likelihood for unilateral liberalization in the individual countries as well.

The Bogor Declaration also includes a standstill commitment. It is a weak commitment that talks about "best endeavors" to avoid any new increases in trade barriers. Standstill agreements have a checkered history: they have often been used in the Organization for Economic Cooperation and Development (OECD), the Group of Seven (G-7), and elsewhere; and they have not always been strictly adhered to. Nevertheless, it is one more element in the Declaration that may contribute to the process of liberalization.

Beyond the whole panoply of major agreements put together recently—such as the Bogor Declaration and the APEC ministerial statement—many practical, though less spectacular steps are being taken to move forward on the issue of trade facilitation. Agreement has been reached on an investment code. Progress is being made on customs harmonization. All of these very practical steps not only further enhance the environment for achieving the trade liberalization commitment, but have concrete implications for business and trade in the region. They are therefore important steps in and of themselves. When you add up all of these developments, it is clear that the Bogor Declaration could indeed be the biggest trade agreement in the history of the world.

It should also be noted that the target date set by the Bogor commitment for trade liberalization is not as far off as it is often said to be. Some of the skeptics have stated that "free trade by the year 2020 is so far away that it is never going to happen." Of the 18 APEC member economies, however, only five or six are developing economies, which have been given until the year 2020 to liberalize. Most of the APEC members are industrial countries, such as the U.S. and Japan, or Asian newly industrializing economies (NIEs). Some of the NIEs (for example, Singapore) have already agreed to join the fast track group, and others (for example, the Republic of Korea) have acknowledged privately that they will be on the fast track and achieve their liberalization by the year 2010, not 2020. An examination of the trade figures reveals that 85–90 percent of the agreed liberalization is called for by the year 2010 since the vast bulk of the trade is carried out by the advanced countries rather than by those countries on the slower track with the 2020 deadline.

It remains unclear which track the People's Republic of China (hereinafter referred to as China) will fall into. China's trade does not now account for a big share of trade within APEC, but this share will of course grow over time. Whether 85 or 90 percent of APEC liberalization occurs by 2010 depends on the course of events in China. Yet, the bottom line is that the great bulk of trade under the Bogor commitment would be liberalized within 15 years, which is not that long a time frame compared with NAFTA and other traditional trade agreements—even the U.S.–Canada agreement, which provided for tariff elimination over a 15-year period.

Another key point to keep in mind is that, historically, trade liberalization commitments have in fact been realized much faster than the governments originally negotiated. The EC, originally in the Treaty of Rome, agreed to eliminate barriers over a 12-year period. In practice, the elimination of barriers was accomplished over a 7-year period. Australia and New Zealand, coincidentally, also agreed to eliminate their trade barriers over a 12-year period—but in practice elimination of barriers was accomplished over a 7-year period. The U.S. and Canada, after laboriously working out 10- to 15-year tariff elimination schedules, had about 600 companies asking to get rid of US$8 billion of the tariffs immediately. After one year the tariff elimination schedules had become redundant because the trade agreement goals had already been accomplished.

Once governments set the course and lay out the basic framework for trade liberalization, the private sectors step in and accelerate the whole process: the private sectors invest on the basis of the expected eventual state of affairs and compete with each other to be the first to exploit the liberalized regime. As usual, governments set a schedule that is too slow—understandably and rightly, because they are worried about the adjustment problems and the domestic politics thereof. In practice the liberalization process happens faster. On the timing of the Bogor commitment, the key points to remember are that the bulk of liberalization, even under the terms of the agreement at this point, would happen in 15 years—not in 25 years—and that in practice the liberalization targets are likely to be achieved over an even shorter period of time.

11.2   The Potential Effects

What impact will the Bogor targets have on the world economy and the individual APEC member countries? To date only a few analyses have been conducted in order to determine the "aggregate payoff" that might accrue from achieving these targets. An Australian study concludes that achievement of the Bogor targets would increase world output by about US$366 billion a year by the year 2010. By comparison, the same study found that the Uruguay Round would increase world output by US$112 billion a year by the year 2020. These findings have led the Australian Prime Minister, Paul Keating, to state that the APEC outcome is worth two to three times as much, for Australia at least, as the Uruguay Round. More recently, Keating has stressed that the APEC benefits will be double the Uruguay Round benefits. It is hard to say at this early stage how much the APEC outcome will be worth exactly, but the study provides a rough estimate of the order of magnitude of its benefits.

The Institute for International Economics in Washington, DC, is conducting a series of studies to quantify the gains that will accrue to individual APEC member countries as a result of trade liberalization. The preliminary results are available for Japan. The bottom line for that analysis is that current Japanese protection is costing the Japanese consumer more than US$100 billion a year. Between 2.5 and 4 percent of Japan's GDP is essentially being wasted as a result of trade barriers. About US$50 billion worth of imports is being kept out of the country as a result of existing barriers. So for Japan alone, moving to trade liberalization would have an enormous impact on the country itself and of course on its trading partners and the world economy as a whole. Again, the preliminary estimates suggest that the potential benefits are very large.

11.3   The APEC Process

The next interesting question is: how did such a far-reaching agreement come about in Bogor? No one would have predicted this outcome a year before. They certainly would not have predicted this outcome before the Seattle summit, which set the APEC process moving in a really intense and extended way. But even after Seattle, it would have been hard to foresee that the APEC leaders would sit down in a meeting as they did at Bogor and declare themselves ready to eliminate all barriers to trade and investment in their countries even over an extended period of time.

Part of the answer lies in the elevation of the trade liberalization issue to the highest political level. The issue was put to the heads of state, not to the ministers or officials or bureaucrats; and the political leaders did in fact exercise leadership on this issue. Without this political step, we would not have seen this outcome.

The APEC summit process has now become institutionalized. The Osaka summit is scheduled for 1995. The Philippines will host the summit the following year, and Canada will do so in 1997. In 1998, Malaysia will chair the summit. It will be very interesting to see if Malaysian Prime Minister Mahathir Mohamad (or his successor by that time) decides to continue to actively participate in the process of summits. It is widely believed that the temptation to contribute to the process will be great even in those quarters, and that the process will continue. But at least the first four or five years of the evolving APEC process have benefited from the leadership of the heads of state and government; and that has been a decisive factor.

Incidentally, support for the APEC process within the U.S. has been bipartisan. American thinking on the APEC process began to evolve toward the end of the Bush Administration. The APEC idea was then picked up and more fully developed during the first year of the Clinton Administration. In short, APEC has a distinct bipartisan background in the U.S.

A particularly crucial element in Bogor was Indonesia's leadership role. In light of Indonesia's key role, no one could argue that the Bogor commitment was foisted on Asia or on poorer countries by the Americans or anybody else that was pursuing hegemonic pretensions. The push for the Bogor commitment was led by Indonesia's President Suharto—the leader of an Asian (and more specifically Southeast Asian) as well as developing country.

Interestingly, President Suharto made a speech in August 1993—one month after he had discussed APEC summitry for the first time with President Clinton and three months before Seattle—in which he said, very explicitly, that Indonesia would be taking the chair of APEC in 1994 and would play a forceful leadership role.

Indonesia chaired and led the summit process at APEC at least as effectively as any G-7 country (including the U.S.) has ever led the G-7 summit process. The Indonesians did a superb job. To give an example, there was a big debate, as the Bogor summit approached, over what "consensus" meant and whether the Malaysians or somebody else would block the process. But President Suharto stated very clearly, and repeatedly, that "consensus did not require unanimity"—particularly when the Malaysian Ministers were within earshot.

The Indonesians also helped to steer participants away from exceptions to the Bogor Declaration. As one might predict, there was a last-minute scramble by various countries to pull some economic activities outside the reach of the Declaration. Japan wanted to pull out agriculture. The Chinese wanted to pull out investment. The Americans also had considered carving out some exceptions of their own. But the Indonesians expressed concern that such efforts could unravel the entire process. They asked the Americans whether they really wanted to exclude agriculture and investment, and lose as well the opportunity to liberalize trade in areas that really interested them. These actions represented a masterful display of leadership by the Indonesians, who happened to be chairing the summit at a particularly key time.

There was strong support for the APEC process by other key governments. The Australians have played an active role from the start, and were instrumental in the creation of APEC back in 1989. The Republic of Korea also played a big role, having pioneered the three-China formula in 1991 that broadened APEC and made the Bogor summit possible. Singapore has also played an extremely helpful role through ASEAN.

The U.S. has also played a major role in the APEC process. However, in Bogor the U.S. skilfully played a supportive backstage role—thereby avoiding charges of pursuing hegemonic pretensions, at least in any credible way, and thereby enabling the process to succeed.

It should be noted that the Eminent Persons Group (EPG) probably also played an important role in the process. The EPG report did in fact, to use President Suharto's words, give a point of reference to those who wanted to move energetically forward on liberalization. The whole idea behind the EPG was to go outside governments and bureaucracies to provide a vision. The group provided a vision, but the crucial thing was that governments made use of that vision as the basis for moving ahead.

In addition, one thing the EPG was able to do—consisting as it did of members appointed by governments but acting as individuals—was to forge compromises on a number of the key issues. The EPG worked out balanced agreements that made room for the different points of view rather than choosing one extreme view or another on such key issues as pursuing unilateral versus negotiated liberalization, adopting a global versus regional strategy, and extending the benefits to nonmembers conditionally or unconditionally. Its work not only demonstrated that it was possible to reach a balanced agreement, but provided a substantive basis that 'enabled governments with different views on these issues to feel they could sign on to the consensus and go ahead without having some of their own preferred policy positions undermined or cut off at the outset.

Perhaps the most important compromise put together by the EPG was the four-part formula for open regionalism. The formula defined open regionalism in a way that would permit individual countries, if they wished, to extend the benefits of APEC liberalization to nonmembers on an unconditional basis but would call for the group as a whole to offer to generalize the benefits on a reciprocal basis. The Indonesians have explained that they sought to include all elements of that formula so that the whole system could proceed as suggested in the EPG report.

One thing they did at Bogor against the recommendation of the EPG was to extend the life of the EPG. Instead of closing it down, the Bogor Declaration gave the EPG a far-reaching new mandate to reinforce the APEC process—and specifically, to monitor the progress of the Declaration, to make recommendations for further steps in the future, and to look particularly at the relationship between APEC and subregional agreements such as NAFTA.

Another key contributor was the Pacific Business Forum (PBF)—a forum agreed upon during the Seattle summit. The PBF (which consists of two businessmen from each of the 18 APEC member countries) presented a report in mid-October, which was very consistent with the EPG report on the broad policy issues but went far beyond it, very thoughtfully and creatively, on the business facilitation issues. That report provided another base of political support—a point of reference, as the Indonesians dubbed it—for the process.

11.4   What Happens Next?

The crucial question now of course, and the final issue, is what happens next? Will the Declaration be implemented? There are many skeptics, and certainly many questions that need to be answered.

One has to say at the outset that the APEC process will face setbacks along the way. The history of European integration has not followed a smooth straight path. The European Defense Community (EDC) failed before the Common Market itself ever got going. The British opted out of the EEC at an early stage. DeGaulle vetoed it for several years. Maastricht and the European Monetary System raise problems today. So in appraising the evolution of APEC, as it proceeds, one should not be discouraged nor give up on it if there are setbacks along the way—especially in the early days.

One factor that we need not worry about is Malaysia's reservations. The first thing to keep in mind is that Malaysia only accounts for 0.4 percent of the output of APEC. (All of ASEAN in fact accounts for only 3 percent of the output of APEC. ASEAN includes seven countries but it accounts for a very small portion of the total APEC process and therefore should not be given undue weight.) In addition, the reservations that Prime Minister Mahathir published the day after Bogor do not raise any intractable issues. Some simply state the obvious: that Bogor is a nonbinding agreement and that liberalization in APEC should be GATT consistent. Others endorse ideas in the EPG report: that individual countries can extend their liberalization on an unconditional basis and that countries can proceed unilaterally rather than necessarily in a negotiated way. None of these reservations need to be regarded as a big problem.

There are three or four big issues that have to be worked out. One is the allocation of countries as between the fast track, which requires trade liberalization by the year 2010, and the slower track, which gives developing countries until the year 2020 to liberalize. President Suharto in his press conference after Bogor stated that there are five countries that are clearly in the industrial category and therefore on the fast track: the U.S., Canada, Japan, Australia, and New Zealand. Subsequently, Singapore's Prime Minister publicly volunteered to have Singapore join the fast track. In private discussions the Republic of Korea has also indicated that it would join the fast track. (The other NICs, Taiwan and Hong Kong, are also likely to join the fast track.) In essence, the bulk of trade—about 85 percent—falls under the fast track liberalization deadline.

As noted in Section 11.1, one sticky issue will be which track China will join. We will need to wait and see how China's economy develops and how the country's entry into the WTO works out. When the actual liberalization begins to kick in (around the year 2000 on the EPG formula, though that has not been agreed yet), China can be placed in the appropriate category.

In this context, some very thoughtful observers have raised the question: does the two track system effectively resuscitate the old discredited idea of special and differential (S&D) treatment for developing countries that had been put to rest in NAFTA? My answer is not at all. First of all, let us consider the impact of the two track system purely in U.S. terms: what would the U.S. gain and lose? Let us assume that five or six countries, including China, fall into the slower track category, which allows countries to take the longer period of time to liberalize. The U.S. will go into the APEC liberalization with an average tariff, after the Uruguay Round, of about 3 percent and virtually no nontariff barriers. So achieving complete U.S. liberalization by 2010, or any other date, does not amount to much.

The developing member countries of APEC, including now for this purpose China, have average tariff levels of 30 or 40 percent. It is difficult to quantify the tariff equivalents of these countries' nontariff barriers, but they are at least as high as the average tariff levels and perhaps push the average protection level up to about 50 percent. Assuming these countries liberalize proportionately, even over a 20-year period, they would eliminate half their barriers by the year 2010. That means they would have reduced their protection by somewhere between 15 and 25 percentage points, while the U.S. would have reduced its protection by 3 percentage points. In other words, there is a five- to tenfold payoff for the U.S. in terms of a meaningful calculation—the reduction of barriers in absolute terms.

The U.S. could of course gain more if every country went on the fast track. This would be a desirable state of affairs, and it may happen anyway because of private market reactions. Nevertheless, the U.S. would gain enormously even if—in the worst case scenario from the U.S. standpoint—a few countries in APEC took ten years longer to liberalize.

Those who point out that the U.S. opted for a different approach in NAFTA simply ignore the dramatic differences between NAFTA and APEC. NAFTA amounted to a 4 percent extension of the American economy to a country that badly wanted the deal and essentially agreed to whatever the U.S. wanted. APEC is a different kettle of fish: the rest of APEC is as big as the U.S., the countries are not as susceptible to U.S. blandishments as was Mexico, and therefore it will be a tougher negotiation. Americans should not let themselves be spoiled (and the author puts it that way purposely) by the success achieved in the NAFTA negotiations. American negotiators, the U.S. Congress, and the American business community must recognize that APEC is very different.

The other key point is that the income gap between the richest and poorest countries within APEC is much greater than the gap was in NAFTA. In NAFTA it was an 8:1 or 10:1 per capita income gap. In APEC it is a 30:1 per capita income gap. Japan's per capita income at current market exchange rates is US$30,000 or more. The U.S.'s is about US$23,000. China's, on most calculations, is about US$1,000. Indonesia's is about US$700. The justification for a slower liberalization track for the developing countries is of course this vast disparity in standards of living and the like. As noted before, the gains to the U.S. and all the industrialized countries on the fast track are still so enormous that they certainly should go ahead with the liberalization process if the possibility exists.

A second issue that needs to be worked out is the question of coverage. As noted in Section 11.3, some countries in APEC are concerned about the inclusion of agriculture in the APEC process, while others are concerned about the inclusion of investment. Prime Minister Mahathir has stated his reservation that APEC should only liberalize "substantially" all trade. This position is consistent with GATT Article 24, but it falls short of the target set by the leaders at Bogor, which was to liberalize all trade—no exceptions were to be made. The question of coverage obviously will have to be worked out with the usual debate about exclusions that one gets in any trade negotiation. Different time paths may have to be adopted for very sensitive economic sectors but there certainly should be a major effort to limit or even avoid such exceptions.

Even more complicated will be the extension of the liberalization to primarily domestic policy measures of the type that are particularly prominent in the current U.S. negotiations with Japan. The EPG report stated very clearly that such measures have to be included in the agenda. The APEC Ministerial Declaration enumerated a number of them as already being on the agenda, with others to be discussed. Dealing with such measures will be difficult and tricky but, to be successful, one clearly has to go beyond border measures at this point in time in world trade negotiations.

A third issue that will need to be worked out is the treatment of nonmembers. Are nonmembers to be given automatic access to APEC liberalization, as some in APEC would have it? Or should they simply be offered the opportunity to achieve access to the APEC market on a reciprocal basis? As noted in Section 11.3, the EPG report suggests a four-part formula that includes both options. The Indonesians, at least, interpret the Bogor Declaration as encompassing that four-part formula. APEC's members, however, have not yet explicitly agreed to adopt the formula.

This raises a major process-related question, which needs to be examined by all the parties interested in the APEC process. What is the best way of implementing the far-reaching political commitment set forth in the Bogor Declaration? The traditional approach would entail sitting down and conducting face to face negotiations over the major issues: timing, duration, treatment of outsiders, and the like. This approach may in fact be the best way of implementing the Bogor commitment.

However, there is an alternative. The individual member countries of APEC could come forward with what amount to unilateral offers that state "we have made the political commitment and here is how we intend to implement it." These countries could lay out their own timetables, and put forward their own ideas on the issues of coverage, the treatment of outsiders, and the like. If four or five of the most forthcoming members of the organization came forward with such offers, with implementation of course contingent on what everybody else did at the end of the day, then these members would have a very good chance of leading the process. Peer pressure and demonstration effects could stimulate other members to move in a similarly aggressive direction on all of these variables. Face to face negotiations over the major issues at this point in time might not yield such a positive outcome. There might be foot-dragging. Consideration should therefore be given to the adoption of a more heterodox "unilateral offer" approach.

11.5   Conclusion

The Bogor Declaration obviously holds enormous promise for trade liberalization. For the reasons discussed above, it will have a substantial effect on the world economy as well as on the individual economies of Asia-Pacific. When we look back at the Bogor and Seattle summits 5, 10, or 15 years down the road, we will likely view them as seminal events that altered the course of world trade policy, and maybe broader economic and social policies as well. Every effort should be made to implement the Bogor commitments as fully and as promptly as possible. One result will be a true community of the Asia-Pacific economies.

Chapter 12

Ippei Yamazawa

ON THE ASIA-PACIFIC ECONOMIC INTEGRATION: A JAPANESE PERSPECTIVE

12.1 Introduction

Regional integration concepts started to mushroom rapidly soon after the Uruguay Round negotiations stalled in 1992. The Uruguay Round is most likely to end with a smaller package of achievements than was expected when it was launched at Punta del Este in 1986. Even if the Round is concluded, it is inevitable that the contracting parties will attempt to pursue their aims by means of alternative routes, that is, through liberalization efforts among like-minded countries in the same region. The strengthened regional integration effort in the Pacific is no exception to this trend.[1] However, it differs from the process of regional integration in Western Europe and North America both in form and scope.

   The aim of this chapter is to analyze the current state of economic integration efforts in the Asia-Pacific region and to convey to readers outside the region that the Asia-Pacific economic integration is not myth but reality notwithstanding the absence of a formal framework. Asia-Pacific integration efforts aim to set up a weak form of regional integration that will not have discriminatory impacts on outsiders. This weak form of integration is expected to help the region realize its high growth potential.

This chapter makes use of the "triad of growth" scenario, but rejects the "triad of protectionism" notion, which is often associated with the growth triad idea. Sections 12.3 and 12.4 provide a statistical overview of the growth that has taken place in the Asia-Pacific region in recent years. It is argued that East Asia lies at the center of growth in Asia-Pacific. Sections 12.3 and 12.4 attempt to characterize the mechanisms underpinning growth in East Asia, and make comparisons between the growth records of East Asia, Europe and North America. In view of the trade-oriented nature of its growth, East Asia needs the global free trade regime to further realize its potential. Section 12.5 notes that there has been no region-wide integration framework in Asia-Pacific, and that the region's several subregional groupings are characterized by informal arrangements. The exception is ASEAN (Association of Southeast Asian Nations). The East Asian nations have supported the Uruguay Round, but the limited scope of its achievement has forced them to explore the possibility of pursuing further liberalization through regional initiatives of their own (see Section 12.6). However, there seems to be a wide consensus in the region that only a loose form of integration framework is needed. The current region-wide framework, the Asia Pacific Economic Cooperation (APEC) process, will be analyzed in this context in Section 12.7. Its official stance of "open regionalism" is examined. This loose integration framework of the Asia-Pacific region is shown to depart from the classical concept of free trade area (FTA). The term "open economic association" is seen as a better label for this loose integration framework. The last section makes some observations about the agenda APEC should adopt.

12.2 Asia-Pacific in the "Growth Triad" Scenario

It is no exaggeration to say that during the first half of the 1990s the economic success of the Asia-Pacific region has kept afloat an otherwise troubled world economy. The collapse of the Soviet Union and the dissolution of the East European communist bloc is straining the economies of Germany and other Western European countries. Although the recession in the U.S. ended in 1992, the slow growth of output in that country provides little evidence that a robust recovery is underway. Further, few African, South Asian or Latin American countries have been able to achieve sustained growth.

In contrast, the Asia-Pacific economies—including the ASEAN countries, the newly industrializing economies (NIEs), as well as China and Japan—have been expanding since the mid-1980s and hold a strong growth potential. Some European and North American analysts argue that East Asia has become one side of a triadic structure supporting the world economy, with Western Europe and North America comprising the other two sides.

European and American analysts praise the Asia-Pacific economic growth but are concerned that the region is forming a giant economic bloc centered on Japan. In the triadic scenario, this bloc would be on a par with two other blocs: the

European Community's (EC's) soon to be integrated market, and the North American free trade area being negotiated by Canada, Mexico and the United States.

The concept of a protectionist-driven triadic structure is nothing but fantasy, however. The integration taking place in each of these three regions differs widely. Furthermore, some feel the stalled GATT talks have actually helped to free regional trade since the regional trading arrangements lower or eliminate barriers to intra-regional trade.

The EC's single market program, for example, is in the process of removing more than 280 physical, technical and fiscal barriers hindering the free flow of goods, money and people in the region. By the end of 1992, nearly 90 percent of such barriers were dismantled. The North American pact also aims to reduce restrictions on cross-border investment and services.

Such steps are recognized under Article XXIV of GATT as fostering global liberalization. Nonetheless, there remains concern that protectionism will raise its ugly head during a prolonged recession. Consequently, the East Asian countries excluded from the EC's single market and from the North American free trade pact, must carefully watch these regional trading arrangements and reject any move running counter to GATT principles or global free trade.

12.3   An Overview of the Asia-Pacific Development

Table 12.1 shows the growth performance of the Pacific countries for the past three decades. Four NIEs achieved high growth rates of 8–10 percent in the 1960s and 1970s, while four ASEAN countries (Indonesia, Malaysia, the Philippines and

TABLE 12.1   Real growth rates of the Asia-Pacific countries (% annual)

	1960–70	1970–80	1980–85	1985–89	1990	1991	1992*
Korea	8.4	8.2	8.4	10.5	9.0	8.6	7.6
Taiwan	9.6	9.7	9.7	9.8	5.0	7.2	6.7
Hong Kong	10.0	9.3	5.6	8.8	2.8	4.0	n.a.
Singapore	9.2	9.0	6.2	7.6	8.3	6.5–7.0	5–7
Indonesia	3.9	8.0	4.7	6.0	7.4	6.6	n.a.
Malaysia	–	8.0	5.1	5.9	9.8	8.6	8.5
Philippines	5.2	6.3	–1.0	5.0	3.7	0.8	3.0–3.5
Thailand	8.3	6.8	5.6	9.9	10.0	7.5	8.0–8.5
China	4.0	5.7	10.1	8.2	5.2	6.8	6–7
Japan	10.5	4.7	4.0	4.4	5.2	3.7	3.0
U.S.	3.8	2.8	2.6	3.4	1.0	–0.5	2.0
Canada	4.8	4.5	2.9	4.2	0.5	–1.0	3.0
Australia	5.3	3.3	3.2	7.5	3.6	–0.9	1.5
New Zealand	3.8	1.8	2.9	0.7	1.3	–0.1	1.7

*1992 values are estimates.

Sources: IMF, *International Financial Statistics*; Asian Development Bank, *Asian Development Outlook 1990*; individual country's statistics.

Thailand) achieved rates of 6–8 percent in the 1970s. Although many of these economies suffered a setback in the first half of the 1980s, they recovered quickly in the second. Hong Kong and the Philippines performed poorly due to special factors of their own. China showed a different growth cycle from other countries in the region due to domestic factors but achieved steady, high growth rates after it conducted domestic economic reforms and adopted an open policy in the 1980s.

The high growth rates attained by the Asia-Pacific economies in the past three decades are contrasted with the 2–4 percent rated attained by the developed economies for the same period. Japan's growth rate declined from a 10 percent level before the oil shock to a 4 percent level thereafter. Despite this drastic decline, Japan's growth rate is still the highest among the developed economies. In the early 1980s many developed economies have in decline—many recorded negative growth in 1991. Japan continued to grow moderately until 1990; but growth slowed down in the middle of 1991. Japan is afraid that the NIE and ASEAN economies will be affected by the recession in their major markets. It is a clear advantage for the Asia-Pacific region to have these dynamic developing economies at its center.

Table 12.2 compares the growth performance of East Asia's market economies (NIEs, ASEAN and Japan) with the performance of North America's economies (the U.S., Canada and Mexico) and the EC12 economies in the latter half of the 1980s. East Asia's economic growth rate remained at the 5 percent level during the latter half of the 1980s, while North America and the EC12 recorded rates of 2–3 percent, except in 1988. In 1990 and 1991 North America's growth rate was negative and that of the EC12 declined to 1–2 percent, while East Asia's growth rate remained at the 5 percent level.

TABLE 12.2 Size and growth performance of the three economic groups

	East Asia (Japan, NIEs, and ASEAN)	NAFTA (USA, Canada, and Mexico)	EC12
Population (million persons)	507	362	343
GNP (1990) (US$ billion)	37,174	62,011	57,083
Real growth rate (%)			
1986	3.9	2.6	2.7
1987	5.5	3.4	2.7
1988	6.8	4.4	4.0
1989	5.3	2.6	3.4
1990	5.6	1.0	2.8
Average 1986–90	5.4	2.8	3.1

Source: Ministry of Finance, Customs Bureau, Tokyo.

The economic size of the European and North American regional groups are about the same. The EC12 falls short of North America in both population and GNP. If we add the six EFTA countries to the EC12, Europe (with a population of 376 million) would have a population 40 percent larger than the North American and East Asian groups. However, even with the addition of the six EFTA countries, Europe's GNP (US$6.514 billion) would still be 40 percent smaller than the combined GNP figure for North America and East Asia. If the recent trend of divergent growth performance continues toward the next century, East Asia will account for a larger share of the world population and GNP than North America by the year 2011 and Europe by the year 2016.

Of course, this prediction is based on a simple extrapolation of recent growth trends. It is unlikely that a radical change in the relative economic size of East Asia will occur. The widening gap in growth performance between East Asia and North America and Europe will inevitably cause friction, which in turn will affect East Asia's growth performance. While the growth of the ASEAN economies will likely continue to be high, that of the Asian NIEs will most likely decrease to a moderate level throughout the 1990s.

The rapid growth of East Asia is reflected in its trade performance. Table 12.3 gives a consolidated trade matrix for Asia-Pacific. It is based on a detailed trade matrix of individual countries in the region. The consolidated matrix will make it easier to identify the larger regional trends. The matrix provides information on the Australia–New Zealand (ANZ) "group," the North America group (U.S., Canada and Mexico) and the EC12 as well as Japan, the East Asian NIEs (Singapore excluded), ASEAN (Singapore included) and China. The trade figures for three years—1980, 1986 and 1990—are shown. Wide fluctuations in the world economy make it hard to distinguish the volatile and stagnant period (1980–86) from the rapid expansion period (1988–90).

The growth in total world trade shown at the bottom right hand of Table 12.3 can be used as a reference rate. Total world trade did not increase during the first half of the 1980s, but increased 1.7 times during the latter half. Since the prices of petroleum and other primary commodities fluctuated widely during the 1980–86 period, these figures exaggerate changes in trade volume. The last column on the right hand of Table 12.3 gives total export figures for individual country groups, while the bottom row gives their total imports. The East Asian NIEs and ASEAN recorded the highest growth rates in both exports and imports. These countries have been catching up with Japan's total export and import volume as shown in Table 12.4.

The trade performance of Japan and China was not well balanced: Japan saw a greater rise in imports than exports, while China saw a greater rise of exports than imports. East Asia's trade volume was comparable with that of North America— the value of their imports was about the same but the value of East Asia's exports was 25 percent higher than North America's.

TABLE 12.3   Consolidated matrix of the Asia-Pacific trades: 1980, 1986 and 1990 (US$ million)

		Japan	EANIEs	ASEAN-6	China	E-Asia	North America	ANZ	EC12	World
Japan	80		15,434	13,069	5,078	33,581	35,309	4,069	18,025	129,542
	86		25,812	12,081	9,856	47,749	87,811	6,331	30,871	209,081
	90		46,487	32,066	6,145	84,698	100,132	8,134	54,045	287,678
	86/80		1.67	0.92	1.94	1.42	2.49	1.56	1.71	1.61
	90/86		1.80	2.65	0.62	1.77	1.14	1.28	1.75	1.38
EANIEs	80	6,114	3,312	4,901	1,253	15,579	17,910	1,369	10,175	56,969
	86	11,619	6,469	5,774	7,552	31,414	47,543	2,353	13,996	109,838
	90	25,548	17,740	16,800	20,335	80,423	64,664	2,526	29,796	208,996
	86/80	1.90	1.95	1.18	6.03	2.02	2.65	1.72	1.38	1.93
	90/86	2.20	2.74	2.91	2.69	2.56	1.36	1.07	2.13	1.90
ASEAN-6	80	21,032	4,975	12,934	693	39,634	12,080	2,042	8,897	71,036
	86	15,004	6,122	12,165	1,253	34,544	14,451	1,667	8,721	66,613
	90	27,000	14,532	27,500	2,268	71,300	29,260	3,113	21,039	137,965
	86/80	0.71	1.23	0.94	1.81	0.87	1.20	0.82	0.98	0.94
	90/86	1.80	2.37	2.26	1.81	2.06	2.02	1.87	2.41	2.07
China	80	4,323	4,401	1,722		10,447	1,362	283	2,748	18,120
	86	5,638	10,462	2,443		18,543	5,682	371	4,098	31,367
	90	9,327	26,243	3,493		39,063	8,132	644	6,720	66,518
	86/80	1.30	2.38	1.42		1.78	4.17	1.31	1.49	1.73
	90/86	1.65	2.51	1.43		2.11	1.43	1.73	1.64	2.12
E-Asia	80	31,469	28,122	32,626	7,024	99,241	66,660	7,763	39,845	275,668
	86	32,261	48,865	32,463	18,661	132,250	155,487	10,722	57,686	416,899
	90	61,874	105,001	79,858	28,748	275,483	202,188	14,417	111,600	701,157
	86/80	1.03	1.74	1.00	2.66	1.33	2.33	1.38	1.45	1.51
	90/86	1.92	2.15	2.46	1.54	2.08	1.30	1.34	1.93	1.68

TABLE 12.3 (continued)

		Japan	EANIEs	ASEAN-6	China	E-Asia	North America	ANZ	EC12	World
North America	80	24,919	12,486	9,413	4,587	51,406	97,641	5,317	66,148	291,431
	86	27,440	15,523	8,700	3,963	55,626	127,440	6,598	57,483	301,630
	90	57,609	36,694	20,246	6,230	120,779	228,611	10,674	112,132	554,520
	86/80	1.10	1.24	0.92	0.86	1.08	1.31	1.24	0.87	1.03
	90/86	2.10	2.36	2.33	1.57	2.17	1.79	1.62	1.95	1.84
ANZ	80	6,109	1,500	2,082	938	10,629	3,514	1,791	4,139	27,439
	86	6,095	2,419	1,484	1,163	11,161	3,208	1,845	4,238	27,775
	90	11,699	5,573	4,910	1,046	23,228	6,526	3,681	6,597	48,341
	86/80	1.00	1.61	0.71	1.24	1.05	0.91	1.03	1.02	1.01
	90/86	1.92	2.30	3.31	0.90	2.08	2.03	2.00	1.56	1.74
EC12	80	6,617	5,894	7,416	2,444	22,371	45,773	5,156	381,562	688,113
	86	11,188	9,988	8,261	6,398	35,835	84,118	6,785	449,592	788,431
	90	28,713	22,233	19,627	6,728	77,301	112,933	10,285	889,742	1,364,346
	86/80	1.69	1.69	1.11	2.62	1.60	1.84	1.32	1.18	1.15
	90/86	2.57	2.23	2.38	1.05	2.16	1.34	1.52	1.98	1.73
World	80	139,892	63,918	63,882	20,020	287,712	327,578	25,385	768,328	1,993,312
	86	119,424	91,009	62,232	43,247	315,912	470,533	30,471	776,627	1,973,600
	90	235,307	205,055	159,441	55,378	855,181	668,864	48,700	1,419,062	3,332,100
	86/80	0.85	1.42	0.97	2.16	1.10	1.44	1.20	1.01	0.99
	90/86	1.97	2.25	2.56	1.28	2.07	1.42	1.60	1.83	1.69

EANIEs consists of South Korea, Taiwan and Hong Kong. E-Asia consists of Japan, EANIEs, ASEAN-6 and China.

Sources: Compiled by Mr. Kazuhiko Yokota, Institute of Developing Economies, Tokyo, from IDE's AIDXT (for 1980 and 1986) and IMF's *Direction of Trade* supplemented by Taiwan's trade statistics (for 1990).

TABLE 12.4   Relative volume of trade of the East Asian NIEs and ASEAN to that of Japan (= 100)

Region	Year	Exports	Imports
East Asian NIEs	1980	44.0	45.7
	1990	72.6	87.1
ASEAN	1980	54.8	45.7
	1990	48.6	67.8

Source: Table 12.3.

This rapid expansion of the Asia-Pacific trade has stimulated trade activities in other groups as well, especially through East Asia's growing demand for imports. North America, the ANZ, and the EC all recorded a growth in exports to the East Asian NIEs, ASEAN and Japan that was as rapid as the growth in trade within East Asia. On the other hand, East Asia's exports to the EC increased greatly, while its exports to North America and the ANZ remained stagnant.

The size of intra-regional trade in the three regions is shown in the boxed areas of the trade matrix of Table 12.3 and summarized in percentage terms in Table 12.5. The share of trade handled intra-regionally in East Asia and North America is almost the same, but it is 50 percent higher in the EC than in East Asia or North America. Intra-regional trade shares grew in all three regions in the 1980s.

However, the volume of trade handled intra-regionally within the APEC group (US$2676 billion in 1990)—which comprises the sum of intra-regional trade shares of East Asia, North America and the ANZ—is almost the same size as the EC12's intra-regional share (US$2.783 billion in 1990). APEC's total trade expanded 26 percent more than that of the EC12 during the 1980s and its intra-group trade share has grown larger than the EC12's intra-regional share.

12.4   Mechanisms Underlying the Asia-Pacific Development

Economic relations among the countries of East Asia are different from those among the countries of the EC12 and North America. Production resources are

TABLE 12.5   Percentage shares* of intra-group trade in total trade

Year	East Asia	North America	EC12	APEC**
1980	35.2	31.5	52.4	55.7
1986	36.1	33.0	57.5	64.5
1990	40.6	37.4	63.9	66.2

*(Intra-group trade x 2) / (Total export + total import)

**To be exact, this group includes APEC plus Mexico.

Source: Table 12.3.

not distributed uniformly, and there are wide differences in industrialization and wage levels throughout East Asia. Exchange rates have fluctuated among these countries and tended to promote cross-border investment. Technology transfers are being actively pursued, and trade patterns are moving steadily toward greater interdependence in East Asia.

The countries of East Asia have achieved their high growth rates because of this growing interdependence. Though the EC's single market and the North American free trade pact are designed to benefit European and North American corporations, respectively, by providing access to larger markets, companies in East Asia are banking on the benefits of interdependence in an economically diverse region.

The Asia-Pacific region as a whole has been stimulated by growth in trade, investment and other activities in East Asia. During the second half of the 1980s, developed economies in North America and Oceania achieved 3–5 percent growth— a moderate level in comparison with the rates achieved in East Asia, but a fairly high rate in comparison to the rates achieved in North America and Oceania in recent years. North America and Oceania absorbed exports from East Asia, fueling further growth in East Asia. This sort of flow also characterizes interdependent growth in the region.

The main mechanism underpinning increasing interdependence in the Asia-Pacific region is the transfer of industries, particularly manufacturing industries, from early-starter to late-comer countries. In fact, there has been a shift in the countries which hold a comparative advantage in mature industries such as textiles and steel; namely, from the U.S. and Japan to the Asian NIEs, and from the Asian NIEs to ASEAN.

This is known as the "flying wild-geese pattern" of industrial development. It has been a catalyst for increasing interdependence in the region. This pattern has been gradually extended up the technological ladder, and is now contributing to the development of the electronics and automobile industries in ASEAN. The continued success of the flying wild-geese pattern of industrial transfer is the key to predicting the future success or failure of industrialization in ASEAN and the Pacific region (Ohkita 1987; Yamazawa 1991).

Two types of enterprises have promoted this process of industrial transfer: local enterprises and multinational enterprises (MNEs). Local enterprises in the late-comer countries have been recipients of industrial transfer. Their entrepreneurship makes them eager to acquire new technology to catch up with firms in the early-starter countries. Thus, local enterprises are prime movers in import substitution. MNEs in the early-starter countries are the source of industrial transfer. After choosing the most appropriate country, these MNEs begin to transfer new industrial technology.

Which type of enterprise becomes the main catalyst for industrial transfer in a certain country is dependent on both the industry and the particular late-comer country receiving that new industry. For industries such as textiles and steel, which are technologically mature, it was mainly the local enterprises of the late-comer countries which carried out catch-up activities. However, in industries such as electronics and fine chemicals, where new products and technologies emerge constantly, the role of MNEs inevitably becomes larger.

Recipient countries blessed with entrepreneurship are capable of catch-up development led by local enterprises. On the other hand, when the demand for new products is limited in the domestic market, late-comer countries will need to adapt an export-oriented industrialization policy from the very beginning. Thus dependence on MNEs becomes necessary as these firms are familiar with overseas markets. There are also some cases where both local enterprises and MNEs actively work together to bring about industrial development.

The rapid introduction of new industries into ASEAN—particularly into Malaysia, Thailand and Indonesia—is striking. In the second half of the 1980s the industrial growth rate of these countries was the highest in the region at 11–14 percent, with the percentage of manufacturing in total domestic production expanding to 19 percent in Indonesia, 27 percent in Malaysia and 25 percent in Thailand in 1990. The transfer of some new industries, such as electrical machinery and parts, precision machinery and chemicals, stands out.

Further, many of these new industries in ASEAN are export-oriented as reflected in the high percentage of industrial products in total exports in 1990: 46 percent in Indonesia, 60 percent in Malaysia and 75 percent in Thailand. This new industrialization process is characterized by the participation of MNEs, particularly in areas which are considered export-oriented. Asian NIEs rank alongside Japan with their large share of MNEs in ASEAN. The number of American MNEs in ASEAN has also begun to increase in recent years.

The large role played by the MNEs in these countries represents attempts to confront rapid adjustments in the exchange rate, wage increases and labor shortages. These enterprises have taken advantage of the large differences in the stages of economic development and wage levels in the region. Industries have relocated from the U.S. and Japan to the NIEs, and then from the NIEs to the ASEAN countries. As wage levels have increased in the ASEAN countries, industries have been attracted to more labor abundant, lower-wage manufacturing locations in Asia—most notably, the neighboring socialist economies of China and Indonesia, but also the South Asian countries.

Policy environments which favor such industrial transfer need to be maintained. In the East Asian NIEs and ASEAN, the governments have been instrumental in fostering industrial transfer through outward-looking policies. This policy commitment to free trade and investment needs to be maintained in order to keep the process of industrial transfer going in the East Asian NIEs and ASEAN. In fact, neighboring countries should also be encouraged to adopt policies that emphasize liberal trade and investment. Further growth in East Asia requires trade and investment liberalization not only within the region but also outside the region as well. The successful conclusion of the Uruguay Round negotiation is needed to provide conditions favorable for trade and investment liberalization inside, as well as outside the region.

12.5   Development without a Formal Framework

Interdependent growth in East Asia was achieved without a formal integration framework. Of course ASEAN is an important exception. Five countries, namely Indonesia, Malaysia, the Philippines, Singapore and Thailand established ASEAN as a formal framework for economic cooperation in 1987, and were later joined by Brunei Darussalam. ASEAN implemented a preferential tariff arrangement (PTA), joint industrial project (which involved sharing large-scale production of selected heavy industrial products for the common ASEAN market), and industrial complementation schemes (which involved developing common supply networks). None of these schemes has been very successful because of limited market opening by ASEAN member countries (Imada 1992). However, the six ASEAN countries succeeded in strengthening their collective bargaining position against developing trading partners outside the region.

The volume of extra-ASEAN trading has expanded more quickly than the volume of intra-ASEAN trade, which has remained at around 21 percent of their total trade. Trade between Singapore and other ASEAN countries accounted for 80 percent of intra-ASEAN trade (Table 12.3). In January 1992 the ASEAN nations agreed to establish the ASEAN Free Trade Area (AFTA) in order to step up economic integration efforts among the member countries. Under the AFTA, a preferential tariff reduction scheme will be extended to 15 selected industrial product groups. All internal tariffs on manufactured goods included in the scheme will be abolished over 15 years (ASEAN 1992a, 1992b). While ASEAN has achieved some success, it has hardly contributed to the spectacular development of East Asia as a whole.

Recently, interest in developing various subregional economic zones or groups has been growing in East Asia. These zones or groups include:

1. The Growth Triangle, centered on Singapore, and including the neighboring state of Johor in Malaysia and the province of Riau (including Batam island) in Indonesia.
2. The Baht Zone which brings together the border areas of Thailand, Laos, Cambodia and Vietnam in the Indochinese Peninsula.
3. The Greater South China Economic Zone, centered on Hong Kong and including China's Guangdong and Fujian provinces, and Taiwan.
4. The Yellow Sea Economic Zone, which includes the coastal areas facing the Yellow Sea of North and Northeast China, North and South Korea and Japan.
5. The Japan Sea Economic Zone, which includes the coastal areas of Northeast China, Far East Russia, South and North Korea and Japan.

These subregional arrangements are at different stages of implementation. The Growth Triangle, the Baht Zone and the Greater South China Economic Zone have developed rapidly since the middle of the 1980s. The Yellow Sea Economic Zone has only recently been launched, whereas the Japan Sea Economic Zone still remains at the proposal stage. None of these arrangements has received a formal commitment from the governments concerned. Each zone or group forms a natural economic territory, where transboundary trade has taken place at one time or another. In the Growth Triangle, Singapore and the neighboring state of Johor have engaged in transborder transactions for many years. Transborder transactions have recently intensified partly due to the flow of foreign direct investments to Malaysia and Singapore since the late 1980s and partly due to land and labor constraints in Singapore. The development of Batam was initially made possible by a tacit agreement in 1988 between Indonesia's President Suharto and Singapore's Prime Minister, Goh Chok Tong. However, market forces have since accelerated the development of Batam just as they contributed to the movement of firms from Singapore to Johor.

The other four zones have a common driving force: all are located along the borders separating Asian market economies from Asian socialist economies. Trade and investment transactions between the economies in these zones was severely restricted. Since the end of the Cold War and the adoption of more open, market-oriented economic policies by the Asian socialist countries, transborder trade and investment transactions have resumed. Indeed the occasional speeches of the Chinese leader Deng Xiaoping and the tacit endorsement by the Taiwan government, have certainly contributed to the favorable atmosphere for free trade and investment within their groups. But these assurances can hardly be compared with the inter-governmental arrangements in ASEAN, let alone the EC. Moreover, there is no central coordinating agent overseeing developments in these zones.

The real driving force for development in these informal subregional groups as well as in ASEAN is active trade and investment based on market forces. As each subregional group expands further, these groups will begin to overlap and come to form a greater East Asian group. The geographical coverage of the greater East Asian group would coincide with that of the East Asian Economic Group (EAEG).

The EAEG was proposed by Malaysian Prime Minister Mahathir in December 1990, immediately after the GATT ministerial meeting failed to conclude the Uruguay Round negotiation as was originally scheduled. The EAEG proposal, however, quickly encountered strong criticism from the U.S. and Australia, which warned against the establishment of a trade bloc of rapidly growing East Asian countries which excludes the U.S. and Australia. The EAEG was renamed the East Asian Economic Caucus (EAEC) so as to emphasize its consultative body function. The EAEC proposal reflected the reality of the rapid economic development and trade expansion in East Asia and the EAEC's function as a consultative body met the need of its member traders. But because of the absence of prior consultation among designated members on the one hand, and the quick criticism by outsiders on the other, it failed to obtain strong support from designated member countries, including Japan and some fellow ASEAN countries. The proposal was put on the agenda for the ASEAN Summit Meeting in January 1992. ASEAN leaders agreed to suspend its consideration and launched the AFTA proposal instead (ASEAN 1992a).

12.6   Impediments to Intra-Pacific Trade

Pacific economists are now seeking a loose form of institutional framework for economic cooperation in order to maintain rapid development in the region into the next century. Why do we need an institutional framework for Asia-Pacific at this stage? Over the past two decades several problems have emerged in connection with the process of rapid development in East Asia. These problems can be summarized as follows:

1. Macroeconomic imbalances are an inevitable outcome of interdependent growth. Some countries tend to incur persistent trade deficits while others incur persistent surpluses. Friction will persist between the deficit-prone and surplus-prone groups of countries. This problem is most evident across the Pacific, between the U.S. on the one hand, and Japan and the East Asian NIEs on the other (Table 12.3). U.S.–Japan trade frictions have led to fears that such frictions may have adverse spillover effects on other Asian countries.

2. Import restrictions are still in use in the region. However, a more significant trend is the increased use of nontariff measures such as voluntary export restraints (VERs) and orderly marketing arrangements (OMAs) to regulate the export of manufactured products to American and European markets. The region's exports of textiles and clothing have been managed tightly for individual product types and markets under the Multifiber Arrangement (MFA). The ASEAN countries were given an export quota far beyond their capacities in the beginning. Consequently, these countries have been able to expand their exports. But sooner or later their quota will be exceeded by their capacity increase and the MFA will deter further export expansion. The further transfer textile and clothing export operations to Asian socialist economies and South Asia will also be restricted under the MFA. The fading out of the MFA under the Uruguay Round is therefore imperative for the further expansion of textile and clothing trades (Yamazawa 1989).

3. Foreign investment flows and trade in services have increased along with commodity trade in the region. However, foreign investment flows and services are still subject to more regulations and restrictions than commodity trade. On the other hand, a variety of incentives cancel out the impact of these restrictions and regulations. The trade-related investment measures (TRIM) negotiation of the Uruguay Round will help to resolve these complications to a limited extent, but progress within the GATT framework has stalled. Therefore, a regional initiative is called for (Guisinger 1991).

4. Rapid changes in trade and production structures have been accompanied by serious adjustment difficulties as well as industrial competitiveness problems and macroeconomic imbalances. These difficulties have generated severe frictions among trading partners. This has led to calls to replace exports with foreign direct investments, which have further promoted closer relationships among countries in the region.

5. Tacit political assurances of a commitment to market reforms and an outward orientation provided the initial basis for the recent development of subregional cooperation zones along the border between socialist and market regimes. However, socialist regimes may withdraw these tacit assurances at any time. Doubts about the prospects for maintaining and strengthening these reforms and outward orientation have halted further development of inter-regime trade. Some form of regional framework may be able to serve as a collective guarantee against unfavorable political changes or disturbances.[2]

This region needs a consultative body that will discuss these problems and find solutions to them. Such a body should include not only East Asia but also North America and Oceania. The latter two are by and large complementary in their resource endowments and provide East Asia with energy, resources and markets. Both North America and Oceania are very keen about strengthening trade and investment ties with East Asia. In view of the aggravated state of trans-Pacific frictions, a consultative body with extensive membership coverage is needed in order to prevent frictions from spreading over the Pacific as a whole and killing the region's growth potential. As we saw in Table 12.5, this greater Asia-Pacific group is comparable with the EC12 in terms of its total trade, but has even higher intra-group trade ratios than the EC12.

A consultative body often takes the form of a bilateral arrangement between the countries concerned. The U.S. and Japan have been implementing several forms of bilateral consultations. The bilateral trade imbalance between the two results from each country's overall trade imbalances—the U.S.'s trade deficit and Japan's trade surplus. These imbalances could be better resolved through the macroeconomic policies of each country. Their bilateral consultation has been extended to a variety of sectoral issues, such as supercomputers, forest products, semiconductors, and automobiles. In 1989 the U.S. used Article Super 301 of the Trade Agreements Act of 1979 against Japan. This unilateral action invited strong protest from the Japanese government. President Bush proposed a new bilateral consultation called the U.S.–Japan Structural Impediments Initiative (SII).

The SII covered a broad range of topics, including the corporate behaviors, distribution systems, saving and investment behaviors and educational systems of the two countries. It aimed to foster mutual understanding of the systems and institutions affecting the economic performance of each country and to coordinate conflicting differences. The SII eased tensions, but has not been free of conflict: pressure has been exerted to obtain the concessions needed to settle conflicting differences. A bilateral agreement between two parties often affects a third country and invites the third country to complain against the two parties to the agreement. This was the case with the U.S.–Japan semiconductor agreement (Baker 1991).

A regional consultation mechanism, if set up effectively and in a timely fashion, will resolve disputes and avoid unnecessary (emotionally charged) confrontations and third party complaints.

12.7   Loose Cooperation Framework Desired

East Asia has not been keen on pursuing formal economic integration of the EC type. Neither a treaty like the Treaty of Rome nor a region-wide free trade agreement has been negotiated in East Asia. Economic cooperation in the Pacific dates back to the late 1980s. Trans-Pacific trade had only started then but both businessmen and economists, stimulated by the formation of the European Economic Community and European Free Trade Area, started discussing regional economic cooperation through two series of region-wide conferences, the Pacific Basin Economic Council (PBEC since 1967) and the Pacific Trade and Development Conference (PAFTAD since 1968).

Discussions involving a wider array of participants—including diplomats, politicians, government officials and journalists—began only after the first oil shock in the 1970s. Prime Minister Ohira of Japan proposed to promote a "Pacific Basin Community" at his inaugural speech in 1978. This proposal focused wider attention on the theme of Pacific cooperation both within and outside the region (Pacific Basin Cooperation Study Group 1980). Prime Minister Fraser of Australia responded actively to this proposal and hosted a seminar at Canberra, which started a series of semi-official regional consultations—the Pacific Economic Cooperation Council (PECC)—in 1980 (Crawford 1981). PECC initially involved 12 countries (U.S., Canada, Australia, New Zealand, Japan, South Korea, and the six ASEAN countries) and the Pacific island nations as a group. It has expanded its membership to 20 countries by including China, Taipei, Hong Kong, Mexico, Peru, Chile and Russia. It now covers all major Pacific countries. It has a small secretariat in Singapore, conducts task force activities on individual cooperation issues, and holds general meetings every year and a half to reach the consensus needed to support the task force recommendations addressed to member governments (JANCPEC 1988).

PECC has a tripartite composition of businessmen, academics, and government officials (in their private capacity). PECC has influence over the policies of member governments but at an informal level. In 1989, Australian Prime Minister Hawke hosted the first formal inter-governmental consultative body, the APEC Ministerial Meeting in Canberra (APEC 1989). The foreign ministers and trade ministers of 15 member countries (PECC's first 12 members plus China, Taipei, and Hong Kong which joined in 1991) have been meeting once every year at some city in the Pacific since then. The ministerial meeting is supported by frequent senior official meetings and several work projects on individual cooperation issues carried out by member country government officials. PECC also tries to input its cooperation efforts into APEC at various levels. A new popular topic for discussion in Asia-Pacific is how to institutionalize the APEC and PECC activities in order to meet Asia-Pacific's emerging needs (Drysdale 1989; CSIS 1991). It is expected that a small permanent secretariat will be established in the near future to strengthen the continuity of its activities.

A hot issue is the extent and degree of coordination of policies among member governments. Here, in the Asia-Pacific region, we cannot implement a joint policy like the EC. We have not reached that stage of integration yet. The coordination of macroeconomic policies has never been attempted among the APEC member governments. However, member economies are already interdependent owing to trade, investment, and service flows in the region—no member economy can insulate itself fully from the impacts of another member's policy. We need to hold on a regular basis policy dialogues on trade, investment and development matters.

Moreover, subtle efforts to improve the policy environment in member countries are needed.

As regards trade and investment policies, many member governments in the region have liberalized their markets on a unilateral basis. All member governments have supported the Uruguay Round negotiation and participated in the coordination of their interests in individual areas. But the limited prospect for its achievement has been encouraging member governments to work on regional trade and investment liberalization initiatives.

Pacific economists have often described the main policy stance of Pacific Asia as one of "open regionalism." However, economists outside Pacific Asia seem to find the concept of "open regionalism" difficult to understand. In contrast with globalism, regionalism focuses its policy implementation on a particular region at the expense of countries outside the region. It tends to discriminate against outsiders, whether intentionally or not. Thus, to talk about "regionalism open to outsiders" seems internally inconsistent. The strong regional measures implemented by the EC tend to divert trade and investment from outsiders to insiders.

On the other hand, a weak type of regionalism that does not discriminate against outsiders will not be able to fuel growth within the region. Pacific cooperation fits into this weak type of regionalism, which does not discriminate against outsiders. However, it has maintained high growth in the region owing to the vigor of insider firms. The Asia-Pacific countries have turned to this weak type of regionalism because of differences in levels of development, in the size of the economy, and in resource endowments. In spite of the increased intra-regional trade, East Asia remains highly reliant on trade with countries outside the region (Table 12.5).

It is worth noting that trade in goods is only one part of Asia-Pacific's liberalization agenda. Today, the countries of Asia-Pacific are engaged in a variety of transborder transactions, including direct investment abroad and trade in services. These transactions are restricted by a variety of national regulations and rules. Harmonizing these rules and making national regulations transparent will encourage cross-border business within the region and will not necessarily entail discrimination against outsiders. Free trade agreements negotiated today go much further than the classic concept of a free trade area (FTA). Today all these agreements include harmonization and deregulation provisions.

A textbook FTA is the lowest stage of regional integration. A customs union has no internal tariffs among member countries; and member countries have a common external tariff. In an FTA only the internal tariffs are eliminated within the grouping; but different external tariffs remain. In the Pacific even a FTA of this classic form has not been proposed for the region as a whole. A proposal made at the first PAFTAD conference in 1968 to reduce tariffs across-the-board while retaining external tariffs for the Asia-Pacific countries was not supported by Pacific economists (Kojima 1968).

The modern version of the FTA is better understood as providing environments in which goods, money, persons and information move across the border and enterprises are encouraged to extend their horizons and promote global operations. Apart from tariffs and nontrade barriers, transportation and communication bottlenecks, inadequate information, a lack of skilled personnel, and environmental protection restrictions discourage such business activities.

The bilateral consultation between the U.S. and Japan is an example of a modern version of the FTA. Over the past decade, a number of U.S.–Japan FTAs have been proposed to ease frictions between the two countries. All of these proposals entailed wider coverage than in the classic FTA. One of the proposals resulted in the U.S.–Japan SII (Matsunaga and Solarz 1992). The continued use of the term FTA to describe a substantively different integration arrangement will confuse the discussion on regionalism by unnecessarily bringing in a negative image of discrimination against outsiders. It may be better to give the new arrangement a new name such as "open economic association" (OEA), which emphasizes its much less discriminatory impacts on outsiders.[3]

12.8   Agenda for APEC

A consensus has emerged in the Asia-Pacific region that its integration should take place through a loose and informal FTA. The APEC/PECC process is best suited to bring about such an FTA. Many member governments and committees seem to favor further institutionalizing and intensifying APEC's activities so as to meet emerging needs in the region even though it is still defining its role. Various experts have already made proposals regarding APEC's agenda for the 1990s (see Elek in this volume). Bearing the preceding discussion in mind, the author puts forward the following five suggestions for the APEC/PECC process agenda:

1. The successful conclusion of the Uruguay Rounds, even if its accomplishments are limited is imperative to the APEC/PECC process. A global free trade and investment environment is the necessary precondition for the further development of the Asia-Pacific integration.
2. During the post-Uruguay Round period, the APEC members will continue their efforts to eliminate those impediments to trade and investment that will be left unresolved by the Uruguay Round. (Impediments in such new areas as services, TRIP (trade-related intellectual property) and TRIM are most likely to remain unresolved by the Uruguay Round.)
3. APEC's post-Uruguay Round efforts should be broadened so as to promote the new OEA in the region through such measures as policy dialogues, the elimination of physical bottlenecks, the reduction of uncertainty, and the harmonization of rules and regulations. The new OEA will have encouraging effects on intra-regional transactions but much less discriminatory impacts on outsiders.
4. APEC will accommodate such subregional groupings as NAFTA, ASEAN and the Australia–New Zealand Closer Economic Relations (CER) as well as such independent trading nations as Japan and Korea. It will keep an eye on these subregional groupings and guide their individual development so that it is GATT consistent. A loose framework of economic cooperation as envisaged by APEC best fits in the with East Asia's continued growth.

5. APEC will be open to outside regions such as Europe, South Asia and Latin America through its OEA approach. It will encourage its firms to participate in the development process taking place outside Asia-Pacific and invite non-Pacific firms to participate in the Asia-Pacific development. In this way, it will contribute to global development.

Notes

1. In its popular usage "integration" may be too strong a word to describe the current trend in Asia-Pacific and be better replaced by the word "cooperation." However, in this chapter the word "integration" is meant to convey the meaning it normally has in economics literature, that is, intensified economic activities across the border either with or without a formal institutional setting.
2. An Australian expert on China suggested that this will also enable the socialist regime to rely on the trade and investment expansion with the market economies, and will thus benefit both the market and socialist regimes.
3. The author owes this terminology to Andrew Elek.

References

APEC I, 1989, *Asia Pacific Economic Cooperation Ministerial-Level Meeting, Chairman's Summary*, Canberra, November.

ASEAN, 1992a, *Singapore Declaration of 1992*, Fourth ASEAN Summit, Singapore, January 27–28.

ASEAN, 1992b, *Agreement on the Common Effective Preferential Tariff (CEPT) Scheme for the ASEAN Free Trade Area (AFTA)*, Singapore.

Baker, J. A. III, 1991, "The United States and Japan: Global Partners in a Pacific Community," *Japan Review of International Affairs*, 6 (special issue).

Crawford, J. (ed.), 1981, *Pacific Economic Co-operation: Suggestions for Action*, Canberra.

CSIS, 1991, *A Policy Framework for Asia-Pacific Economic Cooperation*, Report by the CSIS U.S.–Japan Working Group, Washington, DC.

Drysdale, P., 1989, *International Economic Pluralism: Economic Policy in East Asia and the Pacific*, Allen & Unwin, Sydney.

Guisinger, S., 1991, "Foreign Direct Investment Flows in East and Southeast Asia: Policy Issues," *ASEAN Economic Bulletin*, 8(1).

Imada, P., 1992, "Production and Trade Effects of ASEAN Preferential Trading Arrangements," *Developing Economies*, September.

JNCPEC (Japan National Committee for Pacific Economic Cooperation), 1988, *Review on Pacific Cooperation Activities*, Japan Institute of International Affairs, Tokyo.

Kojima, K. (ed.), 1968, *Pacific Trade and Development*, Japan Economic Research Center, Tokyo.

Matsunaga, S. and J. S. Solarz, 1992, "GATT Revival, Pacific Free Trade Keys to Avoiding Debilitating Conflict," *Nikkei Weekly*, July 4.

Ohkita, S., 1987, "The Outlook for Pacific Cooperation and the Role of Japan," *Indonesian Quarterly*, 15(3).

Pacific Basin Cooperation Study Group, 1980, *Report on the Pacific Basin Cooperation Concept*, Tokyo.

Yamazawa, I., 1989, "The Textile Trade Issue in the Uruguay Round Negotiation," in H. E. English (ed.), *Pacific Initiatives in Global Trade*, Halifax, Canada.

——, 1991, *International Trade and Economic Development: The Japanese Model*, East–West Center, Honolulu, Hawaii.

Chapter 13

Peter A. Petri

HISTORICAL ROOTS OF THE ASIA-PACIFIC INTERDEPENDENCE

13.1 Introduction

The phenomenal expansion of East Asia's[1] intra-regional trade—from US$116 billion to $265 billion in the five years between 1985 and 1990—has raised the prospect of an East Asian economic bloc that could more than match the scale of either the European or North American trading areas. This bloc would be inevitably dominated by Japan, and thus trade frictions between Japan and the United States could be generalized into a massive confrontation among giant economies. Against the background of declining U.S. competitiveness and suspicions about the "fairness" of global markets, some observers see sinister motives behind growing East Asian interdependence. Some alarmist scholars go as far as to argue that Japan's recent investment, aid and trade patterns "cloak political and conquistadorial designs similar to those in the past" (Montgomery 1988: xiii).

These issues are examined here in a historical and analytical context. We will show that East Asia has been, and continues to be, a trading bloc in the sense that its trade is more regionally oriented than would be expected on the basis of random trade patterns. Moreover, East Asian interdependence has intensified in the last five or so years. But we will also show that recent increases in interdependence are small in a historical context, and that the East Asian economy has steadily *dis*integrated during the previous three decades. East Asia is *less* interdependent today than it was for most of the twentieth century, save for short periods of time in the aftermath of World War II and during the mid-1980s. The key long-term story has been the shift of East Asian linkages from regional partners to a more diversified group of countries, including the United States.[2]

Nevertheless, there is reason to see 1985 as a turning point in these trends. East Asian interdependence has not greatly intensified so far, but the break with previous trends is clear. In addition, still larger changes have taken place in investment linkages, and these foreshadow future trade changes. These developments, combined with anecdotal evidence on how individual agents and governments are stepping up investments in regional linkages, suggest that from now on the East Asian trading bloc may be strengthening rather than continuing to dissolve.

The analytical base of this chapter is a simple model of bloc formation. The model begins with the idea that a trading bloc's intra-bloc bias—its preference for inside rather than outside partners—rests on low intra-bloc transaction costs compared to outside-bloc transaction costs. Intra-bloc transaction costs can be reduced by investments in intra-bloc linkages—for example, in transport links, economic policies that facilitate integration, or information about regional business opportunities. These investments, in turn, depend on economic and/or political developments that draw the bloc's countries closer together. The process of bloc formation is dynamic, because a growing volume of intra-bloc trade itself provides incentives for investing in linkages. Thus "historical accidents" that bring economies together may well be amplified and perpetuated by the linkage investments that they induce.

Three major historical developments are important for understanding East Asian interdependence. The first is the development of Asian treaty ports in the nineteenth century, which established a network of trade driven by major ports such as Singapore, Hong Kong, Manila and Shanghai. A second is Japan's imperial expansion, which created a very high level of economic integration among the economies of northern East Asia. Finally, the spectacular growth of the region's economies is emerging as a new force for integration today: as East Asian countries are becoming increasingly important to each other, they are beginning to invest heavily in linkages that are very likely to increase their intra-regional bias.

It is also possible to identify forces that have worked against regional integration in the postwar period. These include the central role of the United States in the postwar Pacific economy, the rapid economic development of the region, which enabled its economies to enter many new global markets, and the general integration of the world economy due to trade liberalization and improvements in transport and communications. This paper attempts to trace how the changing balance of these pro- and anti-regional forces has led to the complex pattern of rises and declines that have characterized East Asian economic integration.

13.2   Measures of Interdependence

There is no single, widely accepted measure of interdependence. As we shall see, the reason for this is that the appropriateness of a particular measure depends on the uses to which it is put. Briefly, three different types of measures are frequently used. Let x_{ij} represent exports from country i to country j, and the subscript "*" (in place of i or j) represent the summation across all i or j, respectively. Thus x_{i*} represents the total exports of country i, x_{*j} the total imports of country j, and x_{**} total world trade. In this notation, the three commonly used concepts of interdependence are:

☐ *absolute* measures of trading intensity, which deflate a particular bilateral (or intra-regional) trade flow with overall world trade:

$$A = x_{ij}/x_{**}$$

☐ *relative* measures of trading intensity, which deflate absolute intensity with *either* the worldwide export share of the exporting country, or the worldwide import share of the importing country:

$$B = A(/x_{i*}/x_{**}) = x_{ij}/x_{i*} \text{ or } B' = x_{ij}/x_{*j}$$

☐ *double-relative* measures of trading intensity, which deflate absolute intensity with *both* the worldwide export share of the exporting country and the worldwide import share of the importing country:

$$C = A/\{(x_{i*}/x_{**})(x_{*j}/x_{**})\} = x_{ij}x_{**}/x_{i*}x_{*j}$$

In effect, measure A compares the scale of a particular bilateral (or intra-regional) trading relationship to worldwide averages, measure B compares it to the trade shares of one or the other of the two partners participating in the relationship, and measure C compares it to the product of the trade shares of both partners. These indexes of trading intensity can evolve quite differently over time. For example, exports from X to Y could grow rapidly compared to world trade (rising A measure), but could still fail to keep pace with X's rapidly increasing share of world exports or Y's rapidly increasing share of world imports (declining C measure). The double-relative measures calculated as the "C" measure in this study are commonly described as "gravity coefficients" in the literature.[3]

Each of these measures of trading intensity is appropriate for answering a particular type of question. For example, if one is interested in the relative stakes or influence of different groups of countries in global trade negotiations, it may make sense to compare their trade volumes to world levels by using an absolute intensity index. Alternatively, if one wants to know to what extent a country will respond to the interests of a particular partner (or group of partners), then the intensity of the bilateral (intra-bloc) trading relationship is best judged using a relative measure (in effect, the share of the partner(s) in the country's trade). Finally, if one wants to assess the extent of trade biases toward particular partners (or groups of partners) relative to the neutral of assignment of trade across all partners, then double-relative indexes, or gravity coefficients provide an appropriate answer.

The evolution of East Asian interdependence is summarized, using each of three measures defined above, in Table 13.1 and Figures 13.1–13.3. The data used represent the longest, consistent time series available on international trade flows, and were assembled from the IMF's *Direction of Trade* and its many precursor publications. The measures shown are all calculated for *two-way* trade, that is, with x_{ij} defined as the sum of both exports and imports between i and j (not just as exports from i to j as in the previous discussion).

In absolute terms (Table 13.1 and Figure 13.1), East Asian intra-trade is only slightly larger than North American intra-trade, and considerably smaller than Western European intra-trade. Indeed, East Asia's share of world trade is still smaller than it was during the height of the Japanese empire before World War II. Nevertheless, over the postwar period East Asian intra-trade has grown very fast, nearly quadrupling its share of world trade.

In relative terms, East Asian intra-trade shows a U-shaped pattern (Figure 13.2). By this measure, East Asian interdependence fell sharply as the Japanese empire was dismantled, and continued to decline well into the postwar period. During this period, despite the rapidly growing absolute volume of East Asian intra-trade, the relative importance of regional trade fell, since the region's third country trade developed even more rapidly. Eventually, the region's rapid growth caught up with the diversification of its trade patterns, and intra-trade began to increase.

Still a third story emerges from the double-relative measure (Table 13.1 and Figure 13.3). This index shows a steady and sharp decline in the regional bias of East Asian trade in all but the last five years of data. It also shows that the level of interdependence was initially very high, and that it remained high even in the initial years after World War II. By this measure East Asia was more highly integrated

TABLE 13.1 Measures of regional interdependence (exports plus imports)

	1938	1955	1969	1979	1985	1990
Absolute measure: Intra-trade as share of world trade						
North America	0.030	0.067	0.069	0.042	0.064	0.053
Western Europe	0.182	0.196	0.287	0.293	0.271	0.338
East Asia	0.100	0.022	0.029	0.042	0.064	0.079
Pacific Rim	0.180	0.135	0.169	0.156	0.248	0.246
Relative measure: Intra-trade as share of regional trade						
North America	0.227	0.334	0.379	0.287	0.330	0.313
Western Europe	0.461	0.491	0.647	0.664	0.654	0.712
East Asia	0.671	0.313	0.293	0.332	0.363	0.407
Pacific Rim	0.583	0.450	0.566	0.545	0.643	0.649
Double-relative measure: Gravity coefficients						
North America	1.73	1.65	2.09	1.95	1.71	1.84
Western Europe	1.16	1.23	1.46	1.51	1.58	1.50
East Asia	4.48	4.45	2.97	2.64	2.05	2.09
Pacific Rim	1.89	1.49	1.90	1.91	1.67	1.71

FIGURE 13.1   East Asian interdependence: absolute

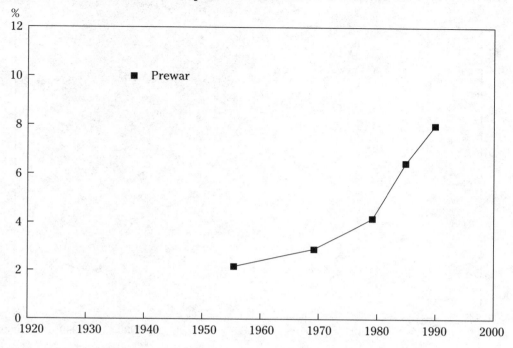

FIGURE 13.2   East Asian interdependence: relative

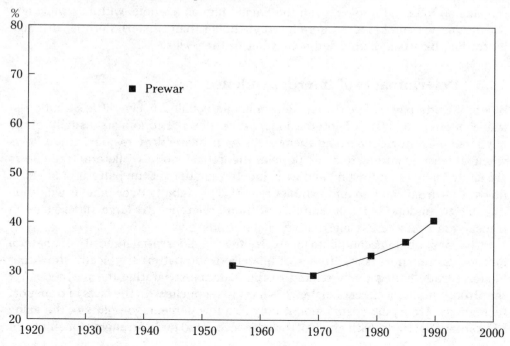

FIGURE 13.3   East Asian interdependence: double-relative

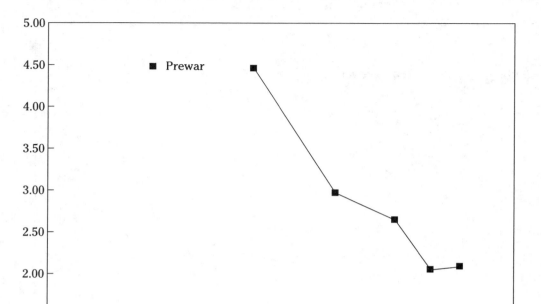

than either North America or Western Europe both before and after the War, and remains so today. Moreover, even the Pacific Rim as a whole, with East Asia and North America combined, is more interdependent than Western Europe, although its trading bias has diminished somewhat in the 1980s.

13.3   Determinants of Interdependence

Bilateral trade patterns and their determinants usually receive little attention in the economic analysis of international trade flows. Economists usually chide noneconomists for concerning themselves with bilateral or regional trade flows when, at least according to some popular theoretical models, bilateral trade flows are analytically uninteresting and even indeterminate[4]. Yet the pattern of bilateral flows is far from random and exhibits remarkable stability over time. It would be difficult to understand this stability without reference to large differences in transaction costs across alternative bilateral linkages.

The most obvious candidate for explaining the differential intensity of bilateral linkages is transport cost. Studies of bilateral trade patterns typically show that bilateral trade is negatively related to the distance separating the partners.[5] Yet the strong empirical effect of distance is hard to reconcile with the facts of transport technology. Transport costs amount only to a few percentage points of the value of international trade, with much of the cost accounted for in arranging for shipment and the loading and unloading of products (Leontief 1973). Thus, while transport costs can vary greatly across products and modes of transport, they do not vary much with distance itself.[6] Nor is there evidence that bilateral flows were much affected by the large fluctuations in transport costs that took place, for example, during the oil price shocks of the 1970s.

So the empirical importance of distance is most likely due not to distance itself, but to factors correlated with distance. Important among these may be human and physical assets that facilitate trade, on both sides of a trading relationship. Investments in such assets are more likely to be made among physically and culturally proximate trade partners.[7] These assets may include knowledge about the partner's language, culture, markets, and business practices. They may also include a network of personal or business relationships and business reputations abroad.

The importance of these factors is underscored by the pervasive role of institutions that economize on transactions costs in international trade. International trade is often intra-firm trade (Lawrence 1991); it is likely to be mediated by international banks (for example, through letters of credit and other instruments that enable the firm to shift the risks and information requirements involved in international deals to banks); and, in many countries, it is dominated by large, specialized international trading companies.

The level of international transaction costs depends in part on past investments in physical infrastructure, information, and education. Often, the investments required to reduce transaction costs involve substantial scale economies, and so transaction costs across a bilateral link will be lower in proportion to the activity across the link. For example, it is generally cheaper (per unit of output) to establish and operate a transport or telecommunications link across a high density linkage. This is even more true for investments in information, which generate an essentially public asset, whose services can be costlessly shared by all. Interestingly, the provision of trading information was an important early objective of Japanese policies in East Asia, and is among the first objectives of APEC (Asia-Pacific Economic Cooperation), the region's new forum for economic cooperation.

In still other cases, intra-bloc transactions costs will be reduced through political mechanisms. For example, a free trade agreement will be easier to negotiate among partners who already have intense linkages. Similarly, the arguments for stabilizing an exchange rate will be much more compelling for countries with substantial bilateral trade than for those that are not highly interdependent. Such mechanisms presume, to be sure, that the trade linkage is valued highly by all of the bloc's countries; asymmetric trade, by contrast, may not lead to reinforcing agreements even if the (one-way) flow is very intense.[8]

The key point is that developments that increase bilateral contacts may trigger strong, positive feedback effects through their impact on trade-facilitating investments. A shock to a bilateral link may be significantly amplified as the initial increase in contacts leads to new investments in the bilateral linkage, which in turn reduces bilateral transaction costs. In some respects, these mechanisms are similar to those that generate irreversible changes ("hysteresis") in trade flows in reaction to exchange rate changes.[9]

The endogeneity of trade-facilitating investments, and thus transaction costs, suggests a simple model of bloc formation. Suppose a relatively loosely connected group of economies becomes more interdependent due to an economic or noneconomic shock. The increased intensity of contacts will make it attractive to invest further in the bilateral relationship. Bilateral transaction costs will fall, leading to further increases in the intensity of the bilateral relationship. The cycle may repeat itself over time. This story is consistent with Europe's integration process in the 1950s and 1960s. After the war, European peace and economic recovery increased the importance of European partners to each other and provided incentives for reducing intra-European trade barriers. The Common Market undertook a massive effort to eliminate trade barriers and later to reduce the volatility of Community exchange rates. These steps substantially raised the regional bias of European trade and, arguably, resulted in further efforts to reduce intra-European barriers.

If international transaction costs are endogenous, then history matters. The extent to which countries are "shocked" into close trading relationships, and the extent to which their periods of rapid growth are parallel, affects their investments in their bilateral trade and shapes their subsequent trading relationships.

This chapter will examine how various historical events have shaped East Asian interdependence. A key piece of the argument is that various "accidents" of history—that is, close international contacts that cannot be traced to market forces alone—have changed the international pattern of transaction costs and have permanently affected East Asia's bilateral trading patterns. Three such accidents appear particularly important. First, the imperialist policies of the Western countries established an initial network of East Asian trade. Later, Japanese imperialism provided an impetus for the integration of East Asia's northern economies. As it was often observed at the time, "trade followed the flag." Finally, the rapid growth of various East Asian countries is now making them loom increasingly large to each other and is providing a new impetus for regional integration.

13.4   East Asian Interdependence before 1931

East Asia has a long history of trade, dating back to Arab and Chinese trade among East Asian countries and with Europe. The volume of East Asian trade in general, and of East Asian intra-trade as well, appears to have gained momentum with the stepped-up involvement of European powers in the nineteenth century. Subsequently, the expansion of Japan's economic sphere of influence became the main force driving interdependence.

13.4.1 The Treaty Port System

Toward the middle of the nineteenth century, prompted by British leadership, a wave of liberalization spread through Europe. Britain sought similar objectives in East Asia: it abolished the monopoly of the East Indies company and moved aggressively to obtain free access to Chinese markets. The Treaty of Nanking, which Britain concluded with China at the end of the Opium War of 1840–42, opened five ports where British subjects could carry on trade "without molestation or restraint" and ceded Hong Kong "in perpetuity" to Her Majesty. Export and import duties were fixed at an average of 5 percent, and consular courts were established to keep British subjects safe from local laws.

As in Europe, Britain also included most favored nation clauses in this and other treaties. Thus it paved the way for "cooperative" imperialism, with France and the United States, and eventually Russia, Prussia, Portugal, Denmark, Holland, Spain, Belgium and Italy all signing treaties guaranteeing access to Chinese and other ports (Beasley 1987).

A surge of trade ensued, both regionally within East Asia, and with Europe. The profitability of this trade led to a lively competition for new ports. The United States focused on Japan, and following Matthew C. Perry's landings eventually concluded a treaty in 1858. Russia, Holland, Britain and France followed with similar treaties of their own. Japan's early trade thus came to be oriented toward the West: silk, tea and coal were exported to France, Italy, and the United States, while textiles, weapons and machinery were imported from Britain and the United States.

Thus, by the turn of the 20th century, when relatively comprehensive regional trade data become available, the level of East Asian regional interdependence was already high. As Table 13.2 shows, by 1913 about 42 percent of the region's trade

TABLE 13.2   East Asian trade as a share of total trade for different countries (exports plus imports)

	1913	1925	1938	1955	1990
China	0.53	0.46	0.70	0.43	0.59
Indonesia	0.32	0.38	0.26	0.32	0.60
Taiwan	–	–	0.99	0.50	0.42
Japan	0.41	0.47	0.70	0.22	0.29
Korea	–	–	1.00	0.35	0.40
Malaysia	0.44	0.39	0.35	0.30	0.37
Philippines	0.18	0.15	0.11	0.17	0.43
Thailand	0.62	0.71	0.65	0.52	0.51
SIMPLE AVERAGE	0.42	0.43	0.59	0.35	0.45
excl. Korea, Taiwan	0.42	0.43	0.46	0.33	0.47
excl. Korea, Taiwan, Japan	0.42	0.42	0.41	0.35	0.50

Source: League of Nations, *Long-Term Economic Statistic of Japan.*

was intra-regional, compared to 46 percent in 1938 and 47 percent today. Most of this trade was mediated by the great ports developed by the European powers—Hong Kong, Manila, Shanghai and Singapore. In addition to maintaining bilateral ties between the colonies and their home countries—between Malaysia and Singapore and England, Indonesia and Holland, and the Philippines and the United States—the ports also played a key role in coordinating the trade of a vast region stretching from India to Japan. Roughly 70 percent of Thailand's trade, for example, was mediated by Singapore, which sent some of Thailand's rice on to China and Japan, in exchange for Indian and British textiles.

13.4.2 Japanese Expansion

A second impetus for the intensification of regional ties came from Japan's industrialization and expanding economic influence. By the end of the nineteenth century Japan had established a role parallel to or surpassing those of other powers in Korea and China. It continued to gain economic and military power in the early 20th century, and began to displace the exports of European powers in their own colonies.

Japan's role in the treaty port system quickly changed from host to protagonist. By 1876 Japan had itself opened three Korean ports and began competing aggressively with China to reexport Western textiles to Korea. In 1895 Japan won a major military victory over China, gaining a large indemnity, further influence in Korea, commercial privileges in China, and two important territories: the Liaotung Peninsula (including Dalien, Manchuria's most important port) and Taiwan. Japan was eventually forced to back down on the Liaotung claims, but its victory had clearly established it as a rising imperial power.

Scholars tend to agree that the conquest of Korea reflected primarily military, rather than economic objectives—as the Japanese Army's Prussian advisor had put it, Korea was "a dagger thrust at the heart of Japan" (Myers and Peattie 1984: 15). But the economic potential of a broader sphere of influence was not lost on the Meiji leadership. Foreign Minister Komura Jutaro explicitly recognized the importance of economic objectives and their relationship to military power:

> Competition through commercial and industrial activity and through overseas enterprises is a phenomenon of grave importance in recent international relations … [Western countries] have been zealous in expanding their rights in mining, or in railroads, or in internal waterways, and in various other directions on the Asian continents, especially in China … However, when we look at the measures [taken by] our own empire, which has the most important ties of interest in the area, separated by only a thin stretch of water, there is not much to be seen yet. Both those in government and those outside it regard this as highly regrettable (Duus 1984: 133).

In any case, Japan's military triumphs in Korea were quickly followed by investments in communications infrastructure related to bilateral trade, and eventually modifications in the Taiwanese and Korean economies that helped to make them more complementary to the Japanese economy. Meiji-style agricultural reforms, such as comprehensive land surveys, were introduced, establishing clear criteria for the ownership and taxation of land, and also facilitating the sale of land.[10] A combination of these administrative measures and new agricultural technologies imported from Japan resulted in a dramatic surge of agricultural production[11]. By the late 1920s Korea and Taiwan supplied 80 percent of Japan's rice imports,[12] two-thirds of its sugar, and substantial shares of other minerals and lumber (Peattie 1984: 32).

But it was China that was regarded as the great prize. In 1905, Japan defeated Russia in Manchuria and acquired control over the Liaotung peninsula (known as the Kwantung Leased Territories), all of Korea, the southern half of Sakhalin Island (Karafuto), and the Chinese Eastern Railway. There followed a substantial wave of investments in communications, coordinated by the Southern Manchuria Railway Company (SMR), a quasi public company which remained a key player also in later phases of Japanese expansion. A key objective of the company was to shape the transport infrastructure of Manchuria—that is, to ensure that the network fed into Dalien, the Japanese-controlled port (Beasley 1987: 90–92).

The Japanese government also moved aggressively to improve information on the Chinese economy. The Finance Ministry proposed a wide-ranging study of Chinese demand, exhibitions in treaty ports, visits by Japanese entrepreneurs, and new ways of disseminating information, including a China Association in Japan that would encourage businessmen to take interest in China. The Minister of Agriculture and Commerce (the precursor of the modern-day Ministry of International Trade and Industry (MITI)) provided a particularly eloquent argument for investments in information:

> There was a time when Japan hoped to find her chief field of commercial enterprise in the west; but today the mind of Japan is all toward China as the commercial hope of our future, not to say anything of our geographical and racial advantages with that country. It is our ambition to be to the East what Great Britain is to the West. We have left no means untried in making a thorough investigation of the present conditions of China ... We think we know a good deal about commercial conditions in China because we know a little more than the merchants of the West; but we really know nothing as we ought to know; and I would advise all those who hope to share in trade with China, to make careful and constant investigation into the conditions prevailing there; for I am sure there is much yet to be learned, if our trade with China is to achieve its best. Instead of our business men staying at home and waiting for orders, let them go or send representatives into central China, and they will find a more remunerative field of demand and consumption than they ever dreamed of, reclining in their offices at home (Whelpley 1913: 247–48).

But as Japan became good at imperialism, the Western powers began to change the rules of the game. The powers started to relax their control over their colonies by revising the treaties on foreign ports; soon after World War I, for example, China was granted substantial tariff autonomy. At the same time, powers moved to control Japan's growing regional influence. The Washington Conference in 1921 sharply limited the size of the Japanese navy, and a period of economic and political frictions ensued.

Despite the strained political circumstances, the sphere of influence established at the turn of the century resulted in a sharp increase in Japan's regional economic role. By the late 1920s Japan had essentially caught up with Western interests in China, and by 1931 the stock of Japanese investments in China equalled those of Great Britain and exceeded those of all other countries combined (Beasley 1987: 133). Japanese investments reached deep into Manchuria; for example, by the end of World War I, the Hanyehping coal and iron company supplied 60 percent of Yawata Steel's iron ore requirements (Beasley 1987: 137). This period of the so-called "Shidehara Diplomacy" was characterized by frequent Japanese-Western clashes, repeated concessions on both military and trade rights, and yet considerable economic gains.

13.5   Interdependence between 1931 and 1945

The era of political compromise ended in 1931. This turn of events was hastened by Chinese resistance to Japan's economic advance and by world depression. Subsequently, Japan's economic strategy dramatically changed. The colonial-style exchange of manufactures for raw materials gave way to a concerted effort to develop independent bases of industrial strength in several parts of Japan's economic empire. The new strategy led to substantial industrial investments outside Japan proper, and eventually gave rise to an increasingly sophisticated economic linkages between Japan, Korea, Taiwan, and eventually China.

13.5.1 Military Expansion

Three factors helped to replace the economic approaches of the 1920s with a strategy based on military power. The first was China's emerging nationalism. By the late 1920s Japan's influence in China came under increased threat from the Kuomintang. In 1927, for example, the northern Chinese warlord Chang Tso-Lin, under Kuomintang influence, withdrew permission for the construction of five new Japanese railway lines into northern Manchuria. A year later, Chiang Kai-shek defeated his Peking rivals and set his sights on the northern Chinese provinces dominated by Japan. Japan's Kwantung Army responded with a complex series of intrigues which eventually led to the invasion of Manchuria in 1931 (Barnhart 1987).

A second factor involved trade frictions which increasingly limited Japan's conventional access to international markets. As the world economy began to decline starting in 1929, Japan's trade relations sharply deteriorated, since many trade partners blamed Japan for the particularly large gains that it had achieved during the previous decade. For example, by 1932 Japan had displaced the

Netherlands as Indonesia's largest trade partner, and had made similar inroads in Malaysia. During the 1930s Japan became embroiled in one trade dispute after another; conflicts with India, the Dutch East Indies, and Canada each resulted in a trade war or reciprocal boycott. As one contemporary writer put it, it was:

> the bad fortune of the Island Empire that it has come of age industrially at a time when economic theory and, still more, economic practice have drifted far away from the ideals of Bright and Cobden ... [Its] export trade has been considerably retarded by a multitude of economic barbed-wire entanglements in the shape of quota restrictions, high tariffs, and other measures designed to check the sweep of 'Made in Japan' products ... More than sixty countries have imposed special restrictions on Japanese textiles; less than thirty have left the door open on equal terms (Chamberlin 1937: 219).

The final factor that pushed Japan toward a military strategy was a severe agricultural recession. Policies designed to generate rice surpluses in Taiwan and Korea coincided with worldwide commodity deflation. As rice prices fell, conditions in Japanese agriculture worsened, and the government rapidly shifted its colonial investments toward industry.

In any case, the 1931 invasion of Manchuria, as previous Japanese colonial moves, was followed by a large wave of public and private investments. But there was little room in this picture for non-Japanese companies; by the early 1930s the Anglo-Dutch Petroleum, Standard Oil, Siemens, Skoda had all liquidated major interests (Jones 1949). Manchuria, Korea, and to a lesser extent Taiwan, became thoroughly transformed. In the meantime, the complementarity of the Manchurian, Korean and Japanese economies came to be based on manufacturing; Nissan, for example, a manufacturer of armaments, airplanes, automobiles, and machinery, moved its headquarters to Changchun, and its president eventually went on to direct the Manchuria Industrial Development Company (MIDC) (Jones 1949). Manchuria was to become a self-sufficient industrial base, supplying basic materials, including coal, iron and steel, electricity and synthetic oil, rolling stock, and ships to itself and Japan in exchange for machinery (Beasley 1987: 216).

Toward the end of the 1930s, Japan's expansion into China became increasingly ominous and continued to accelerate. In 1937, a minor clash between Chinese and Japanese troops provided a pretext for capturing Nanking and much of the Yangtze valley. Soon afterwards, Prime Minister Konoe announced a "New Order" which called for close cooperation ("coprosperity") among China, Japan and Manchuria.

A broad southern advance also began to emerge as part of Japan's increasingly expansionist strategy. In 1939 the Showa Research Institute developed an extensive plan for an East Asian Economic Bloc (Lebra 1975: 100–3), which would be self-sufficient by relying on tin, rubber, bauxite, tungsten, nickel and chromium from Thailand, Philippines, Dutch East Indies, and Malaya (Beasley 1987: 225).

As World War II approached, the scope of Japan's sphere of influence was expanded to include Indochina in the so-called "Greater East Asian Co-prosperity Sphere" (GEACS). In the event, not much economic integration took place during the GEACS period, aside from the diversion of some raw materials to Japan, because the sea-lanes were not safe enough to permit large scale transport. Instead, the region suffered a deep economic decline as its trade with the West collapsed.

13.5.2 Legacies and Parallels

Japan's role in the prewar economy substantially increased East Asian interdependence, particularly between China, Korea, Taiwan and Japan in the 1930s. Japan's activities in these countries focused on developing transport infrastructure and information, and in the end on developing complementarities with the Japanese economy. The result, naturally enough, was a surge in Japan's regional trade, as shown in Figure 13.4. GEACS expanded Japan's influence into Southeast Asia, but the economic connections between this region and Japan were brief and overshadowed by the imperatives of war. The Japanese occupation, however, did drive European colonial governments from Southeast Asia and laid the foundations for independence after the war. Thus the economic links that emerged after the war were more Asian than before.

Japan's intense style of imperialism has left long-lived legacies. Unlike the European imperialistic powers, Japan was close to its colonies and, in Korea and Manchuria, had excellent communications with them through rail transport. Also, because it was concerned not only with the economic exploitation of the colonies

FIGURE 13.4   Partner composition of Japanese trade

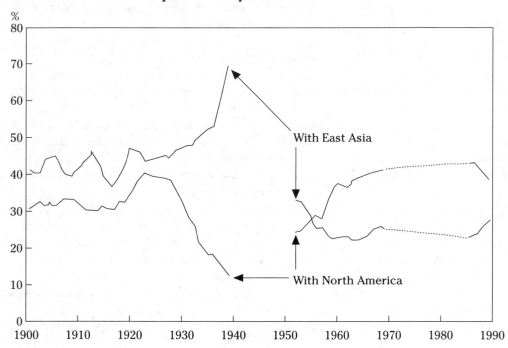

but also their role as buffers against Russian and Western forces, Japan developed dense political and military organizations to control its empire. Finally, given rice exports as a key early objective, Japan could not restrict its economic activities to an "enclave," but was forced to penetrate local economic structures (Ho 1984: 385).

By the early 1930s Japan's style of complementarity differed dramatically from that of other colonial powers; as Cumings (1984) has observed, Japanese imperialism "involved the location of industry and an infrastructure of communications and transportation *in* the colonies, bringing industry to the labor and raw materials, rather than vice-versa" (Cumings 1984: 482). Although the linkage between the Japanese occupation and the subsequent spectacular development of Manchuria, Korea and Taiwan is extremely controversial, there is no doubt that powerful industrial centers developed in each of these areas, and that these centers evolved along the same technological lines as Japan's own industries.

The notion of a large regional bloc that would also include Southeast Asia does not appear to have been a part of Japan's strategy until 1939. Prime Minister Konoe's 1938 announcement made no mention of southern areas, and the inclusion of Southeast Asia did not arise until the fall of France. By that time, GEACS was clearly designed to obtain raw materials needed for war. As Peattie has argued, "GEACS is best seen as a response to a sudden turn in international events ... rather than the consequence of long-considered or widely-held interest in the co-prosperity of Asian peoples" (1991: 42).

13.6   Interdependence from World War II to 1985

As Table 13.1 and Figure 13.4 have shown, World War II thoroughly disrupted the trade patterns established in the prewar years. Trade flows shifted toward the United States, now the leading military power in the Pacific, and the only country with its economy largely intact. Linkages between Japan and Taiwan and Korea were sharply curtailed. China's trade also collapsed as the country sank into civil war. Insurrections erupted also in Indonesia, Indochina and Malaysia. As a result, trade flows declined sharply throughout the Pacific, and especially among China, Japan, Korea and Taiwan, the "core" countries of GEACS.

Postwar U.S. policy recognized that this sharp dislocation in trade patterns would undermine the prospects for economic recovery in all of the countries that once formed the Japanese empire. The influential Institute of Pacific Relations, for example, concluded at its 1947 conference on the reconstruction of East Asia that, for the sake of Japan and the rest of the region, "Japan must be actively helped to regain something of her old position as the mainspring of the Far Eastern economy as a whole" (Institute of Pacific Relations 1949). The United States occupation authorities in turn began to use the leverage provided by their influence over aid and Japanese reparations to China, Korea and Taiwan, as well as in Southeast Asia, to revive these countries' trade with Japan.

The data show the magnitude of this challenge. As Figure 13.4 shows, Japan's two-way trade with East Asia fell from 73 percent of her trade around 1940 to only about 31 percent in 1951. At the same time, the partner composition of this East Asian trade shifted from the "core" economies of GEACS to Southeast Asia. The decline in the importance of East Asian countries in general, and of the core partners in particular, can be traced almost entirely to the general decline of their economies, rather than to a decline in their special gravitational linkages with Japan. The analysis of gravity coefficients suggests that regional biases within East Asian trade remained at essentially the same high level in 1955 as they were in 1938. While East Asian linkages remained strong, they were now driven not by Japanese policy, but by economic structures inherited from the prewar period, and by United States policies designed to restart this group of highly interdependent economies.

The subsequent story of East Asian economic growth is well known and has been recently reviewed by Kuznets (1988), Noland (1990), Wade (1990) and others. What is of interest here is that the spectacular growth of the region's economies was accompanied by a substantial decline in their regional trade bias. As shown in Table 13.3, the gravity coefficients of East Asian trade—coefficients that summarize each country's bias toward East Asian trade partners—which survived World War II at relatively high levels, fell steadily in the following years. The pattern of decline is similar for most East Asian countries, and the few anomalies that do occur (an unusually rapid decline in the case of China, and an unusual increase in the case

TABLE 13.3   Intensity of the East Asian trade linkages of different countries and regions (gravity coefficient measure)

	1938	1955	1969	1979	1985	1990
Japan	4.66	3.13	2.07	2.02	1.46	1.50
North America	0.92	1.16	1.48	1.53	1.48	1.44
Australia, New Zealand	0.53	1.35	2.70	2.85	2.24	2.11
Taiwan	6.63	7.15	4.83	2.82	1.72	2.14
Korea	6.68	4.92	4.83	2.91	1.96	2.04
Hong Kong	3.96	7.55	3.72	3.22	3.09	2.96
Malaysia, Singapore	2.31	4.22	3.34	3.11	2.05	1.88
Thailand	4.34	7.36	5.38	3.64	2.69	2.61
Philippines	0.70	2.45	4.58	3.17	2.54	2.22
Indonesia	1.76	4.60	5.52	4.89	3.34	3.10
China	4.70	6.13	2.91	2.76	3.23	3.04
Western Europe	0.26	0.49	0.33	0.34	0.31	0.36
Middle East	0.46	1.05	1.39	1.84	1.36	1.33
Rest of world	0.30	0.67	0.81	0.62	0.70	0.76
TOTAL IMPORTS	1.00	1.00	1.00	1.00	1.00	1.00
East Asia	4.48	4.45	2.97	2.64	2.05	2.09
Pacific Rim	2.61	1.95	2.05	2.08	1.77	1.80
AVERAGE	2.72	3.51	2.93	2.44	1.94	1.91

of the Philippines) can be understood in terms of major political changes in the countries involved.

Equally remarkable is a parallel decline in the *dispersion* of gravity coefficients (that is, in variations in the intensity of linkages across different trade partners) in the region. As shown in Table 13.4, the standard deviations of the gravity coefficients of most East Asian countries fell steadily during the postwar period. In effect, each country's bilateral trade pattern came to look more and more like the world's trade pattern—the importance of any particular partner to a given country came to resemble the importance of that partner in world trade as a whole. (If each partner's share of a country's trade were equal to that partner's share in world trade, then all gravity coefficients would be one.) Country-specific biases became less and less important in explaining the distribution of East Asian trade, both between East Asia and other regions, and also across different East Asian partners.

Three types of factors help to explain the diversification and homogenization of the region's trade. The first was the general integration of the global economy during most of the postwar period, which was spurred by several successful rounds of trade negotiations, steady progress toward convertibility, and considerable improvements in international communications and transport. All of these factors worked to "pull" East Asia's trade (as well as the trade of all other countries) away from its regional partners toward more global sources and destinations.

TABLE 13.4 Dispersion of gravity coefficients, by country and over time (standard deviations of gravity coefficients by country)

	1938	1955	1969	1979	1985	1990
Japan	5.55	4.25	2.50	1.75	1.26	1.22
North America	1.41	0.85	0.62	0.50	0.55	0.47
Australia, New Zealand	0.65	0.66	0.94	1.19	0.97	1.23
Taiwan	4.08	4.51	2.60	1.53	1.07	1.13
Korea	4.18	5.45	2.01	1.19	0.91	0.97
Hong Kong	6.81	10.22	2.79	2.61	3.36	4.02
Malaysia, Singapore	9.25	4.21	3.78	2.74	1.95	1.24
Thailand	9.59	4.92	3.14	2.18	1.80	1.26
Philippines	1.52	1.42	1.96	1.19	1.23	0.86
Indonesia	3.11	3.53	3.45	2.58	1.49	1.30
China	6.15	9.51	2.77	2.57	3.47	4.09
Western Europe	0.56	0.43	0.33	0.32	0.36	0.33
Middle East	1.12	0.68	0.74	0.63	0.41	0.49
Rest of world	0.41	0.38	0.58	0.48	0.37	0.37
TOTAL IMPORTS	0.00	0.00	0.00	0.00	0.00	0.00
East Asia	2.28	2.52	1.68	1.15	0.88	0.80
Pacific Rim	0.97	0.76	0.77	0.64	0.49	0.46
AVERAGE	3.39	3.19	1.80	1.37	1.21	1.19

A second important factor was the rapid development of the region's economies. The expansion of each economy's overall trade provided the scale needed to justify investments in trading linkages with an increasingly large number of countries. More frequent shipping and air schedules could now be maintained; additional investments could be made in communications; and a greater stock of information could be developed to link firms and their foreign counterparts. All these trends undoubtedly contributed to the broadening of East Asian marketing efforts. These trends presumably operated in all countries, but it is likely that their effect was especially pronounced in the context of East Asia's "miracle" economies.

A third factor driving East Asia's diversification was the similarity of East Asian development patterns. Each country rapidly shifted its output from raw materials to manufactures, and within manufactures, from labor-intensive to more capital- and technology-intensive sectors. These patterns have been described as the "flying geese pattern" of development by the Japanese economists (Akamatsu 1960) and are consistent with Heckscher-Ohlin explanations of how trade patterns are likely to change with the accumulation of human and physical capital.[13]

The similarity in development patterns is important for two reasons. First, it explains how each country acquired an increasingly sophisticated basket of exports, and thus positioned itself to compete in a wider world market. Second, it explains why East Asian countries developed competitive rather than complementary economies, and thus why they had to look to outside markets, rather than regional markets, for new trading opportunities.

An important exception to this story involves linkages based on the importation of intermediate inputs and capital goods. The commonality of East Asian development trajectories has meant that each country would typically look to neighboring countries for appropriate technology. These supply-side linkages in turn gave rise to substantial imports of machinery and components. As a result, several East Asian economies acquired asymmetrical linkages. On the one hand, they relied heavily on the region's more advanced economies—Japan, Korea, Taiwan, Singapore—for imports of machinery and components, and on the other, they looked outside the region to sell their exports.

13.7 Interdependence Today

The intensity of East Asian interdependence appears to have reached a trough in 1985–86. The turning point came at the end of a period when the real value of the U.S. dollar was unusually high; in the preceding years, several East Asian countries had sharply shifted their trade toward the United States. In addition, the high value of the dollar had permitted Japanese companies to maintain their exports despite sharply higher wages and declining competitiveness against other East Asian economies.

The large exchange rate adjustments of 1985 and 1986 affected interdependence in a complex way. Initially, the appreciation of the yen was not matched by other

East Asian currencies; thus other countries became more competitive against Japan in both United States and Japan markets. For a while, East Asian imports surged in both markets, and Korea, Taiwan, and other countries began to run substantial trade surpluses. These export surges also led to accelerating imports from Japan and Singapore. As a result, the level of East Asian interdependence intensified; intra-regional trade expanded very rapidly, and the long-run decline of the region's gravity coefficients ceased.

Many observers assumed at that time that the trade flow adjustments described above represented the beginning of a new historical trend toward the greater integration of the East Asian economy. This may still be the case, but the events of 1985–88 were in large part driven by the staggered adjustment of exchange rates in different East Asian countries. By the late 1980s the second phase of the exchange rate adjustments took hold, as most of the region's currencies appreciated to close the gap that had opened between them and the yen in the mid-1980s. These corrections slowed the surge of Japanese imports from East Asia and stopped the increase in the region's gravity coefficients. To be sure, the absolute volume of East Asian trade continued to expand at a rapid pace due to the high growth of the region's economies.

The more significant impact of the appreciation of the yen was a sharp increase in regional investment flows (see Table 13.5). Malaysia, Thailand and Indonesia had two-thirds as much investment in 1988–89 alone as in all previous years up until then. The cause of this wave is widely accepted; the exchange rate changes of the late 1980s reduced the competitiveness of Japanese firms and led firms to shift some production activities to countries with lower labor costs. While most of these investments went into the United States and other developed countries, a substantial amount also occurred in East Asia.

By the late 1980s, as the NICs also adjusted their exchange rates and began to face similar competitive strains as Japan, they too joined Japan as major investors in East Asia. Thus an entirely new channel of interdependence began to operate: cross-investments among a large number of East Asian countries. This is a natural result of the region's prosperity; it recalls patterns of integration that have evolved in Europe.

The investment wave of the late 1980s differed from earlier investments in developing country production facilities not just in magnitude and origin, but also in structure. Japan's investments in East Asia in the 1970s, for example, were primarily focused on local markets, often encouraged by policies that sought to increase local participation in industry, for example, through the importation of automobile kits instead of assembled automobiles. The recent wave of investments, by contrast, is the product of new, global strategies by regional firms. Nearly all firms have adopted such strategies, and some have gone to some length to plan a comprehensive distribution of their activities across different regional markets. Toyota, for example, has selected locations that will permit it to build a regional automobile, with components produced in different countries depending on the

TABLE 13.5   Foreign direct investment in East Asia (US$ millions)

Host/Source	Total	Japan	U.S.	Korea	Taiwan	Hong Kong	Singapore
Thailand							
Up to 1987	11,536	2,773	1,910	9	675	445	351
1988–89	7,868	4,431	570	66	530	278	408
Malaysia							
Up to 1987	4,200	1,741	202	0	34	262	594
1988–89	3,690	967	179	49	1,314	138	231
Indonesia							
Up to 1987	17,284	5,928	1,244	222	144	1,876	299
1988–89	11,159	1,304	783	728	1,126	867	489
Philippines							
Up to 1987	2,830	377	1,620				
1988–89	275	71	98				
Korea							
1984–88	3,648	1,857	876				
Taiwan							
1984–88	4,170	1,343	1,251				
Singapore							
1984–88	6,529	2,200	2,814				
SUM (Thailand, Malaysia, Indonesia only)							
Up to 1987	33,020	10,442	3,356	231	853	2,583	1,244
1988–89	22,717	6,702	1,532	843	2,970	1,283	1,128
SHARES OF SUM							
1987	1.000	0.316	0.102	0.007	0.026	0.078	0.038
1988–89	1.000	0.295	0.067	0.037	0.131	0.056	0.050

Sources: Tho (1991), Holloway (1991).

advantages of the location in terms of supplier infrastructure and local resources (Figure 13.5).

Since the recent investment wave has been driven by production strategy rather than market considerations, it has included a larger share of export-oriented industries. More so than in the past, the firms established in foreign locations have also been intended to serve home (for example, Japanese) markets. At the same time, since these investments were closely tied to Japanese technologies and suppliers that have remained at home, they have typically required a higher ratio of imported inputs than earlier investments. Because of these characteristics, the recent wave of intra-East Asian investment flows has helped to intensify regional linkages by facilitating exports into Japan and other regional markets and by spreading technologies that require regional inputs and capital goods.

The market forces which have helped to intensify regional linkages through trade and investment have also been supported by government aid policies. Japan's aid program has been always oriented toward Asia, but its growing scale has made it an important factor in recent economic linkages. Japanese aid

FIGURE 13.5   Toyota Motor's ASEAN Regional Interdependence Scheme

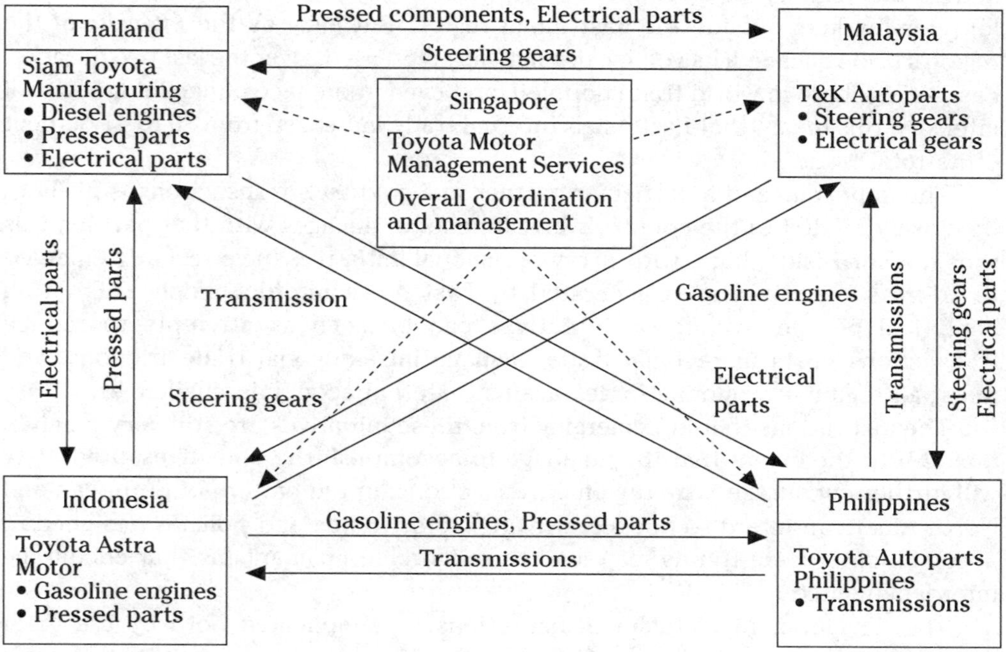

Source: *Nikkei Business*.

flows to East Asia have been substantial compared to private investment flows. These flows have helped to finance the infrastructure that supports private investment.

The volume of intra-regional investment has slackened somewhat recently, but is likely to remain relatively high compared to historical levels. Some of the reasons for the current slowdown are permanent: the investment wave of late 1980s represented, in part, a one-time adjustment in corporate sourcing policies, triggered by the appreciation of the yen and the NICs' currencies. But other reasons are temporary. As a result of the rapid inflow of capital, infrastructure bottlenecks developed in several of the receiving economies (including especially Thailand), and labor and real estate costs rose sharply due to the overheated economy. At the same time, the accumulation of Japanese firms has contributed to the development of an economic infrastructure—consisting of suppliers and service companies—that will make it easier for other firms to invest in the future.

13.8   Policy Reactions

Postwar trends in East Asian interdependence have been driven by market rather than political forces. These forces initially worked to diversify the region's trade, as the growing scale of the region's economies permitted more diversified links, and as the region's competitive development strategies forced each country to look for markets outside the East Asian region. But even as the *intensity* of the region's trade declined, its volume dramatically increased. Over the last two decades, East Asia's share in world trade doubled, and even in the face of declining regional intensity, this meant that East Asia's internal trade increased from 30 to 41 percent of its total trade.

The importance of a particular partner in a country's transactions is likely to be closely related to the country's investments in linkages with that partner. It is thus not surprising that a wide array of regional initiatives have recently emerged to address the new issues generated by East Asian interdependence. From an analytical perspective, these initiatives can be seen as attempts to reduce transactions costs in regional trade, manage intra-regional trade frictions, and marshall regional economic forces against external economic challenges.

The institutions that are emerging from these initiatives are still very much in flux. But to the extent that they manage to accomplish the objectives cited, they will further encourage intra-regional transactions. In the pattern of European and North American interdependence, private sector trends and policies designed to accommodate these trends may lead to reinforcing mechanisms that encourage interdependence.

The development of regional institutions is complicated both by the great diversity of the region's countries, and by the preference of many of the region's countries for informal, negotiated (as opposed to formal, legalistic) approaches to policy. Regional trade policies range widely from the virtual absence of trade barriers in Hong Kong and Singapore, to the relatively liberal regimes of Malaysia and Thailand, the intermediate and more opaque regimes of Korea, Indonesia, and the Philippines, and the still extensive protection in China. The picture is further complicated by the fact that some highly outward countries—for example, Korea and Thailand—still use protection to promote infant industries and exports. And even countries that have little formal protection, such as Japan, have policy and business structures that are difficult to penetrate.

Regional cooperation is also tempered by the "style" of East Asian policy making. At the risk of excessive generalization, many East Asian countries pursue informal and relatively opaque approaches to policy. Relationships among businesses, and between business and government are often characterized by long-term collaboration, reciprocal favors and continuous negotiations, rather than market-mediated transactions and explicit contracts. Most East Asian governments, even in countries with modest trade barriers, actively participate in the management of the economy, and administer complex arrays of incentives and barriers (Arndt 1987). Bureaucrats and influential industrialists have high stakes in maintaining this system of intervention and thus prefer to respond to new policy challenges with administrative instruments such as Voluntary Export Restraints (VERs), Voluntary Export Increases (VEIs) and regulatory interventions.

In this context cooperation on a modest, practical level has proved more possible than the development of large-scale agreements and institutions. Small, local free trade areas (especially Shenzhen and the Singapore Growth Triangle) are especially well suited to this policy setting and appear to be developing very fast. In what follows, each of the region's cooperative structures is reviewed in the context of its history and likely evolution, moving from the least to the most comprehensive.

13.8.1 Mini Trading Areas (MTA)

Though not unique to East Asia, international trading schemes involving small geographical areas of two or more countries have multiplied. These areas feature special provisions to exempt international trade from national tariffs until the products leave the MFTA, as well as transportation and other infrastructure to support international trade and investment. The oldest and perhaps most successful such area is the Shenzhen Free Trade Zone, which forms a bridge between Guangdong Province and Hong Kong. A new initiative along these lines is the "Growth Triangle" formed by Singapore, the state of Johor in Malaysia, and the island of Batam in Indonesia. Similar zones have been proposed to link: (a) China, the Koreas, eastern Siberia and western Japan (North-East Asia Economic Cooperation); (b) Japan, China up to Liaoning, and Korea (Yellow Sea Cooperation); (c) Hong Kong, Taiwan and China south of Shanghai (Southern China Economic Cooperation); (d) Hong Kong, Guangdong, Guangxi and northern Thailand, Laos and Vietnam (Tongking–Mekong Economic Cooperation); (e) Thailand, Cambodia and Southern Vietnam (Southern Indochina Economic Cooperation); (f) Myanmar, Thailand and Indochina (Souvannaphoum); and (g) Thailand, northern Sumatra, and northern Malaysia (ITM Nexus).[14]

Not all of these MTAs will get off the ground, but the proliferation of the idea is interesting. MTAs fit the region's pragmatic approach to policy, and especially its reluctance to adopt more complex agreements than warranted by immediate economic needs. Such pragmatism is likely to be especially helpful in cooperations with the formerly socialist economies, which may not have the institutions to offer credible large-scale agreements for some time to come. So MTAs offer a potentially important model for linking China, Russia, Indochina and North Korea with East Asia's market economies.

13.8.2 Association of Southeast Asian Nations (ASEAN)

This association, comprising Brunei, Indonesia, Malaysia, Philippines, Thailand and Singapore was initially focused on political and security issues. Due to competing industrial objectives, the organization made little progress toward integrating the region's economies until recently. A Preferential Trade Area Agreement was signed in 1977, but the proportion of trade covered by this agreement has remained small.

However, as the association's economies came to pursue more liberal economic strategies, the possibilities for regional cooperation improved.

In February 1992 ASEAN adopted an ambitious program to establish a free trade area in 15 years. Some tariffs have already been lowered with this objective in mind. But ASEAN's internal trade is modest, and the great similarity of ASEAN's economies (Brunei and Singapore aside) raises the possibility of substantial trade diversion within an ASEAN free trade area, particularly if external tariffs remain high. Against this, the opportunity to serve a larger regional market may improve prospects for attracting large-scale foreign investment. Overall, ASEAN's political divisions and the doubtful economic merits of the FTA will tend to limit the influence of ASEAN in the region's institutional framework.

13.8.3 East Asia Economic Caucus (EAEC)

In late 1990, with the Uruguay Round negotiations heading for stalemate, President Mahathir of Malaysia called for the formation of an East Asia Economic Group (EAEG), consisting of Japan, the East Asian NICs, China and the remaining ASEAN countries. Perhaps the plan emerged in President Mahathir's mind as a natural extension of his "Look East" program, which aimed to shift Malaysia's economic perspectives closer to the development models of Japan and Korea. Although the objectives of EAEG were not spelled out, it appeared to create an alliance of East Asian states to counter emerging blocs in Europe and the Western Hemisphere. The plan was strongly opposed by Australia, New Zealand and the United States, because it was viewed as undermining APEC, the emerging OECD-like institution that includes countries from both sides of the Pacific (see below). Japan also publicly opposed the plan, but some Japanese government officials and senior business executives were more positive in private statements.

The opposition of the United States and the lack of a clear agenda for the EAEG eventually led President Mahathir to recast the idea as an East Asia Economic Caucus (EAEC). The concept now calls for periodic consultations among East Asian states—a mission no clearer than that of the EAEG. Three interpretations are possible. First, the EAEC may be a face-saving device for abandoning the EAEG idea. Second, the EAEC may be represent a threat against exclusionist U.S. and European policies. Third, the EAEC could be a step toward accelerating the integration of East Asian economies by promoting the coordination of their policies. Given the conflicting styles of East Asian and Anglo-Saxon policy making, the EAEC may be better suited for this purpose than a broader group such as the APEC, which also includes Anglo-Saxon countries.

13.8.4 Asia-Pacific Economic Cooperation (APEC)

The idea of forming a Pacific region wide organization has been pursued for several decades through informal, quasi-private organizations such as the Pacific Basin

Economic Council (PBEC), Pacific Economic Cooperation Council (PECC), and Pacific Association for Trade and Development (PAFTAD). Since 1989, however, the Foreign Ministers of 12 Pacific Rim countries—Australia, Brunei, Canada, Indonesia, Japan, Korea, Malaysia, New Zealand, the Philippines, Singapore, Thailand, the United States—agreed to meet annually to review issues of mutual interest. APEC's initial work program consisted of a series of tasks, managed by member countries, on cooperation in areas such as the collection of trade and investment data, and the analysis of policies in sectors such as energy, tourism, transportation, and fisheries. At its 1991 meeting APEC also established a modest secretariat.

APEC's mission is still evolving. The organization has been most comfortable with tasks involving technical cooperation and information exchange. Its stiffest challenge has been the "China problem"—resolved by admitting China, Taiwan, and Hong Kong to APEC membership. Beyond this, APEC meetings have dealt with noncontroversial issues such as support for international trade liberalization through the Uruguay Round. It remains to be seen whether APEC can assume functions beyond the technical; for example, whether it can facilitate movement toward regional liberalization, the harmonization of regulations, or the resolution of trade frictions. APEC's membership is very diverse, and few members seem willing to trust this new institution with significant responsibilities.

13.9   Conclusions

This paper has explored the hypothesis that blocs are, in part, the product of historical accidents. Reinforcing mechanisms of integration can be set into motion by military force, or other developments that make countries important to each other. In East Asia, important initial investments in regional linkages were triggered by imperial conquest—first by the Western powers under the Treaty Port System, and then by Japan during its imperialist period. By the advent of World War II, these investments had transformed East Asia into perhaps the most interdependent region in the world.

After World War II, the intensity of East Asian interdependence resumed its prewar level. Subsequently, however, the region diversified its trade patterns, due to the important role of the United States in postwar Pacific relations, and to the growing sophistication of the region's industries. The trend toward diversification has been reversed in the last five or so years. Since 1985, spurred in part by investment and aid, trade flows within East Asia have grown sharply, and have become more regionally biased.

An interesting question is how the recent flurry of regional policy initiatives will affect these trends. It is likely that the institutions created by these initiatives will not be strong enough to liberalize regional trade. Even if growing intraregional linkages create a demand for cooperation, the diversity of the region's policy approaches makes broad, formal agreements difficult and unlikely. So far, collaboration has focused on narrow, highly pragmatic objectives—trade cooperation in the context of mini FTAs and ASEAN, and technical cooperation in the context of APEC.

For the time being, then, much of the region's business will be conducted through bilateral rather than multilateral institutions. Japan is raising its profile in regional diplomacy as well as economic cooperation and consultation. An intense series of Asian visits are scheduled for the Emperor and the Prime Minister. Japanese ministries are also developing country-specific development plans, and are encouraging their implementation with aid, expert advice, infrastructure lending, and support for private investment.

The East Asian trading bloc has a long and complex history. Investments in this bloc, some made more than a century ago, have proved surprisingly durable. Today's developments, likewise, may shape the pattern of East Asian trade far into the future. If there are externalities associated with investments in bilateral trade, as the anecdotal evidence here suggests, then the factors and policies that affect bilateral trade deserve more attention than they usually receive.

Notes

1. The regions referred to in this chapter will be North America (Canada and the United States), East Asia (China, Hong Kong, Indonesia, Japan, Korea, Malaysia, Philippines, Taiwan, Thailand, Singapore), and Pacific Rim (North America, East Asia, Australia and New Zealand).
2. The importance of the United States in the Pacific trade network is examined in some detail in Petri (1992). That study concludes that these trans-Pacific connections make it unlikely that any exclusionist East Asian bloc could develop in the near future.
3. Some of the early studies based on gravity coefficients include Linneman (1966) and Leontief and Strout (1963).
4. For example, the bilateral pattern of trade is indeterminate in a Heckscher-Ohlin model with more products than factors, assuming zero transport costs.
5. For example, Linneman (1966) provides clear evidence of distance effects.
6. Linneman (1966) concludes a survey of transport cost data by saying that "one cannot help feeling that these magnitudes [of transport costs] (for instance in comparison to prevailing profit margins) are in a sense too small to justify the emphasis on transportation costs as the major natural obstacle to international trade."
7. Already in an early empirical study of trade patterns Beckerman (1956) concluded that "while transport costs paid (directly or indirectly) by an Italian entrepreneur on a raw material supplied by Turkey may be no greater (as the material may come by sea) than the same material supplied by Switzerland, he is more likely to have contacts with Swiss suppliers, since Switzerland will be 'nearer' to him in a psychic evaluation (fewer language difficulties and so on) as well as in the economic sense that air travel will absorb less of his time."
8. Petri (1992) argues that strong asymmetries in East Asian trade, including especially the fact that many East Asian countries run large trade deficits with Japan and large trade surpluses with the United States, explain why purely East Asian trading agreements are unlikely.
9. Baldwin (1990), for example, presents a model in which firms establish a "beachhead" (say, an export distribution system) in a foreign market after the appreciation of that

country's currency, and then continue to sell in the market even after the currency depreciates. The argument here subsumes such investments, but especially focuses on investments that affect transactions costs in the bilateral trading relationship.

10. According to some historians, the land surveys made it easier for Japanese investors to acquire land from Korean and Taiwanese owners.

11. Colonial farmers did not benefit, however; despite substantial growth in output, per capital rice consumption was essentially flat in both Korea and Taiwan in the 1920s, and then declined substantially in the 1930s (Ho 1984: 379).

12. In light of the considerable current emphasis on full self-sufficiency in rice, it is interesting to note that Japan depended extensively on rice imports during much of the prewar period, generally importing 20 percent of its requirements.

13. A case can be made that East Asian development trajectories are *more* similar than would be justified by Heckscher-Ohlin considerations because they "follow" a common East Asian development model, as pioneered by Japan. This case is most easily made for Korea, which systematically researched and adopted Japanese policies during its high-growth period. Petri (1988) has shown that the composition of Korean industry resembles the composition of Japanese industry more closely than would be expected on the basis of resource similarities alone. These similarities are in part due to the similarity of external opportunities; for example, the dynamics of foreign protection systematically "capped" import surges from Japan and thus created systematic incentives for Korean producers to move into the same industries in which Japan excelled.

14. Some items on this list are drawn from Noordin Sopiee (1991).

References

Akamatsu, K., 1960, "A Theory of Unbalanced Growth in the World Economy," *Weltwirtschaftliches Archiv*, 86(2).

Arndt, H. W., 1987, "Industrial Policy in East Asia," *Industry and Development*, 22: 1–65.

Baldwin, Richard, 1990, "Some Empirical Evidence on Hysteresis in Aggregate U.S. Import Prices," in Peter A. Petri and Stefan Gerlach (eds.), *The Economics of the Dollar Cycle*, MIT Press, Cambridge, MA, pp. 235–73.

Barnhart, Michael A., 1987, *Japan Prepares for Total War: The Search for Economic Security, 1919–1941*, Cornell University Press, Ithaca, NY.

Beasley, W. G., 1987, *Japanese Imperialism: 1894–1945*, Clarendon Press, Oxford.

Beckerman, W., 1956, "Distance and the Pattern of Intra-European Trade," *Review of Economics and Statistics*, 28: 38.

Chamberlin, William Henry, 1937, *Japan over Asia*, Little Brown, Boston, MA.

Cumings, Bruce, 1984, "The Legacy of Japanese Colonialism in Korea," in Myers and Peattie, pp. 478–96.

Duus, Peter, 1984, "Economic Dimensions of Meiji Imperialism: The Case of Korea, 1895–1910," in Myers and Peattie.

Ho, Samuel P., 1984, "Colonialism and Development: Korea, Taiwan and Kwantung," in Myers and Peattie, pp. 347–98.

Holloway, Nigel, 1991, *Japan in Asia*, Review Publishing, Hong Kong.

Institute of Pacific Relations, 1949, *Problems of Economic Reconstruction in the Far East*, New York.

Jones, F. C., 1949, *Manchuria since 1931*, Oxford University Press, New York.

Kuznets, Paul, 1988, "An East Asian Model of Economic Development: Japan, Taiwan, and South Korea," *Economic Development and Cultural Change*, 36(3): S11–43.

Lawrence, Robert Z., 1991, "How Open is Japan?" in Paul Krugman (ed.), *Trade with Japan: Has the Door Opened Wider?* University of Chicago Press, Chicago, pp. 9–50.

Lebra, Joyce C., 1975, *Japan's Greater East Asia Co-prosperity Sphere in World War II: Selected Readings and Documents*, Oxford University Press, Kuala Lumpur.

Leontief, Wassily, 1973, "Explanatory Power of the Comparative Cost Theory of International Trade and Its Limits," in H. C. Bos (ed.), *Economic Structure and Development: Lectures in Honor of Jan Tinbergen*, North Holland, Amsterdam, pp. 153–60.

Linneman, Hans, 1966, *An Econometric Study of International Trade Flows*, North Holland, Amsterdam.

Montgomery, Michael, 1988, *Imperialist Japan: The Yen to Dominate,* St. Martin's Press, New York.

Myers, Ramon H. and Mark R. Peattie (eds.), 1984, *The Japanese Colonial Empire, 1895–1945*, Princeton University Press, Princeton, NJ.

Noland, Marcus, 1990, *Pacific Basin Developing Countries: Prospects for the Future*, Institute for International Economics, Washington, DC.

Peattie, Mark R., 1984, "The Nan'yo: Japan in the South Pacific, 1885–1945," in Myers and Peattie.

———, 1991, "Nanshin: The "Southward Advance", 1931–1941, as a Prelude to the Japanese Occupation of Southeast Asia," paper presented at the Conference on the Japanese Wartime Empire in Asia, 1937–1945, Hoover Institution, Stanford University, August 23–24.

Petri, Peter A., 1988, "Korea's Export Niche: Origins and Prospects," *World Development*, 16(1): 47–63.

———, 1992, "One Bloc, Two Blocs or None? Political–Economic Factors in Pacific Trade Policy," in Kaoru Okuizumi, Kent E. Calder, and Gerrit W. Gong (eds.), *The U.S.–Japan Economic Relationship in East and Southeast Asia: A Policy Framework for Asia-Pacific Economic Cooperation*, Significant Issues Series, Vol. 14, No. 1, Center for Strategic and International Studies, pp. 39–70.

Soopie, Noordin, 1991, "Introductory Remarks," paper presented at the Fifth Trade Policy Forum, Pacific Economic Cooperation Conference, Kuala Lumpur, August 18–21.

Tho, Tran Van, 1991, "Technology Transfer in the Asian Pacific Region: Some Observations on Recent Trends," paper presented at the NBER Second Annual East Asian Seminar on Economics, Taipei, Taiwan, June 19–21.

Wade, Robert, 1990, *Governing the Market: Economic Theory and the Role of Government in East Asian Industrialization*, Princeton University Press, Princeton, NJ.

Whelpley, James D., 1913, *The Trade of the World*, Century Co., New York.

Yamazawa, Ippei and Yuzo Yamamura, 1979, "Trade and Balance of Payments," in Kazushi Ohkawa and Miyohei Shinohara (eds.), *Patterns of Japanese Economic Development: A Quantitative Appraisal*, pp. 134–58.

Chapter 14

Etsuro Ishigami

JAPANESE–ASEAN BUSINESS LINKAGES: AN EVALUATION

14.1 Background of ASEAN Industrialization

As set forth in the preceding chapters, the Asia-Pacific economies, particularly those of East Asia, form a single high-growth region in the world economy as well as in the developing world. Although the developing countries in the 1970s (or "go-go seventies") also experienced an upward growth trend as did the NICs (newly industrializing countries, hereafter NIEs), it was a short-lived experience.

By now we have more than a nodding acquaintance with the following scenario: A remarkable and continuous economic growth in East Asia is led by the vital increase of manufactures exports in the NIEs, whose policy framework is more open and less restrictive toward foreign capital and technology. The ASEAN countries and China are now following this policy orientation since the late 1980s.[1] On the other hand, Latin America, including Latin American NICs like Brazil and Mexico, was forced to face a severe economic downturn caused mainly by the shrinkage of capital inflow, fixed capital investment and import of capital goods after "the debt crisis in 1982." The 1980s was literally "a lost decade" for these countries and many heavily indebted countries of Africa as well, which recorded negative annual growth rates during the 1980s.[2]

Indeed, the massive export of manufactured goods by the NIEs and the ASEAN countries has been the result of the inflow of foreign direct investment (FDI) and foreign technologies (including capital goods). Therefore one needs to take into account the role of investment, technology and manufacturing by foreign firms (led by Japan and the NIEs), although the growth pattern of East Asia is often defined as:

> Increase of export → Increase of income → Increase of fixed capital investment → Increase of output → Increase of export

However, that foreign firms played a big role in the increase of manufactures exports during the 1980s is not quite a new phenomenon in the world economy. A report by the Organization for Economic Cooperation and Development (OECD 1979) points to foreign firms as one of the main factors underpinning the NICs growth phenomenon:

> New approaches to the organization of production and marketing have also contributed to the expansion of trade in manufactures and to the shift in the commodity composition of manufactured exports of the NICs. Transnational enterprises (and the expansion of intra-firm trade) have been an important feature in the decentralisation and fragmentation of production processes and the development of new forms of the international division of labour. Through sub-contracting for off-shore processing and assembly, they have moved capital, technology, managerial and marketing skills to suitable locations, making use of "potential" comparative advantage deriving from low-cost labour, proximity to major markets and political stability in the host countries (para. 16).

This new evolution of the international division of labor[3] led by multinational enterprises stems from these enterprises overwhelming technological advantage and competitive edge over firms in the developing countries, as well as from a tremendous gap in resource bases. It may be useful to refer to the OECD Report (1979) again, which reflects the advanced countries' self-confidence and discusses the advantage these countries have over the "challenge" of the NICs:

> because the advanced countries are at the frontier of changing tastes and technological progress, their competitive advantage will generally lie in new products, processes and technologies. Also, an important part will consist of services and know-how, only partly embodied in traded goods. Almost by definition, therefore, a large part of the comparative advantage of the advanced industrialised countries lies in products and processes which are hard to describe because they are either rather intangible or do not yet exist (para. 39).

For developing countries, and even for the NIEs, it is very hard to catch up with the state-of-the art technology of advanced countries in the present world order of technology, where technological innovation is concentrated in and owned by the advanced countries.[4] In this context one can see why some international institutes such as the International Labor Organization/United Nations Centre on Transnational Corporations (ILO/UNCTC 1988) and United Nations Industrial Development Organization (UNIDO 1989) advocate a more pragmatic development strategy in tune with the policy orientation of the World Bank and International Monetary Fund. The World Bank has put forward the "Export Processing Countries" concept, while the International Monetary Fund has proposed a "Complementation of Parts" scheme for South-South economic cooperation that will accelerate industrialization.

The underlying logic of East Asian and ASEAN industrialization can be understood in part against the background of the new evolution of the international division of labor that has been led by multinational enterprises. However, one also needs to take into account the specific conditions of each country in terms of its resource endowments, "developmental state" (White 1988), geo-political background and so on. Moreover, the rapid growth of the ASEAN countries since the late 1980s has specific features of its own as well. Put simply, it is the economic link these countries have with Japan, the NIEs (and the U.S.). The outstanding performance of the ASEAN countries in terms of export growth and industrialization can be partly ascribed to the business strategy of Japanese firms (and NIE firms at a later date). The recent rapid upturn of Japan's foreign direct investment (FDI), particularly in the ASEAN countries, has been accelerated by the appreciation of the yen since 1985. Through its massive investment, Japanese firms have developed an "intra-region international division of labor" (Japan–NIEs–ASEAN). We may characterize the main feature of ASEAN industrialization as an "international export processing platform."

14.2 ASEAN's Open Door Policy and Japan's FDI in the Region[5]

The policy change the ASEAN countries underwent in the late 1980s was a necessary precondition for the massive inflow of FDI and foreign technology. Since 1986 most ASEAN countries have extended "open door policies" to foreign export-oriented firms in line with their export-led growth strategy. Indeed, the basic principle followed is one of "the more the exports, the more incentives given." In contrast, in the past restrictions were imposed on foreign capital inflows as well as on export promotion activities. The following factors contributed towards the shift from restrictive to open development policies:

1. The growth rate of most ASEAN countries dropped drastically after the "collapse of commodity prices" in 1985 and 1986. This led to a decline in government revenues, foreign exchange reserves and debt servicing as well as in the overall performance of each economy. Export promotion by foreign businesses was then seen as a cure that would lead to quick recovery.
2. The prices of goods (basic and intermediate) produced by ASEAN "big project" firms were much higher than the international market prices. Apart from other factors, this possibly explains why domestic export firms which used these goods as inputs were not able to maintain their cost competitivenes. Supporting such loss-making enterprises was therefore a huge burden on the public purse. Consequently, some governments were forced to abandon their previous policy of "import substitution-oriented" big projects. Another expression of this is the failure of ASEAN's "joint industrialization project," which aimed for collective import substitution.
3. The foreign firms in the export promotion zones (EPZs) had achieved good results in terms of export performance in manufactured goods. This encouraged Thailand to introduce EPZs in 1987. On the other hand, from the viewpoint of Japanese

businesses, the ASEAN countries were initially very attractive because they offered cheaper and good quality labor, had fewer industrial relations conflicts (sometimes as a result of restrictions imposed by authoritarian regimes) and had better infrastructure (some of which was constructed using Japanese official development aid). The policy shift together with these factors enticed many Japanese firms to invest in the ASEAN countries. Most of these firms were seeking an export base to replace previously established ones in the NIEs.

In the course of Japan's FDI boom the ASEAN countries, particularly Thailand and Malaysia have become major destinations for Japanese FDI in Asia. In 1988 Japan's FDI in manufacturing in ASEAN (US$1360 million) surpassed that in the NIEs (US$776 million). Incidentally, the NIEs have also become suppliers of FDI to the ASEAN countries, with Taiwan leading the way (see Table 14.1).

During 1951–90, the share of manufacturing industry in total Japanese FDI in Asia was 39.3 percent—a much higher figure than its world average (26.3 percent). The main industries involved are the electronics industry (with a share of 22.4 percent), the iron and nonferrous metals industry (15.0 percent), the chemicals industry (14.2 percent), the textiles industry (10.0 percent), the transport equipment industry (9.1 percent) and the machinery industry (8.8 percent). However, for the last four years (1987–90), the share of the electronics industry has risen. It reached 29.8 percent in 1990, which is almost the same as the world average for Japan (29.3 percent) (Ministry of Finance 1992).

Small- and medium-sized businesses as well as large manufacturing firms have played a major role in this FDI boom. The proportion of Japanese FDI in manufacturing is relatively high (more than 40 percent). More than two-thirds of it goes to Asia (for example, in 1988, 31.2 percent went to the NIEs, 26.0 percent to ASEAN and 8.1 percent to China). The number of small- and medium-sized businesses investing in manufacturing in the region in 1986, 1987 and 1988 was 279, 469 and 724 respectively.

If we limit our coverage to firms which are presently engaged in overseas production, the share of small- and medium-sized businesses is 25.6 percent—a higher figure than that of the large firms (15.6 percent). The main stream of investment comes from local and independent small- and medium-sized businesses. The share for subcontracting small- and medium-sized firms in 1988 was 18.8 percent. This figure has been increasing. The main impetus behind this increase was the appreciation of the yen: small- and medium-sized businesses losing their competitiveness in the domestic and/or foreign market rushed into ASEAN to take advantage of cheaper labor. "The White Paper on small and medium enterprises for 1989" points out that "some small- and medium-sized businesses, with dozens of employees, have built up a sort of 'global network,' in which firms not only simply go abroad, but also develop new products, and sources for parts and components, establish assembly and processing units as well as sales networks in the context of optimal location and multinational business" (Small and Medium Enterprise Agency 1989).

TABLE 14.1   Foreign direct investment (FDI) in the ASEAN countries (in millions and percentage composition by country and area)

Investor country	Year	Host country							
		Malaysia		Thailand		Indonesia		Philippines	
		Ringgit	%	Baht	%	U.S. Dollar	%	Peso	%
Taiwan	1986	5.0	1.0	940	6.2	17	2.1	7	0.4
	1987	118.5	15.8	7,696	15.3	8	0.6	186	5.4
	1988	384.3	19.1	21,498	13.6	913	20.7	2,317	23.2
	1989	1,013.0	29.8	22,305	10.9	158	3.4	3,233	18.5
	1990	2,353.4	37.8	19,567	5.4	618	7.1	3,419	14.6
Hong Kong	1986	27.5	5.2	1,178	7.7	−60	−7.5	149	9.3
	1987	27.8	3.7	3,216	6.4	122	9.8	570	16.6
	1988	129.5	6.4	12,008	7.6	259	5.9	567	5.7
	1989	112.5	3.3	14,430	7.0	407	8.6	2,887	16.5
	1990	136.1	2.2	183,412	50.7	993	11.3	5,064	21.7
Singapore	1986	90.0	17.2	250	1.6	105	13.1	5	0.3
	1987	135.4	18.1	1,645	3.3	13	1.0	18	0.5
	1988	172.1	8.6	6,971	4.4	151	3.4	53	0.5
	1989	269.5	7.9	10,570	5.1	166	3.5	514	2.9
	1990	321.3	5.2	15,115	4.2	264	3.0	333	1.4
South Korea	1986	1.6	0.3	23	0.2	22	2.8	1	0.0
	1987	2.0	0.8	333	0.7	16	1.3	15	0.4
	1988	23.3	1.2	2,758	1.7	207	4.7	32	0.3
	1989	78.9	2.3	4,387	2.1	466	9.9	380	2.2
	1990	164.2	2.6	6,889	1.9	723	8.3	515	2.2
Asian NIEs total	1986	124.1	23.7	2,391	15.7	84	10.5	162	10.2
	1987	283.7	37.8	12,890	25.8	158	12.7	789	23.0
	1988	709.2	35.3	43,235	27.4	1,530	34.7	2,963	29.7
	1989	1,473.9	43.3	51,582	25.1	1,197	25.4	7,014	40.1
	1990	2,975.0	47.8	224,983	62.2	2,598	29.7	9,331	39.9
Japan	1986	58.1	11.1	6,593	43.3	325	40.6	454	28.5
	1987	230.8	30.8	24,829	49.5	512	41.3	591	17.2
	1988	561.1	27.9	77,469	49.0	256	5.8	2,015	20.2
	1989	1,065.3	31.3	90,569	44.1	769	16.3	3,428	19.6
	1990	1,777.7	28.5	69,231	19.2	2,241	25.6	7,437	31.8
U.S.	1986	17.1	3.3	1,067	7.0	128	16.0	458	28.7
	1987	61.3	8.2	4,430	8.8	−62	−5.0	740	21.6
	1988	252.6	12.6	17,028	10.8	731	16.6	3,229	32.3
	1989	126.8	3.8	14,123	6.9	348	7.4	2,852	16.3
	1990	187.1	3.0	27,913	7.7	153	1.7	1,445	6.2
World	1986	524.5	100	15,230	100	800	100	1,594	100
	1987	750.0	100	50,138	100	1,240	100	3,427	100
	1988	2,010.5	100	158,066	100	4,409	100	9,983	100
	1989	3,401.1	100	205,496	100	4,719	100	17,480	100
	1990	6,227.9	100	361,470	100	8,750	100	23,369	100

Source: Compiled from statistics of each country. Reproduced from Aoki (1992: 65).

With regard to the "global network," which is an exaggerated term, we should distinguish between transnational corporations and small- and medium-sized businesses. Many Japanese manufacturing companies, led by the electronics companies, have rushed into the ASEAN countries only to face severe shortages of local vendors (supporting industries). Consequently, many *keiretsu* (group) companies (mostly small- and medium-sized businesses) are investing in the ASEAN countries, along with their parent firms. The shortage of local vendors has also provided opportunities for non-*keiretsu* small- and medium-sized businesses— these businesses can now form new trading relationships with the large companies beyond the wall of *keiretsu*, which makes Japanese small- and medium-sized businesses very competitive in the host countries. In addition, Thailand's rapid indigenization policy (which calls for an increase in local content) in the automobile industry has resulted in further investment by Japanese vendors.

Japanese businesses are also investing in Asia in order to take advantage of cheaper wages and to set up a new export-platform. Thus, many Japanese firms have shifted their investments from the NIEs to the ASEAN countries, and then to China.

The amount of FDI in the ASEAN countries (led by Japan) is large enough to make FDI the main contributor to domestic fixed capital formation in some of the ASEAN countries, particularly in Thailand and Malaysia (see Table 14.2). Both countries can be described as "international export-processing platform" countries.

14.2.1 Thailand

One of the most striking features of the "investment-rush" Thailand experienced in the period 1987–90 is the dominance of foreign investors, particularly those from

TABLE 14.2 Percentage share of FDI in the nominal gross fixed capital formation in the Asian NIEs and ASEAN countries

	1985	1986	1987	1988	1989	1990
South Korea	2.0	1.2	2.8	2.5	1.6	0.9
Taiwan	6.0	5.6	7.3	4.7	7.5	6.7
Hong Kong*	28.2	29.7	23.7	23.4	23.2	21.3
Singapore*	5.4	8.3	9.5	9.6	7.9	9.3
Asian NIEs total	**6.9**	**7.2**	**7.7**	**6.7**	**6.4**	**5.4**
Thailand	9.8	10.5	16.9	38.8	37.7	51.1
Malaysia*	4.1	8.9	11.3	22.3	28.6	46.6
Indonesia	4.3	4.3	7.7	20.3	18.3	n.a.
Philippines	2.7	2.0	3.4	7.5	10.5	11.2
ASEAN total	**5.2**	**6.3**	**10.3**	**24.9**	**25.4**	**n.a.**

*Figures for Hong Kong, Singapore, and Malaysia are for manufacturing only.

Source: Compiled from the statistics of each country and Asian Development Bank. Reproduced from JETRO (1992a: 47).

Japan and the NIEs. If one takes the two years of 1987 and 1988, foreign firms accounted for about 60 percent of the number of investments and 75 percent of the investment value amount of the Board of Investment (BOI) base. Japanese firms alone accounted for about half of the value amount of the BOI base. In 1988, Thailand was the second largest destination of Japanese FDI, coming after the U.S. Suehiro (1989) points out the following characteristics of the recent investment boom:

1. Due to the BOI's investment approval requirement that 80 percent of total sales (or production) be destined for exports, most investment changed from a domestic market/import substitution orientation to a foreign market/export orientation.
2. Diversification from textiles and electronics to a wide range of products. From 1986 to the first half of 1988, the total number of investment items reached 241. Japan accounted for 180 items, followed by Taiwan with 80 and the U.S. with 29. (The sum of these figures exceeds the actual total number of investment items due to the presence of overlapping investment item categories among these countries.) Taiwanese and Japanese investment largely focus on different production activities, with Taiwan's concentrating mainly on light-miscellaneous industry such as sports-shoes, plastic Christmas trees and lamps, rubber gloves, synthetic/leather bags, furniture, toys, chopsticks and toothpicks.
3. An increase in the number of investments involving large sums (application base). For example, Toshiba contributed new investments amounting to ¥50 billion (about £200 million) and Minebea contributed investments amounting to ¥37 billion. The Japanese firms approved by the BOI added 84,000 jobs to the Thai economy between 1987 and May 1988. In 1988, 72,000 persons were employed by the 203 Japanese firms in Thailand.
4. Increase in the number of small- and medium-sized businesses from Japan and Taiwan. These businesses can be classified into two types of business according to their motivation for investing in Thailand. One is the export firm which seeks to escape from high labor costs and an uncompetitively highly-valued currency at home. The other is the firm ordered to do business in Thailand by its parent company; most of them are subcontracting and group firms from Japan.
5. Thailand's extension of the privilege of majority equity holding (more than an 80 percent holding), or even 100 percent holding to Japanese and Taiwanese firms, particularly to new firms.
6. Decentralization of location from Bangkok to local areas.

Japanese FDI in Thailand reached its peak in 1989, while NIE FDI peaked in 1990. The 1989 peak was mainly due to the economic downturn in Japan and the saturation in infrastructure facilities in Thailand, while the sudden jump in Hong Kong's FDI (approval base) in 1990 was due to Hong Kong's role in a huge railway development project in Thailand (worth 156 billion baht). In the early 1990s, the NIEs came to invest large sums per unit in industries such as artificial fiber, resins and printers (Tsunekawa 1992).

14.2.2 Malaysia

In Malaysia, the FDI boom is continuing. There was a remarkable surge in FDI levels in 1988–89. Japan is the leading source of FDI, followed by Taiwan, Singapore and the U.S. However, the level of FDI from the NIEs, particularly from Taiwan, has been increasing rapidly. Indeed, in 1990 the NIEs and Taiwan became the largest investor group and investor country, respectively. FDI goes mainly into the electronics and resource processing industries such as rubber, food, chemical, basic metals and timber. During the period 1987–90, 40 percent to 60 percent of the total investment from the top six investors went into the electronics industry, followed by chemicals (mainly plastics). These two industries together accounted for 70 percent of the total investment. In recent years, Japan's investment has flowed into the machinery industry and its supporting industries.

Investments from the NIEs are, in part, diversifying from light industry (for example, clothing and footwear) to assembly-type machine and capital-intensive industries. Although Taiwanese firms entering Malaysia are mostly small- and medium-sized businesses of the OEM (Original Equipment Manufacturing) supplier-type, some of these firms are set up as cooperation firms with Japanese firms trading with them in Taiwan.

As in Thailand, most foreign firms are export-oriented with an export share of 80 percent or more. Japanese and American firms prefer majority equity or 100 percent ownership/holdings, while those from Taiwan and Singapore tend to go for joint ventures either with Malaysian firms or third country firms.

Despite the similarities, there are some differences between Japanese and American FDI firms operating in Malaysia. Those from the U.S. are concentrated in the semiconductor and integrated circuit (IC) sectors, and produce mainly for export to U.S. industries. Those from Japan are also concentrated in the semi-conductor sector and serve as an offshore base for firms in Japan (and in this region). However, Japanese firms are also concentrated in the consumer electronics sector, producing such items as audio sets, color TV sets and air conditioners. It is interesting to note that Singaporean FDI in the electronics sector was not carried out by local Singaporean firms but by the Singapore subsidiaries of transnational corporations (Torii 1989).

14.3   Change of Trade Structure of the ASEAN Countries and Japan's Role

With the establishment of a large number of export-oriented firms in the ASEAN countries since 1986, the ratio of manufactures to total exports has increased very rapidly, particularly that of "machinery" (SITC 7) exports. Manufactured exports classified as "other manufactured goods" (SITC 8) are also growing. The ratio of manufactures in Malaysia's total exports jumped from 18.6 percent in 1985 to 32.4 percent in 1989. That of Thailand jumped from 8.8 percent to 17.8 percent between 1985 to 1989. The corresponding figures for the NIEs are: 37.6 percent to 37.8 percent in South Korea, 27.9 percent to 35.2 percent (1988) in Taiwan, 12.2 percent to 9.9 percent in Hong Kong and 33.0 percent to 49.5 percent in Singapore (ICSEAD

1992). One should note that among the NIEs, only Singapore saw a big jump in its ratio. Singapore's jump will be explained later in relation to her particular position in the intra-regional division of labor of the export-oriented foreign firms.

In Malaysia, new export items behind the increase in machinery exports include, among other things, domestic appliances such as air conditioners and its parts, and color TV sets and audio sets. These new items have diversified Malaysia's "IC and semiconductor centric" machinery export structure. In Thailand, such new export items include ball bearings, TV sets, radio receivers, computer parts and automobiles.

As one expects, foreign firms (led by Japanese firms) play a pivotal role in the increase of manufactures exports in the ASEAN countries. Indeed, no less than 90 percent of Malaysian machinery is produced by foreign firms (Aoki 1992). In Thailand, Japanese firms were responsible for an average of 40 percent of the growth in Thai manufactures exports in the last three years (but imports of machinery and parts from Japan have increased too) (*Far Eastern Economic Review*, May 3, 1990).

The rapid increase in manufactures exports has been accompanied by a massive increase in the import of capital goods, parts and intermediate products and materials, particularly from Japan. Generally speaking, products for export have to be of a higher quality than those for the domestic market. Where supporting industries are in shortage, there is need to import more parts and machines as the export of machinery grows. Under these circumstances, the entry of a whole group of Japanese businesses with a mentality of "group business first" tends to undermine the development of local supporting industries.

As imports grew faster than exports, Thailand's trade deficit widened from 33 billion baht in 1985–86 (average) to 200 billion baht in 1989–90 (average)—an almost sixfold increase. The major import items are capital goods (28.8 percent share of total imports in 1990) and intermediate products (33.3 percent). Japan's export share of capital goods and intermediate products imported by Thailand in 1990 was 62.2 percent and 58.6 percent respectively. Japan was the largest source of these items, followed by the U.S. (TDRI 1992). On the other hand, Malaysia ran into a trade deficit in 1991, mainly because of the growing import of "machines and transport equipment (including parts)." These items constituted some 54 percent of total imports that year. Japan's share of Malaysia's total imports was 38.1 percent (JETRO 1992b).

It is interesting to note that Japan is recreating the same structure of trade with the ASEAN countries that it did with the NIEs, especially with Korea, in terms of manufacturing-related items (that is, Japan exports mainly machinery and parts and imports mainly nonmanufactured products). Indeed, newly investing firms such as in the electronics and automobile industry require continuously increasing investments on equipment, which entails massive capital goods imports. In both Thailand and Malaysia, this relationship cannot be changed easily, as the experience of Korea and Japan clearly demonstrates.

The net trade balance of leading Japanese firms in Thailand and Malaysia is a deficit (see Table 7 in Ishigami (1991) for Thailand). This is also true of the trade in manufactures with the U.S. by American subsidiaries in Malaysia. The more Thailand and Malaysia depend on exports of manufactures by Japanese firms, the more the deficit of the Japanese firms widens.

According to the MITI White Paper (1992), the percentage share of Japan's export of parts in nominal manufacturing GNP for the NIEs and the ASEAN countries is more than 10 percent, while Japan's share of world imports of parts is less than 2 percent. This shows that the region's import dependence on parts from Japan is at an extremely high level (MITI 1992: 148).

At this juncture, Japanese firms also have deeper economic links with the ASEAN countries than American firms in terms of FDI and the export of capital goods and technology (see Table 14.3).

14.4   Formation of a Network of Japanese Firms and the ASEAN Economies

As the yen appreciated, wage costs in the NIEs also increased and so did export prices. Other factors may have been responsible for the rise in export prices: (a) a strong Korean won and Taiwan dollar; (b) NIE "graduation" from the Generalized System of Preferences (GSP) in January 1989; (c) unstable industrial relations in South Korea; (d) rise of environmental problems in Taiwan; and so forth. These factors explain why Japanese firms decided to relocate their export firms from the NIEs to the ASEAN countries which offered access to cheaper labor and/or consumer markets serving a large population with rising disposable income. These factors also explain the decision to upgrade existing plants in the NIEs to produce sophisticated or high value-added goods.

One of the consequences of these changes is the intensification of the intra-firm/intra-region division of labor between Japan and the NIEs and the ASEAN countries in proportion to their levels of value-added and technology. It does not necessarily mean that the ASEAN countries are always allotted the least value-added and least sophisticated goods—allocations depend on the specific strategies of individual firms. For example, Matsushita (Panasonic) recently set up a Research and Development Center for air conditioners in Malaysia.

In line with corporate restructuring in Japan, major Japanese industries led by the electronics industries, have embarked on product-wise specialization of manufacturing for lower-end products among the Asian countries. At the same time, plants in Japan now manufacture exclusively more sophisticated and highly value-added product lines. Matsushita's product-wise specialization represents a typical case:

> Malaysia Matsushita for automatic washing machines, irons and vacuum cleaners; A.P. National (Thailand) for rice cookers and electrical water boiler pots; Philippine Matsushita

TABLE 14.3 Manufactures import,[1] export of capital goods[2] and technology[3] and FDI[4] of Japan and the U.S. in 1990 (US$ million, percentage share)

	Destinations	Import of manufactures[1]	Export of capital goods[2]	Export of technology[3]	FDI (cumulative total)[4]
Japan	World	118,027.7 (100.0)	154,844.1 (100.0)	2,344.1 (100.0)	310,808.0 (100.0)
	NIEs	19,057.8 (16.1)	29,584.5 (19.1)	557.4 (23.8)	23,383.7 (7.5)
	ASEAN	5,831.7 (4.9)	13,485.2 (8.7)	306.0 (13.1)	20,783.9 (6.7)
U.S.	World	385,394.7 (100.0)	161,547.0 (100.0)	15,840.0 (100.0)	421,494.0 (100.0)
	NIEs	60,815.8 (15.8)	16,140.2 (10.0)	752.0 (4.7)	14,874.0 (3.5)
	ASEAN	13,585.0 (3.5)	6,289.6 (3.9)	77.0 (0.5)	8,422.0 (2.0)
Japan/U.S.	World	0.31	0.96	0.15	0.73
	NIEs	0.31	1.83	0.74	1.57
	ASEAN	0.42	2.14	3.97	2.47

1. Figures for the U.S. cover items of SITC 5–8.
2. Figures for the U.S. stand for SITC 7 minus passenger cars.
3. Figures for Japan are calculated using the dollar–yen exchange rate of the financial year base and excluding Hong Kong from the Asian NIEs and the Philippines and Malaysia from ASEAN. U.S. figure for ASEAN excludes Thailand.
4. Figures for Japan are cumulative totals at the end of the financial year.

Sources: Japan: Various statistics of government and JETRO. U.S.: United Nations, *Commodity Trade Statistics*; OECD, *Foreign Trade by Commodities*, *SCB* and *US Direct Investment Abroad Benchmark Survey*. Reproduced from JETRO (1992b: 65).

for oven toasters; Taiwan Matsushita for two-tub washing machines (*Nippon Keizai Shimbun*, October 22, 1992).

This means that each plant focuses on the strategic export of one of the specific item(s) under the logistics policy of the parent company. These plants also accelerate the trade of these goods among the Asian countries, while they continue to export their products to other parts of the world.

Another type of division of labor is the intra-process scheme. Under this scheme, for example, firms procure simple plastic castings, metal parts and structural parts and assemble them in Taiwan, Singapore and Malaysia. Later, these parts are taken for final assembly in the final consumer market, be it Japan, the U.S. or Europe. The "ASEAN car," a product of Mitsubishi Motor company belongs to this category: the car radio is manufactured in Singapore, the doors in Malaysia, the transmission in the Philippines, the wheels in Australia, the engine in Japan, and the chassis in Thailand. Assembly takes place in Thailand. Figure 14.1 illustrates Toyota's intra-ASEAN division of labor. The ASEAN Brand to Brand Complementation scheme for the automobile industry was promoted by Mitsubishi to evade the indigenization policy (which is supported by countries with a strong nationalist orientation) and to achieve de facto an intra-firm division of labor in this region. In addition, specialization in the production of certain car parts could lead to good

FIGURE 14.1   Outline of Toyota's Parts-Complementation in ASEAN

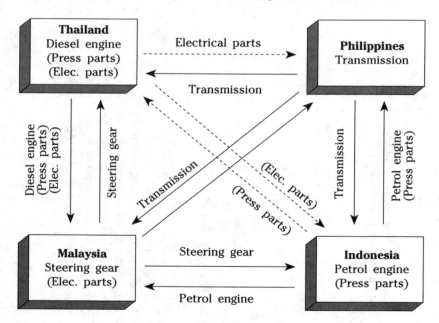

Source: Toyota Motor Corporation. Reproduced from *The Weekly Toyo Keizai*, May 22, 1992, 107.

quality and cost competitiveness, that is, "killing two birds with one stone" (*Nikkei Sangyou Shimbun*, February 21, 1990).

According to a survey on Japanese firms in Asia (mainly on Japanese firms in the electronics, automobile, and machinery industries), 41.7 percent of their exports are destined for Japan, 15.1 percent for the NIEs, 15.1 percent for the U.S., 14.0 percent for ASEAN and 7.3 percent for the EC. These firms reportedly procure 52.5 percent of their input materials from Japan, 33.8 percent from host countries and regions, 10.5 percent from the NIEs and 1.4 percent from ASEAN (*Nikkei Sangyou Shimbun*, April 22, 1992). This implies that Japanese firms in Asia are forming their own economic area in the NIEs and ASEAN—or more precisely, a Japanese business network through FDI, the export of goods and the procurement of input materials. ASEAN's capacity to provide input materials to other regions is still very low.

In the context of this regional division of labor, firms in Singapore (that is, Japanese firms in Singapore) occupy a core position as the center of high value-added and sophisticated parts and components. They control most of the Asian market. Over the last few years, Singapore has received large amounts of FDI for the expansion and upgrading of the subsidiaries of electronics industries from Japan and the U.S. Singapore has been attractive not only because of its good infrastructure, transportation and distribution facilities, but also because it has a skilled labor force, is within easy access to other countries, is a financial center, and offers many incentives to foreign firms such as the "OHQ" (Operational Head-Quarter) scheme. SONIS (Sony International (Singapore)) was the first Japanese company granted OHQ status by Singapore in November 1987. Malaysia is also offering an incentive similar to Singapore's OHQ scheme.

The major problems facing the electronics industry—the largest industry destination for Japanese FDI—is the weakness of supporting industries. This is also the case in the automobile industry. For example, according to data for early 1988, the local content of consumer electronics produced by Japanese FDI firms was only 30 percent. This was the case in spite of the fact that the procurement of local parts came mostly from Japanese firms in Malaysia; indeed, 14 leading Japanese consumer electronics firms, mainly producing TV and audio sets, had 393 local subcontracting firms. Thus, the ratio of Japanese FDI firms to local subcontracting firms was 1/31. Most local subcontracting firms engage in packing materials and in producing small lots of plastics and simply shaped press parts.

Quality control and the accuracy of delivery of these subcontracting firms has also not been good enough. In fact, it has been too low for Japanese firms to take advantage of wage differentials. In the case of dies, while the Japanese firms were fostering the industry, they depended on imports of high-precision and large-sized dies (Small Business Finance Corporation 1989). Also, as mentioned above, some parts and materials are offered by NIE firms, particularly Taiwanese firms, whose technology level lies between that of Japan and the ASEAN countries. However, most of the parts and materials are provided by Japanese firms.

Some of the research on technology transfer by Japanese firms shows that generally Japanese firms are initially reluctant to transfer whole bundles of technology to subsidiaries in the ASEAN countries. So far, they have transferred only a small fraction of technology of a nonadvanced nature, such as operational techniques, maintenance and quality control. Japanese firms are reluctant to transfer advanced technologies, such as dies, designs, new products and processes for the development of manufacturing equipment (Yamashita 1991b; *Nikkei Sangyou Shimbun*, April 22, 1992). In addition, both the change to a stress on manufacturing for the international market and the shortening of the life cycle of products requires better quality and the quicker delivery of parts—requirements which local firms alone cannot handle.

Thailand's experience with export-oriented Japanese FDI in the electronics industry since the yen appreciation illustrates Japanese firms' reluctance to transfer whole bundles of technology to subsidiaries in ASEAN (Shiowattana 1991). As new 100 percent Japanese-holding investments increase, two features have become prominent:

1. New investing firms are more "self-contained."
2. "[T]he width and depth of technology to be transferred will be determined by and for the interest of the multinationals. In comparison to joint venture cases, the role of the technology recipient in the learning process will become trivial. Decisions regarding the breadth and depth of the technologies to be transferred will rest solely with MNCs"[6] (Shiowattana 1991: 191).

However, with the intensification of the intra-region division of labor and the emergence of product-wise specialization, Japanese firms in the ASEAN countries need to localize design and R&D activities. However, only countries possessing a certain level of technology and manpower skills will be able to benefit from this need. Also, as Phongpaichit (1991) and Suehiro ("Comment" in Yamashita 1991a) note, massive Japanese FDI provides Thailand's local firms with an opportunity to diversify their product lines and enter new businesses, making use of joint venture types of businesses.

At this juncture, the policy initiatives of the ASEAN governments need to be directed towards broadening their industrial base and training their manpower resources, as well as inviting Japanese firms into favorable, better-developed industrial sectors. Such initiatives would surely buttress the new regional division of labor.

Notes

1. For example, refer to Chapter 2 of this volume.
2. Average annual growth rates of the export volume by region from 1980 to 1990 are as follows (percentage): world 4.0, developing countries 3.5, Southeast and East Asia 10.0 (East Asia 11.7, ASEAN 7.0, South Asia 4.0), China 15.0, Latin America 3.9, West Asia −2.2, Africa −1.0 (North Africa −0.6, sub-Saharan Africa −1.4) (UNCTAD 1991).

3. Economists of the so-called "New International Division of Labor" and "Regulation" schools attach importance to this particular point in the paradigm of their theories (see Frobel et al. 1980; Lipietz 1985; Prasartset 1991).
4. With regard to the present world order of technology, see Stewart (1991: 61–62).
5. A good and comprehensive discussion of Japanese FDI in and transfer of technology to the ASEAN countries is provided by Yamashita (1991) and Taniura (1989).
6. In this context, Sclair's study (1989: 211–12) on the *maquiladoras* of Mexico, one of the typical and largest bonded areas (a similar facility to the Export Processing Zone) in the world, is interesting to our study. He characterizes the manufacturing activities of foreign firms, mainly American ones, as "technology relocation." By this he means to say that these firms are less inclined to contribute to the local economy in terms of technology transfer.

References

Aoki, Takeshi, 1992, "Nippon no Chokusetsu Toshi to Network no Keisei" (Japan's FDI and Formation of Network), in Kohama, pp. 63–85.

Frobel, F., J. Heinrichs, and O. Kreye, 1980, *The New International Division of Labour*, Cambridge University Press, Cambridge.

ILO/UNCTC, 1988, *Economic and Social Effects of Multinational Enterprises in Export Processing Zones*, ILO, Geneva.

International Centre for the Study of East Asian Development (ICSEAD), 1992, *Asian Data Handbook*, Kita-Kyushu.

Ishigami, Etsuro, 1991, "Japanese Business in ASEAN Countries: New Industrialisation or Japanisation?" *Fukuoka University Review of Commercial Sciences*, 35(4): pp. 821–46.

JETRO, 1992a, *Sekai to Nippon no Kaigai Chokusetsu Toshi* (JETRO White Paper on FDI), Tokyo.

———, 1992b, *Sekai to Nippon no Boeki* (JETRO White Paper on International Trade), Tokyo.

Kohama, Hirohisa (ed.), 1992, *Chokusetsu Toshi to Kogyo-ka* (FDI and Industrialization), JETRO, Tokyo.

Lipietz, A., 1985, *Mirages et Miracles*, Editions La Decouverte, Paris (Japanese translation: *Kiseki to Gen-ei*, trans. F. Wakamori and Y. Inoue, Shin Hyoron, Tokyo, 1987).

Ministry of Finance, 1992, *Zaisei Kin-yu Tokei Geppo* (Monthly Bulletin of Financial and Monetary Statistics), December.

MITI, 1989/1990/1992, *Tsusho Hakusho* (White Paper on International Trade), Tokyo.

OECD, 1979, *The Impact of the Newly Industrialising Countries on Production and Trade in Manufactures*, Report by the Secretary-General, Paris.

Phongpaichit, Pasuk, 1991, "Japan's Investment and Local Capital in ASEAN Since 1985," in Yamashita (1991a), pp. 23–50.

Prasartset, Suthy, 1991, "The Global Context and the New Wave of Japanese Investment in Thailand," in Yamashita (1991a), pp. 55–8.

Sclair, L., 1989, *Assembling for Development: The Maquila Industry in Mexico and the United States*, Unwin Hyman, Boston.

Shiowattana, Prayoon, 1991, "Technology Transfer in Thailand's Electronics Industry," in Yamashita (1991a), pp. 169–93.

Small Business Finance Corporation, Research Division, 1989, *Yakusin suru ASEAN no Sangyo to Kinyu* (Industry and Finance of ASEAN), Toyo Keizai Shinpo Sha, Tokyo.

Small and Medium Enterprise Agency, 1989, *Chusho-kigyo Hakusho* (White Paper on Small and Medium Enterprise), Tokyo.

Stewart, F., 1991, "Technology Transfer for Development," in H. W. Singer, N. Hatti, and R. Tandon (eds.), *Joint Ventures and Collaborations*, Indus Publishing, New Delhi, pp. 57–90.

Suehiro, Akira, 1989, "Thailand," in Taniura, pp. 189–224.

Taniura, Takao (ed.), 1989, *Ajia no Kagyo-ka to Chokusetsu Toshi* (Industrialization and FDI in Asia), Institute of Developing Economies, Tokyo.

Thailand Development Research Institute (TDRI), 1992, *Thailand Economic Information Kit*, Bangkok.

Torii, Takashi, 1989, "Malaysia," in Taniura, pp. 159–88.

Tsunekawa, Jun, 1992, "Thai no Kogyou-ka to Gaikoku Toshi" (Industrialization of Thailand and Foreign Investment), in Kohama, pp. 207–35.

UNCTAD, 1991, *The Least Developed Countries, 1990 Report*, United Nations, New York.

UNIDO, 1989, *Industry and Development, Global Report 1989/90*, Vienna.

White, G. (ed.), 1988, *Developmental States in East Asia*, Macmillan, Basingstoke, U.K.

Yamashita, Shoichi (ed.), 1991a, *Transfer of Japanese Technology and Management to the ASEAN Countries*, University of Tokyo Press, Tokyo.

———, 1991b, "Economic Development of the ASEAN Countries and the Role of Japanese Direct Investment," in Yamashita (1991a), pp. 3–22.

Part IV

Exchange Rate, Finance and Banking

Part IV concentrates on the financial issues, that is, both domestic and international finance-related issues.

Faruqee (Chapter 15) traces the impact of the liberalization process on the capital account as well as on the integration process between domestic and international financial markets. As liberalization in the region gained momentum, restrictions on international capital flows were by and large eliminated. Faruqee's time-varying estimation of return differentials provides strong support for the hypothesis that liberalization raises the level of integration between domestic and international financial markets. The result was that the degree of linkage between regional and world interest rates strengthened. Liberalization encouraged a higher degree of capital mobility. Under such circumstances, departures from interest rate parity induce increasingly responsive market forces which tend to narrow the existing return differential. This leads one to conclude that financial market liberalization leads to integration of the domestic market with the international financial market.

Although the region has remained the fastest growing part of the international economy, growth rates in many cases remained unsteady and fluctuating. The yen-dollar exchange rate has become a major determinant of the level of economic activity in the region. An appreciation of the yen tends to raise the economic growth in the ANIEs but lowers that in the ASEAN countries. This asymmetry is created by differences in the trade structures of the two country groups.

A long-sustained outstanding performance on the economic front, current account surpluses and an appreciating yen turned Japan into the most solvent nation and the leading financial power of the latter half of the 1980s. Japan was known to be a country of highly restricted financial markets. The surge in Japan's status as a leading creditor began after 1980 with financial deregulation and liberalization. By the mid-1980s Japan had become the largest creditor nation in the world and the Japanese banks and security firms became the largest firms and banks in their respective categories.

Since 1980, the yen has gradually internationalized while the significance of the dollar has somewhat declined. However, the dollar remains the dominant international currency because it is impeccably suited to be an international vehicle and intervention currency. Japan's yen-denominated current account transactions have grown a little over the 1980s but the use of the yen in trade between third countries is negligible. The deutsche mark is far ahead of the yen in this respect. In terms of the volume of currency traded on the foreign exchange markets, the yen is well behind the dollar and the deutsche mark. Going by the daily turnover, the importance of Tokyo in the foreign exchange markets is generally regarded as the second largest after London. In foreign exchange trade, likewise, the dollar–yen exchange rate is considered the second busiest after the dollar–deutsche mark rate. Recent growth of trading in the yen–deutsche mark rate has contributed to the progress of yen internationalization (Das 1993).

The strength of the Japanese economy and growing internationalization of the yen created the expectation that a yen bloc would be created in the Asia-Pacific region. With deepening economic interdependence in the region in the recent past, this expectation has heightened. Kwan (Chapter 16) chooses to define the yen bloc narrowly, in terms of currency alignments, that is, where currencies of the regional economies maintain stable exchange rates against the yen. Thus, creating a yen bloc will amount to pegging the regional currencies to the yen. This would lower the risk associated with exchange rate fluctuations and benefits the Asia-Pacific economies by expanding their trade with, and capital inflows from, Japan. This argument holds *a fortiori* with Japan becoming the second largest economy in the world and the U.S. losing its relative importance.

Chapter 17 (Goldberg) begins by examining the internationalization of financial markets. Next, it considers and comments on the theories and empirical evidence related to the formation of international financial centers (IFCs). Some of the imperatives for the creation of an IFC include political stability, geographical suitability, not too stringent regulatory environment, availability of agglomeration economies, advanced transportation and telecommunications network and a high quality of life for the staff of financial service firms. Tokyo is a financial hub and one of the most important IFCs in the world. Beyond Tokyo, several financial centers in the region have developed well and other centers in the region are likely to experience similar development.

Reference

Das, Dilip K. (ed.), 1993, "The Internationalization of the Yen," in *International Finance: Contemporary Issues*, Routledge, London.

Chapter 15

Hamid Faruqee

FINANCIAL LIBERALIZATION AND CAPITAL MARKET INTEGRATION

15.1 Introduction

Over the past decade developing countries in Asia-Pacific have experienced a continuing process of financial market liberalization and growing financial flows. Although individual countries have taken different measures, the region as a whole has moved toward the deregulation of domestic financial markets and the relaxation of restrictions on international capital flows. As liberalization continues in the region, the impact of these developments on the level of integration between local and world financial markets becomes an important consideration. In particular, measuring the changing degree of capital mobility—defined broadly in this context as the degree of linkage between domestic and foreign interest rates—is central to our understanding and assessment of financial liberalization and its consequences.

   Most of the empirical work done in this area has examined capital mobility from a static perspective, estimating either an offset or an openness coefficient. For example, Edwards and Khan (1985) developed an analytical framework for interest rate determination in developing countries, wherein the prevailing interest rate represents a weighted average of open and closed economy rates that would have existed otherwise. Estimation of this weight indicates the relative importance of interest rate parity and domestic monetary factors in determining national interest rates, thus capturing the degree of financial openness. More accurately, however, this approach estimates the *average* degree of openness for a given country over a sample period. Hence, this line of research essentially ignores the *changing* degree of capital mobility and, consequently, the changing roles of stabilization and exchange rate policies over time.

To assess the *dynamic* impact of financial market liberalization on the mobility of capital and the role of policy, this chapter applies autoregressive conditional heteroscedasticity (ARCH) estimation to interest rates differentials between selected Asia-Pacific developing countries and Japan.[1] The purpose is to determine the extent to which these rates have become increasingly interrelated. Specifically, a sustained narrowing in deviations of interest rate differentials from an appropriate measure of interest rate parity indicates an increased level of capital mobility. Using time-series estimation, this chapter details the timing and magnitude of these changes resulting from financial liberalization.

There are many possible explanations for deviations from covered or uncovered interest rate parity. Various frictions, such as information and transactions costs, preclude strict equalization in rates of return across markets. Instead, differentials between exchange rate-adjusted interest rates may exist within some neutral band, indicating a range over which arbitrage opportunities are nonexistent. More generally, the width of the band should reflect all observable *and* unobservable costs involved in relocating arbitrage funds. For example, consider the case of capital controls and risk-averse investors. Beyond the "certainty" or direct costs associated with existing controls, capital restrictions exert "uncertainty costs" concerning future controls (see Otani and Tiwari 1990). Capital controls, differential taxation, foreign exchange controls, and so on, introduce elements of country-specific risk that may drive a wedge between various market rates of return, as captured by a risk premium. Moreover, country risk also reduces the sensitivity of capital supply that would eliminate return differentials beyond the risk premium, leading to a still broader range of speculative inactivity.

Financial market liberalization, which involves changes in various adjustment costs and asset risk, directly affects the size of the neutral band within which return differentials may systematically deviate from interest rate parity. Specifically, liberalization measures that effectively increase financial openness will narrow the implicit band. The effectiveness of these measures ultimately depends on the reputation of the authorities and the credibility of their commitment to liberalization, as perceived by market participants. Moreover, these reputation and credibility effects are likely to be established only gradually over time, *conditional* on past credibility, reputation, and efforts to open up domestic financial markets.

As liberalization takes hold and the band narrows, increasingly confined deviations from interest rate parity will reflect the reduced impact of domestic monetary factors in determining domestic interest rates, corresponding to a heightened responsiveness of internationally mobile capital. Furthermore, the centrality of the band may also be affected by increasing financial market integration, as indicated by a diminishing risk premium stemming from greater asset substitutability.

The chapter is organized as follows. Section 15.2 implements standard autoregressive moving average (ARMA) estimation to represent the time-series behavior of interest rate differentials in the Asia-Pacific. Next, the estimates are revised via the ARCH model to capture any changing variability in interest rate parity deviations. These time-series results are translated into a dynamic representation of capital mobility through the simulation of impulse-response functions using country parameter estimates. Section 15.3 offers conclusions.

15.2 Time-Series Estimation

Monthly data series on domestic money market interest rates were obtained for the Republic of Korea, Singapore, Malaysia, and Thailand.[2] For purposes of comparison, the three-month London interbank offer rate (LIBOR) on Japanese yen deposits was chosen to represent the world rate of interest.[3] The choice of an offshore rate as the reference point was intended to limit the influence of liberalization measures taken in Japan in order to isolate the impact of measures taken domestically on interest rate convergence.

Series on interest rate differentials were then constructed by subtracting the Japan LIBOR from the domestic rate, or $\phi_t = (i - i^*)_t$, expressed in annual percentage terms. Assuming that exchange rates vis-a-vis the yen follow a random walk in the sample,[4] one can relate interest rate differentials to a suitably defined interest rate parity condition, as a means of calibrating deviations from the latter as a measure of capital mobility.

15.2.1 ARMA Estimation

To analyze deviations from interest rate parity, the time-series behavior of interest rate differentials is characterized, using an ARMA representation of ϕ_t, including a constant and a nonlinear time trend. Introducing a constant allows for the presence of a long-run liquidity and/or risk premium, implying a nonzero long-run value of ϕ. An ARMA specification with a time trend permits one to separate transitory fluctuations around interest rate parity, which reflect the degree of capital mobility, from movements in the parity value itself, which reflect underlying changes in asset substitutability.[5]

An ARMA (p, q) model for de-meaned and de-trended interest rate differentials—representing deviations from interest rate parity—can be written generally as

$$A(L) (\phi_t - \mu - \text{trend}_t) = B(L)\epsilon_t \tag{15.1}$$

where μ is the constant, and $A(L)$ and $B(L)$ are the AR and MA lag polynomials of orders p and q, respectively. ARMA estimation results are reported below in Table 15.1.

As shown in Table 15.1, the appropriate time-series representation for interest rate differentials in Singapore, Korea, and Thailand was an AR (1) specification,

TABLE 15.1   ARMA estimation: interest rate differentials in Asia-Pacific

Country	μ	Trend[a]	ϕ_{t-1}	ϵ_{t-1}	Adj. R^2
Singapore	–	–	0.8684** (21.488)	–	0.748
Malaysia	–	–	0.9373** (27.500)	–0.4381** (–4.982)	0.658
Korea	5.424** (10.115)	15.246** (5.287)	0.8170** (16.957)	–	0.916
Thailand	5.553** (5.834)	–	0.8923** (23.850)	–	0.795

Two asterisks indicate significance at the 1 percent level; t-statistics are in parentheses.
[a] Exponential trend$_t = e^{(-0.05t)}$.

whereas for Malaysia, the ARMA (1,1) model was more appropriate. So, for example, the time-series behavior of interest rate differentials in Malaysia is best represented by the univariate model, $\phi_t = 0.9373\phi_{t-1} + \epsilon_t - 0.4381\epsilon_{t-1}$. The Schwarz information criterion (SIC) was used to select the particular order of the model—that is, the number of AR and MA lags—for each country.[6]

Constant terms were found statistically significant for Thailand and Korea only and were omitted elsewhere. Also, a time trend was found to be significant for Korean interest rate differentials. The large estimates (close to 1) for the AR (1) coefficient in Table 15.1 suggest weak mean-reverting behavior in the data, especially in the case of Malaysia and Thailand.[7]

Figure 15.1 presents plots of interest rate differentials, ϕ, and residuals from ARMA estimation for each country. Across all four countries, large residuals generally cluster together, as do small residuals. This observation strongly suggests that an ARCH framework—which models an underlying pattern to the changing variance of residuals—is appropriate in order to improve the initial estimates and to further illustrate the systematic changes in capital mobility in Asia-Pacific.

15.2.2   ARCH Estimation

The purpose of this subsection is to test formally for the presence of ARCH residuals and to revise the original estimates through ARCH estimation. Maximum likelihood estimation (MLE) is applied to the data series to correct for conditional heteroscedasticity. Under an assumption of normality and ARCH errors, the log-likelihood function for the tth observation can be written as follows:

$$l_t = -0.5 \log h_t - 0.5\epsilon_t^2/h_t; \qquad h_t = \alpha_0 + \alpha_1\epsilon_{t-1}^2 + \dots + \alpha_n\epsilon_{t-n}^2 \tag{15.2}$$

where h_t is the conditional variance function for ϵ_t. Maximizing equation (15.2) with respect to the vector of parameters α and those shown in Table 15.1 generates the ARCH-corrected estimates. As discussed in Engle (1982), the MLE

FIGURE 15.1 Interest rate differential versus Japanese LIBOR, September 1978 to December 1990

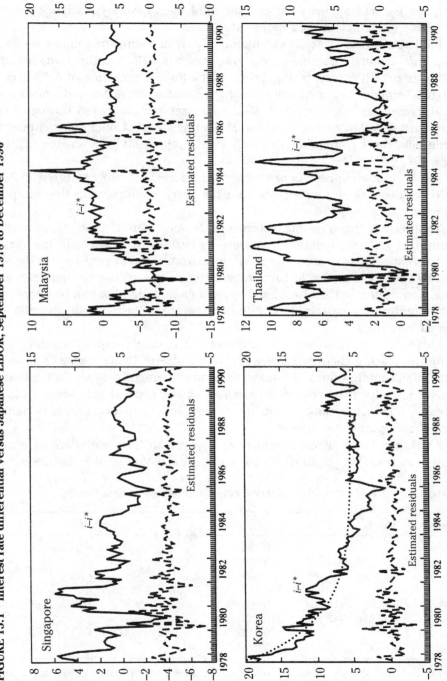

approach generates consistent estimation of the variance-covariance matrix and asymptotically efficient parameter estimates.

Implementation of ARCH estimation to ϕ is accomplished in two steps. First, using the residuals obtained from the previous ARMA estimation, a Lagrange multiplier or ARCH test[8] is applied to check for the presence of ARCH residuals and to determine the appropriate linear specification for h_t. Second, once a suitable ARCH model has been selected, MLE estimates are computed through iterative search, using ARMA estimates as initial starting values. Under sufficient regularity conditions, the iterative solution will yield optimal MLE parameter values (see Engle 1982).

ARCH estimation results are presented for each country in Table 15.2 below. ARCH residuals were found significant for every country, with the exception of Malaysia.[9]

To interpret these results in terms of dynamic capital mobility, note that the conditional variance function h_t represents systematic changes in the variability of disturbances which underlie deviations from interest rate parity. Departures from interest rate parity, in turn, reflect the degree of linkage between interest rates. Consequently, the changing degree of capital mobility can be characterized by the underlying pattern of conditional heteroscedasticity in disturbances to interest rate parity.

Figure 15.2 summarizes the estimates of dynamic capital mobility in Asia-Pacific by tracing this underlying variance pattern. Using residuals from ARCH estimation, sample values of h_t taken as annual averages are calculated. In viewing Figure 15.2, note that movement down along the vertical axis toward the origin indicates increasing capital mobility corresponding to decreasing variability in interest rate parity deviations.

As Figure 15.2 indicates, Singapore appears to have experienced a uniform decline (increase) in conditional variance (capital mobility) over the 1980s, leveling

TABLE 15.2   ARCH estimation: interest rate differentials in Asia-Pacific

Country	μ	Trend	ϕ_{t-1}	ϵ_{t-1}	h_t	ARCH[a]
Singapore	–	–	0.7645** (23.699)	–	$\alpha_0 + \alpha_1\epsilon_{t-2}^2 + \alpha_3\epsilon_{t-3}^2$	6.616*
Malaysia	–	–	0.9086** (39.155)	−0.4271** (−7.610)	$\alpha_0 + \alpha_1\epsilon_{t-1}^2$	1.878
Korea	5.203** (7.351)	18.964** (3.356)	0.8657** (16.283)	–	$\alpha_0\alpha_1\epsilon_{t-1}^2 + \alpha_2\epsilon_{t-2}^2 + \alpha_3\epsilon_{t-3}^2$	12.061**
Thailand	6.190** (3.475)	–	0.9432** (23.274)	–	$\alpha_0 + \alpha_1\epsilon_{t-1}^2$	16.081**

One asterisk indicates significance at the 5 percent level, and two asterisks indicate significance at the 1 percent level; t-statistics are in parentheses.
[a]ARCH test statistic is distributed $x^2(k)$, where k equals the number of lags in h_t.

FIGURE 15.2   Regional interest rate parity deviations (conditional variance averages)

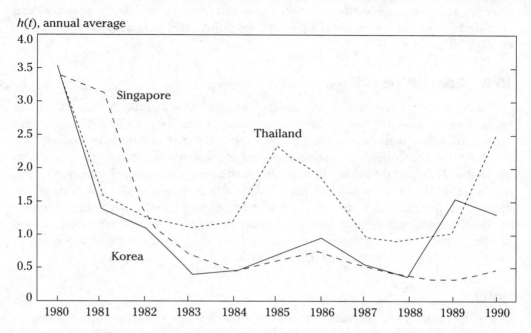

$h(t)$, annual average

off around 1983. Korea's experience was similar to Singapore's, except for an apparent reversal in direction in the latter part of the decade.[10] Thailand showed several episodes of increasing and decreasing financial openness in the 1980s without a clear tendency toward either direction. As for Malaysia, using initial ARMA estimates, a moving average of the sample variance suggests an overall dampening in shocks to interest rate parity with one notable exception. During specific periods in the mid-1980s, Malaysia witnessed extraordinary volatility in interest rate differentials which overwhelmed the detection of any possible underlying ARCH pattern in interest rate parity deviations.

15.2.3   Impulse-Response Simulations

Translating the variability of deviations from interest rate parity as a measure of capital mobility makes implications for policy less readily apparent than, say, an openness or offset coefficient. To better understand policy implications based on this calibration of capital mobility, impulse-response functions were constructed from the time-series estimates in Section 15.2 to simulate the dynamic effects of domestic monetary shocks on interest rate parity deviations. Integrating the changing variability of interest rate parity disturbances with the estimated time-series structure completes the dynamic representation of capital mobility.[11]

Specifically, ARCH parameter estimates and the conditional variance functions are used to track the effects of a one-standard-deviation shock to interest rate differentials in 1980 and in 1990.[12] (See Figure 15.3.) Simulated trajectories are interpreted as departures from trend or long-run interest rate parity values where amplitude is measured in annual percentage points and persistence is measured in months.

15.3 Conclusion

Financial market liberalization in Asia-Pacific has had a significant impact on the region's economic and financial environment over the past decade. Time-varying estimation of return differentials provides strong support for the notion that liberalization measures have raised the level of integration between domestic and international financial markets. Consequently, the degree of linkage between regional and world interest rates has increased. With a higher degree of capital mobility, departures from interest rate parity induce increasingly responsive market forces to narrow existing return differentials. And as rates of return converge across markets, the ability of independent monetary policy to affect domestic interest rates in Asia-Pacific becomes further limited.

Notes

This article is a revised version of "Dynamic Capital Mobility in Pacific Basin Developing Countries," *IMF Staff Papers*, 1992, 39(3): 706–17.

1. The methodology employed in this paper essentially follows that of Engle (1982), here applied to interest rate differentials for the Republic of Korea, Malaysia, Singapore, and Thailand.
2. The disposition between countries and interest rates is as follows: for Malaysia, the overnight interbank rate; for Korea, the daily rate on call money; and for Singapore and Thailand, three-month interbank rates.
3. Although the sample countries float vis-a-vis the yen, one can think of the Japanese offshore rate as a proxy for the rate of return and financial conditions in the "world" market. Given fixed exchange rates at some margin, a small open economy must import its inflation and money growth rates from abroad, fixing its risk-adjusted domestic interest rate in the long run. Using the U.S. LIBOR instead as the international rate of return does not change the findings presented here.
4. An uncovered version of interest rate parity with perfect capital mobility and asset substitutability can be written as

$$\phi_t = i_t - i_t^* - \Delta s_{t+k}^e,$$

where Δs_{t+k}^e is the expected rate of depreciation in the spot exchange rate over maturity, with s being the log spot rate, and k, the length of maturity for i and i^*. Assuming the spot exchange rate follows a random walk, the last term in the expression is set to zero, equating rational with static expectations. Initial exchange rate estimates strongly support a random walk hypothesis in the data. See also Levich (1985).
5. In the case of time-varying risk, this process is approximated with an exponential time trend, representing a smooth, downward convergence in the risk premium to its long-run value, paralleling a process of progressive financial liberalization and integration.

FIGURE 15.3   Impulse-response simulations with ARCH estimates

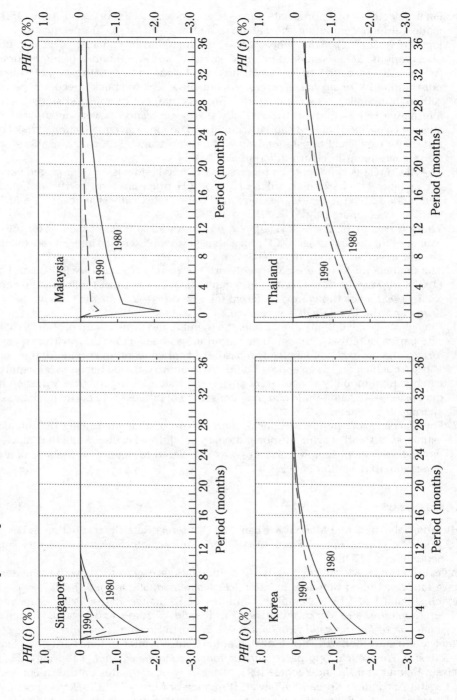

6. Final selections of appropriate time-series models, as reported in Table 15.1, were made through computing the SIC for numerous ARMA (p, q) specifications: $(RSS + \log(NOBS)*SEE^2*K)/NOBS$, where RSS = residual sum of squares, $NOBS$ = number of observations, SEE = standard error of estimate, and K = number of regressors.

7. As the AR(1) coefficient goes to unity (unit root in $A(L)$), the model will exhibit nonstationarity or no mean reversion, and the effect of shocks becomes permanent. Although modeling ϕ as an integrated process may not be rejected statistically as an alternative representation, theoretically this specification is very unappealing, for it suggests a perfectly closed capital account and no long-run equalization of risk-adjusted returns or significant nonstationarity in the risk premium inducing a sizable stochastic trend component in return differentials.

8. The ARCH test is conducted by regressing squared residuals on their lagged values and a constant. The particular order of the ARCH process (form of the h_t function) is determined from the test regression found to be statistically significant. The ARCH test statistic is computed by $NOBS*R^2$.

9. The ARCH statistic for Malaysia has a p-value of 0.170 (significance level). Also, MLE estimates for the first-order ARCH process suggest that Malaysian interest rate differentials are not covariance stationary (estimate on $\alpha_1 > 1$).

10. The findings for Korea are consistent with the results obtained by Reisen and Yèches (1991), who used a time-varying approach to financial openness following Edwards and Khan (1985), even though two different interest rates—a domestic curb market rate for Korea and the U.S. LIBOR—were used.

11. Changing capital mobility affects *both* the impulse and propagation of shocks to interest rate parity. Note that although time variation has been allowed for with respect to the former, the propagation mechanism has been kept constant over time (that is, same AR and MA coefficients) as an approximation. This approximation becomes less appropriate when capital mobility is near zero, suggesting that allowing for time variation in both dimensions—the amplitude *and* the persistence of interest rate parity deviations—may sharpen the results.

12. For Malaysia, the impulse-response functions were simulated using the initial ARMA estimates. Instead of using the nonstationary conditional variance function, an 18-month moving average of sample variances was calculated to determine the size of a typical one-standard-deviation shock.

References

Edwards, Sebastian, and Moshin S. Khan, 1985, "Interest Rate Determination in Developing Countries: A Conceptual Framework," *Staff Papers*, International Monetary Fund, 32 (September): 377–403.

Engle, Robert F., 1982, "Autoregressive Conditional Heteroscedasticity with Estimates of the Variance of United Kingdom Inflation," *Econometrica*, 50 (July): 987–1007.

Levich, Richard M., 1985, "Empirical Studies of Exchange Rates: Price Behavior, Rate Determination, and Market Efficiency," in Ronald W. Jones and Peter B. Kenen (eds.), *Handbook of International Economics*, Vol. 2, North-Holland, New York.

Otani, Ichiro and Siddharth Tiwari, 1990, "Capital Controls, Interest Rate Parity, and Exchange Rates: A Theoretical Approach," *International Economic Journal*, 4 (Spring): 25–44.

Reisen, Helmut and Hélène Yèches, 1991, "Time-Varying Estimates on the Openness of the Capital Account in Korea and Taiwan [Province of China]," OECD Development Centre, Organization for Economic Cooperation and Development, Paris, unpublished.

Chapter 16

Chi-Hung Kwan

A YEN BLOC FOR ASIA-PACIFIC?

16.1 Introduction

A currency bloc for Asia-Pacific will necessarily have to be a yen bloc—that is, a grouping of countries among which the Japanese currency is widely used as an international (or a regional) currency, and where countries maintain stable exchange rates against the yen.[1] This is analogous to such currency blocs as the former Sterling Area and the Economic and Monetary Union (EMU) now taking shape in the European Union (EU).

Interest in the possibility of forming a yen bloc between Japan and its Asia-Pacific neighbors has increased in recent years against the background of growing Japanese economic and financial power, deepening economic interdependence between Japan and the Asian countries, and monetary integration in the EU. The traditional approach to this issue, along the lines of "the internationalization of the yen," has a distinctive Japanese perspective. To deepen our understanding further, we also need to add the perspective of the Asian countries (ANIEs and ASEAN), which are supposed to be potential members of the bloc.

The Asian countries have, up to now, focused on the bilateral rates between their local currencies and the dollar when formulating exchange rate policy, in view of their traditional dependence on the U.S. economy. However, they have experienced drastic changes in their regional composition of trade and inflows of foreign direct investment, and wide fluctuations in economic growth brought about by the global exchange rate realignment since 1985. Indeed, the yen–dollar rate has replaced the U.S. economic growth rate as the major determinant of short-term economic growth in the Asian Newly Industrializing Economies (ANIEs) (Kwan 1991). To adapt to the new international environment, the traditional exchange rate policy of pegging loosely to the dollar may have to be amended, and more emphasis may have to be put on other major currencies, the Japanese yen in particular.

In this chapter, the literature on optimal currency pegs for developing countries is applied to examine the implications for the economic stability of the Asian countries when they choose to peg their currencies to the yen instead of other (baskets of) currencies. Special attention will be paid to the objective of stabilizing output in the face of fluctuating exchange rates among major currencies. At the same time, the role played by economic structures—trade relations with Japan in particular—will also be emphasized.

The conclusion can be summarized as follows. For the ANIEs, which compete with Japan in international markets, pegging to the yen would promote economic stability. For the ASEAN countries, which have trade structures complementary to, instead of competitive with, that of Japan, pegging to the dollar is more compatible with economic stability than pegging to the yen. Other things being equal, the ANIEs therefore have more incentive to join a yen bloc than the ASEAN countries.

This chapter is composed of five sections. To provide a background, we summarize evidence of the use of the yen as a regional currency in Section 16.1 and analytical approaches to a yen bloc in Section 16.2. In Section 16.3 we formulate a model that shows the relations between exchange rate fluctuations and short-term economic growth for a small open economy and test it with Korean data. Based on this model, in Section 16.4 we study the role of exchange rate policy in output stabilization and derive for an Asian country the optimal peg that minimizes output fluctuations. In Section 16.5 we draw implications from our analysis on the possibility of forming a yen bloc in the Asia-Pacific region.

16.2   Use of the Yen Versus the Dollar as a Regional Currency

Parallel to a domestic currency, an international currency performs the functions of a medium of exchange, unit of account and store of value. As a medium of exchange, it is used to settle international trade and financial transactions. As a unit of account, an international currency is used in invoicing international trade, denominating financial instruments, and expressing exchange rate relations. As a store of value, it serves as an investment asset, including foreign exchange reserves of central banks. In addition, an international currency also acts as a peg for the currencies of smaller countries. The evidence of the use of the yen as an international currency is summarized in Figure 16.1.[2]

16.2.1   Exchange Rate Regimes of the Asian Countries

The Asian countries have maintained relatively more stable exchange rates against the U.S. dollar than against other currencies (Figure 16.2). In all the ANIEs (South Korea, Taiwan, Hong Kong and Singapore) and the ASEAN-4 countries (Indonesia,

FIGURE 16.1   Progress in the internationalization of the yen

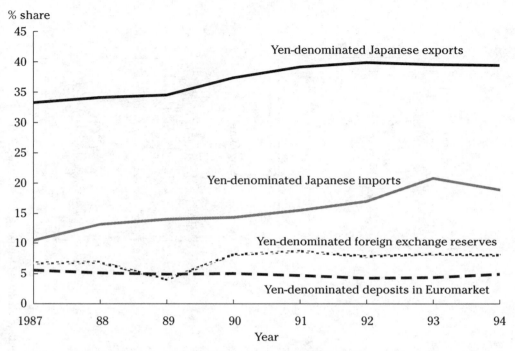

% share

Sources: Japanese Ministry of International Trade and Industry, International Monetary Fund, and Bank for International Settlements.

Malaysia, Philippines and Thailand), local currencies have in general shown higher volatility against the yen and the Special Drawing Right (SDR), as measured by the standard deviations of the month-on-month percentage changes since 1973. Exceptions are the Singapore dollar and the Malaysian ringgit, which have exhibited higher volatility against the dollar than against the SDR.

Consistent with global trends, most of the exchange rate regimes of the Asian countries have gradually shifted from pegging to a single currency (predominantly the dollar) to more flexible arrangements since the breakdown of the Bretton Woods system in the early 1970s. According to the notification of exchange arrangements that member countries furnish to the International Monetary Fund (1994), Thailand currently peg their currencies to currency baskets; Hong Kong,[3] Indonesia, Malaysia, South Korea and Singapore have exchange rate regimes characterized by managed floating; and the Philippines allows its currency to float independently. Taiwan does not notify the IMF about its exchange arrangements (as it is not a member), but if it did, the New Taiwan dollar would probably be classified as independently floating. Back in 1974, the majority of the Asian currencies (Korean won, New Taiwan dollar, Hong Kong dollar, Indonesian rupiah and Thai baht) were pegged to the dollar, and only Malaysia, Singapore and the Philippines

FIGURE 16.2 Volatility of the Asian currencies

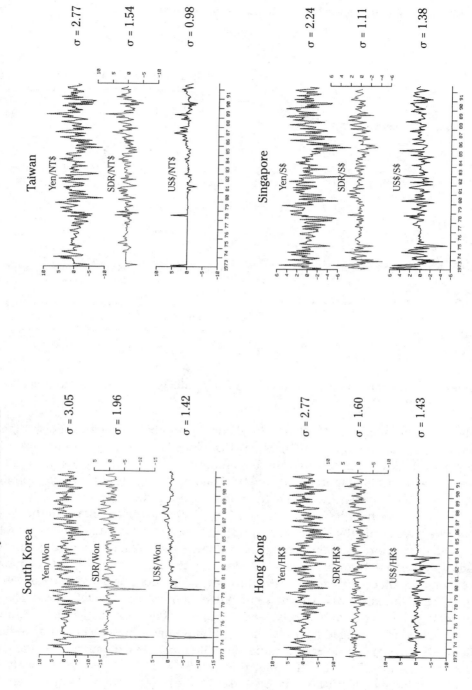

σ denotes standard deviation of month-on-month percentage changes (January 1973 to June 1992).

FIGURE 16.2 (continued)

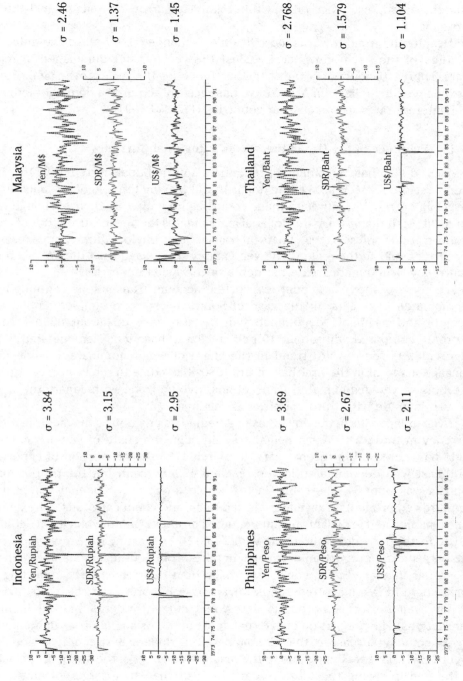

σ denotes standard deviation of month-on-month percentage changes (January 1973 to June 1992).

did not maintain exchange rates within relatively narrow margins against the U.S. currency.

Despite the trend towards more flexible exchange rates against the dollar, the volatility of the Asian currencies against the yen has not diminished in recent years. This casts doubt over the claim that, reflecting the yen's growing importance in exchange rate policies in Asia, Tokyo has recently acquired a dominant influence over interest rates in some Asian countries (Frankel 1991a).

16.2.2 Evidence of the Use of the Yen as a Regional Currency

The U.S. dollar has remained the dominant international currency in the Asia-Pacific region. As seen above, the dollar is still playing the role of an "anchor" for the Asian currencies, although these countries no longer fix their exchange rates against it. At the same time, the dollar also dominates the yen in current transactions (trade in goods and services), financial transactions and foreign exchange reserves of central banks in the region. The yen is more often used than the dollar only as a currency denominating external debts of the Asian countries.

The bulk of the Asian countries' current account transactions continue to be denominated in dollars. In the case of South Korea, for example, visible trade receipts and payments denominated in dollars make up about 80 percent of the total, compared with about 10 percent for transactions denominated in yen (Figure 16.3). The upward trend in the share of yen-denominated visible trade transactions seen in the first half of the 1980s has come to a halt in recent years. The bulk of yen-denominated transactions involve trade with Japan; the use of the yen in trade with third countries is minimal.

Even in Japan itself, the dollar has maintained its position as the major invoicing currency in trade with Asian neighbors, although the share of yen-denominated trade has increased in recent years. In March 1995 the proportion of exports to Southeast Asia denominated in yen reached 47.2 percent, but the proportion of imports was only 34.1 percent. On the whole, there is a tendency for trade in standardized products (raw materials and fuels, and chemical goods, for example) to be denominated in dollars and differentiated products (motor vehicles, machinery, and so forth) to be denominated in yen (Table 16.1). Starting from a very low base of 2 percent, the proportion of Japan's imports from Southeast Asia denominated in yen has increased at a much faster pace than that for exports, reflecting the rising share of manufactured goods in Japanese imports from these countries.

The yen performs better as a regional currency denominating financial transactions. The proportion of external debts of the Asian countries denominated in yen actually surpassed that denominated in dollars between 1987 and 1992 (Figure 16.4). This was due more to the revaluation effect of the sharp appreciation of the yen following the Plaza Accord in 1985 than to a larger proportion of borrowing from Japan.

The proportion of the yen in the foreign exchange holdings of the Asian countries

FIGURE 16.3   Korea's current account transactions by settlement currency

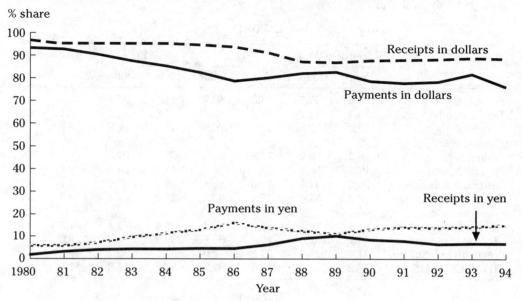

Source: Bank of Korea, *Economic Statistics Yearbook.*

FIGURE 16.4   Currency composition of long-term debt (East Asia and the Pacific)

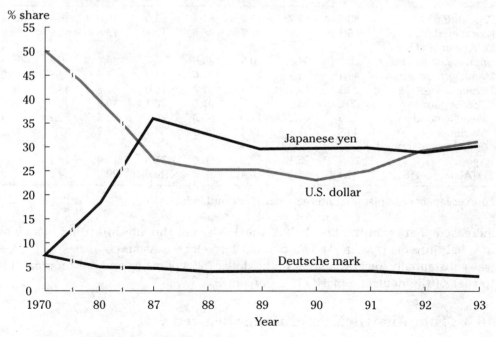

Sources: World Bank, *World Debt Tables.*

TABLE 16.1   Currency denomination of Japanese trade by region and commodity (March 1995) (% share)

EXPORTS

	Southeast Asia		U.S.		EU		All regions	
	Yen	Dollar	Yen	Dollar	Yen	Dollar	Yen	Dollar
Foodstuffs	63.8	35.7	13.8	86.2	46.1	33.1	50.7	45.9
Textile goods	26.3	72.7	17.3	82.7	50.8	11.3	32.1	62.8
Chemical goods	19.2	79.3	29.5	70.5	44.1	16.5	26.0	66.1
Nonmetallic								
mineral products	28.9	68.2	14.9	84.6	53.1	7.0	29.7	64.7
Metallic goods	17.9	80.9	23.2	76.8	43.3	24.0	19.8	77.2
General machinery	66.8	31.6	19.0	80.8	35.9	21.1	45.7	45.0
Electrical machinery	37.0	57.6	17.2	82.5	37.0	7.4	32.0	55.8
Transportation								
machinery	71.5	26.2	12.1	87.8	36.4	2.4	41.5	45.9
Motor vehicles	66.1	22.8	10.4	89.6	30.9	0.4	28.5	53.7
Precision machinery	71.6	25.4	27.8	72.0	37.5	2.2	46.0	35.9
TOTAL EXPORTS	47.2	49.9	17.5	82.3	37.2	11.3	37.6	51.5

IMPORTS

	Southeast Asia		U.S.		EU		All regions	
	Yen	Dollar	Yen	Dollar	Yen	Dollar	Yen	Dollar
Foodstuffs	33.7	65.7	17.9	81.4	53.9	16.9	26.5	69.1
Raw materials	6.1	93.4	1.7	98.3	13.3	72.6	5.2	92.0
Petroleum and								
petroleum products	0.2	99.8	0.5	94.5	–	96.4	0.2	99.6
Manufactured goods	44.1	53.4	22.3	77.0	41.3	15.9	33.8	56.2
Chemical goods	23.1	73.1	37.9	61.0	70.0	11.6	43.2	46.5
Textile goods	60.6	38.9	7.7	91.8	36.1	10.9	40.0	55.5
Metallic goods	51.9	47.2	11.0	88.9	26.9	52.6	22.1	75.4
Machinery	44.8	51.8	22.4	76.9	34.7	11.9	37.7	49.3
Other manufactured								
goods	20.7	75.1	13.0	86.6	31.6	16.4	19.7	66.3
TOTAL IMPORTS	34.1	64.2	18.4	80.9	40.6	20.2	24.3	68.9

Source: Japanese Ministry of International Trade and Industry.

increased sharply in the first half of the 1980s, but this upward trend has come to a halt in recent years. At 17.5 percent for selected Asian countries in 1989, it was substantially lower than that of the dollar (56.4 percent) and only comparable to that of the deutsche mark (15.2 percent).[4]

16.3   Four Analytical Approaches to a Yen Bloc

A yen bloc can be studied from four alternative (and complementary) approaches—

"the internationalization of the yen," "the yen as an international currency," "optimum currency areas," and "optimal pegs for developing countries"—which offer, respectively, Japanese, global, regional and Asian perspectives. The first two approaches place more emphasis on the "yen" aspect, while the latter two focus on the "bloc" aspect of the issue.

16.3.1 Internationalization of the Yen

The literature along the lines of "the internationalization of the yen (*En no Kokusaika*)" can be extended to offer a *Japanese perspective* on the yen bloc. The focus is on the advantages and disadvantages for Japan of increasing the use of the yen as an international currency and its implications for domestic economic policy, including whether the internationalization of the yen should be promoted.

Until the early 1980s, the Japanese authorities were reluctant to internationalize the yen for fear that: (a) larger fluctuations in demand for the currency would destabilize the Japanese economy and make it difficult to conduct monetary policy; and (b) an increase in average demand for the currency would cause it to appreciate and hurt exports (Suzuki 1989: Ch. 4).

With Japan emerging as the world's largest creditor country in the second half of the 1980s, however, the Japanese authorities have changed their attitude. Since almost all of Japan's foreign assets are denominated in US dollars and therefore subject to the risk of exchange rate fluctuations, it would be desirable for Japan to increase its proportion of yen-denominated assets. At the same time, the internationalization of the yen would help promote Tokyo as an international financial center, bringing more business for Japan's banks and other financial institutions. In an attempt to enhance the attractiveness of yen holdings by nonresidents, the authorities have speeded up the development of the Tokyo money market.

Studies along the lines of the internationalization of the yen have so far been formulated in the form of Japan versus the world. Indeed, in the *Annual Report of the International Finance Bureau* (Ministry of Finance 1994), the standard reference for the subject, there is no mention of the Asian countries at all. To be a useful tool for analyzing the yen bloc, the advantages and disadvantages for Japan of forming a monetary union with its Asian neighbors need to be explicitly considered.

16.3.2 The Yen as an International Currency

Studies along the lines of "the yen as an international currency" can be extended to offer a *global perspective* of the issue. As a starting point, the conditions for an international currency and the extent to which the Japanese yen meets these conditions need to be examined. Comparisons are usually made between the roles of the yen and other major key currencies (the dollar and the Deutsche mark in particular) as international currencies.

As summarized in Tavlas and Ozeki (1992) and Frankel (1991b), the principal conditions for an international currency are: (a) a relatively low inflation rate in the issuing country, which contributes to a stable external value of the currency; and (b) deep, open and broad financial markets. Supplementary conditions include a country's share of world exports, the share of its exports comprising differentiated manufactured goods, and the extent of its trade with developing countries. These factors generally imply a growing role for the yen as an international currency.

When applied to a yen bloc, the analysis has been more descriptive than analytical. The focus has been on the use of the yen in the invoicing of trade in the Asia-Pacific region, denominating regional capital flows, and assessing the reserve holdings of the central banks of Asian countries. However, insufficient attention has been paid to the possibility of the yen becoming a currency to which the Asian currencies can be pegged. At the same time, the implications of increasing the use of the yen as an international currency for the international monetary system deserve further study.

16.3.3 Optimum Currency Areas

The theory of optimum currency areas, by studying which areas or countries should adopt (genuinely) fixed exchange rates among themselves, while allowing flexible rates in relation to the rest of the world, can provide a *regional perspective* (and a more direct approach) to a yen bloc. The traditional approach to the theory of optimum currency areas tries to single out a crucial economic characteristic which supposedly indicates where the lines between different blocs should be drawn. The principal criteria determining the domain of an optimum currency area cited in the literature include the extent of factor mobility, the openness of the economies in question, product diversification, the degree of financial integration, similarity in rates of inflation, and the degree of policy integration.[5] A number of studies have attempted to determine the preconditions for a yen bloc by asking whether Asia is an optimum currency area.[6]

Drawing from the European experience, Holloway (1990) identifies a common tariff wall, the free movement of goods, services, labor and capital within a common market, and rough parity among members in their level of economic development as the major preconditions for the formation of a monetary union. Since these preconditions are not currently met in Asia, he concludes that the formation of a yen bloc is unrealistic at this stage. Suzuki (1989: Ch. 4), however, views growing trade between Japan and the Asian countries (intra-industry trade in manufactured goods in particular) as a factor favorable to increasing the use of the yen as an international currency in Asia.

Park and Park (1990) are skeptical about the formation of a yen bloc between Japan and the Asian countries. Unfavorable factors cited include: (a) the still high dependence of the Asian countries on the U.S. market; (b) Japan's limited capacity and willingness to absorb Asian imports; (c) the lead in Japanese technology and the high Japanese savings rate that necessitate frequent devaluations of the Asian currencies against the yen to prevent deterioration in their current accounts; (d) the unwillingness of the Asian countries to lose monetary autonomy and to tolerate a worsening of the inflation–unemployment trade-off; (e) the unlikeliness that a monetary union centering on the yen could narrow inflation differentials among members; and (f) the concern among Asian countries that monetary union could pave the way for political union.

The focus of the theory of optimum currency areas has been limited to relations within a given area. When applied to a situation of fluctuating exchange rates among different currency areas, more attention needs to be paid to the relations with the rest of the world.

16.3.4 Optimal Pegs for Developing Countries

The literature on optimal pegs for developing countries (or small open economies) tries to evaluate the costs and benefits of pegging to some currency or basket of currencies (or participation in a monetary union) from the point of view of the self-interest of the particular region or country.[7] It can provide an *Asian perspective* on the yen bloc if we use the developing countries to refer to the Asian countries, and the currency union uses the yen as the common currency.

A number of criteria have been considered relevant in the economic literature when a developing country decides to which currency or basket of currencies it wishes to peg its local currency. As summarized in Table 16.2, choosing a peg usually aims at minimizing the volatility in one or more of the major macroeconomic variables—output, current account, and inflation, for example—imposed by movements between third currencies. Different rules have been recommended, but usually they involve pegging to a basket of currencies, whose weights depend on the policy objective(s) as well as the economic structure of the country under consideration.

In this chapter, the literature on the optimal pegs for developing countries will serve as the starting point for our analysis of a yen bloc from an Asian perspective.

16.4 Exchange Rate Fluctuations and Short-Term Economic Growth

In this section we examine the relations between exchange rate changes and output fluctuations with a simple economic model. In addition to the exchange rate against the dollar, the yen–dollar rate (and oil prices) will be emphasized. Specific attention will be paid to Japan's dual role as the major competitor and supplier of imports for the Asian countries. Our model is then tested using Korean data.

TABLE 16.2   Aims of exchange rate policy and recommended pegs suggested in the literature

Author(s)	Suggested aim	Recommended peg
Black (1976)	Minimize variance of relative price of traded goods	Basket with weights based on direction of total trade in goods and services (or elasticity weights for country with market power), provided the benefits of pegging to a basket outweigh the costs of inability to intervene in the unit providing the peg
Crokett & Nsouli (1977)	Stabilize balance of trade and output, by stabilizing EER	Peg to import-weighted basket, with consideration as to whether the SDR is a good proxy
Flanders & Helpman (1979)	(a) Minimize variance of the balance of trade subject to a requirement on its expected level, by stabilizing the EER with MERM-type weights	Peg to an elasticity-weighted basket. (Special case with price-inelastic imports and perfectly elastic export demand: export-weighted basket)
	(b) Minimize variance of real income subject to a requirement on its expected level	Peg to a basket with large weights for competitors and small or even negative weights for suppliers
Lipschitz (1979)	Minimize variations in resource allocation and income distribution, by stabilizing REER	Peg to a basket, with weights based on currency of denomination of total trade when the export and import-competing sectors are of similar size
Bacha (1981)	Stabilize REER	(Consider pegging to a basket)
Lipschitz & Sundararajan (1980)	Stabilize REER	Peg to elasticity-weighted basket modified by covariance between inflation and depreciation. (Special case with PPP among trading partners: peg to single currency with preferred inflation rate)
Branson and Katseli-Papaefstratiou (1980)	Stabilize the terms of trade	Peg to basket with weights reflecting market power in export and import markets
Connolly (1982)	Minimize the level and variability of inflation	Peg to the US dollar, or perhaps to the SDR or a trade-weighted basket

Source: Williamson (1982).

16.4.1 Theoretical Analysis

The model that follows takes into account the impact of changes in the exchange rate of the domestic currency on output (Figure 16.5). Here, the nominal wage rate is taken to be sticky in the short run (the Keynesian assumption) instead of moving flexibly to clear the labor market (the classical assumption). In addition to the terms of trade, changes in the real wage rate resulting from movements in export prices provide an additional channel through which fluctuations in the exchange rates of third currencies affect national output. Output stabilization can be achieved by manipulating the exchange rate of the domestic currency, which affects output through its impact on the real wage rate.

Economic growth in the ANIEs tends to rise as the yen appreciates and decline as the yen depreciates, reflecting the fact that Japan is more a competitor than a supplier of imports for them. A stronger yen, for example, tends to raise their export prices more than import prices. The resulting improvement in their terms of trade boosts output. Given the nominal wage rate, this output expansion effect is reinforced by the decline in the real wage rate accompanying the increase in export prices.

In contrast, an appreciation of the yen tends to depress the ASEAN countries' terms of trade, reflecting the fact that Japan is more a supplier than a competitor for them. Assuming that the nominal wage rate is rigid in the short run, an increase in export prices (output prices) resulting from the yen's appreciation also boosts output by reducing the real wage rate. This effect is expected to be smaller for the ASEAN countries than for the ANIEs, whose export prices are more sensitive to changes in the yen–dollar rate.

Put together, an appreciation of the yen tends to raise output in the ANIEs by improving their terms of trade and reducing their real wage rates. In contrast, it tends to reduce output in the ASEAN countries, as the negative effect on output of a deterioration in the terms of trade is likely to more than offset the positive effect of a decline in real wage rates.

In addition to the yen–dollar rate, oil prices are a major determinant of short-term output fluctuations in the Asian countries. An increase in oil prices, which is analogous to an appreciation of the currency of OPEC, boosts output in the oil-exporting countries by improving their terms of trade (and depressing their real wage rates), and depresses output in the oil-importing countries by reducing their terms of trade.

The exchange rate of the domestic currency against the dollar can be considered a policy variable at the government's disposal. Changes in the exchange rate of the domestic currency against the dollar affect output through their impact on the real wage rate. Given the nominal wage rate, a devaluation of the local currency raises output prices in local currency terms and reduces the real wage rate, which in turn boosts output. In contrast to changes in foreign exchange rates (such as the yen–dollar rate), the impact of changes in the exchange rate of the domestic

FIGURE 16.5 Structure of the model

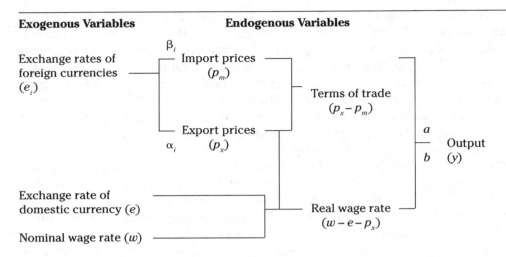

Note: All variables are expressed in natural log form. All exchange rates are measured in terms of domestic currencies per dollar. Import and export prices are measured in terms of the dollar, and the nominal wage rate is measured in terms of the domestic currency. The parameters a and b measure the elasticity of output with respect to the terms of trade and to the real wage rate, respectively, while α_i and β_i measure the elasticity of export prices and import prices with respect to the exchange rate of foreign currency i.

In mathematical terms, the model can be summarized as follows:

$$y = a\,(p_x - p_m) - b\,(w - e - p_x) \tag{1}$$

$$p_x = - \sum_{i=1}^{n} \alpha_i\, e_i \tag{2}$$

$$p_m = - \sum_{i=1}^{n} \beta_i\, e_i \tag{3}$$

with $a > 0$, $b > 0$, and $\alpha_i > 0$, $\beta_i > 0$ for all i. The exchange rate of the dollar (the numeraire) against itself is 0 in log form (that is, when the United States is taken as country n, $e_n = 0$). By the small-country assumption, $\Sigma\alpha_i = 1$ and $\Sigma\beta_i = 1$ (where i includes the United States). Output y can be obtained as a function of the exogenous variables by substituting (2) and (3) into (1) and rearranging. That is,

$$y = - \sum_{i=1}^{n} e_i\,[a(\alpha_i - \beta_i) + b\,\alpha_i] + be - bw \tag{4}$$

currency on output through the terms of trade is negligible in the Asian countries, because they are too small to have price-setting power in international markets (the small-country assumption).

16.4.2 Empirical Evidence

Our model can now be tested using data from South Korea. For simplification, among the foreign exchange rates, we shall limit ourselves to the yen–dollar rate and oil prices, which have the largest impact on the Korean economy. The results, as summarized in Table 16.3, support our formulation of the relations between exchange rate and output fluctuations in the Korean economy. The following points are worth noting.

First, Korean output (as measured by industrial production) tends to be more sensitive to changes in the terms of trade than changes in the real wage rate, rising by 1.071 percent with a 1 percent improvement in the terms of trade and only 0.399 percent with a 1 percent decrease in the real wage rate.

Second, an appreciation of the yen against the dollar tends to raise both Korean export prices and import prices, with the impact on the former being larger than on the latter. A 1 per cent appreciation of the yen raises export prices

TABLE 16.3   Results of estimation

Dependent variables	Time	Terms of trade	Real wage rate	¥/$ rate	Oil prices	$\bar{R}^2$	D.W.
			Independent variables				
Industrial production	0.029 (52.47)	–	–	–	–	0.985	0.390
Industrial production	0.030 (20.68)	1.071 (5.25)	–0.399 (–5.10)	–	–	0.989	0.761
Industrial production	0.025 (34.48)	–	–	–0.220 (–6.28)	–0.141 (–2.81)	0.993	1.064
Export prices	0.003 (3.88)	–	–	–0.394 (–10.54)	0.322 (6.07)	0.936	0.730
Import prices	–0.002 (–2.92)	–	–	–0.261 (–6.43)	0.416 (7.16)	0.754	0.945
Terms of trade	0.005 (8.03)	–	–	–0.133 (–4.07)	–0.094 (–2.01)	0.926	1.377

Sample period: 1980 Quarter 1 to 1990 Quarter 4. Figures for industrial production are seasonally adjusted.
Figures in ( ) denote t-values and D.W. denotes Durbin-Watson statistic.
Except for time trend, all variables are in log form so that the coefficients correspond to elasticities.
Shiller lags of appropriate length used in estimation and figures show cumulative effect.

by 0.394 percent and import prices by 0.261 percent, boosting the terms of trade by 0.133 percent. This reflects the fact that Japan is more of a competitor than a supplier for Korea.

Third, an increase in oil prices tends to raise Korean import prices more than export prices, so that the terms of trade deteriorate as a result. This reflects the fact that South Korea is a net importer of oil.

16.5   Output Stabilization and the Optimal Peg

Based on the analysis in Section 16.4, in this section we examine the role of exchange rate policy in output stabilization and derive the optimal peg for an Asian country seeking to minimize output fluctuations that result from changes in exchange rates and oil prices.

16.5.1   The Role of Exchange Rate Policy in Output Stabilization

Asian governments can offset changes in output resulting from fluctuations in third currencies such as the yen–dollar rate and oil prices (the exchange rate of the Organization of Petroleum Exporting Countries (OPEC)) by manipulating the exchange rates of their local currencies. This can be illustrated by considering an appreciation of the yen. In the ANIEs, an increase in output resulting from a stronger yen can be offset by revaluing the local currency, which reduces output through raising the real wage rate. In contrast, in the ASEAN countries, a decrease in output resulting from an appreciation of the yen can be offset by devaluing the local currency.

The direction and magnitude of the exchange rate adjustment needed to achieve output stability in the face of a changing yen–dollar rate depends on the following four parameters: (1) the responsiveness (elasticity) of output to changes in the terms of trade (a); (2) the responsiveness (elasticity) of output to changes in the real wage rate (b); (3) the responsiveness (elasticity) of export prices to changes in the yen–dollar rate (α); and (4) the responsiveness (elasticity) of import prices to changes in the yen–dollar rate (β).

These four parameters summarize the economic structures of the host country relevant to the formulation of exchange rate policy. The value of α reflects more the degree of competitiveness between the exports of the host country and Japan than Japan's share of the host country's exports, as will be emphasized later in this chapter. On the other hand, the value of β comes closer to Japan's share of the host country's imports. This asymmetry reflects the fact that international prices are largely determined by the exchange rates of the exporting countries rather than those of the importing countries, since countries usually have more monopoly power on the export side than on the import side in international trade.

The impact of fluctuations in oil prices on output can also be offset by manipulating the exchange rate of the local currency. As seen above, an increase in oil prices boosts output in the oil-exporting countries but reduces that in oil-importing countries through its impact on the terms of trade. To stabilize output, an oil-importing country should devalue its local currency to stimulate production as oil prices increase, while an oil-exporting country should revalue its local currency to suppress production. The direction and magnitude of the exchange rate adjustment needed to achieve output stability in the face of changing oil prices will again depend on the four parameters just cited, with α and β interpreted, respectively, as the responsiveness of export and import prices in the host country to changes in oil prices.

16.5.2 Choosing the Optimal Peg

Pegging to a basket of currencies provides an automatic way for the Asian countries to stabilize output fluctuations arising from changes in third country exchange rates, such as the yen–dollar rate. In a multi-currency framework, the weight of a foreign currency in the "optimal basket" can be derived as follows.

The weight θ_i of currency i in the optimal basket that stabilizes output depends on: (1) the elasticity of output with respect to currency i's exchange rate (against the dollar), and (2) the elasticity of output with respect to the domestic exchange rate. In what follows, currency i refers to the yen, so that θ_i denotes the weight of the yen in the optimal basket for the host country.

The elasticity of output with respect to the yen–dollar rate in turn can be calculated as the sum of (1) the product of the elasticity of the terms of trade with respect to the yen–dollar rate ($\alpha_i - \beta_i$) and the elasticity of output with respect to the terms of trade a, and (2) the product of the elasticity of export prices (and thus the real wage rate) with respect to the yen–dollar rate α_i and the elasticity of output with respect to the real wage rate b.

On the other hand, the elasticity of output with respect to the domestic exchange rate is equal to the elasticity of output with respect to the real wage rate b.

The optimal weight of currency i (the yen in the present case) in the currency basket is given by the elasticity of output with respect to currency i's exchange rate $a(\alpha_i - \beta_i) + b\alpha_i$ divided by the elasticity of output with respect to the domestic exchange rate b. That is,

$$\theta_i = \frac{a(\alpha_i - \beta_i) + b\alpha_i}{b}$$

A country whose terms of trade benefit from an appreciation of the yen (with $\alpha_i - \beta_i > 0$), as in the case of South Korea, should include a substantial weight for the yen in its basket. In extreme cases, the yen may have a weight larger than 100 percent.

On the other hand, in a developing country that depends on Japan heavily for imports but does not compete with it directly (with $\alpha_i - \beta_i < 0$), as in the case of Malaysia, the optimal basket may involve a negative weight for the yen. An appreciation of the yen reduces output (as the negative effect on output of the resulting deterioration in the terms of trade is not compensated for by the positive effect acting through the resulting decline in the real wage rate), and thus requires a depreciation of the domestic currency to restore output (through a reduction in the real wage rate).

When country i refers to OPEC, the above equation suggests that an oil-importing country should assign a negative weight to oil prices when considering pegging to a basket of currencies. In contrast, in oil-exporting countries, pegging to a basket of currencies that involves a large positive weight for oil prices may help stabilize output.

The Korean case can be used to illustrate how pegging to a basket can help stabilize output (Figure 16.6). Using the parameters estimated above, the optimal peg for the Korean won would be composed of: yen 75 percent ($\alpha = 0.394$, $\beta = 0.261$, $a = 1.071$, $b = 0.399$), oil – 8 percent ($\alpha = 0.322$, $\beta = 0.416$, $a = 1.071$, $b = 0.399$), and dollar 33 percent (100 percent – 75 percent + 8 percent). When the yen appreciates by 1 percent against the dollar, for example, Korea's export and import prices rise by 0.394 percent and 0.261 percent respectively, so that the terms of trade improve by 0.133 percent. At the same time, given the nominal wage rate and the won rate

FIGURE 16.6   The output stabilizing effect of pegging to a basket of currencies (when the yen appreciates by 1%)

Change in Korean output (%)

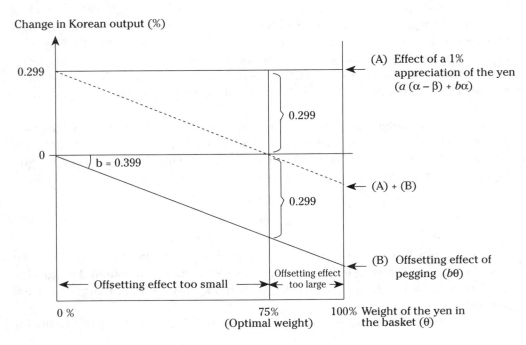

against the dollar, the real wage rate drops by 0.394 percent. As a result, output rises by 0.299 percent (0.133 percent × 1.071 = 0.142 percent through an improvement in the terms of trade, plus 0.394 percent × 0.399 = 0.157 percent through a decline in the real wage rate). To reduce output by the same amount requires raising the real wage rate by 0.75 percent (0.299 percent/0.399) which can be brought about by revaluing the won against the dollar by 0.75 percent. This can be achieved automatically when the won is pegged to a basket of currencies in which the yen carries a weight of 75 percent (the optimal weight for the yen calculated above). Likewise, when the yen depreciates against the dollar by 1 percent, the negative impact on Korean output can be offset by devaluing the won by 0.75 percent. Again, this can be achieved automatically by pegging the won to a basket of currencies in which the yen carries a weight of 75 percent.

When the won is pegged to this "optimal basket" of currencies, a 10 percent appreciation of the yen against the dollar, for example, would automatically lead to a 7.5 percent appreciation of the won against the dollar; the positive effect of the 10 percent appreciation of the yen on Korean output would then be just offset by the negative effect of the 7.5 percent appreciation of the won. Assigning any other weight to the yen in the basket would imply a counterbalancing force either too small (when the weight is less than 75 percent) or too large (when the weight is more than 75 percent) to offset the initial effect.

So far we have concentrated on the policy objective of stabilizing output, but in reality other macroeconomic objectives need to be taken into consideration when deciding which policy mix to adopt. If the objective is to stabilize domestic prices, for example, the optimal peg would involve assigning a (positive) weight equal to α_i to currency i. For an oil importer, this would magnify the decline (increase) in output as oil prices increase (decrease). Since these objectives may contradict one another, the final choice involves striking an optimal trade-off between them.

16.6 An Asian Perspective on a Yen Bloc

Choosing a currency to use in international transactions can be considered conceptually as a two-stage process. The first stage involves choosing an exchange rate regime, which determines the relations of the domestic currency against foreign currencies. This decision is usually undertaken by the government, taking into consideration its policy objectives. The second stage involves the actual choice of currency (currencies) to be used by economic agents in denominating trade and financial instruments under the given exchange regime.[8] While the decision at the first stage usually involves macroeconomic objectives, that at the second stage is mainly based on microeconomic considerations involving balancing risks and returns (or costs). The advantages and disadvantages of joining a yen bloc for the Asian countries need therefore to be considered at both the macro- and micro-levels.

16.6.1 Macroeconomic Considerations

When the policy objective is to stabilize output, our analysis suggests that a country should peg its currency to a basket with large weights for competitors' currencies and small or even negative weights for major suppliers' currencies.[9] When applied to the Asian countries, the ANIEs (Korea and Taiwan in particular), which have export structures similar to that of Japan, may benefit by pegging to the yen (or by raising the weight of the yen in the reference basket of currencies when managing their exchange rates). The reverse may be true for primary commodity exporters that rely heavily on Japan for imports (the ASEAN countries, for example). Other things being equal, the ANIEs have more of an incentive than the ASEAN countries to peg their exchange rates to the yen.

The argument that the Asian countries should peg their currencies to the dollar because the U.S. is their largest export market can be challenged on two grounds. First, being the major market does not usually imply being a competitor, or an unimportant supplier, of the exporter country, so that the weight in the optimal basket of the currency of a trading partner does not need to be proportional to that country's share of the host country's exports.[10] Second, the share of Asian countries' exports to the U.S. has been declining rapidly since 1986 anyway (Figure 16.7). This trend is expected to continue in the future in view of the need for the U.S. to reduce its trade deficit, and in its place, the share of intra-regional trade among Asian countries is expected to increase.

The current rapid pace of industrialization in the Asian countries is expected to continue, and this should favor a more important role for the yen in managing their exchange rate policies. The ANIEs' commodity composition of exports will become increasingly similar to that of Japan, while the ASEAN countries' export composition will approach that of the ANIEs (Kwan 1990). As a result, the benefits—in terms of output stability—for an Asian country of pegging its currency to the yen will increase. This is especially true when other Asian countries are also pegging their currencies to the yen.

Instead of forming a yen bloc, monetary integration in the Asia-Pacific region could also be achieved by pegging exchange rates of member countries to an "Asian Currency Unit" or ACU, analogous to the ECU in the EC. The currency composition of the ECU is broadly in line with the relative economic power of the EC members, with the weight of the Deutsche mark reaching 30.1 percent (Table 16.4). If the same rule applies to the ACU, the Japanese yen should have a weight of over 50 percent.

16.6.2 Microeconomic Considerations

The volatility of the Asian currencies against the yen seems to be the major factor restraining the use of the yen as a regional currency, in contrast to the role the deutsche mark plays in the EC. Should the Asian countries shift from their current

TABLE 16.4 Relative economic size and composition of the common currency basket, 1993

| | GDP or GNP | | | Exports + Imports | | Weight in |
	($ bil.)	Share (%)	Per capita ($)	($ bil.)	Share (%)	ECU (%)
Europe						
Germany	1,712.9	27.5	21,097.4	689.0	25.6	30.1
France	1,250.6	20.1	21,686.6	411.2	15.3	19.0
Italy	991.4	15.9	17,665.7	366.6	13.6	10.2
United Kingdom	938.9	15.1	16,235.5	385.6	14.3	13.0
Spain	478.4	7.7	12,240.6	138.2	5.1	5.3
Netherlands	308.7	5.0	20,176.5	265.6	9.9	9.4
Belgium + Luxembourg	216.4	3.5	20,827.7	248.2	9.2	7.6
Denmark	135.5	2.2	26,112.9	65.4	2.4	2.5
Portugal	74.9	1.2	7,575.6	39.8	1.5	0.8
Greece	73.7	1.2	7,108.4	32.7	1.2	0.8
Ireland	45.8	0.7	12,865.2	50.0	1.9	1.1
ECU total	6,227.2	100.0	17,967.4	2,692.3	100.0	100.0
Asia						
Japan	4,215.5	71.7	33,813.3	603.9	31.3	–
NIEs	726.6	12.4	9,830.2	859.0	44.5	–
Korea	332.8	5.7	7,554.0	166.0	8.6	–
Taiwan	222.6	3.8	10,565.0	161.8	8.4	–
Hong Kong	116.1	2.0	19,618.0	274.1	14.2	–
Singapore	55.1	0.9	19,194.0	257.1	13.3	–
ASEAN	388.8	6.6	1,168.6	269.9	14.0	–
Indonesia	144.7	2.5	765.0	65.2	3.4	–
Malaysia	64.4	1.1	3,347.0	92.7	4.8	–
Philippines	54.4	0.9	828.0	28.8	1.5	–
Thailand	125.2	2.1	2,138.0	83.2	4.3	–
China	544.6	9.3	462.0	195.7	10.1	–
Japan + NIEs + ASEAN + China	5,875.5	100.0	3,435.9	1,928.5	100.0	–

The weight of each currency in the ECU is determined by its physical amount in the ECU basket (composition) and current exchange rates. Figures in the table show the weights on September 21, 1989, after the latest recomposition of the basket.

Sources: Compiled by NRI based on: IMF, *International Financial Statistics*; OECD, *Main Economic Indicators*; and official statistics from individual countries.

FIGURE 16.7   Growing importance of intra-regional trade

Share of total exports, %

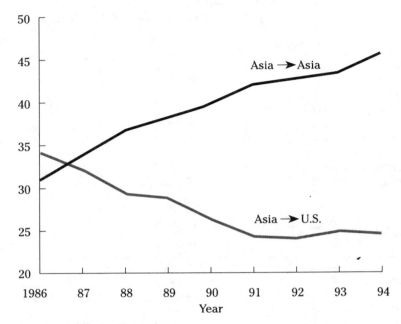

Asia = Japan + China + NIEs + ASEAN

Source: IMF, Direction of Trade Statistics, and Taiwan Trade.

exchange rate regimes of pegging loosely to the dollar to pegging to the yen (or raising substantially the weight of the yen in their current currency baskets), the cost–benefit analysis at the macroeconomic level may favor more extensive use of the yen as a regional currency (other things, as discussed in Section 16.2, being equal). More Asian importers and exporters would then prefer invoicing in the yen instead of the dollar; and borrowers and investors, including governments and central banks, would be more willing to hold a larger proportion of their portfolios in yen-denominated financial instruments.

By lowering the risk associated with exchange-rate fluctuations, pegging to the yen may also benefit the Asia-Pacific countries by expanding their trade with, and capital inflows (foreign direct investment in particular) from, Japan. This has become all the more important now that Japan has replaced the U.S. as the largest investor in Asia, and the U.S. alone can no longer play the role of locomotive for the Asian countries.

Notes

This chapter is largely based on Kwan (1992).

1. Our definition of the yen bloc comes close to the narrow definition suggested by Holloway (1990: 72):

   A yen bloc can mean different things to different people. Among its various guises, however, two stand out:

   The broad definition. In this view, Japan becomes the center of gravity of the West Pacific economy by virtue of its size—it comprises two-thirds of the region's annual output—and technological lead. As the region becomes increasingly integrated, more business activity enters the gravitational pull of Japan and its corporations. Trade and investment with the rest of the world continue to grow, but at a slower rate than within the region.

   The narrower, monetary definition. The Japanese currency is used increasingly for regional trade and financial transactions, to the point where countries find it convenient to peg their currencies to the yen. The eventual result may be some form of monetary union, as is evolving in the EC, in which a common currency emerges.

   Outside academic circles, the broader definition is more commonly used. Typical examples are Maidment (1989) and Powell (1991).
2. For further details, see Tavlas and Ozeki (1991) and Ministry of Finance (1991: Ch. 3). The former also provides data for the use of the yen as a regional currency.
3. Under the current system, certificates of indebtedness (CIs), which the two note-issuing banks are required to hold as cover for the issue of Hong Kong dollar notes, are issued and redeemed by the Exchange Fund at a fixed exchange rate of HK$7.8 = US$1. The two note-issuing banks in turn extend this rate to their note transactions will all other banks in Hong Kong. In the foreign exchange market, the exchange rate of the Hong Kong dollar continues to be determined by forces of supply and demand. However, the interplay of arbitration and competition between banks ensures that the market exchange rate stays close to the official rate (Hong Kong Government Information Services 1991).
4. Figures are from Tavlas and Ozeki (1992).
5. The literature on the theory of optimum currency areas, starting from Mundell (1961), is surveyed by Ishiyama (1975) and Tower and Willett (1976).
6. For an application of the theory of optimum currency areas to monetary integration in Europe, see Eichengreen (1991).
7. For a survey of the literature on optimal pegs, see Williamson (1982). At a more general level, there is also a substantial literature that considers the optimal exchange regimes for developing countries, which usually focuses on the advantages and disadvantages of fixed versus flexible exchange rates (see Aghevli et al. 1991; Balassa 1990). There seems to be general agreement that freely floating exchanges rates are either not feasible or undesirable for most developing countries, which are characterized by limited capital markets, restrictions on capital flows and a prevalence of real shocks that need to be financed from reserves (see Black 1976; Wickham 1985).
8. This is analogous to the two-stage "world money game," with the first stage being the game of agreeing on choosing an international monetary regime and the second stage being the game of monetary interplays under given sets of rules (Hamada 1985).
9. Flanders and Helpman (1979) reach a similar conclusion when considering the policy objective of stabilizing real income (real output adjusted for changes in the terms of trade) in a model that emphasizes the demand side of the economy.

10. When calculating the effective exchange rates for the ANIEs based on competitor weights, Balassa and Williamson (1987) assign weights for the yen ranging from 39.7 percent (in the case of Hong Kong) to 66.9 percent (in the case of Singapore). The U.S. is not even included in the list of competitors.

References

Aghevli, B. B., M. S. Khan and P. J. Montiel, 1991, *Exchange Rate Policy in Developing Countries: Some Analytical Issues*, Occasional Papers, No. 78, International Monetary Fund, Washington, DC.

Bacha, E. L., 1981, "The Impact of the Float on LDCs: Latin American Experience in the 1970s," in J. Williamson (ed.), *Exchange Rate Rules*, Macmillan, London.

Balassa, B., 1990, "Exchange Rate Regimes for LDCs," in E. Claassen (ed.), *International and European Monetary Systems*, Heinemann Professional Publishing, Oxford, pp. 83–96.

Balassa, B. and J. Williamson, 1987, *Adjusting to Success: Balance of Payments Policy in the East Asian NICs*, Policy Analyses in International Economics, No. 17, Institute for International Economics, Washington, DC.

Black, S. W., 1976, *Exchange Rate Policies for Less Developed Countries in a World of Floating Rates*, Essay in International Finance, No. 119, Princeton University, Princeton, NJ.

Branson, W. H. and L. T. Katseli-Papaefstratiou, 1980, "Income Instability, Terms of Trade, and the Choice of an Exchange Rate Regime," *Journal of Development Economics*, 7 (March): 49–69.

Connolly, M., 1982, "The Choice of an Optimum Currency Peg for a Small Open Country," *Journal of International Money and Finance*, 1 (August): 153–64.

Crokett, A. D. and S. M. Nsouli, 1977, "Exchange Rate Policies for Developing Countries," *Journal of Development Studies*, 13 (January): 125–43.

Eichengreen, B., 1991, *Is Europe an Optimum Currency Area?* National Bureau of Economic Research Working Papers, No. 3579.

Flanders, M. J. and E. Helpman, 1979, "An Optimal Exchange Rate Peg in a World of General Floating," *Review of Economic Studies*, 46 (July): 533–42.

Frankel, J. A., 1991a, "Is a Yen Bloc Forming in Pacific Asia?" in *Finance and the International Economy*, Vol. 5: *The AMEX Bank Review Prize Essays*, R. O'Brien (ed.), Oxford University Press, Oxford, pp. 4–20.

———, 1991b, *On the Dollar and the Yen*, Pacific Basin Working Paper Series, No. PB 91-04, Center for Pacific Basin Monetary and Economic Studies, Federal Reserve Bank of San Francisco.

Hamada, K., 1985, *The Political Economy of International Monetary Interdependence*, MIT Press, Cambridge, MA.

Holloway, N., 1990, "Building a Yen Bloc," *Far Eastern Economic Review*, October 11, 72–73.

Hong Kong Government Information Services, 1991, *Hong Kong 1991—A Review of 1990*.

International Monetary Fund, 1994, *Exchange Arrangements and Exchange Restrictions*, Annual Report, Washington, DC.

Ishiyama, Y., 1975, "The Theory of Optimum Currency Areas: A Survey," *IMF Staff Papers*, 22 (July): 344–83.

Kwan, C. H., 1990, "The Emerging Pattern of Trade and Interdependence in the Pacific Region," *Tokyo Club Papers*, Tokyo Club Foundation for Global Studies, Tokyo, No. 4, Pt. 2: 122–55.

———, 1991, "The Impact of Exchange-Rate Realignment on the Asian Economies—An Expanded Analysis," *Asian Club Papers*, Tokyo Club Foundation for Global Studies, Tokyo, No. 2, May: 159–86.

———— 1992, "An Optimal Peg for the Asian Currencies and the Implications for a Yen Bloc," *Asia Club Papers*, Tokyo Club Foundation for Global Studies, Tokyo, No. 3, May: 202–28.

Lipschitz, L., 1979, "Exchange Rate Policies for a Small Developing Country, and the Selection of an Appropriate Standard," *IMF Staff Papers*, 26 (September): 423–49.

Lipschitz, L. and V. Sundararajan, 1980, "An Optimal Exchange Rate Peg in a World of Generalized Floating," *IMF Staff Papers*, 27 (March): 80–100.

Maidment, P., 1989, "The Yen Block—A New Balance in Asia," *The Economist*, July 15, Survey, 1–20.

Ministry of Finance, 1994, *Annual Report of the International Finance Bureau*, Tokyo (in Japanese).

Mundell, R., 1961, "A Theory of Optimum Currency Areas," *American Economic Review*, 51 (September): 657–65.

Park, Y. C. and W. A. Park, 1990, *Exchange Rate Policy for the East Asian NICs*, Korea Development Institute Working Paper, No. 9010.

Powell, B., 1991, "The Yen Bloc—Sayonara, America," *Newsweek*, August 5, 16–17.

Suzuki, Y., 1989, *Japan's Economic Performance and International Role*, Tokyo University Press, Tokyo.

Tavlas, G. S. and Y. Ozeki, 1992, *The Japanese Yen as an International Currency*, Occasional Paper No. 90, International Monetary Fund, Washington, DC.

Tower, E. and T. D. Willett, 1976, *The Theory of Optimum Currency Areas and Exchange Rate Flexibility*, Princeton Special Papers in International Finance, No. 11, Princeton University, Princeton, NJ.

Wickham, P., 1985, "The Choice of Exchange Rate Regime in Developing Countries," *IMF Staff Papers*, 32 (June): 248–88.

Williamson, J., 1982, "A Survey of the Literature on the Optimal Peg," *Journal of Development Economics*, 11: 39–61.

Chapter 17

Michael A. Goldberg

The Development of a Network of Asia-Pacific Financial Centers

17.1   Introduction

The development of Asia-Pacific financial centers needs to be placed in its global context. It is no longer possible to treat financial center development in isolation, even in countries that have historically been isolated by geography and by restrictive and protectionist regulation. Two particular aspects of the globalization of financial markets are relevant here. First, domestic financial markets cannot be dealt with independently of world financial market forces. Second, globalization in financial services has been accompanied by a dramatic growth in the scale of domestic and international financial transactions.

   The chapter begins by examining the internationalization of financial markets. Theories and empirical evidence on the formation and characteristics of international financial centers (IFCs) are then considered as IFCs are the spatial focus of the global financial system. Attention moves next to leading Asia-Pacific IFCs. The chapter closes with a brief summary and look at where the Asia-Pacific financial centers are likely headed in future. The development of an Asia-Pacific network of international financial centers (or indeed the development of any particular financial center) needs to be placed in context. It is no longer possible to treat financial center development in isolation, even in countries that have historically been isolated by geography and by restrictive and protectionist regulation, such as Australia or Japan. Advances in telecommunication and transportation have overcome geographic isolation, while the globalization of markets, particularly financial markets, has served to reduce, and in many instances neutralize entirely, the effectiveness of narrowly conceived nationally based regulatory environments.

17.2 The Globalization of the Financial Marketplace

One of the early forces globalizing capital markets dates from the 1950s when the Soviet Union held its US dollar balances outside the U.S. to avoid possible seizure of these assets (Levi 1989: 263). This was a progenitor of the Euromarket, and the Eurocurrency market was the foundation on which international banking was subsequently built. From about US$110 billion in 1970, the Eurocurrency market is now estimated to exceed US$2.5 trillion. Trade imbalances have also been important contributors to the growth in international lending and Eurocurrency activity. The most cited example is "petro-dollars" which were recycled first through the Eurodollar market, and later through offshore banking centres like Bahrain.

Another major cause of the internationalization of financial markets is, in part, the breakdown of the Bretton Woods agreement with the move to floating exchange rates after 1971. Floating exchange rates increased foreign exchange risks leading to a proliferation of financial instruments (for example, currency futures and options) as hedges. By 1990 foreign exchange transactions were estimated at US$640 billion per day (*Hong Kong Trader* 1990).

Internationalization of finance would have been impossible without the use of advanced technology, particularly in telecommunications and computers (Hamilton 1986). The first such improvement in 1970 was the creation of the Clearing House Interbank Payments System (CHIPS) (*The Economist* 1990). In 1987 roughly 25 million fully automated transactions were handled for 138 member banks. Average daily volumes were US$300 billion (Compton 1987). In 1972 the Society for Worldwide Interbank Financial Telecommunications (SWIFT) was formed for international payments instructions. Starting in May 1977, it carried some 800 banking transactions daily which rose to nearly one million transactions in the late 1980s (Economic Council of Canada 1989).

Telecommunications progress has enabled stock, option and commodity exchanges to link up, thereby facilitating global trading. Since 1984, the Singapore International Monetary Exchange (SIMEX) and the Chicago Mercantile Exchange (CME) have been linked to offer financial futures and options. This allows market players to take a position on one exchange and liquidate it on the other, creating a 24-hour trading day (*The Banker* 1984). Technology created the possibility of a truly global financial market, leading to a more competitive industry by permitting financial institutions to achieve economies of scale (*The Economist* 1990). Technology has fostered new financial instruments and, arguably (Kaufman 1986), greater efficiency via instantaneous global flows of information. For example, globalization has intensified the use of swaps for arbitraging:

> in 1986, 80 percent of yen-denominated bond issues, 95 percent of Australian dollar issues, and 90 percent of New Zealand dollar issues were swapped. The interest-rate and currency swap markets, which were nonexistent in 1980, are estimated to have been above C$889 billion and C$219 billion, respectively, at the end of 1987 (Economic Council of Canada 1989).

A final and key factor in financial market globalization is the deregulation and liberalization of world financial markets in the 1970s and 1980s, including low or no tax havens. Singapore, for example, emerged as an IFC in the 1970s through tax concessions it offered financial institutions in the offshore Asian dollar market (Skully and Viksnins 1987; Tan and Kapur 1986). Deregulation has led to the integration of domestic financial systems into a single global financial system, allowing no country to regulate its financial sector isolated from developments elsewhere (Hamilton 1986: 181). Deregulation has been self-propagating, forcing global harmonization of financial rules and regulations. Britain's "Big Bang" of 1986, the current round of regulatory revision in Canada, and the improved access of foreigners to Japan's capital markets all testify to this fact. So do developments in Thailand, Malaysia, South Korea and Taiwan, which are liberalizing their financial markets. Globalization will intensify as borrowers seek the cheapest sources of funding, no matter where in the world they are located, and investors take advantage of more liberal financial markets for portfolio diversification, yield enhancement and new investment opportunities.

17.3   Theories of IFC Formation and Characteristics of IFCs

Reed (1981) distinguishes between international banking centers (IBCs) and international financial centers (IFCs), a distinction we use below in our discussions of the broader IFC concept. After analyzing nearly 50 such centers over the period 1900–80, he concluded that there are well defined attributes differentiating IBCs from IFCs. Specifically, evolution as an international banking center often predates development as an international financial center. However, this is not an inviolable rule.

> A center's banking infrastructure is obviously important. However, power and influence (preeminence) is derived primarily from the center's global portfolio management activities, which usually requires that the center be successful in attracting relatively large amounts of financial liabilities. Because of the potential volatility associated with international finance ... I believe it is reasonable to conclude that the behavior of and activities of international financial centers cannot adequately be explained or predicted by analyzing international banking centers. Therefore, analyses of international financial centers that focus only on "banking" dimensions are just as inadequate as analyses that exclude banking and focus mainly on "finance" (capital flows and foreign lending) (Reed 1981: 56).

Reed then goes on to develop a five-level hierarchy to describe IFC evolution:

to serve, exclusively, the lowest strata within the nation-state hierarchy (its city, its county, and its state/canton/province, and so forth). The second phase of the process envisions the center serving a geographic area larger than its immediate environs but smaller than the nation itself. In phase three, the center becomes preeminent within the nation itself. In phase four, the center is providing financial and related services to its nation and to a number of other countries that are geographically contiguous. The fifth phase of the evolutionary process places the center at the apex of the hierarchy comprising all financial centers (Reed 1981: 57).

Reed (1981) sees IFCs as being key components in the developing global economy, functioning as communication and management centers. Of particular relevance in the present context, Reed closes his study by stressing that participants in the international economic arena (the "political economy" in Reed's words) often limit the roles of IFCs to those of "providing investment instruments and liquidity to the saver and funds to the borrower" (p. 67). However, he notes that his work suggests that IFCs go well beyond this perception of their traditional role and that the IFC is a key component in the global political economy "because it functions as a communication center and a management center" (p. 67). The ease of access to state-of-the-art telecommunications is just a part of this communication system. Of greater importance is the presence of a dense network of airline connections to other IFCs as is typified by London, Amsterdam, New York and Zurich. Additionally, access to vital management services such as accounting, law, marketing/advertising, printing, and trade are virtually essential adjuncts of both IFC status and IFC functioning, given the relatively high degree of autonomy granted to regional managers located in IFCs and their resulting need for high quality management support services (Reed 1981: 69–74).

Against this background IFC description, we need to look at explanations of IFC growth. Charles Kindleberger, who prompted a renewed interest in the growth of financial centers, has argued that banks and financial markets play an essential role in more than equating savings and investment. Kindleberger (1974) believes that banks and other financial intermediaries are also crucial vehicles for commercial payments, enabling trade and general economic activity to expand. Following Kindleberger's (1974) comparative historical study in which he provided potential explanations of the development of particular cities as financial centers, a number of authors have examined the evolution of banking and financial intermediation. Particularly close attention has been paid to the expansion of international banking because the relative importance of banking in a country is largely determined by how much international banking takes place there. The theoretical contributions to the literature on international financial centers have suggested a number of factors as being tied to the relative importance of banking and associated financial activity. In general, theory suggests that a country will exhibit more banking and financial activity:

☐ the higher its volume of international trade
☐ the greater the degree of financial intermediation

The volume of trade directly influences the activity of banks as they facilitate payments, provide letters of credit, and so on. Trade volume can be measured directly from the value of imports and exports. The degree of financial intermediation affects banks' balance sheets and is a function of such factors as the size of the balance of payments deficits/surpluses, the size of government and private debt, the scale of overall economic activity, savings levels, direct investment from overseas, and so on. Other factors influencing the relative importance of financial activity that have been identified include the degree of regulation, and the availability of telecommunication, transportation and service infrastructure.

With the pace of international financial activity expanding at an extraordinary rate, and with so much income and employment generated by this activity, it is perhaps surprising that so little attention has been paid to evaluating the factors affecting the geographical location of centers of international finance. Indeed, after noting that "it is a curious fact that the formation of financial centers is no longer studied in economics," Kindleberger (1974) hypothesized that this is due to the issue falling between two areas of investigation, urban and regional economics, which is concerned with locational matters, but which concentrates on commerce, industry, and housing rather than finance, and monetary and financial economics, which has little interest in geographical location.

Kindleberger himself made an effort to fill the gap by offering a number of potential explanations of the geographical location of centers of financial activity. However, he offered only a comparative, historical account which in his own words is "qualitative rather than quantitative," and which "derives from the limitations of the writer, the magnitude of the task of deriving comparable data from a wide number of countries, and an interest more in process than in detailed outcome."

A number of empirical studies have attempted to deal with this lack of quantitative evidence, spawned by the renewed interest in the evolution of international banking and more generally by the enormous growth in international financial transactions. However, these studies do not concentrate on identifying which of the many factors suggested by theory are particularly significant. Rather, most empirical research has focused on a particular country or aspect of international banking. An exception is Reed (1981) quoted earlier. His focus though is on the emergence of particular cities as financial centers which restricts his findings considerably, since they cannot be applied to nations as a whole. Given that much urban financial center activity is dependent upon national economic activity, Reed's work casts little light on the role of national economic variables in financial center formation and growth. Accordingly, Goldberg et al. (1989) dealt with national, regional and urban economic variables explicitly to try to overcome the weaknesses of previous work.

Their conclusions can be grouped according to their national and regional levels of analysis:

☐ *Concomitants of financial center evolution—national factors.* In these cross-national analyses surprisingly few factors consistently led the way as concomitants of financial center development. Most important were imports and exports, with imports being positively associated with financial sector development and exports being negatively associated. Foreign trade levels were vitally important in financial sector growth. It was also found that regulation matters as evidenced by reserve requirements (negatively related) and tax breaks (positively related). Finally, but of less importance, the level of national economic development as approximated by GNP/ GDP per capita mattered in several cases.

☐ *Concomitants of financial center evolution—regional factors.* At the regional level, we saw strong reinforcement for the preceding results. Specifically, once again imports are a key variable in the growth of specific urban financial centers. Additionally, regulation matters, as measured by reserve ratios. In keeping with the findings on trade and international finance, the presence of multinational firms and foreign firms is also frequently associated with financial center growth.

These studies found that they could explain the vast majority of the variation in financial activity whether measured by assets, liabilities or employment. The results suggest that any theory of the development of centers of financial activity should take into account the following variables all of which were found significant: income levels and the location of multinational corporate headquarters; the nature of the centers such as their industrial structure, and their importance within a country or time zone; and measures of international trade, separated between imports and exports. Other factors such as city age or status as a national capital do not appear to be important. More specifically, any theory which is developed must be predicated upon a positive influence of imports and a negative influence of exports as repeatedly and strongly demonstrated in all of their empirical findings.

With the previously noted explosion in international financial services, a great deal of attention has been directed to the growth of IFCs. However, relatively little work has been done at a more micro level to understand the factors that affect the location of international banks *per se*. Several studies do exist, though, and their findings are discussed briefly here. Six broad major headings, and two minor ones, span the location criteria that are most frequently mentioned.

First, agglomeration economies are very important both in theoretical work (Markusen 1986), in descriptive work (Gerakis and Roncesvalles 1983) and in empirical studies (Daniels 1986; Choi et al. 1985). Here agglomeration economies are those external to the firm (foreign banks) but internal to the industry (international banking). Choi et al. (1985: 61) note, "to the banks of another country, one good measure of a center's attractiveness is simply the number of banks already there." Kindleberger (1980: 76) also stressed that agglomeration economies help to explain the formation of international financial centers, their location in large urban centers, and their ability to attract international financial firms.

Up to a certain high degree of concentration, positive externalities and economies of scale appear to outweigh diseconomies and favor centralization. The continuous reduction in the costs and difficulties of transport and communication of the last two hundred years has favored the formation of a single world financial market (Kindleberger 1980: 76).

Closely related to the above is a different sort of agglomeration economy, one that is external to both the firm and the industry. Included in this second location factor is the availability of the whole range of producer services (legal, accounting, insurance, real estate, and management consulting) and the associated skilled and unskilled labor market that enables foreign locating banks to staff themselves appropriately. "Infrastructure" is the name given to this sort of agglomeration economy by several studies (Daniels 1986; Gerakis and Roncesvalles 1983; Reed 1981). Reed (1981) focused great attention on this factor as noted earlier. The term however is somewhat ambiguous and at odds with traditional economic usage since infrastructure usually refers to such hard services as roads, sewers, and the like.

Advanced transportation and telecommunication systems comprise the third locational criterion sought by international banks (Gerakis and Roncesvalles 1983; Reed 1981). International banks are particularly interested in ready access to a first class, widely linked international airport, and to state-of-the-art telecommunications capable of handling the most advanced sorts of voice and data transmission equipment.

A fourth factor, and one that is equal in importance to the previous three, is access to foreign bank customers who have located abroad (Daniels 1986; Fairlamb 1986). Banks need to be near their customers wherever in the world their domestic customers are located. With the burgeoning growth in world trade, banks have found it necessary to go to the markets where their domestic clients are going, to service their exports (that is, the imports to the country in which the foreign banks are seeking to locate). This result is strongly supportive of the previously noted work by Goldberg et al. (1989) where imports were found to be strongly associated with international financial activity and employment. Ball and Tschoegl (1982) place considerable importance on this factor as well, noting that: "When its customers go abroad, a bank can follow them and draw on the information about them which it already possesses quickly and at low cost. Thus, it is better able than others to respond to its customers' needs. In fact, if a bank does not follow, it gives other banks an entrée to its customers" (p. 416).

Fifth, foreign banks are also combing the world for cities and regions where they can find new international customers. Thus, cities and regions with buoyant and growing economies, particularly those with strong international trade ties, are especially sought out by foreign banks (Gerakis and Roncesvalles 1983; Choi et al. 1985).

Sixth, and last of the major location factors, is "stability." Here a number of concepts come together. Political stability in the normal sense is important (Gerakis and Roncesvalles 1983). However, and more subtly, of equal concern is the assurance that government regulation will be predictable, consistent and flexible and competitive with other jurisdictions (Fairlamb 1986; Lee 1986).

Two frequently mentioned, but less important location factors are time zone and cost. Several authors (Gerakis and Roncesvalles (1983) for Bahrain; Fairlamb (1986) for New York; and Lee (1986) for Hong Kong) note that the time zones in which each of these cities is located bestows considerable advantages. Thus, New York provides access to North American time zones, Bahrain allows bridging Asia and Europe, and Hong Kong permits easy access to all of Asia and also Europe and the west coast of North America for portions of the working day.

Finally, the cost of doing business has been mentioned in several studies: (Gerard (1985) relative to migration from New York City; and Lee (1986) concerning Chinese-owned banks in Hong Kong). Personal interviews by the author suggest costs are becoming considerably more important than in the past. Previously a minor factor in locational choice, they are likely to play a much more vital role in the future as booming international financial markets are replaced by more stable (and even declining) ones.

In the case of the international financial center (IFC) literature attention focuses on the broad category of financial and producer service firms and their location requirements or preferences. While often difficult to separate from the locational needs of banks (which are after all financial service firms too), an attempt is made below to identify the locational needs of the broader class of producer service firms, first by reviewing the existing literature, and then by summarizing the results of a loosely structured interview survey conducted by the author.

17.3.1 Reviewing the Literature

First, political stability is again extremely important for international financial and producer service activities (Gerakis and Roncesvalles 1983); Lee and Vertinsky 1988; Reed 1981). Indeed, Heenan (1979) in a survey of the locational preferences of Japanese and American multinational corporations (MNCs) found that political stability ranked third in importance out of sixteen location factors cited by American MNCs and fourth in importance by Japanese MNCs, confirming other work done by Heenan and Perlmutter (1978) more broadly on political stability as a criterion and location factor in the development of an urban center as a true international city. The Lee and Vertinsky (1988) survey of bankers in Hong Kong and Singapore showed that political stability ranked fifth in Singapore and eighth in Hong Kong (out of the twelve factors they considered), while the closely related "mature and sound legal system" ranked third in Hong Kong and eighth in Singapore, both giving additional support for the importance of political stability.

Second, financial and producer service firms prefer a "gateway" city when choosing among the major cities of a nation or multination region (Heenan and Perlmutter 1978; O'Connor and Edgington 1987). For example, in Australia O'Connor and Edgington found that in the post-1960 era of airport gateways, Sydney became the predominant international arrival point for visitors, business people, and immigrants. They observe that there are three elements associated with the gateway notion: the nature and vitality of the hinterland served by the gateway; the direction of travel; the technology of travel. In all these areas Sydney dominates explaining in part its dramatic growth in international financial and producer service activities. Heenan and Perlmutter use the analogous concept of "crossroads city" as a "city linking regional blocs with the corporate superpowers" (1978: 108–10). They note that these urban crossroads provide international executives with the best opportunities not only for easy international access, but also provide unique advantages as listening posts to assess the political economy of the linked regions. Lee and Vertinsky (1988) provide further support for the importance of this factor. They rank international transportation access fifth in importance in Hong Kong and seventh in Singapore (again out of the twelve factors they considered). Dunning and Norman (1983) point out that it is not just the linkages with the rest of the world available through the gateway airport, but the "density" of these international connections that is possessed by the international airport.

Third, the regulatory environment matters. Of concern here is not the complete freedom provided by such tax havens as the Cayman Islands. Rather, flexible and enlightened regulation is sought. The "Big Bang" in London showed the locational effects of more flexible regulation (Hamilton 1986). Indeed, Hamilton points out that much of the revolution in financial markets, particularly the trend-setting explosion in the eurodollar market, was "a reaction to regulation within the domestic financial systems of the U.S., Europe, and Japan (1986: 21)." At a strategic level, cities and regions increasingly compete using favourable and flexible regulation to enhance their international attractiveness (Bryant 1987; Lee and Vertinsky 1988; Tan and Kapur 1986). McGahey et al. (1990) stress this in noting that as financial services become more complex, and change accelerates, balanced and well-informed regulation and supervision increase in importance as does the need for a more positive and creative tax policy. Lee and Vertinsky (1988) place considerable emphasis on this point as well when explaining the successes of both Hong Kong and Singapore in attracting international financial firms and transactions.

Fourth, the availability of agglomeration economies and infrastructure in the form of related producer services (agglomeration economies) are almost always deemed to be important in the financial and producer services industries (McGahey et al. 1990, Lee and Vertinsky 1988, Reed 1981). These can occur historically as in London, New York or Tokyo, or be more actively promoted by government policy (Lee and Vertinsky 1988). Thus, McGahey et al. (1990) stress that the concentration of market players in major leading financial centers has reinforced the tendency for financial innovation to be concentrated there, giving firms in these locations a significant competitive edge. Being in innovative centers is crucial for learning quickly about new financial instruments. Moreover, without the skilled financial staff and legal and business support services available in these locations, firms cannot provide customers with the broad range of complex services required. Dunning and Norman (1983) review the international and intranational locational needs of a variety of producer services, including engineering, management consultants, advertising, accounting, legal, and banking and insurance. They observe that concentration in major cities and agglomeration economies are generally important for all the producer services studied, but are especially important in banking, insurance, accounting and legal services (Dunning and Norman 1983: 683–84). Lee and Vertinsky (1988) provide further support here as "a pool of expertise in financial services" (a proxy for agglomeration economies) ranked fifth in both Hong Kong and Singapore out of the twelve factors they used in their survey of bankers. A related aspect of agglomeration economies noted by Dunning and Norman (1983) has to do with the availability of qualified labor resources which are another central aspect of the kinds of external economies generally included under the broader heading of agglomeration economies. A final piece of evidence from Hutton and Ley should be noted here. They note that for producer service firms surveyed in Vancouver "the distribution of inputs was extremely localized in Greater Vancouver, particularly its core area" (1987: 18). This suggests again the existence of agglomeration economies arguing for the location of producer services in the urban core of the major metropolitan area in the economic region.

Fifth, advanced transportation and telecommunication systems are a must for international financial and producer service firms (Gerakis and Roncesvalles 1983). The provision of current and reliable information through face-to-face contact or via electronic media are essential to the conduct of modern financial and producer service businesses. McGahey et al. (1990) quite simply note that these transportation and telecommunications systems must be taken as absolutely essential givens if cities and regions are to attract international financial firms. Lee and Vertinsky (1988) support this strong statement in their comparative study of the assessment of bankers in Singapore and Hong Kong as to the importance of locational attributes of each city. In the views of bankers in both cities, well developed external and internal communication systems ranked first and second (in Hong Kong) and first and third (in Singapore) out of the dozen of factors considered, reinforcing the paramountcy of telecommunications links.

Sixth, and finally, faced with intense global competition, costs are a growing concern. Accordingly, locations that provide high amenities and "quality of life" to firms and their employees are of growing interest (Lee and Vertinsky 1988). In the context of the U.S., Blomquist and his colleagues (1988) actually estimated the value of the quality of life associated with 253 Standard Metropolitan Statistical Areas (SMSAs) in the U.S. in 1980. They suggest that firms locating in these areas can realize savings in the form of reduced wages and salaries from locating in high amenity regions of the U.S. Once again, in the context of New York's experience, McGahey et al. (1990) observe that apart from direct business costs, firms incur indirect costs through the problems imposed by a decline in a location's quality of life. To attract and retain the necessary professional and supporting labor force, financial centers must offer a quality of life which is both affordable and attractive, or risk losing these jobs to other centers.

17.3.2 Some Findings from Structured Interviews

Interviews were conducted in 30 major centers in Europe, Asia and North America with some 130 senior executives of a broad array of financial firms in five major sectors of the financial services industry to ascertain the locational needs of each sector. The findings, briefly, by sector were:

- ☐ *Private banking.* Not surprisingly, private bankers require first and foremost the free movement of capital and people, political stability and strong bank secrecy laws. Tax incentives and a favorable regulatory environment are also of primary importance.

- ☐ *Trade financing.* Financing international trade is closely tied to trade activity itself. It also relies heavily on its time zone, sophisticated support services including advanced telecommunication and international airport access. A favorable regulatory environment is also a plus.

- ☐ *Securities sales and underwriting.* The securities industry was the least bound by specific location criteria requiring a strategic time zone, advanced telecommunications, local liquid capital markets, and a favorable regulatory environment. It also benefited from a growing domestic market.

- ☐ *Funds management.* Fund managers need information to manage. Accordingly, they need a strategic time zone, good telecommunications and international airport access. They also need good people and a high quality living environment. Finally, a growing domestic market, a trusted local stock market, and political stability are also seen as distinct locational benefits.

- ☐ *International commercial banking.* International commercial bankers seek out strategic time zones, tax incentives and strong local capital markets. They also require up-to-date information via telecommunications and international air access. A favorable regulatory environment is also of considerable importance. Lastly, the location of their customers, the presence of a strong and growing domestic economy, political stability and ease in obtaining work permits and visas for moving expatriate staff into a new locale are influential too.

17.3.3 Global Cities and the New International Division of Labor

The micro-location issues above impact directly on the macro-aggregation of financial services in specific nodes of the network of global cities where the global economy is managed. Closely tied to global cities is the new international division of labor (NIDL). The NIDL asserts that production is increasingly being organized and managed on a global scale (Frobel et al. 1980). This new mode of production is closely tied to the emergence of the global firm which: internalizes many specific product markets; allocates capital globally to the most profitable locales; and which gathers, processes and communicates information on a global scale to perform its functions (Thrift 1983). These functions almost force global firms into global cities which in turn foster the global firm—like the link between IFCs and global corporations, most global cities are also IFCs.

Turning to the global city literature itself there are several themes of potential interest and use. First, services need to be seen as key elements in any strategy to develop an internationally competitive urban economy (Hutton and Ley 1987; Friedmann 1986). Not only are services growing very rapidly, especially producer services (Enderwick 1987) but they are also relatively free of the trade barriers that exist in the "goods" market. Moreover, given the growing role played by producer services in job creation in advanced economies, these services need to be stressed in urban and regional economic strategies.

Second, cities (and regions) will have to take an increasingly active role in developing and shaping their economic futures. (Heenan and Perlmutter 1978; Heenan 1979). This is particularly the case in gaining access to the global city network. They will need to plan carefully and draw upon a broad base of community sectors to achieve a coordinated approach to becoming a global city (Heenan 1979), where the micro details of a city's strengths and weaknesses matter enormously.

Third, global cities will be those that provide the necessary infrastructure to attract international firms. Included here is not just state-of-the-art telecommunications, but also a world class airport, high quality educational and health services, and cultural institutions (Heenan and Perlmutter 1978). Such cities need to see themselves as "an urban crossroads, a city linking regional blocs with the corporate superpowers" (Heenan and Perlmutter 1978: 108).

Other factors important for future world cities include: political stability (Heenan and Perlmutter 1978); destination points for international immigrants (Friedmann 1986); a strong healthy central business district and broadly based community commitment (Heenan and Perlmutter 1978).

17.4   Some Leading and Emerging Asia-Pacific IFCs

17.4.1 Singapore

As in most economic developments, Singapore has pursued a more interventionist and government guided approach than Hong Kong's almost classically laissez-faire approach (Hofheinz and Calder 1982). The case of international financial services and Singapore's growth as an IFC typifies these differences in approach between these two ASEAN urban economies.

From the very start in 1968, financial services were seen as a vehicle of economic growth and diversification. It was an artificial market built on a series of well crafted tax and regulatory measures, in sharp contrast to Hong Kong. The Asian Dollar Market (ADM) began in 1968 by eliminating withholding tax on foreign deposits as the initial vehicle for developing Singapore as an IFC (DBS Bank 1987). The ADM led to the creation of "Asian Currency Units"(ACUs) to lend (largely US dollars) outside Singapore at first only. In addition, preferential tax rates applied to profits earned by ACUs (a 10 percent tax rate on ACU profits). In 1978 Singapore eliminated exchange controls. Previously ACUs were exempt in any event. The Monetary Authority of Singapore (MAS) provides strong supervision and enforces strict separation of ACUs and domestic banking activities.

The success of these measures is evidenced by the more than 200 foreign banks operating in 1992 (Balakrishnan 1992) with more than US$350 billion in ACU deposits and over US$390 in total foreign deposits (Yamazawa et al. 1992). Singapore has also stimulated demand for offshore loans through tax incentives to multinationals establishing regional head offices in Singapore "operational head-quarters" (OHQs) and "international procurement offices" (IPOs). The incentive has attracted to Singapore 20 OHQs (as of September 1989) and 61 IPOs (as of June 1989) (Bando 1990) providing the needed capability in Singapore to make borrowing decisions. By 1992 Singapore's share of the US$32.77 loan market was US$6.09 or 18.6 percent up from only 12 percent in 1990 (Economist Intelligence Unit 1992).

Singapore has been aggressive in using its vast Central Provident Fund (CPF) (S$223.9 billion in assets at the end of 1985 (Glorieux and Hedderich 1990)) to lure asset managers to Singapore. Singapore has also been extremely innovative, introducing a host of new financial instruments (*Business Times* 1989). It has developed an active money and foreign exchange market, which is now second only to Tokyo in Asia (DBS Bank 1988), and has established a nonlisted stock trading system (SESDAQ) under the aegis of the Stock Exchange of Singapore (SES) linked with NASDAQ in the U.S. Similarly, the Singapore International Money Exchange (SIMEX) has been extremely actively in developing financial futures and options, and oil (in 1989), and has also established a trading link with a leading U.S. exchange, the Chicago Mercantile Exchange (CME).

17.4.2 Hong Kong

Hong Kong's development as an IFC in the past two decades has benefited greatly from: low taxes; no taxes on profits arising from income earned outside Hong Kong including financial transactions with nonresidents; no exchange controls; an enormous re-export trade requiring great use of and skill in trade finance and foreign exchange; a free money and international gold market; a time zone that splits North America and Europe; a critical location in the center of the booming Southeast Asian region; British Common law; English as its commercial language; the principal stock exchange in the region; and good infrastructure and international air access (Scott et al. 1986).

There has been no special regulatory treatment of offshore activity. Foreign financial institutions have been allowed to locate in Hong Kong, if regulated in their home market by a satisfactory regulator. Thus, a variety of licensing options exist (Ghose 1987). Compared to Singapore, in Hong Kong no separation exists between domestic and offshore markets, which are well integrated. Eliminating withholding tax on foreign deposits in 1982 greatly facilitated deposit gathering. There is much less regulation in Hong Kong—where regulatory responsibility is split among several regulators—than in Singapore. The currency in circulation is mostly bank notes issued by the Hong Kong and Shanghai Banking Corporation (roughly 80 percent) and Standard Chartered Bank (20 percent).

Hong Kong's international financial sector has developed across a number of fronts. Looking at banking, as of July 30, 1989 Hong Kong boasted 171 banks and 246 deposit-taking companies (Glorieux and Hedderich 1990). Foreign currency financial assets booked in Hong Kong equalled US$543 billion in 1990 exceeding Singapore's US$390 billion total and roughly equalling Tokyo's market (Yamazawa et al. 1992). Hong Kong has developed as a center for syndicated loans, partly due to 0 percent tax on income from offshore loans. This contrasts with Singapore's deposit gathering focus.

Economic and political stability and the return of Hong Kong in 1997 to China are also important as are periodic banking and stock market failures and losses of confidence. The 1983 banking crisis and the October 1987 crash both damaged Hong Kong's credibility and led to significant regulatory reforms in the banking system and securities markets. Accordingly, Hong Kong's future as the primary Southeast Asian regional financial center is in question. Its advantages should continue to be those outlined above that allowed it to develop its present preeminent position in the region. Its vulnerability derives from distrust of the People's Republic of China (PRC) and its treatment of Hong Kong as a capitalist island in a communist sea, and from the growing competition from Singapore.

17.4.3 Tokyo

In the 1980s Tokyo emerged as an international financial center, and also came to share a dominant role, with London and New York, in the global financial system. Tokyo's global financial clout is so new, that it is hard to recall that at the start of the 1980s, the Japanese financial system, dominated by Tokyo, was insulated from the outside world. Until 1985 both long and short interest rates were administered (Suzuki 1987). This changed with the birth of money market certificates in March 1985 and the deregulation of interest rates on large deposits of ¥1 billion or more (Viner 1987). The size of such deposits fell continuously by April 1989 to ¥10 million with similar declines in limits on money market certificates and certificates of deposit (Papailiadis 1989b).

Capital and money markets were also largely underdeveloped in 1980 consistent with administered rates. The entire *keiretsu* business organizational form also hampered efficiency because industrial corporations dealt almost exclusively with the *keiretsu* bank (Wright and Pauli 1987). Finally, Article 65 of the Japanese Securities and Exchange Law separates securities and banking businesses rigidly like the U.S. Glass-Steagall Act.

There are several key measures in Japanese deregulation that allow us to track its progress. First there was the pivotally important December 1980 change in the Foreign Exchange and Foreign Trade Control Law. This enabled Japanese banks to lend in foreign currencies and allowed convertibility of the yen. It also gave foreign investors access to Japanese stock markets. It was followed in 1981 by a new Banking Law allowing banks to engage in limited aspects of securities such as the placement of government bonds and dealing in existing bond issues in the secondary market (Suzuki 1987). In 1982 another Banking Law was promulgated further freeing the banks to engage in securities operations and allowing banks to conduct international operations with greater flexibility (Suzuki 1987: 174–91).

Perhaps the best measure of the success of Japanese deregulation is the entry and role of foreign banks and securities firms in Japan and the development of the Tokyo Offshore Banking Center. Before 1970 there were only 18 foreign banks and 38 foreign branch offices in Japan. By May 1988 there were 81 foreign banks registered as branches (Papailiadis 1989a). Meanwhile, foreign bank deposits grew from ¥402.4 billion in December 1971 (0.77 percent of Japanese bank deposits) to ¥2,176 billion in March 1987 (0.80 percent). Foreign banks had done better on the loan side recording ¥722.1 billion of loans in December 1971 (1.47 percent of the loan assets of Japanese banks) and ¥5,601.8 billion of loans (2.04 percent) by March 1987 rising to ¥13,925 billion in 1990 (Statistics Bureau 1991). Thus, foreign banks have had some success in the Japanese bank loan market, but still have difficulty getting low cost deposit liabilities.

The securities industry provides a similar picture. As of December 1984 there were ten foreign securities dealers licensed to carry on their business in Japan and they operated 11 branch offices with another 96 representative offices. Less than four years later in August 1988 there were 45 foreign securities firms operating 49 branches and another 120 foreign representative offices. In February 1986 the first six foreign firms were allowed to become members of the Tokyo Stock Exchange, rising to 22 firms (of 114 members) by December 1988. December 1973 saw the first six foreign issues listed on the TSE rising to 112 by December 1988 (TSE 1989). Recently though, the decline of the TSE and problems with raising capital there has caused a number of the world's largest companies (for example, General Motors, News Corp., and Philips NV) to delist (*Financial Post* 1992).

The Japanese banking and securities sectors have both seen significant penetration of their domestic markets by foreign competitors. However, to become an IFC, a financial center must have significant offshore business. Thus, we turn to look at the Tokyo Offshore Banking Market established in late 1986. Despite opposition from both the Ministry of Finance and the Bank of Japan, the Japan Offshore Market (JOM) was created, modeled on the U.S. "international banking facility" (IBF) legislation of 1981. The JOM did have much higher minimum deposit levels than did the U.S. IBFs. It also had more restrictions, for instance banning securities from the offshore market (Viner 1987). When the JOM opened in Tokyo on December 1, 1986 licenses were issued by the Ministry of Finance to 112 domestic financial institutions and to 69 foreign banks (Viner 1987). On opening day the US$55 billion in deposits that were moved into the Tokyo offshore market exceeded the performance of the first day of New York's IBF six years earlier. The JOM and Tokyo still are a long way from rivalling London as an offshore market, but the development of the JOM has put Tokyo in the first rank of such markets.

In summary, Tokyo has clearly surged to the highest levels of international finance remarkably fast. Despite residual regulation and official and nonofficial barriers to international finance, Tokyo is clearly established as one of the premier IFCs. There is still a long way to go before it is an IFC in the way Hong Kong, Singapore and London are international centers. Tokyo's success to date is a function of the scale of the Japanese economy which it serves. Part of Tokyo's globalization is illusory resulting from foreign firms moving in to tap the Japanese domestic market in Tokyo. This is not to say that Tokyo has not also emerged as a truly global center, which it has. Rather it is to stress that some of the apparent globalization is really attributed to domestic factors and not the result of doing true third party offshore business as is done in London.

17.4.4 Sydney as an Australian IFC

Sydney and Melbourne have long vied for primacy as "the" Australian financial center. Early in the postwar era, Sydney began to assert its dominance which it achieved by the 1980s (O'Connor and Edgington 1987). This dominance was subsequently reinforced with the opening of Australian banking to foreign banks. Thus, 41 of 49 members of the Australian Merchant Bankers Association (AMBA) in 1988 had head offices in Sydney. Of the 8 Melbourne merchant banks, 4 were subsidiaries of Melbourne based institutions, and 4 were foreign. Sydney hosted 37 foreign merchant banks. With Sydney's dominant role the AMBA moved from Melbourne to Sydney in 1988.

Sydney's growing dominance can be traced to a number of factors. First, it is the capital of New South Wales, the largest state economy with the largest population. Second, with air as the dominant mode of international business and tourist travel, Sydney became the gateway city. Third, Sydney is renowned for its livability, moderate sunny winters and magnificent physical setting. Melbourne, in comparison, has considerably poorer weather being colder and greyer with less spectacular scenery. Fourth, Sydney is the primary locale for foreign merchant banks. These banks made it clear that they chose Sydney in part because of air access and livability (Goldberg 1989). With the progressive deregulation of the Australian financial system and the entry of foreign merchant banks in the 1960s, Sydney was the location of choice.

Sydney is basically a domestic center (Goldberg 1989) with little true offshore financial business. Given a history of exchange controls, a low domestic savings rate, and large needs for capital by Australian resource companies and aggressive entrepreneurs, it is clear why foreign firms would have boomed in the 1980s providing international capital for Australian firms. Sydney's evolution as a financial center is linked to the dominance of the New South Wales economy in Australia and to regulation. Australian exchange control and exchange rate policies combined with onerous financial system regulation and protection of local banks from foreign competition at home create openings for largely foreign owned domestic nonbank financial institutions. Therefore, despite the presence of dozens of international financial institutions and their significant scale of operation, the Sydney financial market is basically domestic and driven by domestic demand for capital.

17.5   Aspiring Asian International Financial Centers

17.5.1 Some Examples and the Challenges They Face

Vanuuatu. In many ways Vanuuatu represents the prototypical offshore banking "tax haven" with its relaxed regulatory environment for offshore transactions and its favorable tax treatment of such transactions. It is however, finding the going increasingly tough. One source of difficulty Vanuuatu and other tax havens face are the new Bank for International Settlement (BIS) capital adequacy and accounting standards for banks. These BIS standards greatly curtail the ability of low tax and slack regulatory regimes to attract international banking since banks in essence are being regulated globally under the BIS rules. Another difficulty faced by Vanuuatu and other tax havens is that increasingly, bank clients look for politically stable locales to place deposits as such stability reduces the risks associated with placing deposits in offshore centers by increasing the likelihood that depositors will be able to get their funds back when desired. Finally, as we saw earlier, IFCs increasingly require state-of-the-art telecommunications and ready access to other major financial and business centers around the globe. Relatively remote locales such as Vanuuatu thus should find it increasingly difficult to break into the IFC network when competing centers like Hong Kong and Singapore are so much more accessible and better served with advanced telecommunications, airport and hotel infrastructure.

Given this preamble, it is not surprising that Vanuuatu has realized modest gains in its push to become an IFC. Vanuuatu claimed US$300 million per day in transactions, with US$50 million being a more reasonable estimate (Phinney 1986). Port Vila accounts for roughly 10 percent of the nation's GNP (Phinney 1986). By the end of 1984 (the most recent year available) some 1100 firms had registered to do international financial business in Port Vila. Over 100 banks were registered by 1992 (Deans 1992). However, Vanuuatu is largely of interest to Asian companies, particularly Southeast Asian.

These gains have been offset by a decline in confidence in the country as a result of the political riots of 1988 and competition from competing South Pacific tax havens such as Western Samoa and the Cook Islands (Lowenstein 1989). Pure tax havens like Vanuuatu are vulnerable to competition from similar centers. Also, increasing concern for political stability and strong but flexible regulation clearly disadvantage such centers compared with those located in stable developed countries (Deans 1992).

Taipei. The Republic of China introduced its "Statute for International Financial Business" in 1983. Under the legislation OBUs were established in mid-1984 (Liu 1990). OBUs are jointly regulated by the Central Bank of China (CBC) and the Ministry of Finance (MOF), though they are exempt from a broad array of domestic taxes (including stamp duties and withholding tax), interest rate regulation, foreign exchange controls and reserve requirements (Liu 1990). They are allowed to take deposits from, and make loans to, nonresidents and engage in foreign exchange transactions.

So far the OBU program has not been successful in attracting significant international finance or in raising Taiwan's stature as a growing IFC. Efforts to establish a US dollar inter-bank market are too new to be assessed, although they do add another dimension to Taiwan's ability to attract international financial institutions and transactions (Liu 1990). Despite these moves foreign banks comprise less than 5 percent of the domestic market, and 10 percent of trade finance, with the foreign share accounted for by one major U.S. bank.

With continued stringent controls on foreign ownership of Taiwanese securities, and restrictions on foreign bank operations likely to continue for the foreseeable future, Taiwan is not likely to make much headway in the near term in its goal of becoming an IFC providing a Southeast Asian alternative to Hong Kong and Singapore for the conduct of international finance. With Hong Kong's 1997 deadline nearing, Taiwan is stepping up efforts to attract business from Hong Kong, but the outcome of its efforts will not be known for a decade at least.

Osaka and Kansai region. The dominance of Tokyo in world and Japanese financial markets is such that few ever think of Japan's second financial center, Osaka. Yet Osaka and its surrounding Kansai region is a very large financial center. Some impressive financial statistics will bear this out below.

Osaka is the home of the Osaka Securities Exchange (OSE) which ranked fourth in volume behind only Tokyo, New York, and London in the late 1980s (Osaka Prefectural Government 1989b). As of the end of March 1987, Osaka City banks held 9.2 percent of national bank deposits, made 11.5 percent of national bank loans, cleared 9.7 percent of national checking activity, and traded 12.2 percent of the shares traded in Japan (Osaka Municipal Government 1988). The OSE is generally regarded as the most innovative and aggressive exchange in Japan having pioneered the development of a very successful junior company board in 1983 and stock futures in 1987. In addition, the 1981 census of establishments showed more than 117,000 people employed in the nearly 3900 financial firms which comprise the Osaka City financial services industry (Osaka Municipal Government 1988), obviously a dramatic underestimate of the present scale of financial employment and activity today. A more recent, 1989 estimate, shows that there were 28 foreign banks operating in Osaka as well as all 13 national banks, 74 regional banks (out of 116 in Japan), all three long term credit banks and all seven trust banks (Osaka Prefectural Government 1989a).

Osaka is already a major international financial center. However, with the planned opening in 1995 of the massive Kansai International Airport, the city and its hinterland should become even more global in outlook and activities. While Osaka will undoubtedly continue to be dwarfed and overshadowed by Tokyo as both a domestic and international financial center, Osaka's role in the future Pacific and global financial economy should not be underrated. The increased access noted above and the lower land and building costs as well as the proximity to scenic and historic areas like Kobe and Kyoto, all should combine to move Osaka into the global spotlight in the future.

Manila. Manila is an interesting contrast to Hong Kong and Singapore. First, where both of the former have been enormously successful, Manila has done poorly (*The Banker* 1990). The Philippines established OBUs in mid-1977 in an attempt to stem the flow of funds to other offshore markets and to create a new source of employment and development at the same time (Tan and Kapur 1986). The overwhelming majority of deposits have come from domestic sources with a minority (roughly 10 percent) from the rest of Asia. The funds have also been used domestically by Philippines companies.

The failure of Manila to develop as an IFC can be found mainly in its lack of those market advantages that both Hong Kong and Singapore possess. Additionally, it has been plagued by poor telecommunications infrastructure and a rather inward looking worldview. The absence of a strong and developed domestic financial system, with its attendant agglomeration economies, has further hampered Manila's evolution as an IFC.

Other new or planned Asia-Pacific IFCs. Given the growing importance of the financial sector as a factor in economic growth, a number of countries and states are actively reviewing ways in which they might promote an IFC within their borders. In 1990, Malaysia designated Labuan island (10 kilometers from Sabah) as an IFC, allowing a range of international transactions to be conducted there tax free. Eighteen months later 31 companies, including 2 international banks and 9 trust companies had located in Labuan (Tsuruoka 1992), but business volumes are still small. Thailand is also considering IFC tax concessions to establish Bangkok as an IFC (Handley 1992), while Macau too, is studying IFC policies (Field 1992). Finally, the Cook Islands, Nauru and Western Samoa have also joined the fray with some modest successes being achieved (Deans 1992). Clearly, there is no shortage of aspirants to IFC status, but these and other prospective IFCs will have to battle extant IFCs and overcome infrastructure and locational weaknesses to succeed.

17.5.2 Conclusion

From these Asia-Pacific financial centers some useful lessons emerge for others. First, market forces play an extremely important role. All of the preconditions for market development must be there: excellent infrastructure; good labor market; international orientation: free movement of capital; time zone; English as a working language; political stability; and a strong financial sector. Second, the offshore market must have favorable tax treatment and flexible regulation.

17.6 Summarizing and Concluding

This chapter ties the development of Asia-Pacific financial centers to forces of globalization in financial services. We found diverse factors at work including booming world trade, technological change in telecommunications and financial products, deregulation, and declining barriers to capital flows.

We then moved to the factors shaping the development of those urban centers (IFCs) from which the global financial economy is run. This led us to examine the attributes of successful IFCs. There emerged a clear picture of the underlying factors affecting the growth and development of IFCs.

To wrap up the context of the Asia-Pacific IFCs, we examined the literature on global cities and the related new international division of labor concept. This suggested that IFCs and global cities overlap greatly since financial decisions are closely linked to other global managerial decisions. Given this context, we finally examined major and aspiring Asia-Pacific IFCs.

The discussion on the Asia-Pacific IFCs turned up interesting regularities and anomalies. In the regularity camp, we found that IFCs could grow as a result of natural, trade-related and national economic market forces (Hong Kong) or as a result of concerted government policy efforts (Singapore). We also found that IFCs were important national centers (Tokyo). Less successful centers suffered from a deficiency in one or more requisite attributes: poor access (Vanuuatu); political instability (Manila); or rigid and uncertain regulation (Taipei).

Surprises also arose. Large numbers of foreign financial institutions did not necessarily indicate international financial activity. Large centers such as Sydney and Taipei had significant representation of foreign financial firms, but surprisingly little true offshore financial activity. Smaller centers such as Singapore (and in some specialized areas like trade finance) outdistanced larger domestic financial centers in terms of international financial business. This suggests that success as a dominant national or domestic regional center held back development of international finance in some cases by focusing attention on domestic demand instead of international financial opportunities. Sydney illustrates this point.

Conversely, other centers were forced to adopt an international view because of the limited domestic scope of financial activities (for example, Singapore and Hong Kong). In these cases it would seem that these centers benefited from having to adopt a global view and look for international financial niches.

The continued formation of IFCs around Asia-Pacific is not just a product of the heady days of international finance in the 1980s. IFC status is being sought by an increasing number of locales as we saw above. Despite the decline of major economies in the early 1990s, and despite tumultuous financial market conditions in Japan and Europe in 1992, international financial activity must inevitably increase as does global production and trade. Accordingly, interest in IFC formation in the rapidly growing Asia-Pacific region should increase, not decrease, in the years to come. The present overview of extant and emerging IFCs seeks to provide needed background for potential newcomers to the Asia-Pacific IFC network about both the competition and the rigours of becoming an IFC. For extant IFCs, the discussion aims to clarify key facets of their success and provide some guidance for maintaining their roles in the global financial marketplace.

References

Balakrishnan, N., 1992, "Singapore: Banking by Concession," *Far Eastern Economic Review*, March 5, 34–36.

Ball, Clifford A. and Adrian E. Tschoegl, 1982, "The Decision to Establish a Foreign Bank Branch or Subsidiary: An Application of Binary Classification Procedures," *Journal of Financial and Quantitative Analysis*, 17(3): 411–24.

Bando, Shunsuke, 1990, "The Change in Singapore's Economy and Investment Environment," *RIM*, 1(7): 28–32.

The Banker, 1984, "Singapore Relies on Mutual Offset," May.

———, 1990, "Thriller in Manila," February, 18–22.

Blomquist, Glenn C., Mark C. Berger, and John P. Hoehn, 1988, "New Estimates of Quality of Life in Urban Areas," *American Economic Review*, 78(1): 89–107.

Bryant, Ralph C., 1987, *International Financial Intermediation*, Brookings, Washington, DC.

Business Times (Singapore), 1989, Banking & Finance Special Supplement, May 4.

Choi, Sang-Rim, Adrian E. Tschoegl, and Chwo-Ming Yu, 1985, "Banks and the World's Major Financial Centers, 1970–1980," *Weltwirtschftliches Archiv*, 122: 48–63.

Compton, Eric, 1987, *The New World of Commercial Banking*, Lexington Books, Lexington, MA.

Daniels, Peter W., 1986, "Foreign Banks and Metropolitan Development: A Comparison of London and New York," *Journal of Economic and Social Geography*, 77(4): 269–87.

DBS Bank, 1987, *The Singapore Financial Centre*, Singapore Briefing No. 2, Economic Research Department, DBS Bank, Singapore.

———, 1988, *The Emergence of the Japan Offshore Market: Implications for Hong Kong and Singapore*, Occasional Paper No. 20, Economic Research Department, DBS Bank, Singapore.

Deans, Alan, 1992, "Treasure Islands," *Far Eastern Economic Review*, March 5, 38.

Dunning, John H. and G. Norman, 1983, "The Theory of the Multinational Enterprise: An Application to Multinational Office Location," *Environment and Planning A*, 19(4): 675–95.

Economic Council of Canada, 1989, *A New Frontier: Globalization and Canada's Financial Markets*, Ottawa, Ontario.

The Economist, 1990, "A Survey of International Banking: A Question of Definition," April 7.

Economist Intelligence Unit, 1992, *Country Report No. 2—Singapore*, London.

Enderwick, Peter, 1987, "The Strategy and Structure of Service-Sector Multi-nationals: Implications for Potential Host Regions," *Regional Studies*, 21(3): 215–23.

Fairlamb, D., 1986, "Foreign Banks Take an Increasing Share of the Cake," *The Banker*, March, 87–134.

Field, G., 1992, "The Challenge of Transforming Macau's Financial System," *Euromoney*, May, SS5–6.

Financial Post, 1992, "Five Firms Axe Tokyo Listing," September 17, 12.

Friedland, J., 1992, "How to be Inscrutable," *Far Eastern Economic Review*, March 5, 29–30.

Friedmann, J., 1986, "The World City Hypothesis," *Development and Change*, 17: 69–83.

Frobel, F. J., J. Heinrichs, and B. Kreye, 1980, *The New International Division of Labour*, Cambridge University Press, Cambridge.

Gerakis, A. S. and O. Roncesvalles, 1983, "Bahrain's Offshore Banking Centre," *Economic Development and Cultural Change*, 31(2): 270–93.

Gerard, Karen, 1985, "Why They Fled the Big Apple (And Do They Regret It?)" *Across the Board*, May, 56–63.

Ghose, T. K., 1987, *The Banking System of Hong Kong*, Butterworths, Singapore.

Glorieux, Guy and Sydney Hedderich, 1990, *Building on Success in the Dynamic Asian Markets: Canadian Financial Institutions in Hong Kong and Singapore, A Preliminary Report*, Conference Board of Canada, Ottawa, Ontario.

Goldberg, Michael A., 1989, "Sydney's Evolution as an International Financial Centre: A Brief History and Comparative Analysis and Lessons to be Learned," Faculty of Commerce and Business Administration, University of British Columbia, Vancouver, BC, mimeo.

Goldberg, Michael A., Robert Helsley, and Maurice Levi, 1989, "The Location of International Financial Activity: An Interregional Analysis," *Regional Studies*, 23(1): 1–10.

Hamilton, Adrian, 1986, *The Financial Revolution*, Free Press, New York.

Handley, Paul, 1992, "Banking on Bangkok," *Far Eastern Economic Review*, March 5, 34–35.

Heenan, David A., 1979, "The Regional Headquarters Decision: A Comparative Analysis," *Academy of Management Journal*, 22(2): 410–15.

Heenan, D. A. and H. Perlmutter, 1978, *Multinational Organization Development: A Social Architecture Perspective*, Addison-Wesley, Reading, MA.

Hofheinz, Roy and Kent Calder, 1982, *The East Asian Edge*, Basic Books, New York.

Hong Kong Trader, 1990, "Territory's Foreign Exchange Market Ranks High in Survey," December, 7.

Hutton, Thomas and David Ley, 1987, "Location, Linkages and Labour: The Downtown Complex of Corporate Activities in a Medium Size City, Vancouver British Columbia," Department of Geography, University of British Columbia, Vancouver, BC, mimeo.

Kaufman, Henry, 1986, *Interest Rates, the Markets, and the New Financial World*, Times Books, New York.

Kindleberger, Charles P., 1974, *The Formation of Financial Centers: A Study in Comparative Economic History*, Princeton University Press, Princeton, NJ.

Lee, K.-H. and I. Vertinsky, 1988, "Strategic Adjustment of International Financial Centres in Small Economies: A Comparative Study of Hong Kong and Singapore," *Journal of Business Administration*, 17(1).

Lee, Sheng Yi, 1986, "Developing Asian Financial Centres," in Tan and Kapur, pp. 205–36.

Levi, Maurice D., 1989, *International Finance*, 2nd edition, McGraw-Hill, New York.

Liu, L., 1990, "Brave New World of Financial Reform in Taiwan, ROC—Three Waves of Internationalization and Liberalization and Beyond," *Chinese Yearbook of International Law and Affairs*.

Lowenstein, J., 1989, "Economic Dependence Dies Hard," *Euromoney Special Supplement*, September, 15–18.

McGahey, Richard, Mary Malloy, Katerine Kazanas, and Michael P. Jacobs, 1990, *Financial Services, Financial Centers: Public Policy and the Competition for Markets, Firms, and Jobs*, Westview Press, Boulder, CO.

O'Connor, Kevin and David Edgington, 1987, "The Location of Services Involved with International Trade," *Environment and Planning A*, 19: 687–700.

Osaka Municipal Government, 1988, *Economic Profile of Osaka City*, Economic Affairs Bureau, Osaka Municipal Government.

Osaka Prefectural Government, 1989a, *Economic Performance of Osaka*, Business Innovation Division, Department of Commerce and Industry, Osaka Prefectural Government.

———, 1989b, *Overview of Osaka Prefecture, Japan*, Business Innovation Division, Department of Commerce and Industry, Osaka Prefectural Government.

Papailiadis, Tom, 1989a, *The Canadian and Japanese Financial Services Industries: Opportunities and Prospects from Mutual Access*, Report 46–89 DF, Conference Board of Canada, Ottawa, Ontario.

———, 1989b, *The Japanese Financial System in Transition*, Report 47–89 DF, Conference Board of Canada, Ottawa, Ontario.

Phinney, R., 1986, "Radical Father Nurtures a Safe Home for Funds," *Asian Business*, November, 62–64.

Reed, Howard Curtis, 1981, *The Preeminence of International Financial Centers*, Praeger, New York.

Scott, Robert Haney, K. A. Wong, and Yan Ki Ho, 1986, *Hong Kong's Financial Institutions and Markets*, Oxford University Press, Hong Kong.

Skully, Michael T. and George J. Viksnins, 1987, *Financing East Asia's Success: Comparative Financial Development in Eight Asian Countries*, St. Martin's Press, New York.

Statistics Bureau, 1991, *Japan Statistical Yearbook*, Statistics Bureau, Management and Coordination Agency, Tokyo.

Suzuki, Yoshio, 1987, *The Japanese Financial System*, Clarendon Press, Oxford.

Tan, Augustine H. H. and Basant Kapur (eds.), 1986, *Pacific Growth and Financial Interdependence*, Allen and Unwin Australia, Sydney.

Thrift, Nigel, 1983, "World Cities and the World City Property Market: The Age of Southeast Asian Investment in Australia," Working Paper, Research School of Pacific Studies, Department of Human Geography, Australian National University, Canberra, mimeo.

Tokyo Stock Exchange, 1988 and 1989, *TSE Factbook*, Tokyo.

Tsuruoka, Doug, 1992, "Life on Labuan," *Far Eastern Economic Review*, March 5, 36.

Viner, Aron, 1987, *Inside Japan's Financial Markets*, Tokyo: Japan Times.

Wright, Richard W. and Gunter A. Pauli, 1987, *The Second Wave: Japan's Assault on Financial Services*, St. Martin's Press, New York.

Yamazawa, Kotaro, Yoshiaki Wada, and Taekshi Hachimura, 1992, *Outlook for the Financial Markets of Hong Kong*, Special Report No. 218, Research and Statistics Department, Bank of Japan, Tokyo.

Part V

MACROECONOMIC AND MONETARY ISSUES

This part comprises three chapters. It begins with the introduction of the macroeconomic policy issues in the Asia-Pacific region in Chapter 18 (Treadgold). The objective of the chapter is to provide a selective account and assessment of recent analysis of macroeconomic management in these economies. In the context of the Asia-Pacific economies, there has been little analysis of the macroeconomic issues. The chapter covers both domestic and external aspects of macroeconomic policy. Its five principal themes are: (1) the objective of macroeconomic policies, (2) conflicts constraints and trade-offs, (3) targets and instrument framework used in these economies, (4) monetary policy, and (5) fiscal policy. Macroeconomic stability and rapid export expansion bore fruit in the Asia-Pacific economies. It contributed to an accelerated rate of accumulation, efficient allocation and strong productivity growth in the region. In general these economies adhered to orthodox policy prescriptions, that is, they held the budget deficit to levels that could be prudently financed. Other than fiscal prudence they consciously avoided exchange rate overvaluation. Another characteristic of these economies was their quick and flexible response to changing economic circumstances, both internal and external. Other noteworthy macroeconomic features were: (a) inflation was kept under control; (b) debt, both internal and external, was kept within manageable limits; and (c) whenever macroeconomic crises emerged they were resolved without delay. To be sure, there were periods of recession and policy adjustment which squeezed the private sector. But these were only ephemeral periods. Long recessions did not become built-in into these economies as they did in many other parts of the developing and industrialized world. The World Bank called their macroeconomic policy a "pragmatic orthodoxy."

In Chapter 19 (Fry), first, analyzes the effects of monetary policy and financial opening in several Asia-Pacific economies. Although structural changes can be detected in several of these economies, monetary control was maintained. The monetary and fiscal policies pursued by many of these countries were relatively less accommodative. Secondly, inflation rates were kept from spinning out of control. Several of these countries were committed to low inflation and accordingly they kept their options for activism constrained. International experience suggests that inflation rates lower than 20 percent, a level not breached by any of the Asia-Pacific economies, can be maintained for long periods without generating macroeconomic stability. Low inflation is a corollary of fiscal prudence. There were other self-imposed limits, like those on fiscal policy and on balancing the budget. Each economy had its own reason for its commitment to low inflation but the common element was that they took lessons from their own economic history.

Chapter 20 (Emery) focuses on the central banks' use of money market instruments. Much of the past literature on the control instruments used by central banks in the Asia-Pacific has focused on three main areas: adjustments in commercial bank reserve requirements or liquidity ratios, central bank discount policy and the use of various direct controls such as ceilings on the amount of commercial bank credit expansion. Less attention has been paid to commercial banks' use of money market instruments in the conduct of monetary policy. Many Asia-Pacific economies utilize money market instruments of one kind or another for achieving their monetary policy objectives. This chapter examines the utilization of money market instruments during the past decade.

Chapter 18

Malcolm L. Treadgold

MACROECONOMIC POLICY ISSUES IN THE ASIA-PACIFIC ECONOMIES

18.1   Introduction

Since the early 1970s the external economic environment of the developing countries of Asia and the Pacific has been powerfully disrupted by the collapse of the Bretton Woods international monetary system, two massive oil shocks, world inflation, strong cyclical movements in real activity, high interest rates and the accumulation of large international debts. These countries have also been subjected to a range of domestic shocks of varying degrees of intensity. It has been a difficult and challenging period for their macroeconomic policymakers.

Yet, on the whole, the Asian and Pacific developing countries have adjusted more flexibly and achieved better macroeconomic performances than other developing countries. While there have obviously been individual exceptions and marked intra-group differences, on average, growth rates have tended to be higher, inflation rates lower, and foreign debt problems less pressing.

The aim of this chapter is to provide a selective account and assessment of recent analyses of macroeconomic management in the developing countries of Asia and the Pacific. The paper covers both domestic and external aspects of macroeconomic policy, although greater attention is given to domestic aspects. It is built around five themes:

☐   The objectives of macroeconomic policy
☐   Conflicts, constraints and trade-offs

   ☐   Target/instrument frameworks
   ☐   Monetary policy
   ☐   Fiscal policy

A brief conclusion draws attention to some topics not covered or covered only inadequately under the above headings.

18.2   Policy Objectives

Within the Asian-Pacific context, there has been comparatively little analysis of the nature, choice and formulation of macroeconomic policy objectives and the social preferences, or at least the preferences of policymakers, which underlie these objectives. For the most part, one finds little more than brief statements that accept or assert the desirability of pursuing broad macroeconomic goals measured in terms of target variables such as the price level, the balance of payments, employment, and the rate of economic growth.

To the extent that policy objectives have been more deeply explored, the main regional focus has been on the goals of price stability and balance of payments equilibrium. In the case of price stability, explanations for the degree of priority given to avoiding or reducing inflation in particular countries can sometimes be found in their political and economic history. For example, it has been suggested that the apparently "genuine anti-inflationary attitude" of policymakers in Taiwan is at least "partly based on a belief that the downfall of the Nationalist regime on mainland China was related to ... hyperinflation," and that this attitude "was probably strengthened by Taiwan's own inflationary experience during the years 1946–60" and by the influence of U.S. Agency for International Development (AID) advisers and missions (Lundberg 1979: 260). Correspondingly, the same belief about the role of inflation in the downfall of the Nationalist regime has apparently been shared by the Communist leaders in China, for whom price stability has always been a major goal, although not one that has been achieved recently (Chen and Hou 1986: 831). And in Thailand, anti-inflationary attitudes and a commitment to financial prudence have even deeper historical roots. "The Thai Kings of the nineteenth century saw financial stability as being essential to keeping foreign gunboats—especially the French and British—from forcing colonial rule onto Thailand ... The influence of this tradition continues today" (Warr and Nidhiprabha 1988: 112).

Policymakers elsewhere in the Asian-Pacific region have not always displayed the same degree of concern about inflation. Over much of the 1960s and 1970s the Korean government claimed to be pursuing both price stability and economic growth, but growth was almost continuously given priority. (The pressure to reduce inflation in fact came largely from the U.S. government and the International Monetary Fund.) It was not until the late 1970s or early 1980s that inflation was recognized domestically as a genuine problem, by which time there was "some indication that both the government and the general public would be willing to trade 1 or 2 percent of growth for greater stability of prices" (Cole and Park 1983: 214).

Indonesia provides another case of a shift of preferences towards price stability. Given the availability of a choice "between combinations of two policy options; price stability and resource transfers through the inflation tax," it has been argued that the preferences of the Indonesian authorities in the first half of the 1960s were such that they were prepared to tolerate high and increasing rates of inflation in order to achieve a "politically necessary level of government expenditure" (Grenville 1981: 119). After 1966, however, a new government with a strong commitment to price stability effectively chose a much lower rate of inflation and a lower associated volume of resource transfers (which, incidentally, were redirected towards the business sector and the accumulation of foreign exchange reserves).

In general, investigation of the price stability objective has bypassed issues of definition and formulation. There appears to be a broad, if unstated, consensus that the degree of achievement of this objective can be adequately defined and identified in terms of the behavior of conventional measures such as consumer price indexes and GDP implicit price deflators. By contrast, formulation of the goal (or what is more properly regarded as the constraint) of balance of payments equilibrium or external balance has been widely regarded as a more complex task, involving considerations of both international liquidity and solvency. The former implies a focus on the behavior of international reserves. Subject to familiar reservations, this variable may be used to specify an operational indicator of external balance in the traditional partial sense of a balance between the aggregate autonomous supply and demand for foreign exchange, where the balance is maintained, if not continuously as in a floating exchange rate system, then at least over the duration of normal cyclical disturbances. Very much in this tradition was a 1979 formulation of a balance of payments target for Papua New Guinea (PNG): "maintenance of an adequate stock of foreign currency reserves throughout the commodity price cycle" (Palmer 1979: 6).

This approach neglects, however, the composition of the balance of payments and, in particular, the balance on current account which, of course, measures the change in a country's net foreign liabilities. In an international environment of high interest rates and third world debt problems, current account deficits and the associated extent of foreign borrowing and future debt-service obligations have been seen as adding an extra dimension to the external balance objective. Thus, although in Indonesia it has been the rate of change of foreign exchange reserves to which the authorities "are probably most sensitive in the short run," it seems that by the early 1980s solvency had come to be accepted as a more significant long-term constraint on general policymaking than it had been previously (Rosendale 1981: 164–66).

Likewise, the approach to external balance in a PNG context has been extended to recognize that the concept of external balance should take into account the effects of foreign borrowing on the distribution of income between generations (that is, the future impact of debt service). This has led to the following "working definition" of external balance:

> the maintenance of currency convertibility at all stages of the international business cycle without recourse to external borrowings that are so large that their servicing requires absolute reductions in average living standards at some future time (Garnaut and Baxter 1983: 57).

Concern about the accumulation of foreign debt and the related idea of specifying a current account objective have, however, not gone unchallenged. The counter-argument is based on the fact that the current account deficit is necessarily equal to the algebraic sum of the differences between corporate investment and corporate saving, household investment and household saving, and public investment and public saving (that is, the government deficit or surplus). Using this framework, Corden has suggested that "Provided taxes, subsidies, information flows and various regulations are set at optimal levels, it seems appropriate to let corporate savings and corporate investment be decided on the basis of the normal profit-maximising principles"; and the same type of point can be made with respect to the household sector. In addition, where the structure of the economy rules out domestic stabilization as a consideration, the appropriate fiscal policy (that is, government budgetary balance) is determined by "various considerations concerned with optimal savings, with the expected social rate of return on public investment relative to the world rate of interest and so on." In these circumstances there is no need for a current account target. More generally, 'it is better to go direct to the separate [sectoral] net balances (or the separate elements that yield each balance) to assess the desirability of various policies" (Corden 1984: 34).

Although price stability and external balance have dominated analyses of macroeconomic policy objectives in the region, there has also been some limited recognition and exploration of employment objectives and, relatedly, the goal of stabilization of the volume of real output in the face of exogenous stocks. That the recognition and exploration have been limited is hardly surprising. Even for high-income industrialized countries where the traditional goal of full employment originated (and where it was once frequently tied in simplistic fashion to that of price stability under the composite heading of "internal balance"), the status of full employment as an objective of macroeconomic policy has now become a subject of considerable doubt. This principally reflects widespread acceptance of the notion of a natural rate of unemployment and the associated influence of monetarist and new classical theories that dispute the efficacy of, and necessity for, demand management policies directed at employment targets.

As far as the developing countries are concerned, there is, of course, a much longer history of skepticism about the suitability of full employment as a objective of macroeconomic policy, dating back to V. K. R. V. Rao's (1952) famous paper on the inapplicability of Keynesian economics to underdeveloped countries. This theme has been echoed within the region, specifically in relation to Thailand

(Trescott 1971) and Indonesia (Arndt 1979a). Elsewhere, in some newly industrializing countries (NICs) such as Hong Kong and Taiwan, the very success that comparatively unregulated labor markets have displayed in overcoming or avoiding shortfalls of employment opportunities relative to the aggregate supply of labor has probably served to downgrade interest in employment as an objective of macroeconomic policy. Even in Korea unemployment, or underemployment, which was once among the most urgent problems, no longer seemed to be a pressing issue by the end of the 1970s (Cole and Park 1983: 238).

Singapore, however, is one NIC where interest in employment as a macroeconomic goal has increased sharply in recent years. In large part this seems to be a direct reflection of the major deterioration in labor market performance which accompanied the 1985 recession in that economy. (The unemployment rate rose from only 2.7 percent in 1984 to 6.5 percent in 1986, its highest level since the 1960s.) However, even before this recession the short-run level of employment had attracted attention as a macroeconomic target variable (Corden 1984). One complication in this context was the presence of temporary foreign workers, which implied a close link between any employment objective and migration policy.

For Papua New Guinea also, specification of an employment objective has been complicated by migration. In this case the migration is an internal flow from rural villages, where most people earn their livelihoods in non-wage activities, to urban areas where most wage-employment opportunities, and also most open unemployment, occur. Under these conditions full employment has been defined as:

the state in which the number of people who prefer wage employment to village life, given the level of wages and other factors affecting non-village and village standards of living, roughly balances the number of wage and other non-village jobs available (Garnaut and Baxter 1983: 54–5).

While this definition tends to gloss over the issue of labor utilization in the village sector, it appears to have been readily accepted in a PNG context, presumably because of the politically sensitive and socially disruptive nature of urban unemployment and the apparent absence of significant underemployment in rural areas.

Although employment and growth objectives have sometimes been grouped together (Goodman et al. 1985; Park 1986), the frequent appearance of economic growth in listings of macroeconomic policy goals reflects much more than just a narrow perception that growth has positive implications for the demand for labor. Probably to a greater extent than anywhere else in the third world, the countries of the Asian-Pacific region have espoused the desirability of economic growth on the usual grounds that it brings an increasing range of human choice (Lewis 1955), and thus permits, in particular, rising material standards of living. The questioning of economic growth that has occurred in some developing country literature in relation to social justice or distributional issues (see Arndt 1987 for a recent evaluation), and in the West in terms of the perceived finite nature of natural resource stocks, environmental threats, and social and psychological costs, has been extremely muted in the Asian-Pacific region.

Within this context, the thinking of policymakers in the ASEAN countries seems to have been dominated by the "traditional or neoclassical model of economic growth and development," involving an emphasis on capital formation and adherence to three interconnected ideas: that development is a gradual and continuous process; that the process is harmonious and cumulative; and that growth is beneficial, with significant spread and trickle-down effects (Asher 1985; Yotopoulos and Nugent 1976). Moreover, this is a view not confined to official policy-thinking in the ASEAN countries, but one that appears to have been widely adopted in the Asian-Pacific region. Even for Papua New Guinea, where growth was not specifically cited as a policy objective in the early post-independence period, its omission should not be interpreted as a denial of its importance, but rather as reflecting an assumption that it could be achieved without special effort (Goodman et al. 1985).

In concluding this section, it may be noted that in general regional analysis of policy objectives has focused appropriately on variables that can fairly readily be accepted as ultimate target variables, that is on macroeconomic aggregates which can be assumed "to affect the well-being of individuals or the social well-being of the nation directly or else, for the purposes of policy decisions, are believed to be satisfactory proxies for still more remote and fundamental goals" (Bryant 1980: 12). There have, however, been some exceptions where macroeconomic objectives or targets have in fact been specified in terms of magnitudes that could more accurately be regarded as "intermediate variables," not pursued in their own right, but because they provide links between policy actions or instruments and genuinely ultimate targets. For example, with respect to Singapore, there has been some tendency to specify export volume (Bender 1986) and the related concept of export competitiveness (Lim et al. 1988) as targets. At first glance, these appear to have an almost mercantilist ring to them, although in view of the structure of the Singapore economy export targets are obviously defensible as proxies for more basic welfare-oriented objectives such as real income or employment. Similarly, in Taiwan in the 1950s one of the aims of government policy was to reduce or eliminate large budget deficits, an objective which, however, was really concerned with reducing the rate of money creation and hence ultimately dampening the rate of inflation (Lundberg 1979: 269).

18.3   Conflicts, Constraints and Trade-offs

If all objective functions were monolithic, macro-economic policy-making would be a relatively simple task. Alternatively, if policy objectives were positively correlated ... so that the attainment of any one goal necessarily implied progress toward achieving the remainder, little difficulty would be encountered in the formation of policy. It is the fact that macro-economic objective functions are multi-dimensional and that for the most part the objectives are negatively related with respect to a given policy change, which means the decision-maker's lot is not a happy one (Shaw, 1977: 10).

A pervasive awareness exists within the region of the possibility of conflict between policy objectives. In relation to Indonesia, reference has already been made to a stylized depiction of trade-offs in the 1960s between price stability and resource transfers through the inflation tax, where the transfers serve other policy objectives which have at times dominated price stability. While later Indonesian experience from 1968 to 1981 has been identified as "a striking example of the extent to which demand expansion can be used to promote growth of employment and output, without serious inflationary problems" (Sundrum 1986: 66), it is clear that this absence of conflict between price stability and growth reflected an unusually favorable combination of circumstances involving an elastic supply of wage-goods and abundant supplies of foreign exchange. A new form of trade-off emerged when subsequent declines in the terms of trade and deterioration in the balance of payments led to restrictive demand policies which reduced the rate of economic growth (Sundrum 1988).

The vast "two-gap" literature of development economics attests to the popularity of the notion of external balance as a constraint on growth. Within the region, concern about the conflict has been muted somewhat by the success of export-led economies such as South Korea, Taiwan, Singapore and Hong Kong. Nevertheless, it remains a major preoccupation, not least in relation to Malaysia. General equilibrium analysis using a quantitative model "representative of Malaysia" indicates that without a conscious policy of demand expansion an increased physical capital stock may merely substitute for labor and bring about only a modest increase in output. The trade-off problem is that although exogenous domestic demand expansion will considerably enhance the effects of capital accumulation on the growth of output and employment, it will do so at the cost of a significant deterioration in the balance of payments (Lysy 1980).

Inquiry into the possibility of another trade-off in Malaysia, that between inflation and unemployment, has found some weak support for a traditional, negatively sloped Phillips curve. However, the curve is "extremely steep and almost vertical," leading to the conclusion "that the existence of the trade-off between inflation and unemployment is not borne out by the empirical evidence" (Ariff 1983: 494).

The question of whether there exists a stable empirical relationship of the Phillips type between the rate of money wage or price changes and the rate of unemployment or output growth has also attracted attention in other countries of the region, with mixed results. For Singapore, they have been negative. One study claims to have found for the period 1967–81 a Phillips curve relating the rate of change of wages to unemployment, the lagged inflation rate and incomes-policy dummy variables; but it is noteworthy that the negative coefficient on unemployment is not significant (Chew and Chew 1987). Another study for almost the same period (1968–82) has examined the hypothesis of an expectations-augmented Phillips curve in which the rate of price inflation in Singapore is a function of both excess aggregate demand, represented by the ratio of actual to trend real income, and the expected rate of inflation, represented by an exponential auto-projection of the actual rate. Its finding that there was no statistical relationship between, on the one hand, deviations of the actual rate of inflation from the expected rate and, on the other hand, the ratio of actual to trend real income led to rejection of the hypothesis and, by implication, the existence of a short-run trade-off between inflation and the rate of economic growth.

In the case of Hong Kong, early (1975–81) evidence in support of a negative or inverse relationship between inflation and unemployment depended heavily on one outlying observation (1975). If this were excluded, the trade-off relationship became less clear-cut, with the plot resembling more a long-run vertical Phillips curve than a downward sloping curve (Ho 1983: 368). More observations brought an unqualified assertion that "there is an inverse relationship between the rate of inflation and the rate of unemployment" in Hong Kong, but also a warning against interpreting this as indicative of the existence of a permanently exploitable policy trade-off (Peebles 1988: 277). While this warning seems to have been based implicitly on some notion of adaptive price expectations, the rational expectations hypothesis (arguably, more relevant to Hong Kong than to most economies of the region) suggests, of course, that the relationship may not be exploitable even as a temporary, short-run trade-off.

Subject to reservations about the data, the early evidence for Taiwan seemed to indicate some pattern of regularity of a Phillips curve type, involving an inverse relationship between unemployment and money wage increases (Lundberg 1979: 295–6). More recently, dynamic simulations, using a small econometric monetary model, have suggested that although expansionary monetary policy has comparatively weak effects on price and output variables because of the openness of the economy, it still generates both short and long-run trade-offs between them (Lii 1987).

The quarterly macroeconometric model of South Korea constructed by van Wijnbergen (1982) contains the first rigorous study of the Phillips curve for that country. The model's wage equation is an expectations-augmented form of the curve which also allows for catch-up wage claims when past inflation was higher than anticipated. Unemployment is shown to have a moderating impact on wage demands, which feeds through to domestic price inflation by way of a lagged markup mechanism.

In a later econometric study of South Korea, Chung and Kim (1986) combine an expectations-augmented wage adjustment equation (in which inflationary expectations are influenced adaptively by past inflation) with aggregate supply and demand functions for the goods market. Eschewing long-run considerations and treating unemployment as an exogenous variable, they examine the trade-off relationship between it and inflation. Their results also imply that the short-run Phillips curve is relevant to Korea.

It is no coincidence that inquiry into the possibility of Phillips-type trade-offs between inflation and unemployment has been largely concentrated on the four NICs of the region: Singapore, Hong Kong, Taiwan and South Korea. In a negative sense, this concentration reflects the inadequacy of labor market statistics in most of the other countries of the region and, more fundamentally, recognition of the inappropriateness of open unemployment as an inverse indicator of the pace of real economic activity in these other countries. However, an alternative specification of the Phillips relationship, that between inflation and the rate of growth of real output, has been the subject of wider investigation, most notably by Fry (1981, 1983) who has applied a small-scale model of inflation and growth to seven Pacific basin developing countries—Indonesia, Malaysia, the Philippines, Singapore, South Korea, Taiwan and Thailand.

In this model an acceleration in nominal money growth raises the inflation rate in a conventional quantity theory or monetarist manner. This, in turn, increases the rate of growth of real GNP in the short run because expectations of inflation are treated as lagging behind actual inflation rates so that actual prices come to exceed expected prices:

> entrepreneurs interpret the difference to reflect a real increase in the demand for their products. In response, they raise their rate of capacity utilization to increase output immediately, and also invest more to increase that capacity (Fry 1981: 13).

The result is a short-run Phillips curve displaying the standard positive relationship between inflation and growth.

In the long run, of course, as inflation becomes fully anticipated, this trade-off must disappear. However, in financially repressed economies where institutional rates of interest are fixed below competitive equilibrium levels, growth will not simply return to some normal trend rate but rather will decline below its original rate. In particular, higher expected rates of inflation will reduce real deposit rates of interest, thereby leading to a contraction in the demand for real money balances, where money is broadly defined to include interest-bearing deposits. The resulting contraction in the real size of the banking system will reduce the real supply of domestic credit, producing a credit squeeze which depresses the rate of growth, so that a negative relationship emerges between inflation and growth in the long run.

There remains for consideration what must be regarded in country-specific terms as the politically most significant trade-off issue in the region. It is the alleged conflict between reform and readjustment in China. Reform, in this context, refers to the systemic changes directed towards decentralization of decision-making and increasing reliance on market mechanisms, which have occurred in that country since 1978. Readjustment refers to the attempts to eliminate the macroeconomic disequilibria that have generated inflationary pressures for much of this period. Although readjustment is readily related to conventional Western goals of macroeconomic policy, particularly those relating to price stability and external balance, this is not the case with respect to the concept of reform. It has much broader connotations of which only a part relates to the very substantial changes that have occurred in the Chinese macroeconomic policy environment; but perhaps in terms of recent outcomes it can be very roughly approximated to an acceleration of economic growth and the pursuit of higher living standards.

Arguments supporting the idea of a conflict between reform and readjustment focus on the apparent way that nonagricultural reforms introduced since 1981 have caused a weakening of central control and thus an inability to regulate macroeconomic performance. Evidence of these trends has been found in declining shares of investment within the state plan, "seemingly uncontrollable growth" of extra-budgetary capital spending, and a breakdown of incomes policy, as indicated by inflationary hikes in wages and bonuses (Lin 1988).

On the other side of the debate, however, it has been pointed out that similar trends emerged in previous phases of accelerated growth before market-oriented reforms had been attempted (Lin 1988). More fundamentally, readjustment and reform may not necessarily be in conflict and may even complement each other (Balassa 1982). Although greater freedom in price setting makes it harder to repress open inflation and greater financial decentralization makes it harder to control investment, macroeconomic stabilization can smooth the implementation of reform, while the increases in efficiency expected from reform can soften the severity of trade-offs associated with the implementation of stabilization policy (World Bank 1983: 167).

18.4   Targets and Instruments

The theory of activist policy formation embraces two broad analytical approaches. In the conceptually elegant optimizing approach (Theil 1956, 1964), decision-makers are depicted as selecting settings of policy instruments which maximize an explicit social welfare function, subject to the constraints or trade-offs imposed by the economic system. The alternative, more pragmatic fixed targets approach simply specifies policy goals as given or fixed targets, and then focuses on the assembly and deployment of the policy instruments required to achieve these targets. Its guiding principle is the well-known Tinbergen rule (Tinbergen 1952) that policymakers, faced with multiple independent targets, should in general possess at least an equal number of effective policy instruments if they are to achieve all targets simultaneously. This rule is supplemented by the Principle of Effective Market Classification or assignment rule (Mundell 1960, 1962) which asserts that, in the absence of complete information or the ability to coordinate policies, each instrument should be directed or assigned solely to controlling the target variable on which it has the greatest relative effect.

In terms of practical policymaking, the optimizing approach runs into the overwhelming difficulty of approximating empirically the nature of the social welfare function and, in particular, marginal rates of substitution between target variables.

Presumably for this reason, it seems to have aroused little or no interest in relation to macroeconomic policy in the Asian-Pacific region. On the other hand, the fixed targets approach has figured quite prominently in the analysis of macroeconomic policy formation in two of the smaller and more open (though structurally very different) economies of the region, Singapore and Papua New Guinea.

Extending earlier insights by Kapur (1981), Corden (1984) has presented a simple short-run macroeconomic policy model for "a small open economy rather like Singapore" in which all output is assumed to be tradable, the domestic price level is determined by a given world price level and the exchange rate, the nominal money wage is exogenous, and perfect capital mobility equates the domestic interest rate with the sum of the given world interest rate and the expected rate of change of the exchange rate. The two target variables are employment (which is linked with output by a diminishing returns production function) and the price level; and the two policy instruments are the exchange rate and wages policy, with the former assigned to the price level and the latter to employment. Specifically, Corden argues that the exchange rate should be used to insulate Singapore from foreign inflation and deflation and thus to stabilize the price level or the rate of inflation; while the money wage should be set in the light of exchange rate/price level policy to yield a real wage conducive to the achievement of the employment target.

In this model domestic demand, and hence monetary and fiscal policy, do not have any direct effects on the price level or employment. Their only potential influence is via induced exchange rate variations; but this channel is in fact blocked by the assumption that at any one point of time the Monetary Authority of Singapore pegs the exchange rate at a desired level by open market operations in foreign exchange. Thus the money supply becomes endogenous, while fiscal policy merely helps determine the size of the current account deficit within the overall balance of payments.

There is one major qualification to the assignment rules concerning the exchange rate and wages policies. It arises from the possibility that in some circumstances (notably a decline in the terms of trade) the achievement of the employment target may require a fall in real wages. If wages policy is not strong enough to overcome the usual resistance to cuts in money wages, this fall in real wages will require a rise in the price level. In these circumstances the exchange rate should be targeted on employment, or there must be a trade-off between employment and price-level targets.

For example, assume for simplicity that all employment is in export industries. If the terms of trade decline as a result of a rise in import prices in terms of foreign currency, and if the maintenance of employment takes priority over the avoidance of inflation, then the exchange rate should not be appreciated but held constant, leaving wages policy to focus simply on preventing cost-of-living adjustments in the face of imported inflation. Alternatively, if export prices fall and the same priority holds, the exchange rate should be depreciated to restore the demand for labor, while wages policy should be used to prevent money wages rising in the face of depreciation-induced inflation.

Although a decline in the terms of trade requires a fall in real wages if total employment is to be maintained, Corden also recognizes that in an economy like Singapore where there is considerable reliance on foreign labor, repatriation of the latter could serve to maintain full employment for Singaporean nationals alone without the need for a decline in real wages, provided that the terms of trade decline was not too large. (Exchange rate policy could then revert to the role of preserving price stability.)

In so far as the downward rigidity of money wages limits the scope for wages policy, it highlights the fact that the Tinbergen rule requires that policy instruments should not only be at least equal in number to policy targets but also effective. To this end, considerable attention has been directed in a Singaporean context to the means of making nominal labor costs more flexible in a downward direction. A careful definition of the money wage instrument as "the average level of wage and salary rates, inclusive of employer CPF [Central Provident Fund] contributions, payroll tax and SDF [Skills Development Fund] contributions, *and* bonus payments" (Lim et al. 1988: 315) clearly points to a number of ways of making nominal labor costs more sensitive to policy requirements; and in fact in the Singapore recession of the mid-1980s a 15 percentage point cut in employers' CPF contributions did achieve a significant one-off cut in labor costs.

The analytical simplicity of the Corden approach stems from its assumptions of perfect capital mobility, a given world interest rate, and the absence of nontradable goods and services. Their empirical relevance may, of course, be disputed. However, econometric evidence suggesting that in Singapore local monetary developments have no direct effect on the interest rate, whereas it responds on a one-to-one basis to variations in the foreign interest rate adjusted for the expected movement in the exchange rate (Edwards and Khan 1985: 393) is certainly consistent with the first two assumptions. Moreover, Corden (1984: 36) has defended the third as "a useful first approximation"; although he readily concedes the existence of significant nontradable activities in Singapore and their implication that domestic aggregate demand will, after all, have some direct effect on the price level and (given the money wage) the level of employment. To this extent, fiscal policy may be viewed as a third available instrument, supporting exchange rate and wages policies.

As in the case of Singapore, much of the analysis of macroeconomic policy in Papua New Guinea has been conducted in terms of the Tinbergen/Mundell fixed targets framework. The PNG approach has, however, varied significantly from that in Singapore because of obvious structural and institutional differences. Thus there has been no attempt to impose an assumption of perfect international mobility of capital (indeed, for the most part international capital flows, including aid, have been implicitly treated as exogenously determined); and relatedly the overall balance of payments situation has been an explicit and major concern. Nontradable activities have figured more prominently; and there has been considerable pessimism about the scope for an effective wages policy to influence real wages.

The PNG approach basically derives from the so-called Australian dependent economy model of Swan (1955) and Salter (1959). This incorporates two types of goods and services, tradables and nontradables, the law of one price for tradables, and exogenously determined terms of trade. There are two policy objectives, external balance and internal balance, and two sets of policy instruments. The latter consist of expenditure policy directed at control of aggregate absorption of goods and services and switching policy directed at control of the relative prices of tradables and nontradables.

In the PNG context this model has been modified to provide what is essentially a three targets/three instruments framework (Garnaut and Baxter 1983). The internal balance objective is divided into separate price stability and employment targets, and two different instruments, exchange rate policy and wages policy, replace switching policy. Within this framework or variants of it, the tendency has been to argue that expenditure policy, or more specifically fiscal policy, should be assigned to the external balance objective, while exchange rate policy should be assigned to the price stability objective (Palmer 1979; Daniel and Sims 1986). By implication, wages policy is left for the employment objective.

In practice, however, this last dimension of macroeconomic policy attracted little interest prior to the early 1980s because strong pressures for institutionalized real wage rigidity, with money wages closely linked to the consumer price index, were seen as effectively rendering policymakers powerless to do much about unemployment in the short run. At the same time, real wage rigidity was relatedly viewed as preventing exchange rate policy from permanently affecting relative prices between tradables and nontradables and thus external balance, while correspondingly reinforcing its impact on the price level.

The upshot was a truncated but highly influential version of the targets/ instrument framework which provided the theoretical underpinning for the so-called hard currency strategy pursued in PNG in the latter half of the 1970s. This strategy was based on "a strong preference for a convertible currency and low inflation, and a presumption that, at least in the early years after independence, it would not be possible to sustain significant reductions in real wages" (Daniel and Sims 1986: 24). Its implementation involved government decisions "to direct exchange rate policy to the goal of maintaining price stability and to maintain balance of payments equilibrium by controlling the level and rate of growth of public expenditure" (Goodman et al. 1985: 53).

The hard currency strategy proved controversial, mainly in relation to the use of currency revaluations to combat imported inflation. One strand of criticism was that revaluations were not passed through fully into retail prices (Lam 1979, 1980; Yari 1980), a possibility which could be explained in terms of the opportunities that revaluations provided for the covert exercise of some degree of monopolistic power in importing or distribution. However, a comprehensive examination of the evidence in the early 1980s failed to support the criticism (Garnaut and Baxter 1983). It was found that since the introduction of a separate monetary system at the beginning of 1976, the prices of imported goods in PNG had, on average, risen more slowly than world prices, by about the proportion by which the local currency, the kina, had appreciated against other currencies. Detailed analysis of the price behavior of particular goods pointed to kina appreciations eventually having been fully passed through into domestic prices, although the pass-through had taken some time, especially in the case of durable goods.

The other strand of criticism was that the use of currency revaluations to combat imported inflation tended to have adverse effects on export and import-competing activities, and hence on the balance of payments, employment and growth (Dahanayake 1982; Mannur 1983; Goodman et al. 1985). Subject only to lags in adjustment, this criticism also appears largely to lack substance. The existence of virtually full wage indexation would have ensured that in all but the very short run the competitive position of tradable activities would have been no better in the absence of currency revaluation, while inflation would have been greater.

Although, within its own terms of reference, the hard currency strategy represented a logically consistent and effective approach to macroeconomic policy formulation, its acceptance of real wage resistance as a constraint meant that it lacked the capacity to prevent falling employment and rising unemployment in the face of declining terms of trade. Since the early 1980s rising concern about this problem has combined with a significant weakening of the institutionalized link between prices and money wages to refocus policy analysis in PNG. In particular, attention has been directed to the need and opportunity for switching policies to engineer an increase in the prices of tradables relative to the prices of labor and nontradables, and thus complement restrictions on absorption made necessary, at least in part, by the real income loss associated with deterioration of the terms of trade. The increase in the relative prices of tradables could be achieved either by permitting ongoing international inflation to raise domestic prices of tradables gradually, perhaps with reinforcement from a series of small depreciations, or by a large once-for-all devaluation; but in either case money wages should not rise in a similar proportion (Garnaut and Baxter 1983; Goodman et al. 1985). While the former approach would probably put less strain on PNG's centralized wage determination mechanisms, both are of course to some extent inflationary. However, some additional inflation would be an unavoidable trade-off for the simultaneous achievement of improved performances in employment and the balance of payments, given the continued likelihood of downward rigidity of nominal wages. In short, we have a three target/three instrument policy framework in which the effectiveness of one instrument, wages policy, is clearly circumscribed.

18.5 Monetary Policy

An effective policy instrument is one that is both controllable and reliable. In the case of monetary policy, controllability refers to the extent to which selected monetary aggregates are capable of being controlled by the monetary authorities, while reliability refers to the extent to which these aggregates are reliably linked to (that is, possess close and systematic relationships with) the ultimate target variables of macroeconomic policy. These two dimensions of monetary policy are examined in reverse order.

18.5.1 Reliability

The issue which has probably been most extensively investigated under this heading is the nature of the demand for money functions in the economies of the region. This reflects the fact that a "necessary condition for monetary policy to have a predictable effect on the ultimate economic objectives is that there must exist a well-defined and stable demand for money" (Aghevli et al. 1979: 788). In general, research into the topic has followed the well-established approach of hypothesizing that the demand for real money balances, defined in either narrow (M1) or broad (M2, M3) terms, is functionally related to a scale variable (typically a real income aggregate) and to the opportunity costs of holding money, measured by an interest rate variable and/or a proxy for the expected rate of inflation, with lags introduced into the relationship through a partial adjustment mechanism. Empirical findings have in many cases been supportive.

For Indonesia, an inquiry using quarterly data for the period 1968–73 concluded that the demand for real balances, in narrow as well as broad terms, was a stable function of real income, the inflation rate and lagged real balances, with actual inflation being viewed as a "close proxy" for expected inflation (Aghevli 1977: 46). For the later but overlapping period, 1969–80, a similar conclusion was reached using a narrow concept of money, although the specification of the expectations variable differed (Parikh et al. 1985). In neither study was the rate of interest a significant explanatory variable, possibly because it was an infrequently changed administered rate.

On the other hand, Boediono (1985), using data for the period 1975–84, found indications that the domestic interest rate as well as the current rate of inflation (employed as a proxy for the expected rate) did influence the demand for money. This study is also noteworthy for two other findings: first, a measure of real income incorporating the effects of changes in the terms of trade was a better explanatory variable than the conventional GDP aggregate; and secondly the difference in rates of returns between foreign and domestic financial assets was significant in explaining the time and saving deposit component of broad money. Given the obvious difficulties of forecasting movements in the terms of trade, foreign interest rates and exchange rate expectations, these findings have potentially worrisome implications for the practice of monetary programming.

Relatedly, the ease with which residents in ultraliberal financial entrepots such as Singapore can substitute between domestic and foreign currency deposits makes the demand for money in such economies potentially quite unstable (McKinnon 1981). However, at least so far, currency substitution does not appear to have created serious difficulties in modelling the demand for money in Singapore. Of the many studies of this demand, including Khan (1981), Simkin (1984) and Lee (1984), Khan's is the most comprehensive. Its results indicated considerable support for a standard partial adjustment money demand function in which expectations of inflation are revised adaptively in the light of the difference between lagged rates of actual and expected inflation; but an extended model incorporating a further adjustment mechanism relating to unexpected changes in the nominal money stock fitted the data even better. These results held for both narrow and broad definitions of money, although tests for parameter stability suggested that the functions for narrow money would be more reliable for prediction and policy purposes.

For Malaysia, estimates of broad and narrow versions of a money demand function indicated that the aggregate demand for money balances was influenced by income, the rate of inflation (a proxy for the expected rate) and at least one (short-term) interest rate (Semudram 1981). For Fiji, similar variables were reported to be all statistically significant in the case of narrow money, with overall results indicating "a stable but weak relationship between arguments and demand for real balances" (Karunaratne 1985: 30). For Korea, van Wijnbergen (1982, 1985) found that the demand for real money balances narrowly defined displayed a strong negative dependence on the inflation rate, as did real time deposits which also displayed a positive dependence on their own interest rate and a negative dependence on the curb market interest rate. In neither case, however, was the real income variable significant, a result which is consistent with later work (Choi 1987). Other estimates of demand for money functions for the market economies of the region, including estimates for the Philippines and Thailand, can be found in the multicountry studies of Aghevli et al. (1979) and Khan (1980).

Finally, it is appropriate to draw attention to the nature of the demand for money in the planned economy of China. Historically, the currency component of that demand was of particular significance to the Chinese monetary authorities because currency was the only means of payment for consumer goods. In drawing up the so-called Cash Plan the authorities sought to determine that volume of currency in circulation which, given planned supplies of consumer goods and controlled prices, would maintain market equilibrium and avoid excess demand pressure and repressed inflation. To this end, they resorted to a quantity theory of money approach:

> If the velocity of money is assumed to be constant, prices are fixed, and the volume of retail sales is determined by the national plan, then the quantity equation ($MV = PQ$) provides the stock of money (defined as currency in the Chinese literature) required by the price and output objectives (de Wulf and Goldsbrough 1986: 215).

In this context the assumption of constant velocity is, of course, equivalent to assuming that households' demand for currency is a constant proportion of the value of retail sales. In practice, its *ex ante* value was apparently based on the actual value realized in an earlier benchmark year or period of years considered to have been financially stable (Chai 1981; de Wulf and Goldsbrough 1986).

Irrespective of the degree of accuracy achieved by this crude extrapolative method of estimating retail velocity, there is every likelihood that the usefulness of the whole approach has deteriorated greatly as a result of China's economic and social reforms. The growing importance of household bank deposits, which form a fairly close substitute for currency, plus the greater autonomy achieved by enterprises and local governments indicate a need to use broader monetary aggregates than the currency holdings of households (de Wulf and Goldsbrough 1986: 233).

As yet, little work appears to have been done on the identification and stability of demand functions for these broader aggregates. However, in a pioneering study Feltenstein and Farhadian (1987) have used historical data to estimate a stable real balance demand equation for consumer holdings of broad money, defined as currency in circulation plus household time and savings deposits. Their study involves the assumption that there is an implicit or true price level which would induce consumers, in the absence of commodity shortages, to hold the same quantity of nominal money as they are observed to hold at existing controlled prices and with existing shortages. On this basis, real money balances were found to be explained by real income and the anticipated true rate of inflation, while the actual true rate of inflation was simultaneously determined to be about 2.5 times the official rate.

Although a well-defined and stable demand for money function is a necessary condition for monetary policy to have predictable effects on ultimate target variables such as inflation, employment and real output, and the balance of payments, it is clearly not a sufficient condition. Quite apart from the likelihood that in some circumstances the money supply may be an endogenous variable governed by the behavior of the demand for money (an issue which will be explored subsequently when discussing controllability), the interaction between a policy-determined supply of money and a given demand for money function forms only part of the transmission mechanism linking monetary policy to the ultimate target variables. Within the region, various further possible aspects of the mechanism have also been explored, including the conventional Keynesian idea that it is interest rates (and/or credit availability in financially repressed economies) which are the means whereby money market imbalances impact on aggregate demand for goods and services, and investment demand in particular.

On this topic evidence and opinions are mixed. For Singapore, there do not appear to be any strong econometric relationships between interest rates and the components of fixed investment or, more broadly, between monetary variables and real net investment commitments (Lim et al. 1988). A similar story may apply to Malaysia where there has been scepticism about whether higher costs of credit in times of inflation discouraged investment (Ariff 1983).

On the other hand, for the Philippines and Korea, there are indications that financial market variables do influence fixed investment (Lim 1987; van Wijnbergen 1982). In the latter case, they are described as having a strong impact, "with quantity signals (change in real credit to the private sector outstanding) of relevance in the regulated markets, and price signals (real interest rate in the curb market) in the unregulated curb market" (van Wijnbergen 1982: 141). Moreover, in Korea the real curb rate of interest also appears to exert a strongly negative influence on private consumption.

While interest rates and credit availability have traditionally been viewed as influencing real output and prices through their effects on aggregate demand, there has been increasing recognition in the Asia-Pacific region of the possibility that they may also exert an influence through the supply side of the economy. In particular, to the extent that firms' production and pricing decisions depend on the availability and cost of financial working capital, monetary policy may have an influence on output and prices separate from its influence via spending on final products.

Basically, there are two different but related supply-side approaches. The first centers on a credit availability effect to which Fry (1981, 1983, 1985), building on the work of McKinnon (1973) and Kapur (1976), has several times drawn attention. At the risk of oversimplification, this effect rests on the idea that in financially repressed economies the supply-constrained volume of real bank credit limits real working capital funds and hence output. Consequently, in the very short run the use of monetary policy to reduce the rate of nominal credit expansion will have an immediate negative impact on the aggregate supply of real output; although it is central to the argument that over the long run the demand-side deflationary consequences of this form of monetary policy will lead to an increase in the demand for real money balances and hence an increase in the real supply of credit. Another implication, following McKinnon (1973), is that in pursuing an anti-inflationary monetary policy:

> the monetary authorities should initially raise the average nominal deposit rate paid on money holdings, thereby reducing the excess supply of money by raising the demand for real money balances. Concomitant with this increase in real money balances there will ... occur an immediate increase in the flow of real bank credit and hence in real output. Subsequently, the monetary authorities can proceed to gradually reduce the rate of monetary expansion as inflationary expectations decline, so that the flow of real bank credit need not decline at any time during the stabilization process and the short-run squeeze on working capital and real output be completely avoided (Kapur 1976: 778–9).

The second approach to the supply-side influence of monetary policy focuses on the so-called Cavallo effect, otherwise termed more informatively the working capital cost-push effect. It is based on the argument that where the purchase of variable inputs (labor, intermediate imports, and so forth) used in production is financed by working capital in the form of credit, the cost of this credit (interest) forms an element in the variable costs of production. Consequently, changes in interest rates paid by firms on their working capital will cause shifts in the aggregate supply function for real output. In particular, a tight monetary policy, leading to more expensive credit, will have a negative supply impact, exerting upward pressure on prices and downward pressure on output. This impact is viewed as possessing the potential to offset the short-run demand-side impact of tight monetary policy on inflation, while reinforcing its short-run demand-side recessionary effects on output.

Simulation results from a quarterly macroeconometric model suggest that this potential may be realized in South Korea:

> Monetary restraint has serious costs in terms of lost output and investment, causes an initially perverse response of the inflation rate due to the credit-supply link ... and may take considerable time before it brings inflation down. The initial effect actually comes as an adverse supply shock, increasing inflation and reducing output; later on traditional demand shock effects take over ... This analysis warns ... that initial results may be perverse and the good results slow in arriving, with high costs in terms of lost output and investment (van Wijnbergen 1982: 165).

Relatedly, the Cavallo effect casts doubt on the McKinnon/Kapur prescription of raising rates of interest on deposit money as a means of combating the short-run squeeze on working capital and output associated with reducing the rate of monetary expansion. In Korea, it appears that increases in interest rates on time deposits are contractionary in the short run because they trigger portfolio shifts out of the curb market, leading to a tightening of overall credit conditions and higher costs of financing working capital. Since the latter also temporarily increase the inflation rate, the increase in time deposit rates is actually stagflationary in its initial impact (van Wijnbergen 1985). More generally, it appears that the McKinnon/Kapur prescription may be vulnerable to the extent that the interest-earning component of broad money is a closer substitute for informal sector interest-earning financial assets such as curb market loans than for cash and commodities.

The Cavallo effect has also been identified in a Philippine context. Anecdotal evidence suggests that it operated particularly strongly in the final years of the Marcos regime. The unprecedentedly high interest rates of that period were identified in the business community as a source of increased production costs (Manasan 1988), with manufacturing operations being shut down or scaled down as the cost of financing working capital became prohibitive (Montes 1987). A more comprehensive examination, using a one-sector macro model with 1958–80 data, suggests that while monetary and credit contraction to control inflation will exert a negative effect on aggregate demand via investment demand, this seems to be dominated in the short run by the working capital cost-push effect, giving an immediate stagflationary outcome. Only in the longer run is there a prospect of a fall in inflation (Lim 1987).

15.5.2 Controllability

Turning from the effects of monetary changes on ultimate target variables to the logically prior subject of the controllability of money aggregates, it is possible to discern within it three major regional issues or themes. First, there is the extent to which the money supply is controllable or uncontrollable under fixed or managed exchange rate regimes. Secondly, where exchange rate regimes do not appear to preclude controllability, there is the issue of the extent to which the money supply is in fact controlled and the extent to which it is simply accommodating. And thirdly, there is the extensive topic of the nature and efficacy of the specific means or instruments of control.

The focal point for the first issue is the well-known monetarist proposition that it is not possible to control both the exchange rate and the money supply; or, to put it more specifically, "under a system of fixed exchange rates … domestic monetary policy cannot influence the total money supply, but only its composition between foreign and domestic components" (Aghevli et al. 1979: 813). In the context of the small and very open economy of Singapore, where the last elements of exchange controls were abolished in 1978, where capital appears to be internationally very mobile, and where the authorities have adopted a policy of exchange rate targeting, this proposition has commanded widespread support. Kapur (1981), Corden (1984) as already noted, and Fong and Lim (1985) have all essentially subscribed to the argument that:

> a domestic monetary target that differs significantly from that arising as a byproduct of foreign exchange policy is most difficult to achieve. Since the domestic money stock is largely endogenous, there is only limited scope for independent monetary policy in Singapore (Lim et al. 1988: 323).

Moreover, it is an argument which has gained official acceptance. The Chairman of the Monetary Authority of Singapore is on record as stating that "monetary policy … that is, control of the monetary supply—has no place in Singapore" (quoted in Simkin 1984: 10–11).

By contrast, in the case of Thailand, it appears that the monetary authorities have been able to pursue discretionary monetary policy in at least the short run despite an ongoing tradition of a fixed exchange rate policy, albeit one subject to intermittent devaluations. At first glance, this seems to involve a contradiction. A monetary contraction, by causing an increase in domestic interest rates, should attract capital inflow which returns the money supply and interest rates to previous levels; while a monetary expansion should have the opposite effects. However, the apparent contradiction disappears once it is recognized that the capital account of the balance of payments of Thailand is not fully open. Three major factors have restricted openness and hence hindered induced capital flows: ceilings on domestic interest rates, direct controls on capital outflow, and regulation of the net foreign exchange positions of commercial banks. It is these factors that have been ultimately responsible for the short-run capacity of the Thai monetary authorities to control the money supply (Warr and Nidhiprabha 1988).

For Taiwan also, there is evidence to suggest that the monetary authorities have had some capacity to manipulate the money supply under a fixed exchange rate system, notwithstanding periods of apparent loss of control associated with large balance of payments surpluses (Kuo 1983: 203–5; Kohsaka 1987: 333). Simulation results from the econometric model constructed by Lii (1987) to examine the effects of monetary policy in Taiwan yield a long-run offset coefficient of central bank domestic credit on net foreign assets of about –0.633 (with a lower absolute value in the short run). This implies that while an expansionary monetary policy would cause a substantial loss of international reserves, the latter would have a far from completely offsetting effect on the monetary base. The failure of the offset coefficient to rise to unity even in the long run may, as argued for Thailand, reflect capital account controls.

In South Korea such controls may have become, with the passage of time, less reliable in providing scope for independent control of the money supply. In 1983 it was observed that, despite supposedly strict control of capital movements, businesses had somehow managed to borrow abroad when domestic financial markets had tightened, even if the opposite case had been rather rare (Park 1983: 322, 325).

Perhaps the most wide-ranging evidence, within the region, relating to the controllability of the money supply under fixed exchange rate regimes is that provided by Yenko (1985), using data from the 1970s for the then five ASEAN economies. Initially regression tests on several versions of a monetarist exchange market pressure model are used to establish that in the ASEAN countries exchange market pressure is absorbed mainly by foreign exchange reserve movements rather than exchange rate changes. The two-stage least squares technique is then employed to estimate for each country a simultaneous equation model of the determination of reserve movements and changes in the net domestic credit of the monetary authority. Within this model, consistent with the monetary approach to the balance of payments, changes in foreign reserves are hypothesized to be negatively influenced by changes in net domestic credit of the monetary authority; while, through a policy reaction function, changes in domestic credit are hypothesized to be influenced in part by changes in reserves.

With respect to the latter relationship, there is evidence that reserve flows induce opposite movements in the domestic component of the monetary base, that is, the ASEAN countries sterilize reserve flows. However, it also appears that domestic credit movements induce offsetting movements in foreign reserves. Specifically, the estimated offset coefficients range from –0.64 for Malaysia to –0.72 for the Philippines. These coefficients are high, but they nevertheless suggest that there is some scope in at least the short run for the authorities in the ASEAN countries to vary the monetary base, and hence the money supply, despite the simultaneous pursuit of an exchange rate target.

Indeed, in the case of Singapore the coefficient of –0.68 suggests that the scope is perhaps greater than that implied by the views already canvassed in relation to that economy. However, it should be noted that the study uses data for 1972–79, for much of which period there were still some exchange controls in Singapore. Moreover, the estimated offset coefficients refer to only unlagged quarterly relationships. It follows that the estimate for Singapore is not necessarily inconsistent with an equilibrium value for that country in the 1980s which, perhaps incorporating some allowance for adjustment lags, could well be very close to unity.

Even where controllability of the money supply is not precluded by choice of exchange rate regime, it does not follow that control can or will be exercised by the monetary authorities. The money supply may still exhibit accommodating or endogenous behavior as a result of an inadequate armoury of monetary policy weapons or simply a lack of motivation on the part of the authorities to use them. Within the region this possibility has long attracted attention. Following early insights by Hicks (1967) and Sundrum (1973), it has been argued that money played an at least partly endogenous role in the Indonesian inflationary experience of the 1950s and 1960s as a result of a feedback mechanism whereby inflation tended to increase nominal government expenditure faster than nominal tax revenue. According to one analysis, the origins of the inflation were increases in government expenditures in the late 1950s and the impact of drought on food supplies in 1961. A rising price level then led to further increases in government outlays in nominal terms; and since nominal government revenues lagged behind the rising price level, the resulting budget deficits had to be financed by money creation. This, in turn, caused inflation to accelerate, with the process perpetuating itself, and eventually reaching a state close to hyperinflation in the mid-1960s (Aghevli and Khan 1977).

South Korea is also an economy with a history of some loss of control of the money supply as a result of domestic factors, although unlike Indonesia in the 1960s this has not reflected the direct financing needs of government. In part, the endogenous monetary expansion over the two decades prior to the Korean stabilization success of the early 1980s took the form of accommodation of nonmonetary upward pressure on prices and wages, particularly that arising from the two international oil price hikes. In part also, it was attributable to the use of central bank credit to subsidize loans to exporters (through an automatic rediscount mechanism), to cover the deficits of a grain price support program, and to help fund a massive investment program in heavy and chemical industries (Park 1983; Fry 1985).

Hong Kong provided, during its nine-year floating exchange rate period, probably the purest example of an endogenous money supply which, in at least an immediate sense, was governed entirely by domestic factors. Until 1972 the colony had operated a fixed exchange rate currency board system distinguished by the fact that the note issue was essentially the responsibility of two private commercial banks. These were entitled to issue bank notes subject to the matching purchase, with foreign exchange, of Exchange Fund certificates of indebtedness; and correspondingly they were required to withdraw notes from circulation to the extent that they surrendered certificates of indebtedness to the Fund in return for foreign exchange. Within this system, the money supply adjusted automatically to maintain equilibrium in the balance of payments.

In 1972, however, the system was changed to permit the note-issuing banks to acquire certificates of indebtedness by simply crediting the account of the Exchange Fund held at these banks with Hong Kong dollars, thus breaking the link between net foreign exchange receipts and new issues of notes; and two years later the Hong Kong dollar was permitted to float freely in foreign exchange markets. From then until 1983, when a new fixed exchange rate currency board system was introduced, the behavior of the money supply was unconstrained by either the balance of payments or domestic policy. Floating exchange rates precluded external influences. The fact that the currency issue could be increased on demand by the note-issuing banks creating additional Hong Kong dollar deposit liabilities in favor of the Exchange Fund meant that the monetary base was not subject to any direct policy influence. And attempts by the government to control the total money supply through moral suasion and the threat of credit controls, through its influence on an interest-fixing bank cartel, and through sterilization of fiscal surpluses were all ineffective (Sung 1985: 140–1).

In this period the money supply was market-determined. To the extent that the authorities could be said to be undertaking a monetary policy, it effectively involved adherence to a modern form of the real bills doctrine (Fry 1983; Moreno 1986). As was observed towards the end of the period, "the money supply seems to be determined mainly by the behavioural parameters of banks rather than by the actions of the monetary authority" (Ho 1983: 351).

The conventional criticism of the real bills doctrine is that it can lead to instability, involving money creation causing price increases, and these increases causing further money creation in a self-perpetuating inflationary spiral. The extent to which this process occurred in the case of the Hong Kong monetary experiment is, however, problematical. Granger causality testing for the period December 1978–December 1981, using an M3 definition of money supply, revealed a two-way relationship between money and prices (Ho 1983). On the other hand, a later study for January 1973–February 1979, November 1974–February 1979 and the longer period, January 1973–October 1983 failed to find evidence of Granger causality between past prices and an M1 definition of current money supply. Since a necessary (though not sufficient) condition for instability in the above sense is that inflation should lead to money creation, the results of this study suggest that Hong Kong's monetary regime was stable (Moreno 1986).

The issue of an accommodating money supply of domestic origin has also been canvassed in relation to the People's Republic of China. Traditionally, the Chinese authorities have sought to regulate monetary growth through explicit financial planning:

> The financial plan ... is the counterpart of the physical economic plan. It is composed
> of the Government Budget, the Credit Plan, and the Cash Plan. The Budget needs no
> explanation. The Credit Plan sets out the expected sources and uses of banking funds.
> The Cash Plan specifies the planned change in currency in circulation as a net result
> of cash transactions between the government sector (including enterprises) and
> households (including the farm sector).... All three plans are simultaneously constrained
> by a national flow-of-funds identity, so that increases in currency in circulation must
> equal the increases in banks' net lendings (i.e. net of increases in deposits) to the
> government and enterprises, minus increases in households' time and saving deposits
> (Cheng 1981: 21).

It has been argued, however, that in pre-reform China this planning approach
resulted in no more than a "passive accommodating" form of monetary policy
(Hsiao 1982, 1984). In particular, "the banking system had little choice but to
finance budgetary deficits when they arose" (de Wulf and Goldsbrough 1986: 214);
while strict quantitative control on credit supplied to enterprises was precluded
by the "commodity inventory system" for the provision of working capital, a
procedure which, like the Hong Kong experiment, involved adherence to a form
of real bills principle. Moreover, although credit developments had obvious
implications for currency in circulation, the monetary authorities could in fact do
little to regulate currency flows directly, other than by periodic savings drives to
attract deposits from the household sector (Cheng 1981; Hsiao 1982, 1984; de Wulf
and Goldsbrough 1986).

Over the last decade, the process of reform has seen the Chinese monetary
authorities given greater responsibility for the pursuit of macroeconomic stability
(an objective hitherto pursued mainly through physical planning and administrative
regulation of prices and wages); and to this end they have acquired new policy
instruments to control the credit activities of the specialized banks which have
emerged within a restructured banking system. However, although a more active
monetary policy now seems feasible, it has been recognized that other aspects of
reform have exerted some countervailing influence. Specifically, reductions in direct
administrative controls over enterprise decision making have at times generated
strong demands for credit which have been at least partially accommodated by
the banking system, with consequent rapid monetary expansion and aggregate
demand pressure (de Wulf and Goldsbrough 1986).

There remain for consideration the nature and efficacy of the specific
instruments of monetary control. In so far as the money supply may be viewed
as the product of the monetary base and the money multiplier, instruments may
be classified according to whether they operate upon the monetary base, the
multiplier, or in some cases perhaps both. The principal instruments in the first
category are rediscounting (variations in central bank credit to commercial banks)
and open market operations. Clearly, a necessary (though not sufficient) condition
for their efficacy in influencing the money supply is the existence of a stable and
predictable money multiplier, that is, a stable relationship between the monetary

base and the money supply. This issue has been investigated econometrically for the Philippines, leading to the conclusion that by appropriate manipulation of the monetary base, the Philippine monetary authorities can substantially influence bank credit and money supply (Daquila 1987: 39).

Rediscounting has an immediate effect on the monetary base through its direct impact on bank reserves. Historically, it has been quite common in the region, although it has been employed more as a tool of selective credit policy than as an instrument of aggregate monetary control. Ironically, the former use can and often does jeopardize control over the monetary base (Fry 1985, 1986; Arndt 1979b). However, while this risk has long been present in Thailand, it does not appear to have seriously interfered with that country's pursuit of a counter-cyclical monetary policy in which the main instrument has been the central bank lending rate. The Bank of Thailand normally seeks to influence or regulate the movement of reserve money through its ability to control its credit to commercial banks, with other sources of change in reserve money being "largely beyond control of the central bank's short-term monetary operations" (Wibulswasdi 1986: 29).

It has always been conventional wisdom that while open market operations are the most flexible of monetary policy instruments, they are largely inappropriate to developing countries because of insufficient suitable securities and an absence or lack of depth in secondary financial markets. Moreover, policies intended to encourage the development of a government bond market (for example, the maintenance of stable bond prices) often tend themselves to interfere with the use of open market operations (Khatkhate 1977).

Despite this pessimism, the Philippines has for some time been recognized as an exceptional case. In 1970 the central bank of that country started issuing its own certificates of indebtedness and later began trading in them in order to influence commercial bank reserves. At the end of the 1970s these open market operations were assessed as "fairly successful," and identified as the major instrument of Philippine monetary policy (Aghevli et al. 1979). Subsequently, they played a powerful role in the tight credit regime of 1984 when interest rates on central bank bills and treasury bills reached levels in excess of 40 percent.

Moreover, following the lead of the Philippines, and reflecting a general trend away from financial regulation and direct controls towards deregulation and indirect methods of monetary management, there have been further experiments with open market operations in the region, most notably in Indonesia. In 1984 Bank Indonesia copied the Central Bank of the Philippines by introducing its own debt certificate to be used in open market operations. Together with new discount facilities, these have been judged to have, "in general, proved adequate for day-to-day monetary management" (Balino and Sundararajan 1986: 192).

Other instruments of monetary control include variable reserve requirements, quantitative credit controls, interest rate controls and moral suasion. The first three may all influence the magnitude of the money multiplier, while the last may affect the monetary base and/or the money multiplier.

In recent years the trend within the region toward financial deregulation has led to decreasing reliance on credit and interest rate controls. To some extent the same is true of variable reserve requirements which have long been recognized as a blunt and inflexible policy tool which cannot be changed as often as, say, open market operations. Reserve requirements have, moreover, been subjected to the criticism of ineffectiveness. For example, in both Papua New Guinea and Taiwan, the effectiveness of statutory reserve variations have been impaired by the volume of excess liquidity held by banks; while in Indonesia their use is limited by segmentation of the financial market, which generates wide variations in excess reserve holdings across institutions, and by competition from offshore markets (Balino and Sundararajan 1986: 212).

Regional views on moral suasion, the final instrument to be considered, are mixed. On the one hand, it has been judged effective or likely to be effective in Malaysia (Lee and Jao 1982), Singapore (Lim et al. 1988), Indonesia (Grenville 1981) and Fiji (Luckett 1987). On the other hand, in Hong Kong, with a multitude of highly competitive commercial banks, its effectiveness must be doubted (Sung 1985: 140). Moreover, in at least Singapore and Fiji its apparent effectiveness appears to relate more to selective credit policy than aggregative monetary policy.

To conclude this section, it may be appropriate to raise an issue of which comparatively little has been heard in the region in recent years, that of "rules" versus "discretion" or "monetary targeting" versus "fine tuning". At the end of the 1970s Aghevli et al. (1979) completed their study of monetary policy in selected Asian countries by suggesting that the prospects for fine tuning were poor because of institutional constraints on the flexibility of specific monetary instruments, an absence of well-developed information systems giving rise to relatively long "problem recognition" lags, and a lack of full internal economic integration resulting in only a very gradual spread or dissemination of the effects of policy changes. In so far as a number of countries in the region have subsequently experienced some increase in the flexibility of monetary policy instruments, greatly improved information systems and the emergence of more closely integrated economic structures, the time is perhaps ripe for a comprehensive re-examination of the issue.

18.6   Fiscal Policy

Within the Asia-Pacific region, fiscal policy has tended to receive less attention than monetary policy as a separate tool of macroeconomic management. This tendency, which is by no means unique to the region, probably reflects several factors. First, in so far as underdeveloped domestic capital markets ensure that budgetary imbalances are essentially monetary phenomena, the distinction between fiscal and monetary policies becomes blurred, and may even be regarded as "almost non-existent" (Coats and Khatkhate 1984: 331). Second, the scope for using fiscal policy for purposes of short-run macroeconomic control is restricted by the fact that it also serves other objectives of government policy. In particular, in the developing countries of the Asian-Pacific region various long-term development objectives have exerted a major influence on the determination of the levels and composition of government revenue and expenditure, thereby limiting the scope for adjusting these variables for short-term stabilization purposes (United Nations 1983: 171). Third, much more so than monetary policy, the discretionary component of fiscal policy has been long and widely held to be a cumbersome and inflexible arm of macroeconomic policy, subject to lengthy and uncertain implementation lags associated with institutional rigidities, administrative bottlenecks and political pressures. Lastly, recognition of the links between fiscal deficits and foreign debt problems in much of the third world has generated considerable skepticism, rightly or wrongly, about the feasibility and adequacy of traditional counter-cyclical fiscal policy in relatively open developing economies.

There has, nevertheless, been a not insubstantial concern about the macroeconomic aspects of fiscal policy. Three interrelated issues have been prominent. The first is the impact of the public sector or, more narrowly, the government budget on aggregate demand, and the implications of this impact, particularly for real output. The second is the extent to which fiscal policy has actually been deployed, intentionally or otherwise, as a tool for stabilizing domestic economic activity. And the third is the specifically normative issue of the appropriate design of fiscal policy to combat the effects of export price instability.

18.6.1 Macroeconomic Impact

The convenient but very crude practice of using the budget deficit as an indicator of the effects of the public sector on aggregate demand is as common in Asian-Pacific developing countries as elsewhere. However, within the region, there has also been a widespread appreciation of its inadequacies, especially those relating to the fact that budgets involve external transactions as well as transactions having a direct bearing on the aggregate demand for domestic output. In the case of Indonesia, where oil revenues have been very substantial, Booth and McCawley (1981) addressed this issue in a pioneering series of estimates which separated the overall budget balance into two components, a domestic balance showing "the *first-round* direct fiscal impact of the budget on GDP" and a foreign balance showing the corresponding impact on the balance of payments.

Although the concept of the domestic balance is clearly superior to that of the overall balance as a measure of the domestic impact of the budget, it is not without its weaknesses. In particular, it makes no allowance for the possibility that the marginal propensities of the private sector to reduce spending as a result of taxation and to increase spending as a result of transfer payments from the public sector may be less than unity. Moreover, by definition it ignores any induced income-multiplier effects. These considerations have, however, been taken into account in varying degrees in a number of fiscal leverage studies which seek to incorporate the differential effects of various categories of public outlays and revenues, including multiplier effects, on aggregate demand and income.

For example, for Indonesia, an open-economy multiplier methodology has been used in an attempt to measure the "Total Effects" on domestic demand and real output that resulted from the initial and secondary effects of changes in government expenditures and taxes over the period 1969–83 (Snyder 1985). This methodology distinguishes, on the one hand, between changes in the real volume of government expenditure and changes in government expenditure due to changes in wage rates and prices, and on the other hand between changes in direct taxes and changes in indirect taxes. The results suggest that the "Total Effects" of government budgetary changes accounted on average for as much as half the GDP growth rate over the above period.

For Taiwan, a more complex investigation of fiscal leverage has separated the total effects of budgetary changes on real GDP (inclusive of multiplier repercussions) into those due, directly and indirectly, to discretionary budget measures and those which are automatic, that is, essentially built-in stabilizers (Yu and Chen 1982). For the period 1952–79, the total effects of budgetary changes are estimated to have contributed on average a net 3.77 percentage points to the annual rate of growth of GDP. Discretionary effects contributed as much as 5.14 percentage points, but they were partially offset by automatic effects which exerted a dampening or negative influence of 1.37 percentage points.

Fiscal leverage studies are open to the criticism that, being based on relatively naive and mechanistic Keynesian income determination theory, they abstract from all effects of budgetary operations on aggregate demand and supply except direct and induced income effects. Other possible effects that may need to be taken into account include those that fall under the generic heading of crowding out. Of these, financial forms of crowding out have been the most commonly considered within the region.

For Korea, van Wijnbergen (1982) has argued that, given tax revenues and monetary growth targets enforced by credit ceilings and capital controls, additional government expenditure will reduce credit to the private sector, with an immediate negative impact on private investment. For the Philippines, the financial reform of 1981 has meant that interest rate movements have subsequently provided a better guide to crowding out than changes in the allocation of credit between the public and private sectors. In this case, the very high interest rates of 1984 and 1985 appear to have led to substantial crowding out of private investment (Manasan 1988). For Thailand also, financial crowding out has been judged significant, at least in principle. In the SIAM2 economy-wide multisectoral model:

> The public sector is assumed to decide on its investments (in constant prices) and on its net borrowing from abroad. This leaves an imbalance which needs to be financed by the own savings of the public sector and by borrowing from domestic sources. The larger the public sector borrowing from domestic sources the more private investment is crowded out. The reduced resources left to the private sector, on the one hand force

the formal sector to borrow from abroad to finance its investment needs ... and on the other hand constrain informal sector investment (Amranand and Grais 1984: summary).

Obviously in the last case, which involves the assumption of a fixed exchange rate, full crowding out of the private sector is prevented to the extent that there is access to foreign capital. This factor has been important in Papua New Guinea where substantially increased budget deficits in the early 1980s were funded mainly by overseas borrowing (Garnaut and Baxter 1983: 120). Similarly, the Indonesian government's exclusive reliance on external forms of borrowing seems to have been the reason for a lack of concern about crowding out in Indonesia. In fact, the danger of crowding out private borrowers has been a stated reason for the government's policy of refraining from domestic borrowing (Soesastro et al. 1988: 13).

Finally, in the special circumstances of Singapore, where conditions of close to perfect international mobility of capital appear to prevail, the scope for financial crowding out would appear limited by the dependence of domestic interest rates on world rates (Lim et al. 1988: 361). However, this argument may ultimately depend on the maintenance of a pegged exchange rate. It is at least conceivable that with a freely floating rate a fiscal expansion financed by borrowing could lead to an exchange rate appreciation via capital inflow that crowds out, not private investment, but net exports to the full extent of the fiscal expansion.

Crowding out need not, of course, be limited to its traditional financial forms. Various forms of real or direct crowding out are also possibilities. In the well-known dynamic model of public investment, private investment, saving and growth developed and applied to India and Korea by Sundararajan and Thakur (1980), the crowding-out effect of public investment is specified in a general manner which is recognized to incorporate crowding out in the market for real resources as well as crowding out in financial markets. In this model the immediate crowding-out effect of public investment operates by constraining the availability of resources to the private sector and thus reducing the speed of adjustment of the private capital stock. In addition, however, public investment:

> raises the productivity of private capital stock and, by creating demand for the output of the private sector, raises the output expectations and investment requirements of the private sector. It also raises aggregate output and savings, thereby offsetting part of the initial crowding-out effects (Sundararajan and Thakur 1980: 852).

Dynamic simulations of the model to identify the effects of a one-shot increase in public investment show very different patterns of response in private investment and output in India and Korea. In the former country, there is substantial (though not full) initial crowding out of private investment followed by only weak stimulation in subsequent years, while the increase in public sector output is not sufficient to compensate for the loss in private output "for a considerable length of time". By contrast, in Korea public investment has large, positive effects on private investment, both immediately and in the long run. These result from its strongly positive influence on aggregate output and the output expectations of the private sector (Sundararajan and Thakur 1980: 853). Moreover, the contrast is not only with India, but also with the previously mentioned conclusion drawn by van Wijnbergen (1982) for Korea, which relied on a narrower analytical approach.

18.6.2 Historical Use

The second prominent regional issue concerning fiscal policy has been the extent to which this form of policy has actually been used, intentionally or unintentionally, as an instrument for stabilizing domestic economic activity. One can easily gain a somewhat disconcerting first impression of wide divisions of opinion on this issue in a number of countries within the region, although to a large extent these divisions turn out to reflect simply differences in the time periods under consideration. A more significant general impression is that, at least as far as discretionary actions are concerned, counter-cyclical fiscal policies have consisted mainly of anti-recessionary policies.

These points are well illustrated in the case of Singapore. According to conventional wisdom, Singapore does not practice counter-cyclical fiscal policy. Indeed, one comparatively recent evaluation is that, because of its statutory boards which conduct investment activity outside the traditional budget, "Singapore's fiscal policy has been pro-cyclical in the last several years" (Krause 1987: 11). On the other hand, there is also a substantial body of opinion which argues that in previous periods the government did use Keynesian counter-cyclical fiscal policy in the form of pump-priming expansions of public investment to combat recessions, particularly in the mid-1970s and early 1980s (Fong and Lim 1985; Lee 1987; Lim et al. 1988; Corden 1984).

In contrast to Singapore, the conventional wisdom for Malaysia is that it has used the government budget actively as a macroeconomic policy instrument, particularly to counter externally induced business cycles. Support for the relevance of this view at various times since the early 1970s is found in Chander et al. (1981), Semudram (1987) and Wing (1986). However, it has also been argued that the long practice of using expansionary fiscal policy in slumps was abandoned in the mid-1980s because of perceived external debt constraints (Ariff and Hasan 1987).

Foreign debt problems were, of course, the reason for the downfall of the Philippines' counter-cyclical strategy in the early 1980s. Its attempted use of an expansionary public expenditure, particularly investment, program was intended to offset the domestic effects of the prolonged world recession which followed the second oil shock, with the resulting increase in the budget deficit being financed mainly by short-term borrowing abroad. Unfortunately, the duration and severity of the recession were underestimated; and by 1981–82 debt servicing difficulties had begun to emerge. Thereafter the policy foundered rapidly, leaving behind a full-blown foreign exchange crisis (Remolona et al. 1986).

Taiwan does not have any significant history of active use of fiscal policy as a stabilization tool. A structure of low effective tax rates and relatively inflexible budgetary outlays (of which defence spending has formed a very substantial proportion) would probably have constrained the application of discretionary fiscal policy, even if there had been more inclination to pursue this form of macroeconomic management. It was nevertheless "a nice coincidence" that a major public investment program, which began in 1973 and which was "not designed to counter the business cycle or other such phenomenon," reached its maximum share of nearly 20 percent of total investment in 1975 and 1976. It thus contributed greatly to the fast recovery of the Taiwanese economy from its recession following the first oil crisis (Kuo 1983: 216–7).

It is common opinion that fiscal policy in Hong Kong has not been influenced by Keynesian precepts. Empirical support for this view is found in the fact that in the 1970s government expenditure fluctuated more than GDP, thereby actually contributing to instability (Sung 1986: 138). However, while fiscal policy had been eschewed as an instrument of stabilization before 1979, in that year many public construction projects were postponed in "an unprecedented move" to control inflation (Sung 1985: 141). More recently, Peebles, while rightly rejecting the pro-cyclical behavior of the budget balance as an indicator of fiscal stance, has found evidence to suggest "that the government has been willing to use its investment programme to offset large changes in private investment" (Peebles 1988: 235).

For Indonesia, quantitative evidence of the extent to which fiscal policy has been used, not necessarily deliberately, as a stabilization tool comes from the already mentioned study of fiscal leverage in that economy (Snyder 1985). In that study annual changes in the GDP growth rate are separated into estimates of the "Total Effects" of all budgetary changes and estimates of what is termed the "Pure Cycle." Subject to the assumptions on which the methodology is based, the latter component measures how GDP would have changed in any one year if government expenditures and taxes had remained unchanged from the previous year. It is estimated as a residual by subtracting the "Total Effects" of the budgetary changes (expressed as a percentage of GDP) from the actual GDP growth rate.

Comparison of the time paths of the actual GDP growth rate and the "Pure Cycle" growth rate over the 1969–83 indicates that fluctuations in the "Pure Cycle" component were much sharper than those of the actual GDP growth rate. Hence it is concluded that the budget had a stabilizing effect on the Indonesian economy.

Further evidence on the use of fiscal policy as a stabilization instrument comes from the multi-country studies of Chand and Otani (1983, 1986) involving the construction and use of consistent criteria for measuring the primary (adjusted for feedbacks) impact of demand management policies. Their approach, which is derived from a model that distinguishes between the private, government, external and monetary sectors of the economy, focuses on fluctuations around the trend growth path of the economy. Deviations from the trend, which by assumption are explained solely in terms of demand forces, are attributed to the interaction of three types of impulses: impulses from autonomous expenditures (private fixed investment and exports), policy impulses from budgetary operations, and policy impulses from credit operations.

This methodology was applied to a number of Asian economies, including Malaysia, the Philippines, Thailand and Korea. Using data for 1962–81, it was found that for each of these four countries the variance of the growth rate of output was smaller than that of the autonomous impulses. This was taken to suggest that other factors were exerting a stabilizing influence.

Chand and Otani then examined the associations between the two sets of policy impulses and autonomous impulses. With the exception of Malaysia, credit impulses were found to be positively correlated with autonomous impulses, implying that the former tended to accommodate the latter. By contrast, in all four cases budgetary impulses were negatively correlated with autonomous impulses, suggesting that fiscal policy tended to be an offsetting or stabilizing force with respect to the effects of fluctuations in autonomous variables.

18.6.3 Export Price Instability

The final issue to be considered in this section is the appropriate design of fiscal policy to insulate economies from what are seen as the disruptive effects of exogenous export price instability. Within the region, the geographical focus of this issue is mainly on the small, very open, commodity-exporting island economies of the Pacific, principally Papua New Guinea; while the mainstream analytical focus is more on the use of automatic stabilizers than on discretionary policy actions.

The mainstream position, comprehensively expounded by Garnaut (1980), is that, while the real spending power of an economy will vary cyclically with export price instability and consequent short-term fluctuations in the terms of trade, the authorities should pursue, as a broad policy target, a steady level or rate of growth of real domestic expenditure or absorption. This should be consistent with the achievement of external balance over the commodity cycle as a whole (and will presumably be governed by such factors as long-term trends in productive capacity and the terms of trade).

Fiscal policy is assigned the key role in the pursuit of the real absorption target, operating through both the expenditure and revenue sides of the budget. On the expenditure side, this role reflects the fact that the public sector tends to bulk large in the cash economies of the island states of the Pacific, making a big contribution to total absorption. Moreover, even though public expenditure has a substantial import content, it is also a major source of cash incomes and hence a significant influence on private demand. Therefore, if the government keeps public expenditure on a steady trend consistent with long-term revenue prospects, it will contribute in a major way to the stability of the economy as a whole.

On the revenue side, tax receipts can be expected to behave pro-cyclically. Given stable government expenditure, the result will be that the budget balance also moves pro-cyclically. Subject to budget surpluses being disposed of, and deficits financed, in ways that help to sterilize the monetary effects of export instability flowing through the balance of payments, this movement of the budget balance provides an additional stabilizing influence on absorption. (The exchange rate is assumed fixed, or rather changes in it are reserved for dealing with imported inflation.)

It is recognized that because of political pressures it may well be difficult for a government to keep its outlays on a steady growth path when there are large fluctuations in public revenue. In this respect, a helpful institutional arrangement developed by Papua New Guinea is its Mineral Resources Stabilization Fund. The fluctuating government revenue from PNG's mineral export industry is fed directly into this statutory fund, and then released into consolidated revenue (that is, made available for spending) only at a rate considered to be sustainable over the long-term.

While exerting a significant dampening influence, the policy prescriptions outlined so far may still leave a very substantial residual element of instability in a small economy heavily dependent on cash crop exports. However, fluctuations in incomes from these exports and induced fluctuations in the private component of domestic demand can be reduced by imposing levies on export earnings when commodity export prices rise above trend and by paying bounties when they fall below trend.

Two well-known variants of the levy/bounty direct stabilization proposal have been implemented in the region. One is export taxation at progressive *ad valorem* rates. As practiced in Malaysia and Thailand, this taxation forms part of consolidated government revenue. The other variant consists of separate stabilization funds for individual export commodities, as exist in Papua New Guinea. These funds operate progressive schemes of levies/bounties entirely outside the government budget, with the levies collected in times of booming prices financing income-support payments to growers in times of depressed prices. The stabilizing influence of such funds is obviously enhanced to the extent that the monetary effects of their accumulated balances are sterilized by deposit with the central bank or investment abroad (Guest 1986).

International experience suggests that the identification of an appropriate trend price for use as a benchmark in a levy/bounty scheme, and the gaining of industry/political acceptance of such a price, are likely to be challenging tasks. Especially when the administration of the scheme is in the hands of an autonomous marketing board or industry-managed stabilization fund, there is considerable risk that the benchmark, rather than being related to the trend value of the world price of the commodity, will be established with reference to a markup over some industry-wide "average" or "representative" level of unit costs. If this happens in an industry subject to a long-term downward trend in the relative price of its product, and if there are not matching declines in "representative" costs, the levy/bounty scheme will soon deteriorate into one of continuing subsidization. This will either quickly lead to bankruptcy of the scheme (United Nations 1983) or require ongoing subventions from the government, the effect of which will be to sustain resource misallocation.

Where levy/bounty schemes do not exist or at least fail to stabilize adequately total private income from export production, some fluctuation in the private components of domestic absorption and hence domestic activity can be expected. In principle, it would seem that if this instability were deemed severe enough to constitute a problem, it could be counteracted or offset by discretionary counter-cyclical policies, including variations in government expenditure. Such variations form an alternative to adhering to a steady growth in government expenditure, but are open to criticism on the grounds that they would increase the difficulty of public sector planning and exacerbate uncertainty in the private sector (Guest 1986: 80).

Although these criticisms may have some force, both they and the original proposal for steady growth in public expenditure become less compelling in cases where there are not only marked fluctuations in export prices but in addition these fluctuations induce normal quantity responses. Thus in an export-price slump export production may be cut back, leading to unemployment in the export sector (for example, in a plantation industry where there is some downward rigidity of money wages), which is then spread through the economy by the usual multiplier effects. Correspondingly, in an export-price boom resources may be drawn out of other sectors to contribute to an expanding volume of export production, thereby also contributing to a reduction in the supply of, and hence to excess demand for, nontradables. In these sets of circumstances there is clearly an argument for not maintaining a stable level or rate of growth of total absorption over the cycle but instead actually varying it counter-cyclically to preserve internal balance, that is, to avoid both deficient and excess demand for resources.

18.7 Conclusion

Even when confined to a specific regional context, the treatment of a subject as large as macroeconomic policy involves unavoidable trade-offs between breadth of coverage and depth of treatment. While it is hoped that in this respect some approximation of optimality has been achieved, it is appropriate to point out a number of the areas which have not been covered or covered only inadequately.

First, despite a perennial regional preoccupation with competing monetarist and cost-push import price explanations of inflation, no attempt has been made to include a systematic examination of empirical evidence on the sources of inflation and its associated policy implications. Secondly and relatedly, while the interaction between internal and external balance has been a pervasive concern, this chapter has drawn only peripherally and selectively on the large volume of case study work dealing with macroeconomic adjustment to the global oil crises and related external shocks. A particularly prominent omission in this regard is the Indonesian "Dutch disease" debate. Thirdly, in examining the instruments of macroeconomic management, only monetary and fiscal policy have received extensive treatment. Discussion of wages/incomes policy has been confined to the target/instrument context; no attention at all has been given to direct price control policies; and while exchange rate policy has been considered both in the target/instrument context and in relation to domestic monetary policy, it has certainly not been examined comprehensively.

The gaps in this chapter are, however, by no means solely a reflection of selective decision-making. They also reflect the fact that some topics seemingly relevant to macroeconomic management have so far not been the subject of much inquiry in the region. Thus, with the exception of demand for money functions, comparatively little work seems to have been undertaken on the dynamic aspects of macroeconomic management, and the roles of inside and outside lags in particular. Similarly, notwithstanding a burgeoning Phillips curve industry and an increasing awareness of the significance of nominal and real wage rigidities, empirical work appears to have hardly begun on the macroeconomics of labor market behavior and its implications for policy. Moreover, within the region macroeconomists have so far displayed little more than a token awareness of the rational expectations approach to macroeconomics. The relevance, or lack of relevance, of the new classical idea of policy neutrality (that is, the impotence of systematic demand management policy) awaits comprehensive investigation, as does the rediscovered Ricardian equivalence theorem (which suggests that a bond-financed expansionary fiscal policy will lead to an increase in private saving to provide for future tax liabilities). Finally, despite its *prima facie* appropriateness, there seems to have as yet been no attempt to apply quantity-constrained disequilibrium macroeconomic theory to the problems of stabilization policy in China. All of these items warrant high ranking on any agenda for future research on macroeconomic policy in the Asian/Pacific region.

Note

This article is a revised version of "Macroeconomic Management in Asian-Pacific Developing Countries," *Asian-Pacific Economic Literature*, 1990, 4(1): 3–40.

References

Aghevli, B. B., 1977, "Money, Prices and the Balance of Payments: Indonesia 1968–73," *Journal of Development Studies*, 13(2): 37–57.

Aghevli, B. B. and M. S. Khan, 1977, "Inflationary Finance and the Dynamics of Inflation: Indonesia, 1951–72," *American Economic Review*, 67(3): 390–403.

Aghevli, B. B., M. S. Khan, P. R. Narvekar, and B. K. Short, 1979, "Monetary Policy in Selected Asian Countries," *International Monetary Fund Staff Papers*, 26(4): 775–824.

Amranand, P. and W. Grais, 1984, *Macroeconomic and Distributional Implications of Sectoral Policy Interventions: An Application to Thailand*, World Bank Staff Working Paper No. 627, Washington, DC.

Ariff, M., 1983, "Inflation in Malaysia—An Empirical Enquiry," in *Conference on Inflation in East Asian Countries*, Chung-Hua Institution for Economic Research, Taipei, pp. 483–501.

Ariff, M. and M. M. Hasan, 1987, "Fiscal Strategies and Public Debts: The Malaysian Experience," paper presented at the Seminar on Issues and Challenges in National Development, University of Malaya, December 15–16.

Arndt, H. W., 1979a, "Keynes or Friedman or Both?" *Ekonomi dan Keuangan Indonesia*, 27(3): 383–96.

———, 1979b, "Monetary Policy Instruments in Indonesia," *Bulletin of Indonesian Economic Studies*, 15(3): 107–22.

———, 1987, *Economic Development: The History of an Idea*, University of Chicago Press, Chicago and London.

Asher, M. G., 1985, "Fiscal Policies in ASEAN: An Appraisal," in Jomo (ed.), *ASEAN Economies: Crisis and Response*, Malaysian Economic Association for the Federation of ASEAN Economic Associations, pp. 184–218.

Balassa, B., 1982, "Economic Reform in China," *Banca Nazionale del Lavoro*, 142 (September): 307–33.

Balino, T. J. T. and V. Sundararajan, 1986, "Financial Reform in Indonesia: Causes, Consequences, and Prospects," in H.-S. Cheng (ed.), *Financial Policy and Reform in Pacific Basin Countries*, Lexington Books, Lexington, MA, pp. 191–219.

Bender, D., 1986, "Monetary Stability, Export Promotion, and Exchange Rate Policy: A Macro Model of Exchange Rate Management in NICs and Its Application to Singapore, 1975–83," *ASEAN Economic Bulletin*, 2(3): 196–210.

Boediono, 1985, "Demand for Money in Indonesia, 1975–84," *Bulletin of Indonesian Economic Studies*, 21(2): 74–94.

Booth, A. and P. McCawley (eds.), 1981, "Fiscal Policy," in *The Indonesian Economy during the Soeharto Era*, Oxford University Press, Kuala Lumpur, pp. 126–61.

Bryant, R. C., 1980, *Money and Monetary Policy in Interdependent Nations*, Brookings Institution, Washington, DC.

Chai, C. H., 1981, "Domestic Money and Banking Reforms in China," *Hong Kong Economic Papers*, 14: 37–52.

Chand, S. K. and I. Otani, 1983, "Some Criteria to Evaluate Demand Management Policies in Asian Countries," *Journal of Policy Modeling*, 5(1): 107–23.

———, 1986, "Aggregate Demand and the Coordination of Monetary and Fiscal Action," in P. Shome (ed.), *Fiscal Issues in South-East Asia*, Oxford University Press, Singapore, pp. 173–97.

Chander, R., C. L. Robless, and K. P. Teh, 1981, "Malaysian Growth and Stabilization," in W. R. Cline and Associates, *World Inflation and the Developing Countries*, Brookings Institution, Washington, DC, pp. 208–27.

Chen, N.-R. and C.-m. Hou, 1986, "China's Inflation, 1979–83: Measurement and Analysis," *Economic Development and Cultural Change*, 34(4): 811–35.

Cheng, H.-S., 1981, "Money and Credit in China," *Federal Reserve Bank of San Francisco Economic Review*, Fall: 19–36.

Chew, S. B. and R. Chew, 1987, "Incomes Policy: The Singapore Experience," *South East Asian Economic Review*, 8(1): 53–91.

Choi, J.-B., 1987, "The Quarterly Macro Model of the Korean Economy," *Bank of Korea Quarterly Economic Review*, December: 23–46.

Chung, J. W. and D. Kim, 1986, "An Interactive Causal Analysis of Price Dynamics: A Case Study of Korea," *Economic Development and Cultural Change*, 34(4): 837–53.

Coats, W. L. and D. R. Khatkhate, 1984, "Monetary Policy in Less Developed Countries: Main Issues," *Developing Economies*, 22: 329–48.

Cole, D. C. and Y. C. Park, 1983, *Financial Development in Korea, 1945–1978*, Harvard University Press, Cambridge, MA.

Corden, W. M., 1984, "Macroeconomic Targets and Instruments for a Small Open Economy," *Singapore Economic Review*, 24(2): 27–37.

Dahanayake, P. A. S. (ed.), 1982, "Hard Currency Strategy in a Developing Country: The Case of Papua New Guinea," in *Post-Independence Economic Development of Papua New Guinea*, Monograph 19, Institute of Applied Social and Economic Research, Boroko, Papua New Guinea, pp. 185–205.

Daniel, P. and R. Sims, 1986, *Swings, Shocks and Leaks: The Making of Economic Policy in Papua New Guinea, 1980–82*, Discussion Paper DP211, Institute of Development Studies, University of Sussex.

Daquila, T. C., 1987, *Analysis of Money and Bank Credit in the Philippines: An Application of the Brunner-Meltzer Framework*, Working Papers in Trade and Development, No. 87/3, Research School of Pacific Studies, Australian National University, Canberra.

De Wulf, L. and D. Goldsbrough, 1986, "The Evolving Role of Monetary Policy in China," *International Monetary Fund Staff Papers*, 33: 209–42.

Edwards, S. and M. S. Khan, 1985, "Interest Rate Determination in Developing Countries," *International Monetary Fund Staff Papers*, 32: 377–403.

Feltenstein, A. and Z. Farhadian, 1987, "Fiscal Policy, Monetary Targets, and the Price Level in a Centrally Planned Economy: An Application to the Case of China," *Journal of Money, Credit and Banking*, 19(2): 137–56.

Fong, P. E. and L. Lim, 1985, "Rapid Growth and Relative Price Stability in a Small Open Economy: The Experience of Singapore," in V. Corbo, A. O. Krueger and F. Ossa (eds.), *Export-Oriented Development Strategies: The Success of Five Newly Industrializing Countries*, Westview Press, Boulder, CO, pp. 79–110.

Fry, M. J., 1981, "Inflation and Economic Growth in Pacific Basin Developing Economies," *Federal Reserve Bank of San Francisco Economic Review*, Fall: 8–18.

———, 1983, "Inflation and Monetary Policy in Hong Kong, Indonesia, Korea, Malaysia, Philippines, Singapore, Taiwan and Thailand, 1960–1982," in *Conference on Inflation in East Asian Countries*, Chung-Hua Institution for Economic Research, Taipei, pp. 83–137.

———, 1985, "Financial Structure, Monetary Policy and Economic Growth in Hong Kong, Singapore, Taiwan and South Korea, 1960–1983," in V. Corbo, A. O. Krueger and F. Ossa (eds.), *Export-Oriented Development Strategies: The Success of Five Newly Industrializing Countries*, Westview Press, Boulder, CO, pp. 275–324.

———, 1986, "Financial Structure, Financial Regulation, and Financial Reform in the Philippines and Thailand, 1960–1984," in H.-S. Cheng (ed.), *Financial Policy and Reform in Pacific Basin Countries*, Lexington Books, Lexington, MA, pp. 161–84.

Garnaut, R., 1980, "Economic Instability in Small Countries: Macro-economic Responses," in R. T. Shand (ed.), *The Island States of the Pacific and Indian Oceans: Anatomy of Development*, Development Studies Monograph no. 23, Australian National University, Canberra, pp. 313–31.

Garnaut, R. and P. Baxter, 1983, in consultation with A. O. Krueger, *Exchange Rate and Macro-economic Policy in Independent Papua New Guinea*, Department of Finance, Port Moresby, Papua New Guinea.

Goodman, R., C. Lepani, and D. Morawetz, 1985, *The Economy of Papua New Guinea: An Independent Review*, Development Studies Centre, Australian National University, Canberra.

Grenville, S., 1981, "Monetary Policy and the Formal Financial Sector," in Booth and McCawley, pp. 102–25.

Guest, J., 1986, "Macroeconomic Stabilization Policy with Special Reference to Fiscal Policy," in R. V. Cole and T. G. Parry (eds.), *Selected Issues in Pacific Island Development*, National Centre for Development Studies, Australian National University, Canberra, pp. 71–110.

Hicks, G. L., 1967, "The Indonesian Inflation," *Philippine Economic Journal*, 6(2): 210–24.

Ho, Y.-k., 1983, "An Analysis of Inflation in Hong Kong," in *Conference on Inflation in East Asian Countries*, Chung-Hua Institution for Economic Research, Taipei, pp. 349–77.

Hsiao, K. H. Y. H., 1982, "Money and Banking in the People's Republic of China: Recent Developments," *China Quarterly*, 91: 462–77.

———, 1984, *Money and Banking in the Chinese Mainland*, Chung-Hua Institution for Economic Research, Taipei.

Kapur, B. K., 1976, "Alternative Stabilization Policies for Less-Developed Economies," *Journal of Political Economy*, 84(4), pt. 1: 777–95.

———, 1981, "Exchange Rate Flexibility and Monetary Policy," in Monetary Authority of Singapore, *Papers on Monetary Economics*, Singapore University Press, Singapore, pp. 102–11.

Karunaratne, N. D., 1985, "An Econometric Analysis of the Monetary Sector of a Developing Economy—Fiji," *Asian Economies*, 52 (March): 20–46.

Khan, M. S., 1980, "Monetary Shocks and the Dynamics of Inflation," *International Monetary Fund Staff Papers*, 27(2): 250–84.

———, 1981, "The Dynamics of Monetary Demand and Monetary Policy in Singapore," in Monetary Authority of Singapore, *Papers on Monetary Economics*, Singapore University Press, Singapore, pp. 46–76.

Khatkhate, D. R., 1977, "Evolving Open Market Operations in a Developing Economy: The Taiwan Experience," *Journal of Development Studies*, 13(2): 92–101.

Kohsaka, A., 1987, "Financial Liberalization in Asian NICs: A Comparative Study of Korea and Taiwan in the 1980s," *Developing Economies*, 25(4): 323–45.

Krause, L. B., 1987, "Thinking about Singapore," in L. B. Krause, A. T. Koh, and (T.) Y. Lee, *The Singapore Economy Reconsidered*, Institute of Southeast Asian Studies, Singapore, pp. 1–20.

Kuo, S. W. Y., 1983, *The Taiwan Economy in Transition*, Westview Press, Boulder, CO.

Lam, N. V., 1979, "Imported Inflation in Papua New Guinea, 1972–76," *Developing Economies*, 17: 344–64.

———, 1980, "Monetary Policies and Options for Domestic Economic Stabilization in Papua New Guinea," *Developing Economies*, 18(2): 227–42.

Lee, S.-Y., 1984, "Demand for Money in Singapore 1968–82," *ASEAN Economic Bulletin*, 1(2): 152–71.

Lee, S. Y. and Y. C. Jao, 1982, *Financial Structures and Monetary Policy in South East Asia*, St Martin's Press, New York.

Lee, (T.) Y., 1987, "The Government in Macro-economic Management," in L. Krause, A. T. Koh and (T.) Y. Lee, *The Singapore Economy Reconsidered*, Institute of Southeast Asian Studies, Singapore, pp. 128–73.

Lewis, W. A., 1955, *The Theory of Economic Growth*, George Allen & Unwin, London.

Lii, S.-y., 1987, "A Monetary Model of Taiwan," *Asian Economic Journal*, 6(1): 26–47.

Lim, C. Y. and Associates, 1988, *Policy Options for the Singapore Economy*, McGraw-Hill, Singapore.

Lim, J., 1987, "The New Structuralist Critique of the Monetarist Theory of Inflation: The Case of the Philippines," *Journal of Development Economics*, 25: 45–61.

Lin, C. Z., 1988, "China's Economic Reforms II: Western Perspectives," *Asian-Pacific Economic Literature*, 2(1): 1–25.

Luckett, D. G., 1987, *Monetary Policy in Fiji*, Institute of Pacific Studies, University of the South Pacific, Suva, Fiji.

Lundberg, E., 1979, "Fiscal and Monetary Policies," in W. Galenson (ed.), *Economic Growth and Structural Change in Taiwan*, Cornell University Press, Ithaca, NY, pp. 263–307.

Lysy, F. J., 1980, "Investment and Employment with Unlimited Labour: The Role of Aggregate Demand," *Journal of Development Economics*, 7: 541–66.

Manasan, R. G., 1988, *Financing Public Sector Development Expenditure in Selected Countries: Philippines*, Asian Development Bank, Manila.

Mannur, H. G., 1983, "Papua New Guinea's Exchange Rate Policy: Its Evolution and Evaluation," *Yagl-Ambu*, 10(2): 33–47.

McKinnon, R. I., 1973, *Money and Capital in Economic Development*, Brookings Institution, Washington, DC.

———, 1981, "Offshore Markets in Foreign Currencies and Monetary Control: Britain, Singapore, and the United States," in Monetary Authority of Singapore, *Papers on Monetary Economics*, Singapore University Press, Singapore, pp. 136–64.

Montes, M. F., 1987, *Stabilization and Adjustment Policies and Programmes, Country Study: The Philippines*, World Institute for Development Economics Research of the United Nations University, Helsinki.

Moreno, R., 1986, "Monetary Control Without a Central Bank: The Case of Hong Kong," *Federal Reserve Bank of San Francisco Economic Review*, 2 (Spring): 17–37.

Mundell, R. A., 1960, "The Monetary Dynamics of International Adjustment under Fixed and Flexible Exchange Rates," *Quarterly Journal of Economics*, 74(2): 227–57.

———, 1962, "The Appropriate Use of Monetary and Fiscal Policy for Internal and External Stability," *International Monetary Fund Staff Papers*, 9: 70–9.

Palmer, K., 1979, "Targets and Instruments of Economic Policy in Papua New Guinea," *Yagl-Ambu*, 6(2): 3–20.

Parikh, A., A. Booth, and R. M. Sundrum, 1985, "An Econometric Model of the Monetary Sector in Indonesia," *Journal of Development Studies*, 21(3): 406–21.

Park, Y. C., 1983, "Inflation and Stabilization Policies in Korea, 1960–1980," in *Conference on Inflation in East Asian Countries*, Chung-Hua Institution for Economic Research, Taipei, pp. 287–330.

———, 1986, "Foreign Debt, Balance of Payments, and Growth Prospects: The Case of the Republic of Korea, 1965–88," *World Development*, 14(8): 1019–58.

Peebles, G., 1988, *Hong Kong's Economy: An Introductory Macroeconomic Analysis*, Oxford University Press, Hong Kong.

Rao, V. K. R. V., 1952, "Investment, Income and the Multiplier in an Underdeveloped Economy," *Indian Economic Review*, 1(1): 55–67.

Remolona, E. M., M. Mangahas, and F. Pante, 1986, "Foreign Debt, Balance of Payments, and the Economic Crisis of the Philippines in 1983–84," *World Development*, 14(8): 993–1018.

Rosendale, P., 1981, "The Balance of Payments," in Booth and McCawley, pp. 162–80.

Salter, W. E. G., 1959, "Internal and External Balance: The Role of Price and Expenditure Effects," *Economic Record*, 35: 226–38.

Semudram, M., 1981, "The Demand for Money in the Malaysian Economy: Empirical Estimates and an Analysis of Stability," *Malaysian Economic Review*, 26(2): 53–63.

———, 1987, "Economic Stabilization Policies in Malaysia," in P. B. Rana and F. A. Alburo (eds.), *Economic Stabilization Policies in ASEAN Countries*, Institute of Southeast Asian Studies, Singapore, pp. 79–103.

Shaw, G. K., 1977, *An Introduction to the Theory of Macro-economic Policy*, Martin Robertson, London.

Simkin, C., 1984, "Does Money Matter in Singapore?" *Singapore Economic Review*, 29(1): 1–15.

Snyder, W., 1985, "The Budget Impact on Economic Growth and Stability in Indonesia," *Ekonomi dan Keuangan Indonesia*, 33(2): 139–50.

Soesastro, M. H., D. S. Simandjuntak, and P. R. Silalahi, 1988, *Financing Public Sector Development Expenditures: Indonesia*, Asian Development Bank, Manila.

Sundararajan, V. and S. Thakur, 1980, "Public Investment, Crowding out, and Growth: A Dynamic Model Applied to India and Korea," *International Monetary Fund Staff Papers*, 27(4): 814–55.

Sundrum, R. M., 1973, "Money Supply and Prices: A Re-interpretation," *Bulletin of Indonesian Economic Studies*, 9(3): 73–86.

———, 1986, "Indonesia's Rapid Economic Growth: 1968–81," *Bulletin of Indonesian Economic Studies*, 22(3): 40–69.

———, 1988, "Indonesia's Slow Economic Growth, 1981–86," *Bulletin of Indonesian Economic Studies*, 24(1): 37–72.

Sung, Y. W., 1985, "Economic Growth and Structural Change in the Small Open Economy of Hong Kong," in V. Corbo, A. O. Krueger and F. Ossa (eds.), *Export-Oriented Development Strategies: The Success of Five Newly Industrializing Countries*, Westview Press, Boulder, CO, pp. 111–54.

———, 1986, "Fiscal and Economic Policies in Hong Kong," in J. Y. S. Cheng (ed.), *Hong Kong in Transition*, Oxford University Press, Hong Kong, pp. 120–41.

Swan, T. W., 1955, "Longer Run Problems of the Balance of Payments," paper presented to Section G of the Congress of the Australian and New Zealand Association for the Advancement of Science, Melbourne.

Theil, H., 1956, "On the Theory of Economic Policy," *American Economic Review*, 46(2): 360–6.

———, 1964, *Optimal Decision Rules for Government and Industry*, North-Holland, Amsterdam.

Tinbergen, J., 1952, *On the Theory of Economic Policy*, North-Holland, Amsterdam.

Trescott, P. B., 1971, *Thailand's Monetary Experience: The Economics of Stability*, Praeger, New York.

United Nations, 1983, *Economic and Social Survey of Asia and the Pacific 1982*, Bangkok.

Van Wijnbergen, S., 1982, "Stagflationary Effects of Monetary Stabilization Policies," *Journal of Development Economics*, 10: 133–69.

———, 1985, "Macro-economic Effects of Changes in Bank Interest Rates: Simulation Results for South Korea," *Journal of Development Economics*, 18: 541–54.

Warr, P. G. and B. Nidhiprabha, 1988, "Macroeconomic Policies and Long-Term Growth," Research Project World Bank (RPO 673–99) Thailand, Part II: Revised Draft, mimeo.

Wibulswasdi, C., 1986, "The Formulation and Implementation of the Monetary Policy: The Thai Monetary Experience during 1983–1984," *Bank of Thailand Quarterly Bulletin*, 26(3): 27–35.

Wing, T. W., 1986, "The Impact of U.S. Policy Mix on the ASEAN Economies, 1980–84: The Neglected European-Japanese Connection," *ASEAN Economic Bulletin*, 3(2): 207–24.

World Bank, 1983, *China: Socialist Economic Development*, Vol. 1, Washington, DC.

Yari, M., 1980, "Effects of December 1979 Revaluation on Imported Prices," *Bank of Papua New Guinea Quarterly Economic Bulletin*, December: 19–23.

Yenko, A. L., 1985, "Monetary Base Management and BOP Movements: The ASEAN Countries," *ASEAN Economic Bulletin*, 1(3): 232–49.

Yotopoulos, P. A. and J. B. Nugent, 1976, *Economics of Development: Empirical Investigations*, Harper & Row, New York.

Yu, T.-s. and T.-a. Chen, 1982, "Fiscal Reforms and Economic Development," in K.-t. Li and T.-s. Yu (eds.), *Experiences and Lessons of Economic Development in Taiwan*, Academia Sinica, Taipei, pp. 187–217.

Chapter 19

Maxwell J. Fry

FINANCIAL OPENING AND MONETARY CONTROL IN THE ASIA-PACIFIC REGION

19.1 Introduction

As the developing market economies of the Asia-Pacific region have become increasingly open over the past two decades, they have liberalized capital account transactions. This financial opening has implications for monetary control: perfect international capital mobility means that these economies would be unable to pursue separate exchange rate and monetary targets. Under a managed exchange rate, a restrictive monetary policy would produce overwhelming capital inflows that would completely negate the restrictive effects.

Although there has been substantial financial opening in the Asia-Pacific developing market economies, little attention has been paid to the issue of whether or not monetary control has actually been lost. This chapter examines the issue of monetary control by testing econometrically whether or not there have been significant structural changes in both capital inflow and monetary policy behavior over the past three decades. Structural changes in the capital inflow equations are detected roughly when they might have been expected, but monetary control has not been lost. Indeed, the estimates suggest that the monetary authorities in the larger Asia-Pacific developing market economies have strengthened monetary control over time.

The primary or even the sole objective of monetary policy is price stability. Hence, some indication of the extent to which monetary control has been maintained can be gleaned from a country's inflation record. Inflation was one of the major macroeconomic topics of the 1970s. A decade of accelerating inflation culminated in the double-digit inflation associated with the first oil price shock of 1973–74. A second worldwide inflationary spurt occurred contemporaneously with the second oil price shock of 1980. Refuting a popularly held view that inflation is now under control, Figure 19.1 shows that worldwide inflation accelerated after 1986 and reached a record level in 1990; inflation in the developing countries exceeded 100 percent.

Figure 19.2 shows that inflation declined steadily in the industrial countries from 12 percent in 1980 to 3 percent in 1986, although it then rose to 5 percent in 1990. Figure 19.2 also shows that inflation fell, albeit somewhat more erratically, in eight developing market economies of Asia-Pacific—Indonesia, Hong Kong, Korea, Malaysia, the Philippines, Singapore, Taiwan and Thailand.[1] Over the past two decades inflation in these eight Asia-Pacific economies mirrored the pattern of inflation in the industrial countries. Although inflation in these eight Asia-Pacific economies deviated only occasionally from inflation in the industrial countries, such correspondence is not observed in the rest of the developing world.

Inflation has declined in the industrial countries from 9.1 percent in 1976–80, to 6.3 percent in 1981–85, and to 3.6 percent in 1986–90; it has also declined in the Asia-Pacific economies from 9.0 percent in 1976–80, to 6.9 percent in 1981–85 and to 3.6 percent in 1986–90. The 1974 peak was considerably higher in Asia-Pacific than in the industrial countries, but inflation was subsequently brought down more rapidly and less painfully than it was in the industrial countries. The 1980 peak was also somewhat higher in Asia-Pacific than in the industrial countries, but the difference was not dramatic. The anomalous Asia-Pacific bulge in 1984 was due solely to the political disruptions that year in the Philippines (Figures 19.3 and 19.4).

My own basic tenet is that inflation is always and everywhere home grown. In small open economies, it might be controlled best through exchange rate policy. In larger developing countries that maintain any effective exchange controls, domestic monetary policy takes primary responsibility. Imported inflation can be countered through exchange rate appreciation, as evinced by Singapore. Inflationary pressures emanating from government budget deficits may be neutralized by tight monetary policies that prevent monetization of these deficits, as the United States has demonstrated since 1980.

This chapter addresses two questions about monetary control in the six larger Asia-Pacific developing market economies: (1) Has financial opening eroded the ability of these economies to pursue independent monetary policies? (2) Is inflation lower in these developing economies than it is in other developing countries because of the way in which monetary policy has been conducted?

FIGURE 19.1   Worldwide inflation

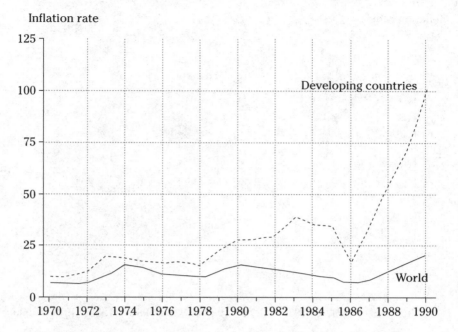

FIGURE 19.2   Inflation in industrial and the Asia-Pacific developing market economies

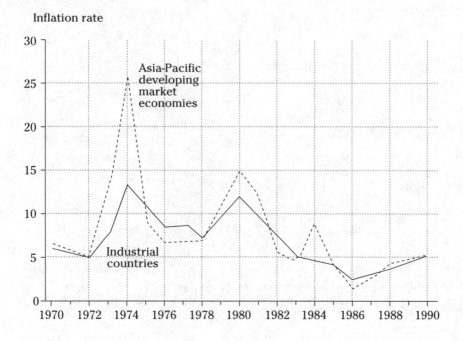

FIGURE 19.3   Inflation in Hong Kong, Malaysia, Singapore and Thailand

Inflation rate

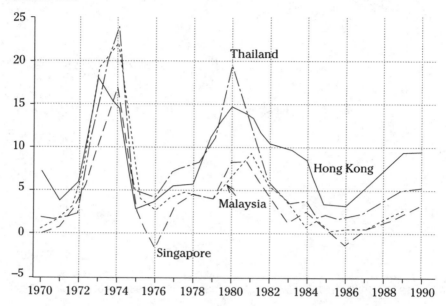

FIGURE 19.4   Inflation in Indonesia, Korea, Philippines and Taiwan

Inflation rate

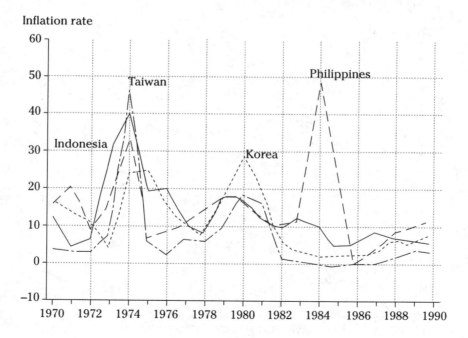

19.2   A Model of Capital Inflows and Monetary Policy Behavior

In its most extreme form, the monetary approach to the balance of payments states that central banks in open economies with fixed exchange rates have no ability to affect the nominal money stock. Among others, Bijan Aghevli et al. (1979: 776) and Lorenzo Bini Smaghi (1982) have used this proposition in more moderate form to assert that Asia-Pacific developing market economies have only a limited degree of monetary policy independence. Even were these developing countries able to pursue independent monetary policies, Michael Connolly and Dean Taylor (1979) find that in general developing countries do not appear to pursue any systematic monetary policy. In this section, therefore, I develop a model to address the question: Can the Asia-Pacific developing market economies pursue independent monetary policies?

The two alternative capital inflow equations examined here are embedded in a macroeconomic model designed for a small semi-open developing economy.[2] In this economy, the government sets or manipulates the foreign exchange rate and uses domestic credit as its target for monetary policy purposes. The assets available to residents of this country are money M, other domestic assets K and foreign bonds B. Net holdings of foreign bonds are negative when foreign borrowing exceeds foreign lending. Some developing countries can borrow abroad by selling dollar-denominated bonds in world financial markets. In practice, developing country bonds are not perfect substitutes for industrial country bonds. Hence, developing countries face a downward sloping demand curve for their bonds on world markets. In such case, both the supply of and the demand for foreign bonds must be specified.

Table 19.1 presents the parts of the underlying model that are of immediate relevance. There are three assets: domestic money M, foreign bonds B and other domestic assets (for example, bonds, productive capital, gold, grain or land) K. The nominal returns on these three assets are zero on money, i_f on foreign bonds (as measured by the rate of return in terms of the domestic currency), and i_d on other domestic assets. The market for other domestic assets is not specified, since it can be derived using Walras's law.

The remaining endogenous variables of the model specified in Table 19.1 are real GNP y, the domestic price level P, the domestic-currency return on foreign bonds (or the domestic-currency cost of borrowing abroad) i_f, the return on other domestic assets i_d, exchange rate depreciation ϵ, expected exchange rate depreciation ϵ^e, the country-specific risk premium ρ, net foreign assets NFA, domestic credit DC, domestic credit to the private sector DCp, capital inflows CF, the current account CA and the cumulated current account ΣCA.[3] The exogenous variables in equations (19.1) to (19.9) are wealth W at the beginning of each period, foreign wealth W^*, foreign inflation (U.S. wholesale price inflation) π^*, the rate of change in the world dollar price of oil π° and net domestic credit to the government sector DCg.

TABLE 19.1   The key elements of the capital inflow model

$$M = \xi(\overset{+}{y}, \overset{+}{P}, \overline{i}_{d}, \overline{i}_{f}, \overset{+}{W}) \tag{19.1}$$

$$M \equiv NFA + DC \tag{19.2}$$

$$DC \equiv DCg + DCp \tag{19.3}$$

$$B = \theta(\overline{y}, \overline{P}, \overline{i}_{d}, \overset{+}{i}_{f}, \overset{+}{W}) \tag{19.4}$$

$$B = \omega(\overline{i_{f} - \epsilon^{e}}, \Sigma\overline{C}A, \overset{+}{W^{*}}) \tag{19.5}$$

$$W \equiv M + K + B \tag{19.6}$$

$$CF \equiv -\Delta B \tag{19.7}$$

$$\Delta NFA \equiv CA + CF \tag{19.8}$$

$$\Delta DC = \mu(\Delta NFA, \pi - \pi^{*}, \pi^{\circ}, \Delta DCg) \tag{19.9}$$

Equation (19.1) is a money demand function. Its determinants include both the return on other domestic assets i_{d} and the domestic-currency return on foreign assets i_{f}. For net debtor countries, this return consists of the dollar yield on foreign bonds or the world interest rate i^{*} plus the country-specific risk premium on foreign borrowing ρ plus the expected exchange rate depreciation ϵ^{e}, i^{*} is exogenous, while ρ and ϵ^{e} are endogenous. Net foreign bond holdings of the majority of the Asia-Pacific developing market economies examined here have been negative for most of the observation period; they have been net borrowers. For net creditor countries and for countries with such small values of international loans outstanding that no country-specific risk premia apply, however, the return on foreign assets consists of i^{*} plus ϵ^{e}.

Equation (19.2) is the money supply function; it takes the form of a simplified balance sheet of the consolidated banking system. The liability—money M—is created by banking system holdings of net foreign assets NFA and domestic credit DC. Equation (19.3) decomposes domestic credit into net domestic credit to the government sector DCg and domestic credit to the private sector DCp.

Equation (19.4), the demand for foreign bonds (net) B, takes exactly the same form as equation (19.1). For net creditor countries, equation (19.4) simply specifies the factors determining the demand for foreign bonds. If foreign bond holdings are negative, however, this equation determines the level of net foreign indebtedness that the country wishes to incur, given the interest rate on the debt in terms of the domestic currency.

Equation (19.5) is derived from work by Jonathan Eaton and Mark Gersovitz (1981), Sebastián Edwards (1986), James Hanson (1974) and Jeffrey Sachs (1984) on the determinants of the country-specific risk premium. For net debtor countries, the net supply of foreign bonds becomes a demand for dollar-denominated developing country bonds. This demand is determined by the world nominal interest rate plus the country-specific risk premium $i^* + \rho$. It is not influenced by the expected exchange rate depreciation ϵ^e, because foreign lenders are unaffected by domestic currency depreciation. Since $i_f = i^* + \rho + \epsilon^e$, it follows that $i^* + \rho$ equals $i_f - \epsilon^e$. The net supply of foreign credit is also affected by the size of a country's cumulated current account position ΣCA.[4] In flow terms, this implies that a large current account deficit makes the rest of the world less inclined to lend more to this developing country. Finally, the net supply of foreign bonds is determined by foreign wealth W^*.

This supply function is appropriate only for negative supplies of foreign bonds or net lending by the rest of the world to the developing country. For positive supplies of foreign bonds or net borrowing by the rest of the world from the developing country, supply is infinitely elastic and purchases are determined solely by demand. For net creditor developing countries, equation (19.5) disappears from the model. This implies that the quasi reduced-form capital flow equation for net creditor countries differs from the capital inflow equation for net debtor countries.

Equation (19.6) indicates that the exogenous wealth at the beginning of each period W can be allocated among money M, other domestic assets K and foreign bonds B. Equation (19.7) defines the capital account or capital inflows CF as the change in the holdings of foreign bonds (which can of course be negative) ΔB. Equation (19.8) uses the balance-of-payments identity to express the change in net foreign assets ΔNFA as the sum of the current account CA and the capital account CF. Equation (19.9), the central bank's monetary policy reaction function determining the change in domestic credit, is discussed in section 19.4.

Combining equations (19.1), (19.2) and (19.8) gives

$$CA + CF + \Delta DC = \Delta[\xi(y, P, i_d, i_f, W)] \tag{19.10}$$

Equations (19.4) and (19.7) produce

$$CF = -\Delta[\theta(y, P, i_d, i_f, W)] \tag{19.11}$$

Equations (19.5) and (19.7) yield

$$CF = -\Delta[\omega(i_f - \epsilon^e, \Sigma CA, W^*)] \tag{19.12}$$

Equations (19.10), (19.11) and (19.12) can be solved simultaneously to eliminate the two price variables, the return on other domestic assets i_d and the domestic return on foreign bonds i_f. The derivation of this quasi reduced-form capital flow equation can be illustrated with a simple linear system in which all coefficients take positive values. For expositional simplicity, W and W^* are omitted. For this illustration, equations (19.10), (19.11) and (19.12) take the specific forms:

$$CA + CF + \Delta DC = a_1\Delta y + a_2\Delta P - a_3\Delta i_d - a_4\Delta i_f \tag{19.13}$$

$$CF = b_1\Delta y + b_2\Delta P + b_3\Delta i_d - b_4\Delta i_f \tag{19.14}$$

$$CF = c_1(\Delta i_f - \Delta\epsilon^e) + c_2CA \tag{19.15}$$

Equations (19.14) and (19.15) can be rearranged in terms of Δi_d and Δi_f:

$$\Delta i_d = CF/b_3 - (b_1/b_3)\Delta y - (b_2/b_3)\Delta P + (b_4/b_3)\Delta i_f \tag{19.16}$$

$$\Delta i_f = CF/c_1 + \Delta\epsilon^e - (c_2/c_1)CA \tag{19.17}$$

Substituting equations (19.16) and (19.17) into equation (19.13) gives the quasi reduced-form capital inflow equation:

$$CF = \frac{-\Delta DC - \left(1 - \dfrac{a_3 b_4 c_2}{b_3 c_1} - \dfrac{a_4 c_2}{c_1}\right)CA + \left(a_1 + \dfrac{a_3 b_1}{b_3}\right)\Delta y + \left(a_2 + \dfrac{a_3 b_2}{b_3}\right)\Delta P - \left(a_4 + \dfrac{a_3 b_4}{b_3}\right)\Delta\epsilon^e}{1 + a_3/b_3 + a_3 b_4/b_3 c_1 + a_4/c_1} \tag{19.18}$$

The qualitative effects on capital inflows of all the variables in equation (19.18), except the current account CA, are unambiguous.

In the case of an infinitely elastic supply of foreign bonds for net creditor countries, equation 19.5 disappears and the quasi reduced-form capital inflow equation is derived solely from equations (19.10) and (19.11); equation (19.14) can still be rearranged in terms of $\Delta\pi^f$. Inserting equation (19.16) into equation (19.13) now provides the alternative quasi reduced-form capital inflow equation:

$$CF = \frac{-\Delta DC - CA + \left(a_1 + \dfrac{a_3 b_1}{b_3}\right)\Delta y + \left(a_2 + \dfrac{a_3 b_2}{b_3}\right)\Delta P - \left(a_4 + \dfrac{a_3 b_4}{b_3}\right)\Delta i^* - \left(a_4 + \dfrac{a_3 b_4}{b_3}\right)\Delta\epsilon^e}{1 + a_3/b_3} \tag{19.19}$$

The qualitative effects on capital inflows of all the variables in equation (19.19) are unambiguous.

The linear versions of equations (19.18) and (19.19) scaled by nominal GNP (not wealth) actually estimated here takes the form:

$$CFY = \bar{b}_{11}\widehat{DDCY} + \bar{b}_{12}\widehat{CAY} + \overset{+}{b}_{13}\widehat{YG} + \overset{+}{b}_{14}\widehat{INF} + \bar{b}_{15}\widehat{EDEXG} \tag{19.20}$$

$$CFY = \bar{b}_{11}\widehat{DDCY} + \bar{b}_{11}\widehat{CAY} + \overset{+}{b}_{13}\widehat{YG} + \overset{+}{b}_{14}\widehat{INF} + \bar{b}_{15}\widehat{IWD} + \bar{b}_{15}\widehat{EDEXG} \tag{19.21}$$

where CFY is the ratio of capital inflows to nominal GNP, $DDCY$ is the change in domestic credit divided by nominal GNP, CAY is the current account ratio, YG is the rate of growth in real GNP, INF is the inflation rate, $EDEXG$ is the expected change in exchange rate depreciation (continuously compounded) and IWD is the change in the six-month LIBOR (London Inter-Bank Offered Rate) dollar deposit rate (also continuously compounded). The hats denote endogenous variables.

If expectations are formed rationally, the change in exchange rate depreciation estimated by variables known at time $t-1$ can be used as the expected change in exchange rate depreciation. Specifically, the expected change in exchange rate depreciation is the change in exchange rate depreciation estimated separately for each country by ordinary least squares (OLS) using lagged values of the change in exchange rate depreciation, the rate of growth in real GNP, money (M2) growth, the gap between domestic and U.S. inflation, the rate of change in oil prices expressed in U.S. dollars, the change in domestic credit as a ratio of nominal GNP and the ratio of capital inflows to GNP.

The offset coefficient is b_{11} in equations (19.20) and (19.21). Its value can lie between 0 and –1. A value of –1 implies that monetary policy is impotent because the private sector reduces its holdings of net foreign assets *pari passu* with any increase in domestic credit. In this case changes in domestic credit, the intermediate monetary policy target for central banks in open economies, have no effect on the money supply.

The changes in income and price in equations (19.10) and (19.11) are converted into the growth and inflation variables in equations (19.20) and (19.21), since first differences of logarithms are used. They exert positive effects on capital inflows through their positive effects on money demand and negative effects on the demand for foreign bonds. The expected change in exchange rate depreciation reduces capital inflows because of an asymmetry between foreign bond demand and supply functions with respect to this variable. A rise in *EDEXG* encourages capital outflows but has no effect on capital inflows. Hence, a rise in *EDEXG* reduces *net* capital inflows in equation (19.20). In combination with the world interest rate, it also deters capital inflows in equation (19.21).

19.3   Some Estimates of Capital Inflows to the Asia-Pacific Developing Market Economies

The first regression estimates presented in this section use 699 observations from 27 developing countries: Algeria, Argentina, Brazil, Chile, Côte d'Ivoire, Egypt, Ghana, Greece, India, Indonesia, Korea, Malaysia, Mexico, Morocco, Nigeria, Pakistan, Peru, Philippines, Portugal, Sri Lanka, Taiwan, Tanzania, Thailand, Turkey, Venezuela, Yugoslavia and Zaire.[5] These countries comprise developing countries with populations over 10 million for which there are reasonably good financial data. The data are taken from the World Bank (1989, 1990), *International Financial Statistics* computer tape and national sources for Taiwan. The observation period is 1960–88, but a full data set for some countries starts only in the mid-1960s.

The regression method is three-stage least squares (3SLS). The 27 individual country equations for capital inflow ratios are estimated as a system of equations with cross-equation restrictions on all coefficients except the intercept. Coefficient equality over countries within a group is imposed in the estimated equation. However, the instruments are allowed to have different coefficients for each country in the first stage of the estimation procedure. The instruments used for the endogenous variables in the capital flow equations are the world real interest rate, world economic growth, the ratio of government sector credit to total domestic credit, *EDEXG*, and lagged values of real GNP growth, money (M2) growth, inflation, the change in the ratio of domestic credit to GNP, and the current and capital account ratios. The coefficient of *EDEXG* was not significant.

Table 19.2 gives estimates of two versions of the capital flow equation. In equation (19.22), the Asia-Pacific developing economies have the same coefficients as the rest of the sample. The estimated offset coefficient in equation (19.22) is –0.23. The size of this offset coefficient is inconsistent with the assertion that active monetary policy cannot be pursued in a representative developing country. Indeed, it is considerably smaller than offset coefficients estimated for most industrial countries. Not surprisingly, capital accounts seem to be more open in the industrial countries than they are in this sample of developing countries. For example, Kouri and Porter (1974: 455–56) estimate offset coefficients averaging –0.57 for Australia, Germany, Holland and Italy, whereas Laskar (1983: 329) reports his preferred offset coefficients averaging –0.64 for Britain, Canada, France, Germany, Holland, Italy and Japan.

The x^2 for the Wald test for equation (19.23) indicates that the six Asia-Pacific developing market economies are significantly different from the control group. Equation 19.23 shows that the Asia-Pacific developing economies have a joint offset

TABLE 19.2   Capital inflow (CFY) estimates for 27 developing countries

Variable	Equation (19.22)	Equation (19.23)
$\widehat{DDCY}$	–0.234	–0.251
	(–24.394)	(–25.288)
$\widehat{CAY}$	–0.760	–0.838
	(–95.144)	(–85.224)
$\widehat{YG}$	0.073	0.063
	(7.163)	(5.820)
$\widehat{INF}$	–0.008	–0.005
	(–2.569)	(–1.387)
Shift parameters for Asia-Pacific developing market economies		
$\widehat{DDCY}$		0.100
		(6.772)
$\widehat{CAY}$		0.256
		(14.047)
$\widehat{YG}$		–0.021
		(–0.942)
$\widehat{INF}$		0.005
		(0.790)
R^2	0.533	0.540
x^2 against equation (19.22)		2031

The hats denote endogenous variables. *t* statistics in parentheses.

coefficient of only –0.15, while the offset coefficient for the control group of developing countries is now –0.25. Again, the size of both these offset coefficients are significantly less than one. Capital flows have by no means completely offset monetary policy action in the form of changes in domestic credit. Hence, the monetary authorities in this sample of developing countries can control their money supplies by controlling or influencing domestic credit in the short run.

The capital inflow estimates indicate that asset markets in this sample of developing countries are not perfectly integrated with asset markets in the rest of the world. This lack of integration permits an independent monetary policy over the short run. In the medium and longer runs, however, arbitrage across goods markets requires consistent monetary and exchange rate policies if balance-of-payments crises are to be avoided. One distinguishing characteristic of the Asia-Pacific developing market economies examined here lies in the general complementarity between their monetary and exchange rate policies. Unlike the majority of developing countries, the Asia-Pacific developing market economies have rarely allowed their currencies to appreciate in real terms solely as a result of domestic inflation. This policy consistency has been rewarded by phenomenal export growth.

For an estimate of capital flow behavior in these six Asia-Pacific developing market economies as a group, I estimate a system of six equations with the same slope parameters but different intercepts for each economy using iterative 3SLS (asymptotically, full-information maximum likelihood) over the period 1960–91:

$$CFY = -0.127 DD\widehat{C}Y - 0.580\widehat{CAY} + 0.134\widehat{YG} + 0.049\widehat{INF}$$
$$ (-3.494) \quad\quad (-18.085) \quad\quad (2.016) \quad\quad (2.451) \tag{19.24}$$
$$R^2 = 0.748$$

The precise starting and ending dates are determined by data availability for each economy—Indonesia, 1967–90; Korea, 1965–91; Malaysia, 1963–90; the Philippines, 1960–91; Taiwan, 1964–91; Thailand, 1960–90. The instruments used in equation (19.24) and for the remaining regressions reported in this section are $EDEXG$, IWD, π^0, $DDCGY$, $DDCY_{t-1}$, YG_{t-1}, INF_{t-1}, CFY_{t-1} and CAY_{t-1}. The variable $DDCGY$ is the change in net domestic credit to the public sector divided by nominal GNP. The figures in parentheses are t statistics. The coefficients of $EDEXG$ plus IWD and $EDEXG$ were not significant.

Equation (19.24) indicates that capital inflows to these six Asia-Pacific developing market economies are affected in the ways predicted by the model. An increase in domestic credit and an improvement in the balance of payments on current account reduce capital inflows, while economic growth and inflation increase capital inflows. The offset coefficient of –0.13 is significantly different from both zero and –1 and is very similar to the offset coefficient of –0.15 derived from equation (19.23) for these six economies. Over the period as a whole, therefore, the monetary authorities of these economies as a group have been capable of monetary control through control over domestic credit expansion.

The x^2 for the Wald test rejects the hypothesis of coefficient equality for *DDCY* and *CAY* in equation (19.24). Therefore, this section now examines separate capital inflow equations for each of these six Asia-Pacific developing market economies. Specifically, test whether equation (19.20) or (19.21) is most appropriate for each of these six economies. I also test for any structural changes that might have occurred over the past three decades.

Separate two-stage least-squares (2SLS) estimates for each economy indicate that coefficient equality for *DDCY* and *CAY* is rejected for Indonesia, Malaysia and Thailand, but is accepted for Korea, the Philippines and Taiwan. The rejection of the equality hypothesis for Indonesia, Malaysia and Thailand indicates that these economies face upward sloping supply curves for foreign capital that are influenced negatively by the size of their current account deficits.

To test for structural change, the regression period must be split. In order to retain some degrees of freedom, potential switch dates near the beginning and end of the regression period are excluded; potential switch dates tested here range from 1970 to 1983. For a structural change that occurred between 1975 and 1976, a dummy variable *AD* takes a value of one for the period 1960–75 and a value of zero for the period 1976–91, while a dummy variable *DA* takes a value of zero for the period 1960–75 and one for 1976–91. The two dummies are then interacted with all the explanatory and instrumental variables, so doubling the number of variables in the system:

$$CFY = b_{10}AD + b_{11}AD \cdot DDCY + b_{12}AD \cdot CAY + b_{13}AD \cdot YG + b_{14}AD \cdot INF$$
$$+ b_{20}DA + b_{21}DA \cdot DDCY + b_{22}DA \cdot CAY + b_{23}DA \cdot YG + b_{24}DA \cdot INF \qquad (19.25)$$

The maximum likelihood functions show that the most likely switch for the capital inflow equations are 1975–76 for Indonesia, 1970–71 for Korea, 1980–81 for Malaysia, 1977–78 for the Philippines, 1982–83 for Taiwan and 1978–79 for Thailand. These regime-switching estimates can be used to test for coefficient equality over two separate periods. The results indicate that coefficient equality for *DDCY* and *CAY* is now rejected for Indonesia and Malaysia, but is accepted for the Philippines, Taiwan and Thailand. In the case of Korea, coefficient equality is rejected for the earlier period 1960–70, but is accepted for the later period 1971–91. In other words, Korea faced an upward sloping supply curve for foreign capital in the 1960s, but has not since 1971.

The estimates discussed so far enable each economy to be classified on the basis of whether or not it has faced an infinitely elastic supply of foreign bonds or foreign lending. The appropriate choice of equation (19.20) or (19.21) can now be made for each country. In Korea's case, a hybrid is used in which equation (19.20) is used for the earlier years and equation (19.21) for the later period. The appropriate model can be estimated using a logistic-switching model.

The step-switching model discussed above forces the structural changes to take place instantaneously. The logistic function provides a more general specification of the switching model (Mankiw et al. 1987). Rather than requiring the values of AD and DA to move instantaneously from one to zero and *vice versa*, the logistic function allows the values of AD and DA to vary gradually over time. Specifically, DA is now defined to equal $e^{\alpha+\delta t}/(1 + e^{\alpha+\delta t})$ and AD equals $1-DA$ as before. The parameters α and δ determine the timing and speed of the regime shift. The logistic curve has its inflection when t equals $-\alpha/\delta$. At this date, behavior is determined by an equal mix of old and new regime parameter values. The value of δ determines the speed with which the switch occurs. In particular, one half of the adjustment takes place within $(\log 9)/\delta$ years. The step-switching function is the limit of the logistic function when δ equals ∞.

Maximum likelihood estimation of the logistic switching model is done in two stages. For a given value of δ, the equations are estimated by 2SLS with alternative values of α that permit structural changes in the period 1970–83. This set of iterations is then repeated for a new value of δ. I tried nine alternative values of δ ranging from 0.220 to 6.592. Table 19.3 presents the maximum-likelihood results of this procedure. Table 19.4 gives the corresponding offset coefficients for both the single- and the two-period maximum-likelihood estimates.

Two important conclusions can be drawn from Table 19.4. The first is that the capital inflow equations' explanatory powers are increased considerably when structural changes are permitted. From rather mediocre explanatory power of the single-period estimates, the regime-switching capital inflow equations provide substantially improved explanatory power. This improvement is most noticeable for Thailand's capital inflow estimate. The second conclusion is that offsetting capital flows have not jeopardised monetary control in any of these Asia-Pacific developing market economies, even in recent years. The three significant offset coefficients for the second period are all significantly less than –1 in absolute terms. In fact, most of these offset coefficients are not significantly different from zero.

TABLE 19.3 Speed and timing of structural changes in capital inflow equations using logistic-switching model

Economy	Years for half of switch	Maximum likelihood value of δ	Maximum likelihood value of α	Maximum likelihood switch date	F statistic for structural change
Indonesia	1/3	6.592	–501	1976.00	3.04*
Korea	1/3	6.592	–459	1969.63	23.49**
Malaysia	2/3	3.296	–279	1984.65	8.31**
Philippines	2/3	3.296	–280	1984.96	3.97*
Taiwan	0	∞	n.a.	1982–83	10.46**
Thailand	0	∞	n.a.	1978–79	11.40**

*Significant at 95 percent confidence level. **Significant at 99 percent confidence level.

TABLE 19.4   Offset coefficients and adjusted correlation coefficients for single- and two-period estimates

Economy	Single period		Two periods		
	Single offset coefficient	$\bar{R}^2$	First offset coefficient	Second offset coefficient	$\bar{R}^2$
Indonesia	−0.265 (−1.674)	0.425	−1.410* (−2.882)	−0.302* (−2.157)	0.626
Korea	−0.238 (−1.880)	0.699	0.123 (1.469)	−0.479* (−4.814)	0.890
Malaysia	0.152 (0.482)	0.563	−0.254 (−1.434)	−1.297 (−1.254)	0.836
Philippines	−0.328 (−1.189)	0.296	−0.385 (−1.459)	0.455 (1.323)	0.462
Taiwan	−0.487* (−7.631)	0.704	−0.157 (−1.563)	−0.499* (−4.570)	0.903
Thailand	0.328 (1.858)	−0.027	−0.072 (−0.480)	0.179 (1.054)	0.605

*Significant at 95 percent confidence level. t statistics in parentheses.

My finding of relatively small offset coefficients contradicts the conclusions of recent work on interest rate linkages in the Asia-Pacific region (Claassen 1992; Faruqee 1991; Fischer and Reisen 1992; Glick and Hutchison 1990; Scholnick 1992). It also challenges the conclusion of Nadeem Haque and Peter Montiel (1990: 11) using an indirect approach that "the degree of openness in developing economies, though it differs across countries, tends to be surprisingly large." Haque and Montiel find that the assumption of perfect capital mobility cannot be rejected for two-thirds of their sample of developing countries. Among those countries are Indonesia, Malaysia and the Philippines.

My finding is not inconsistent with that of Helmut Reisen and Hélène Yèches (1991: 30) who conclude that in Korea and Taiwan: "The capital account of both countries seems still quite closed, with the possible exception of Taiwan's interbank market in very recent years. Therefore, the authorities in both Korea and Taiwan have continued to enjoy considerable scope for an independent short-term monetary policy."

One explanation for these divergent findings may lie in the fact that bank loans differ substantially from bonds (Fama 1985). Most bank borrowers do not have access to the bond market, either at home or abroad. In a sense, therefore, they are captive borrowers from their domestic banking systems. Where there are only a few banks, some of which may well be government-owned, implementation of monetary policy can work through a number of well-known nonprice channels (Lin 1991). As Wanda Tseng and Robert Corker (1991: 34) point out: "the use of indirect instruments of monetary control has been hampered by the thinness of monetary and capital markets and by the large domestic financing needs of governments." Hence, the monetary authorities' ability to influence the volume and direction of domestic credit may not have been eroded by increased interest rate linkages in these bond and interbank markets. The monetary authorities simply do not rely on these markets for monetary policy implementation.

Nonprice rationing can ensure that domestic credit targets are met regardless of interest rate movements. Hence, capital flows could well be influenced by relative interest rates in direct financial markets but not to anything like the same extent by the volume of domestic credit supplied by the banking system. Whether or not this interpretation is accepted, I now turn to the implementation of monetary policy in these economies, having established that offsetting capital flows do not make monetary policy impotent in any of these six Asia-Pacific developing market economies.

19.4 Determinants of Monetary Policy in the Asia-Pacific Developing Market Economies

In the previous section I conclude that, due to capital controls, capital market imperfections or nonprice credit rationing of bank loans, the six Asia-Pacific developing market economies can pursue independent monetary policies even though they peg their exchange rates. In this section I address the question: Do they pursue systematic discretionary monetary policies? The monetary policy reaction function, specified as the change in domestic credit scaled by GNP $DDCY$, is designed to discover whether or not monetary authorities in this sample developing countries have pursued systematic monetary policies.

Equation (19.9) in Table 19.1 is the central bank's monetary policy reaction function determining the change in domestic credit. Following the early work on monetary policy reaction functions by Grant Reuber (1964) and Richard Froyen (1974), central bank objectives have typically been taken to include a balance-of-payments target ΔNFA, an inflation target π or an inflation target relative to U.S. inflation $\pi - \pi^*$, where π^* is the rate of change in U.S. wholesale prices, and possibly some response to exogenous shocks such as oil price inflation π^0. Here, an attempt is also made to determine the extent to which the central bank accommodates the credit requirements of the government sector ΔDCg without squeezing private sector credit availability.

The monetary policy reaction function includes the change in net foreign assets of the banking system ΔNFA scaled by GNP to detect any systematic sterilization of the effects of such asset acquisition on the money supply. The monetary authorities might also squeeze domestic credit in response either to a widening gap between domestic inflation and inflation in the United States $\pi - \pi^*$ or to an increase in oil price inflation π^0. Alternatively, the monetary authorities might accommodate higher oil prices by increasing domestic credit. Finally, the monetary authorities might squeeze domestic credit to the private sector ΔDCp when the credit requirements of the government, ΔDCg increase. A complete neutralization of the public sector's credit requirements would imply a coefficient of zero for ΔDCg. A partial neutralization would produce a coefficient greater than zero but less than 1.

This monetary policy reaction function is specified for estimation in the form:

$$DDCY = b_{30} + \overline{b}_{31}\widehat{DNFAY} + \overset{?}{b}_{32}DNFAY_{t-1} + \overline{b}_{33}\widehat{INFGAP} + \overset{?}{b}_{34}INFGAP_{t-1}$$
$$+ \overset{?}{b}_{35}OILINF + \overset{?}{b}_{36}OILINF_{t-1} + \overset{+}{b}_{37}DDCGY + \overset{?}{b}_{38}DDCGY_{t-1} \tag{19.26}$$

In order to compare monetary policy implementation in the Asia-Pacific developing market economies with monetary policy implementation in a control group of developing countries, I estimate the monetary policy reaction function as a system of 27 country equations by 3SLS with cross-equation restrictions on all coefficients, except the intercept, using 694 observations over the period 1960–88 for the same sample of developing countries used for equations (19.22) and (19.23). Instruments for $DNFAY$ and $INFGAP$ are $OILINF$, $OILINF_{t-1}$, $DDCY_{t-1}$, $DNFAY_{t-1}$, $INFGAP_{t-1}$, $DDCGY$, $DDCGY_{t-1}$, U.S. inflation, the world real interest rate, world economic growth, and lagged values of real GNP growth and money (M2) growth.

Table 19.5 reports two estimates of the monetary policy reaction function. Both equations show that the monetary authorities in this sample of developing countries do appear to react systematically to changes in several economic variables. The results presented here contrast with those of Connolly and Taylor (1979: 287), who find no evidence that developing countries pursue any systematic monetary policies. They also contrast with estimates of substantial or complete sterilization in industrial countries (except for Switzerland) reported by Jacques Artus (1976: 326), Michael Darby (1983: 307–8), Leroy Laney and Thomas Willett (1982: 144–47) and Maurice Obstfeld (1983).

The two sets of policy coefficients in equation (19.28) indicate that the Asia-Pacific market economies adopted entirely different monetary policy stances from the other countries in the sample; the x^2 test for equation (19.28) is highly significant. Of most importance is the finding that the Asia-Pacific developing market economies sterilized 41 percent of the increase in net foreign assets (–0.24 plus –0.17), compared with only 17 percent in the other developing countries. The x^2 for the Wald test accepts the hypothesis of coefficient equality for $DNFAY$ in the same monetary policy reaction function estimated separately for the six Asia-Pacific developing market economies.

The small sterilization coefficient for the non Asia-Pacific countries may well be due to the fact that some countries in this group actually increased domestic credit when net foreign assets rose. Arturo Porzecanski (1979: 434–35) finds in Mexico and Venezuela that higher net foreign assets led to more rapid domestic credit expansion; I detect the same phenomenon in Turkey (Fry 1988: 188–203). In these countries, domestic credit was increased when foreign exchange receipts

TABLE 19.5 Monetary policy reaction functions (*DDCY*) for 27 developing countries

Variable	Equation (19.27)	Equation (19.28)
$D\widehat{NF}AY$	−0.184	−0.168
	(−14.385)	(−12.912)
$DNFAY_{t-1}$	0.066	0.045
	(5.612)	(3.740)
$IN\widehat{F}GAP$	0.090	0.088
	(19.774)	(19.991)
$INFGAP_{t-1}$	−0.015	−0.014
	(−4.059)	(−4.010)
$OILINF$	0.017	0.016
	(6.016)	(6.449)
$OILINF_{t-1}$	0.024	0.032
	(7.431)	(10.973)
$DDCGY$	0.858	0.882
	(81.300)	(86.134)
$DDCGY_{t-1}$	−0.027	−0.033
	(−2.647)	(−3.443)
Shift parameters for Asia-Pacific developing market economies		
$D\widehat{NF}AY$		−0.245
		(−7.822)
$OILINF_{t-1}$		−0.014
		(−2.754)
$DDCGY$		−0.388
		(−8.812)
$DDCGY_{t-1}$		−0.135
		(−3.177)
R^2	0.766	0.769
x^2 against equation (19.27)		1.30

The hats denote endogenous variables. *t* statistics in parentheses.

rose so that a larger volume of capital equipment and raw material imports could be financed. Rather than contracting domestic credit to sterilize foreign exchange inflows, these central banks reacted by expanding domestic credit to stimulate investment and growth.

The developing countries outside Asia-Pacific accommodated domestically generated inflationary pressures *INFGAP*, the increase in oil prices *OILINF* and the government's credit requirements *DDCGY*. Indeed, these countries contracted domestic credit to the private sector by only 12 percent of the increase in the government's credit requirements (15 percent over a two-year period).

In contrast, the Asia-Pacific developing market economies sterilized 41 percent of any increase in the banking system's net foreign assets *DNFAY* and increased domestic credit less than the control group when oil price inflation *OILINF* accelerated. Finally, the Asia-Pacific developing market economies neutralized two-thirds of the effects of the government's credit requirements on the money supply. The monetary authorities of the Asia-Pacific developing market economies increased aggregate domestic credit by only 33 percent (0.85 plus –0.52) of any increase in the government's credit requirements over a two-year period. This implies a reduction in domestic credit to the private sector equal to 67 percent of the increase in the government's credit requirements.

Equation (19.28) demonstrates that the implementation of monetary policy in this group of Asia-Pacific developing market economies is significantly different from monetary policy implementation in the other sample countries. These results support Arnold Harberger's (1988: 177) finding that "when East Asian countries deviate from average behavior, they deviate on the side of prudence ... [their] economic policy was indeed quite different...." The estimates reported in this section suggest strongly that inflation in the Asia-Pacific developing market economies was indeed lower than it has been in other developing countries because of the way in which monetary policy has been conducted.

Separate 2SLS estimates of *DDCY* for each economy indicate that regime switches took place in each of the six Asia-Pacific developing market economies. The maximum likelihood functions show that the most likely switch for the domestic credit equations are 1983–84 for Indonesia, 1978–79 for Korea, 1976–77 for Malaysia, 1983–84 for the Philippines, 1980–81 for Taiwan and 1971–72 for Thailand. Except in the case of the Philippines, the monetary authorities sterilized capital inflows to a greater extent in the second period than in the first period. The estimated coefficients are given in Table 19.6.

Table 19.6 shows that explanatory power is increased considerably when regime changes are permitted. From negligible explanatory power of the single-period estimates, the regime-switching monetary policy equations provide substantially improved explanatory power. The point estimates of the second-period sterilization coefficients suggest that the monetary authorities in all the economies, except the Philippines, sterilize at least three quarters of any capital inflow. Except in the cases of Indonesia and the Philippines, none of the estimated second-period sterilization coefficients is significantly different from –1.

19.5 Conclusion

In this chapter, I examined two questions relating to monetary policy and inflation in a sample of Asia-Pacific developing market economies. The major findings are: (1) financial opening has not reduced the ability of the monetary authorities in these economies to pursue independent monetary policies despite pegged exchange rates; (2) inflation has been lower in the Asia-Pacific developing

TABLE 19.6   Sterilization coefficients and adjusted correlation coefficients for single- and two-period estimates

| Economy | Single period | | Two periods | | |
	Single sterilization coefficient	$\bar{R}^2$	First sterilization coefficient	Second sterilization coefficient	$\bar{R}^2$
Indonesia	−2.884 (−1.904)	−1.465	−0.075 (−0.209)	−2.808* (−4.604)	0.629
Korea	−0.252 (−0.351)	−0.563	−0.381 (−0.625)	−0.754 (−1.608)	0.604
Malaysia	1.300 (1.328)	−0.598	0.584 (1.003)	−0.738 (−1.628)	0.606
Philippines	0.174 (0.481)	0.686	−0.394 (−1.072)	0.346 (1.684)	0.840
Taiwan	1.861 (1.380)	−3.029	0.558 (0.803)	−1.077* (−3.238)	0.802
Thailand	−2.915 (−0.745)	−1.271	0.496 (0.361)	−1.315 (−1.985)	0.605

*Significant at 95 percent confidence level. t statistics in parentheses.

market economies than it has in a control group of 21 other developing countries because of the way in which monetary policy has been conducted.

Monetary policies pursued by these Asia-Pacific developing market economies have been much less accommodative and hence less inflationary than policies followed by the rest of the sample countries. Further support for this proposition is provided by the tests of different sample means in Table 19.7. The means of inflation, domestic credit expansion and the proportion of domestic credit expropriated by the government (reflecting fiscal discipline) are all significantly lower in the Asia-Pacific developing market economies than in the control group of developing countries. In contrast, the rate of economic growth is significantly higher in the Asia-Pacific developing market economies.[6]

Finally, I examine simple relationships between rates of economic growth, inflation and the ratio of net domestic credit to the government sector to total domestic credit for the 27 sample countries; Table 19.8 presents these bivariate regression estimates. They yield a significantly negative relationship between growth and inflation and between growth and the government credit ratio. On the other hand, they indicate a significantly positive relationship between inflation and the government credit ratio. The same relationships can be detected when the country means of the same variables are used instead of the annual observations. These results are consistent with the hypotheses that government deficits raise inflation and lower rates of economic growth.[7]

TABLE 19.7   Sample means for some key macroeconomic variables in 27 developing countries

Variable	Control group mean	Asia-Pacific	Difference	SE of difference
INF	0.209	0.128	−0.081*	0.0237
DDCY	0.089	0.060	−0.029*	0.0050
DCG	0.276	0.215	−0.062*	0.0172
DCGR	0.396	0.160	−0.235*	0.0246
YG	0.040	0.067	0.027*	0.0035

INF – Rate of change in GNP deflator (continuously compounded)
DDCY – Change in domestic credit/GNP (current prices)
DCG – Rate of change in domestic credit (continuously compounded)
DCGR – Net domestic credit to government/domestic credit (current prices)
YG   – Rate of growth in GNP (constant prices, continuously compounded)

*Significant at 99 percent confidence level.

TABLE 19.8   Bivariate relationships between growth, inflation, and government credit ratios in 27 developing countries

	Dependent variable			
	YG		*INF*	
Independent variable	Annual observations	Country means	Annual observations	Country means
INF	−0.049 (−8.231)	−0.040 (−2.136)		
DCGR	−0.009 (−2.496)	−0.028 (−2.273)		
DCGR			0.081 (3.609)	0.075 (0.573)

INF – Rate of change in GNP deflator (continuously compounded)
DCGR – Net domestic credit to government/domestic credit (current prices)
YG   – Rate of growth in GNP (constant prices, continuously compounded)

t statistics in parentheses.

The econometric results and significant differences in means reported here can hardly be used to infer that policy rather than behavioral differences explain the superior economic performance of the Asia-Pacific developing market economies. However, econometric analysis of the rate of economic growth reported elsewhere (Fry and Lilien 1986) indicates that accommodative, discretionary monetary and fiscal policies have negative effects on economic growth in the long run. Monetary accommodation of exogenous shocks adds noise to the economic environment by increasing the variance of money growth shocks. In the same vein, Harberger (1988) suggests that erratic exchange rate policies in Latin America have reduced export supply elasticities in that part of the world.

The conclusions reached by Fry and David Lilien (1986) combined with results reported here are certainly consistent with the hypothesis that greater monetary discipline in the Asia-Pacific developing market economies has been one of the factors contributing to the substantially higher rates of economic growth in this region. Nevertheless, the job of linking the results reported here that detect distinctly different monetary policy stances in the Asia-Pacific developing market economies with work that suggests that these policy differences may explain the distinctly better economic performance in these economies still remains.

Notes

This article first appeared in *Financial Opening: Policy Issues and Experiences in Developing Countries*, Helmut Reisen and Bernhard Fischer (eds.), OECD Development Centre, Paris, 1993, pp. 143–64. © OECD, Paris, 1993. Reproduced by permission of the OECD.

1. The Asia-Pacific inflation rate is the simple average of the eight annual rates of inflation. Inflation rates for other regions are weighted by relative GNPS. Data for Figures 19.1 to 19.4 are taken from *International Financial Statistics*, CD-ROM, June 1992, and national sources for Hong Kong and Taiwan.
2. The capital inflow equations derived here are similar to the quasi reduced-form equations used by Pentti Kouri and Michael Porter (1974: 447–54), Daniel Laskar (1983: 317–21) and Linda Kamas (1986: 471–72). Following Kamas and Laskar, the current account is treated as endogenous, since the full model determines both national saving and domestic investment. My model also recognizes that many developing countries face country-specific risk premia when borrowing abroad.
3. The full model would also treat national saving, domestic investment, the rate of economic growth, terms of trade, income growth attributable to terms-of-trade improvements, the real exchange rate, exports and imports as endogenous. Hence, none of these variables is used as an instrument in the two- and three-stage least-squares estimates reported below.
4. A cumulated current account deficit equals net cumulated capital inflows minus the stock of net foreign assets. It provides a rough measure of the relative exposure of the rest of the world to the vagaries of this country's economic performance.
5. Greece and Portugal are included in this sample, although they are no longer classified as developing countries.
6. The variance of inflation is also lower in the Asia-Pacific developing market economies than in the control group.
7. The variance of inflation also has a significant negative relationship with economic growth.

References

Aghevli, Bijan B., Mohsin S. Khan, Prabhakar R. Narvekar, and Brock K. Short, 1979, "Monetary Policy in Selected Asian Countries," *International Monetary Fund Staff Papers*, 26(4): 775–824.

Artus, Jacques R., 1976, "Exchange Rate Stability and Managed Floating: The Experience of the Federal Republic of Germany," *International Monetary Fund Staff Papers*, 23(2): 312–33.

Claassen, Emil-Maria, 1992, *Financial Liberalization and Its Impact on Domestic Stabilization Policies: Singapore and Malaysia*, Institute of Southeast Asian Studies, Singapore.

Connolly, Michael B. and Dean Taylor, 1979, "Exchange Rate Changes and Neutralization: A Test of the Monetary Approach Applied to Developed and Developing Countries," *Economica*, 46(183): 281–94.

Darby, Michael R., 1983, "Sterilization and Monetary Control: Concepts, Issues, and a Reduced-Form Test," in Michael R. Darby, James R. Lothian, et al., *The International Transmission of Inflation*, University of Chicago Press for the National Bureau of Economic Research, Chicago, pp. 291–313.

Eaton, Jonathan and Mark Gersovitz, 1981, "Debt with Potential Repudiation: Theoretical and Empirical Analysis," *Review of Economic Studies*, 48(2): 289–309.

Edwards, Sebastián, 1986, "The Pricing of Bonds and Bank Loans in International Markets: An Empirical Analysis of Developing Countries' Foreign Borrowing," *European Economic Review*, 30(3): 565–89.

Fama, Eugene F., 1985, "What's Different about Banks?" *Journal of Monetary Economics*, 15(1): 29–39.

Faruqee, Hamid, 1991, *Dynamic Capital Mobility in Pacific Basin Developing Countries: Estimation and Policy Implications*, WP/91/115, International Monetary Fund, Washington, DC.

Fischer, Bernhard and Helmut Reisen, 1992, *Towards Capital Account Convertibility*, Policy Brief No. 4, OECD Development Centre, Paris.

Froyen, Richard T., 1974, "A Test of the Endogeneity of Monetary Policy," *Journal of Econometrics*, 2(2): 175–88.

Fry, Maxwell J., 1988, *Money, Interest, and Banking in Economic Development*, Johns Hopkins University Press, Baltimore, MD.

Fry, Maxwell J. and David M. Lilien, 1986, "Monetary Policy Responses to Exogenous Shocks," *American Economic Review*, 76(2): 79–83.

Glick, Reuven and Michael M. Hutchison, 1990, "Financial Liberalization in the Pacific Basin: Implications for Real Interest Rate Linkages," *Journal of the Japanese and International Economies*, 4(1): 36–48.

Hanson, James A., 1974, "Optimal International Borrowing and Lending," *American Economic Review*, 64(4): 616–30.

Haque, Nadeem Ul and Peter J. Montiel, 1990, *Capital Mobility in Developing Countries—Some Empirical Tests*, WP/90/117, International Monetary Fund, Research Department, Washington, DC.

Harberger, Arnold C., 1988, "Growth, Industrialization and Economic Structure: Latin America and East Asia Compared," in Helen Hughes (ed.), *Achieving Industrialization in East Asia*, Cambridge University Press, Cambridge, pp. 164–94.

Kamas, Linda, 1986, "The Balance of Payments Offset to Monetary Policy: Monetarist, Portfolio Balance, and Keynesian Estimates for Mexico and Venezuela," *Journal of Money, Credit and Banking*, 18(4): 467–81.

Kouri, Pentti J. K. and Michael G. Porter, 1974, "International Capital Flows and Portfolio Equilibrium," *Journal of Political Economy*, 82(3): 443–67.

Laney, Leroy O. and Thomas D. Willett, 1982, "The International Liquidity Explosion and Worldwide Inflation: The Evidence from Sterilization Coefficient Estimates," *Journal of International Money and Finance*, 1(2): 141–52.

Laskar, Daniel M., 1983, "Short-Run Independence of Monetary Policy under a Pegged Exchange-Rate System: An Econometric Approach," in Michael R. Darby, James R. Lothian, et al., *The International Transmission of Inflation*, University of Chicago Press for the National Bureau of Economic Research, Chicago, pp. 314–48.

Lin, See Yan, 1991, "Interaction of Exchange Rate Policy and Monetary Policy: The Case of Malaysia," in Gerard Caprio and Patrick Honohan (eds.), *Monetary Policy Instruments for Developing Countries*, World Bank, Washington, DC, pp. 131–34.

Mankiw, N. Gregory, Jeffrey A. Miron, and David N. Weil, 1987, "The Adjustment of Expectations to a Change in Regime: A Study of the Founding of the Federal Reserve," *American Economic Review*, 77(3): 358–74.

Obstfeld, Maurice, 1983, "Exchange Rates, Inflation, and the Sterilization Problem: Germany, 1975–1981," *European Economic Review*, 21(1–2): 161–89.

Porzecanski, Arturo, 1979, "Patterns of Monetary Policy in Latin America," *Journal of Money, Credit and Banking*, 11(4): 427–37.

Reisen, Helmut and Hélène Yèches, 1991, *Time-Varying Estimates on the Openness of the Capital Account in Korea and Taiwan*, OECD Development Centre Technical Paper No. 42, Organisation for Economic Co-operation and Development, Paris.

Reuber, Grant L., 1964, "The Objectives of Canadian Monetary Policy, 1949–61: Empirical 'Trade-offs' and the Reaction Function of the Authorities," *Journal of Political Economy*, 72(2): 109–32.

Sachs, Jeffrey D., 1984, "Theoretical Issues in International Borrowing," *Princeton Studies in International Finance*, issue 54.

Scholnick, Barry, 1992, "Interest, Rates, Capital Controls and Financial Liberalization," Darwin College, Cambridge, unpublished.

Smaghi, Lorenzo Bini, 1982, *Independent Monetary Policy and Capital Mobility in LDCs: The Case of Malaysia, 1978–1981*, DM/82/72, International Monetary Fund, Washington, DC.

Tseng, Wanda and Robert Corker, 1991, *Financial Liberalization, Money Demand, and Monetary Policy in Asian Countries*, Occasional Paper 84, International Monetary Fund, Washington, DC.

World Bank, 1989, *World Tables 1988–89*, Washington, DC, March.

World Bank, 1990, *World Tables 1989–90: Socio-economic Time-Series Access and Retrieval System, Version 1.0*, Washington, DC.

Chapter 20

Robert F. Emery

CENTRAL BANKS' USE OF MONEY MARKET INSTRUMENTS IN THE ASIA-PACIFIC ECONOMIES

20.1 Introduction

Much of the past literature on the control instruments used by central banks in Asia-Pacific has focused on three main areas. These have been adjustments in commercial bank reserve requirements or liquidity ratios, central bank discount policy, and the use of various direct controls such as ceilings on the amount of commercial bank credit expansion. Less attention has been paid to central banks' use of money market instruments in the conduct of monetary policy. Yet, this is an important area, particularly since six of the eight major Asia-Pacific economies have utilized money market instruments of one type or another since the early 1980s in achieving their monetary policy objectives. This shift to greater use of money market instruments and, hence, open market operations, has been accompanied by the central banks' issuance of their own debt instruments.[1]

This chapter examines the six Asia-Pacific developing economies that have utilized money market instruments during the past decade as either a major monetary policy instrument or as a supplement to other central banking instruments in the pursuit of monetary policy objectives. The six economies covered are the Philippines, Korea, Taiwan, Indonesia, Thailand and Hong Kong. Malaysia and

Singapore are excluded because the central banks in neither of the two countries made much, if any, use of money market instruments in their conduct of monetary policy.

It is hoped that through an examination of the central banks' use of money market instruments in carrying out monetary policy some insights can be gained as to which approaches and instruments are likely to be successful in achieving the authorities' monetary policy objectives. Equally important is to gain an understanding of what conditions are needed in order to undertake successful operations with these money market instruments. The concluding section lists some of the reasons why open market operations in the case of truly viable money market instruments, are more advantageous than the three other traditional instruments mentioned earlier.

20.2   Individual Countries' Use of Money Market Instruments

With the exception of Hong Kong and the Philippines, all of the six economies employ money market instruments that constitute some type of central bank obligation, rather than a national government, or federal treasury, obligation such as a treasury bill. The main reasons for this will be discussed later. Hong Kong, an overseas territory of the United Kingdom, has no central bank. However, in recent years, the territory's Exchange Fund has had its powers of control over bank liquidity strengthened, and in March 1990, the Exchange Fund began to issue its own Exchange Fund bills. Currently the Central Bank of the Philippines uses national government treasury bills in its open market operations, but earlier during 1984–87 the Central Bank issued its own obligations—popularly known as "Jobo" bills after Central Bank Governor Jose B. Fernandez, Jr.—to mop up excess liquidity in the commercial banking system.[2] However, the focus in this chapter will be on the Central Bank's current use of treasury bills in its open market operations, and not on the "Jobo" bills.

The situation in each of the six economies differs, either in terms of the nature of the central bank obligation, the name of such an obligation, or how such an obligation is employed in the pursuit of the central banks' monetary policy objectives. Thus it is appropriate to examine each economy separately. This is done chronologically, depending on the date when the money market instrument was first introduced. The earliest instrument is the Philippine treasury bill (1966) and the most recent is Hong Kong's Exchange Fund bill (March 1990).

20.2.1 Philippines

The Philippine government first began to issue treasury bills on May 16, 1966.[3] Since then the treasury bill market has had an on-again, off-again, history. However, currently the treasury bill market constitutes one of the largest components of the Philippine money market and is roughly equal in size—based on turnover—to the interbank market. It is also a major source of borrowed funds for the government since in recent years treasury bills have accounted for roughly 80 percent of all outstanding national government securities.

The history of the treasury bill market can be divided into three periods. The first period extended from 1966 to 1973. During the early 1970s the authorities began to require the commercial banks to hold treasury bills as part of their secondary reserves. With a somewhat captive market, the yields on treasury bills tended to become less competitive with other nongovernment money market instruments. By 1973, treasury bills had disappeared from most private nonbank portfolios. Treasury bills enjoyed a resurgence in the second period (1977–89) when the government imposed in June 1977 a 35 percent transactions tax on the sale of many private money market instruments. This resurgence continued until a balance of payments crisis occurred in October 1983. Due to this financial crisis, the government suspended treasury bill auctions in 1984 and in March began to issue the "Jobo" bills mentioned earlier. The third period began in October 1986 when the government once more began to auction treasury bills. Since then the treasury bill market has remained an active and viable market. At the beginning of each of these three periods the government had to accredit, or re-accredit, a network of government securities dealers in order to properly start, or re-start, the market.

Although the Philippine central bank has several instruments of monetary control, its main instrument has been the treasury bill auctions and the open market operations—particularly on a day-to-day basis. Occasional use has been made of changes in reserve requirements and in the central bank's discount rate. For example, on November 30, 1990, the central bank raised the reserve requirement on bank deposit and deposit substitute liabilities to 23 percent from 21 percent, and between June 1990 and March 1991 the central bank's discount rate was increased from 9.8 percent to 10.8 percent. But both of these instruments are not well suited for influencing week-to-week or even day-to-day, bank liquidity. The treasury bill market is better suited for that task and it is able to be effective because of its relatively large size. At the end of 1989, treasury bills outstanding totaled 173 billion pesos, which was much larger than the money supply outstanding of 81 billion pesos at the time.

The central bank has used several techniques to influence bank liquidity. For example, in addition to regular open market operations with the treasury bills, the bank has—at times—increased the size of the weekly auction in order to absorb excess bank liquidity. Thus, in mid-August 1989 the weekly treasury bill offering was raised to 10 billion pesos from 6 billion in the previous week. The bank has also frequently used reverse repurchase agreement transactions to absorb commercial bank liquidity. This has involved central bank borrowing from the commercial banks using the central bank's holdings of treasury bills as collateral, with an agreement to repay the loan at a specified maturity date and rate of interest.

The central bank could not have exercised an effective control over bank liquidity in the absence of a well developed treasury bill market, or, similarly, a well developed market in some central bank money market obligation. As indicated earlier, the Central Bank Certificate of Indebtedness, which was phased out in 1987, was not particularly appropriate for open market operations since it was a medium-term instrument carrying a fixed rate of interest. The central bank has continued, on an irregular basis, to issue its own CB bills to reduce commercial bank reserves,[4] but otherwise its main reliance has been on the treasury bill auctions and open market operations.

There are several important factors that have helped to make the central bank's open market operations with treasury bills successful. One is that the interest rates in the treasury bill market have not been controlled since 1983 and have been free to reflect demand and supply conditions. This has helped in the development of an active secondary market in treasury bills—particularly since 1988—and market transactions have also been facilitated by the introduction of a book entry system in February 1989. A second factor is that the central bank has not made treasury bills reserve eligible, that is, they do not qualify for any primary or secondary commercial bank reserve requirement. The danger with making treasury bills reserve eligible is that too much of a "captive market" develops for such bills and the government is tempted to issue the bills at below-market interest rates. Lastly, the Philippine money market is sufficiently flexible that the central bank has been able to use reverse repurchase agreements extensively when it desires to reduce bank liquidity. This has not been the case for most of the other East Asian central banks examined here.

20.2.2 Korea

Although Korea has a treasury bill market, the nature of the market is such that treasury bills have not been a suitable instrument for the Bank of Korea—the central bank—to use in the pursuit of its monetary policy objectives. One reason is that the amount of treasury bills issued and outstanding has not been large enough to conduct open market operations. In some years, such as 1983–85, there were no treasury bills outstanding at year-end and during 1969–76 there were no treasury bills issued at all. In addition, although there is some trading of treasury bills in a secondary market, there is no competitive bidding for the bills in the primary market. Instead, the issue system is administered by the Bank of Korea, with the issues being more or less forced on the underwriters who do not find the bills attractive.

In lieu of using treasury bills to conduct open market operations in order to influence bank liquidity, the Bank of Korea has instead made heavy use, particularly since 1986, of Monetary Stabilization Bonds (MSBs) that are a direct obligation of the Bank of Korea. The issue of these bonds was first authorized in 1961 as a result of the passage of the Stabilization Bonds Act of that year. The Act authorizes the Bank of Korea to issue shorter-term bonds in its own name under terms specified by the Monetary Board, and, if appropriate, to repurchase the bonds prior to maturity. As their name implies, the MSBs are to be used to stabilize monetary conditions. The Bank of Korea also issues Foreign Exchange Stabilization Fund bonds that carry various maturities up to five years.

Although the MSBs are referred to as "bonds", government bonds in Korea can have relatively short maturities. The MSB maturities range between nine weeks and two years, but are mainly one year or less in maturity. Most Korean government bonds other than MSBs have a maturity of about five years or less. There are no issues of national treasury bonds *per se* in Korea, but there are issues of other government bonds, such as national investment bonds and national housing bonds.

Issues of MSBs were relatively small until 1973 when the yield on the MSBs was increased. The MSBs began to be issued in larger amounts after 1982 and in very large amounts in the late 1980s. For example, the amount outstanding rose from 1.9 trillion won at the end of 1985 to 18.0 trillion at the end of 1989, by which time the MSBs were the largest component of the Korean money market. Excluding the interbank call market, MSBs accounted for 49 percent of the outstanding money market balances at the end of 1989.

The main factor contributing to the large increase in MSBs in recent years has been the country's large surpluses in the current account of the balance of payments through 1989. In 1990 there was a deficit of US$2.2 billion. These surpluses were potentially expansionary and the Bank of Korea needed an instrument to absorb the excess liquidity created by the current account surpluses. To offset the expansionary impact from the surpluses, the Bank of Korea sold MSBs heavily during 1986–89. The amount of MSBs outstanding at year-end was as follows: W. 1.9 trillion (1985); W. 4.3 trillion (1986); W. 9.0 trillion (1987); W. 16.3 trillion (1988); and W. 18.0 trillion (1989). To put these amounts in perspective, MSBs outstanding at the end of 1989 were equal to 42 percent of the money supply (M_2A). The Bank of Korea's use of MSBs to reduce liquidity helped to keep the annual rate of increase in consumer prices to single-digit levels through 1990.

Since 1986, the Bank of Korea has had five types of financial institutions serve as underwriters for the issues of MSBs in the primary market. These are commercial banks, investment trust companies, securities companies, insurance companies, and investment finance companies. There is reportedly a compulsory allotment of the bonds by the Bank of Korea to various financial institutions (Ssangyong Investment and Securities 1987: 8). In the primary dealers market for the bonds, the main buyers have been commercial banks, savings institutions, securities companies, insurance companies and various nonbank financial institutions.

As is the case with United States treasury bills, MSBs are sold on a discount basis. However, the Bank of Korea specifies both the price and the amounts to be offered for the respective maturities. While a wide range of maturities are available, most of the maturities are under one year. Because the Bank of Korea generally specifies a below-market rate for the MSBs in the primary market, the bonds are not attractive to most initial buyers—hence the necessity to dispose of the bonds through the Bank's administrative allocation system.

In the secondary market, however, the bonds are sold at a substantial discount and this has made them attractive to various buyers—including the foreign branch banks in Korea. (The foreign banks are not required to participate in the compulsory allotment.) Because of the bonds' more attractive yield in the secondary market, the secondary market for MSBs in Korea tends to be quite active.

It is evident that the rapid growth of the MSB market through 1989 was due primarily to the large current account surpluses which necessitated heavy sales of MSBs by the Bank of Korea to offset the potentially inflationary impact of the current account surpluses. In this regard, the MSBs have been a very important and useful instrument in holding down the rate of inflation in Korea. The amount of treasury bills available would have been too small to do the job.

However, as indicated by the Bank of Korea's annual reports, the large volume of MSB issues impacted adversely on the Bank of Korea's finances in 1986 and 1987, and the Bank experienced negative net profits of 57 billion won and 87 billion won in those years, respectively. Total operating income in those years was 1,036 billion won and 1,327 billion won, respectively. For this, as well as other reasons, it would be unwise to continue to use in the medium- to long-term the MSBs as an important instrument of monetary policy. It would be better to use national government treasury bills for this purpose.

There are several reasons for this. First, it would not be a good long-term policy to have the central bank experience annual losses in its operations. This might be tolerated on a short-term basis, but not in the long run. Such continued losses, which would clearly indicate that something was wrong, are likely to impact adversely on the financial community's confidence in the bank. In addition, the losses might also hamper the central bank's ability to carry out other important operations. Second, for the central bank to carry out *successful* open-market operations, it is crucial in the long run that the yield on the instruments be at market rates. But in some cases, such as in Korea, the central bank's power and authority over the banking system allow it to simply allocate the issues of MSBs to various financial institutions. This contributes to a misallocation of financial resources. If the national government, instead of the central bank, were the issuer of the securities, there would likely be pressure on the national government to sell its securities at market rates, which would be desirable, in order to make the weekly auctions *successful*—particularly if there were no "captive" buyers such as the central bank or other government institutions. With the national government's short-term securities trading at market prices, this would help the central bank greatly in carrying out market-based open market operations.

Relying on national government treasury bills would, of course, involve expanding the volume of issues of treasury bills in Korea and allowing the rate on the bills to move to market levels. At the same time, it would be appropriate to phase out the issues of MSBs. Since the disappearance of the current account surplus in 1990, the outstanding amount of MSBs have leveled off at roughly 16 trillion won.

20.2.3 Taiwan

Like Korea, Taiwan also faced a problem in the 1980s of an excessive expansion of the money supply due to large current account surpluses in the balance of payments. Initially the Taiwanese authorities absorbed the excess liquidity by issuing relatively large amounts of Class B treasury bills in 1983–85. Taiwan's Class B treasury bills are obligations of the central bank and are issued for monetary control purposes. Class A treasury bills are obligations of the government that are issued basically for fiscal policy purposes. With the exception of a single three-month issue in November 1985, Class A treasury bills have not been issued by the government since at least the early 1980s, mainly because the budget has been in balance or nearly in balance during this period. The central bank's Class B treasury bills carried maturities of 91, 182 and 364 days, and trading was very active in the secondary market.

The sharp expansion in the issue of treasury bills in 1983–85 worked for a while to absorb liquidity, partly because the treasury bills were legally acceptable assets that the banks could hold to meet the central bank's minimum liquidity ratio, and the bills could also be used as collateral in commercial bank borrowing from the central bank. The large issues of treasury bills helped to keep the rate of inflation in check. However, eventually the authorities ran into a problem in issuing additional treasury bills in the mid-1980s due to a government law prohibiting the issuance of Class B treasury bills in a total amount greater than 20 percent of the government's expenditures budget. This problem was later eased substantially in November 1987 when the government raised the ceiling from 20 percent to 40 percent. But in the meantime, the Central Bank of China needed some instrument to offset the large current account surpluses which were continuing to rise.

Since the amount of Class B treasury bills that the central bank was permitted to issue was insufficient to absorb all of the excess liquidity, the central bank in 1985 began to start issuing again its own obligations in the form of certificates of deposits (CDs) with maturities of six months, one year and two years. (The central bank first began issuing its own CDs in relatively small amounts back in October 1973, but during 1979–84 there were no central bank CDs outstanding at year-end.) Treasury bill issues began to level off and decline moderately in 1985–87, but central bank CDs outstanding rose from NT$27 billion at the end of 1985 to NT$399 billion a year later, and to NT$948 billion at the end of 1987. This represented a very large year-to-year increase in this instrument, as the money supply (M_1B) at end-1987 was NT$1,568 billion. The operation was generally successful in absorbing excess bank liquidity and in holding down the rate of increase in consumer prices to less than 2 percent per year through 1988.[5]

As time passed, the current account surpluses diminished in size and the amount of treasury bill issues was reduced. However, the amount of central bank CDs remained relatively high through the early summer of 1990 and later declined somewhat as the annual inflation rate rose from 1.25 percent in 1988 to about 5 percent in early 1991. This prompted additional central bank issues of treasury bills and CDs in 1991. Combined with low import prices, the rate of inflation decreased and in December 1991 the consumer price index was 4.4 percent higher than a year earlier. It is apparent that the central bank's operations with its own obligations—treasury bills and CDs—were successful in preventing a high rate of inflation in Taiwan.

20.2.4 Indonesia

Indonesia is one of the more interesting countries of the six examined here since it has experimented actively since 1984 with two money market instruments—one of which is a central bank obligation—in carrying out monetary policy. This use of money market instruments became necessary after the authorities in June 1983: (1) eliminated the direct ceilings on bank credits; (2) abolished a large portion of the interest rate ceilings on deposits; and, (3) assigned Bank Indonesia—the central bank—a new role in providing liquidity to the banking system. It quickly became evident that Bank Indonesia needed some kind of new instrument to control bank liquidity. It was not possible to use government securities, such as treasury bills, since Indonesia has no national government debt securities outstanding due to a parliamentary resolution prohibiting domestic borrowing (except directly from the central bank) by the government to finance budget deficits. Therefore, Bank Indonesia decided to issue its own obligations in the form of central bank certificates.

The customary name for this certificate is SBI, from *Sertifikat Bank Indonesia*. The central bank began to issue SBIs on February 1, 1984. In the beginning the main buyers were the five large state commercial banks that had roughly 70 percent of the assets of the banking system at the time. Although the SBIs are issued in the form of a bearer certificate—a direct obligation of the central bank—Bank Indonesia has declined to redeem any SBIs prior to maturity. Later, in August 1985, holders of SBIs were authorized to discount the SBIs at P. T. First Indonesian Finance and Investment Corporation (FICORINVEST), a financial intermediary owned largely by Bank Indonesia that has served as a market maker for SBIs.[6]

The SBIs were initially offered by Bank Indonesia each Wednesday on a tap basis. But a month and a half later in mid-March 1984, the system was changed to a weekly auction. Although this moved the issue system away from being passive, the interest rate on the SBIs was still controlled as Bank Indonesia mandated a cutoff rate for the SBIs—that is, the maximum yield that purchasers of SBIs could receive. This cutoff rate was not announced to the market and the employment of the cutoff rate system meant that demand, and not supply determined the quantity of SBIs provided to the market. This created problems later in sales of SBIs to absorb bank liquidity as the supply of SBIs was not sufficiently flexible.

As Bank Indonesia gained more experience during 1984 with SBIs, it found that the SBI was not a satisfactory instrument for injecting liquidity into the banking system. This was mainly because of Bank Indonesia's self-imposed restraint to not purchase any outstanding SBIs prior to maturity. Some way had to be found to inject funds into the banking system, both on a short-term and long-term basis, without relying on the central bank's discount window. In addition, Bank Indonesia hoped to broaden the existing money market by adding a new instrument that would, at the same time, be helpful in achieving its monetary policy objectives.

Accordingly, Bank Indonesia introduced the SBPU (*Surat Berharga Pasar Uang*) on February 1, 1985. Indonesia's SBPU is basically commercial paper that has been endorsed by either banks or Indonesia's nonbank financial institutions. There are four different types of SBPUs, but generally the most common has been promissory notes issued by eligible banks and nonbank financial institutions when borrowing from other banks or nonbank financial institutions. The main element that distinguishes an SBPU from other commercial paper is that the SBPU is endorsed by a bank or nonbank financial institution. In addition, regular commercial paper issued by nonbank financial institutions is not used by Bank Indonesia for monetary control purposes.

To make the SBPU attractive to the market, the central bank ruled that SBPUs would not be subject to legal reserve requirements, and during certain periods, SBPUs could be rediscounted at the central bank. FICORINVEST began to trade in SBPUs in February 1985. As time passed, most of the rediscounting of SBPUs was with FICORINVEST, which in turn rediscounted the SBPUs with Bank Indonesia. The central bank, rather than FICORINVEST, turned out to be the main source of funds supporting the SBPU market. For example, of the 1.1 billion rupiah in SBPUs outstanding at the end of 1986, Bank Indonesia had rediscounts of SBPUs outstanding equal to 89 percent of all SBPUs outstanding.

SBIs and SBPUs were used actively by Bank Indonesia to influence bank liquidity. For example, during the 15 months prior to the October 27, 1988 financial reforms, Bank Indonesia auctioned seven-day SBIs on a daily basis to influence the reserve positions of the banks. In conjunction with the October 27, 1988 financial reforms, Bank Indonesia expanded the SBI maturities, increased the range of denominations and changed to a single weekly auction. However, because the central bank has generally invoked a cutoff rate for the SBIs, and since this rate has often been below other money market rates, the SBIs have not always been attractive to potential purchasers.

In retrospect, the use of SBI sales by Bank Indonesia as its main instrument of monetary control has been less than successful. Twice, in June 1987 and again in February 1991, the central bank has had to order the large government enterprises with deposits in the state banks to shift those deposits into SBIs in order to offset speculative capital outflows. This, of course, reduced bank liquidity sharply and raised interest rates, but was generally successful in dampening the previously heavy outflow of capital. However, this is not the most desirable way to conduct monetary policy. In general, it would be much better to utilize open market operations, employing the existing SBIs and SBPUs.

The main problem has been that the interest rate on the SBIs has been controlled at a level below free money market rates. In addition, the total supply of SBIs has, at times, been too low to conduct effective open market operations. In the long run, SBIs are not likely to be a viable instrument for carrying out open market operations unless the supply of SBIs is expanded and the interest rate on the SBI is determined freely by demand and supply in the market.

Another drawback to the SBI arrangement is that it has operated, so far, only to withdraw reserves from the banking system and not to add reserves. This is because of Bank Indonesia's self-imposed restraint of not *buying* SBIs before maturity. This arrangement has prevented the central bank from carrying out bona fide open market operations in SBIs. Bank Indonesia has had to use purchases of SBPUs as its instrument for adding reserves to the banking system. A viable secondary market for SBIs has not developed since their introduction in 1984, partly because FICORINVEST has mainly served as the central bank's agent in the market and not as an active dealer.

There are several lessons that can be learned from Indonesia's use of new money market instruments in the conduct of monetary policy. One important lesson is that it is advisable to first develop a viable money market instrument that can stand by itself without central bank or national government support. If this is not done, the market for the instrument will always be somewhat artificial and poorly suited for open market operations. Bank Indonesia became so absorbed with using SBIs as an instrument of monetary policy that it neglected to develop SBIs as a component of the money market that could stand by itself.

Part and parcel of this aspect is the fact that the interest rate for the SBIs has been too controlled. The rate has not been a true market rate determined by the free forces of demand and supply. Thus, it would be appropriate to move away from the central bank's system of limited supply and cutoff prices to a true auction system for the SBIs.

Because the yields on SBIs have generally been below other money market rates, SBIs have not been popular with brokers or dealers, despite the government's attempt in January 1989 to establish 15 money market makers and two brokers: FICORINVEST and Bank Duta. Viable secondary markets in SBIs and SBPUs have yet to emerge on a medium- to long-term basis. One step which the authorities could take in order to help the SBI play the role of a treasury bill in Indonesia would be for the central bank to discontinue its policy of not buying SBIs prior to maturity. If Bank Indonesia were to freely *buy* and sell SBIs in the open market—and at market rates—this would create the appropriate conditions for undertaking true garden variety open market operations. Given Indonesia's open economy, this would go a long way toward improving Bank Indonesia's control of bank liquidity and hence reducing the danger of occasional flight of capital.

20.2.5 Thailand

Although the Thai central government issues bonds and treasury bills, the market in these instruments is not suitable for use by the Bank of Thailand—the central bank—to carry out direct open market operations in its pursuit of monetary policy objectives. There are several reasons for this. Thailand's government bond and treasury bill market is basically a primary market, and an active, bona fide secondary market does not exist in these instruments. However, the Bank of Thailand does sell treasury bills from its own portfolio, and purchases treasury bills from others before they mature. Second, there are no brokers or dealers making a market in treasury bills, with most of the outstanding bills being held by the Bank of Thailand or the government's Exchange Equalization Fund. (The latter is used by the authorities to stabilize the exchange rate for the baht, the Thai currency.) For the weekly treasury bill auctions, the Bank of Thailand serves as underwriter and purchases the balance of any unsold treasury bills. Because the yields on treasury bills are usually below the interest rates on other money market instruments, treasury bills are not a very popular investment and commercial bank holdings of treasury bills have been low or nonexistent in recent years. Third, there are large fluctuations in the amount of treasury bills outstanding and during 1984–89 there was no growth in the market, with the outstanding amount not exceeding 12 trillion baht. This was because the government has a self-imposed ceiling on the total amount of treasury bills that can be outstanding. An illustration of the sharp fluctuations that can occur happened in 1988 when the total amount of treasury bills outstanding dropped from 12 billion baht at the end of September, to 3 billion baht a month later at the end of October. During February–August of 1990 there were no treasury bills outstanding (*Quarterly Bulletin* 1990: 39).

The Bank of Thailand's main instruments of monetary control have been changes in bank reserve requirements, interest rate ceilings, and, since 1986, the use of repurchase agreements (RPs). Since September 1979, each commercial bank has been required to maintain a cash reserve equal to 7 percent of the bank's total deposits. This reserve consists of a combination of deposits at the central bank, vault cash and government securities. The central bank has the power to vary the proportions that comprise the 7 percent requirement.

The central bank also has the power to set interest rate ceilings for both bank deposits and loans. During 1989–91, however, the central bank generally eliminated the interest rate ceilings for most types of deposits and raised the interest rate ceiling for bank loans. The central bank also sets limits on commercial banks' net foreign asset position and net foreign liability position.

Since the late 1980s, the central bank's main monetary instrument has been the use of repurchase agreements (RPs) with commercial banks in order to influence bank liquidity. As part of a money market development project, the central bank introduced a government bond repurchase market in April 1979, but played a largely passive role in the market until the mid-1980s. Since May 1986, however, the central bank has intervened directly in the RP market—as opposed to merely bringing together borrowers and lenders in the market. This central bank intervention in the RP market was able to reduce, to some extent, bank liquidity in line with the central bank's monetary objectives.

In 1987, however, the Bank of Thailand became concerned that its intervention in the RP market would not be able to absorb all of the bank liquidity that it wanted to absorb. This was partly due to the fact that the central bank's own portfolio of bonds had fallen to such a low level that its anti-inflationary operations in the RP market were threatened. It therefore decided in May 1987 to issue 2 billion baht of its own 180-day obligations in order to absorb the excess liquidity in the banking system. The bonds,[7] which were issued in 100,000 baht denominations at a flat 6 percent interest rate, were mainly sold to the commercial banks and the Government Savings Bank. On the whole, the operation was generally successful in reducing bank liquidity, and consumer prices in 1987 were up only 2.5 percent over 1986. A second set of bonds was issued in February 1988 to absorb excess liquidity in the banking system—again in an amount of 2 billion baht with a 6 percent interest rate—but this time the maturity was set at one year.

Assessing the Bank of Thailand's RP operations, they have added a useful additional instrument to the central bank's arsenal of monetary weapons, and they have been helpful in controlling bank liquidity. However, the RP operations, which generally use bonds rather than treasury bills as the underlying security, fall short of being a full-fledged open market operation. As presently constituted, the operating arrangements are awkward. Because its charter forbids it to act as a broker, the Bank of Thailand has to serve as the principal for each and every RP transaction. This is, of course, not a problem where the central bank is acting for its own account, but the arrangement has restricted a fuller development of the RP market. These arrangements are likely to hinder, in the long run, the development of a viable government securities market. In addition, the interest rate in the RP market has, at times, been subject to control. For example, near the end of 1986 the central bank set a floor RP rate as it was concerned that the general level of interest rates might decline too far.

With regard to the Bank of Thailand's issue of its own obligations in May 1987 and February 1988, these actions appear to have been a largely ad hoc reaction to a situation in which the central bank could not readily use RP operations or some other instrument to mop up bank liquidity. As far as can be determined, the two bond issues appear to have been a one-time arrangement, with no additional central bank bonds having been issued since February 1988. The Bank of Thailand is reportedly disappointed that a secondary market did not develop in its bonds as it had expected.

Thailand's main problem, if it is to use open market operations as an active monetary policy instrument, is to develop a large and viable secondary market in government securities—preferably those with short maturities. Some of the basic steps needed to accomplish this goal involve letting the interest rates on government securities rise to true market levels and expanding the supply of short-term government securities so that there is an adequate supply for conducting open market operations. It is also likely that the central bank would have to encourage active trading in government securities by establishing primary government securities dealers and an active secondary market for the securities.

20.2.6 Hong Kong

Hong Kong does not have a central bank, *per se*, as it is an overseas territory of the United Kingdom. Hence its situation differs from some of the economies cited earlier—such as Korea, Taiwan and Indonesia—where the central banks have issued their own obligations. Some central bank functions in Hong Kong, such as the note issue, have been performed by two private banks: the Hongkong and Shanghai Banking Corporation, and the Standard Chartered Bank. In addition, the government fixes by law a minimum liquidity requirement for banks, but the requirement is largely static and has remained unchanged in recent years. However, Hong Kong does have a government Exchange Fund and the authorities have given it increasing monetary control powers since 1988.

The Exchange Fund was established in 1935, basically to maintain a stable exchange rate for the Hong Kong currency.[8] Prior to July 1988, its main method for influencing bank liquidity was through its purchases or sales of foreign exchange in the foreign exchange market, or through its borrowing or lending of Hong Kong dollars in the interbank market. These measures were not completely satisfactory and in July 1988 the government introduced the New Accounting Arrangement between the Exchange Fund and the Hongkong and Shanghai Bank, the latter having served—and continuing to serve—as a clearing agent for the banks. This arrangement made the Exchange Fund, in effect, the ultimate provider of liquidity to the interbank market. It thus allowed the Fund to exert an important influence over the amount of liquidity and hence the level of interest rates in the interbank market—all with the ultimate objective of maintaining exchange rate stability.[9]

Still, the government desired to enhance further the Exchange Fund's ability to exert monetary control over the economy. In his budget speech in March 1989 the Financial Secretary announced plans for the Exchange Fund to issue short-term bills that would be used for purposes of monetary control and not to finance public expenditures. Appropriate legislation was passed in February 1990 which exempted the new Exchange Fund bills from the profits and stamp duty taxes, and authorized the government to appoint some 118 business firms to serve as dealers in the new Exchange Fund bills market with 14 of these being designated as market makers. The market makers are required to quote both buying and selling prices. The total borrowing limit set on the issue of 91-day Exchange Fund bills was HK$50 billion or about US$6.4 billion.

During the 1980s the Hong Kong government did not issue securities with one exception. In 1984 the government issued a HK$1 billion, 10 percent, five-year bond. Although negotiable, most investors held these bonds to maturity, with the result that no secondary market in the bonds developed.

The government began to issue Exchange Fund bills on March 14, 1990. Issued in weekly amounts of about HK$300 million, the Exchange Fund issued HK$3.8 billion during the first 13 weeks of the operation. These bills had a minimum denomination of HK$500,000 and a 13-week maturity. The bills were sold at a discount in a manner similar to the way that United States treasury bills are issued. The average accepted yield on March 14, 1990 was 8.04 percent, but by June 6, 1990—13 weeks later—the yield had moved up to 9.04 percent. The operation was so successful that in the next 13-week cycle the weekly amount was raised to HK$400 million. Later, on October 30, 1990, the government also began to issue 182-day Exchange Fund bills every two weeks, and in late February 1991, issued HK$200 million of one-year bills. Exchange Fund bills have been well received by the banks, which have been the main purchasers so far. Since March 1990, the government has generally offset the contractionary impact from the sale of bills by injecting approximately the same amount of funds back into the interbank market by means of the New Accounting Arrangement.

The Exchange Fund bills are a direct, unsecured, unconditional, general obligation of the Hong Kong government. They are in a paperless form as they are recorded in a bills register maintained in the Monetary Affairs Branch of the Government Secretariat. The bills are not backed by the general revenue of the treasury and the proceeds from the bills, by law, cannot be used to finance public expenditures. Although holders of Exchange Fund bills do not normally rediscount the bills with the Exchange Fund, the Secretary for Monetary Affairs has given an undertaking to the market makers of the Exchange Fund bills that he will make a bid to them for any bills that they may offer.

Since July 1988, the Hong Kong authorities have made important use of the New Accounting Arrangement, as well as the Exchange Fund bills market, to influence bank liquidity. For example, following the June 4, 1989 crackdown on pro-democracy demonstrators in Tiananmen Square in China, the authorities injected about HK$194 million into the interbank market by means of the accounting arrangement to counter the heavy withdrawal of funds from certain Chinese banks in Hong Kong. After things had settled down, there was a subsequent withdrawal of HK$195 million from the interbank market on August 7, 1989 (see Hong Kong 1989: 36). The issue of Exchange Fund bills since March 1990 has provided the authorities with an additional instrument to influence liquidity in the interbank market. In March 1991, the government described the monetary aspects of its Exchange Fund bill operation as follows:

> With the launching of the Exchange Fund bills programme in mid-March 1990, the Exchange Fund operates more frequently in the local money market. Under normal

circumstances, the operations are either for the purpose of relieving a shortage of liquidity arising from a take-up of Exchange Fund bills or to mop up surplus liquidity arising from a redemption of these bills. But if the need arises, the Exchange Fund may, through under- or over-compensating the effect of the issue or redemption of Exchange Fund bills, or through buying or selling these bills in the secondary market, produce a level of interbank liquidity that is appropriate for ensuring exchange rate stability (Hong Kong 1991: 37).

Unfortunately, official data are not readily available to indicate the extent to which the Exchange Fund has been intervening in the secondary market for the bills, or adjusting its issue and redemption of the bills to influence interbank liquidity. The basic objective of the Exchange Fund's operations, as indicated earlier, is to maintain the stability of the Hong Kong dollar in foreign exchange markets. To date the authorities have been able to maintain the linked exchange rate of HK$7.8 to US$1 that was established in October 1983.

On the whole, the government has managed the introduction of Exchange Fund bills into the local money market well, and it now has an additional monetary instrument besides the three indicated earlier: Exchange Fund borrowing and lending in the interbank market, changes in the net clearing balance under the New Accounting Arrangement, and purchases and sales of foreign exchange by the Exchange Fund. The government's stated objective in establishing the Exchange Fund bills market has been to provide itself with a flexible, low-cost and cost-effective instrument for the conduct of monetary policy. In establishing the Exchange Fund bills market, the government wisely arranged for 14 firms to serve as market makers. These 14, by standing ready to buy and sell Exchange Fund bills at daily quoted prices, have provided liquidity to the market. An additional aspect that has improved the popularity of the bills is the official decision to make the bills tax exempt. Income from the bills is not subject to the profits tax that is imposed on interest income and the Exchange Fund bills are the only financial asset in Hong Kong that have this tax exempt feature.

One advantage that the government has in using the Exchange Fund bills market to influence bank liquidity is that it can act with less publicity than when it acts to change the net clearing balance. The government has continued, however, to supplement its Exchange Fund bill operations with Exchange Fund lending and borrowing in the interbank market, and sales and purchases in the foreign exchange market. All of these operations can be used to influence money market conditions, especially the trend in short-term interest rates, in defense of the linkage of the Hong Kong dollar to the U.S. dollar.

In conclusion, the Exchange Fund bills program has improved Hong Kong's monetary management as it has provided an additional useful instrument for carrying out open market operations to ensure exchange rate stability. The program has also been helpful in that it has provided a benchmark short-term interest rate for government securities than can be used in connection with the issue of private money market instruments. Various reports indicate that a moderately active secondary market has developed in the bills, which will be helpful for the Exchange Fund as it carries out open market operations.

Encouraged by its success with 91-day, 182-day and one-year Exchange Fund bills, the government also began to issue a modest amount of two- to three-year bonds in November 1991. Like the Exchange Fund bills, they have been issued in a paperless form, that is on a book entry basis. In addition to bonds, the May 15, 1991 authorizing legislation, the Loans (Amendment) Bill 1991, will also allow the government to issue promissory notes or other instruments, the proceeds of which can be used to help finance capital expenditures in Hong Kong for such projects as a new airport and port facilities.

20.3   Concluding Observations

As the above cases indicate, there has been a greater use of money market instruments in the conduct of monetary policy by the central banks in the main Asia-Pacific countries in the past decade. Of the eight economies listed at the beginning, the central banks in six of the economies have issued their own obligations at one time or another for purposes of monetary control. For some central banks, these obligations have been their principal means of influencing bank liquidity. Currently central bank money market obligations are continuing to be used actively by the central banks, or their equivalent: in Indonesia (SBIs), Korea (MSBs), Taiwan (TBs and CDs) and Hong Kong[10] (Exchange Fund bills). Even the Philippines, as mentioned earlier, is continuing to make some use of the central bank obligations popularly known as "Jobo" bills, and the Bank of Thailand has twice issued its own short-term bonds to absorb excessive bank liquidity in recent years.

Of the six economies examined here, the central bank in the Philippines is the only one to conduct its open market operations using mainly national government treasury bills. All of the other central banks in the remaining economies have had to depend instead on carrying out open market operations using short-term obligations that the central bank itself has issued. In a sense, the central banks were forced to do this for a variety of reasons. In Indonesia, a parliamentary resolution prevents the issue of national government securities. In Taiwan, Class A treasury bills are rarely issued by the government, mainly because there is little or no deficit financing. In Korea and Thailand, the low and unattractive yield on treasury bills—not to mention the unreliable and erratic supply of treasury bills—has kept the market small. In Hong Kong, the only issue of government securities in the past 12 years—except for the bond issues in November 1991—occurred in 1984 when the government issued HK$1 billion in 10 percent bonds with a five-year maturity. In short, open market operations in national government treasury bills have not been a viable alternative for these central banks, so they have had to fall back on their own central bank obligations.

Not all of the open market operations in central bank obligations have gone smoothly. In Indonesia, the market for the central bank's certificates (SBIs) has remained somewhat artificial due to the central bank's control of the interest rate on the certificates and heavy central bank support, or erratic intervention, in the market. In the Philippines, the central bank requirement in the 1970s that banks hold treasury bills as part of their secondary reserves, and the payment by the government of below-market rates on the bills, caused the treasury bill market to virtually disappear by 1973 (see Skully 1989: 321). It was only after most interest rate ceilings were gradually eliminated during the early 1980s that the treasury bill market was able to become a viable market.

Although the Philippines is the only country out of the six examined here to use *national government* treasury bills as a major instrument in carrying out monetary policy, this is likely to be the best approach in the long run for the other countries. When a central bank is forced to use its own obligations—as in Korea—this has often led to losses and a weakening of the central bank's financial condition as discussed earlier in the section on Korea. In addition, central banks have found it necessary, at times, to force their obligations on certain buyers, and this has tended to create undesirable distortions in the allocation of financial resources.

Measures should be taken, over an extended period of time, to develop a sound and viable *national government* treasury bill market that can be used by the central bank in its monetary policy operations. In the case of Indonesia, this would necessitate some revision of the parliamentary resolution that prevents the issue of treasury bills. While some monetary instruments—such as discount policy, bank reserve requirements, and foreign exchange swaps—can be helpful in achieving monetary policy objectives, a well-developed open market operation is the best instrument for quickly and flexibly controlling bank liquidity.

In the first section of this chapter, the point was made that—assuming a viable money market instrument exists—there are certain advantages that a central bank obtains if it uses open market operations in implementing monetary policy, as opposed to reliance on traditional instruments such as adjusting reserve requirements, imposing direct credit controls, or changing the discount rate. Being market based, open market operations are likely to be less distortionary to the interest rate structure, whereas mandated changes in the level of the discount rate might, at times, cause undesired distortions to the interest rate structure. In addition, open market operations operate indirectly on the amount of liquidity in the financial system and are consequently less intrusive than using direct credit controls or interest rate ceilings. Lastly, there are certain other benefits from using open market operations: (1) it is possible to change liquidity by either small, medium, or large amounts; (2) the central bank is able to act quickly; (3) there are several ways in which open market operations can be carried out, such as through direct purchases, through repurchase agreements (RPs), or through reverse RPs; and (4) the open market operations can be carried out quietly without public fanfare when it is appropriate to do so. All of these enhance the amount of discretionary power granted to the central bank.[11]

Finally, whether national government treasury bills, or some form of central bank obligation is used for the open market operations, it is very important that the interest rate for the instrument be market-determined. This is mainly because it is very difficult to conduct effective open market operations when the yield on an instrument is below free market rates and is thus unattractive to potential buyers. In addition, it is also very important that there be a good, steady supply of the instrument to the market, so that shortages of the instrument do not hamstring the open market operations or create undesirable price fluctuations.

Notes

This article, with minor modifications, first appeared in *Journal of Asian Economics,* 1993, 4(1): 99–116.

1. For additional details on this topic, see Tseng and Corker (1991: 24–33).
2. Even earlier, beginning in 1970, the Central Bank issued CBCIs (Central Bank Certificates of Indebtedness), but these were medium-term certificates and were not necessarily designed for carrying out open market operations. By 1987 the CBCIs had been gradually phased out.
3. For a detailed description of the first year of activity, see Emery (1967).
4. In September 1990, for example, the central bank issued some 60-day CB bills. Eligible holders include banks, public and private corporations and individuals. See *CB Review* (1990: 40).
5. For additional details on the central bank's anti-inflationary operations in the mid-1980s, see Emery (1987).
6. For a more extensive explanation of the SBI and the Bank Indonesia's SBI operations, see Emery (1991: 58–65).
7. The term "bond" is used by various East Asian countries, Korea being another example, for government obligations with original maturities under one year.
8. For additional details on the Exchange Fund and its operations, see Emery (1991: 13–15).
9. For a more complete description of the New Accounting Arrangement, see Emery (1991: 14–15).
10. Hong Kong's Exchange Fund, obviously, is not a central bank. However, it currently engages in operations aimed at controlling bank liquidity and interest rates, and in that sense operates in a manner similar to a central bank.
11. For a more detailed discussion of the benefits from using indirect methods of monetary control, see Caprio and Honohan (1990).

References

Caprio, Gerard Jr. and Patrick Honohan, 1990, *Monetary Policy Instruments for Developing Countries*, Working Paper No. 528, World Bank, Washington, DC.

CB Review, 1990, "CB Sops up Excess Liquidity," Central Bank of the Philippines, Manila, September, 40.

Emery, Robert F., 1967, "The Successful Development of the Philippine Treasury Bill Market," *Central Bank News Digest*, Central Bank of the Philippines, Manila, June 13, 2–7.

——, 1987, *Monetary Policy in Taiwan, China*, International Finance Discussion Paper, No. 313, Board of Governors of the Federal Reserve System, Washington, DC.

————, 1991, *The Money Markets of Developing East Asia*, Praeger, New York.

Hong Kong, 1989, *Third Quarter Economic Report: 1989*, Economic Services Branch, Government Secretariat.

————, 1991, *1990 Economic Background*, Economic Services Branch, Government Secretariat.

Quarterly Bulletin, 1990, Bank of Thailand, Bangkok, December.

Skully, Michael T. (ed.), 1989, *Financial Institutions and Markets in Southeast Asia*, St. Martin's Press, New York.

Ssangyong Investment and Securities Company, 1987, "The Bond Market in Korea," Seoul, mimeo.

Tseng, Wanda and Robert Corker, 1991, *Financial Liberalization, Money Demand, and Monetary Policy in Asian Countries*, Occasional Paper 84, International Monetary Fund, Washington, DC.

Part VI

ECONOMIC STUDIES OF SELECTED COUNTRIES

In the last part of this treatise we take five regional economies and analyze some of their more interesting characteristics and experiences. The first economy we examine is Japan. World War II devastated the Japanese economy. Although Japan's economy appeared to be beyond repair, Japan has been able to rebuild itself as the second largest economy in the world in a very short span of time—a feat admired throughout the world. Chapter 21 (Das) analyzes Japan's ascension from a low economic status to international economic preeminence. After providing a brief overview of the characteristics of the postwar brisk growth period, Chapter 21 examines Japan's two principal growth phases, namely, the *Asahi* and the *Endaka* phases. The liberalization and the deregulation phase of the economy is examined next. Other than the usual macroeconomic features, there were several unique characteristics, practices and institutions that were instrumental in making Japan an economic superpower. To take two examples, the Ministry of International Trade and Industry (MITI) and *keiretsu* are unique institutions which contributed significantly to Japan's economic success story. However, Japan's striking economic performance cannot entirely be attributed to macroeconomic factors alone. Several successful Japanese corporations developed a major international presence by the mid-1960s. These corporations achieved high visibility in products ranging from ball bearings, forklifts and machine tools to a large range of high technology products.

Table 21.4 shows that the nominal GNP growth rate of Japan in 1991 was 6.4 percent. The very next year the economy slid into a recession and recorded a real GNP growth rate of 1.5 percent, the lowest figure since 1974. Similarly, corporate profits in the 1992 fiscal year reached their lowest point since the 1974 recession. The recent 1992–93 recession is unique insofar as its constitutes the first "home-made" recession. It has called into question the fundamental strength of the Japanese economy. There are several interpretations of the characteristics of this slowdown.

One leading explanation posited that the collapse of the "speculative bubble" triggered a deflation in asset values, which led to economic slowdown. Other explanations put forward include the psychological recession theory, the satiated consumption theory, the medium-term growth refraction theory and the theory of stagnation of technological innovation. At this juncture it is hard to judge which theory or explanation is most valid. However, there is little doubt that one of the most important factors behind the 1992–93 recession was the stock adjustment that took place in the wake of the collapse of the "speculative bubble."

A word about the so-called "double bubble burst" in the Japanese economy is needed here. Over the latter half of the 1980s the Japanese economy underwent asset price inflation in the stock and property markets. There was an unprecedented deviation from the historical trend line. The twin-inflation or the double-bubble burst in 1991. The wealth effect of asset price inflation and deflation distorted the cycle of economic development. Demand had been inflated during the bubble formation period. This process of high demand inflation apparently was financed through borrowing on future demand growth. Therefore, the economy will have to endure a couple of years of extremely low growth in domestic demand in order to pay back past debt. This, in turn, should lead to a low growth rate in the Japanese economy over the 1993–95 period.

As mentioned in Chapter 2, the Chinese economy made a U-turn after its adoption of an open door policy, recording double digit growth rates over the decade of the 1980s. Chapter 22 (Ng and Ng) shows that economic reforms and deregulation contributed a great deal to vibrant economic growth and the creation of a "socialist market economy" in China. They conclude that the reform process will continue along with the further opening of the economy. This strategy will attract more foreign investment and involve China more deeply in international trade. This means that China will play an increasingly significant role in the Asia-Pacific region. However, there are several problems that China needs to tackle, such as its poorly performing state enterprise sector. Optimism, therefore, must be tempered with caution.

Although small, the Republic of China (or Taiwan) and the Republic of Korea (or Korea) have operated as two of the most dynamic economies of the Asia-Pacific region. These two countries were natural resource poor and human resource rich, and were endowed with relatively good physical and institutional infrastructure. Like other developing economies, they moved into an early import substitution sub-phase. This sub-phase was, however, short and mild. If there was one key to the East Asian story of economic success, especially Taiwan's, it was the early attention paid to making the agricultural sector work in tandem with the decentralized industrial sector (Ranis 1992). On the human capital front, Taiwan and Korea first emphasized increasing the literacy rate. Later, these economies emphasized vocational training and education. Lastly, they came to emphasize a technology-oriented education attuned to a continuously changing economic structure. Their labor markets behaved competitively, with little government or labor union intervention. Economic policy was consciously and clearly focused on easing the transition from inward- to outward-oriented growth. In operational terms, this entailed providing the necessary infrastructure and externalities for balanced domestic growth and the development of export-oriented industries. Government strategy on export-oriented industries, first concentrated on developing the labor-intensive sectors. More recently, the focus has shifted to the high-technology, capital- and skill-intensive sectors.

The macroeconomic policy adopted by these two economies followed neo-classical economic lines; it remained flexible and adopted rapidly to the changing needs of the economies. An export-oriented strategy allowed these economies to achieve high growth rates, equitable income distribution, and full employment. Conservatism and flexibility marked fiscal and monetary policies. The opening up of the economies and liberalization proceeded slowly but steadily. Exchange rates were maintained at realistic levels throughout the growth phase. Taiwan and Korea only came to introduce market liberalization after they had implemented their other liberalization and market opening reforms. Thus viewed, the economic policy that Taiwan and Korea followed was prudent and flexible. It allowed these economies to withstand internal and external shocks relatively easily.

Helped by its export success, the Taiwanese economy accumulated a large trade surplus. This led to a significant currency appreciation during the 1980s. In 1986, the trade surplus accounted for 19.3 percent of GNP—an all time high for Taiwan and unparalleled figure among the trade surplus non-oil producing economies such as Germany and Japan. This situation weakened the international competitiveness of Taiwanese products, a phenomenon known as the Dutch disease. This term was first used to describe the appreciation of the Dutch guilder that took place after the surge in Dutch natural gas exports during the first oil crisis. This appreciation weakened the international competitiveness of Dutch products and raised the unemployment level.

In many ways Taiwan's development experience was extraordinary. Chapter 23 (Schive) dwells on the unique set of conditions and problems emerging out of a successful experience. He divides the development experience into several stages and discusses Taiwan's varying policy focuses. Taiwan's experience is also important in the regional context because it has made a constructive contribution towards integrating the regional economies. This contribution—along with Taiwan's commitment to economic liberalization—will not only help Taiwan's economy but also the Asia-Pacific economy as a whole. Schive also analyzes Taiwan's Dutch disease which resulted from Taiwan's macroeconomic imbalances in the late 1980s. Taiwan's long-standing policies of export promotion and import substitution had succeeded in bringing about sustained growth and rapid industrialization, but later caused macroeconomic imbalances after two decades of export-led growth.

After 1961, Korea's status in the world economy rose sharply. A series of five-year economic plans were successfully launched and implemented. The first of these was launched in 1962. Korea's productive capacity increased by nearly

9 percent per year, and as a result its GNP grew fast. In 1992, its per capita income crossed US$6,600. Further, in multilateral negotiations (MTNs) under the aegis of the General Agreement on Tariffs and Trade (GATT), Korea is no longer treated as a developing economy. Comparison of real per capita gross domestic products (GDPs), using purchasing power adjusted measures of income, place Korea among the top developing economies, just below Singapore and Taiwan and not much behind Portugal (Das 1992). Korea is scheduled to join the prestigious industrial economy club, OECD (Organization for Economic Cooperation and Development), in 1996. In Chapter 24 Suh discusses the place of the Korean economy in the international arena, and in particular in the Asia-Pacific region. He also addresses the question of the transferability of the Korean experience.

Since the 1950s, Thailand has recorded steady economic growth. Based on its performance during the decade of the 1980s, it has been given the sobriquet "fifth dragon." Over the 1985–90 period, Thailand became the fastest growing economy in the world. To be sure, rapid growth has had its cost. Chapter 25 (Warr) gives a detailed account of Thailand's experience with accelerated economic growth. Both the positive and negative aspects of the Thai growth experience are dealt with in an evenhanded and dispassionate manner. He compares and contrasts the Thai experience with that of the other regional economies.

References

Das, Dilip K., 1992, *Korean Economic Dynamism*, Macmillan, London.
Ranis, G., 1992, "Labour Market, Human Capital and Development Performance in East Asia," Yale University Economic Growth Center, New Haven, CT, mimeo.

Chapter 21

Dilip K. Das

AN INTRODUCTION TO THE JAPANESE ECONOMY

21.1　Introduction

A broad-brush sketch of the Japanese economy, basic facts related to it, its structure and changes therein are presented here. Also, an attempt has been made to give a succinct overview of its operation. The approach, essentially, is that of mainstream economists. Although the treatment is in no way comprehensive, it does cover all the salient aspects of Japanese economic growth during the postwar period. From the ravages of the war, the Japanese economy rose and rebuilt itself into the second largest economy in the world by the early 1970s. It is an achievement lauded by the world at large. A decade or so later it became the largest creditor country in the world, and then, in quick succession, the largest donor and the largest foreign investor. By the mid-1980s, it was generally recognized as an economic, financial and technological superpower. This process of growth from an abjectly low economic level to international preeminence has been analyzed here. Japan's new status has significant international implications, in the post cold war world, economic strength has a great deal of swaying capability. Some even equate it to military strength. This has assigned Japan a meaningful role not only in the Asia-Pacific region but also in the wider international economic arena.

21.2　Aftermath of the War

The Second World War devastated the economic base and created all kinds of shortages, including a severe food shortage. Japan was occupied by the U.S. Army under the Supreme Commander for Allied Powers who held absolute powers. Apparently, therefore, the U.S. dominated efforts to reconstruct and rehabilitate the Japanese economy. The reform measures adopted *inter alia* entailed reduction of concentration of business power and the establishment of more competitive markets. It involved steps like the dissolution of family-owned *zaibatsu* conglomerates, the elimination of cartels and monopolies, and the break up of some extremely large firms.

Since inflation was running menacingly high and the economy badly needed to be stabilized, the Dodge Plan was announced in 1948 by the General Headquarters of the occupation forces. It emphasized measures like balancing the budget, restraining credit, stabilizing wages and increasing domestic production of raw materials and manufactured goods. The austerity programme was faithfully implemented. As a consequence, the volume of currency circulation contracted, black market prices fell and, therefore, after some time, price control measures began to be abolished. Trends in the rationalization of firms and in their efficiency increases were impressive. The Dodge austerity policy also dealt a blow to the labor union movement which was beginning to gather steam.

Since the economic base was devastated, output was increased by eliminating waste caused by bottlenecks and excess capacity in the existing industrial structure. The experience of the war-torn West European countries was identical. Although Japan became a giant supply base serving the American forces during the Korean war (1950–53)—and experienced a mini-boom due to the war—the economy remained impoverished. The Allied occupation of Japan ended in April 1952 and Japan became an independent state. At this point, according to the Organization for Economic Cooperation and Development (OECD) statistics, Japan's GNP was US$16.3 billion and per capita GNP a paltry US$188, which was lower than that of Brazil, Chile, Malaysia and several other developing countries. Structurally the economy was a quaint mix of the characteristics of developing and developed countries.

In the early 1950s, the Japanese economy was widely considered a basket case, one that would have to depend on the Western industrialized economies for a long time before stabilizing at any level. This supercilious evaluation turned out to be incorrect and the economy achieved an outstanding record of recovery and growth, particularly since the adoption of the Yonzenso program. It thrust Japan into a decade-long era of double-digit annual growth rates during the 1960s. This was the beginning of the *asahi* or the rising sun era. Sagacious macroeconomic management, organizational acumen and plain hard work lifted Japan from the ravages of the War to middle income level in little over a decade. By the 1970s, Japan had achieved keen industrial competitiveness in a good number of industries and Herman Kahn prognosticated that it would "not be surprising if the twenty-first century were the Japanese century" (Kahn 1970). The economy continued to expand, the per capita income continued to rise while income distribution in the society grew egalitarian. In 1960, its share of world GNP was 3 percent, in 1980 it grew to 9 percent, while in 1990 it was 13 percent. In relative terms, at the beginning of the 1960s, Japan's GNP was less than 10 percent that of the U.S. By the early 1980s, it was 40 percent of the U.S. GNP, while in 1990 it was 54 percent. In the mid-1980s, Japan became the largest creditor of the world while the U.S. became the largest debtor. Before the end of the decade, as stated earlier, Japan achieved other status milestones. For example, it had become the largest foreign investor and the largest donor economy. It has remained the third largest trading economy throughout the 1980s. The contrast between the Japan of the early 1950s and the mid-1980s is as startling as it is interesting. In what follows we shall see how this contrast was created and what were the principal contributing factors behind it.

21.2.1 The Backdrop of Brisk Growth

Inasmuch as the economic and cultural foundation of the future economic growth of Japan was laid after the collapse of the Tokugawa shogunate and restoration of the reign of Emperor Meiji in 1968, this should be the logical starting point of any study of the contemporary Japanese economy. During the Tokugawa shogunate Japan was an isolationist, semi-feudal and economically backward country. The shogunate was brought down by a remarkable group of reformers and cultural revolutionaries that included rising young merchants and disaffected *samurai* bureaucrats. This group abhorred the erstwhile "box" society and went about the business of modernizing Japan with a missionary zeal. They had an obsession for opening Japan to other influences, particularly for learning from the West. The most influential of Meiji reformers was Yukichi Fukuzawa, an indignant samurai turned scholar-reformer, who was one of the prime movers behind Japan's entry into the modern era. He led an intensely productive, albeit apolitical, life and almost single-handedly introduced and popularized the intellectual culture of the West along with the whole body of ideas of the Western Enlightenment (Gibney 1992). Fukuzawa founded Keio University and led Japan towards empirical learning. He decried Confucianism as irrelevant and promoted "the laws of number and reason" as understood in the West. The wheel has come full circle and Japan is now being fervently lauded for its Confucian legacy in the West. Reformers like Mori Arinori, who followed Fukuzawa, remained equally committed to modernizing and industrializing Japan so that it would catch up with the West. Thus, a national ethos for industrialization was firmly established. Little wonder that the Meiji period has come to be known as the beginning of an era, one of modern economic expansion for Japan.

Textile factories were the first to develop. Family silk farms expanded. Japan had a comparative advantage in producing silk, therefore, silk exports expanded and became a major source of foreign exchange. This status continued until the early 1930s. The Meiji government helped industrialization endeavours by developing a centralized banking system under the Bank of Japan. It went a long way in capital formation, which is indispensable for economic growth. The burdensome land tax was supplanted by broad based consumption and excise taxes. The government also helped develop steel and shipbuilding industries. A large steel mill, called the Yawata Steel, was established in 1901, so that scale economies could be exploited. The first of the *sogo shosha* or the great trading companies, called Mitsui Bussan, was established during this period with the objective of competing with the Western companies in acquiring commodities and raw materials in the international markets. The usual provision of public goods, such as infrastructure creation, was also undertaken by the government. By 1900, over 40,000 miles of railroad tracks were laid linking all major cities. Mining, particularly coal, was paid a good deal of official attention. Working conditions in the mines and factories were unhealthy and they took a heavy toll in terms of human life. Workers worked for long hours in stifling sweatshops for minuscule wages.

Foreign capital was purposively shunned because Japan watched the economic colonization of China next door and disapproved of it. The government and businessmen worked together to make up for the absence of foreign capital. The development of finance institutions such as the Industrial Bank of Japan provided much needed capital. The bond between the business and bureaucracy began to grow stronger until it began to appear that all roads led to Tokyo. By the end of the last century, the foundation for a modern industrial society was in place. It was strengthened by the family-owned *zaibatsu* conglomerates that were subsequently to play a large part in the Japanese economy. At this point, the economy had reached, what in modern parlance is known as, the "takeoff stage." Japan, thus, became the first Asian country to acquire this distinction by a margin of at least 75 years.

Over the last quarter of the last century, Japan exploited its traditional agricultural sector which was the largest in the economy. The revenue provided to the government was utilized in infrastructure building and importing technology. By 1900, the size of the agricultural sector had contracted somewhat and it employed 66 percent of the total labor force. The investment ratio at this time was 13.0 percent of the GNP. During the first quarter of the current century, the economy expanded at the annual average rate of 3.5 percent in real terms. It even experienced a boom period during the first World War years. Cotton textile had become a major industry and, as in the silk industry, Japan had a good deal of comparative advantage in it also. Its textile exports were competitive all over the world. By 1930, employment in agriculture had further declined to 50 percent of the total labor force and the investment ratio had climbed to 17.7 percent. Unlike other industrial countries, Japan posted a high growth rate for the decade of the 1930s. GNP grew at an average annual rate of 5 percent during this decade. This was the time when militant nationalism gripped Japan and in its wake large industrial units in chemicals, metals and machinery were created. They soon dominated the industrial structure. By the end of the 1930s, Japan was considered a relatively advanced economy. Employment in agriculture had further declined to 40 percent of the total workforce and the investment ratio had topped 20 percent. Japan had become an important exporter of manufactured products and importer of industrial raw materials. Although it was a rapidly expanding economy, it retained its so-called dual character which is a characteristic of a developing economy (Ohkawa and Rosovsky 1973). The story of Japan being involved in two military misadventures is too well known.

21.3   The *Asahi* Phase

Over the decade of the 1950s and 1960s, the objectives underpinning economic strategy were clearly defined. Moreover, economic strategies were consistently implemented. Economic growth topped the priority, while secondary emphasis was laid on stability, that is, on reducing the crests and troughs of business cycles and keeping inflation within moderate limits. The size of GDP was too small to attract any external attention. Growth was assisted during the Korean War years (1950–53) by American procurement orders. A tiny upswing of the business cycle began in 1955 and ended in 1957. It was called the *Jimmu* boom[1] and was followed by a shortfall in growth and investment rates. But in 1958 another upswing of the business cycle started. It was a stronger and longer lasting upswing, at a higher level of average growth rate than the previous one, and was called the *Iwato*[2] boom. It lasted for 42 months between July 1958 and December 1961, and like the first boom was followed by a shortfall in real growth and investment rates. In 1961, the Doubling National Income Plan was announced. This Plan envisaged a future growth rate of 7.2 percent. Despite the fact that Japan had experienced two booms in quick succession, skeptics abounded. Japan not only attained this goal, but its long-term (1950–73) average growth rate turned out to be 10.5 percent. This long-term average growth rate was more than twice the growth rate of the world GDP for this period, which was 4.7 percent. Among 11 industrial economies Japan's average was the highest. West Germany came second with 5.5 percent while the U.S. averaged 3.2 percent (Denison and Chung 1976).

   Since saving and investment are so necessary, although not sufficient, for growth, let me first focus on the saving-investment balance. Private sector saving rates, which include the savings of corporate and household sectors, were very high during the rapid growth period. They were 28.9 percent of GNP in 1950, 26.0 percent in 1955, 28.2 percent in 1960 and 27.4 percent in 1965. One possible explanation for the high savings rate could possibly be that the rapid rate of growth produced an unequal distribution of income and raised the savings rate. However, this scenario did not apply to the Japanese economy. Savings rose, instead, as part of the process of income equalization. A wage differential had developed during the latter half of the reconstruction period and a two-tier dual economic structure had become rather prominent. As the economy moved into the rapid growth period, the two-tier structure dissolved and the surplus labor force was absorbed in the expanding economy, which in turn resulted in income equality and higher savings. Over the 1960s, private sector investment regularly exceeded savings. This imbalance was offset by: (a) government surplus; and (b) the current account deficit which occurred frequently during the decade. As Table 21.1 shows, savings in the private sector were high. An equally high investment demand in the corporate sector kept gobbling these savings up as fast as they accumulated. During these years, both savings and investment levels, as a percentage of GNP, were double that in the U.S. The average private sector saving-investment balance for the entire decade showed an excess of investment over savings of 1.9 percent of GNP. Also, the household sector was a consistent net saver, averaging 4.4 percent of GNP, while the corporate sector was a consistent net investor, averaging 6.3 percent of GNP. These figures imply a voracious corporate demand and, therefore, a constant flow of savings from households to the corporate sector (Lincoln 1988). Whenever the household sector was unable to fulfil the total demand of the corporate sector, the deficit was met by the government sector rather than from capital flows from abroad. This brings us to another important feature, that is, government revenues exceeded expenditures. Thus, one can infer that as a net saver government made a direct contribution to investment endeavors.

In the 1970s, the scenario changed and in a way was the opposite of the 1960s. With moderation in growth and decline in investment, the private sector became a net saver (Table 21.1) and the government sector began to record deficits. The private sector began to record a surplus of savings over investment since the early 1970s. It rose rapidly and reached a peak of 6.8 percent of GNP in 1978 (Ito 1992). The outlet for the surplus was long-term capital outflow. Japanese banks expanded overseas and began to contribute to the international syndication of loans. Several leading city banks began to participate in international business. Over the decade of the 1980s and the early 1990s, the private sector savings continued to be at a very high level. By this period, Japan had become a mature industrialized economy. Compared to other mature economies, these rates were four to five times higher, therefore, Japan was accused of "oversaving". This helped fuel long-term capital outflows from Japan after 1981 (Table 21.2). Private sector investment rates between 1988 and 1991 ranged between 24.4 percent of GNP and 26.4 percent of GNP. At the time when the economy entered a recessionary phase in the latter half of 1992, it became obvious that Japan had over invested during these years.

The direct impact of high levels of investment in plant and equipment was that the average age of the capital stock came down, leading to rapid productivity. The K/L ratio, or capital equipment per person ratio, increased by leaps and bounds and so did the average productivity per person (Y/L) (see Table 21.3).

Initially, labor productivity was low because the capital stock per worker was small. This state of affairs continued even after recovery because capital formation in absolute terms was slow. As the statistics above show, after the mid-1950s, capital began to grow more rapidly than the labor force. During the two decades spanning 1952–73, plant and equipment expenditure increased by an average of 14.4 percent per year. Over the 1950s, investment in real terms remained at about 20 percent of GNP, an impressive performance by any measure (Patrick and Rosovsky 1976). The optimism in the business and managerial community was responsible

TABLE 21.1 Savings-investment balances, 1960–91 (as % of GNP)

Year	Private sector			Corporate sector			Household sector			Government sector		
	Savings	Investment	Savings minus investment	Savings	Investment	Savings minus investment	Savings	Investment	Savings minus investment	Savings	Investment	Savings minus investment
1960	28.2	31.1	−2.9	16.5	24.6	−8.1	11.8	6.6	5.2	7.7	4.7	3.0
1965	27.4	27.5	−0.1	15.8	19.1	−3.3	11.6	8.4	3.2	6.0	5.4	0.6
1967	31.4	32.7	−1.3	18.4	23.8	−5.4	13.0	8.9	4.1	6.3	5.1	1.2
1968	32.9	33.0	−0.1	19.7	24.1	−4.4	13.2	8.9	4.3	6.9	5.1	1.8
1969	32.6	34.5	−1.9	19.8	25.3	−5.5	12.7	9.2	3.6	7.5	5.0	2.5
1970	33.3	34.0	−0.7	18.7	27.5	−8.8	14.6	6.5	8.1	6.8	5.1	1.7
1971	31.0	30.0	1.0	16.1	24.8	−8.7	15.1	5.3	9.8	6.2	6.3	−0.1
1972	32.0	29.2	2.8	16.9	23.9	−7.0	14.9	5.2	9.7	7.0	5.8	1.2
1973	32.3	31.7	0.6	15.4	26.2	−10.8	16.9	5.4	11.5	6.9	6.4	0.5
1974	30.0	31.4	−1.4	10.3	23.1	−12.9	19.7	8.3	11.5	6.3	6.0	0.4
1975	29.0	26.8	2.2	8.4	17.9	−9.5	20.6	8.6	11.7	3.3	6.0	−2.8
1976	30.4	26.0	4.4	9.1	16.2	−7.0	21.3	9.8	11.4	2.1	5.8	−3.7
1977	29.5	24.6	5.0	9.5	15.2	−5.6	20.0	9.4	10.6	2.5	6.3	−3.8
1978	30.7	23.9	6.8	11.4	13.9	−2.5	19.4	10.0	9.3	1.5	7.0	−5.5
1979	29.0	25.2	3.8	11.7	16.1	−4.3	17.3	9.2	8.1	2.5	7.2	−4.7
1980	28.4	25.1	3.2	11.3	17.0	−5.7	17.1	8.1	9.0	2.7	7.1	−4.4
1981	27.9	24.2	3.7	10.6	16.9	−6.3	17.3	7.3	10.0	3.3	7.1	−3.8
1982	27.2	23.3	3.9	11.2	16.2	−4.9	16.0	7.1	8.8	3.2	6.8	−3.6
1983	26.9	21.9	5.0	11.0	15.3	−4.2	15.9	6.6	9.3	2.8	6.4	−3.7
1984	26.7	22.3	4.5	11.4	19.5	−4.5	15.3	6.4	9.0	3.9	6.0	−2.1
1985	26.8	22.8	4.0	11.8	17.2	−5.4	15.0	5.6	9.4	4.8	5.6	−0.8
1986	27.2	22.1	5.1	12.6	16.2	−3.6	15.1	5.4	9.7	4.7	5.6	−0.9
1987	26.0	22.6	3.4	12.9	16.7	−3.7	13.9	5.4	8.5	6.4	5.9	0.5
1988	26.0	24.4	1.6	13.3	18.9	−5.6	13.3	4.9	8.6	7.6	6.1	1.5
1989	25.6	25.6	0.0	12.9	20.4	−7.7	13.6	4.4	9.2	8.8	5.9	2.5
1990	25.2	26.4	−1.2	12.4	21.8	−9.4	13.3	3.7	9.4	8.9	6.1	2.9
1991	25.4	25.9	−0.5	12.1	28.9	−8.8	13.9	4.1	9.7	9.2	6.2	2.9

Sources: Economic Planning Agency, *Annual Report on National Statistics*, Tokyo, various issues.

TABLE 21.2   Balance of payments indicators, 1965–91 (US$ million)

Year	Current account balance	Trade balance	Long-term capital flows (net)	Overall balance of monetary movement (net)
1965	932	1,901	−415	405
1967	−190	1,160	−812	−571
1968	1,048	2,529	−239	1,102
1969	2,119	3,699	−155	2,283
1970	1,970	3,963	−1,591	1,374
1971	5,797	7,787	−1,082	7,677
1972	6,624	8,971	−4,487	4,741
1973	−136	3,688	−9,750	10,074
1974	−4,693	1,436	−3,881	−6,839
1975	−682	5,028	−272	−2,676
1976	3,680	9,887	−984	2,924
1977	10,918	17,311	3,184	7,743
1978	16,534	24,596	12,389	5,950
1979	−8,754	1,845	−12,976	16,662
1980	−10,746	2,125	2,324	−8,396
1981	4,770	19,967	−9,672	−2,144
1982	6,850	18,079	−14,969	−4,971
1983	20,799	31,454	−17,700	5,177
1984	35,003	44,257	−49,651	−15,200
1985	49,169	55,986	64,542	−12,318
1986	85,845	92,827	−13,461	−44,767
1987	87,015	96,386	−136,532	−29,545
1988	79,631	95,012	−130,930	−28,982
1989	57,157	76,917	−89,246	−33,286
1990	35,762	63,528	−43,586	−7,234
1991	72,598	103,289	36,628	76,369

Source: Bank of Japan, *Economic Statistics Annual 1991*, Research and Statistics Department, Tokyo, March 1992.

TABLE 21.3   Changes in productivity, 1955, 1965 and 1975

	1955	1965	1975
K/L (in ¥'000)	492	982	274
Y/L (in ¥'000)	443	883	1,867

Source: Kosai and Ogino (1984).

for further improvement in capital formation in the 1960s. No other industrial economy matched this performance. Ploughing back such large proportions with a reasonably low incremental capital–output ratio (ICOR) apparently had an income effect. The high investment phenomenon was economy-wide, therefore, it did not create any situation of industry specific excess capacity.

Japan was determined not to import capital and made up for any gaps through domestic sources. The reason for this lays in its external account. The exchange rate for the yen was fixed at 360 to the dollar under the Bretton Woods system, which made the yen overvalued. At this rate Japan could not export enough to pay for its imports. Under the Bretton Woods system all the adjustments were to be made by the country facing the deficit, if it did not wish to resort to a devaluation. Japan did not want to devalue its currency because it was trying to be seen as a responsible and productive member of the international economic community. It equated devaluation with national humiliation. To ward off any current account deficits, Japan instituted high tariffs, widespread import quotas and prevented corporations from borrowing abroad. Capital control measures were instituted. As a result, up to the mid-1960s the effective interest rates were higher at home than abroad. There was, however, a discretionary policy and industries with large growth potential or firms in high technology areas were allowed to borrow abroad.

Rapid growth of household savings was strongly supported by high growth of household incomes. As stated earlier, this sector continued to be a large supplier of funds even after the slowing of the growth rate over the 1970s. From an average of 15 percent of GNP in the early 1970s, it rose to 20 percent or more in the mid-1970s. Finally, it declined to 15 percent of GNP in the mid-1980s. Excess savings resulted due to a declining trend in private sector investment. That Japan's household savings rate is one of the highest in the world was recognized as early as 1960. An exhaustive survey (Horioka 1985) lists over 30 possible factors that might contribute to Japan's high household savings rate. The four celebrated reasons for the high household savings are: (a) high income growth rate; (b) favorable tax treatment of both small and large savings; (c) an inadequate social security system; and (d) the high prices of land and houses. Bequest has been a strong motive in Japanese society (Hayashi et al. 1987). However, there are disagreements on the nature of saving motives. For instance, Yoshitomi (1989) has argued that expensive land and housing can explain high household saving rates only if the demand for owner-occupied housing was price-inelastic. He demonstrated evidence of price elasticity in the demand of land and housing. Such high rates of savings and investment were instrumental in the rapid industrialization of the war-ravaged economy. When reconstruction began, the Japanese industrial sector was in worse shape than West Germany's and other war-torn European economies' industrial sectors.

Over the years a pattern of industrial growth had evolved. First preference was accorded to basic industries like iron and steel, heavy and chemical industries and power generation. They had a prewar base and contributed to upgrading the industrial structure. In addition, due to lower imported raw material content, chemical industries had greater domestic value-added. Government supported the growth of all three sectors financially. Conversely, inefficient industries like coal, nonferrous metals, paper and pulp were ruthlessly eliminated. There was another set of industries which were considered unsuitable. Japan did not want to become competitive in these industries in the future. The set included industries involved in the manufacture of cotton textiles, as well as industries producing bicycles, sewing machines and the like. These industries were discouraged because strategists saw them as only fit for economies at an early stage of industrialization, such as the economies of China and India. Under official guidance, firms had to release resources, that is, men and materials, for more efficient sectors that buttressed growth. After the basic industries, two groups were sequentially provided official stimulus. The first included shipbuilding, trucks and buses, television and radio, rolling stock and optical equipment. The second group of industries was palpably at a higher technological level and comprised consumer electronics, machinery, precision tools, autos, optics, heavy construction equipment and, later on, computer hardware. Development of these sectors contributed a great deal to Japanese growth efforts, particularly the second list of product lines which comprises what is called second stage industrialization products. Growth in these sectors first met the needs of the growing domestic markets and, therefore, was import substituting. But firms soon had to begin exporting and ensure the competitiveness of their products in the international markets. Consequently, most of these industries succeeded in becoming substantial exporters by the 1960s.

Like economic and industrial strategies, a well-defined technology plan was also adhered to. Since cheap steel was essential for industrial growth, two rationalization plans were implemented in order to upgrade the steel industry in the 1950s. The spread of oxygen converters, which used scrap iron as raw material, greatly helped the steel industry. The second rationalization plan essentially focused on the construction of strip mills that would be used to produce thin steel plates for the production of consumer durable goods. By the early 1960s, steel mills were producing over 5.5 million tons of steel plates a year. This volume of output was greater than that of France and England. In terms of the number of hot strip mills, Japan was second only to the U.S., and in oxygen converter capacity it soon reached the leading position in the world. All along this development, a good deal of attention was paid to quality improvements and new product development, such as the development of high quality steel sheets, light-gauge steel, seamless electrical pipe and high tensile strength steel. By the mid-1970s, Japan's steel industry was widely recognized as being the strongest in the world, producing the finest steel. This was not merely due to the locational advantages of its coastal steel mills. Technological progress had been phenomenal, which in turn had halved the unit cost of production in several plants.

Cheap sources of energy were essential for efficient industrialization. Therefore, to reduce energy prices, steam powered, high-capacity power plants were installed. A fall in the unit price of oil brought the costs further down. This almost started an energy revolution which benefited the industrial sector a great deal. It continued until the oil crisis of 1973 (Kosai 1986). The flip side of this development was that the reliance of the economy on oil grew inordinate. Modernization and technological upgrading in the manufacturing sector in general continued to proceed. Typical was the development of such consumer durable industries as the automobiles, electric machinery and appliances industries. A series of technological advances finally resulted in the mass production of automobiles. It was not without snags, but after they were overcome, they contributed a great deal to mass production. Similar technological upgrading took place in the motorcycle industry. After meeting the explosive domestic demand, a large part of the international motorcycle market was captured by Japan. The auto industry is known for its strong backward linkages. It provided strong stimulus to the steel and machine tool industries. It also supported a wide range of small subcontracting firms because the large auto firms had adopted the just-in-time system. Several of the technological advances were linked and fed on each other. For instance, when the steel industry was able to introduce the automatic, continuous-process stamping machines, mass production in electric machinery, washing machines and refrigerators became possible. In short, rapid industrial growth was constantly underpinned by technological upgrading. These two features together transformed the industrial scene beyond recognition.

Two major reasons account for Japan's success in absorbing Western technology. First, in the beginning, Japan relied on foreign engineers who were subsequently replaced by those trained in the domestic universities. These engineers studied foreign technical treaties and actual imported machinery. They copied what they saw, often adding improvements and modifications of their own. Thus, they were innovative imitators. Secondly, a good deal of research and development (R&D) took place before actual application and absorption of modern technology. The scale of R&D expanded after World War II. In two decades, it became immensely sophisticated. This in turn had a great impact over the industrial sector and, therefore, industrial value-added. A symbolic representation of Japanese technological advancement was the *Shinkansen*, or the bullet train, that began to operate in 1964. This is generally considered the time when the Meiji dream of catching up with the West was attained, and Japan had reached by and large the same stage of industrialization as the West. Its growth was fast-paced because it had a lot of catching up to do.

During its early growth phase, enormous investment was made by Japan in education, particularly engineering education. Japanese corporations are now reaping the benefits of this investment. Technical literacy is more widely diffused throughout Japanese business than elsewhere in the industrial world. Japan had 5,000 technical workers per million people in 1990. The comparable figure for the U.S. was 3,500, and for West Germany 2,500. No other country came close (*The Economist* 1991). Another characteristic of Japanese technological advancement was made without breaking through the boundaries of existing technologies. A large proportion of the innovations made by the Japanese resulted from the fusion of different types of technologies rather than from technological breakthroughs (Kodama 1991). By the mid-1980s Japan had become a frontrunner in industrial technology. Scientific and technological researchers, both academic and industrial, had begun to pay more attention to what was happening in Japan. Japan's strength lay in the mass market technologies. They included video cameras, semiconductors, advanced color televisions and computer displays, semiconductor-manufacturing equipment, computer-controlled machine tools, and since the late 1980s, luxury cars. Although all these are important areas of strength, they are medium value-added technologies. There are, however, several very high value-added products in which Japan does not lead, for instance, satellites, supercomputers, aero engines, and jet aircraft (Emmott 1992). Japan also has weaknesses in biotechnology, chemical engineering and pharmaceuticals.

Although the 8 percent GDP growth rate in real terms which Japan posted for 1955–65 was admirable, the following decade was even better in terms of growth. Japan's phenomenal growth enhanced its international status. In 1963, Japan acceded to Article VIII of the International Monetary Fund. In recognition of its status as an advanced country, Japan was made a member of the OECD in 1964. The latter half of the 1960s was a period of phenomenal growth performance. Kosai called it "a time of record-setting long-term prosperity." The real growth rate over the 1955–60 period was 9.0 percent, it rose marginally to 9.7 percent for the 1960–65 period and further to an unprecedented 13.1 percent for the 1965–70 period. The last part of the upswing of this business cycle lasted for 57 months, from the fall of 1965 to the summer of 1970. It was christened the *Izanagi* boom.[3] This was the period when investment was calling for investment and was instrumental in creating new processes and industries. It made growth autonomous and self-propelled. By the time the *Izanagi* boom ended, Japan was fully established as a respectable— if somewhat envied—member of the community of mature industrial economies.

The Japanese economy adopted an outward-oriented stance since the beginning because after the mini-boom of the Korean war, when its current account was helped by American procurement orders, it was faced with a difficult situation. Overseas assets were lost due to the war. It needed foreign exchange to sustain the recovery which was beginning to take place. Ironically the world economy was showing signs of a downturn at this time. Under these circumstances there was little choice but to turn to exporting in an aggressive manner and, to this end, be as competitive in the international markets as possible. In this venture, Japan received U.S. help in two ways: first, because of its special relationship with the U.S., it found American markets welcoming its exports; second, the U.S. was championing the cause of free trade in the world. It succeeded in trade and exchange regime liberalization, which, in turn, helped Japan expand its export markets.

International trade, following the regulations and discipline of the General Agreement on Tariffs and Trade (GATT), expanded at an unprecedented pace. The decades of the 1950s and 1960s are widely considered the halcyon period of world trade. The two countries that made the most of this free trading environment and rapid trade expansion were Japan and Germany. Japanese exports started from a tiny base of US$2 billion in 1955, doubled to $4.1 billion in 1960 and catapulted to $19.3 billion in 1970. This amounts to an average growth of 16.9 percent for the decade of the 1960s. Import growth kept pace with export growth. These soared from US$2.2 billion in 1955 to $4.5 billion in 1960 and further to US$18.9 billion in 1970 (Table 21.4). Their growth rate averaged 15 percent for the 1960s (Kojima 1977). Japanese export growth was twice as rapid as world trade during this period. As a result, Japan doubled its share of world trade, from 3.2 percent in 1960 to 6.2 percent in 1970.

The silver lining had to have a cloud. Producers in the importing countries found the loss of their own markets disconcerting. Japanese exports also chipped

TABLE 21.4 Foreign trade indicators, 1960–91

Year	Exports ($ million)	% change over preceding year	Imports ($ million)	% change over preceding year	Volume index 1985 = 100 Exports	Imports	Gold and foreign exchange reserves ($ million)	Exchange rate ¥/$
1960	4,055	+17.3	4,491	+24.8			1,824	358
1965	8,452	+26.7	8,169	+2.9			2,107	360
1967	10,442	+6.8	11,663	+22.5			2,005	362
1968	12,972	+24.2	12,987	+11.4			2,891	358
1969	15,990	+23.3	15,024	+15.7			3,496	358
1970	19,318	+20.8	18,881	+25.7			4,399	358
1971	24,019	+24.3	19,712	+4.4			15,235	315
1972	28,591	+19.0	23,471	+19.1			18,365	301
1973	36,930	+29.2	38,314	+63.2			12,246	280
1974	55,536	+50.4	62,110	+62.1	45.8	79.6	13,518	300
1975	55,753	+0.4	57,863	−6.8	45.4	69.8	12,815	305
1976	67,225	+20.6	64,799	+12.0	54.8	76.8	16,604	293
1977	80,495	+19.7	70,809	+9.3	59.2	78.6	22,848	240
1978	97,543	+21.2	79,343	+12.1	59.3	83.4	33,019	195
1979	103,032	+5.6	110,672	+39.5	60.0	94.0	20,327	240
1980	129,807	+26.0	140,528	+27.0	70.6	91.2	25,232	204
1981	152,030	+17.1	143,290	+2.0	78.0	89.9	28,403	220
1982	138,831	−8.7	131,931	−7.9	76.3	89.4	23,262	235
1983	146,927	+3.8	126,393	−4.2	82.3	90.1	24,496	232
1984	170,114	+15.8	136,503	+8.0	95.6	99.6	26,313	252
1985	175,638	+3.2	129,539	−5.1	100.0	100.0	26,510	200
1986	209,151	+19.1	126,408	−2.4	99.4	109.5	42,239	160
1987	229,221	+9.6	149,515	+18.3	99.7	119.7	81,479	122
1988	264,917	+15.6	187,354	+25.3	104.8	139.7	97,662	126
1989	275,175	+3.9	210,847	+12.5	108.8	150.6	84,895	143
1990	286,948	+4.3	234,799	+11.4	114.8	159.3	77,053	135
1991	314,948	+9.6	236,737	+0.8	118.2	164.0	6,880	125

Source: Bank of Japan, *Economic Statistics Annual 1991*, Research and Statistics Department, Tokyo, March 1992.

away their shares in third country markets. Dumping and unfair trade charges became rampant. U.S. textile and steel producers were among the first to make such accusations. The U.S. was Japan's biggest market in several products. When the Japanese economy was tiny, its export expansion was, if anything, admired. However, by 1970 it had grown into a large economy exporting large volumes of manufactured goods and importing massive amounts of raw materials. Japan's trade expansion was far more rapid than that of other industrial economies. By the early 1970s, West Europeans were also disaffected and Japan began to be seen as an economy that was destabilizing the world economy. The accusation took a pungent edge because at 358 yen to the dollar, the yen was undervalued and Japan's domestic markets had protectionist tariffs, quota restrictions (QRs), exchange controls, capital controls, and administrative guidance. Its markets were reputed to be the most difficult to break into for foreign exporters. Japan's distribution system worked as a barrier in its own right. To be sure, consumers around the world benefited from good quality products at internationally competitive prices and international welfare and household welfare in the importing countries rose. However, *vide ut supra* the volume of Japanese exports rose too fast for firms to adjust production and for economies to adjust structurally—both micro- and macro-economic adjustments were rendered difficult. Hindsight reveals that in some product lines the importing countries had lost comparative advantage, therefore, they could not compete with Japanese products in their own markets. Yet, largely for noneconomic reasons, they did not wish to give up on those product lines and turn to areas where they did have a comparative advantage. Consequently, the drumbeats of protectionist lobbies in the industrial countries became increasingly strident.

Comparative advantage is a dynamic phenomenon. In a growing economy, it is always in a state of flux. Japan's comparative advantage shifted from unskilled labor-intensive products in the 1960s to skilled labor-intensive products later and then to high technology products. Balassa and Noland (1988) computed the indices of revealed comparative advantage (RCA) of a range of products for the 1967–83 period to demonstrate changes in international specialization. The RCA is defined as the ratio of a country's share in the exports of a particular commodity to a country's share in total merchandise exports. A value >1 for a particular industry reflects comparative advantage while <1 stands for comparative disadvantage in that industry. In the mid-1960s, Japan's comparative advantage was in products like textiles, apparel, rubber and plastic products, leather and leather products, clay and miscellaneous light manufactured products. These were unskilled labor-intensive products. Japan also had some comparative advantage in human capital-intensive products, such as nonelectrical machinery, electrical machinery, transportation equipment, instruments, and so forth. By the early 1980s, the unskilled labor-intensive products shifted from a position of comparative advantage to one of comparative disadvantage. Skill-intensive and high technology products began to record high points on the RCA index. Japan increased its comparative advantage in 12 out of 19 high technology product categories considered by Balassa and Noland. It also did well in several R&D and science based industries. It did better in industries in which research is product-specific and management of research activities is important (Kodama 1991). This transformation in comparative advantage is clearly visible in Japan's exports. Japanese firms constantly moved upmarket and in 30 years became world leaders in industries as complex as automobiles.

For the first time in 1965, a small surplus was recorded on the current account as well as trade balance. However, by 1967, it had disappeared (Table 21.2). The Nixon "shockoo" of 1971 abruptly discontinued the dollar convertibility into gold. For a considerable time before the Nixon shock, the exchange rate in force was believed to have been undervalued relative to the yen's purchasing power parity (ppp). The fixed exchange rate regime ended and floating exchange rates began. The Bretton Woods exchange rate of the yen was no longer valid and the yen appreciated. It fluctuated between 280 to 310 to the dollar. Despite currency appreciation, Japan recorded current account and trade balance surpluses of a large magnitude. It was essentially due to the poor export performance of other industrial countries, particularly the U.S. This resulted in large amount of dollars and foreign exchange flowing into Japan and its foreign exchange reserves jumped from US$2 billion in 1965 to over $15 billion in 1971 (Table 21.4). The surpluses in the current account and trade balance took everyone by surprise, including the Japanese. The current account moved into the red in 1973 because of several reasons. First, the oil-price hike was a serious shock to the Japanese economy. Second, progress was being made in import liberalization and imports had recorded a large increase in 1973. Third, the adverse impact of the yen appreciation was felt after a time lag. Foreign exchange reserves declined after touching the high-mark of US$18 billion in 1972. Economic growth languished. The oil shock dealt a severe blow to the Japanese economy because its energy sector was based entirely on the availability of cheap oil. It sent the Japanese economy into an inflationary tailspin. However, Japan was not the lone sufferer because the whole of the industrialized world went into a deep recession in the mid-1970s. Japan, unlike the other industrial economies, had only one year of poor growth. After recording GNP growth of 2.9 percent in real terms in 1975, Japan's GNP improved to 4.2 percent in 1976. Japan sustained growth around this level during the rest of the decade (Table 21.5).

There are two noteworthy, if not remarkable, features of the Japanese economy of this period that must not elude our attention. First, as remarkable as the high rate of growth was, it was significant that the wealth that was created was well diffused in the society and unemployment was maintained at a low ebb. The income distribution, measured by Gini coefficient, demonstrated one of the highest degrees of equality among industrial nations (Economist Intelligence Unit 1991). This became possible because of the various forms of protection provided to labor during the U.S. occupation as well as because rapid gains in productivity were rewarded with commensurate wage increases. The latter worked to provide a

TABLE 21.5   Gross national product, 1955–91

Year	Gross national product (billions of yen)	Percentage change over the preceding year	
		In nominal terms	In real terms
1955	8,399	–	–
1960	15,998	21.3	13.1
1965	32,773	11.3	5.8
1970	73,188	17.9	10.2
1975	148,169	10.6	2.9
1976	166,417	12.3	4.2
1977	185,530	11.5	4.8
1978	204,475	10.2	5.0
1979	221,825	8.5	5.6
1980	240,099	8.2	3.5
1981	257,417	7.2	3.4
1982	270,669	5.1	3.4
1983	282,078	4.2	2.8
1984	301,048	6.7	4.3
1985	321,556	6.8	5.2
1986	335,838	4.4	2.6
1987	350,479	4.4	4.3
1988	373,731	6.6	6.2
1989	399,046	6.8	4.8
1990	428,668	7.4	5.2
1991	456,113	6.4	4.4

Source: Ministry of Finance, *Financial Statistics of Japan 1992*, Tokyo.

social consensus in favor of economic growth. Second, although by the early 1970s the Japanese economy had grown to be the second largest in the world and it had earned the appellation of economic "superpower," a fundamental change took place at this point in time, namely, the economy left behind its high growth era and became a moderate growth economy. Although the oil crisis created a massive economic disruption, the economy did not return to its high growth path even after the adverse influence of the crisis was dissipated. The single most important reason why Japan settled to moderate growth was that the technology gap between Japan and the industrial economies was bridged. When the gap existed, Japan had become adept at importing and adapting technology and in the process benefiting from fast productivity gains. This process made private sector investment highly profitable (Lincoln 1988). When Japan caught up with the industrial nations, this process ceased to work and the Japanese economy found itself in a new era. Between 1974 and 1985, the economy suffered no recession, yet its average annual growth rate in real terms was as low as 4.3 percent. This was less than half of the average for the preceding 12 years. However, Japan continued to outperform the other industrial economies, albeit with a smaller margin than that in the past.

As in other industrial countries, the services sector in Japan had enlarged at the expense of the primary and secondary sectors, more at the expense of the former. This expansion of the service sector was rapid between 1955 and 1970. When it began to slow in the early 1970s, it triggered a debate among the Japanese economists regarding shifting of the industrial structure towards "knowledge-intensive industries." The Ministry of International Trade and Industry (MITI) published a report spelling out the new direction that industry should take. The knowledge intensive industries that it recommended were information services, computer software, systems engineering and telecommunications (MITI 1971). Subsequently this list was expanded to include construction services, entertainment related services, technical counselling and the like. MITI took a great deal of initiative in supporting industrial expansion in high technology services and provided "seed money" to firms for R&D, until this sector picked up its own momentum. It considered support and development of the high technology services sector *a fortiori* important because it reduced the dependence of the industrial sector on oil and made it more technology-intensive.

The services sector began expanding faster than in the past and its share of total economic activity, whether measured in terms of the value added to GNP, or in terms of sales or the number of businesses established, or in terms of the labor force employed, rose considerably. These industries accounted for more than half of the GNP in the early 1990s (Fugii 1992). Since growth of the services sector in general is increasingly tied to growth in business and professional services, this sector in Japan has remained increasingly sensitive to activity in the manufacturing sector. The Japanese economy is given a good deal of credit for turning towards the development of the services sector at the appropriate juncture in its growth process.

When the yen left its fixed parity, or its Bretton Woods rate, after the Nixon shock and began to appreciate in 1971, it soon acquired a high place in the demonology of Western economic and financial analysts—although for no fault of its own. If one juxtaposes the current account and trade balance deficits and surpluses in Table 21.2 with the value of the yen, one cannot fail to observe a pattern. Whenever the current account plunged into deficit, the yen depreciated with it (see statistics for 1973, 1974 and 1980). The Japanese were accused of engaging in currency value manipulation for trade revival. To support the accusation, Japan did keep coming out of the red faster and further than other OECD countries. To buttress this conspiracy theory, the yen remained rather weak during 1982–84 when the economy was recording strong trade balance and current account surpluses. The sharp gyrations in the value of the yen and their clear relationships with Japan's current account were hardly the result of deliberate policy. The culprit was Japan's unusual trade structure. During the 1970s, it was dominated by imports of oil and raw materials. First, unlike most industrialized countries, it depended 100 percent on imported oil. Second, raw materials accounted for 75 percent of its imports. This proportion was about 40 percent in France and West Germany and a little higher in the U.S. Manufactured goods accounted for almost the whole (98 percent) of Japanese exports, against 90 percent for France and West Germany, and 70 percent for the U.S. (Economist Newspaper Ltd 1983). Therefore, any changes in the price of oil or raw material had a relatively larger affect on Japan's terms of trade. Following the two oil-price hikes, the adverse terms of trade movement for Japan was much higher—about thrice as much—than other major OECD economies. That led to a deeper swing of current account into the red. During the 1970s, the yen exchange rate was determined by movement in the current account. Therefore, every time the current account dipped in the red, the yen depreciated against other currencies. The late 1970s is a good illustration—the real effective exchange rate dipped by 25 percent in two years. Another reason why the current account bounced back into surplus so quickly after each oil crisis was MITI's determination to export their way out of trouble. Exporters responded to rapid domestic sales by aggressive sales overseas. With improvement in exports, the current account came into surplus, the yen began to appreciate and the cycle was complete. As Table 21.2 shows, this process failed to work in the early 1980s because Japan's trade partners were still in recession. After 1982, the yen was weak, and again the current account surplus began to rise, eventually peaking at 4.5 of the GNP.

By 1976, the economy had recovered fully from the first oil shock as well as the recession. Between 1976 and 1981, when the second postwar recession began, Japanese GNP grew at 4.4 percent in real terms (Table 21.5) while that of its four biggest rivals (the U.S., West Germany, France and the U.K.) grew by an average of 2.5 percent. In 1982, Japan had the largest manufacturing base in the capitalist world, it was the largest producer of memory chips, it overtook the U.S. in production of vehicles, was the second largest producer of steel and overwhelmingly dominated world markets in motorcycles, engines, cameras, calculators, television, photo-copiers and several other product lines. The industries in which it could not compete with the Western firms were: aircraft, drugs and pharmaceuticals, bio-technology, and nuclear power. Although in terms of inflation and unemployment, the worldwide recession of the early 1980s left Japan in a better shape than other industrial nations, the Japanese economy was faced with a dilemma. It had grown so large that its export expansion, which was faster than world trade, was resented and resisted by other industrial economies. Economic growth in Japan had become closely tied to exports at a time when world trade had lost steam. In 1980, the volume of world trade rose by 5 percent against Japan's export volume growth of 17 percent. The very next year the volume of world trade expanded by 2 percent while that in Japan by 11 percent (Table 21.4). Retaliation and retribution were swift. In 1982, for the first time in the postwar period, the value of Japanese exports declined by 8.7 percent and volume contracted by 2.2 percent (Table 21.4). Voluntary export restraints (VERs), orderly marketing arrangements (OMAs) and other ingenious protectionist measures put Japanese exports on a tight lease. Japan could have stimulated domestic demand so that the economy could go on its own steam, however it did not opt to do this. The rate of domestic capital formation also dipped after 1981. Was this the end of the *Asahi* phase? Hardly. Notwithstanding the economic doldrums, Japan was far from heading for a sustained down turn and unmistakably had several elements of sound economic health. For instance, its efficacious manufacturing base and technological powers were as strong as in the high growth era. In 1982, output per man-hour in Japan was 47 percent above its level in 1975. For the U.S. this proportion was 21 percent, France 34 percent, Germany 24 percent and Britain 18 percent (Economist Newspaper Ltd 1983). Another important feature, high productivity growth, was also intact and in 1982 its industrial production was 50 percent above its level in 1975. The comparable proportion for the U.S. was 17 percent, West Germany 8 percent and Britain 5 percent (Economist Newspaper Ltd 1983). By the early 1980s, Japan had become a highly efficient, productive and, therefore, prosperous economy. It was inventive and innovative in ways that seemed marvellous and exemplary. The economy began to loom large in the international economic and financial news.

21.4 The *Endaka* Phase

The Plaza accord was the largest and the most successful exercise of macroeconomics coordination in the international economy. It was made between the Group of Five (G-5) countries in September 1985 to bring the exchange rates of the major industrial economies in line with the economic fundamentals. In keeping with the objectives of the accord, the yen appreciated by 92 percent against the dollar over the 1985–88 period. Its nominal effective exchange rate during 1985–88 escalated by 58 percent while the real effective exchange rate appreciated by 29 percent against the trade-weighted currency basket. Did this create an *endaka*, or high yen, recession? In the first post-appreciation year (1986) the negative effects were strong and the economy showed clear signs of deceleration. The nominal and real economic growth rates made a nose dive to 4.4 percent and 2.6 percent, respectively (Table 21.5). The plant and equipment investment increased by only one quarter of its 1985 increase. The gross domestic capital formation stagnated. The economy absorbed the deflationary impact of the high yen by mid-1986 and the bottom of the *endaka* recession was reached in the third quarter of 1986, thereafter, the economic activity displayed a gradual and sustained recovery led by domestic demand. An extraordinary rebound in capital spending was the other propelling factor. This upswing of the business cycle continued unabated until 1991.[4] In 1990, when the other major economies were sliding into recession, Japanese economists and banking circles were anxious about the possible overheating. It was hardly irrelevant because the economy demonstrated remarkable vigour in the face of recession abroad and high interest rates at home and grew at an astonishing annual rate of 11.2 percent in the first quarter of 1991 (Chandler 1991). This boom exceeded even the *Izanagi* boom to become the longest lasting upswing of a business cycle in the postwar period. It should be named after *Izanami*, the wife of god *Izanagi* and co-creator of the Japanese archipelago. The reason for choosing the goddess' name was that this boom was partly created by domestic demand and led by personal spending which are largely controlled by housewives (Kazutomo 1990).

In the high growth era of the Japanese economy, manufacturing output, labor productivity and export achievements were the building blocks of spectacular economic growth. Down to the first quinquennium of the 1980s, net exports were responsible for almost 40 percent of real GNP growth. Currency appreciation changed this scenario. In the second quinquennium of the 1980s, unlike the first, external demand not only did not contribute to real GNP growth but its contributions were negative. It contributed –1.4 percent to real growth in 1986, –1.0 percent in 1987, –1.7 percent in 1988 and –0.7 percent in 1989 (Economic Planning Agency, various issues). As alluded to earlier, the domestic demand gained strength in 1986 and became stronger thereafter, which led to accelerated growth in 1987 as well as to import expansion. There was a complete reversal of the domestic economy during the post-appreciation period from a supply-oriented to a demand-oriented economy. For the first time excess demand was implanted in the system. As the domestic sales activity expanded with increasing domestic demand, the production structure switched from export-oriented to domestic-demand-oriented. Firms began to aim at achieving scale economies through expansion of sales volumes in the domestic market rather than in export markets. The Bank of Japan estimated the total demand conditions in each industry using inducement coefficients derived from the input-output tables and found that: (a) demand of the manufacturing industries slackened after the yen appreciation on account of weakened export demand; and (b) growth in demand in the nonmanufacturing industries gained momentum reflecting a firm domestic demand, specially from the household sector (Bank of Japan 1987).

As stated earlier, underpinning much of the post-appreciation surge in Japan's economic growth has been an extraordinary rebound in capital spending by industry. In the immediate aftermath of the yen appreciation, investment in plant and equipment fell. However, it soon rebounded to 14.3 percent in 1988, 15.5 percent in 1989 and 13.6 percent in 1990, making these years the period of highest increase in investment during the decade. This investment was supported by a flood of technological innovations and went into high technology sectors. Part of these outlays were also devoted to shifting capacity offshore. The industrial restructuring took place in an environment of declining interest rates and monetary relaxation. There was a monotomic fall in the official discount rate (ODR) and during 1987 and 1988, it remained as low as 2.5 percent, the lowest level during the postwar period. The three-months *gensaki* rate also fell from 7.4 percent in 1985 to 4.2 percent in 1989. Lower interest rates helped in overcoming the initial deflationary impact of yen appreciation and softened its negative impact on the business enterprises.

Import volume growth reflecting the new strength has already been dealt with. The large market made available for export expansion of the other economies worked towards stabilizing the international economy. It is known as the locomotive role and until recently it was performed only by the U.S. economy. While the increases in imports took place in the context of a stronger yen, the fact that their growth continued even in 1989, when the yen had weakened to 143 to the dollar, indicated that import expansion had taken roots as a stable trend in the economy.

The increased manufactured goods imports included semi-finished goods used by processing industries as well as durable and non-durable consumer goods. The shift away from the import of raw materials to that of manufactured goods was first noticed in a small way in 1980 when upgrading of technological levels and progress in industrialization had created substantial supply capacity in the Asian newly industrializing economies (ANIEs). The appreciation of the yen brought this shift to light and accelerated it. The domestic suppliers of several semi-finished goods were forced out of market. In short, Japanese trade shifted its axis from vertical to horizontal specialization.

The yen appreciation had a wealth effect through terms-of-trade improvement. The size of the terms-of-trade gain was estimated to have amounted to ¥12 trillion annually in 1986 and 1987 (Bank of Japan 1988). Domestic demand increased in 1986 despite slower economic growth because real purchasing power increased and the real income of the household sector expanded. This was the income effect of the yen appreciation.

Somewhat paradoxically the trade surplus as well as the nominal current account surplus coexisted with the appreciated yen for some time. This seeming incongruity could be explained by the following factors:

1. Terms of trade improvement leading to real income effect.
2. Continued growth in demand of the other industrialized countries.
3. Several areas of Japanese exports consisted of products of strong nonprice competitiveness; their sales volumes did not decline even after dollar prices were readjusted for these export products.
4. Wide differences in the starting bases of exports and imports.
5. The pass-through coefficient of Japanese export prices was low, therefore full impact of currency appreciation was not felt by importers.
6. Oil and raw material prices were bearish and the yen appreciation magnified this decline for Japan.
7. Low interest rates and falling unit labor costs helped.[5]
8. Intra-company exports were not affected by the yen appreciation.

Currency appreciation polarized the Japanese firms into those benefiting from the strong domestic demand and those suffering from the deflationary impact created by adjustment in import and export volumes. Profits improved for the former category of firms and declined for the latter group. In general, the price stabilizing effect of yen appreciation had a favorable impact on corporate finances. Some of the exporters brought down their fixed costs and succeeded in re-establishing an improved profit structure, allowing them to be profitable without large increases in sales.

As the economy began to slow down in the latter half of 1991, demand and production began to contract and the rate of investment recorded a decline. The economy was seriously jolted by the emergence and burst of "the bubbles" (that is, the steep rise in stock and land prices, well above the level consistent with economic fundamentals, and then the sharp fall in these prices). GDP fell in both the second and the third quarters of 1992, in line with the textbook definition of a recession. It is now widely believed that the economy is shifting from an expansion phase to an adjustment phase—that is, the economy is undergoing the stock adjustment and adjustment in plant and equipment that occurs after a period of high growth (Economic Planning Agency 1992). This kind of recessionary stock adjustment period has followed all the three booms in the past, namely, the *Jimmu*, the *Iwato* and the *Izanagi* booms. All three booms recorded falling investment rates at the end. Thus, the current recession has resulted from autonomous endogenous factors.

21.5   Trade Liberalization and Financial Deregulation

Japan has had a long-enduring protectionist stance and, therefore a history of tariffs, quota restrictions (QRs) and nontariff barriers (NTBs). Together these restrictions firmly controlled imports and managed to capture the domestic market for domestic producers. Initially all imports, agricultural and manufacturing, were protected from foreign competition on balance of payments and infant industry grounds. Agricultural imports were restricted by stringent QRs while manufactured products were largely protected by tariffs. One of the consequences of this was that when Japan became a contracting party (CP) of GATT in 1955, 14 industrial countries invoked Article XXXV, withholding most-favored nation (MFN) treatment. Several British and French colonies, after becoming independent, followed the metropolitan powers and withheld their application of the agreement to Japan, bringing the number of countries that invoked Article XXXV to 30.

Although trade liberalization began in 1960, it progressed at a snail's pace. It was believed that after the 1965 trade balance surplus was attained, rapid liberalization would follow. But policymakers considered this an inadequate signal. Besides, the economic community was convinced that the protectionist policy had served Japan well and had led it to record an export expansion almost twice as rapid as world trade. Therefore, it was argued that protectionism should not be abandoned until the export surplus became a steady economic trend. Hesitation on this count was not given up until 1969, rankling Japan's trade partners. Joining the Kennedy Round of multilateral trade negotiations (MTNs) was the first firm-footed step in the direction of trade liberalization. Japan benefited considerably from the "free ride", that is, other countries' general tariff reduction during the MTNs. After the Kennedy Round, Japan began to record large trade surpluses, they were partly attributed to the Round. Complying with the Kennedy Round recommendations, Japan brought average tariff levels on durable manufactured goods down to 12.7 percent in 1972. The comparable levels in the U.S. and the EC were 8.8 percent and 8.2 percent respectively. On semi-manufactured goods, Japanese tariffs averaged 6.3 percent while those in the U.S. and the EC averaged 5.6 percent and 4.8 percent, respectively.[6] However, tariffs on finished consumer goods remained high even after the Kennedy Round.

Japan incurred the ire of its trade partners because of its use of NTBs (such as the steep tax on luxury goods, large cars and high-quality whisky), government procurement practices that were based on the noncompetitive selection of supplying firms and resulted in the exclusion of foreign suppliers, and technicalities (such as customs valuations, industrial standards and safety regulations, the anti-dumping restrictions and countervailing duties). All these inconveniences deterred exports to Japan. Exports were also said to be obstructed due to strong "administrative guidance" or government pressure without the backing of statutes. This guidance, for instance, worked in the following manner: in the case of large thermo-electric generators, importers were advised to import the first one and then meet the domestic needs by manufacturing them using the imported one as a prototype. Practices like administrative guidance or buying cartels, effectively manage to work like quotas. Price changes by exporters did not affect imports under these cases because they failed to affect imports that were barred by quotas. Other practices led to higher domestic prices of imported products and effectively managed to work like tariffs. These imports, however, were sensitive to price changes by exporters (Lawrence 1991). For instance, if an imported product is sold by a firm having monopoly over its distribution, its profit markup will be higher than the markup during competitive distribution. These informal market practices managed to decelerate imports considerably.

Japan had to pay the price of its protectionist stance. Countries that were large markets for Japan frequently resorted to OMAs and VERs. By the mid-1970s, the number of products which were under VERs imposed at the request of importing countries and reported to the GATT by the Japanese government reached 264 (Kojima 1977). Some of these restraints were put in place without government intervention, like VERs on steel exports to the U.S. Many a time VERs were put in place jointly by the importing country and Japan after sharp increases in Japanese exports in some product category and after Japan was convinced that an accusation of market disruption was about to be made, or felt that the importing country would erect some trade barriers. Japan also accepted VERs because they were less damaging than the possible trade barriers and allowed Japan some discretion in determining export volume ceilings. In addition, VERs improved its terms of trade.

The issue of markets not being open enough for trading partners continued to be contentious and Japan was frequently accused of being mercantalistic. In the early 1980s, the EC sought redress through the GATT and the U.S. forced Japan's hand to have a set of extensive bilateral negotiations. In 1985, the U.S. started negotiations with Japan in order to open Japan's telecommunications, electronics, forest products, medical equipment and pharmaceuticals markets. The U.S. sought many wide ranging changes in Japanese markets through the so-called Structural Impediments Initiative (SII).

Several studies have examined why Japan's imports to GNP ratio is abnormally low (Balassa 1986, Bergsten and Cline 1988, Lawrence 1987, Noland 1990, Saxonhouse 1983). A subset of these studies focused only on the manufactured imports. The structures of their models varied widely and depended upon the assumptions made and the methodology followed. In addition, there were serious divergences in the definitions of the variables. The common thread that ran through them was that they all believed that countries that are located far away from their trading partners, tended to trade less because of higher transport costs. But they all had their distinctive manner of calculating the transport costs. Some of them inferred that Japan's import behavior is not significantly different from that in the other OECD countries when all the relevant explanatory variables are taken into account. The other studies reached the opposite conclusion. A recently concluded OECD study concluded that while Japan's merchandise imports were well explained, a significant negative factor lowering the manufactured imports was found which could have been either due to: (a) Japan's comparative advantage, or (b) trade barriers (Barbone 1988). If one juxtaposes these results, one finds that these empirical studies are inconclusive.

From time to time Japan has taken measures to fend off criticism of its trade partners. In 1982, three extensive lists of measures were prepared to dismantle tariff and nontariff measures, and quota restrictions. Japan also has an excellent record of implementing the Tokyo Round recommendations. Japan's trade structure underwent a dramatic market driven change after the post-Plaza yen appreciation. Its imports recorded a sharp surge from US$129 billion in 1986 to $237 billion in 1991. In terms of volume, the index showed a jump from 100.0 to 164.0, a 64 percent rise in a span of six years. Traditionally, Japanese manufactured imports were a smaller share of its domestic use of manufactured goods compared to other industrial countries. After the yen appreciation, it was no longer so. Imports of manufactured goods increased from US$40.16 billion to $106.11 billion in four years between 1985 and 1989. In terms of volume, they grew by 102.1 percent. In addition, the SII negotiations with the U.S. were not only wide ranging but also addressed some deep changes in the traditional market practices that effectively obstructed imports. The resulting changes benefited all the trade partners, developed and developing, of Japan. Thus viewed, a good deal of adjustment was made to liberalize the markets during the 1980s.

The highly regulated financial markets of the 1950s and the 1960s had served the economy well. Interest rates were controlled by the monetary authorities. The financial authorities exercised control over financial institutions and emphasized functional separation. For instance, banks and securities companies had to be separate entities, somewhat on the lines of the U.S. Glass-Steagall Act. Its Japanese parallel was called Article 65. Clear lines were drawn between banks that lent to large corporations and the financial institutions meant for small business. Loans from financial institutions to firms financed plant and equipment expenditure according to the priority of the government. Thus finance was channelled to sectors considered important for growth. Firms generally remained highly leveraged. The moderate growth rates of the 1970s created pressure to deregulate the tightly controlled financial system by reducing the dependence of firms over banks. Also, when government wanted to start floating bonds to finance deficits, control over interest rates appeared to be an obstruction. The current account surpluses created external pressure to deregulate external transactions so that more surpluses could flow to capital-scarce regions of the world. In response to these developments, the financial system was diversified and more financial instruments came to be developed. Moreover, the market began to have a greater influence over interest rates. Yet no sweeping deregulatory measures were adopted overnight and the Ministry of Finance remained committed to gradualism. The pace of deregulation, however, picked up after 1985. Likewise, deregulation in the external transactions began in 1980 with the revision of the foreign Exchange and Foreign Trade Control Law. It entailed drastic liberalization of all foreign exchange transactions. Similar deregulatory measures began to unfold more rapidly after 1984 and eventually helped Japan become a financial superpower. The international financial liberalization was important for many reasons, not least because it forced the pace of domestic liberalization.

21.6   Unique Practices and Institutions?

One of the ways to explain growth is to examine trends in the principal factors of production, namely, labor, capital and productivity growth which encompasses a variety of elements. Denison and Chung's extensive empirical work on the macro explanations of postwar growth in Japan concluded that of the 8.77 percent average annual rise in real national income over the 1950–70 period, productivity gains contributed 4.82 percent, capital 2.10 percent and labor 1.85 percent. There are myriad explanations for such a high contribution of productivity gains to economic growth. Some believe that there are certain culturally derived unique characteristics of the Japanese society that were responsible for it, while others think that it was mere superior working out of market forces and "situational" responses and motivations that have led to Japan's miraculous emergence as a first-rate economic power. Still others think that it was an extraordinary combination of the two. A list of these unique practices can be effortlessly made: strong Confucian influence, life-long employment system, seniority wage system, enterprise unionism, domestic saving system, the multi-tier distribution system, the *keiretsu* system, subcontracting, business-government relationship and the role of the Ministry of International Trade and Industry (MITI). All these were thought to have a constant of Japaneseness. It was believed that all these unique practices, or some of them, coalesced to create the economic "miracle." Did all these unique practices and institutions make unique contributions in making Japan a developmental state? Did they assist the economy in working on neoclassical economic lines? Were they, or some of them, irrelevant to its postwar evolution? Let us look for the answers.

First, Confucianism which is known for striving for *chowa* or harmony, respect for elders as well as for those higher up in the hierarchy, and for putting the group before the individual, is considered to have had two favorable influences of economic significance: it led to an amicable relationship between (a) business and government and (b) managers and workers. The first cooperative relationship, as alluded to earlier, dates back to the post-Meiji era when government assisted with large investments so that appropriate scale of economies could be reaped and modern technology imported. In addition, before World War II, whenever the economy was on a war footing, the relationship between large business conglomerates and government strengthened. Initiatives were taken from both sides. During the postwar reconstruction phase, government assisted industries in procuring raw materials and their transportation. It also protected the domestic markets for their output. The high tariffs and QRs created large rents for business. Under these circumstances, making minor sacrifices, like giving up sales, at the behest of the government, was not difficult for the firms and Confucian harmony could be attained anywhere.

Second, life-time employment and cordial manager–worker relationships also have an economic rationale. When Japan was industrializing in the 1950s and 1960s, master and apprentice relationship still existed. This relationship helped bind the skilled worker to the firm, *a fortiori* because this was a period of skilled labor shortage. However, the majority of other workers and female workers had no employment security. Trade unions, other than company unions, did develop but they had to remain weak because the labor force was divided into long-term, potentially long-term, and casual workers, and because there were large volumes of unskilled and semi-skilled workers. Since productivity gains were rapid and were being shared with the workforce, their living standards grew steadily. This took the wind out of the sails of the trade union movement. The old customs of nonmonetary incentives as well as monetary rewards kept the worker–manager relationship nonconfrontational (Hirono 1988).

Third, the three reasons why domestic savings have remained high have already been explained. Fourth, the seniority pay system began to change in the 1970s. Firms have increasingly started paying on the basis of merit rather than on the basis of seniority.

Some clairvoyantly thought-out patterns of industrial organization and economic behavior enormously strengthened Japan's economic base. These patterns are far from being old traditions. They grew up over the past 30 years and include the following:

1. It started a microelectronics-based industrial revolution and laser control of production processes. It reduced the need for production-line workers, increased flexibility in manufacturing, reduced costs and gave Japan a competitive edge over other countries. Japan could apply the new manufacturing technology because it produced more electrical engineers than any other OECD country (Vogel 1986).

2. It has rapidly expanded its R&D investment in terms of manpower and money for the development of new electronics-related areas and new materials and products in order to develop new business areas. After the *endaka*, they were spurred on further in the same direction by economic restructuring and fear of losing international economic competitiveness due to the yen's strength against other major currencies. All through the 1980s, Japan had the largest industrial robot population in the world. In 1990, it was 274,210 in Japan, 41,304 in the U.S., 28,240 in Germany and 12,500 in Italy. France and the U.K. came next with 8,551 and 6,418 robots, respectively, operating in their industries.[7] According to a U.S. National Science Foundation study, Japan had achieved parity in semiconductor technology, silicon product technology and high-definition television by 1989 and was pulling ahead in superconductivity research.[8] This commitment to R&D reinforced a well-established industrial foundation and went a long way in making the economic superstructure sounder than that of other competing economies.

3. Subcontracting is another distinctive Japanese practice which is widely used in Japan. Because of difficulties of diversification, firms tended to specialize narrowly and therefore were generally smaller than their Western counterparts. However, by supplying parts or sub-assemblies, they became vertically integrated in the system. It allowed them the benefits of specialization without the drawbacks of excessive size.

4. Shareholders' rights mattered less in Japan than in other major industrial economies. In joint-stock companies, there is always a potential for conflict between the shareholders who own assets and the company as a group of people having their own objectives. In Japan, shareholders take the back seat because stocks are traditionally held for capital gains not for earnings from dividends. Institutional investors hold stocks to cement other relations with it, like managing its pensions, lending in times of need and acting as large buyers or suppliers. This has two important consequences: (a) firms are free to plough back a higher proportion of their earnings and short-term profit fluctuations concern them less; and (b) there is a near-impossibility of buying and selling firms on the stock market. Consequently growth and diversification in Japan is more gradual than in other major industrial economies where firms often tend to expand and diversify by buying out competitors or even firms in entirely different industries. In Japan, therefore, firms focus on incremental improvements in their own production and profits (Economist Newspaper Ltd, 1983).

5. The *kanban* system, or the zero defect movement, has made Japanese products extremely competitive in world markets. Under the *kanban* system program and schemes for improvements in work methods were established in various industries to suit their specific needs. Larger firms encourage and assist their subcontractors to adopt improved work methods constantly and reduce the unit cost of production. Also, government has devised assistance schemes for small business enterprises to adopt the *kanban* system.

It is time to answer the clutch of questions we asked, at the beginning of this section, regarding the uniqueness of practices and institutions. If by unique we mean a distinctive characteristic or practice, yes, these were unique practices and institutions profitably used in Japan during its postwar economic evolution. They were born as perceptive, rational and pragmatic situational responses and immensely facilitated successful operation of the economy on neo-classical economic lines.

If by unique we imply being without a like or equal or matchless, no, they were not unique because several of them have been used in the other Western, East Asian or now Southeast Asian economies in one form or the other with varying degree of success. A constant of Japaneseness about them is hard to vindicate. However, there are two Japanese institutions that played a vital role, were distinctive to Japan and have remained by and large matchless. Only a scanty resemblance of their roles can be seen elsewhere. They are the MITI and the *keiretsu*—a closely tied structure of industrial and financial corporations.

Noted scholars like Edward Chen (1979) and Hugh Patrick (1977) credited private individuals and enterprises for Japanese economic growth, who, in their view, exploited the opportunities provided by free markets while the government created an environment of growth. Their claims lacked convincing arguments. If one examines the role of the MITI, their claims ring more hollow. MITI has long been considered the most effective economic bureaucracy in the world. It comprises the most cerebral of Japanese bureaucrats, the *creme de la creme*. For a long time, it had an absolute control over *sangyo seisaku* or industrial policy, although now large enterprises are known to challenge it. MITI saw the creation of "those powerful interests in the economy that favor shift of energy and resources into new industrial and economic activities" as its primary duty. It was convinced that market forces alone would never succeed in producing the shifts. It used familiar tools to implement its industrial policy. For instance, on the protection side, it used discriminatory tariffs, preferential commodity taxes, import and foreign exchange restrictions and discretionary foreign currency allocations. For growth purposes, it used low interest financing of targeted industries through government financial organs, subsidies, special amortization benefits, duty drawbacks on capital equipment, the licensing of imported technology, and the provision of industrial parks and infrastructure facilities for business (Johnson 1982). MITI worked closely with big business and perfected a system of "nurturing" new industrial sectors. It was called *ikusei* and included the following steps:

1. Formulating basic industrial policies based on a close examination of trends
2. Promoting the selected sectors and financing them through cheap Japan Development Bank loans and when needed making foreign currency allocations
3. Facilitating technology imports
4. Granting accelerated depreciation allowances for strategic industries
5. Creating cartels to regulate competition and coordinate investment

MITI's Industrial Structure Council, a joint government–industry advisory body, coordinated *ikusei*.

In the case of many late starters, the state took on itself the developmental function. Japan was no different. The operation of MITI, as stated above, and other economic ministries turned Japan into a developmental state. Japan, *à la* Chalmers Johnson, is a plan-rational state as against a market-rational state like the United States. In the former, the government gives precedence to an industrial policy while in the latter it may not even exist. Thus, Japan grew as a developmental plan-rational state, where industrial policy was designed and implemented by the powerful and talented MITI bureaucracy. This system depends upon the existence of a widely agreed upon set of overarching goals for the society. For instance, for Japan the overarching goals *vide ut supra* were growth, growth with stability and catching up with the West. When a consensus on goals exists, the plan-rational system can well outperform the market-rational one, as Japan outperformed all the other OECD economies. To be sure, MITI was the font of a large majority of ideas on economic growth and industrialization and played a role of unique significance, but it cannot be considered a source of all the bright ideas. Sony and Honda succeeded despite having tenuous ties with MITI. Also, the many-faceted participation of the MITI leads one to believe that the Japanese economic model was over deterministic because the MITI seems to be virtually behind every significant event. Was there nothing left for private initiatives? Were Edward Chen and Hugh Patrick completely wrong? Hardly, any casual observer can see that a vigorous private economy did and does exist, that market forces operate almost freely and that they picked the signal from the MITI to grow in the direction indicated by it. MITI's intervention in the market did not smother them, if anything, it was market-conforming intervention.

Rapid growth provoked "excessive competition" in Japan which tended to work in favor of large firms because they could capitalize on their scale of economies and internalize important externalities. Their finances were in generally sounder shape. Because of this reason, firms formerly affiliated to the prewar *zaibatsu* were re-integrated anew as *keiretsu*. There were six of these groups. The difference between them and *zaibatsu* is that they are essentially horizontally integrated groups having overtones of oligopolies, while the *zaibatsu* system was vertically integrated. A *keiretsu* is a loose federation of independent firms, clustered around a bank and a general trading company. Cross-shareholding is common among the members of a *keiretsu*. The group members are provided priority funds by the core bank of the group. Also, trading companies like Mitsubishi and Mitsui are flush with funds and have hundreds of subsidiaries (Fujigane and Ennis 1990). The *keiretsu* system evolved out of the old *zaibatsu* system because of a strong economic rationale. The stability of long-term relationships between firms promoted by the system contributed to free flows of information, tightly coordinated production schedules, wide dissemination of technology and made long-term strategic planning more meaningful. Prima facie it did appear to be a closed organizational system but it allowed Japan to produce higher quality goods at lower prices and enhanced its competitiveness in the international markets.[9] This is not a trivial contribution of the *keiretsu* system.

21.7 Corporate Strategy and Structure

The foregoing exposition is likely to lead one to believe that the striking performance of the Japanese economy was essentially due to macroeconomic reasons. However, the role of business corporations, or the *kaisha*, was no less significant in building up Japan's competitiveness and enabling Japan to acquire a dominant position in a respectable array of industries. In several industries, *kaisha* rose from the debris of the war, like the Phoenix, to hold leading or important positions. In several industries, Western firms find it hard to compete against Japanese firms. In several major sectors like auto, steel, electrical appliances, electronics, construction equipment, photography, semiconductor, and mainframe computers, Japanese firms are the market leaders or among the largest in the world. This leadership role is not limited to manufacturing. Japanese firms also lead in services sectors like banking, insurance, telecommunications and airlines.

Japanese firms operate in a hierarchical and disciplined manner under their *keiretsu* arrangement. Many of them, certainly the successful ones, have a growth bias which has a imprint over their behavior pattern. They display a strong, unfaltering commitment to the pursuit of growth and are known to create capacity ahead of demand. Prices are not set at the level that the market can bear but at the lowest level to fit the available production capacity. Costs are programmed to come down to support the pricing policies, and investments constantly rise in keeping with the projected demand (Abegglen and Stalk 1985). When the market response is strong, the *kaisha* adopt "doubling strategies" which enable them to double capacity and output in a short span of two to four years. The *kaisha* with a strong growth bias are also known to step up output and investment when the market is weak. In this case product variety is increased, prices are cut and distribution is expanded. Some of the Western companies also behave like a *kaisha* with a growth bias, like Apple Computer and IBM.

Invariably, *kaisha* define their goals in terms of volume and market shares so that fixed investment costs (like labor) can be met without any problem. But it also reflects their belief in scale economies and an intense desire to outperform rivals. Indeed, there are variations in responses to a competitor's initiatives. Some *kaisha*, while driving for volume, may not aim at market dominance. Others may try to differentiate themselves by matching their competitors' product. However, their competitor's initiatives hardly ever go unresponded.

Once a comparative advantage and competitive advantage is located, it is exploited to the fullest. Initially, low-cost manufacturing was used as competitive tool. Low wages allowed Japanese firms to be keenly competitive in textiles and shipbuilding. When wages rose to international levels, new weapons like product line variety, high quality, and technological innovation, were found. A strong belief in R&D and in the most modern facilities and equipment has helped *kaisha* sharpen their competitiveness. With emphasis on R&D, over the years *kaisha* have succeeded in creating a technology-based comparative advantage (Porter 1990). This turn of events was natural because most top managers were technically trained, and therefore, had the advantage of having a technically oriented perspective. Consequently, as alluded to in another context, investment in the key, leading-edge technologies has been on the rise since the early 1980s. Due to this mode of operation, successful *kaisha* were able to develop major positions in the international markets since the mid-1960s, in products ranging from ball bearing, forklifts and machine tools to a large array of high technology products like computer hardware, robots and unmanned production systems.

21.8 The International Role

21.8.1 The Perception Gap

When Japan acquired the appellation of economic "superpower" in the early 1970s, it was confounded, nonplussed and did not recognize its position and power in the world economy. Perhaps because of the rapidity of growth, Japan could not adjust to its new status right away. While Japan did not consider a powerful nation, to the rest of the world, its new found economic status was a stark reminder of its economic prowess. This created a perception gap, which was to endure. Refusing to recognize its place in the international community, Japan remained wrapped up in itself, paying attention only to matters that affected it directly and judging them entirely in term of their impact on Japan (Okita 1990). In 1978, Japan's per capita income was close to that of the U.S. Its current account surplus was US$16.5 billion while the U.S. deficit stood at the same level. Japan's economy was growing and so was its significance in the international economy. Yet, the perception gap persisted. Japan remained economically strong but internationally passive. The society had single-mindedly devoted its energy to developing economically and becoming the most competitive in the world. It seemed that like the Venetian and the Dutch of the mediaeval period, Japan envisioned becoming only a unidimensional economic power. As Japan become more economically successful, this notion strengthened.

As set forth earlier, the Japanese economy entered a new phase of maturity characterized by moderate growth rates over the 1970s. For the decade of the 1980s, its new GDP growth rate averaged at 4.4 percent. Forecasting exercises put the future growth rates at the same or lower levels. According to one such exercise the Japanese economy is to grow at the rate of 4.5 percent over the 1990–2000 period and at 3.7 percent over 2000–10 (Japan Center for Economic Research 1992). In 1990, world GDP was US$23 trillion. If the future exchange rates for all countries against the dollar are taken as being determined by their purchasing power parities, the forecast GDP of the world for the year 2000 comes to US$44.4 trillion and for 2010 $91.3 trillion. Another forecast (Sekiguchi 1991) which stopped at 2000, estimated it at $41.7 trillion, not very far from the first forecast. The 2010 GDP of the world is four times the 1990 GDP and may appear inexplicably inflated. However, if one looks back, world GDP rose from $3.7 trillion to $23 trillion over the 1970–90 period. The forecast exercise takes the world GDP rising in real terms by a factor of 1.8 and the global wholesale prices in dollars terms rising by a factor of 2.2. Therefore, the nominal GDP over the 1990–2010 period will increase by a factor of 4. In the years 2000 and 2010, the U.S. will continue to be the leading economic power, with Japan coming closer to it. In 1990, Japan's GDP was 12.8 percent of the world GDP, in 2000 it was forecast to be 16.7 percent and in 2010 17.5 percent. This means that the importance of the Japanese economy will continue to grow. Despite some possibility of a labor shortage and continuing economic friction, the Japanese economy is expected to continue on its growth path. The per capita GDP of Japan was forecasted to be US$57,786 in the year 2000, the highest in the world. This forecast was made with the yen/dollar exchange rate of 120.90. Japan's external surplus has been projected to decline due to currency appreciation against the major currencies, domestic wage hikes and further growth in manufactured imports due to the opening of domestic markets and the rising strength of the yen. Standardized manufactured imports will rise more than other manufactured imports and the Asia-Pacific economies will be Japan's most likely source of imports. In addition, a labor shortage and the yen's appreciation will force the domestic economy to further shift away from the traded goods to the non-traded goods sectors and to resort to offshore production. It happened perceptibly after *endaka*. Imports of agricultural products and foods will rise with the decrease in domestic production.

Notwithstanding the fact that the external surplus may dip, as the forecasting exercise revealed, Japan's GDP will be absolutely and relatively larger in the foreseeable future. It has to see and perceive that the world of the future will be led not so much by military might as by economic and technological power. Economic power can potentially sway the world and have lasting influence on several areas of international life. In the post-cold war world, when the international economy is measuring the peace dividend, economic principles will have a greater say in the world than ever in the past. The Japanese society has to begin to believe that the language of economic principles is the language of rational and optimal resource allocation, profits and living standards (Fujii 1989). It transcends national boundaries, cultural differences and race relations. Therefore, in an increasingly interdependent world of tomorrow, Japan will have an enormous role to play. Its internationally-minded opinion leaders like Okita (1990) and Morita (1993) have exhorted Japan to take its commensurate place on the international stage and perform like a global actor. Being stage shy for too long may not help Japan retain its superpower status. It is never too late for Japan to change its perception of itself.

The U.S. is, and will continue to be, the dominant economic and strategic power. However, its relative economic decline compared with Japan and the large European economies will entail an erosion of its "rule making" authority or in somewhat coarse language, the end of the *Pax Americana*. This assigns Japan an opportunity to plan an increasing role in the Asia-Pacific and in international economic affairs. To be sure, Japan is not destined to attain hegemony status. For that matter, no single nation could attain the preeminence attained by the U.S. in the postwar period. However, time is ripe for Japan to assume Asia-Pacific economic leadership and be one of the leading lights of the multipolar or pluricentric world of today.

21.8.2 Role in the Asia-Pacific

Japan has been playing a role of increasing significance in the growth and industrialization of the Asian newly industrializing economies (ANIEs) as well as helping the ASEAN grow fast. The economic structure that has developed in the Asia-Pacific in the recent past worked as follows. Capital and intermediate products were received by these country groups from Japan which facilitated transfer of Japanese technology to them. The output of these countries was exported largely to the U.S. and to Japan, the EC and the other countries of the Asia-Pacific region. Thus, the U.S. played the role of a significant export absorber for these two country groups while Japan became an important supplier. In the first half of the 1980s, these economies recorded strong export driven growth. It was largely due to Japan-aided supply-side developments, particularly in capital accumulation and technology transfer (Watanabe 1988). To a great extent this growth had depended on the U.S. for import demand, in that, it was assisted by the U.S. deficits. This pattern is evidently unsustainable because the U.S. deficit has declined. Takenaka (1991) developed an econometric model of the global economy to see the effects of a 2 percent drop in the U.S. GNP on the economic growth in the Asia-Pacific region. Since these economies have a large dependence on the U.S. market, the deflationary effect on them will be large. Korea and Malaysia will experience a contraction of 4.6 percent and 4.4 percent, respectively, in their economies. Singapore GNP will contract by 3.4 percent and Thailand by 2.6 percent. Likewise, Indonesia and Japan will experience a deflation of 1.4 percent and 1 percent, respectively. As opposed to this, a 2 percent expansion of the Japanese economy will have a substantial impact on these economies. But Japan cannot pick up the slack and compensate for a decline in the U.S. demand totally. The expansionary fiscal policy followed by Japan since 1987 has helped inflate demand.

By what degree the Japanese markets will be able to replicate the role of the U.S. markets for the Asia-Pacific countries will essentially depend on the success of structural adjustment measures affecting consumer goods markets and the removal of whatever NTBs that still persist. A reference needs to be made again to post *endaka* import escalation, particularly the rise in manufactured imports. Imports from the ANIEs doubled over 1986–88. This trend was assisted by changes in the exchange rates of the Asia-Pacific countries after the *endaka*. Although the extend of change varied from country to country, the general direction was as follows: (a) relatively mild appreciation against the US dollar, and (b) significant depreciation against the yen. The second change helped bring about the horizontal division of labor between Japan and the Asia-Pacific countries.

New patterns of outsourcing and original equipment manufacturing (OEM) with the ANIEs increased and so did intra-industry trade. It may take time to establish a similar relationship between Japan and ASEAN but it is already under way (Noguchi 1988). While these trends will affect the basic nature of the impact of Japan's economic policies and business cycles on the Asia-Pacific countries, they are also of vital importance for Japan's future. Although market forces are responsible for these trends, there are certain nonmarket developments that are still forcing Japan to make retrograde motion. For instance, Korean steel products were held off by Japan and as recently as June 1989 Korea announced imposing VERs on shipments of knitwear to Japan. Another example is protection of the agriculture sector, where Japan has enormous comparative disadvantage. This protection has continued despite *Keidanren*'s, Japan's federation of economic organizations, vocal opposition. If Japan wishes to be the trade policy leader for the region, dispelling these impediments is a small cost.

Japan is highly susceptible to bilateral political and economic leverage from the U.S. since it has a special relationship with the U.S. and the U.S. has also been Japan's largest trade partner. Japanese negotiators have acceded too easily to U.S. demands for greater market access to Japanese beef and chicken markets. This had a trade diversion effect and adversely affected exports of countries like Australia and Thailand. This was also a case of clear compromise of Article 1 of the GATT. At first sight, Japan's move appeared correct but it turned out to be an abrogation of the international trade discipline as well as injurious to the regional economies. As a future regional leader, this should be a lesson to Japan, something never to be repeated.

The deep-seated rancor of the past in the Asia-Pacific region against Japan has faded away. In April 1992, the *Nihon Keizai Shimbun* conducted an opinion survey among the corporate managers and academics of China, South Korea, Taiwan, Hong Kong, Singapore, Malaysia, Thailand, Indonesia, the Philippines and Australia.[10] According to 70 percent of respondents, Japan should play the role of regional leader in the Asia-Pacific region. On the question of what form Japan's regional leadership should take, investment in the region topped the list with 26.7 percent, followed by market opening and greater provision of technical assistance, including technology transfer.

21.8.3 International Economic Leadership

Growing into an economic superpower has generated special patterns of relationships with the rest of the world economy as well as new perspectives for the Japanese. The Japanese need to locate a leadership role within the pluralist structure of world economic power, while representing the broader global interests of the Asia-Pacific region. Japan's international economic interaction has expanded over the years and has diversified in every field. Its relationship, both macroeconomic and microeconomic, with the other industrialized economies has deepened considerably. Under the stable postwar system governed by GATT and the International Monetary Fund (IMF), Japan established strong ties with other economic areas. The deepening interdependence has enhanced the influence of the Japanese economy on other economies and vice versa. For instance, Japan's fiscal and monetary policies will have a pervasive effect on the industrial environment in other economies. Analogously, changes in the other countries will imminently affect Japan. As the international financial and capital markets are becoming increasingly integrated through deregulation of the domestic market, they will influence each other through exchange rates, interest rates as well as capital movements. Thus, the deepening of interdependence has made macroeconomics policy coordination under collective economic management all the more important, if not indispensable. Japan needs to become a partner in this collective management exercise. In this respect, the Plaza and the Louvre accords show that Japan has made a steady headway. In future, Japan's role in coordinated intervention in exchange markets will have to continue.

The domain of international public goods *inter alia* includes economic assistance, refugee relief, maintaining and lubricating the systems of free trade, international investment and international finance. The supply of these goods in the international system is not assured by any government body and is, therefore, not so well institutionalized. The supply is undertaken or regulated by either supranational organizations or by countries willing and capable of assuming the burden. If Japan sees itself as one of the principal supporters of the collective management system, it will have to actively assume the burden of providing international public goods as well as work for the maintenance of a stable international economic system. This will not only ensure Japan's future prosperity but also stable growth of the international economy (Murakami and Kosai 1986). The relationship will be symbiotic. Furthermore, active involvement in the global collective management system will mean making a commitment to harmonize national economic strategy with international interests, which in turn may call for reforms and adjustment of the domestic systems, somewhat on the lines of the Maekawa committee recommendations.

The four domains of public goods in which Japan can step in forthwith or step up the ongoing involvement are:

1. During the high growth era, Japan had benefited immensely from free trade. Now that the GATT discipline has eroded considerably and the Uruguay Round has been floundering after collapsing once, Japan's support for the GATT, in general, as an institution will rejuvenate free trade. Although it is too late, it would have been ideal for Japan to play the same role in the Uruguay Round as the U.S. did during the Kennedy Round. Now with the U.S. back-tracking, turning protectionist, Japan needs to move forward and support the free trade system in the manner in which the U.S. had supported it over the 1950s and 1960s.

2. Enhance mutually beneficial direct investment, particularly in the developing economies. It will promote the transfer of production and skills and put Japanese economic and industrial vitality to work in the world at large.

3. Since Japanese industries are well-known for their prowess in applied research,

science- and technology-related exchanges at various levels (such as student, researcher, technologist and business leader exchanges) need to be stepped up.

4. In the late 1980s, Japan became the largest donor country in the world. It can further its involvement with the developing economies by lending support to their fragile trade structure and make their former slogan of "trade, not aid" meaningful. This endeavor will also integrate the developing economies better into the international economies. Problem-ridden developing economies can be helped in their debt-related and structural adjustments–related endeavors through the Bretton Woods institutions. A great deal of scope exists for enlarging this channel of support for the developing economies.

21.9 Conclusion

The U.S. rendered assistance in reconstructing and rehabilitating the Japanese economy. It applied several reform measures. The Dodge plan was formulated to stabilize the economy. Japan experienced its first boomlet during the Korean War. During the same decade two more booms followed. Japan's savings and investment rates were much higher that those in other industrial countries. The household saving rates were particularly high and met the large investment needs of the corporate sector. The economy was determined not to rely much on external finances for growth. Large dosages of investment renewed the old capital stock and created new capital stock, which in turn, raised labor productivity as well as the efficiency of capital.

While planning industrialization, first priority was accorded to basic industries like iron and steel, and heavy and chemical industries which had some prewar base. Industries that were considered unsuitable were eliminated. Modernization and technological upgrading in the manufacturing sector continued constantly. Next, development of consumer durable goods such as automobiles, electrical appliances and electronics was emphasized. A well-developed basic sector, like steel, helped in the growth of the consumer durable industries. Japan successfully absorbed western technology, first with the help of Western engineers and then through the efforts of its well-trained, technology conscious managers and labor force. A great deal of attention was paid to R&D. Technological advancement showed through in industrial value-added. Japan opted for export-led growth out of sheer necessity. It was one of the two countries that benefited the most from the liberalization of international trade under the aegis of the GATT. Its exports grew at a staggering pace. By the mid-1960s, Japan had had a decade-and-a-half of brisk growth and in recognition of its status as an advanced economy, it was made a member of the OECD in 1964. The following five years turned out to be a period of record-setting growth.

The economy became exceedingly competitively in several product lines and Japan became successful, if somewhat aggressive, exporter. The importing countries found the loss of their own markets as well as the loss of their third country markets disconcerting. Dumping and unfair trade practice charges became frequent.

VERs, OMAs and other protectionist measures began to be applied against Japanese exports. Japan's own record of market liberalization was poor. By the early 1970s, Japan had grown into the second largest economy in the world exporting large volumes of an array of products. The 1973–74 oil-price hike had a massive adverse affect on the oil-based Japanese economy. Japan's era of high growth ended and one of moderate growth began. This was not entirely due to the oil shock. The economy was, however, faced with a dilemma. It had grown so large that its export expansion, which was faster than world trade, was resented and restricted by other industrial economies. Economic growth in Japan had become closely tied to exports at a time when world trade had lost steam. This is not to say that the economy had lost its vitality. Its efficacious manufacturing base and technological prowess were as strong as they were in the high growth era and it survived the two recessions, of the mid-1970s and the early 1980s, much better than the other industrial countries.

Japan's current account surpluses began to rise in the early 1980s, peaking at 4.5 percent of the GNP. The undervalued yen was squarely blamed for this by the other industrial economies. The Plaza Accord attempted to bring the surpluses down by appreciating the yen in an internationally coordinated manner with the other SDR currencies. The yen appreciation created a year long *endaka* recession in Japan but the economy was pulled out of it by domestic demand and a very high rate of investment. The economy entered an upswing of the business cycle which became the longest lasting boom in Japan's postwar economic history. *Endaka* changed both the production structure and the trade structure. The economy became domestic-demand-oriented instead of export-oriented. Its imports increased enormously, particularly the import of manufactures, and the axis of trade structure changed from vertical to horizontal. The restructuring of the economy was helped by low interest rates, which assisted in softening the deflationary effect of the currency appreciation.

Although the liberalization of the trade regime began in 1960, it was done in a very slow manner which rankled Japan's trade partners. Joining the Kennedy Round was the first firm-footed step. Yet, several NTBs continued to obstruct imports. From time to time Japan took measures to dismantle trade barriers, like offering to implement three lists of such measures in the early 1980s. It also has an excellent record of implementing the Tokyo Round recommendations. The post-Plaza yen appreciation also gave a tremendous boost to imports. In addition, the SII negotiations with the U.S. were not only wide-ranging but also addressed some deep changes in Japan's traditional market practices. Likewise, Japan's highly regulated financial markets were liberalized in the 1980s to a great extent.

It was widely believed that there existed some culturally derived unique characteristics of the Japanese society that were responsible for high productivity gains in the economy. However, there are few such practices which cannot be explained by the superior working of market forces and "situational" responses and motivations. Perhaps, two exceptions to this could be the two important institutions, namely, the MITI and the *keiretsu. Kaisha* or business corporations, played a significant role in making the economy competitive in a respectable array of industries. The striking performance of the economy cannot entirely be attributed to macroeconomic factors. The successful ones among the *kaisha* were able to develop major positions in the international markets since the mid-1960s in products ranging from ball bearing, forklifts and machine tools to a large array of high technology products.

Although Japan acquired the appellation of economic "superpower" in the early 1970s, it did not consider itself a powerful nation and refused to take its rightful place in the international economy. It remained wrapped up in itself, paying attention only to matters that affected it directly and judging them entirely in terms of their impact on Japan. The rest of the world expected it to play a role commensurate to its economic status in the internal arena. Its absolute and relative strengths in the international economy are growing and in two decades it is projected to be a larger economic power, although the U.S. will continue to be the largest economy and geopolitical power. Two significant roles await Japan:

1. regional economic leadership role in the Asia-Pacific region
2. international leadership role within the pluralist structure of the world economy, which will entail being ready to bear the burden of providing international public goods

Notes

1. It was named after the first mythical Emperor of Japan.
2. Iwato was the cave in which the goddess of the sun, Amaterasu, hid because she was offended by the misdeeds of her younger brother.
3. It was named after the god who created the Japanese archipelago by dipping his spear into the sea.
4. This part draws on (Das 1993).
5. For a detailed treatment see Das (1993: Ch. 1).
6. GATT statistics cited by Kojima (1977: Table 1.3).
7. The industrial robot population figures were obtained from the Japan Industrial Robot Association in Tokyo.
8. This survey was cited in Tatsuno (1990: Ch. 1).
9. For the detailed treatment refer to Helon (1991).
10. The results of this survey were reported in the *Nikkei Weekly*, April 25, 1992.

References

Abegglen, J. C. and G. Stalk, 1985, *Kaisha: The Japanese Corporations*, Basic Books, New York.

Balassa, B., 1986, "Japan's Trade Policies," *Weltwirtschaftliches Archiv*, 112(4): 745–90.

Balassa, B. and M. Noland, 1988, *Japan in the World Economy*, Institute for International Economics, Washington, DC.

Bank of Japan, 1987, *Adjustment of the Japanese Economy under Strong Yen*, Special Paper No. 149, Tokyo.

———, 1988, *Balance of Payments Adjustment Processes in Japan and the United States*, Special Paper No. 162, Tokyo.

Barbone, L., 1988, "Import Barriers: An Analysis of Time-Series Cross-Section Data," *OECD Economic Studies*, 11 (Autumn): 44–80.

Bergsten, C. F. and W. R. Cline, 1988, *The United States–Japan Economic Problems*, Institute for International Economics, Washington, DC.

Chandler, C., 1991, "Japanese GNP Grew in Quarter at Rate of 11.2 Percent," *Asian Wall Street Journal*, June 19.

Chen, E., 1979, *Hypergrowth in Asian Economies*, Holmes & Meier Publishers, New York.

Das, Dilip K., 1993, *The Yen Appreciation and the International Economy*, Macmillan, London.

Denison, E. F. and W. K. Chung, 1976, *How Japan's Economy Grew so Fast?* Brookings Institution, Washington, DC.

Economic Planning Agency, *Annual Report on National Accounts*, Tokyo, various issues.

———, 1992, *Economic Survey of Japan 1991–1992*, Tokyo.

The Economist, 1991, "What Makes Yoshio Invent," January 12, 71.

Economist Intelligence Unit, 1991, *Japan in the 1990s*, Special Report No. 2083, London.

Economist Newspaper Ltd, 1983, *Japan*, London.

Emmott, B., 1992, "Japan's Global Reach after the Sunset," *Pacific Review*, 5(3): 232–40.

Fugii, H., 1992, "The Growing Weight of Services in Economic Growth," *Japan Research Quarterly*, Autumn: 28–34.

Fujigane, Y. and P. Ennis, 1990, "Keiretsu: What They Are Doing," *Tokyo Business Today*, 26–30.

Fujii, H., 1989, "Japan's Foreign Policy in an Interdependent World," *Japan Review of International Affairs*, 3(2): 119–44.

Gibney, F., 1992, *The Pacific Century*, Maxwell Macmillan International, New York.

Hayashi, F., T. Ito, and J. Slamrod, 1987, *Housing Finance Imperfections and National Savings: A Comparative Simulation Analysis of the U.S. and Japan*, National Bureau of Economic Research Working Paper No. 2272, Cambridge, MA.

Helon, A., 1991, "The Nature and Competitiveness of Japan's Keiretsu," *Journal of World Trade*, 99–131.

Hirono, R., 1988, "Japan: Model for East Asian Industrialization," in H. Hughes (ed.), *Achieving Industrialization in East Asia*, Cambridge University Press, Cambridge, pp. 241–59.

Horioka, C. Y., 1985, "A Survey of the Literature on Household Saving in Japan: Why is the Household Saving Rate so High in Japan?" Kyoto University, Kyoto, mimeo.

Ito, T., 1992, *The Japanese Economy*, MIT Press, Cambridge, MA.

Japan Center for Economic Research (JCER), 1992, *The Coming Multipolar Economy*, Tokyo.

Johnson, C., 1982, *MITI and the Japanese Miracle*, Stanford University Press, Stanford, CA.

Kahn, H., 1970, *The Emerging Superstate*, Prentice Hall, Englewood Cliffs, NJ.

Kazutomo, I., 1990, *Changes in the Japanese Economy*, Research Institute of International Trade and Industry, Discussion Paper No. 90, Tokyo.

Kodama, F., 1991, *Analysing Japanese Technologies: The Techno-paradigm Shift*, Printer Publishers, London.

Kojima, K., 1977, *Japan and a New World Economic Order*, Westview Press, Boulder, CO.

Kosai, Y., 1986, *The Era of High-Speed Growth*, University of Tokyo Press, Tokyo.

Kosai, Y. and Y. Ogino, *The Contemporary Japanese Economy*, Macmillan, London.

Lawrence, R. Z., 1987, "Imports in Japan: Closed Markets or Minds?" *Brookings Papers on Economic Activity*, 3(2): 517–54.

———, 1991, "How Open is Japan?" in P. Krugman (ed.), *Trade with Japan: Has the Door Opened Wider?* University of Chicago Press, Chicago, IL, pp. 168–210.

Lincoln, E. J., 1988, *Japan Facing Economic Maturity*, Brookings Institution, Washington, DC.

Ministry of International Trade and Industry (MITI), 1971, *The Basic Direction of Trade and Industry*, Tokyo.

Morita, A., 1993, "Japan Should Globalize on Its Own Initiative," *Nikkei Weekly*, January 28, 7.

Murakami, Y. and Y. Kosai, 1986, *Japan in the Global Community*, University of Tokyo Press, Tokyo.

Noguchi, Y., 1988, "Japan's Economic Policies and Their Regional Impact," in R. A. Scalapino et al. (eds.), *Pacific-Asian Economic Policies and Regional Interdependence*, University of California, Berkeley, CA.

Noland, M., 1990, "An Econometric Investigation of International Protection," Institute for International Economics, Washington, DC, mimeo.

Ohkawa, K. and H. Rosovsky, 1973, *Japanese Economic Growth in Trend Acceleration in the Twentieth Century*, Stanford University Press, Stanford, CA.

Okita, S., 1990, *Approaching the 21st Century: Japan's Role*, Japan Times, Tokyo.

Patrick, H., 1977, "The Future of the Japanese Economy," *Journal of Japanese Studies*, Summer: 230–59.

Patrick, H. and H. Rosovsky (eds.), 1976, "Japan's Economic Performance: An Overview," in *Asia's New Giant*, Brookings Institution, Washington, DC, pp. 1–46.

Porter, M. E., 1990, *The Competitive Advantage of Nations*, Macmillan, London.

Saxonhouse, G. R., 1983, "The Micro- and Macro-economics of Foreign Sales to Japan," in W. R. Cline (ed.), *Trade Policies in the 1980s*, Institute for International Economics, Washington, DC, pp. 259–304.

Sekiguchi, S., 1991, "The International Economy and Japan in 2000," Japan Center for Economic Research, Tokyo, mimeo.

Takenaka, H., 1991, "The Japanese Economy and the Pacific Development," in M. Ariff (ed.), *The Pacific Economy*, Allen & Unwin, Sydney.

Tatsuno, S. M., 1990, *Created in Japan*, Harper and Row, New York.

Vogel, E. F., 1986, "Pax Nipponica," *Foreign Affairs*, Spring: 752–67.

Watanable, T., 1988, "Japan, the U.S. and the NICs in the Age of Western Asia," *Toyo Keizai*, May (in Japanese), cited in Takenaka.

Yoshitomi, M., 1989, *Japan's Savings and External Surplus in the World Economy*, Occasional Paper No. 26, Group of Thirty, New York.

Chapter 22

Siang Ng and
Yew-Kwang Ng

THE EFFECTS OF CHINESE ECONOMIC REFORMS AND REGIONAL ECONOMIC COOPERATION

22.1 Introduction

After the Tiananmen incident, mainland China (simply China from here on) moved quickly through "the year of damage control" in 1990 (Shambaugh 1990) to a year of rather impressive growth (real GNP grew by 7 percent, total foreign trade grew by 18 percent, and foreign reserves grew by US$40 billion) in 1991. More recently, China has seen spectacular growth (12 percent in real GNP in 1992, 13.4 percent in real GNP in 1993 and 11.6 percent annual growth for the first half of 1994) and promises of more far-reaching economic reforms. After the pro-reform "whirlwind" created by the speeches made by Deng Xiaoping early in 1992, a proposal to build a socialist market economy was made at the Fourteenth Party Congress held in October 1992 (see section 22.5 for further details). Hong Kong commentators interpreted the "deeper reforms," the introduction of the share system, the adoption of the socialist market economy concept, and the further opening of China to foreign investment and joint ventures as "taking the capitalist road."

22.2 Some Effects of Reforms and the Opportunities for Trade and Investment

Changes effected by economic reforms in China since 1978 have been quite phenomenal. Since then, China's real GNP has been growing at an average rate in excess of 8 percent per year. The real GNP in 1994 was more than four times that of 1978. Thus, the stated objective of quadrupling GNP by the year 2000 was achieved six years ahead of schedule. Moreover, the economy is currently growing strongly (11.6 percent in the first half of 1994). The growth in foreign trade is even more spectacular, as shown in Table 22.1. According to an International Monetary Fund (IMF) projection, by the year 2000, China's foreign trade will be as large as that of Japan in 1990. Looking at more recent figures, this projection is likely to be far exceeded. In fact, by 1992 China had already become the eleventh most important trading nation in the world. (See Kueh (1992) for a recent analysis of the importance of foreign investment and trade in China.)

The failure of the communist system, the need to reform by adopting effectively "capitalist" methods and the success of such reforms helped to seal the fate of the disintegrated communist movements in Southeast Asia. Liberated from the threat

TABLE 22.1   Foreign trade of China (in billion US dollars, on a customs basis)

Year	Exports	Imports	Trade balance
1974	6.9	7.6	−0.7
1975	7.3	7.5	−0.2
1976	6.9	6.6	0.3
1977	7.6	7.2	0.4
1978	9.8	10.9	−1.1
1979	13.7	15.7	−2.0
1980	18.1	20.0	−1.9
1981	22.0	22.0	0
1982	22.3	19.3	3.0
1983	22.2	21.4	0.8
1984	26.1	27.4	−1.3
1985	27.4	42.2	−14.8
1986	30.9	42.9	−12.0
1987	39.4	43.2	−3.8
1988	47.5	55.2	−7.7
1989	52.5	59.1	−6.6
1990	62.1	53.4	8.7
1991	71.9	63.8	8.1
1992	85.0	80.6	4.4
1993	91.8	104.0	−12.2
1994	121.0	115.9	5.1
1995*	143.28	121.92	21.36

*Estimates based on actual figures for the first ten months.

of communism internally and externally, economies in this part of the world have been growing rapidly, increasing the prospect of lucrative trade and investment with East Asia for countries like Australia. In fact, such opportunities might be underestimated judged from the GNP figures alone, for the following reasons.

First, the GNP figures for China as well as those for its growth are probably gross underestimates of the true figures. The GNP figure was understated to begin with.[1] The understatement of the growth rates might also arise from the fact that a significant part of growth comes from the private sector which understates its growth for taxation purposes. (This factor probably more than offset factors contributing to overestimation. See Yeh 1992: 502n.) Recent visitors to China witnessing the spectacular spending abilities of the Chinese will find it hard to believe that it is a country with a per capita annual GDP (1993) of RMB 2648 (less than US$460 at the average 1993 official exchange rate and less than US$300 at the unofficial market rate). This is partly explained by the big disparities in per capita incomes between coastal and inland provinces, between cities and rural areas (discussed in Section 22.3), and between private proprietors, high officials, and those with lucrative sources of income over their formal salaries on the one hand and others who have to rely mainly on their low salaries on the other. However, it is difficult to believe that the understatement of the official GNP figure is not an important explaining factor. It has been estimated that there are now 70 million people with an annual income in excess of US$7,700 each, providing a big market for highly priced imports such as Rado watches at prices averaging US$1,700 each (Li 1992). Another estimate puts the number of millionaires as being in excess of a million (reported in *People's Daily*, Foreign Edition, March 11, 1993).

Secondly, the willingness to buy expensive imported goods cannot be explained alone by the fact that the true GNP figure is much higher. Even at an income many times that of US$7,700, we would not dream of spending US$1,700 on a single watch! The willingness of the Chinese consumers to do this may be explained by a number of factors, including a rampant desire for conspicuous consumption, perhaps as a psychological reaction to a long period of material deprivation. The tendency to regard imported goods as superior must also play a part. The incomplete security with respect to private property and the inadequate outlets for private investment are probably also accountable for the lavish consumption, especially by the Chinese traditional standard of thriftiness.

Thirdly, the opportunities for profitable investments have increased spectacularly now that China has adopted Western management and market oriented ways of doing things. A state enterprise in Shanghai entered into a joint venture with an English company. The state enterprise provided the original plant and employees. Well before the English company had been able to introduce any new technology, imported equipment, export avenues, and so on, its provision of a single managing director and the mere fact of the commencement of the joint venture reversed the collapse in profits of the state enterprise in the previous three years. All performance indicators increased sharply (S. M. Chen 1992). This incident indicates that a proper management system and a market orientation may be decisive. Foreign companies may be able to make good profits without even committing any substantial amount of investment.

Furthermore, the system of foreign trade will be significantly liberalized after 1993. This expected liberalization is related to China's attempt to gain admission to GATT (General Agreement on Tariffs and Trade). It is expected to include movements toward full convertibility of the renminbi or RMB (Chinese dollar or yuan) and decentralization of the authority for exports to the enterprise level, including enterprises involving foreign investment (Guo 1993).

While opportunities for trade and investment with China are ample and growing, there are also some important difficulties, including those of dealing with the Chinese bureaucracy. (On some practical experience on trade and investment in China, see Lai 1991.)

22.3   Rural–Urban Migration

Ever since the 1950s, the Chinese Communist Government has implemented and maintained a policy of urban–rural segregation which disallows agricultural residents and their descendants to stay permanently in cities or to find jobs in urban areas. "People in the cities enjoy special treatment in employment, public medical care, retirement security, housing and food subsidies, as well as cultural and educational advantages" (Yan 1990). The policy has been enforced by allocating coupons for foods and fuel to nonagricultural residents and prohibiting the commercial exchange of these coupons.

Some years after the reforms introduced in the late 1970s, agricultural residents began to break the rural–urban segregation policy by moving to urban areas looking for job opportunities. This trend is termed "blind flood" (also translated nonliterally as "floating population") in the Chinese press and regarded as a major problem. In fact, this rural–urban movement is certainly not blind but can be seen to be an inevitable consequence of the success of reforms. However, if the problem is not tackled properly, it may undermine the stability of the whole country.

The success of reforms leads to increases in agricultural productivity and higher per capita income. As per capita income increases, demand for agricultural products increases but less than proportionately (Engel's law). Given an unchanged proportion of people engaging in agricultural production, the increase in demand falls short of the increase in supply of agricultural products. There is thus a pressure to transfer resources (including the agricultural labor force) from primary to secondary and tertiary production activities which are concentrated in the urban areas. Thus, the rural–urban migration trend is a natural consequence of economic growth. The Chinese government has attempted to address the problem through the development of rural industries. This has alleviated the problem to some extent but not completely. There are scale of economies in the cities and most people prefer to live in cities. In countries with high per capita income, a small percentage of the population works in agricultural production and the majority of the population lives in major urban areas. In Australia, for example, more than one-third of all people live in Sydney and Melbourne.

Beyond the effect explained above (which is related to Engel's law), economic reforms and openness have also led to a relaxation of controls, the availability of more information, and higher mobility. The emergence of a rural–urban migration trend is thus not surprising. However, this does not mean that the migration can be permitted without control. There is some general agreement (even among those who are against the rural–urban segregation policy) that a sudden complete elimination of controls would lead to an unmanageable situation—"the flooding of the cities by rural people."

Before the communists rose to power, China did not have the rural–urban segregation policy. However, the rural people did not flood the cities even though the situation then was far from ideal in the countryside.[2] Why is the situation different now? It might be thought that this change is due to a big increase in population since then. However, the increase in population that China experienced was not really higher than the normal increases countries usually experience during peace time. Moreover, in areas like Taiwan and Japan where the population density is much higher, no segregation policy is being practiced. In our view, the answer lies in the following factor: the implementation of a rural–urban segregation policy over many decades has aggravated the rural–urban disparity in living standard. This disparity is only partly reflected in the ratio of wages of urban to rural enterprises (statistics on urban wages are more readily available from official sources since urban residents enjoy special advantages). Even concentrating on this ratio, it was as high as 2.08 in 1978. The success of reforms in agriculture reduced this ratio between 1978 to 1983, but the ratio has fluctuated around 1.65 since then until 1990 (see Table 22.2). More recent data show that the ratio has increased to near its pre-reform ratio of about 2. In terms of the expenditure income ratio between urban and rural residents, the figure of 2.54 in 1993 is in fact higher than that of 2.37 in 1978 (*Inside China Mainland*, 1994, 16 (April): 42).

The rural–urban segregation policy is not only extremely unfair,[3] it cuts against the requirement of economic efficiency since it impedes the movement of factors seeking higher returns. Even if we forget about fairness and examine the policy purely in terms of efficiency, the segregation policy is still questionable. If an agricultural resident wants to move to a city, on what ground can he or she be prevented from doing so? Presumably, the answer is that, due to congestion in the city, the movement will reduce the welfare of people in the city by reducing job availability and increasing the degree of congestion in public facilities. (On some other relevant factors, see Ng 1991.)

Many people, seeing that rural (or foreign) residents move to the city (migrate to a country) for jobs, reckon that such jobs would otherwise be available to local urban (local) residents and hence conclude that immigration reduces the job opportunities for local people. This is an incorrect conclusion which is based on

TABLE 22.2   Wage ratio between urban and rural enterprises

Year	Urban wages (RMB)	Wages of rural enterprises (RMB)	Ratio
1978	615	296	2.08
1979	668	367	1.82
1980	762	398	1.91
1981	772	440	1.75
1982	798	492	1.62
1983	826	543	1.52
1984	974	622	1.57
1985	1,148	726	1.58
1986	1,329	764	1.74
1987	1,459	909	1.61
1988	1,747	1,106	1.58
1989	1,935	1,230	1.57
1990	2,140	1,321	1.62

Source: Calculated from Zhang (1991: 6) which is based on official Chinese publication such as the *Statistical Yearbook of China*.

readily observable direct effects and ignores indirect effects. The usefulness of economic training is that it allows us also to see the indirect effects.

Some immigrants may take away jobs that would otherwise be available to local residents. However, immigration also increases job opportunities for local residents through:

1. increased demand for products (including housing) of the urban (domestic) economy
2. some entrepreneurial immigrants setting up enterprises employing local residents
3. some immigrants taking up jobs not readily (either due to lack of the required skill or lack of interest) filled by local residents, hence helping to create complementary jobs

If rural–urban and inter-country migrants only took away jobs but did not help to create jobs, cities and countries like Hong Kong and Australia would have over 90 percent unemployment. Studies that look into the effects of immigration on unemployment conclude that immigration does not increase unemployment (for example, Norman and Meikle 1985; Withers and Pope 1985).

In the presence of uncorrected external costs like road congestion, it is true that immigration, by increasing the unpriced usage of roads and other public facilities, may make existing residents worse off. However, this problem is due to the lack of efficient pricing. It might be argued that public facilities like roads are too costly to price. However, efficient road pricing may to a large extent be effected through petrol taxes. With appropriate pricing of public facilities, it can be shown that immigration, even if it increases the level of congestion and pollution, actually makes existing residents better off economically since the taxes paid by the new residents must exceed the additional congestion costs and pollution borne by existing residents (Clarke and Ng 1993).

It might be argued that the poor cannot afford to pay congestion and pollution taxes. However, this is confusing the problem of income distribution with that of efficient taxes to control pollution and congestion. Society may want to help the poor. However, instead of allowing a poor person not to pay say $1000 congestion taxes, it is better to give him $1000 cash and then require him to pay the congestion taxes. He may still find it worthwhile to stay in the city and use the facilities. But it is also possible that he may find the use of the facilities not worth the $1000 taxes and decide to reduce the usage or even move elsewhere. Everyone, whether rich or poor, has to pay for the costs of his consumption of goods or usage of facilities to make him take proper account of efficiency. Equality objectives are better achieved by the general tax/transfer policy rather than through specific subsidies on food or public facilities. While a progressive tax/transfer system may generate disincentive effects, a system of specific equality-oriented subsidies also has disincentive effects and has specific distortive effects, and is hence inferior. (See Ng (1984) for a full argument for "a dollar is a dollar.")

Due to the existing large rural–urban disparity, a sudden and complete dismantling of the rural–urban segregation policy is not feasible. However, both to achieve efficiency and fairness and to prevent the problem from getting out of hand as further reforms and liberalization progress, a policy of gradually narrowing the disparity is imperative. The success or otherwise in the implementation of such a policy will have a significant impact on the future political stability of China (see Section 22.7).

22.4   China and East Asian Economic Groupings

Chinese economic reforms have also helped to transform the former Soviet Union and to end the cold war between the East and the West. The various economies in the world now seem to be grouping themselves into three major trading blocs. The European bloc will comprise the EC and the European Free Trade Area. The East European countries including CIS (that is, the Commonwealth of Independent States, formerly the Soviet Union) or its constituents will likely be joining the European bloc after their successful transition to market economies. The U.S. is entering into a trading arrangement with Canada and Mexico to form the North American bloc. This leaves East Asia as a potential third bloc. While proposals like APEC (Asia-Pacific Economic Cooperation) and EAEC (East Asia Economic Caucus) have been floated, this third bloc is the least developed so far. The situation is further complicated by the fact that countries like the U.S. and Australia want to belong to more than one bloc. With the increasing importance of the Chinese economy and its foreign trade, China can be expected to play a significant role in the East Asia or the Asia-Pacific bloc. This is especially so since Hong Kong, a sizable economy and a major player in the international economic scene, will be returned to China by early 1997 and the prospect for a Chinese Economic Cooperation System (comprising the Mainland, Hong Kong, and Taiwan) looks good.

For Australia, the increasing importance of the East Asian connection is hardly debatable (Garnaut 1989). Recent figures show that 72.4 percent of Australia's exports of goods in the 1992/1993 financial year were directed to Asia and the South Pacific, compared with 60 percent three years earlier. Australia also enjoyed a trade surplus in trade with Asia. The share of Australian exports to mainland China, Taiwan, Hong Kong, South Korea and the six ASEAN countries (Malaysia, Singapore, Thailand, the Philippines, Indonesia, and Brunei) increased from 24 percent in the second half of 1989 to 33.2 percent in 1992/1993. Exports to these ten East Asian economies (1992/1993) far exceeded exports to Europe (12.34 percent), the United States and Canada (10.03 percent) combined. Exports to China, Hong Kong, Taiwan, and Korea increased by 63.51 percent to US$11.52 billion in 1992/3 compared to 1989/1990. In 1992/1993, mainland China became Australia's tenth largest export market. With China's two other economies (Hong Kong and Taiwan), China has become Australia's second largest export market (after Japan). (Figures in this paragraph were taken from *International Merchandise Trade, Australia*, March Quarter, 1994.)

The increasing importance of regional economic cooperation and the opposition by the U.S. to the EAEC raise the issue of the desirability of economic groupings. In academic economics, this issue has been analyzed in the literature on customs unions. (See Corden 1975 and 1986: Section 11 for surveys. See also Beladi and Samanta 1990; Parai and Yu 1989.) The basic message of this literature has been that the formation of a customs union involves both a desirable trade creation effect and an undesirable trade diversion effect such that the net effect is ambiguous and thus depends on specific cases.

Without challenging the traditional result, we think that a general proposition may be accepted.

> *Proposition*: Ignoring administrative costs, the formation of a non-inward looking customs union or other form of trade grouping may be taken as efficiency-improving from a world viewpoint at least in a probabilistic sense, in the absence of sufficient information to indicate otherwise.

Here, non-inward looking is defined to be the absence of an increase in the degree of external economic barriers to the outside world. A rigorous proof of this proposition may be suitable for a doctoral dissertation and is beyond the scope of this chapter.[4] However, the rationale for the proposition may be briefly sketched. Imagine that we start with a world of 128 countries each with heavy external economic barriers. As a first step, each pair of two neighboring countries then group themselves into a customs union. The world would then consist of 64 trading regions. If we repeat the process another six times (six steps), the world would become a completely unified market with no barriers. Assuming that inefficiencies created by external effects, and so forth are appropriately tackled by taxes/subsidies, we will then achieve the first best outcome. However, according to the customs union theory, all of the seven steps, except the first one, of the union formation process may be efficiency-reducing. In the absence of specific information, we do not know which one (or more) step(s) is the efficiency improving one. Nevertheless, since the seven steps taken as a whole must be efficiency-improving, in the absence of specific information, we may take each step as likely to be efficiency-improving, at least in a probabilistic sense.

The rationale for the proposition may also be seen in the reverse way. Suppose that it is proposed that Australia erect trade barriers between its various states. Obviously, virtually all economists would regard this as a very inefficient move which should be reversed. However, the reversal of the barriers is equivalent to the formation of a customs union. Looked in this way, the validity of the above proposition seems transparent. However, it has some significant implications. For one thing, provided a regional economic grouping is non-inward looking, the burden of proof lies with its opposer, not with its proponent, at least from the viewpoint of world efficiency.

For those who regard the above proposition and argument as trivial, consider the following argument. Obviously, the above argument on the validity of the proposition cannot be correct. In the whole argument, the proviso "non-inward looking" has not been or at least need not be invoked. (Thus, in the seven steps of union formation, if external barriers were doubled each time, the eventual outcome would still be first best.) If the argument were correct, the proposition would be true even for inward looking unions. This is obviously false. Hence, the argument must be incorrect.

We know how to refute the above argument so as to defend the validity of the proposition with respect to non-inward looking unions but not with respect to inward looking ones. However, we will not discuss here our refutation in order to make the reader think more about the proposition. The authors hope this will make the readers realize that the proposition is not trivial.

In the East Asian and Asia-Pacific contexts, it seems that either EAEC or APEC or both will be efficiency-improving provided they are not inward-looking, since there exist ample complementarities between the economies in these regions. (On the potential big gain from Asia-Pacific liberalization alone, see Stoeckel et al. 1990: xiii.) If the formation of an outward-looking EAEC will not hamper a broader grouping such as APEC, objections to it seem unfounded.

22.5   A Socialist Market Economy

The most remarkable aspect of the latest Party Congress in China (the Fourteenth, held in the middle of October 1992) is the formal proposal (advanced in the report by Jiang Zemin, the Party boss, at least formally; the ultimate power being still held by Deng Xiaoping) of building a "socialist market economy." Just before the Congress, there had been articles in the *People's Daily*, *Economic Daily* and other newspapers proposing and expounding on the concept of a market economy. The People's Press in Beijing also published a monograph entitled *Chinese Economists Discuss "Socialist Market Economy."*

The proposal to build a socialist market economy marks a further significant advance in the road of economic reforms. Before this Congress, the Chinese officially spoke of building a "socialist commodity economy." Why is the replacement of the word "commodity" by "market" an important advance? A "commodity economy" might merely entail producing goods and services for sale mainly under the system of public ownership and central planning. The coordination of the allocation of resources need not be mainly by the market. On the other hand, a "market economy" signifies a much smaller role for central planning and a greater consumer orientation not only in the sale of goods but also in the allocation of resources for the production of goods and services.

In his report to the Congress, Jiang said:

> The socialist market economic system we want to build is to enable the market, under the macro coordination and control of the socialist state, to have a fundamental role in the allocation of resources; to enable economic activities to follow the requirement of the law of value and to be consistent with changes in supply and demand. Through the function of the lever of prices and competition mechanism, allocate resources to places of higher efficiency. Provide pressures and motivation to enterprises in order to realise the survival of the fittest. Utilize the advantage of the market in its quicker responses to various economic signals to promote the timely coordination of production and demand (*China Daily*, October 12, 1992).

Such an economic system will be inconsistent with traditional central planning. For example, suppose the planned production of a certain good is X units but the supply and demand situation requires a much lower amount. Should the planned amount be abandoned or should supply and demand be ignored?

However, the proposed "market economy" is qualified by the requirement that it be "socialist." What does this mean? According to Jiang, "The socialist market economic system is united with the socialist fundamental system." This unification rests on three conditions. Firstly, "in the structure of ownership, it is mainly based on public ownership, including state ownership and collective ownership, supplemented by individual economy, private economy, and foreign investment." Secondly, the method of distribution is mainly based on "to each according to his/her labor," supplemented by other methods. Thirdly, state planning is an important instrument of macro-coordination and control.

The above three conditions ensure the socialist nature of the economy. However, they may be seen to be inconsistent with the spirit of a market economy as outlined by Jiang (above). Nevertheless, the actual degree of inconsistency is much smaller than might otherwise appear due to the following factors.

First, there is a subtle but very important change in the original Chinese wording for state enterprises. The term originally used, fully translated, is "state-managed enterprises." The new term used by Jiang in his report to the Party Congress is "state-owned enterprises." This signifies that, though state-*owned* enterprises will still remain the base of the economy, they may largely be managed by private entrepreneurs. Moreover, while the term "state ownership" may remain for a long time, the ownership rights of the state could effectively be reduced. For example, in many (former) British colonies, including Hong Kong and Australia, pieces of land are formally owned by the Queen but are held under very long-term or permanent leases by private individuals who have effectively all rights of normal ownership. This provides a model to which the Chinese may turn to in order to effectively have a private economy while retaining the public ownership in name only.

Secondly, Jiang's report talks about state planning as "an important instrument of macro coordination and control," not as the *main* instrument. One could argue that, even in an economy like the U.S. and Australia, government planning is an important instrument of macro coordination and control.

Thirdly, the insistence on socialism is partly a way of paying lip service to ideology and partly a way of achieving a compromise with the more conservative faction within the Party. While the actual effectiveness of the insistence on socialism will largely depend on which faction that dominates, the general tendency towards further reform and openness seems unlikely to alter in the foreseeable future. (See Section 22.6.)

Many commentators in Hong Kong regard the push for further reforms by Deng in early 1992 and the formal proposal of a socialist market economy as "taking the capitalist road" and "hanging the head of socialism while selling the meat of capitalism." They see this stance as being internally inconsistent. In our view, whether the new proposed market economy is consistent with socialism depends on the interpretation of "socialism." The official Chinese line is to regard public ownership, distribution in accordance to labor, and central planning as the essence of socialism. Strictly speaking, this interpretation of socialism is inconsistent with the requirement of a market economy. However, to some extent, the inconsistency can be and has been reduced, as mentioned above, by replacing public management with public ownership, and by interpreting central planning as an instrument rather than the main instrument of coordination. With respect to the method of distribution, a market economy really requires reward factors in accordance to the values of their marginal products rather than in accordance only to the amount of labor performed. However, before the 1950s, the official Chinese Communist interpretation of socialism with respect to the method of distribution was "to each in accordance to the value of his/her contribution" instead of the current (unchanged since the 1950s) "to each in accordance to his/her labor." Obviously, the former interpretation is more consistent with, or at least is more easily interpreted in a way to be more consistent with the requirement of a market economy. We hope and will not be surprised if the Chinese revert to the former interpretation.

We do not believe that "socialism" will (or should, for that matter) be interpreted to entail effective public ownership and central planning. Socialism was a movement concerned primarily with the improvement of society—making society a better place for all people to live in. At a certain point in time, some socialists believed that public ownership and central planning were essential preconditions for the improvement of society, and hence defined a socialist system accordingly. However, now most people in and outside of the socialist countries have realized that public ownership and central planning are really inimical to the welfare of the people. Thus, if we turn to the more fundamental objective of the early socialists, we should really define socialism as "a system that is conducive to a better livelihood for people in the society" (see Ng 1986). Thus defined, it is clear that most people will divorce socialism with public ownership and central planning.

This may appear to be purely a quibble on words. However, it is relevant to the success of further reforms in China. Most Chinese communists now realize the serious impediments posed by public ownership and central planning but cannot emotionally and politically accept the word "capitalism" and reject "socialism." Describing the proposed new reforms as "taking the capitalist road" is to give ammunition to the conservative faction.

Probably as a countermeasure against the conservative faction, Deng himself recently emphasized the futility of the debate on capitalism versus socialism. Rather, he proposed three ultimate criteria:

1. Benefits to the livelihood of the people
2. Conduciveness to raising the productive capacity
3. Conduciveness to raising the comprehensive power of the country

Such more practical criteria are more consistent with the requirement of a market economy.

Before the Tiananmen incident, Ng and Yang (1989) published an article in the *World Economic Herald* in Shanghai, advocating the adoption of the shareholding system to privatize inefficient state enterprises. After the June 4 incident in 1989, that article was criticized several times in the *People's Daily* (for example, October 16, 1989: 6). Following speeches made by Deng early in 1992, the mass media in China has come to view the shareholding system (including trading in shares) very favorably. The shareholding system has been adopted in Shanghai and Shenzhen, and may possibly be extended throughout the country. This change in attitude is probably related to the dismal performance of the state enterprises in contrast to the spectacular success of the private sector.

22.6   Withering State Enterprises

The lackluster performance of the state enterprises probably accounts for the surprising statistical result that total factor productivity in the industrial sector is a decreasing function of time in recent years (Siang Ng 1993). Siang Ng analyzed the relationship between productivity growth and trade dependence by examining the economic performance of the Chinese industrial sector since the implementation of the open policy. He found that trade increased total factor productivity and contributed 17.5 percent to the output growth during 1985–90. Though inputs, openness, and trade significantly contribute to growth, there is evidence indicating that the total factor productivity is a decreasing function of time. Since the importance of trade (as measured by the trade dependence ratio) has increased over time, this serves to offset the negative effect of time on total factor productivity.

At first, the negative effect of time appears to be surprising since the open policy should lead to the adoption of better technological and management skills. One would expect a positive growth in total factor productivity over time as part of the success story of China's very high growth rates in recent years. However, repeated checking of the data and re-running of the regression relation based on alternative models failed to eliminate the negative relationship. This leads the authors to believe in the real existence of the decrease in total factor productivity with time and to try to search for an explanation.

The industrial sector is dominated by the state enterprises which have been very sluggish: the official publication, *Liaowang*, reported that two-thirds of the state enterprises are either loss-making or "neither alive nor dead" (December 16, 1991).[5] China's rapid growth since the introduction of reforms and adoption of an open policy has taken place mainly in the private sector, including agriculture (which has effectively been almost completely privatized), small private operators and enterprises (mainly in trade and services not included in the industrial sector), and enterprises involving foreign investment and/or cooperation. The growth rate of the state enterprises in 1992 was 8.62 percent while it was 17.89 percent for the collective-owned enterprises and 24.0 percent for the private enterprises. The figure for the joint venture and foreign owned enterprises was as high as 50.11 percent (SBS 1992). (The latest State Bureau of Statistics (SBS) figures for January–March 1993 indicate a widening trend. As reported in *China Daily* (April 25, 1993) the industrial production of the state sector registered a growth of 8.7 percent, the collective sector a growth of 42.4 percent and the private and foreign sectors a growth of 63.6 percent. The latest figures reported in *China Daily* (July 3, 1994) were 4.9 percent, 31.1 percent, and 44.38 percent respectively for the period January–March 1994.) Table 22.3 provides the growth rate of the Chinese industrial enterprises in the 1980s. It is obvious that the individual, the joint venture, and foreign-owned enterprises performed best. While the real growth rate of the individual owned enterprises has been very much higher than that of the collective-owned enterprises, the latter's performance has been better than the state-owned enterprises.

The falling contribution of state-owned enterprises and the increasing contribution of other enterprises to the industrial output can be seen from Figure 22.1. While the production share of the state-owned enterprises fell from 77.64 percent in 1978 to 48.1 percent in 1992, the contributions of the collective-owned, the individual-owned and joint venture/foreign-owned enterprises increased from 22.37 percent, 0 percent and 0 percent in 1978 to 38.04 percent, 6.76 percent and 7.11 percent respectively. It is thus not surprising to see that the forecasted

TABLE 22.3   Index of gross value of industrial output by ownership (1980 = 100)

Year	State	Collective	Individual	Joint/Foreign
1981	102.6	109.0	234.6	131.6
1982	110.3	119.4	419.8	168.1
1983	120.6	138.0	926.0	225.1
1984	131.4	186.0	1,828.5	352.9
1985	148.4	246.8	3,466.8	492.5
1986	159.6	291.1	5,809.4	660.7
1987	175.4	358.8	9,096.9	1,099.4
1988	197.5	459.8	13,403.4	1,775.9
1989	205.1	508.0	16,589.4	2,533.8
1990	211.2	553.8	20,091.4	3,530.3
1991	229.4	652.9	24,913.3	5,299.3
1992	273.4	912.9	38,812.2	8,724.9

Source: *Statistical Yearbook of China*, various issues.

FIGURE 22.1   Industrial production by ownership of enterprises

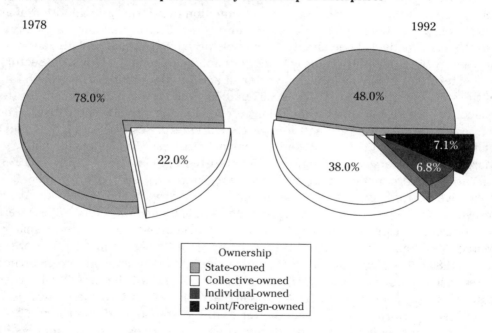

contribution of the collective-owned enterprises will be ahead of the state-owned enterprises in the year 2000 as shown in Figure 22.2. It may be added that these data and estimates based on official figures probably underestimate the true importance of the individual and collective sectors.

Xiao (1991) found that from 1985 to 1987, the state sector had a stagnant growth in total factor productivity and low allocative efficiency whereas the collective

FIGURE 22.2   Gross output value

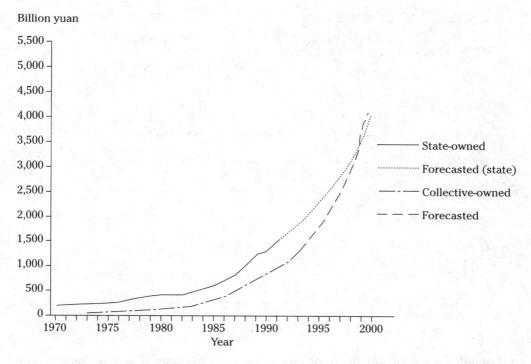

Billion yuan

sector had achieved a rapid growth of total factor productivity and high allocative efficiency. Siang Ng's study shows that the growth of total factor productivity in the industrial sector (which is dominated by state enterprises) since 1986 has been a negative function of time in most provinces.

In order to revitalise the poor performance of the state enterprises, the Chinese government has poured an enormous amount of investment into the state sector. This can be seen from Figure 22.3. However, the problems state enterprises face are not due to a lack of investment. Their problems are due to the state's ownership of the enterprises, which results in a lack of incentives, competition and market orientation. Even though output increased somewhat with the increased investment, the increased investment failed to revitalize the state enterprises. This in turn dragged down total factor productivity despite some technological progress. As noted by the Chinese State Bureau of Statistics, "in 1992 problems causing state-owned firms to lose money were still quite serious, as on-going massive investments failed to lead to an expected increase in economic efficiency" (reported in *China Daily*, March 2, 1993).

This phenomenon of lagging state enterprises in contrast to the fast growing, more efficient collective and private enterprises has also been demonstrated in other studies. Field (1992) shows that rapid industrial growth was not accompanied

FIGURE 22.3   Investment in fixed assets of stated-owned enterprises

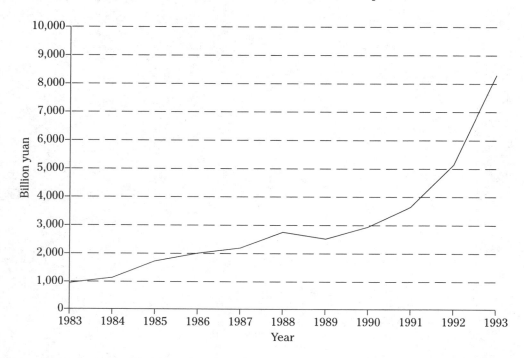

by significant improvements in productivity, especially after the mid-1980s and he predicts a declining rate of industrial growth in the 1990s. Wu (1992) found that in the 1980s the growth rate of total factor productivity of rural enterprises was much greater than that in the urban state industrial sector. In his study of Shanghai's state-owned cotton industry, R. Chen (1992) showed that technical efficiency of the firms deteriorated from 69.04 percent to 62.05 percent during 1987–90. Wan (1992) also concluded that the average rates of technical change were 35.5 percent and 25.9 percent per year for the periods 1952–59 and 1962–66 respectively. However, for the period 1978–88 the rate of technical progress was only 2.8 percent which is much lower than has been claimed or anticipated. It has been revealed that recent growth in the industrial sector is largely due to the injection of physical inputs. This points to the existence of great problems in the utilization of foreign technologies.

22.7   Future Prospects

From an economic viewpoint, the prospects for trade with and investment in China seem to be excellent. This is so since China has a big and fastly expanding market eager for foreign goods and there are excellent opportunities for foreign investments. From a purely economic analysis, China is poised to achieve further substantial growth, further expansion of the private sector and more opportunities for trade and investment. More uncertain is the possible political turmoil that may disrupt both China's domestic economy and its external economic relationships. Let us consider this issue briefly.

The following developments seem inevitable in the foreseeable future:

1. The continued growth of the market and the private sector not only absolutely, but also relative to the state sector. A glimpse of this trend is provided by the spectacular growth of the number of workers in Southern China employed by Hong Kong enterprises which have transferred much of their operation to the Pearl River delta and the surrounding areas in the last few years. According to recent figures, 3.4 million workers are employed by Hong Kong enterprises in Southern China—a figure about 4.5 times larger than the comparable figure for the whole of Hong Kong (see Qi 1992).

2. Growing absolute and relative strength of certain regional economies, especially the Pearl River and the Yangtze River deltas. (This tendency has been enhanced by Deng's pro-reform speeches in early 1992.) This might lead to friction with the central authorities and to difficulties in the exercise of controls. If the Chinese government has enough foresight, an appropriate federal system should be introduced which would also solve the long acclaimed problem of "huge difficulties in managing a big country."

3. The increasing desire for freedom and democracy.

4. The increasing corruption of the party and government bureaucracies. This problem is difficult to avoid before the full transition to a market economy takes place. A full market economy would reduce the scope for corruption and the effective rule of the law and freedom of the press would give effective check to bureaucratic power.

The above developments will lead to the intensification of the conflict between the old (state ownership, controlled economy, bureaucratic power) and the new (private ownership, market mechanism, freedom and democracy). Changes will be inevitable. The question is whether changes can be effected without a major disturbance like a chaotic civil war. The avoidance of chaos is not only important from the viewpoint of investment security, but also crucial for the smooth growth of the economy, the welfare of the ordinary people, and that of individuals in the current government.

A recent development is the mass voluntary transfer of government officials and intellectuals to the private business sector. In the early years of reform, "individual operators" were regarded as inferior to such "iron-bowl holders" as government officials and enterprise employees. Indeed, individual operators even had difficulties in finding wives. Now, with many millionaires emerging in the private sector, many government officials and academics have resigned their tenured positions to "go into the sea" of private business. This movement will probably be favorable to further growth by supplying a group of highly qualified entrepreneurs with good connections. However, the good connections, if abused excessively, may increase the perception of social injustice. That is, it may give rise to sentiments similar to the anti-corruption sentiments which partly fueled Tiananmen movement in 1989. The extent to which the rule of law can prevail and the freer press can be relied on to exercise some check and balance on government officials and former officials will be important in preventing a major political disturbance.

The possibility of avoiding a chaotic disturbance also depends on the following:

1. Whether the more liberal reformers will remain dominant and be able to carry out further necessary reforms. One of such desirable reforms is the privatization of inefficient state enterprises through the issue of shares. This would simultaneously solve the problems of excessive private liquidity (private saving deposits at banks total RMB 800 billion), insufficient government revenue,[6] revitalizing inefficient enterprises, and introducing foreign technology and management skills (since some of the enterprises could be sold to foreign enterprises).

2. Whether those seeking changes have learned from the repeated failure of revolutionary movements (including the Nationalist, the Communist, and to a lesser extent, the 1989 democracy movement), thus opting to use pressures instead of revolutionary methods. From our stay in Beijing in February–May 1993, we understand that this may well be so at least for tertiary students (who led the 1989 incident). Students are now classified into those preparing to go overseas, those wishing to "go into the sea," those playing mahjong, and those sleeping a lot; no one is interested in politics.

3. Whether an appropriate solution to the rural–urban segregation issue is implemented.

Due to the lack of further improvements since the mid-1980s (increases in output being offset by price falls) and the prevalence of deferred payments to farmers, the rural sector is potentially a trouble spot. This has attracted much official attention in recent months, as is obvious in daily radio broadcasts.

In the current climate of fast growth, a natural question is whether the economy will become overheated, leading to a destabilizing rate of inflation. The inflation rate in 1993 was 14 percent. Though officials claimed that "inflation will be kept under 15 percent", the first half of 1994 already registered a rate of 19.8 percent (in comparison to the same period in 1993), and July 1994 registered a rate of 21.4 percent. Also, private savings in banks declined in March 1993 for the first time since 1988 (*China Daily Business Weekly*, May 2–8, 1993). In anticipation of inflation, people withdraw their deposits to buy goods, securities, gold, and foreign currencies. The last explains the spectacular depreciation of the Chinese yuan in the black market, which hit 11 yuan to one US dollar in 1993. However, after the dismantling in early 1994 of the difference between the official rate and the market rate, the rate settled to around 8.4 in the middle of 1994. We also understand that, as most people, including those on fixed salaries, have found ways to supplement their incomes, a moderate rate of inflation may not be socially intolerable.

Moreover, we may be cautiously optimistic about the likelihood of avoiding a chaotic disturbance due to:

1. the traditional Chinese belief in "grand unification"
2. the central control of the military

3. solid economic growth and its likely continuation
4. recent developments favorable to further reforms
5. the general worldwide trend toward liberalization and a market orientation

The inefficiencies of the rigid system of central control and public ownership accentuated by the excesses of various notorious "movements" (including the Great Leap Forward of 1958–61 and the Cultural Revolution of 1967–76), and the big economic success of the reforms introduced since 1978 make the momentum for reform and openness irreversible. Even if there is a political turmoil a hundred times more devastating than the Tiananmen Incident, it seems unlikely that it would pose a great threat to foreign investment.

Notes

1. For estimates of China's GNP, see Eckstein (1980), Liu and Yeh (1973), Wu (1991). Recently, some researchers, using real purchasing power rather than official exchange rates, produced figures for China's *real* per capita GDP six to seven times higher than the conventional measure; see Maddison (1989), Summers and Heston (1991), and Wong (1991).
2. Similarly, the crowded situation in many Indian cities is also far from ideal. This problem may be partly explained by the conflict between equity and efficiency versus freedom and fairness, a conflict related to nonconvexity in the presence of the urban–rural distinction which in turn is related to scale economies in cities, see Ng (1985) or Ng (1990b: Ch. 4).
3. The racial segregation policy of South Africa attracted worldwide condemnation, but the equally repugnant rural–urban segregation policy in China has hardly attracted much attention.
4. The proof of the proposition might follow the approach of proving "the enrichment of a sector generally benefits others", using homothetic preferences and balanced growth, see Ng (1990a).
5. On the behavior of Chinese enterprises under the reforms, see Gordon and Li (1991) and Yin (1994).
6. The problem of insufficient government revenue was aggravated by the decentralization reforms in the 1980s. Following these reforms the government still has had to subsidize loss-making enterprises while profit-making ones can keep much of their profits. The government's net income (pre-tax profits of state-owned enterprises minus pre-tax losses of unprofitable state-owned enterprises) from state industrial enterprises as a proportion national income fell from 24.9 percent in 1978 to 8 percent in 1991. Total government budget revenue as a proportion of national income fell from 37.2 percent in 1978 to 20.5 percent in 1993. Total government expenditure as a proportion of national income fell from 36.9 percent in 1978 to 21.4 percent in 1993. Private saving deposits at banks as a proportion of national income increased from 7 percent in 1978 to 59.3 percent in 1993.

References

Beladi, Hamid and Eubarnak Samanta, 1990, "Foreign Technology and Customs Unions: Trade Creation and Trade Diversion," *Journal of Economic Studies*, 17: 27–35.
Chen, R., 1992, "Technical Efficiency of Large and Medium-Sized Enterprises: Shanghai

Cotton Industry, 1987–1990," paper presented at the Chinese Economic Association Annual Conference, University of Adelaide, November.

Chen, S. M. 陈继明, 1992, "Sino-foreign Joint Venture: A Way to Vitalize," *The Nineties*, 265 (February): 38–40.

Clarke, H. and Y.-K. Ng, 1993, "Immigration and Economic Welfare: Resource and Environmental Aspects," *Economic Record*, 6(206): 259–73.

Corden, W. M., 1975, "The Costs and Consequences of Protection: A Survey of Empirical Work," in P. B. Kenen (ed.), *International Trade and Finance*, Cambridge University Press, Cambridge, pp. 51–91.

———, 1986, "The Normative Theory of International Trade," in R. W. Jones (ed.), *International Trade: Surveys of Theory and Policy*, North-Holland, Amsterdam, pp. 63–130.

Eckstein, Alexander, 1980, *Quantitative Measures of China's Economic Output*, University of Michigan Press, Ann Arbor, MI.

Field, Robert M., 1992, "China's Industrial Performance Since 1978," *China Quarterly*, 131: 577–607.

Garnaut, Ross, 1989, *Australia and the Northeast Asian Ascendancy*, Australian Government Publishing Service, Canberra.

Gordon, Roger H. and Wei Li, 1991, "Chinese Enterprise Behavior Under the Reforms," *American Economic Review*, 81 (May): 202–6.

Guo, Pu 郭普, 1993, "Wither the Mainland Economy in 1993?" *The Nineties Monthly*, January, 32–34.

Kueh, Y. Y., 1992, "Foreign Investment and Economic Change in China," *China Quarterly*, 131: 637–90.

Lai, R. T. 赖初定, 1991, "Experience Problems of Factory Investment in China," *The Nineties*, 254 (March): 102–5.

Li, S. C. 李秀娟, 1992, "Taping Chinese Consumer Market," *Hong Kong Economic Journal*, 15(11): 36–42.

Liu, Ta-chung and Kung-chia Yeh, 1973, "Chinese and Other Asian Economies: A Quantitative Evaluation," *American Economic Review*, 63 (May): 215–31.

Maddison, Angus, 1989, *The World Economy in the 20th Century*, OECD Development Centre Studies, Paris.

Ng, Siang, 1993, "Trade and Productivity: The Case of China," School of Banking and Finance, Working Paper Series No. 1, Monash University, Australia.

Ng, Yew-Kwang, 1984, "Quasi-Pareto Social Improvements," *American Economic Review*, 74(5): 1033–50.

———, 1985, "Equity and Efficiency Versus Freedom and Fairness: An Inherent Conflict," *Kyklos*, 38: 495–516.

———, 1986, "Chinese-Style Socialism from the Viewpoint of Modern Economics," *Mirror Monthly* 镜报月刊, January, 56–60.

———, 1990a, *The Enrichment of a Sector (Individual/Region/Country) Benefits Others*, Department of Economics Seminar Paper No. 11/90, Monash University, Clayton.

———, 1990b, *Social Welfare and Economic Policy*, Harvester-Wheatsheaf, London.

——— 黄有光, 1991, "Democratization and the Rural–Urban Conflict," *Cheng Ming* 争鸣, March, 57–59.

Ng, Yew-Kwang and Yang Xiaokai 杨小凯, 1989, "China Should Privatize in One Giant Step," *World Economic Herald* (Shanghai), February 6, 12–13; February 20, 15.

Norman, N. R. and K. Meikle, 1985, *The Economic Effects of Immigration on Australia*, 2 volumes, Committee for Economic Development of Australia, Melbourne.

Parai, Amark and Eden S. H. Yu, 1989, "Factor Mobility and Customs Unions Theory," *Southern Economic Journal*, 55 (August): 842–52.

Qi, S. 齐辛, 1992, "The Chinese Communists Taking the Capitalist Road," *The Nineties*, 265 (November): 32–35.

Shambaugh, David, 1990, "China in 1990: The Year of Damage Control," *Asian Survey*, 31: 36–45.

State Bureau of Statistics (SBS), *Zhongguo Tongji Nianjian* (Statistical Yearbook of China), Statistical Publishing of China, People's Republic of China.

Stoeckel, Andrew, David Pearce, and Gary Banks, 1990, *Western Trade Blocs*, Centre for International Economies, Canberra.

Summers, Robert and Alan Heston, 1991, "The Penn World Table (Mark 5): An Expanded Set of International Comparison, 1950–1988," *Quarterly Journal of Economics*, 106 (May): 327–68.

Wan, G. H., 1992, "Technical Change in Chinese Industry: A New Approach," paper presented at the Chinese Economic Association Annual Conference, University of Adelaide, November.

Withers, Glen and David Pope, 1985, "Immigration and Unemployment," *Economic Record*, 61: 554–63.

Wong, John, 1991, *What is China's Per-capita GNP?* Institute of East Asian Philosophies Background Brief No. 18, National University of Singapore.

Wu, Harry X., 1991, *The 'Real' Chinese Gross Domestic Product (GDP) in the Pre-reform Period 1952–1977*, Working Paper No. 91/7, Chinese Economy Research Unit, University of Adelaide.

Wu, Y., 1992, "Productivity Performance of Chinese Rural Enterprises: A Comparative Study," paper presented at the International Conference on Trade, Investment and Economic Prospects in China's Three Economies: Mainland, Taiwan, Hong Kong, Monash University, February.

Xiao, G., 1991, "Managerial Autonomy, Fringe Benefits, and Ownership Structure: A Comparative Study of Chinese State and Collective Enterprises," *China Economic Review*, 2(1): 47–73.

Yan, Zhen 颜真, 1990, "The Third Path: The Rational Choice of the Chinese Race," *Cheng Ming* 争鸣, November.

Yeh, K. C., 1992, "Macroeconomic Issues in China in the 1990s," *China Quarterly*, 131: 502–44.

Yin, Xiangkang, 1994, *A Micro–macroeconomic Analysis of the Chinese Economy with Imperfect Competition*, Department of Economics Seminar Paper No. 22/94, Monash University, Australia.

Zhang, Xiaohe, 1991, *The Urban–Rural Isolation and Its Impact on China's Production and Trade Pattern*, Working Paper No. 91/4, Chinese Economy Research Unit, University of Adelaide.

Chapter 23

Chi Schive

TAIWAN'S ECONOMIC RESTRUCTURING AND ITS ROLE IN ASIA-PACIFIC

23.1 Introduction

Looking back at Taiwan's development experience during the past 40-odd years, one sees that each stage of Taiwan's economic development has its own unique set of conditions, and new problems often spring up in the wake of past successes. Therefore each stage was distinguished by a specific policy focus. In the 1950s, it was import substitution to achieve self-sufficiency while in the 1960s the emphasis shifted to the active promotion of exports to boost industrial expansion and help raise foreign reserves. In the 1970s, export promotion was continued and further supplemented by the secondary import substitution of upstream industries. In the 1980s, the Taiwan economy was confronted with two phenomena (like the two sides of a coin): escalating excess savings and mounting trade surpluses. The situation is just the opposite of what Taiwan faced in the early postwar years: a shortage of foreign exchange and inadequate domestic savings. In the mid-1980s, the value of the New Taiwan (NT) dollar had been under tremendous upward pressure, and its sharp appreciation had eroded Taiwan's international competitiveness. This chapter is concerned with how the economy adjusted at the microeconomic level to the macroeconomic imbalances and how the restructuring process turned out to be the force that has forged Taiwan's new era of economic progress and its new role in the Asia-Pacific region.

23.2 Great Transition in the 1980s

23.2.1 Macroeconomic Imbalances

During the first half of the 1980s, Taiwan's trade surplus had multiplied as exports had developed much faster than imports. The exports/GNP ratio remained at 52 percent between 1980 and 1983, but increased to 56 percent in 1986 and 1987, while the imports/GNP ratio declined steadily until 1987 (Table 23.1). Between 1982–86, the average annual growth rate of goods-and-services exports was 13.6 percent, while that of goods-and-services imports was only 4.5 percent or one-third of the former.

Although Taiwan's merchandise trade surplus (US$15.6 billion) in 1986 was much lower than that of Japan (US$83.2 billion) and that of West Germany (US$52.5 billion), as a percentage of GNP (19.3 percent), it was unparalleled among non-oil producing countries, Germany and Japan included. And its goods-and-services trade surplus amounted to as much as 22.1 percent of GNP, far more than those of Japan and Germany, which were both less than 5 percent of GNP.

The mounting trade surplus exerted a great degree of upward pressure on the NT dollar. On September 22, 1985, the G–5 nations intervened to depress the value of the U.S. dollar, and the NT dollar went through a steep appreciation. By the end

TABLE 23.1   External imbalance in Taiwan's economy, 1980–94 (%)

Year	Exports/GNP (1)	Imports/GNP (2)	External Imbalance (3) = (1) – (2)
1980	52.6	53.8	–1.2
1981	52.2	50.2	2.0
1982	50.2	45.0	5.2
1983	53.0	44.4	8.6
1984	55.6	44.5	11.1
1985	53.3	39.8	13.5
1986	56.7	37.4	19.3
1987	56.4	39.3	13.1
1988	53.4	41.6	11.8
1989	49.2	41.2	8.0
1990	46.6	40.7	5.9
1991	47.3	42.4	4.9
1992	43.6	41.2	2.4
1993	44.6	42.7	1.9
1994	43.6	42.2	1.4

Sources: Directorate-General of Budget, Accounting and Statistics, Executive Yuan, Taiwan, *Quarterly National Economic Trends*, various issues.

of 1987, it had already appreciated 42 percent against the U.S. dollar, the highest rate recorded among Asia's major currencies during the same period.

Although foreign exchange controls were almost completely removed in July 1987, except for those imposed on inward remittances, the Central Bank had to continue to absorb a large amount of foreign exchange in order to maintain the stability of the foreign exchange market. At the end of 1987, the Central Bank's foreign exchange reserves exceeded US$76.7 billion, up US$68.2 billion from US$8.5 billion five years earlier. Despite various sterilization measures, the money supply grew at an annual rate of more than 20 percent during the 34 months from March 1986 to the end of 1988, and by more than 30 percent during 24 of those months. During the second half of 1988, the money supply expanded about 30 percent, placing strong inflationary pressures on domestic prices.

The counterpart of the huge external imbalances of the economy is the enormous amount of excess savings, signifying a shortfall of domestic demand. During the 1980s, Taiwan's GNP continued to expand while domestic demand slowed down substantially. Between 1982 and 1986, GNP at current prices rose 10.7 percent a year on average, while domestic demand (national consumption and domestic investment) increased only 5.7 percent. This implied rapidly expanding excess savings over investment, which rose to 21.4 percent of GNP in 1986. And between 1981 and 1986, investment had dropped from 30 percent to 17 percent of GNP, retreating to the level it held in the 1950s.

Besides allowing the NT dollar to appreciate substantially, the Taiwan government undertook a series of liberalization steps to reduce the trade surplus:

☐ Removing almost all foreign exchange controls in June 1987, except for restrictions on inward remittances to avoid the influx of foreign hot money to Taiwan.

☐ Cutting down import tariffs. A series of comprehensive tariff reductions brought the average nominal tariff rate down to one-half of the previous level and the real import tariff rate (total customs duties/total imports) to 4.99 percent in 1993.

☐ Relaxing on a large scale import restrictions. Most restrictions on the issuance of import documents and the origin of import were eliminated in May 1987. And only 1.5 percent of all commodities on import manifests, mostly weapons, drugs and a few agricultural products, were banned, controlled or delayed.

☐ Opening the domestic market for services to outside competition. Access to domestic markets were given to fast food, supermarket, banking, insurance, leasing, and marine shipping services of foreign concerns. And foreign firms already in Taiwan were allowed to expand the scope of their operations.

23.2.2 Microeconomic Adjustments

The rapid appreciation of the NT dollar forced labor costs calculated in U.S. dollars to rise at an extremely rapid rate. The unit labor cost, standardized in terms of the U.S. dollar, also adjusted for exchange rate variations. Changes in wage rates and labor productivity, remained relatively stable in Taiwan between 1981 and 1985 (Table 23.2). Since 1986, the unit labor cost index has sharply increased, recording

TABLE 23.2 Unit labor cost in U.S. dollars: selected countries, 1980–91 (%)

Year	Taiwan	Japan	Korea	U.S.	W. Germany
1980	87	107	104	87	124
1981	97	114	100	94	104
1982	100	100	100	100	100
1983	97	103	94	98	95
1984	108	99	90	96	86
1985	112	97	88	97	85
1986	127	142	83	97	120
1987	160	157	91	94	156
1988	170	173	112	92	160
1989	192	161	153	93	150
1990	199	–	160	–	–
1991	200	–	163	–	–

Sources: U.S. Department of Labor, Bureau of Labor Statistics, *Monthly Labor Review*; Directorate-General of Budget, Accounting and Statistics, Executive Yuan, Taiwan, *Monthly Bulletin of Earnings and Productivity Statistics*, various issues.

the fastest rate of increase relative to all industrialized economies. Based on 1982=100, Taiwan compares very adversely because of her rising labor costs in the late 1980s. The international competitiveness of Taiwan's traded products appears to have eroded significantly, other things being equal. Much of this negative impact is due to the exchange rate revaluation.

Previously, the weaker NT dollar facilitated export expansion because of a very stable domestic price level relative to that of its trading partners in the early and middle 1980s. Since then, export growth has decelerated in response to the currency revaluation. Pushed by the concern over rising labor costs eroding their competitiveness, and encouraged by the government's liberalization measures, Taiwan's manufacturers were quick to make a series of adjustments. Among the adjustments Taiwan's manufacturers could have persued are: relocating production of the least competitive products by increasing overseas investment; speeding up automation; restructuring export composition away from labor-intensive goods, promoting the production of high value-added products; and employing inexpensive foreign laborers. Since overseas investment played a pivotal role in Taiwan's recent transition and helped develop Taiwan's new role in the Asia-Pacific region, it will be examined in the next section.

23.2.3 Automation

Although the theoretical discussion of automation can be linked to the concept of technical progress or the phenomenon of learning, the static version of introducing automated techniques in production entails capital deepening and the substitution of labor. One measure of the degree of automation is the ratio of number of machines with automatic control devices relative to the total number of machines in use. Take five industries, foods, textiles, plastic products, machinery and electronics, for example. There was a clear increasing trend of the usage of automatic machinery in these industries in the 1980s (Table 23.3). The food industry attained a high degree of automation, while four other industries show varying degrees of achievement over the period, particularly since the mid-1980s. Another set of data showing the value of automatic machinery per worker in operation also reveals the same result, although the observation period was between 1985 and 1989. Evidently, Taiwanese industries have moved to progressively introduce automation in the 1980s in order to offset the rising unit labor cost, and more rapidly since 1986 in order to absorb the shock of domestic currency appreciation.

TABLE 23.3   Automation in Taiwan's manufacturing sector, 1981–89

Year	Foods	Textile	Plastic product	Machinery	Electronics
		Ratio of automatic machinery over total (%)			
1981	–	29	8	21	27
1983	66	24	10	28	38
1985	56	55	26	36	46
1987	73	65	41	55	59
		Automatic machinery per worker (NT$ thousand/person)			
1985	203	284	131	360	158
1987	357	369	205	349	241
1989	291	641	574	347	310
1991	832	796	517	603	616

Automation machinery denotes that a machinery can operate within a work period without the care of worker.

Sources: Automation Commission, Executive Yuan, Taiwan, *Industrial Automation, A Survey Report (1982, 1984, 1986 and 1988)*; Ministry of Economic Affairs, *Industrial Automation Survey Report*, June 1993.

Another set of data further supports the argument. Between 1987 and 1991, Taiwan's manufacturing employment fell 16 percent from 2.62 million to 2.20 million. However, the manufacturing production index posted a 14 percent increase over the same period. Automation must have made its contribution to the change, enabling the manufacturers to produce more with less labor employment, that is, a gain in productivity.

23.2.4   Quality Improvement

Another effective way to counter a loss in competitiveness is to upgrade product quality rather than lowering prices. Over the period between 1986 and 1989, the export price index in NT dollars displayed a declining trend, implying that Taiwan exporters lowered their prices for the same product exported. If we take the unit export price, deflated by the export price in NT dollars in order to remove the price effect, the deflated curve revealed an increasing trend between 1986 and 1990. This points to quality improvements and product-mix changes in Taiwan's export products. Taiwan obviously exported higher quality products and exported more of these products (Figure 23.1).

FIGURE 23.1   Taiwan's export quality index, 1986–91

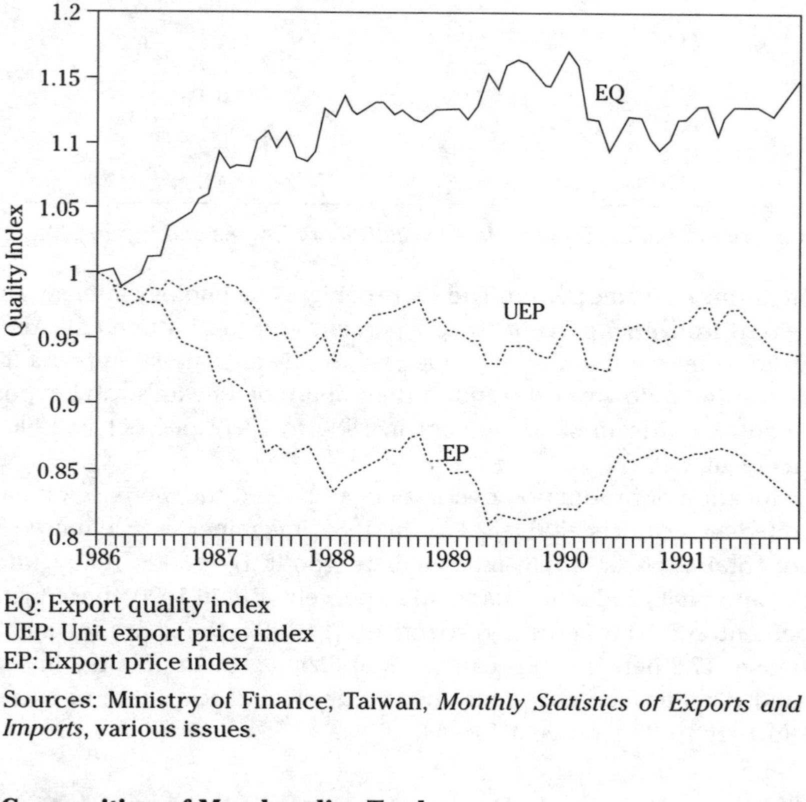

EQ: Export quality index
UEP: Unit export price index
EP: Export price index

Sources: Ministry of Finance, Taiwan, *Monthly Statistics of Exports and Imports*, various issues.

23.2.5   Composition of Merchandise Trade

Labor-intensive export industries are significantly affected by the rising cost of labor and the strong NT dollar. By turning to labor-saving methods of production, Taiwan manufacturers shifted their traditional labor-intensive production overseas and concentrated on capital- and technology-intensive products and/or activities. In 1986, products with high labor intensity accounted for 47 percent of total exports (Table 23.4). The share fell quickly to 41 percent in 1990 and further to 38.8 percent in 1993. With regard to capital intensity, the share of highly capital-intensive products increased from 22.9 percent to 28.9 percent and further to

TABLE 23.4   Taiwan's exports by technology level, 1983–94 (%)

Year	Technology intensity		Heavy industries	High-tech products
	High	Medium and low		
1983	18.2	81.8	35.4	26.0
1984	18.3	81.7	36.4	27.2
1985	18.8	81.2	36.5	27.0
1986	18.4	81.6	35.6	27.6
1987	19.4	80.6	37.9	30.0
1988	22.6	77.4	42.8	33.7
1989	24.2	75.8	44.5	33.9
1990	26.7	73.3	46.7	35.9
1991	27.2	72.8	46.7	36.3
1992	29.5	70.5	49.1	37.9
1993	31.4	68.6	52.6	40.1
1994	32.5	67.6	54.8	42.1

Source: Ministry of Finance, Taiwan, *Monthly Statistics of Exports and Imports*, May 1995.

32 percent during the same period. The share of highly technology-intensive products also increased from 18.4 percent to 26.7 percent and to 31.4 percent. Also, labor-intensive consumer nondurable goods, once Taiwan's most important export products, showed a downward trend in their share of Taiwan's total exports. The segment contracted from 35.61 percent in 1986 to 23.72 percent in 1990, and to 19.79 percent in 1992.

The relocation of production overseas has boosted the increase of machinery and intermediate exports (Table 23.5). In 1986, machineries accounted for 10.8 percent of total exports, while intermediate goods B—goods ready for further processing into final products—made up 26 percent. But in 1990, these figures rose to 16.3 percent and 34.0 percent respectively. In 1992, the share for machineries rose further to 17.2 percent, suggesting a stabilizing growth of initial investments. But demand for intermediates continued to grow, and the share of these goods widened further to 39.1 percent in 1992.

23.3   Taiwan's Economic Restructuring and Regional Integration

23.3.1   Outward Investment

In the 1980s Taiwan has turned from a capital-poor, DFI(direct foreign investment)-importing country to a capital-rich, DFI-sourcing country. Taiwanese entrepreneurs have been attracted to Southeast Asian countries and mainland China since 1986. Besides economic factors, cultural factors and the high degree of complementarity between these economies and Taiwan are behind the wave of Taiwan's outward investment in these areas.

TABLE 23.5 Taiwan's exports by industry classification (%)

Year	Agriculture, forestry, fishery, livestock and hunting products	Processed food	Beverage and tobacco preparation	Energy and minerals	Construction materials
1981	2.69	4.90	0.10	0.10	0.44
1982	2.28	5.18	0.10	0.00	0.66
1983	2.17	4.61	0.10	0.00	0.77
1984	1.97	4.03	0.00	0.00	0.55
1985	1.76	4.32	0.04	0.08	0.50
1986	1.68	4.72	0.03	0.06	0.40
1987	1.40	4.54	0.03	0.11	0.32
1988	1.61	3.75	0.04	0.07	0.32
1989	0.96	3.58	0.03	0.06	0.27
1990	0.84	3.52	0.03	0.05	0.28
1991	0.91	3.62	0.05	0.04	0.23
1992	0.87	3.31	0.06	0.04	0.22
1993	0.80	3.20	0.10	0.10	0.20
1994	0.70	3.20	0.10	0.00	0.10

Year	Intermediate goods* Sub-total	A	B	Consumer non-durable goods	Consumer durable goods	Machineries	Transportation equipments
1981	36.45	9.92	26.53	35.27	11.90	6.16	1.90
1982	35.72	10.44	25.28	35.56	11.13	6.16	2.99
1983	35.41	9.51	25.90	36.14	11.61	6.93	1.90
1984	34.68	9.09	25.59	36.81	11.03	9.03	1.63
1985	35.72	8.73	26.99	35.85	9.08	10.39	1.72
1986	33.64	7.45	26.19	35.61	11.01	10.93	1.87
1987	33.56	6.90	26.66	33.48	11.42	13.21	1.87
1988	36.56	8.77	27.79	29.77	10.08	15.42	1.54
1989	40.06	8.99	31.07	27.46	10.16	15.45	1.89
1990	44.48	9.49	34.00	23.72	8.70	16.34	2.11
1991	46.45	9.45	37.00	21.95	8.52	16.11	2.12
1992	48.56	9.45	39.11	19.79	7.95	17.24	1.96
1993	51.20	10.00	41.20	17.00	7.80	17.40	2.30
1994	54.80	11.30	43.50	14.60	7.30	16.80	2.30

*Intermediate products A are the products that can be used for consumer goods or producer goods after processing. Intermediate products B are the products that can be used for consumer goods or producer goods without processing.
Industry classification follows the World Bank model.

Sources: Ministry of Finance, Taiwan, *Report on the Characteristic Classifications of Tradable Commodities*, 1993; Ministry of Finance, Taiwan, *Monthly Statistics of Exports and Imports*, various issues.

Based on approval basis figures, Taiwan's outward investment totaled only US$7.5 million in the 1960s, and US$51.7 million in the 1970s. But since 1986, it roughly doubled every year from US$56.9 million to US$1,552 million in 1990. These figures were much higher according to data from host countries. The disparity between the two sets of figures is more than 100-fold in some cases. For instance, while Taiwan's officially approved investment to Indonesia totaled US$1.9 million in 1988, the Indonesian statistics recorded US$913 million (Table 23.6). Host countries' data also indicated that by the end of 1992, Taiwan was Vietnam's largest foreign investor, Malaysia's second, Indonesia's and the Philippines' third, and Thailand's fourth (Table 23.7). It is very likely that some of Taiwan's investment has been made through Hong Kong, since the latter has been an important financial center in the Asia-Pacific region. Such investments are covered neither in Taiwan's nor the host countries' records under the name of Taiwan.

Traditional manufacturing industries such as textiles, electronic and electrical appliances, paper products and printing, chemical products, and metal and nonmetallic products, are the areas that have received most of Taiwan's overseas investment in Southeast Asian countries, with the exception of Hong Kong and Singapore (Table 23.7). For Taiwan's investment in the latter two, service industries such as trade, banking and insurance, and wholesale and retail, have had the lion's share.

The surge of Taiwan's investment in Southeast Asia and mainland China, however, should not be seen as proof that Taiwan's capital is concentrated only in these areas. As a matter of fact, the official data show that the U.S. used to be the most attractive country for Taiwanese investors and comprised 72.6 percent of Taiwan's total outward investment during the 1980–86 period. But the share went down to 32 percent during the 1987–91 period, despite the investments by large Taiwan-based companies (such as the Formosa Plastic Group and Acer) in many well-known projects in the U.S. On the other hand, in the East European region, including the former Soviet Union, newly opening markets are creating abundant opportunities for Taiwan's investors. Several local personal computer producers, as well as traders, have already responded actively to market signals. Although the absolute level of investment is still modest, the growth rate has been incredible. Taiwan's investors have built up a global view quickly in planning their next operations.

23.3.2 Trade

Taiwan's trade with its westbound and southbound neighbors has been expanding rapidly since the second half of the 1980s, thanks to Taiwan's growing investment in these economies. The impact of outward investment on trade can be analyzed from two perspectives: the composition and direction of trade. The commodity structure of trade has been discussed earlier. The geographic distribution of trade is discussed in this section because the latter affects significantly the economic integration of the East Asia region.

TABLE 23.6   Taiwan's investment in ASEAN countries and mainland China (US$ million; number of cases in parentheses)

Year	Thailand		Malaysia		Philippines		Indonesia		Mainland China (contract basis)
	Taiwan approved	Local approved	Taiwan approved	Local approved	Taiwan approved	Local approved	Taiwan approved	Local approved	
1987	5.4 (5)	300.0 (102)	5.8 (5)	47.4 (37)	2.6 (3)	9.0 (18)	1.0 (1)	7.9 (3)	100.0 (80)
1988	11.9 (15)	842.0 (308)	2.7 (5)	307.3 (111)	36.2 (7)	109.9 (86)	1.9 (3)	913.0 (17)	420.0 (355)
1989	51.6 (23)	871.0 (214)	158.6 (25)	815.0 (191)	66.3 (13)	148.7 (190)	0.3 (1)	158.0 (50)	517.0 (547)
1990	149.4 (39)	761.0 (144)	184.9 (36)	2,383.0 (270)	123.6 (16)	140.7 (158)	61.9 (18)	618.0 (50)	984.0 (1,117)
1991	86.4 (33)	567.6 (69)	442.0 (35)	1,314.2 (182)	1.3 (2)	11.6 (109)	160.3 (25)	1,056.5 (57)	1,392.3 (1,735)
1992	83.3 (23)	289.9 (44)	155.7 (13)	602 (137)	1.2 (3)	9.3 (27)	39.9 (20)	563.3 (23)	5,547.9 (6,430)
1993	109.2 (19)	215.0 (61)	64.5 (18)	346.5 (86)	6.5 (12)	5.4 (21)	25.5 (11)	131.4 (21)	9,965.0 (10,948)
1994	57.3 (12)	492.5 (91)	101.1 (17)	1,149.6 (100)	9.6 (10)	292.4 (42)	20.6 (12)	2,487.5 (48)	n.a.

Sources: Investment Commission, Ministry of Economic Affairs (MOEA), Taiwan; BOI, Thailand; MIDA, Malaysia; BOI, the Philippines; BKPM, Indonesia; EDB, Singapore.

TABLE 23.7 Taiwan's investment in ASEAN* (approved by host countries, 1959–94)

	Singapore	Malaysia	Thailand	Indonesia	Philippines
Amount (US$ million)	90.08	7,064.70	5,000.72	6,829.60	734.69
Number of cases	62	1,252	1,190	337	730
Ranking among all investing countries in the host country	13	2	4	7	4
Countries with higher ranking	Japan United States and others	Japan	Japan Hong Kong United States	Japan Hong Kong and others	United States Japan Hong Kong
Major industries of interest	1. Textile 2. Electronic and electrical products 3. Clothing 4. Plastic processing 5. Nonferreous metals	1. Electronic and electrical products 2. Textile and products 3. Rubber products 4. Wood and woodworks 5. Alloy forging	1. Machinery hardware 2. Electronics and telecommunications 3. Plastics and rubber 4. Textile 5. Chemicals	1. Textile 2. Metal products 3. Chemicals 4. Wood 5. Food	1. Trading 2. Textile and products 3. Electronic and electrical products 4. Food 5. Raw materials for chemical engineering

*Excluding Brunei.

Source: Investment Commission, MOEA.

The U.S. has been Taiwan's most important trade partner since the late 1960s. It has been Taiwan's largest export market and second largest source of imports. The dependence on the U.S. market increased sharply in the first half of the 1980s. The U.S. share of Taiwan's exports increased from 34.1 percent in 1980 to 48.8 percent and 48.1 percent in 1984 and 1985, respectively. But by 1990, a combination of falling exports to the U.S. and rising exports to ASEAN and mainland China, as well as to Europe had pushed this figure down to 32.4 percent in 1990 and further to 28.9 percent in 1992 (Tables 23.8 and 23.9). For example, exports to Hong Kong accounted for 18.9 percent of Taiwan's total exports in 1992, more than double the ratio of 6.9 percent in 1984.

Taiwan's overseas investments have had a large role to play in this shift. Many Taiwanese firms, while continuing to be important exporters to the U.S. market, have now located their factories overseas. As a result Taiwan has become an important exporter of capital and intermediate goods to neighboring economies who then produce goods for the U.S. market (Table 23.10).

Taiwan's trade with ASEAN has displayed increasing cooperative relations between Taiwan and the ASEAN members. The intra-industry trade coefficient indicates that industrial integration among these economies has expanded greatly. The coefficient suggests vast vertical integration—trade of final or semi-final products within the same industry—or horizontal integration when its value approaches to one. Between 1985 and 1991, the figure for Taiwan–ASEAN intra-industry trade increased from 19.7 percent to 36.5 percent (Table 23.11).

The technological impact of Taiwan's overseas investment is obvious and worth mentioning. By planting their production in the host countries, Taiwanese entrepreneurs are also sending technology, engineers and managers. Because of the limitation of data, it is difficult to measure the overall impact. But there is no doubt that investment by Taiwanese has helped upgrade and expand the industrial sector of the host countries.

23.4   Taiwan as a Regional Operations Center

23.4.1   A Conceptual Framework

There are two major trends emerging over the past few years: the globalization of corporate businesses and the proliferation of regional economic integration arrangements. In this Information Age, both governments and corporations need to plan globally to capture the greatest comparative advantages and economies of scale available and further enhance their competitive edge in the world marketplace. On the one hand, entrepreneurs are going beyond national and regional borders in an effort to minimize costs and maximize profits. On the other hand, governments are working together to eliminate trade restrictions within their regions and to facilitate intra-regional trade, investment and other economic transactions. Even if the aim is not to establish a free trade area, free trade is

TABLE 23.8 Taiwan's trade in the Pacific region (US$ million; in %)

(a) Export

| Year | Total in the world | Total in the area | U.S. | NICs | | | | ASEAN (excluding Singapore) | | | | |
				Japan	Korea	Hong Kong	Singapore	Sub-total	Thailand	Malaysia	Philippines	Indonesia	Sub-total
1980	19,810.6 (100.0)	12,145.5 (61.3)	6,760.3 (34.1)	2,173.4 (11.0)	266.5 (1.3)	1,550.6 (7.8)	545.2 (2.8)	2,362.3 (11.9)	176.3 (0.9)	169.9 (0.0)	195.0 (1.0)	478.2 (2.4)	849.5 (4.3)
1985	30,725.7 (100.0)	22,864.2 (74.4)	14,773.4 (48.1)	3,460.9 (11.3)	253.8 (0.8)	2,539.7 (8.3)	885.2 (2.9)	3,678.7 (12.0)	236.2 (0.8)	194.9 (0.6)	239.2 (0.8)	280.9 (0.9)	951.2 (3.1)
1986	39,861.5 (100.0)	28,982.2 (72.7)	19,013.9 (47.7)	4,559.8 (11.4)	351.6 (0.9)	2,921.3 (7.3)	930.9 (2.3)	4,203.8 (10.5)	278.6 (0.7)	205.7 (0.5)	328.6 (0.8)	391.8 (1.0)	1,204.7 (3.0)
1987	53,678.7 (100.0)	38,384.7 (71.5)	23,684.8 (44.1)	6,986.0 (13.0)	638.2 (1.2)	4,123.3 (7.7)	1,350.5 (2.5)	6,112.0 (11.4)	424.6 (0.8)	272.1 (0.5)	459.7 (0.9)	445.5 (0.8)	1,601.9 (3.0)
1988	61,667.4 (100.0)	42,864.8 (69.5)	23,467.2 (38.1)	8,771.7 (14.2)	917.3 (1.5)	5,587.1 (9.1)	1,682.7 (2.7)	8,187.1 (13.3)	753.7 (1.2)	451.1 (0.7)	601.4 (1.0)	632.6 (1.0)	2,438.8 (4.0)
1989	66,304.0 (100.0)	46,769.0 (70.5)	24,036.2 (36.3)	9,064.9 (13.7)	1,132.8 (1.7)	7,042.3 (10.6)	1,975.6 (3.0)	10,150.7 (15.3)	1,110.2 (1.7)	694.8 (1.0)	778.1 (1.2)	934.1 (1.4)	3,517.2 (5.3)
1990	67,214.4 (100.0)	46,640.7 (69.4)	21,745.9 (32.4)	8,337.7 (12.4)	1,212.8 (1.8)	8,556.2 (12.7)	2,203.7 (3.3)	11,972.7 (17.8)	1,423.6 (2.1)	1,103.6 (1.6)	811.4 (1.2)	1,245.8 (1.9)	4,584.4 (6.8)
1991	76,178.3 (100.0)	52,596.4 (69.0)	22,320.8 (29.3)	9,188.9 (12.1)	1,287.3 (1.7)	12,430.5 (16.3)	2,403.5 (3.2)	16,121.3 (21.2)	1,444.9 (1.9)	1,464.9 (1.9)	848.4 (1.1)	1,207.2 (1.6)	4,965.4 (6.5)
1992	81,470.3 (100.0)	57,183.9 (70.2)	23,571.6 (28.9)	8,893.7 (10.9)	1,150.4 (1.4)	15,415.0 (18.9)	2,505.2 (3.1)	19,070.6 (23.4)	1,809.6 (2.2)	1,600.3 (2.0)	1,023.4 (1.3)	1,214.8 (1.5)	5,648.0 (6.9)
1993	84,916.6 (100.0)	61,040.8 (71.9)	23,484.5 (27.7)	8,964.1 (10.6)	1,271.5 (1.5)	18,444.3 (21.7)	2,876.0 (3.4)	22,591.8 (26.6)	2,017.1 (2.4)	1,668.0 (2.0)	1,030.8 (1.2)	1,284.5 (1.5)	6,000.4 (7.1)

TABLE 23.8 (continued)

(b) Import

Year	Total in the world	Total in the area	U.S.	Japan	NICs				ASEAN (excluding Singapore)				
					Korea	Hong Kong	Singapore	Sub-total	Thailand	Malaysia	Philippines	Indonesia	Sub-total
1980	19,733.1 (100.0)	11,878.5 (60.2)	4,673.5 (23.7)	5,353.2 (27.1)	208.5 (1.1)	249.9 (1.3)	221.7 (1.1)	680.1 (3.4)	89.9 (0.5)	424.9 (2.2)	117.3 (0.6)	539.6 (2.7)	1,171.7 (5.9)
1985	20,102.0 (100.0)	12,223.7 (60.8)	4,746.3 (23.6)	5,548.8 (27.6)	186.6 (0.9)	319.7 (1.6)	275.9 (1.4)	782.2 (3.9)	146.9 (0.7)	481.5 (2.4)	104.2 (0.5)	413.8 (2.1)	1,146.4 (5.7)
1986	24,181.5 (100.0)	15,908.2 (65.8)	5,432.6 (22.5)	8,254.7 (34.1)	328.7 (1.4)	378.7 (1.6)	339.9 (1.4)	1,047.3 (4.3)	162.9 (0.7)	500.7 (2.1)	152.7 (0.6)	357.3 (1.5)	1,173.6 (4.9)
1987	34,983.4 (100.0)	22,988.2 (65.7)	7,648.0 (21.9)	11,840.6 (33.8)	532.7 (1.5)	753.8 (2.2)	522.1 (1.5)	1,808.6 (5.2)	200.4 (0.6)	729.0 (2.1)	194.4 (0.6)	567.2 (1.6)	1,691.0 (4.8)
1988	49,672.8 (100.0)	33,535.4 (67.5)	13,006.7 (26.2)	14,825.4 (29.8)	900.1 (1.8)	1,922.1 (3.9)	740.1 (1.5)	3,562.3 (7.2)	341.9 (0.7)	943.4 (1.9)	242.3 (0.5)	613.4 (1.2)	2,141.0 (4.3)
1989	52,265.3 (100.0)	34,589.8 (66.2)	12,002.8 (23.0)	16,031.0 (30.7)	1,239.0 (2.4)	2,205.2 (4.2)	889.4 (1.7)	4,333.6 (8.3)	390.2 (0.7)	887.5 (1.7)	238.5 (0.5)	706.2 (1.4)	2,222.4 (4.3)
1990	54,716.0 (100.0)	35,414.6 (64.7)	12,611.8 (23.0)	15,998.4 (29.2)	1,343.6 (2.5)	1,445.9 (2.6)	1,406.0 (2.6)	4,195.5 (7.7)	448.0 (0.8)	1,003.0 (1.8)	236.3 (0.4)	921.6 (1.7)	2,608.9 (4.8)
1991	62,862.5 (100.0)	41,576.9 (66.1)	14,113.8 (22.5)	18,858.3 (30.0)	1,747.0 (2.8)	1,946.8 (3.1)	1,445.9 (2.3)	5,139.7 (8.2)	586.1 (0.9)	1,409.4 (2.2)	235.3 (0.4)	1,234.3 (2.0)	3,465.1 (5.5)
1992	72,007.0 (100.0)	47,681.1 (66.2)	15,771.0 (21.9)	21,766.6 (30.2)	2,300.9 (3.2)	1,781.4 (2.5)	1,694.9 (2.4)	5,777.2 (8.0)	824.6 (1.1)	1,829.2 (2.5)	305.2 (0.4)	1,407.3 (2.0)	4,366.3 (6.1)
1993	77,061.2 (100.0)	50,941.2 (66.1)	16,722.6 (21.7)	23,186.1 (30.1)	2,537.3 (3.3)	1,728.6 (2.2)	1,865.9 (2.4)	6,131.8 (8.0)	973.0 (1.3)	1,938.9 (2.5)	364.8 (0.5)	1,624.0 (2.1)	4,900.7 (6.4)

Sources: Ministry of Finance, Taiwan, *Monthly Statistics of Exports and Imports*, various issues.

TABLE 23.9   Taiwan's Trade with ASEAN countries* and mainland China, 1987–94 (US$ million)

Year	Thailand		Malaysia		Philippines		Indonesia		Mainland China**	
	Export	Import	Export	Import	Export	Import	Export	Import	Export	Import
1987	424.6	200.4	272.1	729.0	459.7	194.4	445.5	567.2	1,226.5	288.9
1988	753.7	341.9	451.1	943.4	601.4	242.3	632.6	613.4	2,242.2	478.7
1989	1,110.2	390.2	694.8	887.5	778.1	238.5	934.1	706.2	2,896.5	586.9
1990	1,423.6	448.0	1,103.6	1,003.0	811.4	236.3	1,245.8	921.6	3,278.3	765.4
1991	1,444.9	586.1	1,464.9	1,409.4	848.0	235.3	1,207.2	1,234.3	4,667.2	1,125.9
1992	1,809.6	824.6	1,600.3	1,829.2	1,023.3	305.2	1,214.8	1,407.3	6,287.9	1,119.0
1993	2,017.1	973.0	1,668.0	1,938.9	1,030.8	364.8	1,284.5	1,624.0	7,585.4	1,103.6
1994	2,440.2	1,108.8	2,224.2	2,326.9	1,222.5	460.7	1,433.0	2,114.4	16,022.5	1,858.7

*Excluding Singapore and Brunei.
**Referring to indirect trade through Hong Kong. Export data are adjusted by the Mainland Affairs Council according to both Hong Kong and Taiwan customs.

Sources: Ministry of Finance, Taiwan, *Monthly Statistics of Exports and Imports*, various issues; Mainland Affairs Council, Taiwan, *Monthly Statistics of Cross-Strait Economic Activities*, various issues.

TABLE 23.10   Taiwan's exports of capital goods to ASEAN (excluding Brunei) (%)

	Machinery and transportation equipment[1]					Manufactures[2]				
	1981	1985	1988	1990	1991	1981	1985	1988	1990	1991
Singapore	32.12	25.76	47.16	51.96	51.86	88.97	85.10	94.83	96.82	95.86
Malaysia	32.45	35.47	49.93	54.76	52.78	91.44	89.50	95.20	97.23	97.38
Thailand	40.80	26.55	41.24	43.41	45.04	89.09	72.68	91.18	91.57	93.09
Indonesia	40.53	38.51	41.87	45.71	45.25	80.73	82.12	85.43	92.33	93.13
Philippines	18.50	14.70	26.74	26.00	26.55	71.63	86.81	89.64	93.33	93.60
Total[3]	33.01	27.40	42.59	43.39	46.72	84.32	83.74	92.00	94.55	94.91

1. SITC code 7.
2. SITC code 5,6,7,8.
3. Figures represent ratios of Taiwan's exports of listed products to ASEAN (excluding Brunei) over Taiwan's total exports.

Source: Council for Economic Planning and Development, Taiwan, "Bilateral Relations between Taiwan and ASEAN," internal report, 1992 (in Chinese).

TABLE 23.11   Coefficient of intra-industry (manufacturing) trade between Taiwan and ASEAN*

SITC	Item	1981	1985	1988	1990	1991
5	Chemicals	25.39	34.72	45.15	43.33	47.82
6	Manufactures (classified by raw materials)	10.85	10.75	20.57	19.66	24.01
7	Machinery and transportation equipment	29.18	28.55	35.34	42.51	41.47
8	Miscellaneous products	21.28	8.86	29.95	29.23	35.10
5–8	Manufacturing	20.87	19.68	30.71	34.40	36.47

*Excluding Brunei.

Sources: International Monetary Fund, *Direction of Trade Statistics Yearbook*, various issues.

pursued by all. Meanwhile, business globalism calls for governmental talks on economic cooperation at a very broad level, such as the recently concluded Uruguay Round trade talks, and the trend of worldwide liberalization encourages the globalization of companies.

In globalizing their activities, corporate planners are very well aware that the Asian-Pacific region is too important to be ignored. With its burgeoning economic strength, the Asia-Pacific region has become known as the world's production house and the world's hottest market is just bubbling up in this region. Indeed, the failure to get into Asia would be the greatest danger for any global competitor. Alert companies are spreading operations around the region. And as the region is gaining momentum, sooner or later these companies will have to set up regional operations centers (ROCs) to take care of decision-making, not only in production activities, but also in distribution, financing, R&D, and all other regional business activities.

The basic idea behind a regional operations center is the decentralization of decision-making of the parent company to a local division or subsidiary which is responsible for all regional business including production, distribution, and R&D. Such decentralization allows companies to use local information more efficiently, particularly when there are coordination problems between or among regions. Moreover, decentralization of decision-making to the regional level promotes the deepening of international specialization and division of labor and stimulates regional coordination such as in building transportation networks. A step further from a regional operation center is the regional or multiple profits center. By establishing profits centers in different parts of the world (for example, in Europe, Asia Pacific, and North America), the parent company will no longer be vulnerable to the developments in the economy where it is located: it can diversify the risk while holding shares of its profits center corporations in other countries. Moreover, the parent company can benefit significantly by listing the financially independent yet profit-earning subsidiary in the local stock market, or simply by raising funds in the local market.

Regional operations centers become desirable when the prospect for intraregional trade is growing, and when there are significant institutional and behavioral differences between markets in the West and the East. Since in Asia intraregional trade is increasing, and rapidly changing market conditions call for a fast response, it is more profitable to set up a regional operations center than build various divisions across the region that report separately to the parent company.

23.4.2 Blessings

Given its central position in Asia-Pacific, its close links with the West, and the strength of its local economy, Taiwan emerges as an attractive site for companies contemplating setting up Asia-Pacific regional operations centers.

As stated earlier, Taiwan's great transition since the 1980s was rooted in the sharp appreciation of the NT dollar and the economy's adjustment efforts to macro imbalances, namely, the extraordinarily high level of trade surplus and declining investment growth. Led by their second sense for comparative advantage, Taiwan's industrialists were quick to develop their new advantage in order to survive intensifying world competition brought on by an appreciating local currency. They achieved their new advantage by investing increasingly in the neighboring economies and improving the productivity of home-based products. These entrepreneurs were unaware that they were actually equipping Taiwan with the capability and skills to perform regional operations.

Important position. Taiwan's important position in the region has geographic, cultural and economic dimensions. Geographically, Taiwan is in a superior position to serve as a flywheel in East Asia. It is well situated for coordinating trade among China, Southeast Asia, Japan and North America. Culturally, Taiwan is a Chinese society that has much in common with Singapore, Hong Kong, mainland China, and the enormous overseas Chinese communities across Southeast Asia. It is also similar to other Confucian economies that do not use Mandarin or other Chinese dialects, such as Japan and Korea.

Extensive economic ties with other member economies of the region. As noted earlier, these include trade, investment, and technological exchanges. Taiwan's trade with Asia amounted to US$69.2 billion for the first 11 months of 1993, with Japan and Hong Kong taking the lion's share. Indirect trade with mainland China has been growing by leaps. Trade across the Taiwan Straits through Hong Kong had increased thirtyfold from US$0.2 billion to US$7.4 billion in the ten years starting from 1983. Trade with ASEAN members also expanded remarkably. Between 1986 and 1992, ASEAN's share of Taiwan's total exports rose from below 5 percent to 10 percent, while its share of Taiwan's total imports increased from 6 percent to 8 percent.

The rapid growth in trade with the mainland and ASEAN is believed to have been fueled by Taiwan's growing investment in these areas. In the face of the rising value of local currency and spiralling wages, land prices, and other costs of production, Taiwanese entrepreneurs have been attracted to Southeast Asia and mainland China since 1986. Besides economic factors, cultural factors and the high degree of complementarity between these economies and Taiwan are also behind such capital flows. In 1992, investment in the mainland by Taiwan businessmen totaled US$5.5 billion. Almost one-third of Taiwan's outward investment is directed to ASEAN. The cumulative amount of investment surpassed US$2 billion in August 1993, with the information industry taking the lead. Unlike Hong Kong's ventures which have invested heavily in mainland China, Taiwan's ventures have invested more evenly across the region. Thanks to close and extensive trade and investment ties between Taiwan and its regional neighbors, and growing partnerships that have taken other forms, Taiwan is more than ready to coordinate regional operations in Asia-Pacific.

Although Hong Kong and Singapore also have important links in the region, Taiwan is distinguished by the fact that it is not just a city-state but a highly industrialized, integrated economy with a medium-sized population base. As such Taiwan's trade with the rest of the region is more than entrepôt and service trade. Rather, it involves the connection between local industries and other industries in the region. Instead of withering away like Hong Kong's manufacturing industries, Taiwan's industries have survived intensifying regional competition by quickly shifting from labor-intensive methods of production to more capital- and technology-intensive methods.

Close Links with the West. Whereas Taiwan's assumption of a pivotal role in Asia-Pacific is recent, Taiwan has a much longer history of close ties with Western countries and is still expanding on them. Western companies have invested greatly in Taiwan, bringing in advanced technology at the same time. This has contributed to Taiwan's swift industrialization, broad links with the West, and experience with Western management. The latter two virtues will make Taiwan a good intermediary between Western parent companies and their Asian affiliates. Taiwan's close historical ties with Japan and the United States have also in recent years been supplemented by growing ties with European economies.

Resilient Domestic Economy. A foreign magazine correspondent once wrote: "Taipei has always succeeded where others thought it would fail." Taiwan emerged from hopeless circumstances 40 years ago when the economy was in chaos with rampant inflation, serious unemployment, a huge fiscal deficit, insufficient capital for investment, and an extreme shortage of foreign exchange. But the economy took off and enjoyed an annual average rate of growth of nearly 9 percent. This has been accompanied with price stability, industrialization, modest unemployment, and a more equitable distribution of income. Despite its recent slowdown, which is common among maturing economies, Taiwan was able to grow 6.3 percent in

1993 and 6.5 percent in 1994. Companies that are locating their regional operations centers in Taiwan will benefit not only from the host economy's resources they directly use but also its resilient strength.

With per capita GNP of US$11,000, Taiwan's 21 million people represent an enormous consumer market with strong purchasing power. Private consumption has been expanding by double-digit rates since 1987, the year when the New Taiwan dollar began to rapidly appreciate and the opening of the domestic market started to quicken. This year, private consumption is targeted to grow 11 percent in nominal terms. The ongoing six-year infrastructural plan (although scaled down somewhat this year) and a promotion program for private investment certainly provide great opportunities for foreign capital goods and services.

23.4.3 Challenges and Limitations

For all the blessings, Taiwan has its drawbacks. The most often heard criticisms are: (1) infrastructural hardware (such as transportation and communications) needs to be strengthened, and (2) laws and regulations need to be updated to facilitate rather than hamper trade, investment, and financial activities.

23.4.4 Infrastructural Development

The six-year National Development Plan was launched in 1991 to provide Taiwan with the infrastructural software and hardware needed to increase overall productivity and improve the national quality of life. The comprehensive plan proposes a series of public construction projects that will strengthen infrastructural development, boost industrial growth, and balance development among counties and cities. These projects are concerned mostly with the development of transportation and communications, public utilities, urban construction and housing, manufacturing industries, environmental protection, and medical care.

The transportation sector seems to have fallen behind economic development in recent years. To make Taiwan an ideal site for regional operations centers, Taiwan must provide a comprehensive telecommunications network for domestic and international exchanges of information. This calls for the acceleration of network digitalization and the promotion of optical fiber transmission.

Another important theme that will help boost Taiwan's candidacy as a regional operations center is the modernization of the service sector. High-quality services will be required to meet a wide range of demands by increasing regional business operations. The six-year plan's design for services development includes the updating of laws and regulations, manpower planning, and spatial programming of services distribution. The output and employment in the service sector is targeted to grow 7.8 percent and 3.4 percent during the six-year period (1991–96). Growth targets for insurance services and financial services (excluding insurance) are 14.8 percent and 9.1 percent, respectively.

23.4.5 Institutional Reform—Deregulation and Reregulation

The direction of Taiwan's economic policy has been set clearly toward liberalization and internationalization. Its current theme is trade and financial liberalizations—these appear to be appropriate themes in every aspect. And this is a manifestation of the outward-looking strategy pursued by Taiwan ever since it began its rapid development at the turn of the 1960s. Also, prospective investors in Taiwan should be assured of an increasingly more open host economy for their operations.

In July 1993, Taiwan's Cabinet launched an action plan, the so-called Economic Revitalization Program, for the promotion of private investment. One of the program's two objectives is developing Taiwan into an Asia-Pacific regional operations center. The other aim is to accelerate Taiwan's industrial upgrading.

This program sets forth immediate actions to remedy the shortages of land and manpower, increase and improve technological resources, and better Taiwan's financial environment. Its land programs include opening up land owned by the government and public enterprises, converting farmland for use by industry and public works, and accelerating the development of industrial zones. High technology industries will enjoy a five-year exemption from business income tax and more tax credits are offered for plant and office automation. Reform of the government administration as well as government enterprises is also listed in the program. This means that laws, regulations, and other measures will be put in place to modernize the civil service, attain full administrative coordination, and improve the efficiency of government enterprises.

Last but not least, Taiwan's relations with mainland China have changed dramatically after half a century of military and political confrontation. The high degree of resource complementarity and division of labor, and the fading of the Cold War has helped forge the recent warming of the relations between the two sides across the Taiwan Straits. The increasing economic and trade exchanges between Taiwan and the mainland have become a trend beneficial to both parties. Therefore, the Revitalization Program calls for clear and realistic policies on such relations. It proposes a step-by-step relaxation of cross-straits exchange restrictions, support measures for Taiwanese investors in the mainland, the promotion of cross-strait technological exchanges, and the recruitment of talent from the mainland.

23.5 Taiwan's Role in the Asia-Pacific Region

The last few years have witnessed remarkable political and economic changes throughout the world. The fading of the East-West Cold War; ethnic strife raging in Africa, Central Europe, and the Middle East; the European Community moving towards economic unification; the expansion of the North American Free Trade Agreement (NAFTA); the burgeoning power of the Asia-Pacific economies; and the recent signing of the new GATT rules—all these developments are part of a new agenda of global issues.

TABLE 23.12 Intra-regional trade within 12 East Asian countries

	1970*		1980		1985		1990		1992	
	Amount of trade (US$ m)	% of total trade	Amount of trade (US$ m)	% of total trade	Amount of trade (US$ m)	% of total trade	Amount of trade (US$ m)	% of total trade	Amount of trade (US$ m)	% of total trade
Japan	8,836	23.13	77,141	28.39	90,881	29.54	169,949	32.50	204,785	35.73
Korea	1,313	46.58	13,965	35.09	20,808	33.88	53,981	40.03	67,810	42.81
Taiwan	1,377	46.58	14,218	35.95	18,371	36.14	55,067	45.16	76,903	50.11
Singapore	2,120	52.80	23,848	54.98	26,628	54.24	59,823	52.64	69,866	51.50
Hong Kong	1,654	30.52	20,006	47.48	33,977	56.73	99,585	60.49	151,686	62.44
Thailand	1,010	50.27	6,636	42.22	7,701	47.06	28,035	49.66	37,064	50.66
Malaysia	1,482	47.88	12,960	54.63	16,882	60.85	34,372	58.58	48,327	59.93
Indonesia	1,226	58.10	21,245	64.88	17,176	59.53	29,426	61.94	36,880	65.12
Philippines	1,021	44.94	5,824	41.49	4,546	45.16	9,280	43.96	11,940	45.20
Australia	2,847	30.57	17,789	41.99	21,455	46.41	37,380	47.47	43,441	52.19
New Zealand	673	27.27	4,529	41.57	5,283	45.11	8,954	47.15	9,406	49.44
Mainland China	–	–	17,800	46.79	40,232	57.60	72,187	63.44	106,950	68.18
Total	23,559	31.55	235,961	38.42	303,940	41.09	658,039	45.28	865,058	49.16

*In 1970, mainland China was not included in the calculation.

Sources: IMF, *Direction of Trade Statistics Yearbook*, 1969–75, 1987, 1991, 1993; Department of Statistics, Ministry of Finance, Taiwan, *Monthly Statistics of Exports and Imports*, various issues; Korea Foreign Trade Association, *Major Statistics of Korean Economy*, various issues.

23.5.1 New Order in the Region

More than ten regional trade bodies have been set up around the world. The EC has been the most successful of these efforts. Though East Asia has been the fastest growing region of the world over the past ten years, no formal or effective arrangement has been adopted to set up a cooperative economic organization in the region. This points to an interesting yet grave fact that dismantles the myth of the need to form a trade bloc in order to achieve rapid trade expansion. A legitimate trade integrating body is not necessarily the premise for rapid trade development and its existence does not necessarily mean it can effectively promote trade.

By observing the development history of individual economies, one finds a common feature: an outward orientation. Trade has been the engine of growth for the East Asian economies. There is almost no exception. Whether it is a cross-section study among countries or time-series analysis of a country over time, all show that openness helps speed up growth. Another feature worth noting is that Japan's and Taiwan's efforts to remedy unusual external imbalances have increased their ties with the other members of the Asia-Pacific region and helped promote the region's economic integration.

One could reason from the above that the openness of the economy will benefit its development and that the industrial division of labor within a region is good for the region's development. This was the case for Japan, which led the push to rapid development in the region in the 1960s. It was followed by the "four little dragons" in the 1970s, the near-NICs in Southeast Asia in the late 1980s, and mainland China and Indonesia in more recent years. These countries have established an exemplary model for the international specialization and division of labor. And soon Vietnam and Burma will join the party and catch up quickly.

As the process of economic integration proceeds in the region, we need to be prepared for a couple of possible challenges: mainland China's policies toward openness and conflicts arising from the emergence of new international cooperations arrangements.

Within mainland China, there are vast ethnic and economic disparities that determine different paces and sequences of economic development and thus various stages of development. In other words, the patterns of division of labor and specialization that are spread throughout the East Asia region should take place within the mainland economy itself. This means mainland China has to pay more attention to a more balanced approach in its external and internal development. In this regard, Taiwan's development experience in the 1950s and 1960s may have something to offer.

23.5.2 Taiwan's New Role

Taiwan has tried hard and actually succeeded to a considerable extent in merging its economy with the outside world. As the new era of globalism and regionalism arrives in the 1990s, Taiwan is ready to play an expanded role in this region. Consider the following developments:

☐ Mainland China is confirming its commitment to the market economy, no matter what term they choose to use to describe their economy. The mainland economy has been growing at a rate of 8.8 percent per year since 1978, which must be a record in history for an economy of that size.

☐ Meanwhile Taiwan has been investing heavily both in mainland China and the booming economies of Southeast Asia, ensuring Taiwan's leading role in the rising Asia-Pacific economy.

☐ NAFTA has been formed and in the future might be expanded to include, in some way, Taiwan and some other East Asian countries.

These developments and Taiwan's close links with both the regional economy and the North American economy could make it the best location for a coordination point between these regions.

While thousands of Taiwan manufacturing companies have moved their production lines wholly or partly abroad in recent years, the manufacturing sector still remained strong, even continuing to grow steadily as domestic industry develops its new niche in the regional economy. Thus, indigenous multinationals have already played an active role in the progress and prosperity of the region.

Foreign investors coming to Taiwan will not focus just on Taiwan but on the future of the whole region. Taiwan is making an all-out effort to enhance its regional role by fostering the development of the most favorable environment to host regional operations centers. Foreign investors are welcome to take advantage of Taiwan's position in the booming regional economy. These developments will shape Taiwan's economic landscape in the 1990s.

23.6 Dutch Disease Symptom in Taiwan[1]

Taiwan's macroeconomic imbalances in the late 1980s, which were described in Section 23.2, seem to bear much resemblance to a development model termed the "Dutch Disease." That term was first used in *The Economist* (November 16, 1977) to refer to problems resulting from surging exports in the Netherlands. During the first oil crisis, the Dutch export of national gas increased significantly, causing a sharp appreciation of the Dutch guilder in a short period of time. The international competitiveness of Dutch products, other than oil products, was then weakened. The price level of Dutch products was rising because of expanded government spending. What had started out as a blessing—the rapid accumulation of a country's foreign exchanges—had turned into an undesirable result in the following years.

Similarly, Taiwan's long standing policies of export promotion and import substitution had succeeded in bringing about sustained growth and rapid industrialization, but later caused macroeconomic imbalances after 20 or more years of export-led growth. The internal imbalances arose from the shortfall in domestic investment, which was the consequence of long-term emphasis on foreign demand, while the external imbalances sprang from the hefty trade surplus, which was, again, the result of long-term export promotion efforts.

In addition to the features mentioned in Section 23.1, the macroeconomy and the social environment of Taiwan in the 1980s was also characterized by the following:

☐ The export-oriented manufacturing sector attained a commanding share in total output: 39.7 percent in 1986, a much higher rate than all other countries with the exception of a few, such as Belgium, which reflects the pivotal role of the export-oriented manufacturing sector.[2]

☐ The Labor Law promulgated in 1984 nurtured a new relationship between labor and management.

☐ Environmental protection began to be emphasized and environmental laws began to be more strictly enforced.

☐ A rapid democratization process began to take place in the mid-1980s.

All these developments had placed Taiwan in a position of great transition. The Dutch disease was an important element in this environment of change.

Let us examine the causes of, and the impact of, the Dutch disease, and whether Taiwan did in fact suffer exactly from the same disease as the Dutch. First, Taiwan did not earn foreign exchange from exporting any kind of natural resources, but from a variety of manufactures. Second, Taiwan's trade surplus did not come from any unexpected favorable change in the price of natural resources, such as oil in the Dutch case. Rather, it came from Taiwan's long-term improvement in international competitiveness and an export-promotion scheme conceptualized as early as 20 years ago. These facts may shed light on why Taiwan ended up in a different position than the Netherlands.

Taiwan's responses to its currency appreciation problem can be summarized as follows:

☐ Achievement of industrial restructuring away from labor-intensive to high technology and higher value-added production.

☐ Achievement of high levels of production automation and product quality improvement at the firm level during a relatively short period of time. This might not have come true without the mounting pressure of currency appreciation.

☐ Overseas investments relocated declining industries to countries where they enjoy a comparative advantage. This facilitated the great restructuring process.

☐ The export market shifted away from its concentration on the U.S. market. Efforts were made to spread export activities across the East Asian economies.

☐ Public investment in infrastructures increased.

☐ Institutional reforms: such as liberalization, internationalization and deregulation were carried out.

☐ Economic revitalization programs aiming for the long-term improvement of the investment climate through the creation of a more flexible and efficient factor market were pursued.

☐ Taiwan suffered from symptoms similar to those associated with Japan's bubble economy. These symptoms appeared in the late 1980s on the heels of the Dutch disease problem. It took a series of tough government measures to ensure a soft landing after the bubble burst.

Taiwan's efforts to cure the Dutch disease, if one can call it that, have been manifold, multidimensional, and successful. The challenge posed by the disease forced Taiwan to restructure its economy. Its adjustment efforts should put Taiwan back on the track of a more balanced long-term development.

23.7 Conclusions

With its burgeoning economy, Taiwan has made a constructive contribution to regional integration while adjusting its domestic imbalances. Taiwan is committed to emphasizing economic liberalization and regional integration and to providing active hardware and software infrastructural support. This approach will yield respectable growth and greater overall welfare over the long run.

The World Trade Organization (WTO) started life on January 1, 1995, to implement the Uruguay Round accords, which are expected to boost global income by more than US$200 billion in the next ten years, according to most quantitative analyses. The Asia-Pacific region has demonstrated great success in integrating member economies with the guidance of market forces. This implies that regional integration does not have to be inconsistent with WTO arrangements. Since a trade bloc will not likely emerge in Asia-Pacific, the region's economic integration is a praiseworthy model of "open regionalism." How regional members will share their resources and work together for the prosperity and progress of the whole world, is the greatest challenge that lies ahead for them.

Notes

This article first appeared in *Industry of Free China*, 1994, 82(2): 29–50. The present chapter has been updated and expanded.

1. For a more detailed study, see Schive (1994).
2. See Schive (1994: 189).

Reference

Schive, Chi, 1994, "How Did Taiwan Solve Its Dutch Disease Problem?" *Research in Asian Economic Studies*, Vol. 5, JAI Press, Greenwich, CT, pp. 183–202.

Chapter 24

Chung-Sok Suh

KOREA IN THE 1990S: LITTLE DRAGON OR NEW GIANT?

24.1 Introduction

The economy of the Republic of Korea (hereafter Korea) has achieved a remarkable rate of growth over the last few decades. It has been transformed from one of the poorest countries in the world, in the beginning of the 1960s, to a country with a prospect in the near future of joining the Organization for Economic Cooperation and Development (OECD) countries in terms of income per capita. In the General Agreement on Tariffs and Trade (GATT) negotiations, Korea is no longer regarded as a developing country. Nevertheless, there remain many imbalances and obstacles in the economy which need to be tackled before a successful transition into a mature industrialized economy can be assured. The momentum developed during the past 30 years clearly indicates the potential of the country to continue its growth toward maturity. However, it is widely agreed that substantial changes and restructuring of the economy are necessary. Some of these changes are already beginning to take place. The way the country overcomes challenges in the 1990s will shape the future of the Korean economy. In this context, the focus of this chapter lies in the examination of the challenges faced by the Korean economy in the early 1990s in the Asia-Pacific region.

This chapter is organized as follows. Section 24.1 briefly surveys the history of Korean industrialization, Section 24.2 discusses the place of the Korean economy in its international setting, especially in the Asia-Pacific region. Section 24.3 identifies the sources of past growth and asks to what extent the Korean experiences can be transferred to other developing countries. Major challenges faced by the Korean economy in the 1990s are explained in Section 24.4, followed by some concluding remarks.

24.2 From Poverty to Prosperity

After World War II, following the defeat of Japan, the Korean peninsula was divided into two parts along the 38 degree latitude line. South Korea became a politically independent country as the Republic of Korea in 1948, but North Korea invaded it in 1950, greatly disrupting the post–World War II economic development of the South Korean economy. When the truce was signed in 1953, South Korea had a very small industrial base and the agricultural sector was hard-pressed to feed the population, which had been growing due to substantial migration from North Korea to South Korea since 1945.

The rest of the 1950s was devoted to recovering from the war and beginning an industrialization drive. This drive was promoted by an import-substitution policy, but the results were not impressive. Although the rate of gross national product (GNP) growth for the rest of 1950s was approximately 5 percent per year (Bank of Korea (BOK) 1970), this was largely financed by foreign aid. The value of manufactured exports declined from US$49 million in 1953 to US$9 million in 1959, measured in 1970 constant dollars (BOK 1973). When the period covered by the first Five Year Economic Development Plan (FYEDP) started in 1962, Korea remained one of the poorest countries in the world.

However, two important policies in the pre-1960s period deserve special mention. One was the education policy, the other land reform. Although educational aspirations have always been important in Korean culture, the government placed education as a high priority after decolonization. Having received continuous support from the government, the highly educated workforce provided a strong base for economic development from the 1960s onward. Land reform took place in 1949, limiting the maximum size of a holding by any one household to three hectares. As a result, approximately 23 percent of the total arable land was redistributed, and in the 1960s there was a strong sense of egalitarianism with no marked income disparities in the agricultural sector, which could otherwise have served as a major constraint on development.

The performance of the Korean economy in the 1960s and 1970s placed the country among the group of successful newly industrializing economies (NIEs) in East Asia. Looked at from a long run perspective, the two oil shocks in the 1970s did not affect the economy's performance a great deal. Even more impressive was the way the economy overcame the severe recession which occurred in the early 1980s. In the second half of the 1980s, Korea became one of a few countries in the world which continued to record a very high rate of growth. Table 24.1 compares major economic indicators in the years since 1960.

TABLE 24.1   Real rates of growth of GNP and its components and inflation rate (%)

Years[a]	GNP	Consumption	Investment	Government expenditure	Exports	Imports	Inflation[b]
1962–66	7.8	5.9	23.2	4.0	26.2	17.4	–
1967–71	9.6	10.6	18.5	10.6	30.3	26.6	12.6
1972–76	9.6	7.1	12.7	4.9	27.6	15.4	17.8
1977–81	5.9	5.6	8.0	7.0	12.3	10.9	18.4
1982–86	8.7	5.7	9.4	4.4	11.8	7.7	3.6
1987–91	10.4	9.5	17.0	10.5	16.4	21.0	6.8

a. These years show each Five Year Economic Development Plan period.
b. Measured by the consumer price index (CPI)

Sources: Bank of Korea, various issues.

A student revolution in 1960 was followed by a military coup in 1961. Although a civilian government was established in 1963, the first FYEDP was launched in 1962 by the military government. Ever since, the government has played an extremely active role in economic development. All financial institutions were nationalized and access to both domestic and foreign credit was totally controlled by the government. The main thrust of the growth strategy from the 1960s onward was export promotion. Exporters were granted unrestricted and tariff-free access to imported intermediate inputs. All exporters also automatically gained access to bank loans. Major policy reforms relating to the exchange rate, trade controls and the financial sector were adopted around 1965, to promote exports.

The agricultural sector was protected from foreign competition and provided with price supports. Due to an increase in productivity in the 1970s and the effects of the price support program, income levels in farm and nonfarm households were quite close, toward the end of the 1970s (Amsden 1991). Consequently, industrialization could proceed in the context of a politically pacified countryside. On the other hand, the agricultural sector was the major source of additional labor supply for the urban manufacturing sector. The government tightly controlled labor markets also, forbidding the emergence of labor union movements. Although the level of real wages continued to increase, due to productivity increases, the labor market was repressed and industrialization was able to proceed with little industrial action from labor unions until the mid-1980s.

During the past three decades, the process of rapid economic growth has transformed Korea's traditional agrarian economy into a modernized industrial economy. During the period, the most remarkable change is that primary industry (agriculture, forestry and fisheries) production, as a percentage of GNP decreased from 40 percent in 1960 to 9 percent in 1990, while secondary industry (mining and manufacturing) production, increased from 19 percent to 28 percent. The Korean industrial structure reflects the poor natural resource endowments of the economy and the export oriented growth strategy. The rapid increase in the share of the manufacturing sector is due largely to the need to export manufactured products to earn foreign exchange for capital goods and raw material imports. The change of employment structure was slower than that of industrial output.[1] In the 1980s the agricultural sector was relatively ignored by the government. As a result, in 1990 agriculture's share of total output was 9 percent while its share of total employment was 20 percent. This reflects the relative poverty of the rural area in the 1980s, as well as the political difficulty of structural adjustments in the 1990s.

Overall, the economic development of Korea has been heavily dependent on the rapid growth of international trade, especially the growth of exports. Before the implementation of the Five-Year Plans the total amount of annual exports were in the order of US$30 million. As shown in Table 24.1 exports grew very rapidly throughout the past 30 years although growth has slowed down from the fourth FYEDP period onwards. However, the ratio of exports to GNP has increased steadily: from 8 percent in the First Plan period to 40 percent in the Sixth Plan period. The rate of growth of imports was lower than that of exports. Until 1985, the balance of trade was always unfavorable, and the trade deficit was offset by a capital account surplus, mainly foreign debt. As a result, the accumulated foreign debt in 1985 was US$60 billion, which amounted to 54 percent of GNP in that year, making Korea the fourth largest debtor country in the world. For four consecutive years, 1986–89, Korea enjoyed large surpluses in its current account balance of payments due to the so-called "three lows": the fall in oil price, the low exchange rates (that is, the appreciation of the Japanese yen), and the low international interest rate. In response, the government chose to repay nearly US$3 billion in foreign loans in 1986 and US$5 billion in 1987, before these loans became due.

Economic growth changed the internal structure of the manufacturing sector as well. Until the mid-1960s growth of the manufacturing sector was led by light industries such as flour, sugar and cotton textiles, based on imported or surplus agricultural products from the U.S. Investment in heavy industry began in the late 1960s for items such as iron and steel, petroleum, chemicals and electronics. After 1972 when President Park Chung-Hee's power was consolidated, investment in the "six main heavy and chemical industries"—iron and steel, shipbuilding, non-ferrous metals, heavy chemicals, machinery, and electronics industries—was emphasized in order to restructure the industrial sector and to develop the defense industry. As a result, the share of heavy manufactures increased from 40 percent of manufacturing output in 1972 to 62 percent in 1984, and from 21 percent of manufacturing exports to 60 percent in the same period. Among these, the steel, cement and shipbuilding sectors were the fastest growing industries in the 1970s. As a result, Korea became the third largest cement exporting country in the world. It also accounted for 20 percent of international ship exports by the early 1980s. Consumer light goods accounted for 59.5 percent of total manufacturing output and 86.3 percent of total merchandise exports in 1971, but fell to 43.7 percent and 60.1 percent respectively in 1980. The proportions declined further in the 1980s.

However, by the end of the 1970s, a number of structural imbalances emerged in the economy. Substantial concessionary loans resulted in the creation of excess capacities in some industries, particularly those in power generation, transport equipment and heavy machinery. On the other hand light industries such as the textile industry were neglected and the lack of investment and technical improvement resulted in the deterioration of competitiveness of major export items. Meanwhile, a rapid expansion of housing and an investment boom accompanied by domestic credit expansion resulted in an acceleration of inflation. In addition, the previously abundant supply of excess labor from the agricultural sector was exhausted by the mid-1970s, raising real wages rapidly despite the high rate of inflation. Gradually, external competitiveness was eroded and export growth declined.

In order to overcome these difficulties, a series of stabilization measures was introduced in April 1979. However, with the second round of oil price increases in July, the assassination of President Park in October of that year, and the political turmoil that followed, these measures did not show any significant effect. In 1980 both the internal and external environments were not favorable to Korea. Internally, political turmoil, a severe drought, and the extremely high rate of inflation all caused difficulties. High international interest rates and the deterioration of Korea's terms of trade alone increased the debt burden by approximately 6 percent of GNP during 1979–80, while the worldwide recession contributed to the slowdown of Korea's economic growth. The result was a decrease in GNP by 3.7 percent for the first time since 1953, and an increase in the consumer price index (CPI) by 34.6 percent and the wholesale price index (WPI) by 39.0 percent.

As the world economy started to show recovery in 1983, the Korean economy also entered a recovery period. Macroeconomic policies during the 1960s and 1970s had been mainly expansionary. The average inflation rate was 16 percent during the 1960s and 1970s. However, the focus of macroeconomic policies moved to price stability and a decrease in reliance on foreign borrowing. Fiscal and monetary policies were extremely tight, to reduce the public sector deficit and monetary expansion. With the help of a flexible exchange rate policy external competitiveness was gradually restored. The effects of this tightening were threefold: (a) long-term external debt as a percentage of total external debt rose from 62 percent in 1982 to 68.8 percent in 1984, (b) the domestic savings ratio increased from 23 percent in 1982 to 28 percent in 1984, reducing the current account deficit considerably, and (c) inflation was eliminated (Chenery 1986). As a result, the economy completely recovered from the recession after 1985. Although financial markets are still strongly influenced by the government, there has been a movement toward a more market oriented system. In 1982 the government abolished the direct credit ceilings in the banks and took less direct measures, relying more on open market operations, reserve requirements and the rediscount mechanism. Preferential interest rates for priority sectors were eliminated in 1982, but directed loans remained an important feature of Korea's financial system, though the share in total loans declined from 20 percent in 1980 to 16 percent in 1982 and showed a decreasing trend.

The second half of 1985 witnessed another turning point in the Korean economy due to favorable external conditions. With domestic inflation completely controlled, the export market succeeded in gaining greater shares in world markets, especially in the U.S. For the first time in 25 years, the economy recorded a current account surplus for four consecutive years from 1986. The sixth FYEDP, which started in 1987, reflected a desire to move toward more balanced socioeconomic growth. Since the current account balance showed surpluses, and the debt burden was no longer a major constraint, areas which had been entirely neglected in the past received relatively more attention. These areas include development in the agricultural sector, small- and medium-sized firms in the manufacturing sector, income inequality and the labor market, the social welfare system, and further research and development programs. Another major change is the liberalization of the economy along with political democratization. This will be explained in detail in Section 24.3.

24.3   A Little Dragon in a Big World

24.3.1   The Structure of Korean Trade

As Korea who is a late-comer to the international world is poorly endowed with natural resources but has been pursuing export promotion policy, its trade structure has been mainly vertical in nature, that is, major export and import items do not overlap much. Due to a paucity of natural resources the share of primary products in total imports has always been as high as one-third. The most important primary products are crude oil, foodstuffs, and minerals. Capital goods, such as machinery and parts are imported mostly. As a result, the share of consumer goods in total imports was only 10 percent even in 1990, the remainder consisted of imports used for production. The import share of machinery is about one-third. Japan is the largest supplier of machinery. Tables 24.2 and 24.3 show the composition and direction of Korean exports and imports.

Exports in the early 1960s were dominated by primary products such as silk, tungsten, and fish. As industrialization proceeded, manufactured products emerged as the dominant export items. The export share of primary products was 86 percent in 1960, but dropped to 6 percent in 1990. As the share of manufactured products in exports changed, the leading exports have also changed. During the 1960s the leading items were labor-intensive products such as plywood, wigs, and sweaters, in the 1970s. This changed to more capital intensive goods such as shipbuilding and steel plate.[2] In the 1980s technology-intensive items such as color TV sets, computers and cars became the leading export items as shown in Table 24.2. Another important feature is that Korea's trade balances differ widely according to its trade partners as shown in Table 24.3. Korea suffers trade deficits with

TABLE 24.2   Composition of ten largest export and import items (1990)

Exports			Imports		
Item	Amount (US$ million)	%	Item	Amount (US$ million)	%
Electronics	17,816	27.4	General machinery	9,579	13.7
Textiles	14,670	22.6	Mineral fuels	7,676	11.0
Footwear	4,307	6.6	Agricultural products	6,787	9.7
Iron and steel	4,237	6.5	Electronics parts	5,824	8.6
Ships	2,799	4.3	Organic chemicals	4,928	7.1
Chemical products	2,336	3.6	Iron and steel products	4,090	5.9
Automobiles	2,128	3.3	Oil products	3,229	4.6
General machinery	1,775	2.7	Industrial electronics	2,959	4.2
Fishery products	1,515	2.3	Precision machinery	2,014	2.9
Plastic products	1,292	2.0	Pharmacy	2,008	2.9
Sum of 10 items	52,875	81.3	Sum of 10 items	49,458	70.8
Total export	65,016	100.0	Total import	69,844	100.0

Source: BOK (1992).

TABLE 24.3   Ten largest trading partners of Korea (1990) (US$ million)

Country	Exports (Ex)	Imports (Im)	Ex + Im	Ex − Im
U.S.	19,360	16,943	36,303	2,417
Japan	12,638	18,574	31,212	−5,936
Germany	2,849	3,284	6,133	−435
Hong Kong	3,780	614	4,394	3,166
Australia	956	2,589	3,545	−1,633
Canada	1,731	1,465	3,196	266
U.K.	1,750	1,226	2,976	524
Singapore	1,805	897	2,701	908
Taiwan	1,249	1,452	2,701	−203
Indonesia	1,079	1,600	2,679	−521
Southeast Asia (total)	10,405	7,157	17,562	3,248
EC (total)	8,844	8,410	17,254	434
Sum of 10 countries	47,197	48,644	95,841	−1,447
Total import/export	65,016	69,844	134,860	−4,828

Source: BOK (1990).

countries possessing natural resources and advanced technology, while it may have trade surpluses with countries which are good customers for consumers goods. Recent trade friction with advanced countries has reflected these bilateral trade characteristics.

The U.S. has played the most important role for Korean economic development. Through military protection, technology transfer, and a relatively open market, the

U.S. enabled Korea to pursue an active export promotion policy. The U.S. has been the largest trading partner of Korea since World War II. The share of Korean exports to the U.S. market reached approximately 35 percent in 1990. Korea has recorded a trade surplus with the U.S. starting from 1981, with its peak amounting to US$9.5 billion in 1987. However, it returned to deficits in 1991. These surpluses caused severe trade friction between the two countries, but negotiations have become easier since the surplus declined after 1987. This decline was partly a result of the appreciation of the Korean won, but it is also due to the weakened competitiveness of Korean exports resulting from high domestic wages.

Currently, the major Korean export items, such as cars, color TV sets, and VCRs, are experiencing severe competition in the U.S. market, for a variety of reasons, including changes in the U.S. market, the nature of Korean industry, and the international strategy of multinational enterprises. When NIEs including Korea started penetrating the U.S. market with color TV sets and VCRs, for example, the U.S. market had a large stock of end users who were price-elastic. But as products become mature, the customers also become less price responsive and more sensitive to quality and product differentiation. On the other hand, wage hikes and the devaluation of the U.S. dollar relative to the Korean won had undermined the price competitiveness of Korean exports. Also, Japanese foreign direct investment (FDI) into the Association of Southeast Asian Nations (ASEAN) and China resulted in a substantial increase in the exports of those countries to the U.S. market. But a more fundamental reason for increased pressure faced by Korean exports may be found in the very factor which helped Korean exports to penetrate the OECD market. Major export industries in Korea are still assembly industries which require large production runs to enjoy economies of scale. But large scale assembly industries are usually not capable of adjusting easily to a changing market environment which requires diversity. Another factor is the global strategy of multinational corporations. Multinational corporations try to dominate all levels of markets with differentiated products produced in various countries. For example a Japanese multinational corporation produces the highest quality products in Japan, the medium quality products in the U.S., and the lower quality product in Mexico. With these differentiated products the corporation tries to dominate most of the differentiated market in the U.S. Therefore, the entry barrier is very high for a new comer. To expand its export share in the U.S. and EC markets, Korea has to have new strategies to overcome these difficulties, including technology improvement, market research, and development of new competitive products.

Japan is the closest country to Korea in various senses. Japan's role in Korean development has been unique. Because of the historical rivalry between Korea and Japan, Japanese economic success has been a strong stimulus to Korea. Also, Japan has been the most important source of industrial technology, machinery and information as Koreans were more easily able to understand Japanese society, culture and industries. Japan is the biggest market for Korean primary products such as vegetables and marine products, light industry products such as synthetic products, and heavy industry products such as iron and steel products. Since the late 1980s exports to Japan have been diversified to electronics and electric products. But most technology-intensive products are exported in buyer's brand names, and specifications and marketing of the products are controlled by the buyers. Japan is the biggest supplier of machinery for Korean manufacturing plants, and technology-intensive semi-processed materials for export industries. So far the Korea–Japan international division of labor is still vertical. Therefore, if the demand increases for Korean products from the rest of the world, import requirements (for example, machinery) from Japan tend to increase accordingly. Thus, Korea has suffered from chronic trade deficits against Japan, even while it recorded substantial surpluses with the U.S. and EC. Therefore, it is important that more attention is paid to research and development (R&D) to reduce the trade imbalance, so that Korea need not import such a large percentage of its industrial input.

The NIEs started their industrialization based on the export of labor-intensive commodities, and hence they have been mainly competitors in major export destinations. As the industrial structure diversifies in NIEs, the international division of labor has become more important, and mutual trade within the NIEs has been increasing. The ASEAN countries are following the NIEs in economic development with a short lag. And as all NIEs are relatively high-wage economies now, the ASEAN countries have now become close competitors of the NIEs in the markets of the U.S., EC, and Japan. One of the important consequences is the rapid relocation of labor-intensive industries from the NIEs to the ASEAN countries, which induces an increase in trade between the NIEs and the ASEAN countries. Therefore, Korea's trade with the other NIEs and ASEAN has been increasing faster than its trade with the advanced countries. As direct investment from Korea to the ASEAN countries increases, Korean exports of semi-processed products to Thailand, Indonesia, and Malaysia are increasing rapidly too.

Since 1979 when China started to actively implement its open-door policy, the amount of two-way trade between Korea and China has been increasing, albeit with some fluctuations. Starting from US$19 million in 1979 the amount increased to US$3,821 million in 1990. In 1992 China became Korea's third largest trading partner. The trade structure reflects a sort of vertical division of labor, with the export of manufactured goods such as electronics products, textiles, and mineral products, and the import of primary products such as agricultural products and mineral fuel. Direct investment from Korea to China increased rapidly since 1989. The total licensed amount of investment by the end of 1990 was US$81 million and 44 percent of these projects had been implemented by the same date.

Korean trade with the former Soviet Union amounted to US$200 million in 1987, and the amount increased rapidly since then, reaching US$889 million in 1990. Korea's major exports to the Soviet Union comprise electronics products and shipbuilding. Its major imports from the Soviet Union comprise mineral fuel and agricultural products. Direct investment to the Soviet Union has not been so conspicuous. But various kinds of projects are under negotiation in connection with the development of natural resources and import of technology from the Soviet Union. Trade with Eastern Europe began in the 1970s, initially with Yugoslavia. It has increased rapidly since 1980, with a growing number of different Eastern European destinations. In 1990 the two-way trade amounted to US$541 million, with a trade surplus of US$328 million. Major trading partners in the region are the former Yugoslavia, Poland, and Hungary. Major Korean export items to these countries are electronics products, textiles and machinery, and import items from these countries consist of steel products, machinery and agricultural products. Korean FDI to the east European region is not active yet. But negotiations on investment in construction of hotels and factories are under way with reasonable prospects. However, it will be a long while before Korea's trade with the former Soviet Union and Eastern bloc countries expands considerably due to these countries' internal problems and shortage of hard currency.

Australia and Korea have become important trading partners to each other. Korea is the third largest trading partner of Australia and Australia the fifth of Korea. In 1990 the size of the two-way trade between Korea and Australia was US$2.5 billion. The major import items from Australia are meat, cereals, hides and skins, textile fibers, metalliferous ores, coal, and metals, and the major export items to Australia are chemical products, rubber manufactures, textile products, iron and steel, manufactures of metals, office machines, telecommunications equipment, electric machines, road vehicles, footwear, and miscellaneous manufactured articles. But the balance of trade so far has been unfavorable to Korea.

24.3.2 Economic Cooperation in the Asia-Pacific Region

The international economic order of the post–World War II world economy was established and maintained under the predominant power of the U.S. economy. This economic order has been undergoing significant structural change with the diversification of economic power through the globalization of the world economy, the emergence of Japan, the EC and the NIEs as economic powerhouses, the relative weakening of U.S. economic power, and the weakening of the IMF–GATT system. The U.S. led the post–World War II world economy with 40 to 45 percent of the world's GNP. But the U.S. has now become the largest debtor country in the world, and its role as a leader in the international economy has significantly declined, although the U.S. is still the largest economic and military power in the world. Japan and Germany have emerged as new super economic powers. The process of multi-polarization in the 1990s will proceed with the integrated and extended EC and Japan as the new major poles. With the collapse of the Soviet Union, the world economic system has become a tripolar system made up of the U.S., the integrated EC and Japan.

Economic regionalism started first in western Europe and spread to the developing countries. But until the 1970s economic integration gained little momentum, due to U.S. dominance and the relative weakness of the relevant regions. In the 1980s the uncertainty of the world economic environment increased and countries began to feel their vulnerability in dealing with international economic problems. In response, countries started to pursue cooperation with other countries suffering from similar problems. In this context, the EC has strengthened its integration throughout the 1980s, the U.S. organized the North American Free Trade Area (NAFTA) with Canada and Mexico, and the countries in the Asia-Pacific region formed or suggested alternative organizations such as the Asia-Pacific Economic Cooperation (APEC) and East Asian Economic Caucus (EAEC).

The Asia-Pacific region houses many diverse countries with a high potential for cooperation. A diverse range of countries can be found in the Asia-Pacific region: industrialized countries, newly industrializing economies, and semi-emerging industrial countries. Diversity in economic structure tends to increase the possible benefits from economic cooperation. However, too high a degree of cultural and historical difference has been a factor which has made it difficult to achieve closer cooperation in the region. Theories of economic integration tell us that trade creation will be larger, the larger the proportion of intraregional trade to total trade. Currently, the U.S. and EC countries are the principal export destinations of the NIEs. Also, both the ASEAN countries and China have been following the NIEs and trying to expand their manufactured exports. However, because the markets in Japan and the NIEs are not large enough to absorb most of the exports from those countries, the ASEAN countries and China must rely on the large markets of the U.S. and EC in order to expand their exports. FDI from Japan and the NIEs have flowed into the ASEAN countries and China. These investment flows have increased intra-regional trade. However, most of these investments are in labor-intensive industries which moved their production bases looking for low wages in order to compete in the markets of the U.S. and EC. Consequently, these investments tend to increase inter-regional trade as well as intra-regional trade. Access to the markets of the U.S. and EC are vital for the successful operation of these labor-intensive industries. So far, the U.S. has shown a relatively passive attitude toward the development of APEC, and concentrated on the formation of NAFTA. And Japan has shown only a lukewarm attitude to assuming a leadership role. Therefore, it is very difficult to expect that APEC or any other form of Asia-Pacific regional cooperation will develop into a trading bloc such as NAFTA. Hence bilateral negotiations and cooperation will continue to be important in the region.[3]

The importance of the Asia-Pacific economies is well understood by Korea and trade within the region will continue to increase. Korean FDI into the ASEAN countries and China has been increasing rapidly. Table 24.4 shows the industry composition of Korean FDI as at 1990. Most Korean FDI outflows lie in the areas of manufacturing and international trading. Both of these are associated with exports. International trading companies are mainly the subsidiaries of the home export industries, handling marketing, service and maintenance. Most FDI in the manufacturing industry flowed out looking for low wages in the ASEAN countries or involved assembly industries in the U.S. and EC. Table 24.5 shows the regional

TABLE 24.4   Industry distribution of foreign investment from Korea (end of 1990)

Industry/Sector	No. of projects	%	Amount (US$ milion)	%
Mining	21	1.7	447	13.4
Forestry	11	0.9	78	2.3
Fishery	48	3.9	88	2.6
Manufacturing	500	40.2	1,061	31.8
Construction	61	4.9	52	1.6
Transportation	36	2.9	7	0.2
International trading	450	36.2	410	12.3
Real estate	17	1.4	38	1.1
Miscellaneous	99	8.0	155	4.6
Total	1,243	100.0	2,335	100.0

Source: Korea Trade Association, *Annual Trade Statistics*, 1991.

TABLE 24.5   Regional distribution of foreign investment from Korea (end of 1990)

Region and country	Number of projects	%	Amount (US$ million)	%
Asia	**522**	**42.0**	**715**	**30.6**
Japan	92		51	
NIEs	102		43	
ASEAN	248		546	
West Asia	33		31	
China	30		22	
North America	**394**	**31.7**	**1,106**	**47.4**
U.S.	364		807	
Canada	30		30	
Europe	**98**	**7.9**	**152**	**6.5**
U.K.	26		41	
Hungary	1		1	
Germany	34		17	
Ireland	1		23	
Turkey	5		19	
Portugal	2		2	
Latin America	**104**	**8.4**	**121**	**5.2**
Middle East	**34**	**2.7**	**56**	**2.4**
Oceania	**66**	**5.3**	**141**	**6.0**
Africa	**25**	**2.0**	**45**	**1.9**
Total	1,243	100.0	2,335	100.0

Source: Korea Trade Association, *Annual Trade Statistics*, 1991.

distribution of FDI from Korea. Investment into North America is expected to increase further as NAFTA increases the minimum component of production inside the region, that qualifies for the exemption from tariff imposition. This will also decrease FDI into the ASEAN countries somewhat. However, in 1991 the amount of exports to Southeast Asia surpassed that to Japan, let alone the EC, and Southeast Asia became the second major destination for exports. The increase of trade with Southeast Asia will continue and its pace will be faster than that for FDI outflows to the region.

24.4 Explaining the Miracle: A Model for Other Developing Countries?

What can be learned from the Korean experience? To students of economic development it is an extremely important task (1) to identify what are the sources of a country's growth, and (2) to analyze to what extent the experiences of a country can be repeated in another country by adopting similar economic policies. In order to do so, it is important to distinguish the given conditions, both economic and noneconomic, and the choices made by economic planners.[4]

There exist two approaches with which economic growth of a country can be examined; a historical perspective and/or an analytical perspective.[5] Within the analytical perspective, neoclassical analysis and structural analysis are two often competing approaches. The neoclassical growth model has been widely used to analyze the sources of economic growth since it was first put forward by Solow and Swan in the 1950s. Although it is a useful tool, the assumption of full employment in the model limits the analysis to the supply side of an economy, and does not deal with the problems associated with the lack of demand, especially unemployment and underemployment, which most developing countries are currently experiencing. The neoclassical approach identifies the sources of a country's growth as: capital accumulation, increase in labor quantity and quality, increase in other intermediate inputs and total factor productivity caused by technical progress. The structural approach identifies as major sources those used in the neoclassical approach, but adds some sources of its own: reallocation of resources to higher productivity sectors, economies of scale and learning by doing, and the reduction of internal and external bottlenecks. The Korean experience can be explained quite well with the structural approach, as summarized by Chenery (1986).

For capital accumulation, Korea relied entirely on foreign savings at the initial stage. As shown in Table 24.6 domestic saving was always lower than gross domestic investment except for the 1986–89 period. This is one of the major differences between the Korean and Taiwanese experiences.[6] Taiwan used a tight monetary policy which kept interest rates high with low inflation, so the saving rate was very high. Yet, Korea used expansionary policies throughout the 1960s and 1970s, consequently the inflation rate was very high. Although it created forced savings in the economy, the saving rate was generally lower than that for investment,

TABLE 24.6   Savings and investment from 1962–86 (as percentage of GNP)

Year	Gross domestic investment	Domestic saving	Net capital inflow
1962	13.0	1.7	11.3
1970	28.0	16.8	9.9
1980	31.3	19.8	10.1
1990	36.2	35.3	0.9

Source: BOK, various issues.

which was reflected in chronic balance of payment deficits. Until the end of the 1970s, international interest rates were very low, and often negative. This encouraged borrowing by the business sector and foreign savings were used to fill the gap. As mentioned in Section 24.1 tight monetary and fiscal policies were adopted in the early 1980s, which succeeded in fighting inflation. In the mid-1980s domestic savings surpassed domestic investment. Most of the foreign capital was injected in the form of loans, and foreign direct investment was strictly controlled until the mid-1990s. This partially reflects the attempt to minimize foreign control—a policy preference which may be grounded in the colonial experience. Korea relied on imported technology and took advantage of the technological backlog available under low wage rates. The low level of foreign direct investment was not a problem in Korea until the mid-1980s when labor-intensive commodities were major exports because the technology used in these industries was easily available internationally. However, FDI will play a greater role in the 1990s as R&D becomes more important.[7]

Korea was abundantly endowed with a well-trained and highly motivated workforce when the country started its first FYEDP in 1962. On the other hand, rural–urban migration provided a continuous supply of unskilled labor until the mid-1970s. Without any industrial disputes, the urban wage rates were kept low. This was an important source of international competitiveness for labor-intensive exports. The price of rice was kept below the market price in order to support the low urban wages. It is interesting to note that the assumptions in the two sector model put forward by Lewis were quite relevant in the Korean case (1954, 1958). The promotion of exports of labor-intensive products eradicated the problem of unemployment and underemployment in the mid-1970s, and since then the unemployment rate has been kept around or below 2 percent.

These factors explain the supply side. Then how did Korea create the demand for its products? Obviously, the answer can be found in its export promotion policy. Unemployment and underemployment were cured through the expansion of labor-intensive industries, which sold mostly in overseas markets. If the access to the international market especially that in the U.S. had been restricted, it would have been very hard to expect such a continued growth as occurred in Korea.

Apart from the well-trained and highly motivated labor force, the conditions identified above were present in many other developing countries as well. Then why did other countries, which enjoyed much better conditions than Korea and the other NIEs, not grow as fast? We must turn to the economic policies adopted by these governments. Most developing countries in the 1960s adopted an import-substitution policy. However, many economists argue that the Korean experience is a success story grounded in an export promotion policy (which is based on the principle of comparative advantage). Yet, Korea did more than just utilize its existing comparative advantage. By combining import substitution and export promotion, Korea created comparative advantage at the initial stage. Since the mid-1980s, however, most protection has been eliminated, except for that of agricultural products.

So far, most of the major economic variables and economic policies, which contributed to the success of Korean development have been described. Apart from these, there exist many other noneconomic factors and/or other exogenous conditions, without which Korea may not have achieved such a high rate of growth. Three important factors are shown below (Australian Department of Foreign Affairs and Trade 1992: Section 2.4):

1. *Enthusiasm for education.* Among household expenditure items, expenses for education have been the highest priority in Korean households. The literacy rate is extremely high, with the average level of education among Koreans being almost the same as that of the most advanced countries (Bai 1992). This high level of education in Korea was also recognized as one of the reasons for the more equal distribution of income (Adelman 1975).
2. *Favorable international environment.* Easy access to world markets for capital, raw materials and technology, and easy access to worldwide markets for export of manufacturing products, were indispensable in Korea's pursuit of an export promotion policy and helped the country to overcome the limitations of the domestic market.
3. *Strong but conscientious government.* In underdeveloped countries, one of the most important prerequisites of economic development is the existence of innovators who can combine natural and social resources available in an economy into an effective and productive system. In Korea the government has been one of these innovators. It has played a leading role in economic development and planning in the early stages of industrialization. Perhaps the scarcest factor for development in most developing countries would be the existence of a conscientious government. By and large, the Korean government was conscientious as far as its pursuit of economic policies was concerned, especially in the 1960s and 1970s.

In the process of industrialization the Korean economy exhibited a set of unique structural traits which reflected the development-oriented government will. The principal goal of economic policy for the first two decades since 1962 was to achieve a self-sustained economy. Major strategies used for this goal can be summarized as follows, although these policies were implicit and have not officially been documented.

1. Most resources should be used to achieve industrialization, which should proceed from light industry to heavy industry.

2. Major processes of economic development should be under the control and leadership of government.
3. In principle, firms may be owned and managed privately, but the government should participate in the process of determination and operation of major investment projects.
4. Foreign capital should be actively induced to meet the needed investment, and exports should be promoted to repay foreign loans and to increase national income and employment.
5. The first priority of development should be rapid economic growth. Some unfavorable side-effects should be tolerated for the time being.[8]

These policies were by and large successful, though they created imbalances, as we shall see in the next section.

It is clear that a mixture of endogenous and exogenous factors produced the success story of Korean industrialization. In a sense, it is significant that all the Asian NIEs which grew fast since the 1960s were poorly endowed with natural resources. To economies with a small land mass and high population density, an outward looking policy was the only choice available. Fortunately, the international trading environment was extremely favorable. Now other countries such as the ASEAN countries (excluding Singapore) and China have been following the NIEs model, and adopted export expansion policies. Countries with abundant natural or agricultural resources are in a much better placed than Korea in terms of achieving economic growth. Although the international trading environment is not so favorable as in the 1960s, provision of the noneconomic factors outlined in this section and careful management of economic policy will create good prospects for the future growth of those countries.

24.5   Today's Little Dragon, Tomorrow's Giant?

The Korean economy has achieved a very high rate of continuous growth over the past 30 years. Korea now has the prospect of joining the group of OECD countries. However, Korea is currently facing many challenges which need to be overcome before it can be successfully transformed into a mature developed economy. These challenges have arisen partly as a result of changes in the international economic environment. More importantly, however, they stem from the consequences of past government economic policies. This section discusses the current problems and challenges faced by the Korean economy in the early 1990s.

24.5.1   Is Small Beautiful?

An active role of government would be indispensable at the early stage of economic development of most developing countries. The leadership of the government has been exceptionally strong during the process of rapid industrialization in Korea. Considering the total devastation of the economy due to the Korean War, this strong leadership certainly was vital in rebuilding the economy. Also, experiences in other developing countries reveal that a successful transition from an import-substitution policy to export promotion is likely to occur under strong governmental leadership since the protected industries tend to lobby governments to prevent or delay the transition process.

However, strong intervention by the government was not without its own adverse effects, namely, creating distortions and imbalances in the economy. The most significant imbalances can be found in the inefficient agricultural sector, which has been protected by tariffs and other import restrictions, but generally neglected during the entire process of industrialization since the 1960s. Also, due to strong government intervention, the Korean financial sector has not been able to develop efficiently and is still in its infancy in the 1990s. Similarly, factor market distortions due to credit rationing, have been reported to be substantial until recently (Hong 1988). As mentioned before, the government has encouraged conglomerates called *chaebol* to expand, especially in the areas of heavy and chemical industries. This has resulted in significant industry concentration, and small- and medium-sized industries have been relatively disadvantaged.

As the economic structure has become diversified and economic scale enlarged, the merit of direct government intervention has decreased in Korea. Recent changes in the political and economic environment also call for the adoption of new roles that will enable the government to cope with newly emerging problems. More attention should now be paid to the areas of promoting technical development; checking stagflation; maintaining a competitive environment for economic activities; securing a steady supply of energy resources; and securing the steady accumulation of effective and high-quality social overhead capital befitting the demands of the changing economic society. Also, new roles will include the promotion of measures to open up the domestic market; and implement smooth industrial coordination. In this sense, the announced plan by the new government in 1993, to decrease the size and the role of the government, is expected to be a turning point.

In the future, a major reason for expanding the government's financial scope will be increases in social security related costs. The social security system, if poorly managed, may affect private sector incentives and damage the vitality of society. In this regard, it will be necessary to take a renewed look at the government's outlays including social security payments and investment in public works projects. In the long run, the social security system must expand in Korea. However, considering the difficulties, encountered by some Western countries, in terms of the inefficient management of the system, cautious steps need to be taken.

24.5.2 Unbalanced Development of Economic Power: *Chaebol*

The Korean government supported the emergence of *chaebol* by assisting a few groups of corporations to dominate exports and build heavy and chemical industries, including the defense industry. In the 1960s the size of each *chaebol* was relatively small, but they started to grow rapidly after 1972 and grew into economic giants in the 1980s.

In addition to all the measures already adopted to promote exports, the government took one more step to establish general trading companies in 1976. Ten large groups were chosen, and each was designated to establish a general trading company and given a variety of incentives to increase exports. The same groups were called upon to take major parts in the designated investment projects within the ambitious program of establishing heavy and chemical industries. To accelerate these projects the government took the risks associated with these large investments by arranging bank credits, guaranteeing foreign loans, and bailing out bankrupt companies. Under these measures the chosen groups could get more returns, at virtually no risk, with ever increasing investments, and each group expanded very rapidly. Failures in some of the investment projects did not stop them from expanding further.

On the other hand, the government was aware of the importance of encouraging small- and medium-sized businesses in the early 1960s. The implementation of policies encouraging small- and medium-sized businesses failed to live up to their spirit. In the 1970s the government tried to support small- and medium-sized firms in order to counter the impact of the enormous expansion of large business groups. The government began to recognize that as heavy and chemical industries were developed, the role of small- and medium-sized firms became more and more important as suppliers of parts and intermediate goods for large companies. But, throughout the 1970s policies to support small- and medium-sized firms were effectively cancelled out by the policies in favor of heavy and chemical industries and the export drive. Consequently, cooperation between small and large companies has not been established to a desirable extent.

The most important difference between Korean *chaebol*s and conglomerates in other countries is their ownership structure. Most of *chaebol*s are owned by a small number of families and, in most cases, the founders of *chaebol*s still own and operate the enterprises. As government regulation decreased in the 1980s the market power of the conglomerates has increased.[9] Trade liberalization initiated since the second half of the 1990s did not reduce their market power significantly, as *chaebol*s themselves became importers. Table 24.7 shows the relative sizes of the 30 largest *chaebol*s in 1990.

As this industrial concentration has been perceived as one of the most problematic areas of the Korean economy, the government initiated a series of laws to aid small- and medium-sized companies, and introduced various measures including tax policies to control the ownership structure of *chaebol*s. It will be a long while before any major results can be seen. However, it should be remembered that *chaebol*s contributed positively to the growth of the Korean economy. The past and future roles of the *chaebol*s remains an important area that demands further extensive research.

TABLE 24.7   Size of the largest 30 conglomerates in the manufacturing sector in South Korea

Largest groups	Number of firms	Employment (%)[a]	Output (%)[a]	Value added (%)[a]	Fixed capital (%)[a]
5 groups	94	9.7	23.0	18.7	20.4
10	147	11.7	30.2	24.2	27.9
15	190	14.4	33.9	27.3	31.6
20	218	15.5	36.4	29.5	34.4
25	246	16.6	38.5	31.4	36.8
30	270	17.6	40.2	33.1	39.6

[a] Percentage of the manufacturing sector total.

Source: Cho Dongsung (1990).

24.5.3   Balance between Social and Economic Development

Income distribution in Korea has been exceptionally equal in comparison with other developing countries. Various reasons can be found for this. The first is the land reform, implemented in the late 1940s. From the early 1960s, export promotion policy pursued through the expansion of labor-intensive industry helped the economy to reduce unemployment, which again helped to reduce poverty and income inequality. Since then, the wage income share of total income has increased fairly rapidly in Korea. Although the big push into heavy and chemical industry increased the Gini coefficient from 0.332 in 1970 to 0.391 in 1976, this decreased to 0.357 by the mid-1980s (Choo 1987). Real wage rates also increased, keeping pace with productivity changes. Due to increases in the real wage rate among blue-collar workers by more than 30 percent from 1987 to 1989, the wage differentials across different classes of workers have decreased substantially. The government so far has not consciously attempted to reduce income inequality. But this self-correcting mechanism has worked to maintain or correct income distribution despite the presence of various factors which might worsen the situation: the tax system, inefficient trade union activity, and concentration of economic power.

However, the distribution of wealth, especially land ownership, is far from equal. Each *chaebol* is largely owned and controlled by one or a few families. Land ownership has become extremely concentrated in the 1980s due to the strong preference for land among the wealthy. Considering the rapid increase in land prices, the distribution of enormous capital gains from land ownership would be much more unequal than the income distribution (Lee 1991). Although there have been some studies in this area, further extensive research is needed.

As the standard of living rises, the economy should cope with the diversified demands of people, hence social development as well as economic development are required. To reflect this requirement, the Korean government changed the title of the FYEDP to "Five Year Economic and Social Development Plan" from the Sixth

Plan, 1987–91, onward. Since the second half of the 1980s, some improvements have been made in the area of health insurance. However, a comprehensive social welfare system including, pensions, unemployment benefits and workers compensation schemes is still beyond reach. A gradual move will be made in this area, but comprehensive studies and careful planning need to be done to avoid unfavorable results.

As living standards improve, the consumption pattern will change accordingly. Changes have already started to take place in the second half of the 1980s, particularly in relation to the opening of markets for manufactured products internationally. Markets for high quality products will be prospering in the 1990s and beyond. Demand for high quality agricultural products (such as health food, high quality dairy products and so on), will also increase. In general, food expenses will decrease significantly, clothing expenses are expected not to show any major changes in terms of its proportion in total expenses but, cultural and entertainment expenses will increase substantially. Among cultural and entertainment expenses, overseas travel is an area which will expand considerably in the 1990s.

During the process of rapid industrialization, environmental concerns were not on the priority agenda. However, investment decisions without environmental considerations are not feasible any longer, as the voice of the public becomes stronger. It has now become extremely difficult to find sites for coal-fired electric power generation plants, let alone nuclear plants. Environmental concerns are now gradually being considered in policy formation, but still remain an area to be improved substantially.

24.5.4 Trade Policy

The growth of the Korean economy owes much to imports of foreign capital and foreign technology. The government has made strenuous efforts to encourage foreign capital and foreign capital inflows that surpass the planned amount most years. Korea has followed the rule of free trade only partially. With a view to increasing exports and restricting imports as much as possible, the government intervened in setting the relative prices both in the commodity markets and the factor markets. In the commodity markets both tariffs and subsidies were used, combining export promotion policy with import restriction policies. Import of consumer goods was subject to severe restriction, whereas exporting firms had nearly automatic access to tariff-free imported inputs. The effect of price setting by the government was most apparent in the financial sector. Exporting companies received easy access to generous loans, both domestic and foreign. This was possible because the financial sector was totally controlled by the government, hence the direction of flow of funds, as well as the interest rates, was determined by the government. With these measures, industrialization through import substitution proceeded rapidly and many of the protected infant industries have now become mature export industries with international comparative advantage.

Some import liberalization policies were adopted as early as 1967. But these policies involved tariff and quota reductions for intermediate inputs only. The import of final goods continued to be strictly controlled. Trade policy in the 1960s and the 1970s was mercantilistic, and the speed of import liberalization was very slow in the 1970s. It was not until the 1980s that comprehensive import liberalization began to be carried out. This was the most important strategic aspect of policy during the intermediate phase in Korean economic growth. As the trade balance recorded huge surpluses, pressures from trading partners mounted in the second half of the 1980s. Since 1987, bold steps have been taken to liberalize trade. Tariffs on manufactured imports have already been reduced substantially, and are now quite close to the rates in OECD countries. Several conflicting voices are heard regarding the opening of the agricultural market. However, overall, a step by step opening of the agricultural market should be inevitable. As an intermediate policy we may need some assistance system for this sector. The assistance should be given for education, training and technological improvement designed to increase productivity and competitiveness in the agricultural sector, not for price supports.

Internationally, the new protectionism which emerged in the 1980s is still prevailing and the international trading environment is not expected to improve significantly, at least in the short and medium run. Participants at the Uruguay Round are trying hard to avoid the regionalization of the world economy and the formation of several trading regions or blocks. Yet, it may be hard to expect significant improvements in the trading relations until the domestic economic conditions in the developed countries improve substantially. Regardless of the outcome of the Uruguay Round, Korea is no longer able to enjoy the privileges of a developing country.

24.5.5 Liberalization of the Korean Economy and the Agricultural Sector

A decrease in the regulating role of the government means a further liberalization of the economy. Liberalization of the banking sector is needed most urgently for the efficient allocation of scarce resources. As the financial sector in Korea has been strongly influenced by the government since the beginning of the First FYEDP, the domestic financial market has not been well developed. The responsibility and authority of financial institutions should become more independent of government control and, management of foreign exchange should also be liberalized.

Korea has opened its market substantially since the mid-1980s, and measures for trade liberalization and tariff reduction have been implemented. Further liberalization is expected and this will improve the overall efficiency of the Korean economy. Of course, there will be industries which will experience difficulties due to liberalization and changes in trade structure. For example, many textile and footwear firms have already gone bankrupt. It is, therefore, necessary to coordinate appropriate industrial policies for the maintenance and strengthening of market functions, and for smooth adjustment in the labor market. This is important in order to maintain the vitality of the economy, without undermining the potential for continued growth. In this context, trade reform will continue, and research is needed on the implications of further trade reforms for income distribution, on how the cost of adjustment should be born, and on what would be appropriate policies for declining industries.

The most difficult area of adjustment is the agricultural market. Gradual and cautious plans have been prepared for opening the agricultural market, and Korea has been quite firm in negotiations at the Uruguay Round regarding the opening of the rice market. However, farmers are still dissatisfied, as the pains from the expected opening will be very severe. In response, the government has changed part of its agricultural policy from price supports to education and restructuring. The restructuring plan focuses on promoting greater specialization, more economical use of land, education, alternative crops, and so forth. However, a more comprehensive national plan needs to be established to minimize the cost of adjustment and to reduce the effect on the welfare of nearly 20 percent of the total population.

24.5.6 International Competitiveness and R&D

Although domestic demand as a factor affecting the overall performance of the Korean economy is more important than before, exports will still set the pace of economic development in Korea. Until the mid-1980s Korean exports enjoyed favorable treatment under the GATT system. The international trading environment has changed in the 1990s. An increase in exports from low wage countries in Southeast Asia and China resulted in the loss of competitiveness of Korean exports in the area of labor-intensive products. Yet, Korean exports are not ready to compete with Japanese exports in terms of quality. Therefore, this challenge is a real trial for the Korean economy. Although the increase in wage rates in the second half of the 1980s is one of the major causes, wages are bound to increase as the economy develops, and in the long run high wages are not to be blamed for the loss of competitiveness. It is the technology improvement that needs attention.

The Korean manufacturing industry has been depending heavily on imported technology. The ratio of imported parts and components is still high for major export items in the electronics and automobile industries. So far, imported technology has been used mostly for the mass-production of standardized products. But technology in the future should be able to cater for an increasing demand for differentiated products. Such technology has to be internally generated as much as it is imported. Therefore, technological innovation should be encouraged in every field of the economy. Technical improvement has lagged behind substantially, considering the growth of the manufacturing sector and the size of exports in the overall GNP. Also, R&D and technological improvement have not been the areas of long-term commitment from either the public or the private sector.

The way in which technological innovations take place is not independent of industrial structure and management style. If the status of small- and medium-sized firms is weak, innovations for intensive development cannot be stimulated within these firms. Without diversification of ownership of *chaebol*s and other large firms, and changes in management style in an efficiency-oriented direction, large firms cannot encourage innovations at every echelon of the firms. In the Seventh Socio-Economic Development Plan for 1992–96, R&D is the top priority. Foreign direct investment, both into Korea and also to other countries, also needs to be carefully considered to assist technical improvement. In this area, joint development with countries with advanced technologies will be desirable. So far, the major links in technological development have been the U.S. and Japan, and to a lesser extent Germany, France and other EC countries.

24.5.7 Labor and Human Resources

Industrialization in Korea began with no organized labor movement in 1962. However, as political democratization proceeded rapidly in the second half of the 1980s industrial conflicts exploded for several years from 1987 and became one of the major concerns of the economy. Average real wages increased by more than 30 percent in the three years from 1987 to 1989, though the process by which this was achieved damaged heretofore valuable labor-management cooperation (Bai 1992). Both workers and employers did not have any previous experience in dealing with labor conflicts on such a large scale, and often labor-management confrontations ballooned into emotional conflicts. Both labor and management still need to learn how to resolve conflicts more skilfully without undermining the cooperative spirit of workers. This will take time. In the early 1990s, labor pressures have subsided considerably and are not likely to be the major stumbling block for continued growth of the economy.

Due to the current labor supply shortage, better human resource management is desired. While the working hours of male workers are quite long, the female labor participation rate is low. Efforts are expected to be made to increase the rate of female labor participation and also to better utilize workers close to retirement age, to alleviate the shortage of labor due to the current tight labor market in Korea. In order to achieve technological improvement and increase the productivity of workers, the education system also needs to be upgraded. The quality of education needs to be improved and more emphasis will be given to technical and vocational training in secondary and tertiary education.

24.5.8 Social Overhead Capital and Energy Issues

The development of infrastructure has been generally satisfactory so far, but for the continued development of the economy in the 1990s and beyond, it needs to be strengthened. Major improvements are needed in the transport system and electricity generation capacity.

The transport system in Korea, both for passengers and for commodities is overutilized, causing undue delays in some major routes. The roads in large cities, especially in the vicinity of Seoul, are notoriously congested, requiring long-term comprehensive solutions. For goods transport, construction of some goods terminals are included in the Seventh Socio-Economic Development Plan. Two oil crises in the 1970s created serious difficulties in the Korean economy, which depends entirely on imported energy resources for industrial use. Since then, major diversification from oil has occurred, to coal and nuclear energy. Toward the end of the 1970s, excess capacities in power generation facilities were often subject to criticism. However, a shortage of electricity was experienced in the summer of 1991, due to the rapid expansion of the economy in the second half of the 1980s along with an improvement in the living standards of people. Yet, construction of power generation plants requires much more caution due to growing environmental concerns and also due to the difficulties in obtaining construction sites.

24.6 Concluding Remarks

During the past 30 years, Korea has witnessed a remarkable transition from an agrarian economy to a newly industrialising economy. The unified efforts of the people and the government combined with a favorable international environment drove the country out of poverty and into relative prosperity. GNP in Korea is estimated to be US$384 billion, and GNP per capita US$8,483 in 1994. In international trade negotiations, Korea is no longer regarded as a developing country.

In the 1990s, Korea stands at the crossroads. Serious challenges are ahead but the international environment has become less congenial. How the current challenges are met will determine how soon the country will successfully move to a mature industrialized economy. On the other hand, Korea's role in the Asia-Pacific region has increased. So far, Korea has enjoyed the benefits as a late-comer, yet it is time to redefine the role of the country in the Asia-Pacific region, and to consider how harmonious regional development can be achieved. Just as the whole region faces new challenge in the 1990s, so does every country in the region, including its policymakers, economists and especially students, who will shape the world of tomorrow.

Notes

1. This is the normal pattern according to Chenery (1986).
2. However, textiles continued to be an important item until the late 1980s.
3. See Park (1989) for a salient exposition of this issue.
4. There exist many studies which identify the sources of Korean economic growth. See Haggard (1991), Amsden (1991), Song (1990) and Cho Soon (1988).
5. The classification and definition used by Meier (1989) is followed here. See Chapter 2 in Meier for detailed explanation.
6. See Scitovsky(1985) for a comparison of the Korean and Taiwanese experiences.

7. This will be explained further in the next section.
8. See Cho Soon (1988) for a detailed explanation.
9. See Cho Donsung (1990) for detailed analysis of the Korean *chaebol*.

References

Adelman, I., 1975, "Growth, Income Distribution and Equity-Oriented Development Strategies," *World Development*, 3(2 and 3): 67–76.

Amsden, A., 1991, *Asia's Next Giant: South Korea and Late Industrialization*, Oxford University Press, New York.

Australian Department of Foreign Affairs and Trade, 1992, *Korea to the Year 2000: Implications for Australia*, East Asia Analytical Unit, Australian Government Publishing Service, Canberra.

Bai, Moo-ki, 1992, "Recent Developments of Korean Labor Conditions," in C. S. Suh and J. Zerby (eds.), *Recent Developments in the Korean Economy*, Centre for Applied Economic Research, University of New South Wales, Sydney, pp. 1–23.

Bank of Korea, *Economic Statistics Yearbook*, Seoul, various issues.

Chenery, H., 1986, "Growth and Transformation," in Hollis Chenery, Sherman Robinson, and Moshe Syrquin (eds.), *Industrialization and Growth*, Oxford University Press, New York.

Cho, Dongsung, 1990, *Study of Korean Conglomerates*, Maeil-Gyungje-Shinmunsa, Seoul (in Korean).

Cho, Soon, 1988, "The Development of the Korean Economy During the Last Forty Years: Its Characteristics and Problems," *Kyung-Je-Non-Jip*, Institute of Economics Research, Seoul National University, Seoul, 27(4): 405–38 (in Korean).

Choo, Hak-Chung, 1987, "Income Distribution," in Cho Soon and Choo Hak-Chung (eds.), *The Theory and Reality of the Korean Economy*, Seoul National University Press, Seoul, pp. 55–80 (in Korean).

Haggard, S., 1990, *Pathways from the Periphery*, Cornell University Press, Ithaca, NY.

Hong, W., 1988, "Growth and Trade Patterns: Korea vs. Japan," in T. Mizoguchi (ed.), *Comparative Studies of Korea and Japan*, Hitotsubashi University Press, Tokyo, pp. 1–34.

Hong, Wontack, 1988, *Market Distortions and Trade Patterns of Korea: 1960–85*, Working Paper No. 8807, Korea Development Institute, Seoul.

Lee, Kunwoo, 1991, "The Wealth in Korea, Capital Gains and Income Inequality," *The Economic Development in Korea, Appraisal and Prospects*, symposium proceedings, Institute of Economic Research, Seoul National University (in Korean).

Lewis, W. A., 1954, "Economic Development with Unlimited Supplies of Labour," *Manchester School*, May.

———, 1958, "Unlimited Labour: Further Notes," *Manchester School*, January.

Meier, G. M., 1989, *Leading Issues in Economics Development*, 5th edition, Oxford University Press, New York.

Park, Yung Chul, 1989, "The Little Dragons and Structural Changes in Pacific Asia," *World Economy*, 12 (June).

Scitovsky, T., 1985, "Economic Development in Taiwan and South Korea, 1965–81," *Food Research Institute Studies*, 19(3).

Song, Byung-Nak, 1990, *The Rise of the Korean Economy*, Oxford University Press, Hong Kong.

Chapter 25

Peter G. Warr

THAILAND: THE NEXT NIC

25.1 Introduction

In 1950, after an entire century of zero growth of output per head of population, Thailand was one of the poorest countries in the world.[1] In the following four decades, the economy was transformed. Rapid and sustained growth of output was achieved simultaneously with low inflation and only moderate growth of external debt. The incidence of poverty fell dramatically. Despite the international turmoil caused by the two oil price shocks of the 1970s, Thailand has not experienced a single year of negative growth since 1970, even in per capita terms—an achievement unmatched by any other oil-importing developing country. In recent years, the story has become even more dramatic. Over the four years to 1990, Thailand was the fastest growing economy in the world.

The sustained growth of the Thai economy has come at a cost, both in social and environmental terms, but the achievement is nevertheless remarkable. Along with Malaysia and Indonesia, Thailand is one of what Schlossstein (1991) has called "Asia's new little dragons" and is now well advanced towards joining East Asia's exclusive, if imaginary, club of NICs (newly industrializing countries), presently consisting of Korea, Taiwan, Hong Kong and Singapore. The rest of the world needs to learn about Thailand and its economy, and learn it quickly, if it is to do business successfully with this booming neo-NIC.

The structure of the Thai economy, and its trade with the rest of the world, is changing rapidly—from that of a relatively backward exporter of agricultural products to that of an economically progressive state with exports dominated by manufactured goods and services. The growth of the urban middle class, heavily concentrated in the capital, Bangkok, has led to political problems. But political trouble is nothing new for Thailand. Historically, authoritarian military governments have alternated with brief periods of democracy or semi-democracy, all combined with repeated coups, attempted coups and political violence. The paradox is that after a long period of economic stagnation, economic progress has occurred in an extraordinarily rapid and stable manner, and in spite of apparent political turmoil.

How did this puzzling combination of events happen? Can Thailand's economic progress be sustained? What lessons, if any, might other countries learn from Thailand's experience? This chapter attempts to provide the background within which answers to these questions might be sought.[2] We begin with a brief profile of Thai social and economic data. The following section surveys the structure of Thailand's product markets, labor markets and financial markets. The role and structure of the public sector is discussed next. We then review Thailand's economic performance, both over the long-term and then in more depth over the period since 1970. The final section briefly discusses Thailand's economic linkages with other Asia-Pacific economies.

25.2 Social and Political Profile

25.2.1 Population

In mid-1990, Thailand's population was 55.8 million and in the decade prior to that had been growing at an average annual rate of 1.8 percent, down from 2.7 percent over the decade before. Population density was 107 persons per square kilometer of total area and 275 persons per square kilometer of cultivable land. In 1990 the urban population was 23 percent of the total, compared with 13 percent in 1965. In 1990, 70 percent of the population worked in agriculture, compared with 6 percent in industry and 24 percent in services (Table 25.1). The corresponding data for 1965 were: agriculture 82 percent, industry 5 percent, and services 13 percent. For countries in Thailand's income group, its degree of urbanization is unusually low and the importance of agriculture in total employment is high. For example, in the Philippines in 1990, urbanization was 43 percent and the 1990 distribution of employment in agriculture, industry and services was 41 percent, 10 percent, and 49 percent, respectively. Even more unusual is the degree to which the urban population is concentrated in a single city, Bangkok. For countries of Thailand's .size, the concentration of the urban population in the capital city is surely unique.

In 1990, 60 percent of the population were of working age (15–64 years), compared with 50 percent in 1965. Life expectancy at birth was 63 years for males and 67 years for females, increases of about nine years each from 1965. The crude birth rate and crude death rates in 1990 were 22 and 7 per thousand, respectively, compared with 43 and 12 per thousand, respectively, in 1965.

The majority of the Thai population is Buddhist, with Islam an important force in the southern provinces. There is a large population of Chinese origin, concentrated

TABLE 25.1   Basic indicators of Thailand and some other East Asian countries

	Average annual growth of population (%) 1980–90	GNP per capita (US$) 1990	Average annual growth of real GNP per capita (%) 1965–90	Average annual rate of inflation (%) 1965–90	Life expectancy at birth (years) 1990	Employment (% total) 1986–89		
						Agricultre	Industry	Services
Thailand	1.8	14.20	4.4	5.08	69	70	6	24
China	1.4	370	5.8	2.14	70	74	14	13
Indonesia	1.8	570	4.5	24.66	62	54	8	38
Philippines	2.4	730	1.3	12.8	64	42	10	49
Malaysia	2.6	2,320	4.0	3.58	70	42	19	39
Korea, Republic of	1.1	5,400	7.1	13.08	71	18	27	56
India	2.1	350	1.9	7.66	59	63	11	27

	Expenditure on education as % GNP 1989	Secondary school enrolment (% age group) 1988–89	Urban population as % total 1990	Percent urban population in largest city 1980	Income distribution		Poverty (% population below poverty line) 1980–89	
					Lowest 20% share of total (% year)	Gini coefficient	Total	Rural
Thailand	3.2	38	23	69	4.0 (1988)	0.47	30	34
China	2.4	44	33	6	n.a.	n.a.	n.a.	n.a.
Indonesia	0.9	47	31	23	8.8 (1987)	0.31	39	44
Philippines	2.9	73	43	30	5.5 (1985)	0.45	58	64
Malaysia	5.6	87	72	41	4.6 (1987)	0.48	27	38
Korea, Republic of	3.6	87	72	41	n.a.	0.36	16	11
India	3.2	43	27	6	8.1 (1983)	0.42	48	51

n.a.: not available

Source: World Bank, *World Development Report*, 1992.

in Bangkok. Ethnic and religious conflicts have occurred but are of minor importance by international standards.

25.2.2 Social Indicators

Table 25.1 provides comparative social data on Thailand compared with several other Asian countries. Thailand's expenditure on education as a proportion of GDP is normal for countries at its income level (the exceptional Southeast Asian case is Indonesia). Its adult literacy rate in 1990 was 93 percent. However, the pattern of expenditures on education was skewed heavily towards the tertiary level. In 1989 the percentage of persons in the relevant age groups who were enrolled in formal education were: primary school 86, secondary school 28, and higher education 16. The low participation rate at the secondary school level is especially significant. The comparable statistic for the Philippines was more than twice as high in 1989, at 73 percent. In 1965, the participation rates in Thailand were (percent): primary school 78, secondary school 14, and higher education 2. It is clear that educational investment has been concentrated at the higher level, at the relative expense of secondary school education.

Thailand's infant mortality rate was 27 per thousand live births in 1990, compared with 90 per thousand in 1965. Comparable data for the Philippines were 41 and 73 per thousand, respectively. Data on income distribution are available for 1988. The percentage share of household income by quintiles, beginning with the lowest, was: 4.0, 8.1, 12.5, 20.5 and 54.9. The percentage share of the highest 10 percent was 34.8. Comparable data for the Philippines (relating to 1985) were: 5.2, 8.9, 13.2, 20.2 and 52.5, with the highest 10 percent, 37.0. These data suggest a marginally more unequal distribution in Thailand than the Philippines. The Gini coefficients reported in Table 25.1 also suggest this conclusion (the higher the Gini coefficient, the more unequal the distribution). Thai data for 1981 suggest a somewhat less unequal distribution than the above Philippine data or the 1988 Thai data. Income inequality in Thailand appears to be widening. The data in Table 25.1 also show that, as in most Asian countries, poverty in Thailand is particularly concentrated in rural areas.

25.2.3 Political Stability?

Thailand's political history is one of a succession of authoritarian military governments alternating with brief periods of democracy or quasi-democracy. This political record would hardly lead one to predict stability of either economic policy or performance. But that is exactly what happened. How can it be explained? The facts are indeed puzzling, but four points can be mentioned in partial explanation.

First, Thailand's political history has not been as turbulent as it may seem. Although power has often changed hands through violence, or the threat of violence, the various contending forces have had a great deal in common. Political leaders must in general be acceptable to the military or at least to some powerful factions within it. Most potential political leaders either are, or have recently been, senior military men. The degree of military involvement in political affairs in Thailand surprises many foreign observers, as does its wide public acceptance within Thailand as a normal state of affairs. Strong military connections are indispensable for aspiring political leaders. This means that politicians espousing views that conflict strongly with the conservative outlook shared by most Thai military men can expect trouble.

Second, partly because of the military factor, Thailand's political life is not characterized by wide ideological differences. Thai politics is highly competitive but the major parties share acceptance of the importance of preserving Thai traditions and institutions, and especially a loyalty to the present monarch, King Bhumipol. In these respects, the fact that Thailand was not colonized by European powers is clearly very important. Thai traditions and institutions were not trampled upon or discredited by the militarily superior Europeans in the way that they were in most former colonies. The Thai intelligentsia have little difficulty in identifying with their country's past.

Third, over the last 30 years, most political leaders in Thailand have recognized a military threat from communist Vietnam. This had a unifying effect and encouraged caution in domestic and foreign policy.

The final point relates to the Thai bureaucracy. Not only do the above three points apply at least as much to the bureaucrats as to the politicians, but Thailand's conservative bureaucracy exhibits a surprising degree of independence from political control. For our purposes, the most interesting example is the central bank, the Bank of Thailand. The Bank has a reputation for attempting to preserve its independence from political control and for using that independence to pursue conservative monetary policies, almost regardless of the government of the day.

25.3   Market Structure

25.3.1   Macroeconomic Overview

Before describing Thailand's product, labor, financial and capital markets in detail we shall provide a simplified description of the macroeconomic environment operating within the Thai economy. Thailand has followed a fixed exchange rate policy since the end of World War II. The baht has been pegged to the US dollar. The trading system is relatively open, but the capital account is less so. Movements of foreign exchange and Thai currency out of Thailand are regulated, although some of these regulations have recently been relaxed. Large conversions of Thai currency into foreign exchange, for the purpose of capital export, require Bank of Thailand approval (Robinson et al. 1991).

Interest rates within Thailand are regulated by ceilings set by the Bank of Thailand. These apply to both borrowing and lending rates. Throughout most of

Thailand's recent economic history interest rates have remained at these ceiling levels. Wages within Thailand are officially subject to minimum wage controls, but these controls are effective only within the public sector and among large business enterprises. Elsewhere—in agriculture, small industrial enterprises and in much of the service sector—the minimum wages cannot be enforced. The minimum wages, in any case, seem to follow market forces, remaining somewhat above wages seen in the small private manufacturing enterprises.

Thailand's macroeconomic policies have been conservative for most of the last century and for all of the post-war period. Maintenance of a stable exchange rate backed by secure international reserves and, most especially, avoidance of domestic inflation have been central policy objectives. The postwar Thai policy environment has also been characterized by the relative independence of the central bank, the Bank of Thailand.

A central issue in understanding the Thai macroeconomic experience relates to the combined implications of its fixed exchange rate, partially controlled capital account and domestic interest rate controls. These variables determine the extent to which the domestic money supply can be controlled by the Bank of Thailand versus international capital flows. Monetary and fiscal policies both appear to have been counter-cyclical and stabilizing in the past suggesting that capital flows are not fully free. But recent capital account reforms will enhance capital mobility and hence reduce the Bank of Thailand's ability to exercize this stabilizing role.

25.3.2 Product Markets

As with most low and middle income developing countries, Thailand's product market policies imply taxation of agriculture and subsidization of industry. Export taxes have historically been applied to several agricultural export commodities, but have been slowly phased out. Rubber is now the only commodity subject to an export tax. Tariffs and quantitative import restrictions are used to protect part of the manufacturing sector. The production of these commodities is highly competitive, with a couple of exceptions mentioned below.

Rice is by far the most important agricultural commodity and a major export revenue earner for Thailand. Until recently, rice exports were taxed by a combination of instruments: the rice premium (a specific export tax), an export duty (an ad valorum export tax), and a reserve requirement (equivalent to an ad valorum export tax). The effect was to keep both consumer prices and prices received by farmers well below international prices. Chirmsak (1984) calculated that the combined effect of these policies was equivalent to a 31 percent export tax in 1970 and a 67 percent export tax in 1973–74, using the free-on-board export price as a base. These were years of very high international prices. The combined effect of these policies then declined to 13 percent by 1984. The rice premium was suspended in early 1986 in response to the low international prices for rice, and has not been reinstated (Ammar and Suthad 1989).

In addition to these policies, the government assigns export quotas to individual export agents, the effect of which is to introduce a noncompetitive element into the rice export market. The government annually announces target prices for paddy, but this is generally understood to be cosmetic. Some farmers are able to sell at support prices above current market prices with funds derived from the Farmer Aid Fund (whose funds in turn originate from the proceeds of the rice premium). The majority of farmers derive no benefit from this provision. The major exception to the general story of taxation of smallholder agriculture for the benefit of urban consumers occurs with sugar. Domestic sugar prices are held above international prices. In the mid-1980s, domestic prices were at least three times as high as international prices. The sugar industry is characterized by some large farmers and a greater number of smaller ones. The small farmers are dependent on the larger ones for their markets because the large farmers typically hold supplier contracts with the small number of large sugar mills. These large farmers and the mill owners act jointly to form a powerful political lobby.

Parts of the manufacturing sector are highly protected and inefficient, but the manufacturing sector is generally competitive and less highly regulated than the manufacturing sectors of some of Thailand's Southeast Asian neighbors (Juanjai et al. 1986).

25.3.3 Labor Markets

Thailand's labor markets can be divided into four major sectors: the civil service, the public enterprises, large private firms and small private firms. Average wages are higher in the first two sectors, but so are the educational requirements for jobs in those sectors. The data on wages in Thailand are very unreliable. Under the Labor Relations Act of 1975, trade unions are not permitted in the civil service, but are legal elsewhere. In practice, trade unions are strong only in the public enterprises. The public enterprises have a long history of labor organization. These firms generally enjoy monopolies in their industries, and commonly have only a single large plant, located in Bangkok. This makes it relatively easy for unions to organize the workforce. Large private firms have a history of opposing the formation and operation of unions. In this, the firms have generally received government support. A variety of tactics, including physical intimidation, have been used against workers attempting to organize. The unions cannot expect much help from the government.

Small private firms, which includes almost all of agriculture, most of manufacturing and almost all of the service sector, obviously employ the bulk of the workforce. The employees are not organized as the cost of organizing workers in scattered small firms would be very high. Labor markets in this, the dominant part of economy, are generally competitive, and wages appear to be flexible in response to variations in labor supply and demand (Bertrand and Squire, 1980).

The evidence presented by Bertrand and Squire does not support the "dual economy" hypothesis in regard to Thailand's labor markets. Minimum wage legislation exists, but is effective only within the public sector and some, but not all of the large private firms. The legislated minimum wages tend to be marginally above the wages paid by small private firms. The discrepancy is greatest among the youngest, least skilled employees.

There is considerable geographical mobility of labor. In recent decades, this has largely meant migration to Bangkok, where the new jobs have been heavily concentrated. Nevertheless, seasonal migration among agricultural regions is also important. Official statistics on unemployment rates are very unreliable, but nevertheless open unemployment seems to be a rare phenomenon in Thailand, except among the most highly educated.

25.3.4 Financial Markets

As with many other developing countries, Thailand's financial markets include both substantial organized and unorganized sectors. The organized sector can be broadly defined to include all legally registered institutions. The unorganized sector refers to financial transactions which do not go through organized financial institutions, of which the most prevalent form is borrowing and lending among individuals and the rotating credit societies.

Thailand's organized financial markets are made up of seven main financial institutions: commercial banks; finance, securities, and credit companies; specialized banks; development finance corporations; insurance companies; saving co-operatives; and other mortgage institutions. The commercial banks comprise the largest component in terms of total assets, credit extended, and savings mobilized. The second largest is the finance companies which began operation in 1969. There are three specialized banks—the Government Saving Bank (GSB), the Bank of Agriculture and Agricultural Cooperatives (BAAC) and the Government Housing Bank (GHB)—and two development finance corporations, the Industrial Finance Corporation of Thailand (IFCT), and the Small Industries Finance Office (SIFO). These specialized institutions are either owned or partly owned by the government.

The financial market is dominated by the activities of commercial banks which absorb roughly three-fourths of all deposits placed with financial institutions. They are, therefore, the central actors in Thailand's financial system. The current structure consists of 16 local (Thai-owned) banks and 14 foreign banks. The role of foreign banks is very limited. As noted earlier, the 1962 Commercial Banking Act restricted entry to the banking business. Licensing permits are required. The last permit was granted in 1965. Of the 16 local commercial banks, one is a state enterprise (the Krung Thai Bank), one is owned by the Crown Property Bureau (Siam Commercial Bank), and another is partly owned by the government (the Sayam Bank).

A significant feature of the commercial banking industry in Thailand is the high degree of concentration in ownership. Ownership is dominated by 16 families of Chinese origin. In the past, Thai monetary authorities have attempted to diversify bank ownership by means of special legislation to limit the concentration of shareholding. The Stock Exchange has been used as a main venue for ownership transfer, by limiting the number of shares a person may hold. The legislation proved ineffective, however, as banks were unable to meet the deadlines for ownership diversification and the deadlines had to be extended repeatedly.

The Thai commercial banking industry has a cartel-like structure with the 16 banks organized loosely under the Thai Bankers Association, whereby they collectively set the standard rates of service charges and loan rates. This oligopolistic practice makes interest rates (loan and deposits) respond relatively slowly to market conditions as it takes time for all banks to agree on the same adjustment, particularly in the downward direction. An important corollary of this is that the Thai bankers, as a collective body, possess substantial power in dictating the cost and the allocation of domestic credit and in influencing the effectiveness of monetary policies.

A number of important government regulations affect the financial market, especially the banking industry. The main features are the stipulation of interest rate ceilings for loans and deposits, control of new entry, agricultural credit policy, and compulsory bond holding for branch expansion. The Bank of Thailand adjusts the ceiling rates to keep the domestic rates in line with foreign rates, to smooth out liquidity problems, or to deliberately carry out monetary policy. Another important control is the stipulation of a compulsory minimum to the banks' capital fund to risky assets ratio. This measure is designed to prevent excessive expansion of bank credit to ensure the soundness of the banking system. In some years, this measure has acted as a major restraint on banks' abilities to reduce excess liquidity through loan expansion.

A novel feature of monetary policy which is administered through the banking system is the use of rediscount facilities. The basic idea has been to assist priority sectors by providing low-cost funds. The use of the rediscount facility, which first appeared in 1960 to finance rice exports, has been extended throughout industry, agriculture, and construction.

Private foreign borrowing is relatively free. Although a withholding tax on foreign borrowing exists, it plays little role in influencing the inflow of international credit. From the mid-1970s, local commercial banks and large companies have used foreign borrowing as a means of adjusting their liquidity positions. This feature makes local liquidity highly responsive to changes in foreign interest rates and the exchange rate. What has been observed is that when the foreign interest rate was high and/or when there was speculation of a baht devaluation, there would be a slowdown in capital inflow. Capital outflows, while officially requiring Bank of Thailand approval, occur through quasi-legal channels such as transfer pricing. Domestic interest rates, constrained by the ceilings set by the Bank of Thailand, do not rise correspondingly. This results in tight liquidity in the domestic money market. The reverse is observed at times of low foreign interest rate and/ or a strong baht.

An important implication of the above structure is that Thailand's financial system is prone to excess liquidity when the world interest rate declines, and this excess liquidity problem is prolonged. This occurs because local commercial banks have a rather limited portfolio choice as the country's capital markets are not well developed and capital outflow, in the form of investing in foreign assets, is tightly regulated. Most banks therefore hold substantial amounts of government bonds and investment in short-term money markets such as treasury bills and bonds in repurchase markets. Another factor prolonging excess liquidity is the rigidity in interest rate adjustment, as noted earlier.

25.3.5 Capital Markets

Capital markets are a recent phenomenon in Thailand. The Securities Exchange of Thailand (SET) began operation only in 1975 as a way of offering savers alternative means of investment, including common and preferred stocks, straight bonds, debentures and unit trusts. The market—as measured in terms of number of listed companies and securities, types of securities, trading volume, and market value—is relatively thin by international standards. Thailand still lacks a well developed institution that can facilitate financial mobilization for long-term investment. A number of factors can be mentioned to explain the problems faced by the SET. On the demand side, stock investment is not a popular portfolio choice in Thailand. This point is reflected by the low volume of trading turnover. Thai investors are conservative. The fact that the local financial markets have been dominated for a long time by commercial banks makes investors feel more accustomed to investments whose yields are known with relative certainty. Knowledge of stock market trading mechanisms, risks, and yields is not widespread. These elements build up an uncertainty which makes stock investment less attractive and more troublesome than bank deposits.

On the supply side, the limited number of instruments offered by the SET is unattractive to investors. The problem is further exacerbated by the uneven distribution of securities by industry. Most companies in Thailand still rely on debt, instead of equity, as a means of raising finance. Secondary markets for government and state enterprise bonds have developed well. These markets, which started in 1982, are hosted by large commercial banks and active finance companies. The hosting institutions offer post-issued government bonds for sale to the general public. They adjust prices daily in line with market conditions. It is not surprising to observe a growing popularity of the market as the degree of risk involved is minimal, yields are relatively certain, and there is flexibility for immediate liquidity.

25.4 The Public Sector

Compared with most other developing countries, the role historically perceived for the public sector in Thailand was strictly limited. This view had roots in the traditional conservatism of Thai ruling elites. The Thai aristocracy of the 19th and early 20th centuries held a virtual monopoly of government affairs. Avoidance of domination by the European colonial powers and maintenance of the existing social order domestically were given overriding priority. The maintenance of financial stability at home was seen as a necessary condition for both of these ends. Accordingly, the domestic role of government was severely constrained by these attitudes, which continued well into the 20th century.

By the 1980s, the influence of the public sector—particularly the core agencies of macroeconomic policy—had increased as the government became more active in economic affairs. This was partly the result of a change in political leadership, and partly due to the perceived macroeconomic difficulties facing the economy. There were increasing demands by the educated public for the government to be more active in initiating and coordinating economic development.

This section reviews the role of the public sector in Thailand. It discusses its current structure and its modes of intervention in the economy. The latter take a variety of forms and they are often used in combination. After describing the institutional background we then discuss the methods of intervention: fiscal measures, sectoral interventions, regulation, public provision of infrastructure, and the public enterprises.

25.4.1 The Institutional Framework

The basis for the current system of administration was laid over a century ago during the reign of King Chulalongkorn (Rama V). The system, which was modelled along British lines, modified the traditional functions of the court into a hierarchical system of government agencies, with administrative power assumed principally by the central government, reflecting the highly centralized political structure then prevailing. This administrative centralization has survived, surprisingly without radical modification, to this day.

The system of government is organized at three levels: the central government, the local governments, and the state enterprises.

Central government. By far the largest public sector body is the central government. It is made up of 12 ministries, the Office of the Prime minister, the Office of University Affairs, and seven independent government agencies including the Parliament and the Bureau of Crown Property. Apart from supervising the work of departments, offices, and publicly funded agencies directly under them, the central government also supervises the work of local governments and state enterprises.

The finance of the central government rests on the distinction between budgetary and non-budgetary transactions. The national budget requires approval of the parliament. Its expenditure is supported by incomes from six main sources: (1) tax revenue, (2) contributions from state enterprises, (3) fines, fees, and proceeds from sales of goods, (4) domestic borrowings, (5) issue of new coins, and (6) use of treasury cash balances. Items (1) to (3) are budgetary revenues whereas items (4) to (6) involve the financing of budgetary deficits. Note the absence of foreign borrowing as a source of budgetary finance; it is legally prohibited.

Nonbudgetary transactions occur outside the annual budget and take two basic forms: (1) expenditure financed by external grants and loans; and (2) expenditure financed by advances from the state treasury deposits. The latter is a special case and is possible only with the approval of the parliament, in the form of a special Act. Being nonbudgetary, expenditure financed by foreign borrowings does not require approval of the parliament. It was through this channel of expenditure that the growth in public sector spending of the early 1980s occurred.

Three regulations governing central government expenditure are notable. First, in any fiscal year, the amount of budgetary deficit may not exceed 25 percent of the expected revenue. Second, direct foreign borrowing by the Ministry of Finance in any fiscal year (October 1 to September 30) must be within 10 percent of the expenditure budget. And third, foreign loans for state enterprises which are guaranteed by the Ministry of Finance in any year must not exceed 10 percent of the expenditure budget.

Local governments. Local governments are the administrative arms of the central government in the provinces. Their administration is the responsibility of the Ministry of Interior, through the Local Government Department (LAD). At present, local governments consist of 126 municipalities, 795 sanitary districts, 72 Changwat (provincial) Administrative Organizations (CAOs), the Bangkok Metropolitan Administration, and the Pattaya City Administration. The main administrative power rests with the CAOs whose heads, with the exception of the cities of Bangkok and Pattaya, are elected. Provincial governors are civil servants appointed by the Ministry of Interior. This direct line of command means that local government administration is closely controlled by the central government.

Local government finance has a relatively small weight in overall public sector finance—less than 5 percent in terms of expenditure. Its main source of income is revenues from local taxes, revenue from shared tax with the central government, own income from property, fines, fees and permits, contributions from the central government, and domestic borrowings. Foreign borrowing by local governments is legally possible but must be organized on its behalf by the Ministry of Interior. To date, no such borrowing has occurred.

The core agencies of economic policy. Within Thailand's system of government, decision-making on macroeconomic policy issues is in the domain of Ministers. Policy decisions at the ministerial level, either made individually by a Minister or by Ministers acting collectively, usually as a cabinet, rely a great deal on information and analyses made available to them by the departments concerned and the core agencies. The latter includes the National Economic and Social Development Board (NESDB), the government's major economic planning agency, the Fiscal Policy Office (FPO) of the Ministry of Finance, the Bank of Thailand (BOT), and the Bureau of the Budget (BOB). The directors of these core agencies sit permanently in the Council of Economic Ministers.

Prior to discussion at the ministerial level, policy options are formulated through coordination and consultation between departments and experts from the core agencies. In recent years, the role and the influence of the core agencies have increased significantly as the government has become increasingly reliant on them for opinions and analyses. The heads of these core agencies are the central actors in formulating Thailand's economic policies.

The development plans. Planning for economic development became a formal process of the Thai government in 1959 when the National Economic Development Board (NEDB)—now the NESDB—was established. Since then, seven national development plans, each covering a five year period, have been drawn up and the first six of these have now been implemented. The underlying philosophy of economic planning in Thailand is a commitment to a market economy. Planning has been directed mainly towards securing a smooth functioning of markets with minimum direct government intervention or controls.

It would be easy to overstate the importance of the development plans in Thailand's economic policy formulation. Circumstances change quickly, and plans made five years or more in advance must always be modified. The plans are almost never implemented in the form described in the plan documents, and often not at all. The plans are more useful as indicators of the policy directions the government viewed as appropriate at the time the plans are drawn up. In reviewing the plans, it is helpful to relate them to the economic outcomes that were actually experienced over the plan periods. In this light we shall briefly discuss the most recent development plan to have been implemented, the Sixth Plan, covering the period 1987 to 1991.

The years 1982–1986 coincided with slowed growth as a result of the world recession of the early 1980s. By 1985 Thailand suffered from serious macroeconomic problems. Largely as a result of the international oil price increases of the 1970s and early 1980s, Thailand had suffered a severe deterioration in its terms of trade—from an index of 100 in 1973 to 51 in 1985 and 56 in 1987. Although it had avoided the economic collapse that these external events had produced in other developing countries—including the Philippines—by 1985 Thailand was experiencing serious macroeconomic problems. These macroeconomic imbalances could be summarized as:

    ☐ A persistent and unsustainable balance of payments deficit on current account equivalent in 1985 to 5 percent of GDP.

    ☐ An investment-savings gap of a similar magnitude. This represented mainly a decline in savings as a proportion of GDP from 20–22 percent in the late 1970s to 16–17 percent in 1985.

☐ Foreign exchange reserves had fallen, as a proportion of GDP, from 12 percent in 1970 to 3 percent in 1985. This required a US$500 million International Monetary Fund (IMF) standby loan in mid-1985. Its renewal was negotiated a year later.

☐ External debt had risen to US$16 billion by 1985, equivalent to 40 percent of GDP and 146 percent of exports. US$12 billion of this was long-term debt, of which US$8 billion was public or publicly guaranteed. An additional US$4 billion of short-term debt was held mainly in the private sector. The debt service ratio in 1985 was around 26 percent, up from 17 percent in 1980.

☐ The government's budget deficit had remained at over 5 percent of GDP over the previous five years. Total public expenditure, comprising central and local governments and state enterprises was around 40 percent of GDP. The central government just managed to finance its current expenditures from its revenues. Virtually all capital expenditures were financed by borrowing. General government savings had fallen from 3.7 percent of GDP (average of 1970 to 1977) to less than 1 percent in 1985.

☐ The overall rate of growth of GDP in real terms was lower in the 1970s than the 1960s, and lower still in the 1980s. Growth in the years 1985 and 1986 was the lowest of any two consecutive years since the 1950s; but this was a decline from a long-term real rate of growth of almost 7 percent to "only" 5 percent.

The Sixth Plan was drafted in response to the above problems. Its objectives were:

☐ To promote the economic growth rate to at least 5 percent per year.

☐ To improve the administrative structure of the government and review its role. The private sector was to play a greater role, thereby reducing the burden of the government.

☐ To increase the mobilization of domestic saving from both private and public sectors from the target of 18.2 percent under the previous Plan to 23.7 percent.

☐ Continuation of the privatization process and improvement of the administrative efficiency of the state enterprises. The proportion of their foreign borrowing was also to be reduced.

☐ The use of fiscal and monetary measures to support economic growth and to reduce the deficit in the trade and current accounts. One fiscal measure was the restructuring of the taxation system to increase government revenues and to attract foreign investment.

From 1986 onward, Thai macroeconomic policy adjusted sharply to the imbalances described above. The adjustments included a striking fiscal contraction. The fiscal deficit described above was transformed into a surplus equivalent to 1.3 percent of GDP in fiscal year 1988 and 4.9 percent in 1990. Cuts in public investment expenditure were a major source of this adjustment. Public sector fixed capital formation declined by three percentage points of GDP from fiscal years 1985 to 1988 (to 5.8 percent of GDP). Simultaneously, Thailand was experiencing an export boom, concentrated in manufactures.

The boom appears to have been a consequence of two mutually reinforcing events, neither of which can reasonably be attributed to deliberate acts of policy on the part of the Thai government. The first was a 30 percent depreciation of Thailand's real effective exchange rate from 1986 to 1990 resulting from the baht being pegged to a depreciating US dollar. The second was the international relocation of light manufacturing industries from Taiwan, Hong Kong, Korea and Singapore, where labor costs were rising rapidly, to lower wage countries like Thailand, Malaysia, Indonesia and the southeastern corner of China. The magnitude of the boom was as much a surprise to the Thai economic planners as to anyone else. But the reduction in expenditure on basic infrastructure—roads, ports, telecommunications, and so forth—threatened the medium-term sustainability of the boom because these facilities were becoming badly congested.

25.4.2 The Tax System

Responsibility for planning and managing taxation policy rests with the Ministry of Finance, specifically its Fiscal Policy Office (FPO). The overall tax system includes both central government and local government tax, but the former is dominant. In 1990 the tax revenue (central and local) to GDP ratio was 20 percent, which is low by international comparison. The composition of tax revenues has changed markedly since the 1960s.

The relative importance of international trade taxes (import and export taxes) has declined, both in relation to GDP and as a share of total taxes (from 30 percent of total tax revenue in 1970 to 22 percent in 1990), a result of a reduction in the reliance on export taxes and the reduced average import taxes. This has been balanced by increases in the relative importance of income-based and consumption taxes. The decline in the relative importance of international trade taxes has made the present tax system more dependent on indirect domestic taxes. Despite the increasing importance of income-based taxes (personal and corporate), direct tax revenues are of limited importance by international standards.

The main features of the current tax system include:

☐ A high proportion of indirect taxes which are inelastic with respect to GDP and have a small tax base. This feature tends to reduce the average tax rate automatically as GDP increases.

☐ The personal income tax is progressive and is the only tax which has an income elasticity greater than unity. The progressive tax schedule has limited effects on the top income earners, however, as many types of income—including income from bequests and income from interest on bank deposits—are exempt from taxation. As a result, the ratio of tax to assessable income is not steeply progressive.

☐ Corporate income tax is losing its relative importance as close to half of all corporations declare losses for tax purposes. In 1990, less than 1 percent of all corporations paid three-quarters of corporate tax revenues. Without substantial improvements in collection, corporate income tax will become an increasingly unreliable revenue measure.

☐ Domestic consumption tax (business and excise taxes) has a regressive structure and the tax base is relatively small. At present, state enterprises do not have to pay business tax and the excise tax covers only nine commodities. This feature makes revenue mobilization costly to the general public as tax rates frequently require adjustment upwards for revenue purposes. The tax burden is therefore passed on to all consumers regardless of their income positions.

☐ Despite the reduced relative importance of international trade taxes there exists a large diversity in the tariff rates, ranging between 5 to 60 percent ad valorem.

☐ Direct transfer payments by the government have a small role in Thailand's fiscal structure. No welfare system exists. Most of the transfers are between public sector agencies and not between households and the government.

In January 1992 the government introduced a new value-added tax (VAT) system. The new tax was designed to overcome some of the problems identified above. The cascading effect of the existing business tax system—the fact that the rate of the tax effectively increases along the chain of production—was stressed as a motivation for implementing the VAT. The rate of the VAT was set at 7 percent, except for industries which were specifically exempted. The latter included all of agriculture and industries producing inputs for direct use in agriculture, such as fertilizer, animal feeds, pesticides, and so forth. Businesses with total revenue less than 600,000 baht (approximately US$24,000) were also exempt. Exporters were entitled to a refund of VAT on proof of export of goods having been completed.

In summary, despite the VAT reform the existing tax system remains handicapped by a structure which hinders effective revenue mobilization. It is necessary for the government to continue to reform the existing tax system so that additional revenue can be raised without seriously distorting private incentives and without creating further inequality in the distribution of income.

25.4.3 Sectoral Interventions

Until the late 1960s, the role of the public sector was limited largely to tax collection, direct production through the public enterprises and public provision of infrastructure. As the economy expanded, the price system came increasingly to be seen within the bureaucracy as distorted and as an unreliable guide to resource allocation. This perception resulted in more direct interventions by the public sector. Some of the interventions were designed to modify the pattern of resource utilization consistently with overall economic policy but many clearly had more to do with the generation of economic rents benefiting particular interest groups. In this section, we briefly discuss government interventions in three important areas: agriculture, industry, and trade.

Interventions in agriculture. The main impetus of Thailand's economic growth in the 1960s and the 1970s had been the growth of agriculture. The momentum of agricultural growth was lost in the late 1970s as the land frontier was exhausted, and the relative importance of agriculture in production declined. Nonetheless, agriculture remains the largest source of employment and the largest provider of income for the majority of the population. Moreover, Thailand's poorest citizens are disproportionately concentrated in the agricultural sector (Ammar and Suthad 1989).

Although growth in agriculture has come mainly from private initiative, government interventions in agriculture, particularly in the pricing system, have had considerable impact. The most important, which also has the longest history, had been the taxation of rice exports. As noted above, the *rice export tax*, introduced immediately after the end of the World War II as a way of raising government revenue, was suspended in 1986. Over the previous three decades, the heavy export tax on rice had depressed rural incomes by reducing the farm-gate prices of paddy and rural wages. It also impeded technological change by altering the price-cost ratio in the rice sector. Rubber remains subject to an export tax (15 percent of the free-on-board price).

The *compulsory rice reserve scheme* had a similar effect. The scheme came into effect in 1973 (a period of rice shortage) and ended in 1982. Under the scheme, exporters were required to sell a proportion of their rice to the government at a price set lower than the domestic price. The quantity of these compulsory sales was fixed in relation to the amount of rice exported. The policy was intended to enable the government to obtain cheap rice for resale to the general public. It was thus similar to an ad valorem export tax, and further depressed farm-gate prices for paddy.

The government has occasionally imposed periodic *export quotas* on agricultural products. In the past, both rice and maize were occasionally subject to such controls. At present, only cassava is affected by this policy, due to the government decision to self-restrict its cassava exports to the European Economic Community (EEC). The allocation of export quotas is under the responsibility of the Ministry of Commerce. It is said that the quota allocation system is often politically motivated.

Apart from rice, maize, cassava, and rubber, other agricultural products such as swine, castor oil seeds, and tobacco are subject to government regulation. In most of these cases, government regulations have introduced monopolistic elements into the markets, resulting in inefficiency. For example, the Animal Slaughtering and Meat Sale Control Act of 1960 requires a transfer of property rights on land and buildings to the local governments as a condition for setting up a private slaughterhouse. This is tantamount to handing monopoly power to public slaughterhouses managed by local governments.

Intervention in industry. The main feature of government intervention in industry has been the promotion of private investment administered through the Board of Investment (BOI). The BOI, established in 1959, uses a combination of various investment promotion schemes, tariff policies, tax regimes, and trade and price controls to direct the pattern of private investment. During the 1960s and the early

1970s, industrial policies strongly favored import substitution. Import tariffs were raised significantly to protect local industries, with incentives being strongest for production of final products based on imported intermediate and capital goods. The emphasis of industrial promotion policy was shifted towards exports with the passage of the Investment Promotion Act of 1972.

To earn a BOI promotion certificate, prospective investors apply for privileges according to the BOI's regulations. A list of industries eligible for promotion privileges is drawn up by the BOI using the national development plan as a broad framework. The incentives offered typically include tax and tariff exemptions, guarantee of government protection from nationalization and from direct competition by state enterprises, and guarantees of rights of profit and capital repatriation. The range of incentives differs between industries, reflecting priority rankings in the promotion policy. The main criticism of the promotion policy is that policy measures are frequently changed and the BOI often exercises discretionary powers in the granting of promotional privileges and the extent of incentives given. It has been observed that the incentives offered differ among firms within the same industry.

In addition to the BOI, the Ministries of Industry, Commerce, and Finance, as well as the Bank of Thailand also formulate and administer policies which directly affect industrial development. The FPO of the Ministry of Finance operates a comprehensive tax refund system for all taxes incurred in the production process. The Bank of Thailand provides a rediscount facility at subsidized interest rates to export- oriented firms. The Ministry of Commerce provides technical assistance through its Export Service Center.

Important regulations administered by the Ministry of Industry are the controls on establishing and expanding factories and production plants, and the regulation on the use of local contents in production. At present, there are 23 categories of industry which are subjected to factory control and four industries are subjected to local content requirements, that is, motor vehicle assembly, motor cycle production, electric wire and cable, and steel production.

Protection policy. Apart from tariffs and export taxes, the trade regime in Thailand includes a number of restrictive measures such as quantitative import and export controls. Currently, there is an import ban on 18 commodities, and special permission is required to import another 30. The Ministry of Commerce imposes and supervises import controls. Commodities under control include those produced in the socialist countries, weapons and strategic firearms, rice, and sugar. The controls on rice and sugar are to prevent re-importation after the products have been exported. Export controls are placed on 38 commodities, 16 of which are outright bans. The export controls are meant to ensure domestic supplies for local consumption at low prices. Items such as paper, pesticide, flat iron sheet, polyfibre, and cement are regulated to ensure local supplies.

Besides direct controls on imports and exports, the Ministry of Commerce also administers price controls on "essential products". This has been possible with the passage of the Price Setting and Anti-Monopoly Act of 1979. In 1986 there were 34 commodities under price control. Such control has helped to keep down the cost of living but at the expense of shortages of these products in retail stores.

Thailand does not practice free trade, but its protection levels are moderate and relatively stable. Since the 1960s empirical studies of effective rates of protection (ERPs) in Thailand have used different sets of data, different product definitions, as well as different methodologies. For example, some studies use the official tariff rates, while others use tariff rates estimated from customs duty collections or from price comparisons. It is thus difficult to compare the results of these studies over time. Nevertheless, studies on the effective rate of protection show the same pattern over the past three decades. The protective system has been biased against the agro-based industries and towards the manufacturing sector, both import competing and non-import competing goods. This is the typical pattern of protection found in developing countries. Tables 25.2 and 25.3 summarize the results of these studies.

Trairong (1970) studied Thailand's ERPs in 23 manufacturing industries in 1964 using input coefficients from Belgium and the Netherlands data derived from Balassa's standardized input-output table. Using official tariffs and the 1962 Investment Promotion Act as measures of the protective system, his results showed that the system of protection was biased towards consumption goods, followed by intermediate goods, and biased against capital goods (Juanjai et al. 1986).

TABLE 25.2 Effective protection of industry groups by levels of fabrication and end uses, 1964–84 (%)

Industry group	1964	1969	1974	1984
Processed food	47	–33	–19	8
Beverages and tobacco	215	241	2,281	27
Construction materials	n.a.	47	47	17
Intermediate goods I	82	3	16	18
Intermediate goods II	60	79	49	242
Consumer nondurable goods	71	33	91	24
Consumer durable goods	64	69	201	19
Machinery	37	31	30	32
Transport equipment	118	35	354	46

n.a.: not available

Sources: The effective rates of protection (ERPs) for 1964 and 1969 were obtained from Juanjai (1986). The ERPs for 1974 and 1984 were obtained from Narongchai (1977) and Paitoon et al. (1989), respectively. The weights used to aggregate products for 1974 and 1984 were value added at market prices of 1975 and 1985, respectively, obtained from the Thai input–output tables.

TABLE 25.3 Effective rates of protection of the manufacturing sector classified by trade oriented group, 1969–87 (%)

Sector	1969[1]	1974[2]	1984[3]	1987[3]
Export group	−43	−35	2	4
Import competing group	54[a] (648)[b]	63	21	39
Non-import competing group	187	77[c] (812)[d]	53	55

a. Tyres and tubes are excluded.
b. Tyres and tubes are included.
c. Cigarettes and soft drinks are excluded.
d. Cigarettes and soft drinks are included.

Products are classified, based on Narongchai's studies (1973, 1977), into three groups: export oriented, import competing and non-import competing, according to their trade orientation. A product is classified as export if its export level is greater than 10 percent of its domestic production and its net export is positive. It is import competing if its import is greater than 10 percent of its total consumption and if its net import is positive. The rest are classified as non-import competing.

The 1975 value added at market price of each industry are used as weights to estimate the aggregate effective rate of protection of each product group of all years.

Sources: 1. Calculated from Narongchai (1973). 2. Calculated from Narongchai (1977). 3. Calculated from Paitoon et al. (1989).

Narongchai (1977) estimated the ERPs of 58 industries for 1969, and of 80 industries for 1971 and 1974 using input-output coefficients obtained from industrial surveys. When tariffs were used as the main instrument of trade policy and industries were classified by trade orientation, his results showed that over the period the import competing and nonimport competing industries received highest protection. When the industries were classified by end use and level of fabrication, the effective protection system was biased in favor of beverages and tobacco and processed food, followed by transport equipment and consumer goods.

Pairote (1975) estimated the ERPs of 58 industries for 1964, and of 82 industries for 1971 and 1974 using the input-output coefficients obtained from industrial surveys. The results showed that the protection system over the period of study was inward-looking, favoring firms selling on domestic markets. Import competing and non-import competing industries received greatest protection. The structure of protection was biased against export industries. When industries were classified by end uses and levels of fabrication, the incentive effects were strongly in favor of consumer goods, especially beverages and tobacco, and transport equipment, followed by consumer goods (Juanjai et al. 1986).

Paitoon et al. (1989) estimated ERPs in Thailand's manufacturing sector for 1981, 1984 and 1987 using input coefficients from the 180-sector input–output tables of 1982 and 1985. The protective instruments covered in the study were mainly tariffs, import surcharges, export taxes, tax rebates and refunds, and royalties. When industries were classified by trade orientation, the results showed that the effective protection was biased against export industries. The non-import competing industries received the highest protection, followed by the import competing industries. From Table 25.3 it may be concluded that over the period 1969 to 1987 the export industries received the lowest effective protection, followed by the import competing industries, while the non-importing industries received the highest effective protection.

In 1969 and 1974, most of the export industries were agro-based, such as rice milling, frozen seafood and canned fruit, which use agricultural products as raw materials. From 1980 onwards, there have been more diversified export industries. The new export industries, in addition to the traditional agro-based ones, include canned fish and crustaceans, garments, rubber sheets and rubber products, wood products, jewelry and footwear. A dominant characteristic of the new export industries is that they are labor-intensive, such as garments and footwear. But these have generally *not* been the industries favored by the system of protection. The protected industries, as well as those favored by the BOI's promotion policies, have in general continued to perform poorly.

Exchange rate policy. Since 1955, when the multiple exchange rate system was abolished, until the devaluations of 1981, the baht was maintained virtually at a fixed parity with the U.S. dollar, at between 20 and 21 baht per U.S. dollar. The main argument for the peg with the dollar was the stability and the confidence it was believed to provide (Corden and Richter 1967). Between 1955 and 1977, the dollar depreciated in relation to other currencies and the baht–dollar rate was adjusted to a minor extent five times, to maintain parity with the depreciated dollar.

The volatility of the dollar and the enlarged trade deficits in the late 1970s following the second oil shock (1979–80) led to a reconsideration of exchange rate policy. Although much of Thailand's trade is denominated in U.S. dollars, less than 20 percent of exports and imports are with the United States. The overvalued dollar in the late 1970s had worked to increase the country's balance of payments deficits. In March 1978, the Bank of Thailand announced that the baht would no longer be tied to the dollar but would be linked to a basket of currencies in which the dollar would be a major component. The new system was short-lived. In November, 1978, a system of daily fixing was introduced, in effect putting the baht back in parity to the dollar at 19.8 baht per dollar. There have been four devaluations since, as summarized in Table 25.4.

The announced objectives of the 1981 and 1984 devaluations were to reduce the existing current account deficits. The devaluations relative to the U.S. dollar of 1981 and 1984 were small relative to the exogenous movements in Thailand's effective exchange rate induced by movements in other countries' exchange rates

TABLE 25.4 Dates and magnitudes of devaluations

Date	Rate of devaluation (%)
May 1981	1.1
July 1981	8.7
November 1984	14.9
December 1985	1.9

Sources: Bank of Thailand, *Annual Report*, 1981 to 1985.

relative to the dollar. Thus, even taking the devaluations into account, Thai exchange rate policy since 1955 was essentially that of fixity relative to the U.S. dollar.

Devaluations have been avoided whenever possible because they undermine the Bank of Thailand's central objective of controlling inflation. They also have unpopular political consequences. They create hardships for those who depend on imported raw materials as well as those holding debts denominated in foreign currencies. In Thailand, devaluations are usually employed only after other methods of coping with trading imbalances have already been used. These other means include raising import tariffs, contractionary fiscal and monetary policies, and credit controls.

An example of such a policy response was the limit on commercial banks' credit growth which began in 1984. This was a major shift in monetary policy since it was the first time that a quantity control was imposed together with a price control, that is, the interest ceiling. The shift in policy stance was attributed to the conditions set by the IMF for the stand-by arrangement loans negotiated in 1984. The Bank of Thailand, alarmed by the huge deficits in the balance of trade in 1983, decided to take this drastic measure against the expansion of imports. The commercial banks were subject to a maximum credit expansion of 18 percent of the 1983 level of credit.

Devaluations can be costly for the politicians who implement them. The 1981 devaluation led to political attacks from opposition parties as well as some members of the governing coalition. Fear of inflation was one of their major concerns. However, some members' opposition to devaluation stemmed from lack of understanding. The record of the parliament in July 1981 indicated that some MPs expressed the fear that the budget would be invalid because the value of the baht had been eroded by 8.7 percent. Others suggested alternative policies such as totally banning imports, increasing tariffs, or asking the Bank of Thailand to assume a monopoly role of foreign exchange dealer. Other MPs even regarded the devaluation as equivalent to *lèse majesté* since the value of the bank notes bearing the King's picture had been reduced. There was also strong opposition from the press. The deputy finance minister, Paichitr Uathavikul pictured as the main culprit, resigned.

While the 1981 devaluation was opposed mainly by politicians, the 1984 devaluation produced a confrontation between the prime minister and the commander-in-chief of the army. The army commander, in a public broadcast, called for the cancellation of the devaluation and a reshuffling of the cabinet. The latter implied the removal of the finance minister, who was responsible for the devaluation. He had also angered the military by opposing the airforce plan to purchase new tactical fighters, pointing out that it would substantially increase Thailand's external public debt. Devaluation was seen as a threat to the plan to modernize the Thai military since the jet fighters would now cost 14.9 percent more. Prime minister Prem satisfied the military by promising to find the 3 billion baht needed to shield the cost of the aircraft from the impact of devaluation. The government also introduced new controls on the price of petroleum and some other necessities, so as to placate the opposition to devaluation. Five days later, the army commander backed away from his opposition, announcing that the dispute had been a "misunderstanding."

After the 1984 devaluation the fixed exchange rate system was officially replaced by a "flexible exchange rate system." Under this, the baht is said to be tied to a basket of currencies to provide greater flexibility in the management of foreign exchange. In fact, the close relationship to the U.S. dollar has been maintained, in spite of the dollar's realignment relative to other currencies. Clearly, the "basket" of currencies is dominated by the U.S. dollar.

25.4.4 Public Provision of Infrastructure

Provision of infrastructure has been a central theme of the Development Plans. During the first two Plans public investment was concentrated on roads, irrigation, power, and telecommunications. The expansion of the road network in 1960s, which was tacitly linked to an American supported counter-insurgency programme, had a considerable impact on agricultural development and overall economic growth. It provided farmers with direct access to external markets, which significantly increased farm-gate prices for cash crops, as well as access to vast uncultivated land. The extension of the land frontier was instrumental to agricultural growth in the 1960s and the 1970s.

Investment in irrigation took the form of building large dams and waterways. Irrigation investment, which provided a source of power supplies, also provided a basis for investment in power, telecommunication, and electrification. There were also significant developments in airports, harbors, and telecommunication. The security risks associated with the Vietnam war partly motivated these developments. From the very poor infrastructure facilities of the 1950s, by the middle of the 1970s Thailand was regarded as possessing a basic infrastructure that compared favorably with most other developing countries.

The military coup of 1976 placed control of the economy's finances under the direct influence of the military and the bureaucrats. In 1977, a special decree was announced, increasing the public sector's access to foreign borrowings. The state enterprises, for the first time, were able to borrow directly from abroad with government guarantees to finance their capital investment. The passage of this decree led to a dramatic expansion in defence expenditure and in the role of state enterprises. Between 1978 and 1983, there was a steady increase in expenditure by the state enterprises, financed in particular by foreign borrowing. The bulk of this was spent on energy related activities, intended to develop an alternative local energy source and reduce dependence on imported energy.

There was no definitive policy on the management of public debt when the decision to liberalize the public sector's foreign borrowing was made in 1977. Regulations on foreign debt merely limited the amount each state enterprise could borrow but not the aggregate for the public sector. The enlarged foreign debt commitment became a serious policy problem in the early 1980s as the economy went into a recession following a slump in primary commodity exports. The current account deficit reached 7.1 percent of GDP in 1983 and the debt–service ratio reached 23.3 percent and was still rising. This development, which was considered a threat to the country's financial stability, prompted the government to revise its foreign borrowing policy and led to the establishment of the National Debt Reform Committee and new policy guidelines on foreign borrowing were announced. The guidelines set annual limits on the public sector's foreign borrowing. Although this decision was welcomed on financial grounds, it affected the economy's long-term growth potential. Several of the large development projects being planned, most of which relied on foreign funds, were either scaled down or postponed due to lack of foreign exchange.

By the early 1990s the export-led boom of the late 1980s had left Thailand's infrastructure facilities severely congested. Ports, roads and telecommunications all required upgrading if the growth was to be sustained. The heavy concentration of economic activity in Bangkok made improvement of road transport, in particular, extremely difficult.

25.4.5 Public Enterprises

Public enterprises play an important role in the Thai economy, as they do in many other less developed countries (LDCs). The activities of state enterprises in Thailand stretch into many areas of business. This includes infrastructure, manufacturing, transport, hotel, service, trade and finance. The central bank, the Bank of Thailand (BOT), is also a state enterprise, as is the national air carrier, Thai International. At present, there are 68 state enterprises, 17 of which operate in infrastructure. Most state enterprises began as special projects (revolving funds) under central government departments with their own staffs and financial accounts, then slowly graduated to the status of state enterprises when their activities enlarged.

The growth of the public enterprises has been haphazard (IBRD 1959). Not only was there little economic rationale for the choice of industries entered by the public enterprises, but by the 1980s their operation, finance and investment behavior was out of control. The practice of public enterprises lending public funds to one another made their accounts difficult to interpret. The public enterprises had become major vehicles for the purchase of political patronage, and remain so today. This was especially important for those Chinese businessmen whose interests were directly threatened by the public enterprises, but the political importance of the public enterprises went well beyond this. The looser budgetary and operational control over the public enterprises, in comparison with the central government, facilitated their political patronage function.

The management of a state enterprise comes under the jurisdiction of its parent ministry, making its chairman a political appointee. Increased participation of civilian politicians in assuming ministerial portfolios, also led to increased political influence in state enterprises. By 1986, 56 out of 68 chairmanships of state enterprises were held by members of political parties. This means that political parties, through their control of state enterprises, had gained a widening influence on economic decisions. Previously, the chairmanships of state enterprises had been dominated by senior bureaucrats and military officers.

The Thai public's perception of the public enterprises is that they incur huge losses, but this is only partially correct. It is true that some important public enterprises regularly lose large sums. The main examples are in the transport sector: notably the Bangkok Mass Transit Authority, annually losing an average of US$30 million and the State Railway of Thailand, annually losing around US$23 million. Nevertheless, in most years, the public enterprises' aggregate revenues exceed their aggregate expenditures. The problem with these calculations is that the expenditures of the state enterprises do not include proper allowance for a return on the public sector's capital investment in them. In any case, some of the state enterprises included in these statistics operate as profit-maximizing monopolists and generate large operating surpluses. Examples are the Thailand Tobacco Monopoly and the State Lottery Bureau.

Each public enterprise has a board of control and is under the supervision of a government ministry. Generally, the board has responsibility for setting prices, but the supervising ministry may also play a role. The more important the enterprise, the greater the role of the ministry. A few of the most important enterprises must have any changes in their prices approved by the cabinet. This makes it politically difficult to raise prices in key public enterprises. In addition to the transport sector mentioned above, this applies to the water, electricity and telephone utilities. The cabinet also approves the price structure of all petroleum-related products. For these key public enterprises, the redistributive effects of changes in prices, and the political implications of these effects, dominate discussions of tariff rates. Decisions to change prices are made only rarely—long after economic circumstances have changed. This slowness to adjust prices, combined with inefficiency, largely accounts for the losses of the key public enterprises.

Public enterprises account for about two-thirds of the public sector's outstanding foreign debt. Servicing this debt absorbs roughly half the total debt servicing burden of the public sector. In recent years, recognition of this problem has caused the investment plans of all public enterprises to come under close scrutiny from the NESDB. The implications of enterprises' investment plans for foreign debt receive the closest examination. Not only are public enterprises now required to have foreign and domestic borrowing plans examined by the National Debt Policy Committee, but all such loans are then negotiated and signed by the Finance Ministry's Fiscal Policy Office.

25.5 Economic Performance

25.5.1 Economic Growth

Long-term changes in Thai real income can be estimated from data provided in Sompop (1989). From these data it is possible to estimate real GDP per capita in baht, expressed in 1950 prices, as shown in Table 25.5. These data imply growth over the 80 year period from 1870 to 1950 at an average annual rate of a mere 0.2 percent per year. Growth since World War II can be estimated more reliably. Figure 25.1 shows this information, from 1951 to 1991, calculated from national income data provided by NESDB. Quite unlike the century before, growth per capita has been impressive. The average annual rate of growth of measured real GDP per capita over this period was 4.3 percent.

Thai national income data before 1970 are considered questionable and the NESDB has released a revised national income series for the period since 1970. Thailand's annual rate of GNP growth from 1970 to 1990 calculated from this new series, is shown in Figure 25.2. A fuller statistical summary of Thailand's macroeconomic performance from 1970 to 1991 is provided in Table 25.6. The annual fluctuations around the average rate of growth of real GDP of 7.1 percent principally involved external phenomena. Domestic political events have had remarkably little apparent effect on aggregate economic performance. Thailand experienced an export commodity boom from 1972 to 1974. This boom affected Thailand mainly through the price of rice. Exports surged and economic growth rose sharply in 1973. This event was quickly followed by the first OPEC-induced international oil price increases of 1973–74 (known as OPEC I). Since Thailand is a substantial petroleum importer, the rise in oil prices slowed Thai growth in 1974 and 1975. Recovery occurred from 1976 to 1978, but the second round of oil price increases of 1979–80 (OPEC II) slowed growth again.

Other oil-importing countries, including the Philippines, were devastated by these petroleum price increases, but Thailand experienced only a "growth recession"—from around 9 percent to around 6 percent. Having borrowed internationally to finance the increased cost of petroleum imports during the mid to late 1970s, Thailand suffered again from the high international interest rates of the early 1980s. By 1985 serious macroeconomic problems were evident, as described above.

TABLE 25.5 Gross domestic product per capita for 1870–1950 (at constant 1950 prices)

Year	Agriculture (million baht)	Manufacturing (million baht)	Services (million baht)	GDP (million baht)	Population	GDP per capita (baht)
1870	2,417	678	2,524	5,619	5,775,000	973
1890	2,959	828	3,035	6,822	6,670,000	1,023
1900	3,222	883	3,274	7,379	7,320,000	1,008
1913	4,459	1,245	4,281	9,985	8,689,000	1,149
1929	5,735	1,603	5,749	13,087	12,058,000	1,085
1938	7,490	2,091	7,337	16,918	14,980,000	1,129
1950	10,196	2,794	9,559	22,549	19,817,000	1,138

Source: Calculated from data provided in Sompop (1989).

FIGURE 25.1   Thailand: per capita GDP at constant 1972 prices, 1951–92

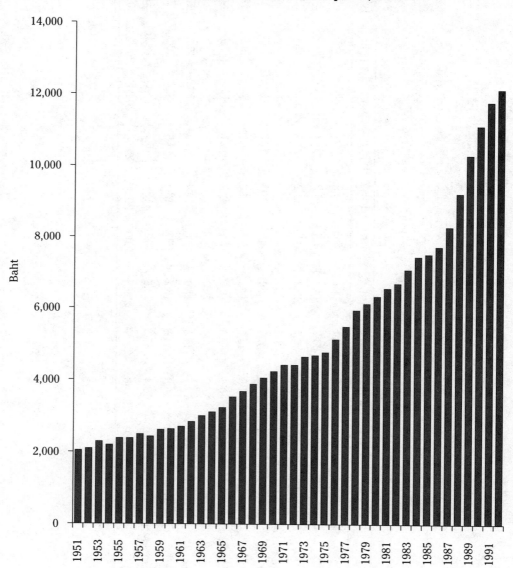

Source: National Economic and Social Development Board, Bangkok.

TABLE 25.6 Thailand: macroeconomic summary, 1970–91

Variable	1970	1971	1972	1973	1974	1975	1976	1977	1978	1979	1980
GNP, real (% growth rate)	7.4	4.6	5.4	9.1	4.1	5.0	8.9	9.8	9.3	5.9	6.2
Exports (% growth rate)	0.3	10.7	26.6	33.2	44.9	−7.8	24.9	14.9	21.7	29.4	27.0
Imports (% growth rate)	4.0	1.2	13.8	36.1	49.2	3.8	12.2	30.3	15.9	38.4	23.2
Terms of trade (export unit value/ import unit value)	100	101	111	155	130	116	107	101	102	105	100
Inflation (% growth rate)	0.8	0.4	4.8	15.6	24.3	5.3	4.2	7.1	8.4	9.9	19.7
Current account balance/GDP (%)	−3.8	−2.5	−0.6	−0.5	−0.7	−4.1	−2.7	−5.7	−1.5	−7.7	−6.2
Money supply (M1), real (% growth rate)	9.7	11.0	17.7	17.9	13.0	11.0	12.4	9.0	17.1	17.0	13.8
Total debt/GDP (%)	16.6	17.2	16.8	14.3	13.2	15.5	13.1	14.8	18.5	20.2	25.7
Total debt service/exports (%)	17.1	18.9	17.4	15.3	14.8	15.1	12.8	16.7	17.4	19.1	14.5
Exchange rate (baht/US$)	20.80	20.80	20.80	20.40	20.00	20.00	20.00	20.00	20.34	20.42	20.48

TABLE 25.6 (continued)

Variable	1981	1982	1983	1984	1985	1986	1987	1988	1989	1990	1991
GNP, real (% growth rate)	5.2	4.8	7.1	6.3	3.0	4.6	9.7	13.3	12.4	10.3[a]	7.4[b]
Exports (% growth rate)	14.1	6.0	-4.6	14.1	10.5	20.7	28.8	33.9	27.7	14.4	23.6[a]
Imports (% growth rate)	14.3	-9.6	20.1	3.8	4.6	-3.0	39.0	46.1	29.8	28.5	16.6[a]
Terms of trade (export unit value/import unit value)	87.0	79.0	85.0	83.0	80.0	89.0	89.0	86.0	83.0	81.0	80.0[a]
Inflation (% growth rate)	12.7	5.2	3.8	0.9	2.4	1.9	2.5	3.8	5.4	6.0	5.7
Current account balance/GDP (%)	-7.1	-2.7	-7.3	-5.1	-4.1	0.6	-0.7	-2.7	-3.6	-4.9	-4.9[b]
Money supply (M1), real (% growth rate)	6.5	12.0	10.3	5.4	8.4	18.2	24.9	8.0	11.7	8.5	n.a.
Total debt/GDP (%)	31.0	34.2	35.0	36.4	46.9	44.6	35.9	30.1	28.2	31.3	31.6[b]
Total debt service/exports (%)	14.4	16.0	19.1	21.5	25.3	25.4	17.1	13.7	12.4	9.8	15.2[b]
Exchange rate (baht/US$)	21.82	23.0	23.0	23.64	27.13	26.3	25.7	25.3	25.8	25.6	25.6

a. Preliminary, from Bank of Thailand, *Quarterly Bulletin*, December 1991.
b. Forecast, from Asian Development Bank, *Asian Development Outlook*, 1991. The 1991 real GNP growth rate estimate relates to GDP.
n.a.: not available.

Sources: Bank of Thailand, *Quarterly Bulletin*, various issues; World Bank, *World Development Report*, various issues; Asian Development Bank, *Asian Development Outlook*, 1991.

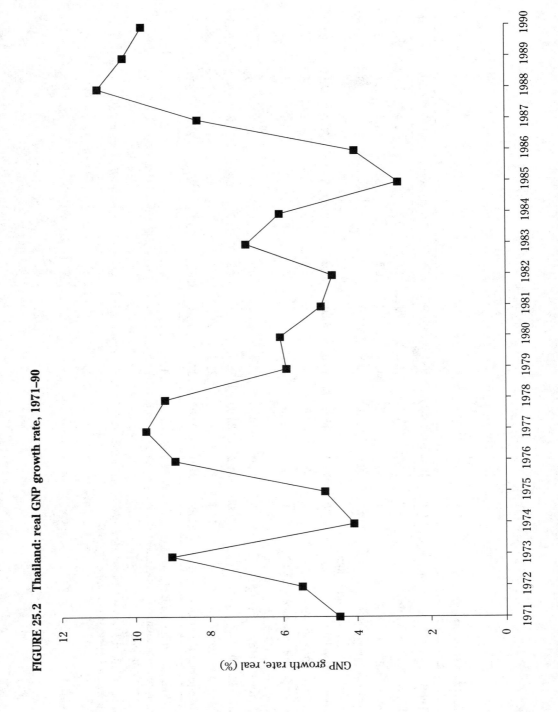

FIGURE 25.2   Thailand: real GNP growth rate, 1971–90

The boom which began in 1987 surprised Thai observers as much as outsiders. It was argued that the boom was driven by two forces:

- [ ] The depreciation of the U.S. dollar relative to other currencies and the fact that the baht was pegged to it made Thai exports more competitive internationally.
- [ ] Foreign investment, especially from the present NICs, Taiwan and Hong Kong, motivated by the desire to avoid rising labor costs in their own countries.

In explaining Thailand's remarkable growth boom of the late 1980s, it would be easy to give too much weight to Thai-specific causes. Similar foreign investment-led booms were occurring in Malaysia and Indonesia, and even more significantly, the southeastern corner of China, adjacent to Hong Kong and Taiwan. The foreign investment did not flow to the Philippines. Its unreliable infrastructure, labor unrest and high level of political uncertainty were enough to discourage that.

External events seem to explain most short-term fluctuations in Thailand's growth rate, but what about the long-term rate? To what extent can Thai economic growth be explained by the growth of conventional factors of production, capital and labor, or alternatively, by other factors, such as technological change, external price movements, and so forth? The standard techniques of growth accounting are applied to Thai data below to attempt to answer this question.

The derivation of our estimating equation is as follows. Let the aggregate production function be

$$Y = f(K, L, t) \tag{25.1}$$

where Y is the GDP at constant prices, K is the aggregate capital stock at constant prices, L is the aggregate labor force and t denotes time. Now

$$\frac{d\ln Y}{dt} = \alpha_K \frac{d\ln K}{dt} + \alpha_L \frac{d\ln L}{dt} + \alpha_0 \tag{25.2}$$

where $\alpha_K = f_K(K/Y)$ and $\alpha_L = f_L(L/Y)$, the elasticities of output with respect to K and L, respectively, and α_0 is a constant.

We attempt to estimate the parameters of this equation using annual data for Thailand for 1961 to 1989, drawn from the World Bank's *World Tables*. The Cochrane-Orcutt autoregression technique was used to correct for autocorrelation. Constant returns to scale was imposed and the estimating equation was

$$\frac{d\ln(Y/L)}{dt} = a_0 + a_1 \frac{d\ln(K/L)}{dt} \tag{25.3}$$

where the variables are formed by

$$\frac{d\ln(Y/L)}{dt} \equiv \ln(Y/L)_t - \ln(Y/L)_{t-1} \tag{25.4}$$

and so forth.

The estimated parameters and relevant diagnostics (t-statistics in parentheses) were

$$\frac{d\ln(Y/L)}{dt} = 0.024 + 0.682\frac{d\ln(K/L)}{dt} \tag{25.5}$$

$$(2.40)\ (25.73)$$

$$\bar{R}^2 = 0.96;\ DW = 1.93$$

These estimated parameters are related to the parameters of (25.2) by

$$\alpha_K = a_1 \text{ and } \alpha_L = 1 - a_1 \tag{25.6}$$

Using these estimated parameters it is now possible to study total factor productivity growth on an annual basis by applying the equation

$$F_t = \frac{d\ln Y}{dt} - \alpha_K\frac{d\ln K}{dt} - \alpha_L\frac{d\ln L}{dt} \tag{25.7}$$

where F_t denotes estimated rate of total factor productivity growth in year t.

These results are summarized in Table 25.7, where the annual results are averaged over four periods: 1961 to 1972, the period before Shock I; 1973 to 1979, capturing the impact of Shock I; 1980 to 1985, capturing the impact of Shock II; and 1986 to 1989, capturing the impact of Shock III. The results are striking. The impacts of the two negative terms of trade shocks caused by OPEC I and II are clearly evident by comparing the results for 1973 to 1979 (Shock I) and 1980 to 1985 (Shock II) with the other two periods—before and after the two oil price shocks, respectively. Total factor productivity (TFP) growth was significantly reduced by the two oil

TABLE 25.7   Growth accounting for Thailand, 1961–89 (% per year)

Variable	1961–72	1973–79	1980–85	1986–89
Growth in GDP	11.3	7.7	5.5	10.0
Growth of labor force	2.6	4.1	2.9	3.3
Growth of capital stock	8.7	8.8	7.0	4.2
Contribution from capital to overall growth	76.0	92.9	95.1	35.9
Contribution from labor to overall growth	8.5	18.4	18.0	12.2
Contribution of TFP to overall growth	15.5	−11.3	−13.1	51.9
TFP growth	1.7	−0.9	−0.7	5.2

Source: Own calculations, as described in text, with data drawn from World Bank, *World Tables*, various issues.

price shocks. From an annual rate of TFP growth of 1.7 percent prior to Shock I, this rate fell to –0.9 and –0.7 percent during Shocks I and II, respectively. In the late 1980s, TFP growth recovered to a startling 5.2 percent per year.

The TFP growth contribution to overall growth from 1986 to 1989 can be interpreted to mean that the growth of conventional factors of production does not explain this period of economic expansion well. External forces seem to have been important, but the causes of this remarkable boom are still not sufficiently well understood.

25.5.2 Structural Change

Figures 25.3 to 25.5 compare the long-term patterns of structural change in Thailand with those observed in Korea and Indonesia. Korea is, of course, ahead of Thailand in the process of economic growth and structural transformation, while Indonesia is somewhat behind. The data show the GDP shares (at constant prices) of agriculture and manufacturing, and also the share of the agricultural labor force in total employment.

Manufacturing overtook agriculture as a share of GDP in 1985 in Thailand and in 1974 in Korea. The same transition seems likely in 1992 in Indonesia. Agriculture's share of the total labor force is also declining in all three countries, but lags well behind agriculture's declining share of national income (Martin and Warr 1990). These issues are further brought out by Figures 25.6 and 25.7, which compare Thailand's GDP shares and labor force shares in 1965 with the latest available data. From Figure 25.6, the decline of agriculture's share of GDP coincided with an expansion of industry's GDP share. The share of services barely changed, but still exceeded industry's share. But turning to the structure of employment in Figure 25.7, the (much slower) decline in agriculture's share of employment was matched by a rise in services share, not that of industry. Clearly, although the services sector is widely neglected by economists, it is very significant, especially for employment.

Table 25.8 shows that the structural change that has occurred in Thailand is not atypical insofar as it involves a decline of agriculture's share of GDP. What is unusual is the high share of services in GDP.

25.5.3 Exports and the Terms of Trade

From Table 25.9 it is clear that the growth rate of Thailand's merchandise exports accelerated through the 1980s. The composition of these exports moved away from primary commodities and toward manufactured goods. By 1990 total manufactured goods exports exceeded those of primary goods, and exports of textiles and clothing alone exceeded that of rice, Thailand's traditional export commodity.

Thailand's external terms of trade (the ratio of the average international prices of its exports to those of its imports) are shown in Figure 25.8. Two points are

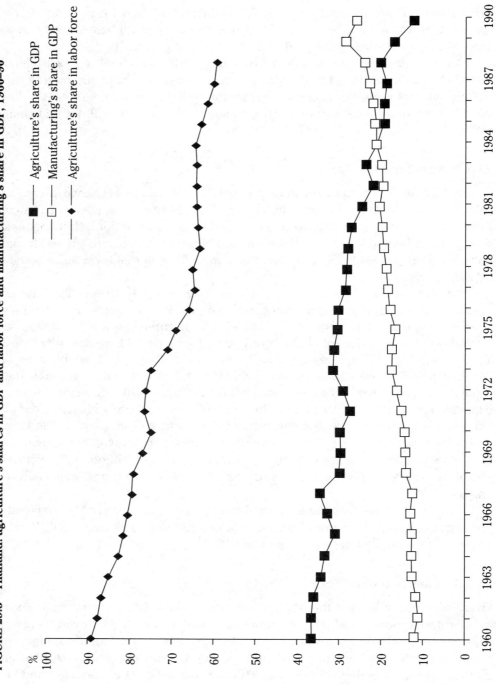

FIGURE 25.3   Thailand: agriculture's shares in GDP and labor force and manufacturing's share in GDP, 1960–90

FIGURE 25.4   Korea: agriculture's shares in GDP and labor force and manufacturing's share in GDP, 1953–90

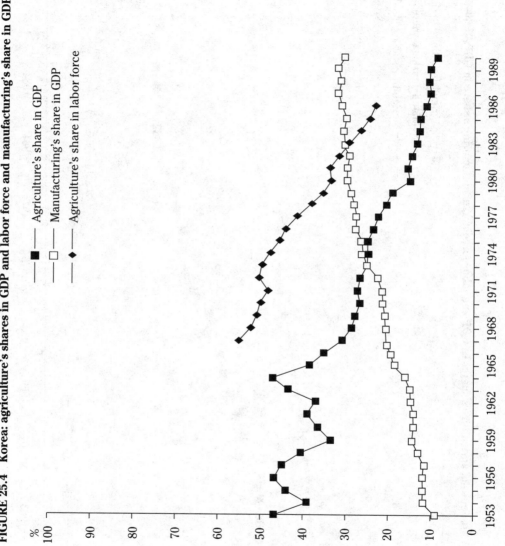

- ■   Agriculture's share in GDP
- □   Manufacturing's share in GDP
- ◆   Agriculture's share in labor force

FIGURE 25.5   Indonesia: agriculture's shares in GDP and labor force and manufacturing's share in GDP, 1960–90

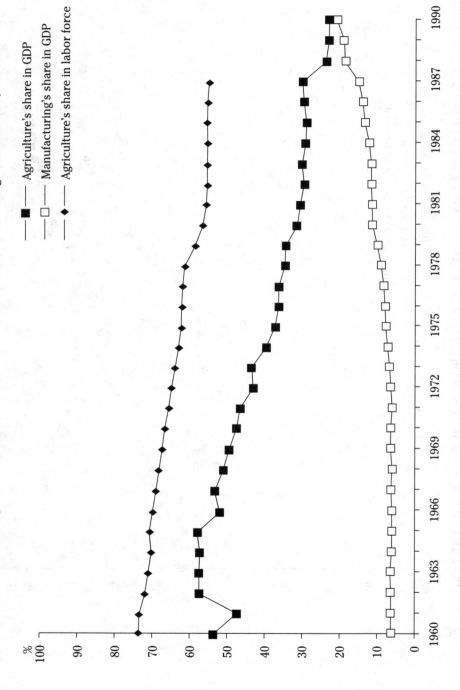

FIGURE 25.6   Sectoral GDP shares, 1965–90 (% current prices)

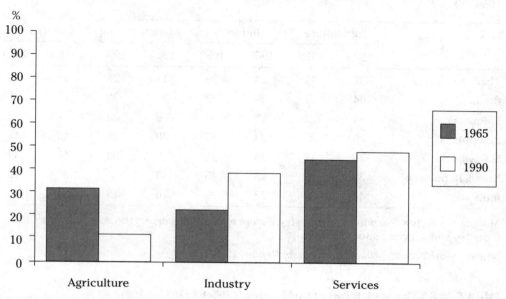

Source: World Bank, *World Development Report 1992*, Oxford University Press, 1992.

FIGURE 25.7   Sectoral labor force shares, 1965 and 1986–89

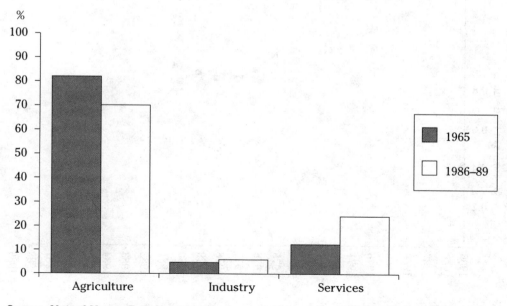

Source: United Nation Development Programme, *Human Development Report 1992*, Oxford University Press, 1992.

TABLE 25.8   Structure of production: distribution of gross domestic product, 1965 and 1990 (%)

	Agriculture		Industry		Manufacturing		Services, etc.	
	1965	1990	1965	1990	1965	1990	1965	1990
Thailand	32	12	23	39	14	26	45	48
China	44	27	39	42	31	38	17	31
Indonesia	56	22	13	40	8	20	31	38
Philippines	26	22	28	35	20	25	46	43
Malaysia	28	19	25	42	9	32	47	39
Korea, Republic of	38	9	25	45	18	31	37	46
India	44	31	22	29	16	19	34	40

Manufacturing is a component of industry. Except for rounding errors the shares of agriculture, industry and services should sum to 100.

Source: World Bank, *World Development Report*, 1992.

FIGURE 25.8   Thailand: terms of trade index, 1965–89 (1971 = 100)

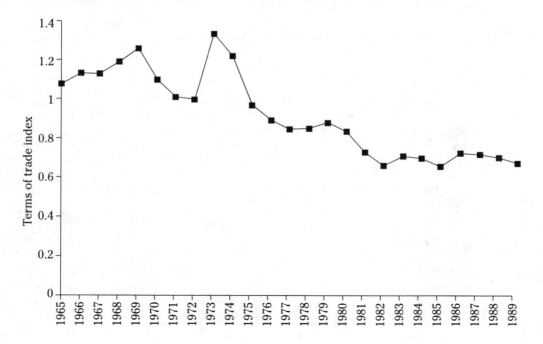

TABLE 25.9 Growth and structure of merchandise trade, 1965–90

| | Annual growth rate of exports | | Percentage share of merchandise exports | | | | | | | | | |
| | | | Fuels, minerals, metals | | Other primary commodities | | Machinery, transport, equipment | | Other manufacturing | | Textiles, clothing | |
	1965–80	1980–90	1965	1990	1965	1990	1965	1990	1965	1990	1965	1990
Thailand	8.6	13.2	11	2	86	43	0	20	3	44	0	16
China	n.a.	11.0	15	10	20	16	9	17	56	56	29	27
Indonesia	9.6	2.8	43	48	53	16	3	1	1	34	0	11
Philippines	4.6	2.5	11	12	84	26	0	10	6	52	1	7
Malaysia	4.6	10.3	34	19	60	37	2	27	4	17	0	5
Korea, Republic of	27.2	12.8	15	2	25	5	3	37	56	57	27	22
India	3.0	6.5	10	8	41	19	1	7	47	66	36	23

n.a.: not available

Source: World Bank, *World Development Report*, 1992.

notable. First, the terms of trade have declined, from an index of 100 in 1965 to an index of 65 in 1990. Second, the terms of trade surged upwards following the 1973 commodity price boom and then fell with each of the two OPEC petroleum price shocks (1973–74 and 1979–80).

25.5.4 Inflation

Thai economic policy has been characterized by a strong aversion to inflation. This is especially true of the monetary policies implemented by the Bank of Thailand since World War II. How well has this goal been achieved? Figure 25.9 shows the annual rate of inflation for the period since 1938. From 1938 to 1948 the data are based on rice prices. Since 1948, cost of living surveys have been conducted and these data are used in the construction of Figure 25.9.

The data show a rapid inflation during and shortly after World War II. Since then, inflation has been below 5 percent except for two brief surges, associated with each of the two OPEC petroleum price increases of 1973–74 and 1979–80. It is notable that after each of these episodes, inflation was quickly brought under control by stringent monetary contractions. It is well understood in Thai financial circles that the Bank of Thailand will contract monetary policy whenever inflation rises above 6 percent, and persist with this policy until the rate falls below 6 percent. Monetary policy thereby has credibility. Inflationary expectations do not

FIGURE 25.9   Thailand: inflation rate, 1938–90

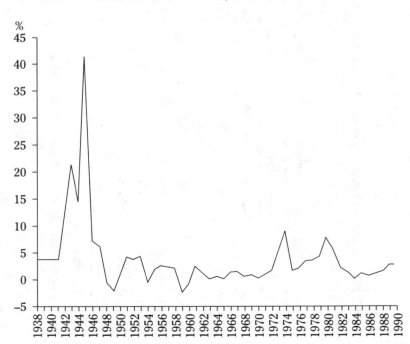

become a serious obstacle to the achievement of the goal of low inflation. The outcome is a superb record of monetary management.

25.5.5 External Debt

Thailand largely avoided the "debt crises" experienced by many developing countries in the 1980s, but by Thailand's conservative standards its levels of debt were a problem. Table 25.10 shows that in 1990 total debt service as a proportion of exports of goods and services was moderately high by East Asian standards. The stock of debt relative to GDP and the annual volume of exports were large, but manageable, because of the high volume of exports. Nevertheless, the level of debt means that Thailand now could not afford a significant decline in the value of exports.

Thailand's adjustments to the oil price shocks of the 1970s, and the high interest rates of the early 1980s were financed to a large extent by foreign borrowing. This is sustainable, so long as the borrowed funds are invested wisely, enabling the loans to be repaid. The major difference between Thailand and the Philippines in this respect is that in the Philippines the borrowed funds were not invested well. Indonesia is more heavily indebted than either of these two countries but appears to have used the borrowed funds in productive ways.

25.5.6 Balance of Payments

As with all countries operating with fixed exchange rates, Thai economic policy discussion is dominated by concern about the balance of payments. This preoccupation is almost certainly excessive, but it does act as a restraint on policies which would imply unsustainable external deficits. Thailand's international reserves are satisfactory, relative to its level of imports and GDP (Table 25.11). In 1990 these reserves were equivalent to 4.4 months of import coverage, compared with 1.5 months for the Philippines, 3.2 months for Indonesia and 1.9 months for India. For many African countries, reserves are equivalent to less than one month's import coverage.

25.6 Asia-Pacific Economic Linkages

Thailand has clearly benefited from its close economic relationships with the dynamic economies of Northeast Asia—Japan, Korea, Hong Kong, Taiwan and China. Nevertheless, Table 25.12 shows that exports to the United States have grown, as a proportion of total export, from 13 percent in 1970, to 23 percent in 1990. The absolute rate of growth of Thai exports to the United States grew at the astounding annual average rate of 24 percent over this 20-year period, compared with 18 percent annual growth of exports to Japan and 20 percent annual growth of total exports.

TABLE 25.10 Total external debt and total external debt ratios, 1980–90

| | Total external debt (US$ million) | | Total external debt as % of: | | | | Total debt services as % of exports of goods and services | |
| | | | Export of goods and services | | GNP | | | |
	1980	1990	1980	1990	1980	1990	1980	1990
Thailand	8,257	25,868	96.3	82.0	25.9	32.6	18.7	17.2
China	7,972	52,555	22.1	77.4	1.5	14.4	4.6	10.3
Indonesia	20,888	67,908	94.2	229.4	28.0	66.4	13.9	30.9
Philippines	17,386	30,456	212.5	229.2	49.5	69.3	26.5	21.2
Malaysia	5,195	19,502	44.6	55.9	28.0	48.0	6.3	11.7
Korea, Republic of	29,749	34,014	130.6	44.0	48.7	14.4	19.7	10.7
India	20,560	70,115	136.0	282.4	11.9	25.0	9.3	28.8

Sources: World Bank, *World Development Report*, various issues.

TABLE 25.11 Balance of payments and reserves, 1970 and 1990

| | Current account balance (US$ million) | | | | Gross international reserves (US$ million) | |
| | After official transfers | | Before official transfers | | | |
	1970	1990	1970	1990	1970	1990
Thailand	-250	-7,053	-296	-7,235	911	14,258
China	-81	12,000	-81	11,935	n.a.	34,476
Indonesia	-310	-2,369	-376	-2,430	160	8,657
Philippines	-48	-2,695	-138	-3,052	255	2,036
Malaysia	8	-1,672	2	-1,733	677	10,659
Korea, Republic of	-623	-2,172	-706	-2,181	610	14,916
India	-385	-9,304	-591	-9,828	1,023	5,637

n.a.: not available

Source: World Bank, *World Development Report*, 1992.

TABLE 25.12 Direction of Thai exports

Country of destination	% of total exports					Annual growth rate (%)			
	1970	1975	1980	1985	1990	1970–75	1975–80	1980–85	1985–90
U.S.	13.4	11.0	12.6	19.7	22.7	20.1	27.6	17.7	28.6
Japan	25.5	27.6	15.1	13.4	17.2	26.9	10.1	5.1	31.5
Europe	17.9	15.1	24.8	17.8	19.6	20.8	37.2	0.9	27.3
France	1.0	0.8	1.6	1.9	2.4	20.2	43.0	10.4	31.9
Italy	1.9	0.5	2.0	1.7	1.8	-4.3	62.4	4.4	27.1
Netherlands	8.6	10.1	13.2	7.1	4.8	28.9	31.1	-4.8	15.6
Switzerland	n.a.	n.a.	1.9	1.0	1.3	n.a.	n.a.	-5.5	30.8
U.K.	2.7	1.2	1.9	2.4	4.1	6.0	36.3	13.5	38.4
W. Germany	3.6	2.5	4.1	3.7	5.2	15.9	37.7	5.5	33.3
Asian NICs	19.3	17.5	14.9	15.4	15.2	22.5	20.4	8.5	24.6
Hong Kong	7.5	6.0	5.1	4.0	4.5	19.5	20.0	2.9	27.7
S. Korea	n.a.	n.a.	0.8	1.8	1.7	n.a.	n.a.	28.8	23.1
Singapore	6.9	9.0	7.7	7.9	7.3	31.9	20.4	8.3	23.1
Taiwan	4.9	2.4	1.3	1.6	1.6	8.2	10.9	11.8	25.1
Australia	0.5	0.9	1.1	1.7	1.6	41.1	27.5	18.7	23.1
Others	23.4	27.9	31.5	32.0	23.8	29.5	27.3	8.1	17.8
World	100.0	100.0	100.0	100.0	100.0	25.0	24.2	7.7	25.0
Total exports									
(billion baht)	14.8	45.0	133.2	193.4	589.8				
(billion US$)	0.71	2.16	6.40	7.13	21.74				

Sources: Bank of Thailand, *Monthly Bulletin* and *Quarterly Bulletin*.

Thailand's imports have increasingly been sourced from East Asia (Table 25.13). East Asia's share of total imports rose from 42 percent in 1970 to 48 percent in 1990, but the more significant point is that the Asian NICs' share of these East Asian imports rose from 5 to 17 percent.

The foreign investment story is the most interesting. In the late 1980s Thailand became a major recipient of direct foreign investment. The magnitude of this foreign investment boom is shown by Figure 25.10, which shows net private foreign investment in Thailand each year from 1970 to 1991. Table 25.14 shows that by 1990 the composition of this foreign investment had shifted away from Thailand's traditional sources—especially the United States and Europe—and toward Northeast Asia. In 1990 Northeast Asia accounted for 78 percent of the US$2.6 billion total net direct foreign investment in Thailand, ASEAN 13 percent, Europe 8 percent and the United States 9 percent. The dramatic change was the new importance of Hong Kong (12 percent), Taiwan (11 percent) and Singapore (10 percent). These three sources together accounted for one-third of total foreign investment in Thailand, twice the total from Europe and the United States combined.

Established NICs were looking for new places to invest. Labor-intensive manufacturing industries were becoming less profitable in the old NICs because of rising labor costs. Thailand was seen as an attractive host. The importance of this source of investment for Thailand is indicated by the fact that in 1990 total

FIGURE 25.10   Net private foreign direct investment in Thailand, 1971–91

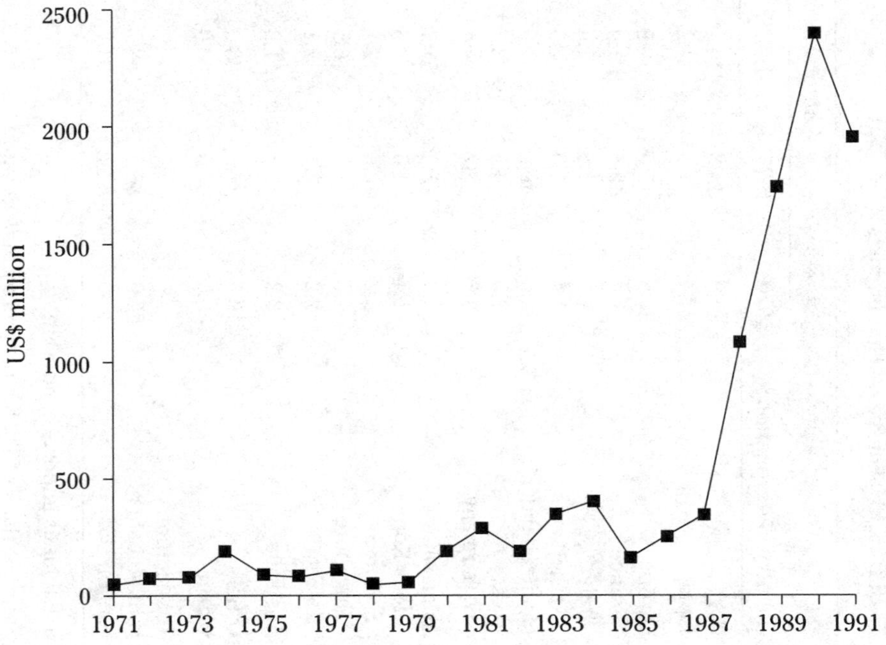

TABLE 25.13 Source of Thai imports

Country of destination	% of total imports					Annual growth rate (%)			
	1970	1975	1980	1985	1990	1970–75	1975–80	1980–85	1985–90
U.S.	14.9	14.3	14.4[a]	11.3	10.9	19.0	23.3	0.9	26.4
Japan	37.4	31.5	21.2	26.5	30.7	15.8	13.7	10.7	31.2
Europe	20.5	15.0	12.8	14.2	13.1	12.7	19.2	8.1	25.4
France	1.4	2.4	1.0	2.7	1.9	33.6	3.2	28.8	18.6
Italy	1.8	1.8	1.4	1.2	1.3	20.2	16.8	1.9	30.0
Netherlands	1.4	1.0	2.5	1.0	0.7	13.1	47.0	−11.9	20.0
Switzerland	n.a.	n.a.	0.9	1.4	1.9	n.a.	n.a.	16.6	35.2
U.K.	7.5	4.5	2.7	2.5	2.4	8.5	10.7	4.7	25.8
W. Germany	8.5	5.2	4.4	5.4	4.9	8.8	18.7	10.6	25.0
Asian NICs	4.6	5.3	11.7	13.8	17.1	23.5	44.0	9.4	33.2
Hong Kong	1.4	1.0	0.9	1.2	1.3	11.3	22.9	10.3	29.4
S. Korea	n.a.	n.a.	2.1	2.0	3.2	n.a.	n.a.	4.6	39.4
Singapore	1.0	2.0	6.5	7.5	7.5	37.9	56.4	8.9	27.5
Taiwan	2.2	2.4	2.1	3.1	5.2	21.7	19.7	14.5	41.5
Australia	3.2	2.3	1.9	1.7	1.7	12.5	18.2	3.2	28.1
Others	19.5	31.5	38.0	32.6	26.5	32.0	27.8	2.7	22.3
World	100.0	100.0	100.0	100.0	100.0	19.9	23.1	5.9	27.4
Total imports									
(billion baht)	27.0	66.8	188.7	251.2	844.4				
(billion US$)	1.30	3.21	9.07	9.26	31.12				

a. Excludes imports of aircraft.

Sources: Bank of Thailand, *Monthly Bulletin* and *Quarterly Bulletin.*

TABLE 25.14   Direct foreign investment (DFI) in Thailand

Country of destination	1970	1975	% of total DFI 1980	1985	1990	Annual growth rate (%) 1980-85	1985-90
U.S.	39.7	28.6	18.9	53.8	9.3	26.7	19.6
Japan	25.8	37.0	23.7	34.5	44.5	10.7	78.5
Europe	15.2	24.7	15.7	11.4	8.1	-3.7	58.7
France	2.9	0.1	0.3	3.2	1.3	61.8	41.2
Italy	0.8	6.2	4.0	0.3	0.1	-40.8	32.1
Netherlands	2.8	1.5	0.6	-0.9	1.0	n.a.	n.a.
Switzerland	2.0	2.2	1.9	1.8	1.3	1.3	58.5
U.K.	6.0	9.1	2.1	2.7	1.8	8.1	55.4
W. Germany	0.8	5.7	6.8	3.7	1.8	-8.7	47.0
Asian NICs	16.1	11.3	36.2	-6.9	33.7	n.a.	n.a.
Hong Kong	10.3	4.5	28.7	14.6	12.0	-10.2	63.2
S. Korea	0.0	0.0	0.3	-0.1	0.8	n.a.	n.a.
Singapore	5.5	6.9	7.2	-25.3	9.5	n.a.	n.a.
Taiwan	0.3	-0.0	0.0	3.8	11.4	145.8	111.1
Australia	0.9	0.0	1.0	-1.8	0.2	n.a.	n.a.
Others	2.2	-1.7	4.5	9.0	4.1	17.8	45.3
World	100.0	100.0	100.0	100.0	100.0	2.8	69.7
Total foreign investment							
(billion baht)	2.2	1.5	3.9	4.4	62.5		
(billion US$)	0.11	0.07	0.19	0.16	2.30		

Source: Bank of Thailand.

foreign investment (direct plus portfolio) accounted for 41 percent of Thailand's total net private investment (Bank of Thailand 1991).

25.7 Conclusions

The Thai economy is growing very rapidly. Although the rate has recently accelerated, high growth performance has been sustained over a long period. Rapid economic growth leads to structural transformation and in Thailand, agriculture's share of national income has decreased very significantly since 1960. Agriculture's share in total employment has also declined, but not by as much; it seems to lag behind the changes in the structure of production. The difference between these two sets of facts gives us a good starting point for understanding the persistence of rural poverty in Thailand in spite of rapid economic growth.

There are two structural issues that must be distinguished. The first is how rapidly the adjustment of output and employment from agriculture to nonagriculture will occur, and the second is where the expanding nonagricultural economic activities will be located. It is important not to identify rural areas with agriculture. The production occurring in rural areas includes agricultural activities but also manufacturing and services. Where nonagricultural economic activities will be located depends partly on government policies, including the provision of economic infrastructure and provision of education and health facilities in rural and urban areas.

Until now, Thailand has managed reasonably well the transition from a slow-growing agricultural exporter to a rapidly growing industrializing NIC. Social tensions have resulted from the rapid change and these could threaten the sustainability of the growth process. The possibility of continued political conflict—between the pro-democracy, urbanized and Westernized middle class versus the traditional, authoritarian military elite—is ominous.

Education policy is critical for Thailand. For economic growth to be sustained, the education system must generate the educated workforce required for constantly upgrading the composition of output toward more skill-intensive economic activities, generating higher value-added. The most worrying point is the low school enrolment rate at the secondary level. The dropout rate at the primary level is particularly high. This phenomenon is especially significant in Thailand's rural areas. Further reductions in rural poverty are principally dependent on providing rural people with opportunities outside agriculture. On the supply side, there is a well-known bias toward government expenditure, including education, in urban areas.[3] On the demand side there is the difficulty for rural people of financing secondary education. Secondary education can be more costly for them than for urban people because the rural children must often relocate to urban areas, away from their families, in order to attend secondary schools. Even more important is the fact that secondary education is perceived as being of low economic value to rural people. The latter is partly a consequence of the uniform and somewhat archaic curriculum imposed by the Thai Ministry of Education.

Infrastructure policy is also very important when the economy is changing rapidly. But Thailand's infrastructure facilities in existing urban areas are already heavily congested.[4] This is especially true of roads, ports and telecommunications; Bangkok's traffic jams are world famous. It is desirable that the movement of labor out of agriculture, which is inevitable, not consist entirely of migration from rural to urban areas. This is especially important in a country like Thailand where "urban areas" can largely be identified with a single city—Bangkok. The fact remains that, for the foreseeable future, sustained economic growth in Thailand will continue to be concentrated in Bangkok. It is urgent that its overburdened public infrastructure be upgraded. Otherwise, Thailand's continued industrialization and its ascendancy to NIC status will surely be jeopardized.

Notes

This paper draws partly on material from the author's introductory chapter to *The Thai Economy in Transition* (Warr 1993). It has benefited from the author's earlier collaborations with Bandid Nijathaworn, now of the Bank of Thailand, and Bhanupongse Nidhiprabha, of Thammasat University, Bangkok. The author is responsible for all views presented and any errors.

1. Sompop (1989) provides estimates of Thailand's GDP for 1870 and 1950. Sompop also estimates Thailand's population for these years. When the GDP estimates are converted to per capita terms, the result implies virtually zero growth per capita over this period.
2. For a recent survey of economic literature in the Thai language, see Warr and Bandid (1987).
3. If the transformation in Thailand's employment structure does continue to coincide with urban expansion, then the current lower utilization of educational facilities in urban areas compared with rural areas may cease; empty schools in the countryside and crowded schools in Bangkok may become the norm.
4. The problem is made more serious by the fact that since 1986 public investment in infrastructure has been contracting, rather than expanding as required.

References

Note: In accordance with Thai custom, Thai names are cited by first name, rather than by family name.

Ammar Siamwalla and Suthad Setboonsarng, 1989, *Trade, Exchange Rate and Agricultural Pricing Policies in Thailand: Comparative Studies on the Agricultural Pricing Policy*, World Bank, Washington, DC.
Bank of Thailand, 1991, *Quarterly Bulletin*, December.
Bertrand, T. J. and L. Squire, 1980, "The Relevance of the Dual Economy Model: A Case Study of Thailand," *Oxford Economic Papers*, 32(3): 480–511.
Chirmsak Pinthong, 1984, "Distribution of Benefit of Government Rice Procurement Policy in 1982/1983," *Thammasat University Journal*, 13(2): 166–87 (in Thai).

Corden, W. M. and H. V. Richter, 1967, "Trade and the Balance of Payments," in Silcock, pp. 151–69.

International Bank for Reconstruction and Development, 1959, *A Public Development Program for Thailand*, Johns Hopkins Press, Baltimore, MD.

Juanjai Ajanant, Supote Chanuantham, and Sorayuth Meenaphant, 1986, *Trade and Industrialisation of Thailand*, Social Science Association of Thailand, Bangkok.

Martin, Will and Peter G. Warr, 1990, "Explaining Agriculture's Declining Share of Thai National Income," *Chulalongkorn Journal of Economics*, 2 (August): 178–224 (in Thai).

Narongchai Akrasanee, 1973, "The Manufacturing Sector in Thailand: A Study of Growth, Import Substitution, and Effective Protection, 1960–1969," Ph.D. Dissertation, Johns Hopkins University, Baltimore, MD.

————, 1977, *The Structure of Effective Protection in Thailand: A Study of Industrial and Trade Policies in the Early 1970s*, report prepared for the Ministry of Finance, the National Economic and Social Development Board of the Government of Thailand, and the International Bank for Reconstruction and Development, Washington, DC.

Pairote Wongwuttiwat, 1975, "The Structure of Differential Incentives in the Manufacturing Sector: A Study of Thailand's Experience during 1945–1974," M.A. Thesis, Thammasat University, Thailand.

Paitoon Wiboonchutikula, Rachain Chintayarangsan, and Nattapong Thongpakde, 1989, "Trade in Manufactured Goods and Mineral Products," in *The 1989 TDRI Year-End Conference*, Thailand Development Research Institute.

Robinson, David, Yangho Byeon, and Ranjit Teja, 1991, *Thailand: Adjusting to Success, Current Policy Issues*, Occasional Paper No. 85, International Monetary Fund, Washington, DC.

Schlossstein, Steven, 1991, *Asia's New Little Dragons: The Dynamic Emergence of Indonesia, Thailand, and Malaysia*, Contemporary Books, Illinois.

Silcock, T. H. (ed.), 1967, *Thailand: Social and Economic Studies in Development*, Australian National University Press, Canberra.

Sompop Manarungsan, 1989, *Economic Development of Thailand, 1850–1950*, Chulalongkorn University, Bangkok.

Trairong Suwankiri, 1970, "The Structure of Protection and Import Substitution in Thailand," M.A. Thesis, University of the Philippines.

Warr, Peter G. (ed.), 1993, *The Thai Economy in Transition*, Cambridge University Press, Cambridge.

Warr, Peter G. and Bandid Nijathaworn, 1987, "Some Thai Perspectives," *Asian-Pacific Economic Literature*, 1: 60–74.

INDEX

CONTRIBUTORS

The Editor

Dilip K. Das, EXIM Bank Professor at the International Management Institute, New Delhi, was recently a visiting professor at the Graduate School of Business, University of Sydney. He has also been associated with some of the leading business schools around the world, including the European Institute of Business Administration (INSEAD), Fontainebleau, France; the Australian National University, Canberra, Australia; l'Ecole Superieures des Sciences Economique et Commerciales (ESSEC) in Paris; and Webster College in Geneva. He has worked as consultant to international organizations like the World Bank, the World Commission on Development and Environment in Geneva, and the United States Agency for International Development.

He was educated at St. John's College, Agra, India and l'Institut Universitaire des Hautes Etudes Internationale, University of Geneva, Switzerland, where he completed his M.Phil. and Ph.D. He is a specialist in the areas of international economics, international finance and the Asia-Pacific economies.

Professor Das has written extensively and contributed to international professional journals. He has written 9 books and 12 monographs and edited a volume on international finance.

Chapter Contributors

Kym Anderson is Professor of Economics and Foundation Director of the Centre for International Economic Studies at the University of Adelaide in South Australia. His previous appointments include Research Fellow in Economics, Research School of Pacific and Asian Studies, Australian National University, Canberra (1977–83) and Counsellor, Economic Research, GATT Secretariat, Geneva (1990–92). He has traveled widely in East Asia, and spent a period as Ford Foundation Visiting Fellow in South Korea (1980–81). He has authored and edited ten books and numerous articles in the areas of international trade and development, agricultural and environmental economics, and the economics of politics. The first of his contributions to this volume grew out of a project that culminated in a book he edited called *New Silk Roads: East Asia and World Textile Markets* (1992); the second from his work at the GATT Secretariat.

C. Fred Bergsten is Director of the Institute for International Economics in Washington, DC. He is the representative of the United States on, and Chairman of, the Eminent Persons Group created in 1992 by the Asia-Pacific Economic Cooperation (APEC) organization. He is also Chairman of the Competitiveness Policy Council chartered by the U.S. Congress to advise the President and Congress on American competitiveness. He was Assistant Secretary of the Treasury for International Affairs during 1977–81 and functioned as Undersecretary for Monetary Affairs in 1980–81. He was previously Assistant for International Economic Affairs to the National Security Council (1969–71). Dr. Bergsten has held positions with the Brookings Institution, the Carnegie Endowment for International Peace and the Council on Foreign Relations. He has authored 25 books on international economics, including most recently *Reconcilable Differences? United States-Japan Economic Conflict* and *Pacific Dynamism and the International Economic System*, and his forthcoming *The Demise of the G-7*.

Andrew Elek is Executive Director of Bellendena Partners, an economic consultancy specializing in Asia-Pacific economic cooperation issues. He is also a Research Associate of the Economics Division of the Research School of Pacific and Asian Studies at the Australian National University. He has worked extensively in development economics in South Asia and the South Pacific, including with the Government of Papua New Guinea and as a Senior Economist with the World Bank. From 1987 to 1990, Dr. Elek was head of the Economic and Trade Development Division of Australia's Department of Foreign Affairs and Trade. In 1989, he was the inaugural chairman of APEC Senior Officials, with a central role in the establishment of the Asia-Pacific Economic Cooperation process. From 1990 to 1994, he was a Senior Research Fellow at the Australian National University.

Robert F. Emery is a consultant and a former international economist at the Board of Governors of the Federal Reserve System. He has published three books: *The*

Financial Institutions of Southeast Asia; The Japanese Money Market; and *The Money Markets of Developing East Asia.* He is currently writing a book, *The Bond Markets of Developing East Asia.*

Hamid Faruqee is an economist at the International Monetary Fund in Washington, DC. A former lecturer in the Woodrow Wilson School of Public and International affairs, he received his PH.D. in Economics from Princeton University. He recently served in the IMF's South East Asian Department working on Malaysia, Singapore and Thailand. Currently, he is in the IMF's Research Department and has written several papers on real exchange rates and is currently doing research on the long-run determinants of saving.

Maxwell Fry is Tokai Bank Professor of International Finance at the University of Birmingham. His research on monetary and financial aspects of economic development has been published in numerous journals; he has also written ten books, including *Money, Interest, and Banking in Economic Development* (1988, 1995). Assignments in over 30 countries, as well as with the Asian Development Bank, the European Commission, the International Monetary Fund, the Organization for Economic Cooperation and Development, and the World Bank, provided the practical experience on which much of his academic work is based.

Michael A. Goldberg is Dean of the Faculty of Commerce and Business Administration at the University of British Columbia and Professor of Urban Land Policy. His recent research has explored international real estate and financial markets; investment and business issues; the economics of the Canadian constitutional debate; and "Cascadia" as an increasingly important economic region. His emerging research activities look at international investment and its linkages to international immigration flows and ethnic business networks.

Gabriel Hawawini is Yamaichi Professor of Finance, and former Associate Dean of INSEAD and Director of the Euro-Asia Centre. His research interests include the structure and dynamics of the financial services industries, the modeling and estimation of risk in financial markets, and Euro-Asian business relationship.

Etsuro Ishigami is a professor at Fukuoka University. He was educated at Tohoku University, Sendai, Japan. He has published on various aspects of the Indian economy as well as the Asian economy, including *Industrialisation of India: A High-Cost Economy at Crossroads* (in Japanese), and "Japanese Business in ASEAN Countries: New Industrialisation or Japanisation" in *IDS Bulletin.*

Chi-Hung Kwan is Senior Economist at the Nomura Research Institute in Tokyo. He has extensive research experience in Japan and Asia's developing countries. His most recent book is *Economic Interdependence in the Asia-Pacific Region* (1994).

Siang Ng is currently subject leader and lecturer in Economics in the Department of Banking and Finance, Monash University. Her fields of interest include international trade and economic development. Born in Penang, Malaysia, Mrs. Ng did her undergraduate study in Singapore, her Master of Economics in Sydney and her Ph.D. at Monash University.

Yew-Kwang Ng holds a personal chair in Economics at Monash University and is a Fellow of the Academy of Social Sciences in Australia since 1981. He has published articles on economics, philosophy, psychology, biology, mathematics, and has written monographs on welfare economics, mesoeconomics, Chinese economic reform, and new classical microeconomics (with Xiaokai Yang).

Peter A. Petri is Dean of the Graduate School of International Economics and Finance and Director of the APEC Study Center at Brandeis University. He received his B.A. and Ph.D. degrees from Harvard University and specializes in international trade and investment, with applications to the Pacific Rim. As a frequent consultant to the World Bank, he participated on the research teams responsible for the *East Asian Miracle* project and the *East Asian Trade and Investment* report. He is the author or editor of 5 books and more than 50 articles, and serves on the Board of Editors of the *Journal of Asian Economics* and *Singapore Economic Review*.

Jocelyn Probert is Research Analyst at the INSEAD Euro-Asia Centre. Her main research area is the Euro-Asian business relationship, with special emphasis on foreign direct investment between the two regions. Recent work includes a study on the entry strategies of Japanese pharmaceutical firms to Europe, a survey of human resource management practices among European firms in Asia, and the process of change in Vietnam.

James Riedel is Professor of International Economics at the Paul H. Nitze School of Advanced International Studies of the Johns Hopkins University and a consultant to the World Bank and other organizations. He is a board member of the American Committee for Asian Economic Studies and the Hong Kong Centre for Economic Research and has been a fellow of the Kiel Institute fur Weltwirtschaft (Germany), Nuffield College of Oxford University, and the National Centre for Development Studies at the Australian National University. He has written several books and numerous articles in the fields of international trade and finance and economic development.

Chi Schive is Vice Chairman of the Council for Economic Planning and Development of the Executive Yuan (the Cabinet), Republic of China; and Professor of the Department of Economics, National Taiwan University. He is also a member of the National Income Committee, Directorate General of the Budget, Accounting, and Statistics, Executive Yuan. Educated at Case Western Reserve University, Ohio, and

National Taiwan University, Dr. Schive has written numerous papers on the economic development of Taiwan and the region, especially in the areas of industrial and trade development, technology transfer, foreign direct investment, and regional economic integration. His recent publications include *Taiwan's Economic Role in East Asia* (1995) and *The Foreign Factor: The Multinational Corporation's Contribution to the Economic Modernization of the Republic of China* (1990).

Chung-Sok Suh is Lecturer in Economics at the University of Wollongong, Australia. He studied at Seoul National University and received his Ph.D. in Economics at the University of New South Wales. His research interests and publications are in the areas of international trade, development economics with emphasis on Asian newly industrializing economies, and resource economics.

Yoshio Suzuki is Chief Counselor in Nomura Research Institute, former Director of the Institute for Monetary and Economic Studies, and former Executive Director in charge of researches of the Bank of Japan. He is also Member of the Tax Commission and of the Price Stabilization Policy Council of the Japanese Government. He is the author of 38 books in Japanese, English, Chinese and Korean mainly on monetary policy and financial system, the most recent being *Future Picture of the Japanese Economy* (in Japanese, 1994). He received his Doctor of Economics from Tokyo University.

Shigeki Tejima is Senior Economist and Deputy Director General (since June 1995), Research Institute for International Investment and Development of the Export–Import Bank of Japan. He joined the Export–Import Bank in 1972 after obtaining a B.A. in Economics from Yokohama National University. He obtained an M.A. in Economics at Yale University in 1977.

Malcolm L. Treadgold is Professor of Economics at the University of New England. He has held research positions at the Australian National University, and is a former Commonwealth Fellow of St. John's College, Cambridge. Professor Treadgold is the author of *Bounteous Bestowal: The Economic History of Norfolk Island* and *The Economy of Fiji: Performance, Management and Prospects*. He is also a co-author of *A Guide to the Australian Economy: Structure, Performance and Policy*.

Peter G. Warr is the John Crawford Professor of Agricultural Economics at the Australian National University. He is a graduate of the University of Sydney, the London School of Economics, and Stanford University where he obtained his doctorate in 1975. He has worked in the areas of international economics, benefit–cost analysis and general equilibrium modeling, applying these fields to the study of the economies of Indonesia, the Philippines and, most recently, Thailand. His recent books include *The Thai Economy in Transition* and *Thailand's Macroeconomic Miracle*.

Ippei Yamazawa is Professor of International Economics at Hitotsubashi University, Tokyo. He has also taught at Thammasat University in Thailand and Sheffield University in England. He was educated at Hitotsubashi University and the University of Chicago. He specializes in international economics, especially trade, investment, industrial adjustment, and trade policy. He has published several books and articles including *Economic Development and International Trade: The Japanese Model* (1990), *Vision for the Economy of the Asia Pacific Region in the Year 2000 and Tasks Ahead* (1992), and *Economic Integration in the Asia-Pacific Region and the Options for Japan* (1993). He is Advisor to the Japanese government and is Japan's representative on the APEC Eminent Persons Group. He has been working on the Pacific Economic Cooperation since 1968, and is a regular member of the Pacific Trade and Development Conference (PAFTAD) and the Pacific Economic Cooperation Council (PECC).